ROUTLEDGE HANDBOOK OF ENTREPRENEURSHIP IN DEVELOPING ECONOMIES

T0361093

The *Routledge Handbook of Entrepreneurship in Developing Economies* is a landmark volume that offers a uniquely comprehensive overview of entrepreneurship in developing countries. Addressing the multi-faceted nature of entrepreneurship, chapters explore a vast range of subject areas including education, economic policy, gender and the prevalence and nature of informal sector entrepreneurship.

In order to understand the process of new venture creation in developing economies, what it means to be engaged in entrepreneurship in a developing world context must be addressed. This handbook does so by exploring the difficulties, risks and rewards associated with being an entrepreneur, and evaluates the impacts of the environment, relationships, performance and policy dynamics on small and entrepreneurial firms in developing economies.

The *Handbook* brings together a unique collection of over forty international researchers who are all actively engaged in studying entrepreneurship in a developing world context. The chapters offer concise but detailed perspectives and explanations on key aspects of the subject across a diverse array of developing economies, spanning Africa, Asia, Latin America and Eastern Europe. In doing so, the chapters highlight the heterogeneity of entrepreneurship in developed economies, and contribute to the ongoing policy discourses for managing and promoting entrepreneurial growth in the developing world.

The book will be of great interest to scholars, students and policy-makers in the areas of development economics, business and management, public policy and development studies.

Colin C. Williams is Professor of Public Policy and Associate Dean (Research) at Sheffield University Management School (SUMS) at the University of Sheffield in the UK.

Anjula Gurtoo is Associate Professor at the Indian Institute of Science, Bangalore, India.

ROUTLEDGE HANDBOOK OF ENTREPRENEURSHIP IN DEVELOPING ECONOMIES

Edited by Colin C. Williams and Anjula Gurtoo

LONDON AND NEW YORK

First published 2017 by Routledge
4 Park Square, Milton Park, Abingdon, Oxon OX14 4RN

605 Third Avenue, New York, NY 10017

Routledge is an imprint of the Taylor & Francis Group, an informa business

First issued in paperback 2020

British Library Cataloguing in Publication Data
A catalogue record for this book is available from the British Library

Library of Congress Cataloging in Publication Data
Names: Williams, Colin C., 1961– editor. | Gurtoo, Anjula, editor.
Title: Routledge handbook of entrepreneurship in developing economies / edited by Colin C. Williams and Anjula Gurtoo.
Description: Abingdon, Oxon; New York, NY: Routledge, 2016.
Identifiers: LCCN 2016003992 | ISBN 9781138849143 (hardback) | ISBN 9781315725826 (ebook)
Subjects: LCSH: Entrepreneurship—Developing countries. | Small business—Developing countries. | Economic development—Developing countries.
Classification: LCC HD2346.5. R68 2016 | DDC 338/.04091724—dc23
LC record available at http://lccn.loc.gov/2016003992

ISBN: 978-1-138-84914-3 (hbk)
ISBN: 978-0-367-66008-6 (pbk)

Typeset in Bembo
by Keystroke, Station Road, Codsall, Wolverhampton

CONTENTS

Contents

Contents

FIGURES

TABLES

CONTRIBUTORS

Kwame Adom, Enterprise Development Services, University of Ghana Business School, University of Ghana, Accra, Ghana

Minha Akber Allibhoy, Department of Economics, Lahore University of Management Sciences, Lahore, Pakistan

Will Bartlett, Honorary Professor, London School of Hygiene and Tropical Medicine and Senior Research Fellow, European Institute, London School of Economics, United Kingdom

Safal Batra, Assistant Professor, Strategy Management, Indian Institute of Management Kashipur, India

Balbir B. Bhasin, Ross Pendergraft Endowed Professor of International Business, University of Arkansas, Fort Smith and Reykjavik University, Iceland

Matthew Bird, Assistant Professor, School of Business, Universidad del Pacifico, Lima, Peru

Sutana Boonlua, Mahasarakham Business School, Mahasarakham University, Thailand

Carol M. Bresnahan, Professor, History Department, College of New Jersey, Ewing, USA

Jürgen Brünjes, German Centre for Research on Higher Education and Science Studies

Elisa Calza, Research Scholar, UNU-MERIT, Maastricht, The Netherlands

Sutapa Chattopadhyay, Research Scholar, UNU-MERIT, Maastricht, The Netherlands

Tanya Chavdarova, Associate Professor, Department of Sociology, Sofia University, Bulgaria

N. S. Cooray, Professor, International University of Japan, Japan

Mario Curcija, Business Administration Department, University of Shkodra "LuigjGurakuqi", Shkodër, Albania

Léo-Paul Dana, Professor of Entrepreneurship, Montpellier Business School, Montpellier, France

Elvisa Drishti, Business Administration Department, University of Shkodra "LuigjGurakuqi", Shkodër, Albania

Adnan Efendic, Associate Professor, School of Economics and Business, University of Sarajevo, Sarajevo, Bosnia and Herzegovina

Nezameddin Faghih, UNESCO Chair in Entrepreneurship, Faculty of Entrepreneurship, University of Tehran, Iran

Cristina I. Fernandes, Researcher, Polytechnic Institute of Castelo Branco and NECE – Research Unit, Portugal

Joao Ferreira, Associate Professor, Management and Economics Department, Universidade da Beira Interior, Covilha, Portugal

Micheline Goedhuys, Research Fellow, UNU-MERIT, the Netherlands

Anjula Gurtoo, Associate Professor, Department of Management Studies, Indian Institute of Science, Bangalore, India

Taehyun Jung, Assistant Professor, Technology and Innovation Management, Hanyang University, Seoul, Korea

Eldrede Kahiya, Lecturer, Faculty of Agribusiness and Commerce, Lincoln University, New Zealand

Esra Karadeniz, Associate Professor, Department of Economics, Yeditepe University, Turkey

Rebecca Kennedy, Assistant Lecturer, Department of Financial and Business Systems, Lincoln University, New Zealand

Jungbu Kim, Associate Professor, Kyung Hee University, Seoul, Korea

Drita Kruja, Professor, Business Administration Department, European University of Tirana, Tirana, Albania

Joseph A. Kuzilwa, Professor, Economics, Mzumbe University, Mzumbe, Tanzania

Andrés Marroquín, Professor of Economics, Francisco Marroquin University, Guatemala, and Visiting Professor of Entrepreneurship, UNOGA, Jérémie, Haiti.

Tamas Medovarszki, Researcher, sti4change, Bangalore, India

Tomasz Mickiewicz, Professor, Aston Business School, Aston University, Birmingham, UK

Mehrangiz Najafizadeh, Associate Professor, Department of Sociology, University of Kansas, Lawrence, Kansas, USA

Alan A. Ndedi, Dean, School of Business and Public Policy, Saint Monica University

Lee Keng Ng, Assistant Professor, Singapore Institute of Technology, Singapore

Ganka D. Nyamsogoro, Professor, Mzumbe University, Tanzania

Ahmet Özçam, Associate Professor, Department of Economics, Yeditepe University, Turkey

Özlem Özdemir, Professor, Middle East Technical University, Ankara, Turkey

Michael J. Pisani, Professor of International Business and Jerry and Felicia Campbell Endowed Professorship for Research, College of Business, Central Michigan University, USA

Shyama Ramani, Brunel Business School, Brunel University, UK

Vanessa Ratten, Associate Professor, La Trobe Business School, La Trobe University, Melbourne, Australia

Veena Ravichandran, Senior Program Officer, Innovation Policy and Science at the International Development Research Centre (IDRC), Ottawa, Canada

Anna Rebmann, Lecturer, Economics, Finance and Entrepreneurship, Aston Business School, Aston University, UK

Javier Revilla Diez, Professor, Institute of Geography, University of Cologne, Germany

Leyla Sarfaraz, Instructor, School of Economy, Management, and Social Science, Shiraz University, Shiraz, Iran

Halima Shehryar, Research Associate, The Competitive Grants Programs, Pakistan Strategy Support Program (PSSP), Lahore, Pakistan

Muhammad Shehryar Shahid, Associate Professor, Suleman Dawood School of Business, Lahore University of Management Sciences, Lahore, Pakistan

Michelle J. Stecker, Director, Lucy Cross Center for Women, Rollins College, Florida, USA

Tulus T.H. Tambunan, Professor, Centre for Industry, SME and Business Competition Studies, Trisakti University, Indonesia

Nobin Thomas, Assistant Professor, Indian Institute of Management, Indore, India

Ajay Thutupalli, Affiliated Researcher, UNU-MERIT, Maastricht, The Netherlands

Sivakumar Venkataramany, Professor, Richard E. and Sandra J. Dauch College of Business and Economics, Ashland University, Ohio, USA

Neharika Vohra, Professor, Organizational Behavior, Indian Institute of Management, Ahmedabad, India

Tonia L. Warnecke, Associate Professor, Social Entrepreneurship and Business, Rollins College, Florida, USA

Lorraine Warren, Professor of Entrepreneurship, Massey University, Palmerston North, New Zealand

Chandani Wijebandara, Statistician, Department of Census and Statistics, Columbo, Sri Lanka

Colin C. Williams, Professor of Public Policy, Sheffield University Management School (SUMS), University of Sheffield, UK

1

INTRODUCTION AND OVERVIEW

Colin C. Williams and Anjula Gurtoo

Across the world, facilitating entrepreneurship is viewed as a key means of promoting economic development and growth. Consequently, entrepreneurship is now a focus of attention worldwide. This is especially the case in developing countries which are perceived to be at the 'back of the queue' in terms of their levels of economic development and growth. Harnessing entrepreneurship is commonly viewed as one of the means by which they might speed up their economic development and growth. To achieve this however, understanding is required not only of current levels of entrepreneurship in different contexts but also of who engages in entrepreneurial endeavour, the characteristics of this endeavour, the motives for becoming entrepreneurs and barriers that prevent the development of an enterprise culture that can act as a motor for economic development and growth. Unless these various facets of entrepreneurship in developing countries are understood, then it will not be known whether the policy approaches and measures being developed to harness entrepreneurship and enterprise culture are the most effective ones to pursue in any particular context. The *Routledge Handbook of Entrepreneurship in Developing Economies* seeks to provide a compendium of the scholarship being conducted to understand entrepreneurship in what are variously called developing or emerging economies, the majority world or the global South. Indeed, this handbook marks one of the first attempts to bring together within one cover the emergent array of scholarship being conducted on entrepreneurship in developing countries.

Until now, entrepreneurship in developing countries has been dominated by various widely held beliefs about the characteristics of entrepreneurship and enterprise culture. These, however, have been on the whole based on assumptions rather than evidence-based findings about entrepreneurship and enterprise culture in developing countries. One of the most common of these assumptions is that entrepreneurship in developing countries is largely undertaken by marginalized populations who, excluded from the formal labour market, have no other options available to them but to engage in necessity-driven entrepreneurship as a last resort and survival practice. Such necessity-driven entrepreneurship is thus viewed to be an unproductive, labour-intensive and inefficient endeavour conducted by poorly educated and low-skilled entrepreneurs and at best, to contribute little to economic development and growth and at worst, to hinder development and growth (La Porta and Shleifer, 2008, 2014). Much of this unproductive entrepreneurship is seen to take place in the informal economy, which is consequently seen as deleterious to economic development and growth.

The consequent policy approach is to seek to eradicate such entrepreneurship and to instead focus upon harnessing legitimate opportunity-driven entrepreneurship. Women's entrepreneurial endeavour in developing countries, meanwhile, has sometimes been hidden from view or else denigrated as endeavour that simply helps households to 'make ends meet'.

In this handbook however, the intention is to put under the spotlight these widely held representations and policy discourses regarding entrepreneurship in developing countries. Each part and every chapter in this handbook addresses one or more of these widely held assumptions and begins to unravel the need for a more nuanced and evidence-based understanding of entrepreneurship in developing countries. In this introductory overview, therefore, we commence by reviewing these assumptions about entrepreneurship in developing countries that are addressed in each part of this handbook. The intention in doing so is to provide the reader with a clear guide to where discussion can be found within this handbook on some of the more widely held assumptions regarding entrepreneurship in developing countries as well as information on the more nuanced understandings that are emerging.

Institutional environment of entrepreneurship

Entrepreneurship does not arise in a vacuum devoid of context. Rather, entrepreneurship is a socially constructed behaviour which is a product of the social environment, or what can be termed the institutional context, in which it takes place (Sine and David, 2010). As such, the importance of understanding the institutional context within which the entrepreneurship takes place in developing countries, cannot be over emphasized. Institutions provide 'the rules of the game' and norms which govern businesses in general and the nature of entrepreneurial endeavour more particularly (Baumol and Blinder, 2008; Denzau and North 1994; North, 1990). They prescribe the acceptability of activities (Mathias et al., 2014). On the one hand, all societies have formal institutions (i.e., codified laws and regulations) that define the legal rules of the game (and prescribe what we here term 'state morality'). On the other hand, all societies also have informal institutions which are the 'socially shared rules, usually unwritten, that are created, communicated and enforced outside of officially sanctioned channels' (Helmke and Levitsky, 2004: 727) and prescribe what we here term 'civic morality'.

Reviewing institutional theory, two schools of thought exist in relation to explaining the prevalence and nature of entrepreneurship in any context. In the first school, studies identify the relationship between the quality and intensity of formal institutions and the prevalence and nature of entrepreneurship. For example, when considering developing countries, the emphasis is often placed in this school of thought on discussing issues like how easy it is to register a new venture, the legal bureaucratic impediments to doing so, the various barriers to entry for nascent entrepreneurs, the level of property rights protection and the quality of services available. From this viewpoint, there are often deemed to be numerous formal institutional constraints that hinder the development of entrepreneurship in developing economies, including the costs of establishing a formal business venture, the existence of over-burdensome regulations, high taxes and corruption in the public sector (De Soto, 1989; Nwabuzor, 2005) but also formal institutional voids such as relatively weak or inadequate legal systems and contract enforcement regimes (Khan and Quaddus, 2015; Puffer et al., 2010; Sutter et al., 2013).

A second school of institutional thought however, turns away from studying solely the role and quality of the regulatory institutional framework. Instead, this investigates the cognitive and normative institutions (Scott, 1995), which can be joined within the broad category of the informal institutions. Seen through this lens, the relationship between formal and informal institutions matters (Vu, 2014; Webb et al., 2009, 2013, 2014). Viewing informal institutions as either 'complementary' if they reinforce formal institutions, or 'substitutive' if their rules are incompatible with those of the formal institutions (Helmke and Levitsky, 2004; North, 1990), the argument states that entrepreneurial endeavour is often hindered and/or takes place in the informal sector when they are substitutive. As Webb et al. (2009: 495) put it, 'the informal economy exists because of the incongruence between what is defined as legitimate by formal and informal institutions'. The consequent argument states that when symmetry exists between formal and informal institutions, entrepreneurship may prosper and the level of informal sector entrepreneurship will be small since the socially shared norms, values and beliefs of informal institutions ('civic morality') are aligned with the codified laws and regulations of formal institutions ('state morality'). However, when asymmetry exists between the formal and informal institutions, such as due to a lack of trust in government, the result is that entrepreneurship is hindered and/or informal sector entrepreneurship emerges, which although socially 'legitimate' in terms of the informal institutions, is deemed 'illegal' in terms of the formal rules (Kistruck et al., 2015; Siqueira et al., 2014; Sutter et al., 2013; Webb et al., 2009).

Part I of this handbook addresses issues related to this institutional context within which entrepreneurship is embedded in developing countries. Each of the chapters in Part I of the book thus reveal how entrepreneurship is a socially constructed behaviour conditioned by the institutional context in which it takes place.

Entrepreneurs' motivations in developing countries

Although there has been widespread recognition in the entrepreneurship literature that multifarious factors feed into the decision to start up a business (Baty, 1990; Bolton and Thompson, 2000; Brockhaus and Horowitz, 1986; Burns, 2001; Chell et al., 1991; Cooper, 1981; Kanter, 1983), and there have been repeated warnings not to over-simplify the complex rationales driving entrepreneurship (Rouse and Daellenbach, 1999), since the turn of the millennium, entrepreneurship scholarship has widely adopted a rather simple classificatory schema. Entrepreneurs have been classified as either 'necessity' entrepreneurs pushed into entrepreneurship as a survival strategy in the absence of alternative means of livelihood, or as 'opportunity' entrepreneurs pulled into this endeavour more out of choice (Aidis et al., 2007; Benz, 2009; Harding et al., 2005; Maritz, 2004; Minniti et al., 2006; Perunović, 2005; Reynolds et al., 2001, 2002; Smallbone and Welter, 2004). This structure/agency binary, which views some entrepreneurs as 'necessity' entrepreneurs and others as 'opportunity' entrepreneurs, has become ever more dominant (Acs, 2006; Bosma et al., 2008; Williams, 2007, 2008, 2009; Williams et al., 2006, 2009, 2010; Williams and Lansky, 2013).

In developing countries, the commonly held assumption in both popular portrayals and policy-making circles is that entrepreneurs are largely from marginalized populations and participate in such endeavour out of necessity as a survival practice and last resort in the absence of alternative means of livelihood. This, nevertheless, is an *a priori* assumption rather than an empirical finding. In recent decades, however, as the chapters in Part II highlight, this has begun to be put under the spotlight and questions raised about whether this is indeed the case (Cross, 2000; Gërxhani, 2004; Maloney, 2004; Snyder, 2004). There has been an emergent recognition that many entrepreneurs in developing countries act out of choice, not least due to the flexible hours such endeavour allows, especially for women with family caring responsibilities, but also due to the economic independence, better wages and avoidance of taxes and inefficient government regulation offered by this sphere, as well as the fact that some entrepreneurs are in formal jobs and engage in entrepreneurship as an additional income-earning opportunity (Maloney, 2004; Perry and Maloney, 2007; Williams and Gurtoo, 2013).

The outcome is that studies of developing countries have started to gauge the ratio of necessity-to-opportunity entrepreneurship in different developing country contexts, as well as who engages in such entrepreneurial endeavour out of necessity and who does so voluntarily, and to decipher how the activities that they engage in differ. As the chapters in Part II will reveal, there appears to be a socio-spatial contingency of entrepreneurs' motives in terms of the ratio of necessity-to-opportunity entrepreneurship with greater proportions of necessity-driven entrepreneurship, for example in deprived populations and opportunity entrepreneurship in more affluent populations. When considering the motives of individual entrepreneurs there has also, as will be revealed, been a recognition that necessity and opportunity drivers can often combine and a recognition that entrepreneurs' motives can change over time, such as from more necessity-oriented to opportunity-oriented rationales.

It is not just the recognition that some entrepreneurs in developing countries voluntarily engage in entrepreneurial endeavour for opportunity-oriented rationales which opens the debate on re-representing the entrepreneurship in developing countries. In recent decades, the view that entrepreneurship is always and everywhere a profit-driven endeavour has also begun to be challenged. A growing literature has displayed how entrepreneurship is not always purely a profit-driven endeavour and how many entrepreneurs engage in not-for-profit activity (Austin et al., 2006; Defourny and Nyssens, 2008; Galera and Borzega, 2009; Hynes, 2009; Lyon and Sepulveda, 2009; Nicholls and Cho, 2006; Thompson, 2008). In other words, besides 'commercial entrepreneurs' who engage in entrepreneurial endeavour for a primarily for-profit objective, there are also 'social entrepreneurs' who pursue primarily social and/or environmental objectives and reinvest the surpluses for that purpose in the business or community (e.g., Austin et al., 2006; Dees, 1998; Dees and Anderson, 2003; Defourny and Nyssens, 2008).

Until now, and grounded in the depiction of entrepreneurship in developing countries as necessity-driven and thus motivated by monetary gain, the literature on social entrepreneurship has been relatively absent compared with the burgeoning social entrepreneurship literature in the developed world. Nevertheless, as chapters in Part II of this handbook reveal, there is an emergent literature on social entrepreneurship in developing countries which reveals not only the need for, but also the existence of, social entrepreneurship in the developing world.

Gender and entrepreneurship

Part III of this handbook turns its attention to the issue of the gendering of entrepreneurship in developing countries. Until now, scholarship and discourse on entrepreneurship in developing countries has sometimes 'written out' women. Even when it has included them, however, women have been commonly portrayed as necessity-driven and engaging in entrepreneurial endeavour simply in order to earn some extra income for their families (Bhatt, 2006; Carr and Chen, 2002; ILO 2006; Mehrotra and Biggeri, 2002).

Women entrepreneurs in developing countries are seen to be heavily reliant on their day-to-day profits for survival due to little or no access to institutional credit (Bhatt, 2006; Carr and Chen, 2002; Charmes, 1998; ILO, 2002, 2006; Nelson, 1997), their entrepreneurial endeavour is asserted to be less often constituted as a separate legal entity independent from the household (Chen et al., 1999, 2004; Fawzi, 2003) and the activities in which they engage locked into traditional gender roles such as selling flowers or fruit (Bhatt, 2006; Charmes, 1998). Whether the nature of, and rationales for, entrepreneurship of men and women differ in this manner has so far seldom been evaluated. The chapters in Part III start to do so by unravelling not only the variations in women's and men's entrepreneurship in the developing world but also the gender disparities.

Examining the lived practices of entrepreneurship in developing countries through a gender lens, the chapters in Part III thus start to provide an evidence-based analysis of how the gender disparities in the wider labour market are often mirrored and reinforced when studying the gendering of entrepreneurship. Not only are recorded participation rates in entrepreneurship sometimes lower for women, but so too do women commonly receive lower incomes from their entrepreneurial endeavour than men despite being better educated, and often face additional barriers to engagement in entrepreneurship and developing their new ventures not suffered by many men.

Informal sector entrepreneurship

It is now widely recognized that the majority of entrepreneurs in the developing world operate wholly or partially in the informal sector. Part IV of this handbook addresses this important topic of entrepreneurship in the informal sector, which refers to those starting up and/or owning and managing a business venture that does not register with and/or declare some or all of their production and/or sales to the authorities for tax, benefit and/or labour law purposes when it should do so (Ketchen et al., 2014; Siqueira et al., 2014; Williams and Martinez-Perez, 2014).

For much of the twentieth century, informal entrepreneurship in developing countries, akin to the informal sector in general, was considered unimportant and unworthy of study. All countries were viewed as on a universal and linear trajectory towards formalization. Endeavour in the informal sector was thus viewed as a minor and declining remnant of an earlier mode of production which would naturally and inevitably disappear, and was associated with 'underdevelopment' and 'backwardness' (Geertz, 1963; Gilbert, 1998; Lewis, 1959).

Over the past few decades however, it has been widely recognized that the informal sector in general and informal entrepreneurship in particular, is an extensive and persistent feature in many developing countries (Autio and Fu, 2015; Williams, 2014a, 2014b, 2015a, 2015b). In recent years, therefore, a new sub-discipline of entrepreneurship scholarship has emerged focused on informal entrepreneurship (Dau and Cuervo-Cazurra, 2014; Kistruck et al., 2015; Siqueira et al., 2014; Thai and Turkina, 2014; Webb et al., 2009, 2013, 2014; Williams and Martinez, 2014). This literature has analyzed not only the nature of entrepreneurship, including who participates (Hudson et al., 2012; Thai and Turkina, 2014; Williams and Martinez-Perez, 2014) and their motives, including whether they are necessity-and/or opportunity-driven (Adom, 2014; Barsoum, 2015; Franck, 2012; Maloney, 2004; Perry et al., 2007), but also its magnitude, including the varying prevalence of informal entrepreneurship cross-nationally (Autio and Fu, 2015; Thai and Turkina, 2014), the differing degrees of informalization of such entrepreneurs (De Castro et al., 2014; Williams and Shahid, 2015) and the determinants of informal sector entrepreneurship (Dau and Cuervo-Cazurra, 2014; Siqueira et al., 2014; Thai and Turkina, 2014).

There has also been a turn away from examining solely the negative impacts of informal sector entrepreneurship and towards highlighting some of the more positive contributions made by this realm. A catalyst for recognizing these more positive impacts has been the recognition that informal entrepreneurship is not always a necessity-driven endeavour, but often a matter of choice (Cross, 2000; Franck, 2012; Gërxhani, 2004; Maloney, 2004; Perry and Maloney, 2007; Snyder, 2004). The outcome has been a resultant shift in some developing economies away from an eradication approach and towards a policy approach which seeks to facilitate the formalization of informal entrepreneurship. In Part IV, the various chapters address different aspects regarding the magnitude and character of informal entrepreneurship in various countries, the varying views on its contributions to economic development and growth and the different policy approaches and measures being pursued in different contexts.

Entrepreneurship education and learning

In recent years, in recognition that fostering entrepreneurship and an enterprise culture is a key means of promoting economic development and growth, many developing countries have sought to shift beyond the traditional conception that entrepreneurs are born and not made, by developing entrepreneurship education. Part V contains chapters on entrepreneurship education in various countries and global regions.

These deal with how entrepreneurship education, which seeks to provide people with the knowledge, skills and motivation to encourage entrepreneurship, is being implemented in a variety of settings across the developing world from the primary and secondary school level to graduate university programmes. The intention in doing so is to enhance the level of entrepreneurship in recognition that wealth and a large proportion of jobs in economies are created by small businesses started by entrepreneurial individuals, and that entrepreneurship is therefore a key driver of economic development and growth.

The intention in doing so is not only to create an entrepreneurial mind-set amongst a greater number of individuals but also to increase an entrepreneurial intention as well as the skill-sets required by entrepreneurially minded individuals. How this entrepreneurship education and learning has been implemented in different contexts, as well as the barriers to implementing such entrepreneurship education, is therefore the subject matter of the chapters in Part V of this handbook. These chapters deal with multifarious issues ranging from organization learning in family firms and the role of social networks, through the problems involved in developing the capacity for entrepreneurship education in war-torn conflict zones, to how entrepreneurship education is taught and whether it has any real impact on the learners regarding their entrepreneurial intentions and business creation. The somewhat worrying finding, albeit from a limited range of developing world contexts, is that entrepreneurship education programmes currently appear to have an insignificant impact on the attitudes and entrepreneurial intentions of those subject to them. Whether this is due to the client groups served, the nature of the entrepreneurship education programmes being offered or other barriers is now badly in need of investigation.

Policy implications and synthesis

The final and concluding Part VI of this handbook provides a synthesis of the findings regarding entrepreneurship in developing countries and the implications for policy of the findings. The key finding demonstrates a need to move away from adopting what might be seen as western ideal-type conceptualizations of entrepreneurs as heroic super-hero figures and instead, to adopt a more lived practice approach to understanding entrepreneurship in developing world contexts.

Unless greater understanding is developed of the magnitude and distribution of entre-preneurship across populations, the multifarious forms that entrepreneurial endeavour takes in different contexts, who engages in what kinds of entrepreneurial endeavour, along with their motives and the barriers to participation, then it will be difficult for developing country governments to know what needs to be done to foster entrepreneurship in their countries. Given that entrepreneurship is widely recognized as a key driver for economic development and growth, and developing countries are so defined precisely because they are lagging behind the developed world in terms of their economic development and growth, this is far more important than some 'academic' issue (in the derogatory sense of little importance of value). Hopefully, this handbook will provide academics, policy-makers and others interested in fostering entrepreneurship in the developing world with an important primer that not only improves understanding of entrepreneurship but also what needs to be done about it. If the *Routledge Handbook of Entrepreneurship in Developing Economies* succeeds in doing this, then it will have achieved its objective.

References

Acs, Z. J. (2006). How is entrepreneurship good for economic growth? *Innovations*, 1(1), 97–107.

Adom, K. (2014). Beyond the marginalization thesis, an examination of the motivations of informal entrepreneurs in Sub-Saharan Africa: Insights from Ghana. *International Journal of Entrepreneurship and Innovation*, 15(2), 113–125

Aidis, R., Welter, F., Smallbone, D. and Isakova, N. (2007). Female entrepreneurship in transition economies: The case of Lithuania and Ukraine. *Feminist Economics*, 13(2), 157–183.

Austin, J., Stevenson, H. and Wei-Skillern, J. (2006). Social and commercial entrepreneurship: same, different or both? *Entrepreneurship Theory and Practice*, 31(1), 1–22.

Autio, E. and Fu, K. (2015). Economic and political institutions and entry into formal and informal entrepreneurship. *Asia Pacific Journal of Management*, 32(1), 67–94.

Barsoum, G. (2015). Striving for job security: the lived experience of employment informality among educated youth in Egypt. *International Journal of Sociology and Social Policy*, 35(5/6), 340–358.

Baty, G. (1990). *Entrepreneurship in the nineties*. London: Prentice Hall.

Baumol, W. J. and Blinder, A. (2008). *Macroeconomics: principles and policy*. Cincinnati, OH: South-Western Publishing.

Benz, M. (2009). Entrepreneurship as a non-profit seeking activity. *International Entrepreneurship and Management Journal*, 5(1), 23–44.

Bhatt, E (2006). *We are poor but so many: the story of self-employed women in India*. Oxford: Oxford University Press.

Bolton, B. and Thompson, J. (2000). *Entrepreneurs: talent, temperament, technique*. Oxford: Butterworth-Heinemann.

Bosma, N., Jones, K., Autio, K. and Levie, J. (2008). *Global entrepreneurship monitor: 2007 executive report*. London: Global Entrepreneurship Monitor Consortium.

Brockhaus, R. H. and Horowitz, P. S. (1986). The psychology of the entrepreneur. *Entrepreneurship Theory and Practice*, 23(2), 29–45.

Burns, P. (2001). *Entrepreneurship and small business*. Basingstoke: Palgrave.

Carr, M. and Chen, M. (2002). Globalization and the informal economy: how global trade and investment impact on the working poor. Geneva: The Informal Economy Working Paper No. 1, Policy Integration Department, International Labor Office.

Charmes, J. (1998). Informal sector, poverty and gender: a review of empirical evidence. Background paper for World Bank, World Development Report 2000. Washington, D.C.

Chell, E., Haworth, J. and Brearly, S. (1991). *The entrepreneurial personality: concepts, cases and categories*. London: Routledge.

Chen, M., Sebstad, J. and Connell, L. (1999). Counting the invisible workforce: The case of homebased workers. *World Development*, 27(3), 603–610.

Chen, M., Carr, M. and Vanek, J. (2004). *Mainstreaming informal employment and gender in poverty reduction: a handbook for policymakers and other stakeholders*. London: Commonwealth Secretariat.

Cooper, A. C. (1981). Strategic management: new ventures and small businesses. *Long Range Planning*, 14(5), 39–45.

Cross, J. C. (2000). Street vendors, modernity and postmodernity: conflict and compromise in the global economy. *International Journal of Sociology and Social Policy*, 20(1), 29–51.

Dau, L.A. and Cuervo-Cazurra, A. (2014). To formalize or not to formalize: entrepreneurship and pro-market institutions. *Journal of Business Venturing*, 29(4), 668–686.

De Castro J. O., Khavul, S. and Bruton, G. D. (2014). Shades of grey: how do informal firms navigate between macro and meso institutional environments? *Strategic Entrepreneurship Journal*, 8(1), 75–94.

De Soto, H. (1989). *The other path: the economic answer to terrorism*. London: Harper and Row.

Dees, J. G. (1998). *The meaning of social entrepreneurship*, Durham, NC: Duke University Press.

Dees, J. G. and Anderson, B. B. (2003). For-profit social ventures. *International Journal of Entrepreneurship Education*, 2(1), 1–26.

Defourny, J. and Nyssens, M. (2008). Social enterprise in Europe: recent trends and developments. *Social Enterprise Journal*, 4(3), 202–228.

Denzau, A.T. and North, D. (1994). Shared mental models: ideologies and institutions. *Kyklos*, 47, 3–30.

Fawzi, C (2003). Gender, poverty and employment in the Arab region. Geneva: Capacity-Building Program on Gender, Poverty and Employment, Discussion Paper, International Labor Office.

Franck, A. K. (2012). Factors motivating women's informal micro-entrepreneurship: experiences from Penang, Malaysia. *International Journal of Gender and Entrepreneurship*, 4(1), 65–78.

Galera, G. and Borzega, C. (2009). Social enterprise: an international overview of its conceptual evolution and legal implementation. *Social Enterprise Journal*, 5(3), 210–228.

Geertz, C. (1963) *Peddlers and princes: social change and economic modernization in two Indonesian towns*. Chicago: University of Chicago Press.

Gërxhani, K (2004). The informal sector in developed and less developed countries: a literature survey. *Public Choice*, 120(3–4), 267–300.

Gilbert, A. (1998). *The Latin American city*. London: Latin American Bureau.

Harding, R., Brooksbank, D., Hart, M., Jones-Evans, D., Levie, J., Reilly, J. O. and Walker, J. (2005). *Global entrepreneurship monitor United Kingdom 2005*. London: London Business School.

Helmke, G. and Levitsky, S. (2004). Informal institutions and comparative politics: a research agenda. *Perspectives on Politics*, 2(4), 725–740.

Hudson, J, Williams, C. C., Orviska, M. and Nadin, S. (2012) Evaluating the impact of the informal economy on businesses in South East Europe: some lessons from the 2009 World Bank Enterprise Survey. *The South-East European Journal of Economics and Business*, 7(1), 99–110.

Hynes, B. (2009). Growing the social enterprise: issues and challenges. *Social Enterprise Journal*, 5(2), 114–125.

ILO (2002) *Decent work and the informal economy*. Geneva: International Labour Office.

ILO (2006). *Decent work for women and men in the informal economy: profile and good practices in Cambodia*. Geneva: International Labor Office.

Kanter, R. M. (1983) *The change masters*. New York: Simon and Schuster.

Ketchen, D. J., Ireland, R. D. and Webb, J. W. (2014). Towards a research agenda for the informal economy: a survey of the Strategic Entrepreneurship Journals Editorial Board. *Strategic Entrepreneurship Journal*, 8, 95–100.

Khan, E. A. and Quaddus, M. (2015) Examining the influence of business environment on socio-economic performance of informal microenterprises: content analysis and partial least square approach. *International Journal of Sociology and Social Policy*, 35 (3/4), 273–288.

Kistruck, G. M., Webb, J. W., Sutter, C. J. and Bailey, A. V. G. (2015). The double-edged sword of legitimacy in base-of-the-pyramid markets. *Journal of Business Venturing*, 30(3), 436–451.

La Porta, R. and Shleifer, A. (2008). The unofficial economy and economic development. *Brookings Papers on Economic Activity*, 47(1), 123–135.

La Porta, R. and Shleifer, A. (2014). Informality and development. *Journal of Economic Perspectives*, 28(3), 109–126.

Lewis, A. (1959). *The theory of economic growth*. London: Allen and Unwin.

Lyon, F. and Sepulveda, L. (2009). Mapping social enterprises: past approaches, challenges and future directions. *Social Enterprise Journal*, 5(1), 83–94.

Maloney, W. F. (2004). Informality revisited. *World Development*, 32(7), 1159–1178.

Maritz, A (2004). New Zealand necessity entrepreneurs. *International Journal of Entrepreneurship and Small Business*, 1(3–4), 255–264.

Mathias, B. D., Lux, S., Crook, T. R., Autry, C. and Zaretzki, R. (2014). Competing against the unknown: the impact of enabling and constraining institutions on the informal economy. *Journal of Business Ethics*, http://dx.doi.org/10.1007/s10551-013-2030-6. Accessed 16 May 2015.

Mehrotra, S. and Biggeri, M. (2002). Social protection in the informal economy: Home-based women workers and outsourced manufacturing in Asia. Florence: Innocenti Working Paper no. 97, UNICEF Innocenti Research Unit.

Minniti, M., Bygrave, W. and Autio, E. (2006). *Global entrepreneurship monitor: 2005 executive report*. London: London Business School.

Nelson, N. (1997). How women and men get by and still get by, only not so well: the sexual division of labor in the informal sector of a Nairobi squatter settlement. In *Cities in the developing world: issues, theory, policy*, J. Gugler (ed.), 141–165. Oxford: Oxford University Press.

Nicholls, A. and Cho, A. (2006). Social entrepreneurship: the structuration of a field. In *Social entrepreneurship: new models of sustainable social change*, A. Nicholls, (ed.), 99–118. Oxford: Oxford University Press.

North, D. C. (1990). *Institutions, institutional change and economic performance*. Cambridge: Cambridge University Press.

Nwabuzor, A. (2005). Corruption and development: new initiatives in economic openness and strengthened rule of law. *Journal of Business Ethics*, 59(1/2), 121–138.

Perry, G. E. and Maloney, W. F. (2007). Overview – informality: exit and exclusion. In *Informality: exit and exclusion*, G. E. Perry, W. F. Maloney, O. S. Arias, P. Fajnzylber, A. D. Mason and J. Saavedra-Chanduvi (eds.), pp. 1–20. Washington DC: World Bank.

Perry, G. E., Maloney, W. F., Arias, O. S., Fajnzylber, P., Mason, A. D., and Saavedra-Chanduvi, S. (2007). *Informality: exit and exclusion*. Washington DC: World Bank.

Perunović, Z. (2005). Introducing opportunity-based entrepreneurship in a transition economy. Michigan: Policy Brief 39, William Davidson Institute, University of Michigan.

Puffer, S. M., McCarthy, D. J. and Boisot, M. (2010). Entrepreneurship in Russia and China: the impact of formal institutional voids. *Entrepreneurship Theory and Practice*, 34(3), 441–467.

Reynolds, P., Camp, S. M., Bygrave, W. D., Autio, E. and Hay, M. (2001). *Global entrepreneurship monitor: 2001 executive monitor*. London: London Business School.

Reynolds, P., Bygrave, W. D., Autio, E. and Hay, M. (2002). *Global entrepreneurship monitor: 2002 executive monitor*. London: London Business School.

Rouse, M. and Dallenbach, U. (1999). Rethinking research methods for the resource-based perspective: isolating sources of sustainable competitive advantage. *Strategic Management Journal*, 20, 487–494.

Scott, W. R. (1995) *Institutions and organizations*. Thousand Oaks, CA: Sage

Sine, W. D. and David, R. J. (2010). Institutions and entrepreneurship. In *Institutions and entrepreneurship: research in the sociology of work*, W. D. Sine and R. J. David (eds.), pp. 1–26. Bingley: Emerald.

Siqueira, A. C. O., Webb, J. and Bruton, G. D. (2014). Informal entrepreneurship and industry conditions. *Entrepreneurship Theory and Practice*, doi: 10.1111/etap.12115.

Smallbone, D. and Welter, F. (2004). Entrepreneurship in transition economies: necessity or opportunity driven? www.babson.edu/entrep/fer/BABSON2003/XXV/XXV-S8/xxv-s8.htm. Accessed 9 April 2013.

Snyder, K. A. (2004). Routes to the informal economy in New York's East village: crisis, economics and identity. *Sociological Perspectives*, 47(2), 215–240.

Sutter, C. J., Webb, J. W., Kistruck, G. M. and Bailey, A. V. G. (2013). Entrepreneurs'. responses to semi-formal illegitimate institutional arrangements. *Journal of Business Venturing*, 28(5), 743–758.

Thai, M. T. T. and Turkina, E. (2014). Macro-level determinants of formal entrepreneurship versus informal entrepreneurship. *Journal of Business Venturing*, 29(4), 490–510.

Thompson, J. L. (2008). Social enterprise and social entrepreneurship: where have we reached? A summary of issues and discussion points. *Social Enterprise Journal*, 4(2), 149–161.

Vu, T. T. (2014). Institutional Incongruence and the Informal Economy: an Empirical Analysis. Paper presented at the European Public Choice Society meeting, Cambridge. http://www.econ.cam. ac.uk/epcs2014/openconf/modules/request.php?module=oc_programandaction=summary.phpan did=54. Accessed 18 May 2015.

Webb, J. W., Tihanyi, L., Ireland, R. D. and Sirmon, D. G. (2009). You say illegal, I say legitimate: entrepreneurship in the informal economy. *Academy of Management Review*, 34(3), 492–510.

Webb, J. W., Bruton, G. D., Tihanyi, L. and Ireland, R. D. (2013). Research on entrepreneurship in the informal economy: framing a research agenda. *Journal of Business Venturing*, 28(5), 598–614.

Webb, J. W., Ireland, R. D. and Ketchen D. J. (2014). Towards a greater understanding of entre-preneurship and strategy in the informal economy. *Strategic Entrepreneurship Journal*, 8(1), 1–15.

Williams, C. C. (2007). Entrepreneurs operating in the informal economy: necessity or opportunity driven? *Journal of Small Business and Entrepreneurship*, 20(3), 309–320.

Williams, C. C. (2008). Beyond necessity-driven versus opportunity-driven entrepreneurship: a study of informal entrepreneurs in England, Russia and Ukraine. *International Journal of Entrepreneurship and Innovation*, 9, 157–166.

Williams, C. C. (2009). The motives of off-the-books entrepreneurs: necessity- or opportunity-driven? *International Entrepreneurship and Management Journal*, 5(2), 203–217.

Williams, C. C. (2014a). Out of the shadows: a classification of economies by the size and character of their informal sector. *Work, Employment and Society*, 28(5), 735–753.

Williams, C. C. (2014b).. Explaining cross-national variations in the commonality of informal sector entrepreneurship: an exploratory analysis of 38 emerging economies. *Journal of Small Business and Entrepreneurship*, 27(2), 191–212.

Williams, C. C. (2015a). Explaining cross-national variations in the scale of informal employment: an exploratory analysis of 41 less developed economies. *International Journal of Manpower*, 36(2), 118–135.

Williams, C. C. (2015b). Out of the margins: classifying economies by the prevalence and character of employment in the informal economy. *International Labour Review*, 154(3).

Williams, C. C. and Gurtoo, A. (2013). Beyond entrepreneurs as heroic icons of capitalism: a case study of street entrepreneurs in India. *International Journal of Entrepreneurship and Small Business*, 19(4), 421–437.

Williams, C. C. and Lansky, M. (2013). Informal employment in developed and emerging economies: perspectives and policy responses. *International Labour Review*, 152(3–4), 355–380.

Williams, C. C. and Martinez-Perez, A. (2014). Is the informal economy an incubator for new enterprise creation? A gender perspective. *International Journal of Entrepreneurial Behaviour and Research*, 20(1), 4–19.

Williams, C. C. and Shahid, M. S. (2015). Informal entrepreneurship and institutional theory: explaining the varying degrees of (in)formalization of entrepreneurs in Pakistan. *Entrepreneurship and Regional Development*, dx.doi.org/10.1080/08985626.2014.963889.

Williams, C. C., Round, J. and Rodgers, P. (2006). Beyond necessity- and opportunity-driven entrepreneurship: some case study evidence from Ukraine. *Journal of Business and Entrepreneurship*, 18(2), 22–34.

Williams, C. C., Round, J. and Rodgers, P. (2009). Evaluating the motives of informal entrepreneurs: some lessons from Ukraine. *Journal of Developmental Entrepreneurship*, 14(1), 59–71.

Williams, C. C., Round, J. and Rodgers, P. (2010). Explaining the off-the-books enterprise culture of Ukraine: reluctant or willing entrepreneurship? *International Journal of Entrepreneurship and Small Business*, 10(2), 65–80.

PART I

Institutional environment of entrepreneurship

2

THE INSTITUTIONAL ENVIRONMENT OF ENTREPRENEURSHIP IN DEVELOPING COUNTRIES

An introductory overview

Colin C. Williams and Anjula Gurtoo

Both the prevalence and nature of entrepreneurship are heavily influenced by its institutional context. Entrepreneurship, after all, is a socially constructed behaviour which is a product of the social environment, or what is here termed the institutional context, in which it occurs. If there is no culture of entrepreneurship in a population for example, and no role models for others to learn from, then the prevalence of entrepreneurship may be low. Consequently, it is crucial to examine the institutional context, especially given that this may markedly vary across the developing world. By institutions, we here follow institutional theory in defining these as 'the rules of the game' and norms which businesses in general and entrepreneurial endeavours more particularly operate within (Baumol and Blinder, 2008; Denzau and North, 1994; North, 1990). These institutions prescribe the acceptability of activities (Mathias et al., 2014) and importantly, these are of two distinct varieties. First, all societies have formal institutions (i.e., codified laws and regulations) that define the legal rules of the game. Second, all societies also have informal institutions which are the 'socially shared rules, usually unwritten, that are created, communicated and enforced outside of officially sanctioned channels' (Helmke and Levitsky, 2004: 727). Formal institutions thus prescribe what we here term 'state morality' about what is acceptable, whilst informal institutions prescribe what we here term 'civic morality'.

Until now, the study of the institutional context within which entrepreneurship takes place has been approached in two different ways. A first school of thought explains the extent and character of entrepreneurship in any context by asserting that this is associated with the quality and intensity of formal institutions. For instance, when considering developing countries, this school of thought often discusses the ease of registration, the existence of legal bureaucratic impediments, barriers to entrepreneurship, the level of property rights protection and the quality of government institutions and formal services available to entrepreneurs. The outcome is to pinpoint various formal institutional constraints which hinder the emergence and growth of entrepreneurship in developing economies, such as the high costs of establishing a formal business venture, the over-burdensome regulations, high taxes and extensive corruption prevalent in the public sector (De Soto, 1989; Nwabuzor, 2005), as well as the formal institutional voids including the inadequate or weak legal systems and contract enforcement regimes in existence in developing countries (Khan and Quaddus, 2015; Puffer et al., 2010; Sutter et al., 2013).

Rather than focus upon the role and quality of the formal regulatory institutional conditions, a second school of institutional thought instead explores the cognitive and normative institutions by examining the informal institutions in existence (Scott, 2008) and how these inter-relate with the formal institutions. Indeed, in this school of thought, the relationship between formal and informal institutions influences the prevalence and nature of entrepreneurship in any particular context (Vu, 2014; Webb et al., 2009, 2013, 2014). When formal and informal institutions are in symmetry, state morality and civic morality will complement each other. When informal institutions are not fully in symmetry with formal institutions however, what is deemed acceptable in terms of the norms, values and beliefs of the population may differ from what is deemed legal from the viewpoint of the formal institutions. In other words, some entrepreneurial activities may be deemed illegal from the viewpoint of formal institutions but socially legitimate in terms of the informal institutions of the society in which they take place (Kistruck et al., 2015; Siqueira et al., 2014; Sutter et al., 2013; Webb et al., 2009).The consequent argument is that when symmetry exists between formal and informal institutions, entrepreneurship may prosper.

Part I of this handbook addresses issues related to understanding the institutional context within which entrepreneurship is embedded in developing countries and what types of institutional contexts enable entrepreneurship to thrive and what institutional contexts lead to the emergence of different types of entrepreneurship. Each chapter thus reveals how entrepreneurship is a socially constructed behaviour conditioned by its institutional context.

In chapter 3 entitled 'Entrepreneurship, development and economic policy in Haiti' by Andrés Marroquín, how both formal institutions and informal institutions have shaped the prevalence and nature of entrepreneurship in Haiti is explored, including a review of the main obstacles that entrepreneurs face in this developing country. This includes pinpointing the weak formal institutions that hinder entrepreneurship and also the important role played by informal institutions, especially particular forms of religious belief found in Haiti, in shaping entrepreneurship.

Chapter 4, 'Entrepreneurship and SME development policy in a least developed country: lessons from Laos', by Balbir B. Bhasin, Sivakumar Venkataramany and Lee Keng Ng, reveals how the institutional context affects the prevalence and character of entrepreneurship in a one-party communist state. Although the government of Laos recognizes the important role that entrepreneurs play in the development of the economy and country, the infrastructure and formal institutions that might create a supportive environment for entrepreneurship are relatively undeveloped. There is shortage of power supply, many parts of the country do not have proper roads and transport access, and poverty and literacy are still a challenge, as the government makes the transition from a government-controlled to a privately held open system. Processes and procedures, control mechanisms and the legal structures to facilitate entrepreneurship are yet to be fully in place.

In chapter 5, 'Mapping entrepreneurial activities and entrepreneurial attitudes in Turkey', Esra Karadeniz and Özlem Özdemir reveal that not just institutions at the national level require investigation but also those at the regional and local level. Reporting one of the first analyses of entrepreneurial activity in Turkey at the sub-national level, this chapter presents, for the first time, data on regional variations in entrepreneurship and the different types of entrepreneurial activity (early stage entrepreneurial activity, opportunity-motivated entrepreneurial activity and necessity-motivated entrepreneurial activity) as well as entrepreneurial attitudes for the NUTS 2 level regions (Eurostat Nomenclature of Territorial Units for Statistics). Revealing the significant variations in entrepreneurial activity and attitudes at the national and regional levels in this country, the strong intimation is that there is a need to also consider the institutional context at a regional and local level when examining entrepreneurship.

Chapter 6, 'Regulative environment and entrepreneurial activity: insights from Sub-Saharan Africa', by Eldrede Kahiya and Rebecca Kennedy, explores the connection between the regulative institutional environment and the capacity for entrepreneurship. To do so, they test the hypothesis that the better the quality of the regulative institutional environment, the higher is the level of entrepreneurial activity. Reporting cross-national data from the World Bank's Ease of Doing Business database, they find support for this hypothesis, and call for further studies of the normative and cognitive dimensions of the institutional environment, as well as how the institutional environment influences the types of entrepreneurial activities.

In chapter 7, 'Nascent enterprises and growth aspirations in a post-conflict environment: the role of social capital', Anna Rebmann, Adnan Efendic and Tomasz Mickiewicz relate social capital to the growth aspirations of owners and managers of young firms in a post-conflict economy. They argue that social capital is best understood as a multi-dimensional construct and introduce the idea that ethnic pluralism is a key component of social capital in ethnically diverse societies. Testing hypotheses on data from nascent enterprises in Bosnia and Herzegovina, they find that ethnic pluralism, entrepreneurs' trust in institutions and having strong social ties outside the family are associated with higher firm growth aspirations. Moreover, the relationship between social capital and entrepreneurial aspirations is also found to vary across local contexts.

Chapter 8 by Safal Batra and Neharika Vohra then deals with 'Planning as a means to innovation in entrepreneurial innovation in India'. While it is widely understood that organizations can improve their performance by becoming more innovative, research on what supports innovation is still underdeveloped. Drawing upon the literature, it was proposed that as simple a tool as strategic planning could support innovation in small and medium entrepreneurial firms. A study was designed to collect data from 123 small and medium entrepreneurial firms in Punjab on their planning processes. It was found that an emphasis on strategic planning was positively correlated with new products, processes, services, suppliers and markets, as well as new ways of organizing. The impact of strategic planning was also higher on radical as compared to incremental innovations. The implications of this research on the theory and practice of innovation for entrepreneurs in emerging economies is then discussed.

Chapter 9 on 'The failure of government policies to drive entrepreneurial performance in Croatia' by Will Bartlett examines how since the onset of the current economic crisis, Croatia has experienced six years of recession associated with low international competitiveness and a weak culture of entrepreneurship. This chapter discusses the failure of government policies to promote an entrepreneurial economy. While governments of all hues have tried to promote the spirit of entrepreneurship, given the context of clientelistic capitalism none of the measures has succeeded in driving forward an entrepreneurial economy with a high innovative potential and improved competitiveness on international markets. The entry of Croatia into the EU may bring about some improvement through new interventions to support entrepreneurship.

In chapter 10, 'Economic aspects of entrepreneurship: the case of Peru', by Matthew Bird, the challenges Peru has faced transitioning from a low-income to middle-income entrepreneurship policy is examined, with a focus on remaining contract enforcement challenges. In doing so, it offers a critical overview of entrepreneurship policy in Peru, while exploring the emerging area of middle-income entrepreneurship policy in general.

Finally, in chapter 11, 'Developing an entrepreneurship climate in Indonesia: a case study of batik as a cultural heritage', Vanessa Ratten examines the role of batik entrepreneurs by focusing on the Solo region located in Central Java as an area promoting cultural-based entrepreneurship that links social and sustainability initiatives. The role of artisans in making the batik in combination with the business development of the batik industry on a global scale is analyzed, along with the attachment of the Javanese people to making batik and their desire to keep the traditional weaving and batik techniques. Implications for developing country entrepreneurs interested in harnessing the informal institution of their cultural heritage as a way to grow businesses are discussed along with the theoretical implications for cultural entrepreneurship in developing countries.

References

Baumol, W. J. and Blinder, A. (2008). *Macroeconomics: principles and policy*. Cincinnati, OH: South-Western Publishing.

De Soto, H. (1989). *The other path: the economic answer to terrorism*. London: Harper and Row.

Denzau, A. T. and North, D. (1994). Shared mental models: ideologies and institutions. *Kyklos*, 47, 3–30.

Helmke, G. and Levitsky, S. (2004). Informal institutions and comparative politics: a research agenda. *Perspectives on Politics*, 2(4), 725–740.

Khan, E. A. and Quaddus, M. (2015). Examining the influence of business environment on socio-economic performance of informal microenterprises: content analysis and partial least square approach. *International Journal of Sociology and Social Policy*, 35 (3/4), 273–288.

Kistruck, G. M., Webb, J. W., Sutter, C. J. and Bailey, A. V. G. (2015). The double-edged sword of legitimacy in base-of-the-pyramid markets. *Journal of Business Venturing*, 30(3), 436–451.

Mathias, B. D., Sean, L., Crook, T. R., Autry, C. and Zaretzki, R. (2014). Competing against the unknown: the impact of enabling and constraining institutions on the informal economy. *Journal of Business Ethics*. doi 10.1007/s10551-013-2030-6. Accessed 16 May 2015.

North, D. C. (1990). *Institutions, institutional change and economic performance*. Cambridge: Cambridge University Press.

Nwabuzor, A. (2005). Corruption and development: new initiatives in economic openness and strengthened rule of law. *Journal of Business Ethics*, 59(1/2), 121–138.

Puffer, S. M., McCarthy, D. J. and Boisot, M. (2010). Entrepreneurship in Russia and China: the impact of formal institutional voids. *Entrepreneurship Theory and Practice*, 34(3), 441–467.

Scott, W. R. (2008 [1995]). *Institutions and organizations* (3rd ed.). Thousand Oaks: Sage.

Siqueira, A. C. O., Webb, J. and Bruton, G.D. (2014). Informal entrepreneurship and industry conditions. *Entrepreneurship Theory and Practice*. DOI: 10.1111/etap.12115.

Sutter, C. J., Webb, J. W., Kistruck, G. M. and Bailey, A. V. G. (2013). Entrepreneurs' responses to semiformal illegitimate institutional arrangements. *Journal of Business Venturing*, 28(5), 743–758.

Vu, T.T. (2014). Institutional incongruence and the informal economy: an empirical analysis. Paper presented at the European Public Choice Society meeting, Cambridge. http://www.econ.cam.ac.uk/epcs2014/openconf/modules/request.php?module=oc_programandaction=summary.phpandid=54. Accessed 18 May 2015.

Webb, J. W., Tihanyi, L., Ireland, R. D. and Sirmon, D. G. (2009). You say illegal, I say legitimate: entrepreneurship in the informal economy. *Academy of Management Review*, 34(3), 492–510.

Webb, J. W., Bruton, G. D., Tihanyi, L. and Ireland, R. D. (2013). Research on entrepreneurship in the informal economy: framing a research agenda. *Journal of Business Venturing*, 28(5), 598–614.

Webb, J. W., Ireland, R. D. and Ketchen D. J. (2014). Towards a greater understanding of entrepreneurship and strategy in the informal economy. *Strategic Entrepreneurship Journal*, 8(1), 1–15.

3

ENTREPRENEURSHIP, DEVELOPMENT AND ECONOMIC POLICY IN HAITI[1]

Andrés Marroquín

The French colony of St. Domingo [now Haiti] was established by pirates and free-booters, who, for a long time, neither required the protection, nor acknowledged the authority of France; and when that race of banditti became so far citizens as to acknowledge this authority, it was for a long time necessary to exercise it with very great gentleness. During this period the population and improvement of this colony increased very fast. Even the oppression of the exclusive company, to which it was for some time subjected, with all the other colonies of France, though it no doubt retarded, had not been able to stop its progress altogether. The course of its prosperity returned as soon as it was relieved from that oppression. It is now the most important of the sugar colonies of the West Indies, and its produce is said to be greater than that of all the English sugar colonies put together. The other sugar colonies of France are in general all very thriving.

Adam Smith ([1776] 1904)

Introduction

Entrepreneurship plays a key role in economic development and growth (Baumol and Strom, 2008). Innovation and creativity are its main features. Economic historians such as Ashton (1964) and Mokyr (2004) have examined the transformation of the industrial revolution and stressed the causal effect of invention and creativity on economic growth. Entrepreneurs create jobs, and they also produce goods and services and find new combinations of products and new sources of raw materials. Schumpeter (1982) wrote about a dynamic economy where new products displaced existing products from the market. He called this a process of 'creation-destruction'.

On the one hand, therefore, we have the 'Schumpeterian entrepreneur' – the individual who innovates, creates, and in the process, destroys. On the other hand, there is the 'Kirzenian entrepreneur' (after Kirzner, 1978) who is alert to opportunities in the market and takes advantage of disequilibria to make profits. Entrepreneurs matter not only for innovation and market satisfaction, but also because they pay taxes that are essential for the provision of basic public goods and services, given the presence of a government that manages resources with some level of efficiency and economic rationality. In the extreme hypothetical case of a

17

country without entrepreneurs, the treasury is empty and the government has to borrow to provide public goods and services, innovation is nil, jobs depend entirely on the government, and long-term economic growth is zero or negative.

This chapter describes entrepreneurship in Haiti and links it to economic development from two points of view: first, a comparative economics perspective, which presents different indicators and variables of Haiti and contrasts them with those of other countries in the region and the world, and second, an anthropological perspective, which looks at qualitative research and informal institutions in the country.

Haiti: a brief history

Haiti has a unique history. It was the richest colony in the western hemisphere and now is often called the poorest country in the same region (Marroquín, 2005). Slaves brought from Africa to work in the sugar plantations initially populated Haiti and to some extent spoke different languages. Campos (2010: 7) argues:

> The boom in the importation of slaves from Africa along the 18th century shows that about 20,000 slaves lived in Saint-Domingue in 1701. In 1753, this number surpassed 165,000 and in 1791, there were more than 600,000 slaves sustaining the whole process behind Saint-Domingue's sugarcane production. At this time, almost half of all sugar produced in the world was produced in the French colony of Saint-Domingue, one of the wealthiest in the Caribbean.

One of the few connections with Africa were religious institutions such as Voodoo. Voodoo was a new religion which helped unify the diversity of beliefs and has its origins among the slaves (Michel, 1996). Labour was exploited in an unimaginable way. Haiti became independent in 1804 and became the 'second new nation in the New World, after the USA' (Crist, 1952: 107). After that, political conflicts led to numerous coups, social unrest and various changes of constitution – around 23 different constitutions since 1804 (Marroquín, 2005: 75). Post-independence Haiti started as a society of peasant cultivators (Murray, 1980).

Haiti has been severely affected by natural disasters and strong government centralization in Port-Au-Prince. The official language in Haiti is French, which hardly 20 per cent of people speak. The prevalent language is Creole, which is not spoken by any of the neighbouring countries. The distinctiveness of the language is a barrier to trade across borders, even though farmers' markets on the border with the Dominican Republic are vibrant and many of the transactions between Dominicans and Haitians are undertaken via hand gestures.

In the next section a comparative economics perspective will be presented, which assumes that it is possible to compare different variables related to entrepreneurship and the way businesses operate in Haiti with other countries in this region and the rest of the world.

Entrepreneurship in Haiti: a comparative economics perspective

Haiti is a low-income country with a population of approximately 10.3 million people. The GDP per capita in current US$ is 820.[2] The Haitian economy mainly exports textiles: knit t-shirts (39 per cent of GDP), knit sweaters (24 per cent), non-knit men's suits (13 per cent), scrap iron (3.8 per cent), and non-knit men's shirts (2.3 per cent).[3] The top five imported products are rice (8.2 per cent), heavy pure woven cotton (5.5 per cent), knit t-shirts (5.5 per cent), raw sugar (3.1 per cent), and poultry meat (2.8 per cent).[4] The country ranks

Table 3.1 Haiti in the Doing Business Ranking[†]

Topics	DB 2015 Rank	DB 2014 Rank
Starting a business	188	187
Dealing with construction permits	132	188
Getting electricity	94	95
Registering property	175	176
Getting credit	171	169
Paying taxes	142	137
Trading across borders	142	147
Enforcing contracts	89	89
Resolving insolvency	189	189

[†]Doing Business: http://goo.gl/gW19TG.

123rd out of 144 in the Index of Economic Complexity. The infant mortality rate per 1,000 live births in 2010 was 70.4.[5] About 10.6 per cent of Haitians have access to the internet.[6]

Given the structure of the Haitian economy, most entrepreneurs operate in the agricultural and trade sectors, rather than manufacturing industry (see, for example, Nedje et al., 2013). Based on his study of a village in eastern Haiti, Murray (1980: 303) argues that males were gardeners and that most women were traders. The family economy however was mainly based on gardening. Table 3.1 presents where Haiti ranks in different categories of the World Bank *Doing Business* report among the 189 countries included.

According to the *World Bank* (2015) Doing Business Report, Haiti is ranked 188 out of 189 countries in the 'Starting a business' category. Only Myanmar has an inferior performance (see Table 3.2).

The *2014 Index of Economic Freedom* reports, moreover, that 'completing licensing requirements takes over 1,000 days'.[7] Therefore, there are significant institutional constraints on starting a legitimate business in Haiti.

Barriers to entrepreneurship in Haiti

There are several barriers to entrepreneurship in Haiti that in turn, affect one another. For example, political instability affects the investment climate and weakens economic institutions. In this section, these barriers are reviewed.

Table 3.2 Starting a Business in Haiti, Doing Business 2015[†]

Indicator	Haiti	Latin America & Caribbean	OECD
Procedures (number)	12	8.3	4.8
Time (days)	97	30.1	9.2
Cost (percent of income per capita)	246.7	31.1	3.4
Paid-in min. capital (percent of income per capita)	17.6	3.2	8.8

[†]Doing Business: http://goo.gl/gW19TG.

Problems with electricity

The lack of reliable electricity is the source of problems in many parts of Haiti. It impedes refrigeration. People cannot store food and as a consequence, they make more trips to shops that have generators. More importantly, Haitians have to cook every meal. As a result, they use charcoal intensely, which is the main cause of forest depletion.

The lack of electricity also increases the costs of doing business in Jérémie. Some entrepreneurs use several sources of energy: generators, batteries, solar panels and others, which can be very expensive. *The 2014 Index of Economic Freedom* indicates: 'The state-owned and -subsidized electrical utility consumes 12 percent of the national budget but serves only 25 percent of the population.'[8]

Unreliable electricity also affects education. The use of computers in schools is limited. Students cannot study at home at night. In fact, the main study area at night in several towns is the central park. At around seven and eight at night, many students gather under the solar-powered lamps to read their books and notebooks. It is a charming sight but also a sad one.

The lack of electricity has other hidden costs that might not be obvious but do affect productivity. The heat is dry and intense. During the high temperatures in the day, say from eleven to five in the afternoon, the heat is tiring. No matter what one is doing, the heat slows things down. One could say that Haitians have lived in these temperatures for hundreds of years. But they complain often about the heat.

Weak institutions

Institutions are the rules of the game that dictate how social life is organized (North, 1990). They can be formal (written in the legal codes) or informal (common practices that are not written in the legal codes). Institutions can facilitate conflict resolution and the respect for property rights is conducive to entrepreneurial activity and economic development (Harper, 2007).

In Haiti, formal institutions to solve conflicts do not work properly. The courts can be very slow, if they work at all. Entrepreneurs have scant legal mechanisms available when others do not comply with business agreements. This is one of the reasons why the credit market is limited. Formal contracts are scarce. Due to political reasons, the limited resources of the state are unevenly distributed across the country, being overrepresented in the capital, Port-au-Prince (Gros, 2011).

The *2014 Index of Economic Freedom* points out: 'Most commercial disputes are settled out of court if at all. There is no comprehensive civil registry. Bona fide and undisputed property titles are virtually nonexistent.'[9] In both dimensions of the rule of law (property rights and freedom from corruption), Haiti ranks as a 'repressed' country.[10] Haiti scores 19 out of 100 in the Corruption Perceptions Index (CPI), and it ranks 161 out of 175 countries (7 per cent percentile rank).[11]

Weak institutions are a cause and effect of what Marroquín (2005: 75–76) calls the political economy of dictatorship in Haiti. He argues:

> During the almost 200 years of its existence, the Haitian Republic has witnessed the swearing-in of 42 chiefs of State. Out of these 42, 7 remained in power for more than 10 years, 9 declared themselves presidents for life, 11 remained in power for less than one year, and 29 were either assassinated or forced to seek exile. Paraphrasing Gordon Tullock the relevant question is 'why so much instability?' As suggested by

Tullock (1974), successions in dictatorial regimes are particularly violent, and this has been the case in Haiti. Almost every dictator has been a 'selfish dictator' (including the Duvaliers—'Papa Doc' and 'Baby Doc') all with the purpose of maximizing benefits in the short run paying the costs of less security in the long run.

Marroquín (2005) argues that institutions in Haiti are weak because the supply and the demand of institutions are low (or relatively low). The supply of institutions comes in part from the government (e.g., institutional enforcement). The problem, however, is that Haiti's history has been plagued with political instability and conflict for power between political incumbents and various opposition groups. Without peace, as Adam Smith rightly said, there is no basis for prosperity. The demand for good institutions comes in part also from civil society. However, the level of education in Haiti is low and their knowledge of what good institutions look like is somewhat limited, hence the demand of good institutions is also low. As a result, the interaction of the supply and the demand of good institutions in Haiti is much lower than other countries in the region. Sparse entrepreneurial activity is an important result.

Secure property rights is one of the main components of an institutional arrangement. Property rights are linked to other aspects of the economy such as credit, investment, and of course, entrepreneurship. The land tenure in Haiti is characterized by three arrangements: (1) land fragmentation, which takes place after successive inheritance across generations, (2) sharecropping, which happens when several people, besides the owner, work the land, and (3) renting (Dolisca, 2003). Sharecropping and renting are different in the sense that renters have ownership over the harvest, and they have to pay the rent. Sharecroppers usually do not pay rent but they have to share the harvest with the owner (Dolisca, 2003: 23). In his study of a forest located in southern Haiti Dolisca (ibid.) argues:

> residents in Forêt des Pins Reserve who depend on government land to reside, farm and graze perceive that they do not have secure rights on that land. As such, they hesitate to make long-term investment of planting trees and management. Insecure and ill defined land rights will prevent farmers to get credit because they cannot use insecure land as guarantee to acquire low interest and long-term institutional credit. As a result, households may not be able to make long-term investments such as ecosystem management.

Lack of credit

Institutional weakness has negative consequences in other markets, such as the loanable funds market. Indeed, the lack of clearly defined property rights limits the capacity of land and other tangible assets to serve as a guarantee for formal credit in the financial sector (De Soto, 2003). In Haiti, property rights are not clearly defined (Marroquín, 2005), there are tensions over land ownership and in general there is no certainty of who owns what. Kushner (2015: 3) describes the current situation:

> The tension [over land control] played out over the past two centuries with governments often bequeathing parcels of land to various groups, only sometimes to take them back later, subsequent disputes over territory, and little regard for formal title throughout. Peasants in rural Haiti generally worked the land under an informal system of tenancy, in which they established de-facto ownership over small plots of land, then joined their plots with their neighbors', usually members of their extended

families, and farmed the land collectively. The land would typically remain under the name of just one family member—but no records of these arrangements were provided to the state.

Many people have sometimes claimed to own the same parcel of land, while other plots of land had no identifiable owner. Cases in which title could be established are rare. A 1997 study, conducted by the U.N. Food and Agriculture Organization and Haiti's agriculture ministry, estimated that 95 per cent of all land sales in rural Haiti had been conducted without going through legal formalities.

In their assessment of women's entrepreneurship in Haiti, Nedjé et al. (2013: 64) argue:

> Financing businesses is one of the biggest issues for entrepreneurs in Haiti. Thus, many women, existing or aspiring entrepreneurs, affirm that the lack of credit is the major problem for developing small and medium enterprises (SME) in the development stage. There are not many types of credit at the commercial banks that are available to small businesses.

The credit gap has been partially covered by microfinance organizations. Microcredit, however, goes to retail and not production. About 74 per cent of microcredit goes to women (Nedjé et al., 2013, 65). Low financial education and skills to prepare business plans are an important barrier to get credit. To the barriers mentioned above, we should add a complicated tax system, high transaction costs, and lack of trust.

A non-traditional anthropological view of entrepreneurship in Haiti

In this section, we go beyond the numbers and see what entrepreneurs do on the ground and how the economy works in very harsh circumstances – at least for the external observer. The situation in Haiti is difficult, but we have to remember that for the 'typical' Haitian, Haiti is the only country s/he has lived in. The only standard of comparison is his/her society. Given the circumstances, people do the best they can. In fact, even in difficult and unstable socioeconomic, political and environmental circumstances people do what is within their means to become innovative entrepreneurs in Haiti (Campos, 2010).

With Haitian history in mind, we should resist the desire to compare Haiti with other countries. It would be like comparing apples and oranges. To understand Haiti and the Haitian entrepreneurs, what we can do is the following:

1. Measure the socioeconomic performance of Haiti in relation to itself.
2. Measure the entrepreneurial success with a different scale. A successful entrepreneur in Haiti might be considered an average, or below average, entrepreneur in another country.
3. Informal economy and informal interactions dominate in Haiti – according to one estimate 95 per cent of businesses are informal (Barrau, 2013) and Marroquín (2005: 67) indicates 'Nearly 75 per cent of the Haitian labor force is engaged in small-scale subsistence farming', and other sources claim '60 percent of households depend on farming for their livelihood' (Trade in Haiti, 2013).Therefore we should concentrate on the informal mechanisms available to people to make a living in Haiti.
4. The starting point of an individual in Haiti is very different from the starting point of a person in many, or most, countries. Just by being born in Haiti, the person is in relative

disadvantage. Their cognitive abilities might be affected by the lack of clean water, malnutrition, etc. That means that surviving in Haiti and succeeding is more difficult than in many other countries in the world.

5.   The state in Haiti is very weak and weaker than in almost any other country in Latin America (Gros, 2011). This means that most of the socioeconomic transactions happen outside the realm of the state. The informal mechanisms are the only means to navigate society, its economic and social environment.

6.   The level of entrepreneurship in Haiti should be higher, but given the factors already mentioned, what exists now is probably the most efficient level of entrepreneurship.

Case examples of entrepreneurship in Haiti

There has been an effort to promote entrepreneurship in Haiti. Some of the initiatives come from the private sector. For example, Digicel, the largest foreign investor in the country and a phone company with headquarters in Jamaica and operations in the Caribbean, Central America and Oceania gives the 'entrepreneur of the year' award. The 2013 winner was the founder of health care centres that provide micro-health insurance for a cost of US$ 10 a month to around 400,000 clients.[12] Other successful entrepreneurs have businesses in the apparel industry, which is the main exporter in Haiti, and mango processing (Fairbanks, 2010).

Some successful entrepreneurs have established insurance businesses. Such is the case of Alternative Insurance Company which targets high-income individuals, families and businesses (Fairbanks, 2010; The Power Of Insurance, 2013). The company has 102,000 clients and creates 102 direct jobs.[13] GaMa is another successful business that sells computer hardware and internet services (Loten, 2010). Its founder, Mathias Pierre, has been featured in several newspapers and magazines as someone who overcame the obstacles of poverty and became a millionaire businessperson. He tells his story in the book, *The Power of a Dream: One Man's Determination to Pursue his Ideals* (Pierre, 2011). More recently Pierre started a business, KayTek, which offers affordable housing in Haiti (Moloney, 2012).

Another successful start-up is the information technology company Solutions, SA. They support other companies with information technology (IT) solutions. The company has received many awards and the founder, Kurt Jean-Charles, creates software applications for over a million cell phone subscribers in Haiti (Fairbanks, 2010).

Most of the larger entrepreneurs run their operations from Port-au-Prince. For the sake of balance, I also include below some brief entrepreneurship cases from the city of Jérémie in southwest Haiti. Most of the businesses in Jérémie are intermediaries who buy and sell consumption goods. Agriculture is the main production activity. The province of the Grand'Anse is located in a part of Haiti where there are forests. Some argue that in Haiti only 2 per cent of the territory has tree cover and this is located in the Grand'Anse. The presence of an intense rainy season makes production of goods and vegetables possible. Mangos, bananas, pineapples, as well as several vegetables are available in the market.

The religious entrepreneur

The entrepreneur is a Catholic Priest who runs several shops that sell grains, cereals, vegetables, and much more to people in the rural areas. He sees himself as a manager, and tries to run the shops in the most efficient way possible without affecting the mission of service. 'A manager is hired to solve problems,' he says, 'which I have to do without blaming those who were before me and caused the problems. The past is gone and one has to perform without looking back.' He says that self-discipline made him accomplish his goals.

The intermediary of consumption goods

An entrepreneur who imports consumption goods received us in his apartment. His business is located by the main road that enters the city. It is a busy area of Jérémie, and a bit chaotic during the day. His apartment is on the upper floor of one of the houses by the main street. The serene atmosphere inside the apartment was in striking contrast with the loud and hectic outside. He told us that one of the main challenges of doing business in Jérémie was the difficulty of finding people he can trust, and people who can accomplish what is needed.

He started off with a small amount of capital when he was in his twenties. Nowadays he has several stores and storage facilities, and his family owns a boat that he uses to transport merchandise from Port-au-Prince, Jamaica and other places. In the storage facilities downstairs he had oil, rice, sodas and juices. In the back room there were a few bags of cement; they were part of a large lot he had imported from Jamaica, most of which had been sold. He stressed that he imports large quantities. For example, he imports containers of 400 boxes of soda. He is not interested in importing small amounts. In a few days he is out of products and has to import more.

The senior entrepreneur

We interviewed the oldest entrepreneur in town. He owns a hotel and a convenience store. He is over 90 years old, and came to Jérémie from Port-au-Prince without much money. He was a founder member of the first association of entrepreneurs in town, and proudly showed us the 'Annales de la Ville de Jérémie'.

The entrepreneur returnee

Another entrepreneur had returned from Montreal and started a pizza business in Port-au-Prince. Crime in the capital was high and he decided to come to Jérémie, his hometown, where he saw business opportunities and found a more relaxing way of life. He is making repairs to his big restaurant that will have a bar and a dancing floor. He also owns a gas station.

The bank manager

We also interviewed the director of a large Haitian bank. He said that currently the bank is not offering credit in Jérémie. He was exploring the market to start loan operations in the town, but it sounded uncertain. In other parts of Haiti the bank gives credit but only to owners of existing businesses. The bank does not take the risk of lending to start-ups. This might be due to the failure rate being high and credit warrantees being scarce. In all of Haiti, land tenure is unclear. This is an area where more research is needed.

The ice cream entrepreneur

Another entrepreneur owns the only ice cream shop in Jérémie. He brings the ice cream from Port-au-Prince by boat. He has developed a way for the ice cream to last the three-day trip without melting; this technology is the key to his success he said. The lack of electricity is his main problem. In his shop he keeps the ice cream from melting using a gasoline-powered generator and batteries. To the question of what he thought about Jérémie having 4G communications technology but not electricity and water, he said: 'this is Haiti, anything is possible.'

The computer intermediary

We interviewed the owner of a hardware and software store. He sells computers, printers, USBs, etc. He obtained a B.A. in agriculture in the US, but during his studies he became interested in computer sciences. He went back to Haiti and started working for an international NGO in the agriculture sector. After some time he decided that he wanted to do something on his own. He noticed that no computer or repair shops existed in Jérémie and decided to import computers and equipment from the US, and started repairing computers as well. In some cases, he takes them to the US for repair. He also noticed the need for more training on computing and software and opened an academy. He started with very few students, now he has over one hundred. He said that the lack of electricity is the main difficulty. In fact, at the beginning he lost some computers due to high fluctuation in the electricity supply. He had to buy electric generators. Like the ice cream vendor, he said that the best way to solve the electricity problem is to let the private companies offer the service.

Micro-entrepreneurs

There are countless micro-entrepreneurs in town. We interviewed several micro-entrepreneurs who had a relatively little working capital – more than US$ 100 but less than US$ 500. For example there are several *motowashes*. In Jérémie the main means of transportation is the *moto-taxis*. Most of the motorcycles are imported from China, at a small fraction of the price of a Japanese one. Some of the roads are unpaved, and they can get muddy, especially in the area where the farmers' market is located; therefore the need for a *motowash*.

Another unique business is letting people watch a soccer game for a price. By the time of my fieldwork in 2012, energy was available in the town only from 7:00 PM to 9:00 or 10:00 PM, or two or three hours per day. Even though many people have TVs in Jérémie, many cannot watch it during the day. A 'tv-theater' responds to the high demand of watching soccer and the low supply of broadcasting due to lack of electricity. By the time we were in Jérémie, the European Cup of Nations was in full swing, and the advertisement for the TV games appeared in a green board in one of the busiest streets.

The micro-entrepreneurs argued that their business provides for daily subsistence but not more. One of them said that he used to be a schoolteacher, and then he retired and opened his business selling consumption goods such as oil and rice.

Conclusions: informal institutions

Given the weak Haitian state, there are certain institutions that have more influence on the economic life of the individuals. One of them is religion. Like any religion and set of beliefs, Voodoo changes and evolves, and throughout its evolution it has affected the economy in different ways. According to Murray (1980), with the population pressure of the late twentieth century, Voodoo fosters the circulation of land within members of the community, as families are pressed by other members of society to sell their land to pay for rituals such as funerals and burials. These pressures persist today. In fact, the largest insurance company in the country, namely Alternative Insurance Company – AIC, offers funeral insurance, and describes the product as: '[F]or mainly freeing the family from the economic burden of organizing funeral arrangements after an accident or natural death of the insured, by relying on an extensive network of high quality funeral service providers all over the country.'[14]

Michel (1996: 281) argues that 'Vodou became not only the means for revitalization through ancestral traditions but also the channel par excellence to organization and to resistance.' Murray (1980) similarly asserts that Voodoo ceremonies played a central role in the early stage of the revolution that led to independence of the country. To some extent Voodoo and Catholicism merged. Historically, the followers of the spirit as Voodoo have been persecuted, so as a protection strategy many of them adopted Catholicism (Michel, 1996). Michel describes Voodoo as a religion that in terms of its organization is decentralized, bottom-up and without a hierarchy. Michel (1996: 282) writes:

> Voodoo is more than rituals of the cult, temple, and family. As a comprehensive religious system, it ties together the visible and invisible, material and spiritual, secular and sacred. It is a philosophy, a way of life for the majority in Haiti that permeates and sustains their entire being and brings coherence where there might otherwise be chaos.
>
> While Haitian Voodoo offers sorcery as one of its ritual options, by no means is it a cult exclusively (or even principally) for ritual violence. The rather abundant literature on Haitian Voodoo (see Murray, 1980) clearly signals that this is a folk-religion or folk-cult, involving beliefs in a pantheon of spirits, rituals performed to influence and interact with these spirits, and specialists who are turned to for theological consultations and certain types of ritual leadership. The contexts in which interaction among believer, specialist and spirit occur ordinarily have little or nothing to do with the black magic of the type symbolized by the pin-riddled doll.

As Murray (1980) asserts, the word 'voodoo' elicits images of a doll riddled with pins, and this identification of voodoo with illness-or death-inflicting sorcery has even made its way into the anthropological literature in discussions of magically induced sickness or death. However, Murray (1980: 302) argues regarding the burial places of people in the village he studied in Eastern Haiti: 'What is more impressive, however, is the quality of the burial monuments. The tombs where many peasants are buried literally cost more to construct than the wattle-doub cottages in which they spend their lives.' He asserts that stonemasons who build the tombs are paid from US$ 200 to 400 (Murray, 1980: 315). In fact, in his study of land tenure, cropping and land 'circulation' in Haiti, Murray concludes that most (75 per cent) of the land is traded due to ritual reasons, such as paying for burials and healing sicknesses, which are directly or indirectly related to Voodoo.

This, however, is not exclusive to Haiti. Comparative research of the extreme poor shows that they often spend money on religious festivals (Banerjee and Duflo, 2007: 146). Financing rituals is a priority over entrepreneurial investment, especially in rural areas.

Thus, evidently, there are many obstacles for entrepreneurs in Haiti. These involve on the one hand, weak formal institutions. Lack of electricity, for example, is a key problem. Therefore a discussion on the possibility of opening the electricity market for private provision is worthwhile. It is puzzling to see some parts of Haiti with 4G Internet but no electricity. Lack of credit exists as well. Banks are reluctant to lend to start-ups. The reason for this could be that property rights on land are not clearly defined. Providing training on financial literacy is one way to support the local entrepreneurial community, as well as offering seminars on the role of the entrepreneurs in society regarding innovation and creativity. On the other hand, informal institutions also represent a constraint. Building trust is a key to promoting entrepreneurial activity. One of the best ways to do this is perhaps to promote the creation of clubs and voluntary associations. Akin to elsewhere, therefore, it is important not only to focus upon developing the formal institutions conducive to entrepreneurship but also to ensure that the informal institutions are in place that foster entrepreneurial endeavour.

Notes

1 This chapter draws upon the unpublished working paper, 'Entrepreneurship and Economic Development in Jérémie, Haiti' by the author. Available at http://goo.gl/C3EPRc, accessed 30 December 2014. The chapter is based on a two-month stay in the city of Jérémie in 2012, where the author taught a class on entrepreneurship and economic development at the University of the Nouvelle Grand'Anse (UNOGA), http://universitynouvellegrandanse.org, accessed 10 April 2015.
2 The World Bank, http://goo.gl/6HGZpu, accessed 21 January 2015.
3 Observatory of Economic Complexity, http://goo.gl/1utVno, accessed 10 April 2015.
4 Ibid.
5 Transparency International, http://goo.gl/eQsSm0, accessed 10 April 2015.
6 Freedom House, http://goo.gl/6iZcJr, accessed 10 April 2015.
7 *2014 Index of Economic Freedom*, http://goo.gl/CeBzRc, accessed 27 December 2014.
8 Ibid.
9 Ibid.
10 Ibid.
11 Transparency International, http://www.transparency.org/country/#HTI, accessed 10 April 2015.
12 http://goo.gl/V3IMyR and http://en.wikipedia.org/wiki/Digicel, accessed 10 April 2015.
13 http://goo.gl/Zfgdmj, accessed 21 January 2015.
14 http://goo.gl/7l5jaE, accessed 21 January 2015.

References

Ashton, T. S. (1964). *The Industrial Revolution, 1760–1830*. Oxford: Oxford University Press.
Baumol, W. and Strom, R. (2008). Entrepreneurship and Economic Growth. *Strategic Entrepreneurship Journal*, 1 (3–4): 233–237.
Banerjee, A. V. and Duflo, E. (2007). The Economic Lives of the Poor. *Journal of Economic Perspectives*, 21(1): 141–168.
Barrau, O. (2013). Powering Haitian Entrepreneurs Through Risk Management, Inc. November 20. Available online at http://goo.gl/dJjsRk. Accessed 20 January 2015.
Campos, N. M. (2010). Entrepreneurship in Socioeconomic and Political Instability. Florianopolis. Paper presented at the VI Encontro de Estudos Organizacionais da ANPAD. Available online at http://bit.ly/1yJXxY6. Accessed 20 January 2015.
Crist, R. (1952). Cultural Dichotomy in the Island of Hispaniola. *Economic Geography*, 28(2): 105–121.
De Soto, H. (2003). *The Mystery of Capital: Why Capitalism Triumphs in the West and Fails Everywhere Else*. New York: Basic Books. Reprint edition.
Dolisca, F. (2003). Population Pressure, Land, Tenure, Deforestation, and Farming Systems in Haiti: The Case of Forest Des Pins Reserve (Doctoral dissertation). Available at http://goo.gl/yV7AX0. Accessed February 3, 2015.
Fairbanks, M. (2010). A Business Solution to Haiti's Poverty. *The Christian Science Monitor*, July 12.
Gros, J. G. (2011). Anatomy of a Haitian Tragedy: When the Fury of Nature Meets the Debility of the State. *Journal of Black Studies*, 42(2): 131–157.
Harper, D. (2007). *Foundations of Entrepreneurship and Economic Development*. London: Routledge.
Kirzner, I. M. (1978). *Competition and Entrepreneurship*. Chicago, IL: University of Chicago Press.

Kushner, J. (2015). Who Owns What in Haiti? *The New Yorker*, January 18. Available at http://goo.gl/aXUgl4. Accessed 5 January 2015.

Loten, A. (2010). Running a Business in a Disaster Zone. *The Wall Street Journal*, December 30. Available at http://goo.gl/YXCIVx. Accessed 23 January 2015.

Marroquín G. A. (2005). A Supply and Demand Approach to the Institutional Performance of Haiti. *Revista Latinoamericana de Desarrollo Economico*, 4, 65–81. Available at http://goo.gl/9oM4x5. Accessed 5 January 2015.

Michel, C. (1996). The Educational Character of Haitian Vodou. *Comparative Education Review*, 40(3), 280–294.

Mokyr, J. (2004). *The Gifts of Athena: Historical Origins of the Knowledge Economy*. Princeton, NJ: Princeton University Press.

Moloney, A. (2012). Haitian Millionaire Determined to Build Back Better. Thomson Reuters Foundation. February 24. Available at http://goo.gl/MX33ac. Accessed 24 January 2015.

Murray, G. F. (1980). Population pressure, land tenure, and Voodoo: The Economics of Haitian Peasant Ritual. In E. Ross (ed.), *Beyond the Myths of Culture* (pp. 295–321). New York: Academic Press. Available at http://goo.gl/Vt09Bt. Accessed 12 January 2015.

Nedjé, M., Emile, E. S. and Paul, B. (2013). Women and Economic Development: Women Entrepreneurship Situation in Haiti. *Haiti Perspectives*, 2(3), 61–67.

North, D. C. (1990). *Institutions, Institutional Change, and Economic Performance*. Cambridge, UK: Cambridge University Press.

Pierre, M. (2011). *The Power of a Dream: One Man's Determination to Pursue his Ideals*. CreateSpace Independent Publishing. 140 pages.

Schumpeter, J. A. (1982). *The Theory of Economic Development: An Inquiry into Profits, Capital, Credit, Interest, and the Business Cycle*. New Jersey: Transaction Publishers.

Smith, A. ([1776] 1904). *An Inquiry into the Nature and Causes of the Wealth of Nations*. London: Methuen & Co., Ltd.Edwin Cannan, ed. Available at http://goo.gl/SWx4tI. Accessed January 27, 2015.

The Power of Insurance: Why Haiti's Future Depends on Planning for the Worst. (27 August 2013). Forbes. Available at http://goo.gl/bZNBZO. Accessed 20 January 2015.

Trade in Haiti: Chickens and Eggs. (2013). *The Economist*, August 24. Available at http://goo.gl/gr27E9. Accessed 29 January 2015.

Tullock, G. (1974). *The Social Dilemma: The Economics of War and Revolution*. Blacksburg, VA: University Publications, 143 pages.

World Bank (2015). Doing Business. http://goo.gl/gW19TG. Accessed 10 April 2015.

4

ENTREPRENEURSHIP AND SME DEVELOPMENT POLICY IN A LEAST DEVELOPED COUNTRY

Lessons from Laos

Balbir B. Bhasin, Sivakumar Venkataramany, and Lee Keng Ng

Introduction

As with most growing economies, Laos needs to develop its small and medium-sized enterprises (SMEs), which are the key engine of growth for all Southeast Asian countries and developing world nations. Laos is the one of the few remaining communist countries in the world, and has recently transited to a market economy like its neighbor Vietnam. A relatively small country, about the size of the US state of Utah, almost 70 percent of the terrain in Laos is forested. The country has a rising population of some 7 million but is still one of the least densely populated countries in Asia. Laos is rich in natural resources and much of these remain untapped due to the lack of capital and technology. The resources include wood, gold, copper, tin, aluminum, rattan, coffee, and hydroelectricity. However, the country remains poor and underdeveloped due to lack of infrastructure and human capacity (Bhasin, 2010).

Background

Laos emerged from the domination of Thailand in the eighteenth century and remained part of French Indochina until the Second World War after which it was occupied by the Japanese. In 1946, the French reoccupied Laos but had to grant full sovereignty after their defeat by the Vietnamese and the subsequent Geneva Peace Conference in 1954 (US Department of State, 2015). The country saw little stability as a civil war ensued between the Royalists, the Communists, and the Neutralists. The 1961–1962 second Geneva conference finally provided for the neutrality and independence of the country. Laos, one of the few remaining one-party communist states, began decentralizing control and encouraging private enterprise only in 1986. The country had remained mostly closed with the government controlling all industrial sectors since declaring independence as the Lao People's Democratic Republic (LPDR) on December 2, 1975 (World Bank, 2015).

The Lao government started encouraging private enterprise in 1986 and is transiting now to a market economy but with continuing governmental participation. Prices are generally determined by the market, and import barriers have been eased and replaced with tariffs. The private sector is now allowed direct imports and farmers own land and sell their crops in the markets. From 1988 to 2013, the economy has grown at an average 6–8 percent annually. Despite being rich in natural resources, the country remains underdeveloped and around 75 percent of the population lives off subsistence agriculture, which contributes roughly 25 percent of GDP. In addition to rice, the main crops are sweet potato, corn, coffee, sugarcane, tobacco, cotton, tea, ginger, soybeans, vegetables, and peanuts. Animal husbandry includes rearing of cattle, pigs, water buffalo, and poultry. Industry is a growing sector (11 percent) and contributes 32 percent of the GDP. The main activity is in the extractive industry with mining of tin, gold, and gypsum. Other industries are timber, electric power, agricultural processing, construction, garments, cement, and tourism. The services sector accounts for around 44 percent of GDP as illustrated in Figure 4.1.

Poverty has reduced substantially from 45 percent in 1992 to 23.2 percent in 2012. Exports in 2013 included wood products, coffee, electricity, tin, copper, gold, cassava, and were mainly to Thailand (33 percent), Vietnam (12 percent), and China (25 percent) as illustrated in Figure 4.2. Imports were mainly machinery and equipment, vehicles, fuel, and consumer goods. The country is rich in hydropower generation, which provides almost 90 percent of electricity. There are no indigenous sources of oil and natural gas but Petro Vietnam is exploring for oil and gas jointly with Laos. There are considerable deposits of minerals and these are largely untapped. There are also ample sources of gemstones, especially high quality sapphires, agate, jade, opal, amber, amethyst, and pearls (World Fact Book, 2015).

Infrastructure development, streamlining business regulations, and improving finance have been identified as the main priorities for the government. Construction of roads and buildings for the Southeast Asian Games in December 2009 and for the celebration of the 450th anniversary of Vientiane as the country's capital in 2010 has helped infrastructure

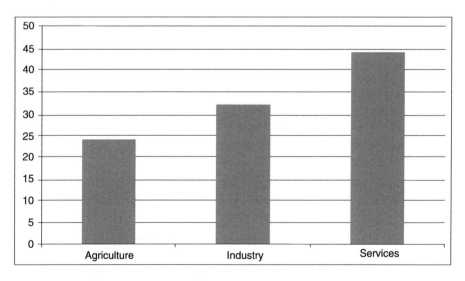

Figure 4.1 GDP by Sector in Laos (2014)

Source: Adaptation from The World Factbook (2015).

Table 4.1 Net Official Development Assistance (ODA) and Official Aid Received

South East Asia Countries	2010	2011	2012	2013
	Current US$ millions			
Cambodia	733.73	790.94	807.41	804.81
Indonesia	1392.51	419.27	67.81	53.33
Laos	413.79	392.48	408.92	421.00
Thailand	2940.08	3595.51	4115.78	4084.77
Vietnam	−11.40	−153.67	−134.79	−23.71

Source: Adaptation from The World Bank (2015).

development. A mini construction boom is being experienced around Vientiane. The manufacturing and tourism sectors are seen as the key sectors for private sector growth. The garment sector has created employment for over 20,000. There is a need to focus attention on improving transportation and skill levels of workers. Laos continues to remain dependent on external assistance to finance its public investment. Table 4.1 illustrates the official financial flows of the Lao economy in comparison to the other Southeast Asian countries. In 2009, investment procedures were simplified and bank facilities expanded for small farmers and entrepreneurs. Inflation is in check and has averaged at around 5 percent, and the currency, the Lao kip, has been rising steadily against the US dollar. In practice, the Lao economy is highly dollarized. Laos' oil import bill remains large.

The country's international reserves have been strengthened through investments in hydropower and mining. The government maintains controls of the price of gasoline and diesel. The economy is expected to continue to grow by around 7–8 percent annually (Bhasin, 2010).

SME policy evolution in Laos

Subsequent to the proclamation of the Lao PDR in 1975, the country remained a socialist centralized planning economy until 1986 when President Kaysone Phomvihane initiated "Chintanakanmay" (New Imagination) as the pragmatic way forward. The market economy was called "New Economic Mechanism" and trade liberalization began in 1987. The tax system was restructured. Export taxes were eliminated and replaced with profit taxes. By 1989, a new tax system was implemented. By 1995, there was unification of exchange rates and a floating rate was adopted. Deregulation measures included the reduction of the number of public employees, autonomy and rationalization of public enterprises and privatization (Nouansavanh, 2005).

Laos joined the Association of Southeast Asian Nations (ASEAN) in 1997 and the ASEAN Free Trade Area (AFTA) in 1998. The net result has been the requirement for Laos to reduce tariffs. Consequently, business and industry need to become more productive and competitive. The burden falls mainly on the SMEs as they are the mainstay of the national economy. In 2004, the prime minister issued Decree No. 42 defining directions and policies for development of SMEs in Laos. In October 2005, the National Assembly approved a new Enterprise Law which was enacted. The intent was to create a level playing field for private businesses by simplifying regulations and procedures.

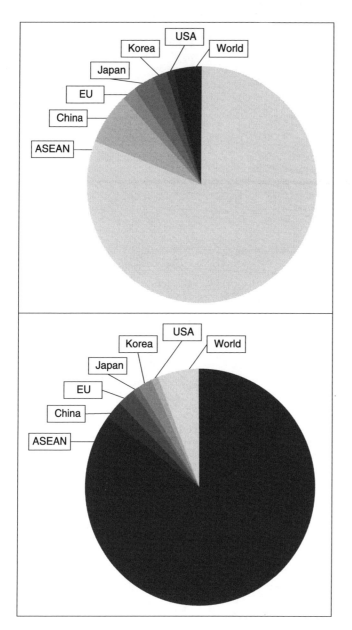

Figure 4.2   Major Trading Partners of Laos, Import and Export (2013)

Source: Adaptation from Asian Development Bank (2015).

A four-dimension definition of SMEs was created, taking into account the number of employees, the turnover or total assets, the business registration, and the independency of the business: SMEs are business units, independent and legally registered in accordance with the law of Lao PDR, and whose sizes are determined by the following criteria as illustrated in Table 4.2:

Table 4.2 Definition of SMEs

Enterprise category	Number of employees	Annual turnover (mil kip)	Asset value (mil kip)
Small	< 20	< = 400	< = 250
Medium	< 100	< = 1000	< =1200

Source: Adaptation from Laos SME Promotion and Development Office (2004).

Small enterprises are those with an annual average number of employees not exceeding 19 persons *or* total assets not exceeding 250 million kip *or* annual turnover not exceeding 400 million kip.

Medium-sized enterprises are those with an annual average number of employees not exceeding 100 persons *or* total assets not exceeding 1.2 billion kip *or* an annual turnover not exceeding 1 billion kip.

Although the private sector in Laos remains small, it dominates the economy in terms of the number of enterprises. In 2005/6, 85 percent of all enterprises were privately owned, 79 percent were small, 16 percent were medium and 5 percent were large. There were a total number of 126,913 enterprises that employed 245,000 people, of which SMEs accounted for 99.8 percent and 83 percent respectively (Phoumilay and Douangsavanh, 2008).

The targets for SME development by 2015 are:

1. Growth of SME sector – 13 percent annual growth
2. Growth in domestic products of 15 percent per annum
3. Existing SMEs to grow by 10 percent in terms of employment or turnover
4. Employment creation – SMEs to generate 85 percent of net job creation

Literature review: SME policy and performance in Laos

Literature and research on SME Development in Laos is predictably limited as the country remained a closed economy for a long time and academics and institutions had minimal interest in the economy. Data about the economic sectors is also dated and often inaccurate.

In 2003, the Laotian government's Deputy Director of Industry presented a self-evaluation of the SME Development Framework in Laos to the OECD-sponsored Regional Workshop on "Trade Capacity Building and Private Sector Development in Asia" in Phnom Penh, Cambodia (Inmyxai, 2003), and reported that:

1. The Lao Expenditure and Consumption Survey (LECS 2) carried out by the National Statistics Center in 1997/1998 indicated 165,000 households involved in operating small businesses in Laos and only 7 percent employed paid labor.
2. An industry survey carried out by the Ministry of Industry and Handicrafts and the United Nations Development Organization (UNIDO) revealed small businesses accounting for 98.1 percent of manufacturing, while medium and large businesses made up 1.5 percent and 0.4 percent respectively. The survey also estimated small businesses having created employment for 57 percent of the industrial labor force. Medium and large enterprises employed 7 percent and 37 percent respectively. SME contribution to GDP could not be ascertained.

3. The major problems faced by SMEs were: inability to compete with neighboring countries due to the poor investment and business environment; SME regulations were not fully developed; lack of service institutions; lack of sources of financing; and poor policy formulation and implementation leading to lack of cooperation between public and private sectors.

In order to improve the situation, an SME Development Framework and SME Development Fund were created. These and other training programs were adopted so as to create an enabling business environment for SMEs, enhance competitiveness of SMEs, and provide services to improve SME performance.

In the first of its kind study on "Development of Excellent Entrepreneurs in Small and Medium Enterprises in Laos and Cambodia" presented to the International Conference on Sustainable Development: Challenges and Opportunities for GMS on December, 2007, in-depth interviews were used to "explore the similarities and differences of the SMEs entrepreneurial characteristics, business experiences, problems and supporting requirements in Laos and Cambodia" (Southiseng et al., 2007). The findings were that the performance of SMEs had improved due to an increase in the number of entrepreneurs. However, both countries faced the same challenges:

1. Unclear and uncertain rules and regulations for establishment of SMEs
2. Lack of accessible credit and
3. Shortage of entrepreneurial and managerial training facilities and programs

The study recommended the systemic training of entrepreneurs, improvement and development of adequate infrastructure, provision of credit for start-ups and reduction of tax rates to stimulate to increase daily revenue for the many in need.

A joint 2007 study by academics from the national University of Laos and Hiroshima University, Japan on "Corporate Financing and Performance of SMEs" empirically investigated the "moderating effects of ownership types and management styles to corporate financing on the performance of SMEs" (Xayphone and Kimbara, 2007). The study collated and analyzed data of 160 trading SMEs in Vientiane, the capital of Laos over the period 2002–2004. The results led the authors to argue for both internal financing (retained earnings) and external financing (debt equity) as the main factors influencing the performance of trading SMEs in Laos.

In a related paper by the same two researchers (Xayphone and Kimbara, 2008) and specifically aimed at SMEs in Laos, 146 trading SMEs were examined to determine (1) financial performance and relationship to managerial types; and (2) relationship between managerial types and financial performance in relation to the size of the firm. Using the MANOVA method to prove defined evidence, we found no difference between founder-CEO and professional-CEO on financial performance of the firms, though the size of the firm does have direct impact on performance. Larger firms outperformed smaller ones to a certain level (sales in excess of USD 500,000) and the study recommended control be handed from founder-CEO to management-CEO.

A study was done to evaluate the impact of FDI and trade liberalization on SME development in Laos as part of a series of research projects at the Economic Research Institute for ASEAN (Association of South East Asian Nations) and East Asia (ERIA) in 2007. Challenges faced by SMEs in Laos were identified as: high taxes, high inflation, unstable exchange rate, and inadequate funding (Kyophilavong, 2007). Additional problems discovered were: need for innovation, lack of competitive capability, lack of market and opportunity, and need for networking. Furthermore, though FDI does provide SMEs with opportunities to increase production, trade liberalization had a negative rather than a positive impact.

Recommendations made for changes in policy to address these issues were to improve collection of data and its analysis; annual monitoring of policy implementation; increase in SME capacity in productivity, quality, and quantity; better coordination of training activity; and the reduction of the tax rate, controlling inflation and the foreign exchange rate.

A study was conducted by the ERIA in 2009 (No. 8) to understand the issues Lao SMEs face during the economic integration process. The economic integration for the ASEAN region has accelerated growth for the region but some economies (including Laos) are still lagging. The national development goal of Laos is to remove itself from the group of Least Developed Countries (LDC) by 2020. SME development is crucial to reaching this goal. The barriers identified prior to this study were:

1. Lack of data on enterprises in Laos
2. SMEs dominated the economy and there were few large firms in the economy
3. Lack of access to capital
4. Lack of skilled technical labor
5. Lack of business service providers

A survey of SMEs was conducted using personal interviews. The constraints of SME growth included:

1. Most sectors faced constrained financial access except for garments, wood processing and handicrafts and most of these products are sold domestically
2. Most sectors failed to meet international standards as they lacked capacity to improve business processes, adopt new production methods, and introduce new products to markets
3. The external barriers identified were the poor economic conditions and high taxes in the domestic market
4. The internal barriers were poor distribution and logistical support including availability of warehousing facilities and excessive costs involved in transportation
5. Shortage of working capital to finance new business start-ups
6. Insufficient trained personnel for market expansion

Table 4.3 illustrates the type of household and government expenditure as a percentage of GDP over the last three years since 2010. An assessment was done to ascertain current government assistance to SMEs and the survey found little support had been forthcoming from government or NGOs. Only 20 percent of SMEs received some form of assistance overall and the lowest ranked categories where support was received from government and NGOs were: financing, technology development and transfer and business linkages and networking. The study concluded that action should be taken by the government to address these issues, in particular the shortage of working capital and the need to meet international standards (Kyophilavong, 2009).

The most recent study on SME Development in Laos was conducted in 2010 by Southiseng and Walsh of the School of Management at the Shinawatra International University in Bangkok, Thailand (Southiseng and Walsh, 2010). The study analyzed competition and management issues of SMEs in three provinces of Laos: Vientiane, Sawannakhet,

Table 4.3 Type of Expenditure as a Percentage of GDP

Type of expenditure	2010	2011	2012	2013
Household consumption expenditure (including NPISH)	61.3	60.1	57.8	59.7
General government final consumption expenditure	12.6	12.6	14.3	13.1
Gross capital formation	25.8	27.0	31.7	28.1
Exports of goods and services	23.6	23.8	22.6	23.3
Imports of goods and services	24.4	26.8	29.3	26.8
Agriculture, hunting, forestry, fishing	29.7	28.0	25.0	24.1
Industry	28.9	31.4	36.0	34.1
Services	41.4	40.5	39.0	41.7

Source: Adaptation from UNCTAD (2015a).

Table 4.4 Real GDP Growth Rates Per Capita

South East Asia Countries	2010	2011	2012	2013
Cambodia	4.33	5.30	5.39	4.99
Indonesia	4.82	5.13	4.91	4.43
Laos	5.97	5.96	5.90	6.02
Thailand	7.13	0.08	6.10	2.65
Vietnam	5.41	5.22	4.23	4.19

Source: Adaptation from UNCTAD (2015b).

and Luang Prabang. The study used qualitative research as well as secondary data. Fifty-two in-depth interviews were conducted. The SME sector is important to the Lao economy and 74 percent of enterprises were family owned. These concentrated on food processing, garment production, construction materials, wooden furniture, tourism, education, trading, transportation, internet services, and others. Increases in the SME sector have certainly contributed to job growth and overall GDP growth. Table 4.4 illustrates the overall incremental increase in real GDP growth rates per capita over four years from 2010 to 2013 relative to Cambodia, Indonesia, Thailand, and Vietnam.

The results find entrepreneurs unable to access modern technology and finance, have limited resources in terms of capital and skill, and receive unfair treatment from government officials. Management styles usually focused on short-term day-to-day objectives and few were able to consider longer-term considerations or business sustainability. Skills management and capacity building in these SMEs were narrowly conceived. Training and development of human resources was seen as a cost rather than an investment. Recommendations for enhancement of SME productivity and capacity included:

1. Income tax rates should be reduced substantially so as to allow for greater capital availability for reinvestment
2. Credit and financing need to be increased and the process made easy and more accessible
3. Training should be increased to provide capacity in product design, quality improvement, and product presentation and packaging

4.   Training be provided to entrepreneurs about complying with laws and commercial regulations, international insurance policies, payment and financing methods, and ways of entering international markets
5.   E-commerce systems be developed, introduced, and implemented

Lessons: policy considerations for Laos

The value of contribution from the SME sector to the national economy must be recognized more substantially. Most Southeast Asian governments do recognize the importance of SME development as essential and necessary for the overall health of each country's economy. The SME sector accounts for upward of 90 percent of all firms outside the agricultural sector and the biggest source of employment, providing livelihood for three-quarters of the region's population (Bhasin and Venkataramany, 2010). This is true for Laos as the country attempts to free itself from the label of a least developed country by 2020. Table 4.5 illustrates Laos as having the highest percentage of labor force in the agriculture sector as compared with the other Southeast Asia countries.

In spite of the importance of SMEs to the national economy, the country still lacks an established, well-crafted, and effectively managed policy for the development of a strong base of corporate and entrepreneurial leaders. First a comprehensive strategy, followed by a detailed plan and then its implementation becomes a priority for the country. Discussed below are some policy considerations.

Though the country is eager to develop the private sector and increase business activity, there are difficulties in running a business in Laos. In a World Bank 2015 report, Laos ranked 148th out of 189 countries for ease of doing business and of the nine ASEAN countries profiled, Laos ranked last. It takes roughly 92 days and six procedures to start a business in Laos. With regard to protecting investors, the country ranks 178th of 189 countries surveyed (World Bank, 2015). Corruption remains a problem although the government at the highest level has made combating corruption a priority. Laos is listed 140 of 177 nations in Transparency International's (2015) Corruption Perception Index (CPI).

The Proposed ASEAN Policy Blueprint for SME Development 2004–2014 (Asasen et al., 2003) used the following objectives for development and integration of SMEs:

1.   Higher income growth
2.   Fuller deployment of domestic resources
3.   Gainful integration through global and regional trade and investment, and
4.   Greater equity in access, distribution, and development

Table 4.5 Percentage of Labor Force in the Agricultural Sector

South East Asia Countries	2010	2011	2012	2013
Cambodia	63.3%	63.1%	62.9%	62.7%
Indonesia	42.2%	41.6%	41.1%	40.5%
Laos	77.1%	77.4%	77.6%	77.8%
Thailand	47.0%	46.0%	44.9%	44.0%
Vietnam	58.1%	57.6%	57.2%	56.8%

Source: Adaptation from UNCTAD (2015c).

The report notes the vital contribution of SMEs to economic development. SMEs remain the largest source of domestic employment. They remain "poor cousins of large firms" and yet SMEs have "driven the emergence of world-class industries." A new development context has been ushered in by trade and investment liberalization in combination with rapid advances in many fields. These include information processing, telecommunications, transportation, bio-technology and engineering, and the new material sciences. As a result there have been fundamental changes in the pace, patterns, and processes of interaction within and between independent economies and enterprises (Asasen et al., 2003).

This paradigm shift highlights the need and importance of networks, linkages, and alliances. Prerequisites of efficiency and competitiveness are also required as cornerstones of policy formulation.

Entrepreneurship is the foundation for gainful progress in the market economic system. Higher levels of efficiency and flexibility in product quality, cost, and delivery punctuality are other determinants of sharpened competitiveness at the domestic and external levels. Strategic considerations for policy formulation must be:

1. The promotion of a culture of entrepreneurship, networking and innovation; and ensuring that SMEs become and remain a learning organization where productivity and innovation are constantly improved.
2. SME participation should be enhanced in borderless e-commerce, and to overcome bottlenecks in bank and supplementary financing for SMEs.
3. Creation of SME-friendly governance by the public sector, which has a major role to play in policy liberalization, administrative deregulation, and asset privatization. Good governance must be conducive to promotion of entrepreneurial initiatives.
4. Establishing a strong public–private sector partnership in favor of SMEs.

In this age of globalization and with an increase in regional trade and transactions, SMEs must be capable of competing in the global marketplace. Exports provide the economy with valuable foreign exchange as well as providing higher returns and new markets. They also serve to increase employment which is a priority for Laos. The major tool to help develop local capacity is sub-contracting. SME policies to help compete were outlined in a discussion in a project by the Economic Research Institute for ASEAN and East Asia (ERIA). The study "Asian SMEs and Globalization" reports the current status and challenges of Asian SMEs (Lin, 2007) as follows:

1. SME policies have tended to have contradicting objectives—protecting and promoting SMEs at the same time
2. SME policies must also consider private sector initiatives and not only targets defined by government—few local SMEs are able to qualify as sub-contractors and need help
3. In Laos, SMEs face challenges of high taxes, high inflation, an unstable exchange rate, and a lack of funding

The following recommendations are relevant for the development of SME policy:

1. SME policies must be long-term based and need effective coordination and implementation—this is not always the case and inconsistencies often exist.
2. Best practices must be developed for the business environment, subcontracting and networking, and a monitoring mechanism put in place

Table 4.6 FDI as a Percentage of GDP

South East Asia Countries	2010	2011	2012	2013
Cambodia	7.0	6.3	10.3	9.0
Indonesia	1.9	2.3	2.2	2.1
Laos	4.1	3.7	3.2	2.8
Thailand	2.7	1.0	2.8	3.2
Vietnam	6.9	5.5	5.4	5.2

Source: Adaptation from UNCTAD (2015d).

3. Local governments must create a SME database and use this to coordinate between owners and supporting organizations
4. SME database needs to be streamlined and quality improved
5. A quality certification system is needed to improve quality and competitiveness
6. Anti-monopoly regulations need to be enacted and implemented
7. SME incubators to encourage new entrants in a competitive environment
8. Joint technology centers with FDI providers can help disseminate information and provide training for local SMEs—an example is the Japan-Singapore Technology Center.

Table 4.6 illustrates the potential of FDI in the Laos economy. The Laos economy, in the earlier years, demonstrated very low percentage of GDP gradually increasing until the market downturn in 2008.

A 2005 study of the factors affecting Lao SMEs as they attempt to integrate with the regional economies (Nouansavanh, 2005) noted the overall effects of joining AFTA as positive as exports would increase. However, measures need to be taken to increase competitiveness. The following problems were highlighted and must be taken into account in formulating SME policy:

1. The problems of red tape and bureaucratic obstacles persist and need to be addressed on an urgent basis. They erode entrepreneurial energies. Rules and regulations need to change to meet standards set in the neighboring countries.
2. Low entrepreneurial spirit and lack of managerial skills and knowledge are common. Management-related education, therefore, needs improvement.
3. There is a strong need to improve technology transfer so as to increase productivity of the manufacturing sector.
4. People have limited access to information and information technology in Laos. The issue needs to be addressed by disseminating business information from different agencies to interested parties. Lack of knowledge of English is a serious concern.
5. Access to financing for SMEs is a major problem.

Recommendations for policy formulation and implementation include the need to create a conducive and enabling business environment starting at the micro-level. The government and the private sector need to work closely as genuine partners in this regard. The existing regulations need to be reviewed and made more business-friendly and attractive to both local and foreign investors. Especially with regards Laos, regulations must be "simplified in terms of content, procedures and coherence" (Nouansavanh, 2005). Coordination between different levels of public administration and the various stakeholders needs to be improved. Good managerial and technical support services require attention. New instruments of financing need to be developed and the overall infrastructure of the country needs to be developed at a faster rate.

The legal system in Laos is based on French legal norms and procedures, socialist practice, and traditional customs. The judiciary is poorly trained and rather inefficient, even corrupt. Judges are all LPRP members and appointed. Laws have been enacted to protect citizens against arbitrary arrest and detention. In rural Laos, disputes are handled by village committees. Inter-village disputes in turn are handled by the district administration in line with local customs and socialist practices (Bhasin, 2010).

The legal environment lacks transparency and is "saddled with red tape, inefficiencies and ambiguous practices that allow abuse" (RAM Consultancy, 2005). Areas for reform are: weak secured transaction law and other commercial laws, lack of titles to property, absence of a transaction registry, and the existence of a large number of unregistered small businesses in the country as the criteria for registration are ambiguous, cumbersome, and costs are too high.

In a presentation to the Regional Forum on Trade Facilitation and SMEs in Times of Crisis, organized by the World Bank's Development Research Group in Beijing on May 20–22, 2009, the president of the Young Entrepreneurs Association of Laos (LYEA) Ousavanh Thiengthepvongsa noted that being a landlocked developing country (LLDC), Laos had special challenges in development. Landlocked countries are dependent on trade and transport in neighboring and coastal countries. Imports and exports have to travel long distances which increases transaction costs and reduces competitiveness. The country must find more creative ways to make domestic enterprises more competitive in a globalized world. Recommendations include adopting an integrated, holistic approach. Strategy should encompass reforms in the areas of: a comprehensive, realistic and targeted agenda; facilitation of transport and transit including physical infrastructure; legal and regulatory reform including implementation and enforcement; regional cooperation needs to be one of the priorities in order to overcome problems related to LLDC. Finally, in order to achieve any or all of these, a strong political will is a prerequisite without which nothing of consequence can be accomplished (Thiengthepvongsa, 2009).

Conclusion and recommendations

Laos is one of few one-party communist states, but the drive to open markets and develop private enterprise has taken off. The Government of Laos (GoL) recognizes the important role that entrepreneurs and SMEs play in the development of the economy and country. The country now needs to put much more effort into creating the infrastructure and institutions. The immediate priority is to ensure macroeconomic and financial stability and continue developing closer commercial links with neighboring countries that provide greater access to outside markets, capital, and technology. Shortage of power supply is common, many parts of the country do not have proper roads and transport access, poverty and literacy are still a challenge, and there continues to be dependence on small sectors of the economy mainly agriculture, mining, forestry, hydropower, and some tourism. The country is still transitioning from government-controlled to a privately held open system. Processes and procedures, control mechanisms, and legal structure are yet to be fully in place. The country has applied for membership to the WTO (expected in 2010 and overdue) and this will pave the way for the opening of new markets and increase in trade.

For SMEs in Laos to take advantage of opportunities arising from globalization, they must develop capacities for allowing them to compete in global markets. Harvie (2004) proposes a clear and well-defined SME development policy inclusive of:

1. Access to markets
2. Access to financing
3. Access to information, and
4. Access to technology

Laos is well poised to benefit from regional markets through its membership of the ASEAN Free Trade Area (AFTA) and of global markets as and when it becomes a full-fledged member of the World Trade Organization (WTO). The country needs to structure and implement a more sound financing mechanism to help new start-ups gain access to capital as well as provide avenues for existing SMEs grow and prosper. This includes a positive tax regime encouraging local and foreign investment. There is a dire need to provide information for promoting and supporting SME development and a systematic approach and proper implementation is needed. Finally, in order to benefit from the advantages new technology brings, proper training and transfer of skill is essential. Laos needs to bolster its education system with a total onslaught on preparing the people to be more entrepreneurial and to create a risk-taking culture. We recommend Laos can learn much from the neighboring countries like India, Singapore, Thailand, and Vietnam. These countries have succeeded in dealing with similar challenges.

References

Asasen, C., Asasen, K. and Chuangcham, N. (2003). A Proposed ASEAN Policy Blueprint for SME Development 2004–2014, Regional Economic Policy Support Facility (REPSF) of the ASEAN-Australia Development Cooperation Program, REPSF Project 02/2005.

Asian Development Bank (2015). Key Indicators for Asia and the Pacific 2014 (45th ed.). Retrieved May 30, 2015, from http://www.adb.org/sites/default/files/publication/43030/ki2014_0.pdf.

Bhasin, B. (2010). *Doing Business in the ASEAN Countries*. New York: Business Expert Press.

Bhasin B. and Venkataramany S. (2010). Globalization of Entrepreneurship: Policy Considerations for SME Development in Indonesia. *International Business and Economics Research Journal*, 9(4), 95–103.

Harvie, C. (2004). East Asian SME Capacity Building, Competitiveness and Market Opportunities in a Global Economy Department of Economics, University of Wollongong, Working Paper 04–16, 2004.

Inmyxai, Somdy (2003). Small and Medium Enterprise (SME). Development Framework, in Lao PDR, Regional Workshop on Trade Capacity Building and Private Sector Development in Asia, sponsored by the OECD Development Co-operation Directorate and the Development Center, Phnom Penh, Cambodia, December, 2–3, 2003.

Kyophilavong, P. (2007). SME Development in Lao PDR, Economic Research Institute for ASEAN and East Asia (ERIA), ERIA Research Project No. 7, 2007, Jakarta, Indonesia.

Kyophilavong, P. (2009). Integrating Lao SMEs into a More Integrated East Asia Region, Economic Research Institute for ASEAN and East Asia (ERIA), ERIA Research Project No. 8, 2009, Jakarta, Indonesia.

Laos Small Medium Sized Enterprise Promotion and Development Office (SMEPDO) (2004). Definition of SMEs. Retrieved August 25, 2014 from http://www.smepdo.org/info/9/?lang=en.

Lin, H. (2007). SMEs in Asia and Globalization, Economic Research Institute for ASEAN and East Asia (ERIA). ERIA Research Project No. 5, 2007, Jakarta, Indonesia.

Nouansavanh, K. (2005). *Laotian Small and Medium Size Enterprises and the regional economic integration*. Osaka, Japan: Asian Community Research Center.

Phoumilay, P. and Douangsavanh, B. (2008). Country Paper – Lao PDR: Best Practices on SME Development and Management presented at the Joint Workshop on SME Development and Regional Economic Development, September 22–26, 2008, Tokyo, Japan.

RAM Consultancy (2005). SME Access to Financing: Addressing the Supply Side of SME Financing Final Main Report, REPFS Project 04/2003, Asean Secretariat, Indonesia. Retrieved May 12, 2010 from atwww.aseansec.org/aadcp/repsf/docs/04-003-FinalMainReport.pdf.

Southiseng, Ty, Walsh, J. and Anurit, P. (2007). Development of Excellent Entrepreneurs in Small and Medium Enterprises in Laos and Cambodia, GMSARN International Conference on Sustainable Development: Challenges and Opportunities for GMS, December 12–14, 2007.

Southiseng, S. and Walsh, J. (2010). Competition and Management Issues of SME Entrepreneurs in Laos: Evidence from Empirical Studies in Vientiane Municipality, Savannakhet and LuangPrabang. *Asian Journal of Business Management*, 2(3), 57–72.

Thiengthepvongsa, O. (2009). Facilitating landlocked and least developed country SMEs participation in trade, Regional Forum on Trade Facilitation and SMEs in Times of Crisis, organized by the World Bank's Development Research Group in Beijing, China on May 20–22, 2009.

Transparency International (2015). Corruption Perceptions Index. Retrieved April 15, 2015 from https://www.transparency.org/cpi2014/results.

United Nations Conference on Trade and Development (UNCTADSTAT) (2015a). National Accounts. GDP by Type of Expenditure and Value Added by Kind of Economic Activity, annual, 1970–2013, as a Percentage of GDP. Retrieved May 30, 2015 from http://unctadstat.unctad.org/wds/Report Folders/reportFolders.aspx?sCS_ChosenLang=en.

United Nations Conference on Trade and Development (UNCTADSTAT) (2015b). National Accounts. Real GDP Growth Rates, Total and Per Capita, annual, 1970–2013. Retrieved May 30, 2015 from http://unctadstat.unctad.org/wds/ReportFolders/reportFolders.aspx?sCS_Chosen Lang=en.

United Nations Conference on Trade and Development (UNCTADSTAT) (2015c). Population and Labor Force. Total Labour Force and Agriculture Labour Force, annual, 1980–2020. Retrieved May 30, 2015 from http://unctadstat.unctad.org/wds/ReportFolders/reportFolders.aspx?sCS_ ChosenLang=en.

United Nations Conference on Trade and Development (UNCTADSTAT) (2015d). Foreign Direction Investment. Inward Foreign Direct Investment Flows, annual, 1970–2013. Retrieved May 30, 2015 from http://unctadstat.unctad.org/wds/ReportFolders/reportFolders.aspx?sCS_ChosenLang=en.

US Department of State (2015). Background Notes of Countries. Retrieved February 1, 2015 from: http://www.state.gov/r/pa/ei/bgn/index.htm.

World Bank (2015). Doing business 2015 [PDF Reader version]. New York, NY: Palgrave Macmillan. Retrieved January 22, 2015, from http://www.doingbusiness.org/data/exploreeconomies/lao-pdr.

World Fact Book (2015). Retrieved April 15, 2015 from https;//www.cia.gov/library/publications/ the-world-factbook/goes/la/html.

Xayphone, K. and Kimbara, T. (2007). Corporate Financing and Performance of SMEs: The Moderating Effects of Ownership Types and Management Styles. *Malaysian Management Review*, 42, 119–133.

Xayphone, K. and Kimbara, T. (2008). Financial Performance of Founder-managed and Professionally-managed SMEs: An Empirical Investigation of Lao Trading Firms. *The Journal of International Development and Cooperation*, 14, 13–25.

5

MAPPING ENTREPRENEURIAL ACTIVITIES AND ENTREPRENEURIAL ATTITUDES IN TURKEY

Esra Karadeniz and Özlem Özdemir

Introduction

Entrepreneurship has been shown to be one of the key drivers of economic growth for nations. However, similar arguments also apply at the sub-national level. Entrepreneurship can be seen as a major driver of economic growth for localities and regions (Bosma, 2009). It is important, therefore, to understand the sub-national variations in the level of entrepreneurship, just as is the case at a cross-national level, as a prelude to identifying the institutional environment required in order to facilitate growth in regions and localities where it is lacking. In this chapter, therefore, we first examine the level of entrepreneurship in Turkey at the national level compared with other developing countries and then turn our attention to the regional variations in the level of entrepreneurship. This study is the first attempt to investigate the level of entrepreneurship in Turkey at the regional level. The data used in this study were collected by means of the national Adult Population Survey (APS) from the Global Entrepreneurship Monitor (GEM) project (Reynolds et al., 2005) conducted in Turkey since 2006. The dataset consists of about 2,400 interviews conducted each year between 2006 and 2012 and 32,000 interviews conducted in 2013 with a representative sample of adults (18–64 years old) covering 26 regions.

The GEM broadly defines entrepreneurship as any attempt at new business or new venture creation. This definition encompasses a broad scope of entrepreneurial behaviors. As such, the GEM breaks down the entrepreneurial business cycle into several stages. For this chapter we focus on two stages which are of particular relevance to Turkey. The first stage of entrepreneurship involves the respondents' readiness to begin an entrepreneurial venture or their intent to start a business within the next three years (termed "Entrepreneurial Intention"). The second stage is the Total Early-Stage Entrepreneur Activity (TEA) rate. The TEA is an indication of how many individuals in an economy are currently participating in entrepreneurial activities. This stage of entrepreneurship is further broken down into two categories, namely Nascent Entrepreneurs and New Firm Entrepreneurs. Nascent entrepreneurs are those actively involved in a startup who expect to own all or part of the new firm and no wages have been paid for more than three months. New Firm Entrepreneurs, meanwhile, are the individuals who are involved as an owner or manager in new firms and wages have been paid for between three to 42 months.

43

The next section of this chapter explains the overall level of entrepreneurial activity in Turkey by breaking down entrepreneurship into the different stages described above. The third section then seeks to outline the entrepreneurial activities in different regions of Turkey, which is the first attempt to depict regional variations in entrepreneurship in Turkey. Finally, the last section summarizes the findings of the GEM data collected for Turkey between the years 2006 and 2013.

Entrepreneurial activities in Turkey

Turkey, as a developing country, is strategically located at the crossroads of Europe and Asia, and is considered to be a geographical and cultural bridge between East and West. Turkey's location clearly makes it a country of geo-strategic and cultural importance. When the Turkish Republic was founded in 1923, the level of entrepreneurship was arguably weak because of the social and cultural legacy inherited from the Ottoman regime in which entrepreneurial activity was under the control of foreign ethnic and religious minorities. Most commerce, finance, and the existing small industry was in the hands of Greeks and Armenians, who were exempted from military service and had their taxes remitted.

Since the establishment of the Turkish Republic, government policies have been designed to encourage private enterprise and to promote industrial development. However, the weakness of entrepreneurship amongst the Turkish population, and the impact of the world depression in 1929 resulted in slow economic development. Hence, the Turkish government embarked in 1934 upon a policy of industrialization which it pursued directly through the establishment of state-owned enterprises. After World War II, the Turkish economy became more liberal in orientation. There was a mixed economy consisting of both public and private enterprises. The rapid growth of entrepreneurship amongst the Turkish population induced rapid industrialization.

During the 1970s, the Turkish economy increasingly relied on a free market approach. The share of public enterprises in the manufacturing and service sectors started falling. Since the 1980s, moreover, Turkey has gradually opened up its markets through economic reforms by reducing government controls on foreign trade and investment and the privatization of publicly owned industries, as well as the liberalization of many sectors to private and foreign participants.

Today, Turkey has the world's 17th largest GDP by personal purchasing power (PPP) and 18th largest nominal GDP and is among the founding members of the OECD and the G20 major economies. Indeed, Turkey was one of the fastest growing economies in the world from 2002 to 2007, a period which witnessed a real GDP growth rate averaging 6.8 percent per annum. However, growth slowed to 1 percent in 2008, and in 2009 the Turkish economy was affected by the global financial crisis, with a reduction of 5 percent. The Turkish economy then bounced back and achieved a growth rate of 9.2 percent and 8.5 percent in the years 2010 and 2011 respectively. However, Turkey's rate of economic growth has slowed down again since 2012.

There has been a dramatic shift from a predominantly agriculture-based economy to an increasingly industrialized and service-based economy. The share of agricultural output which was about 43 percent of GNP in early 1920 has decreased to a level of only 14.5 percent today, while services have increased to 57.8 percent. Turkish industry is now rapidly changing in favor of private enterprises. Turkish firms generally are small and medium-sized enterprises (SMEs) operating in the traditional manufacturing sector rather than in new technology-based sectors. SMEs constitute 99.9 percent of the total number of enterprises, 76 percent of employment, 53 percent of wages and salaries, 63 percent of turnover, 53.3 percent of value added at factor cost, and 53.7 percent of gross investment in tangible goods. SMEs account for 62.6 percent of exports and 38.5 percent of imports (TUİK, 2014). In 2005, Turkish SMEs only had a total share of 38 percent in total investments, 6.5 percent of value added and 10 percent of exports. These numbers clearly demonstrate that the internationalization of Turkey's SMEs has been increased and SMEs have been making significant contributions to the Turkish economy.

Examining entrepreneurial activity in Turkey, a significant difference exists between two time periods, 2006–2008 and 2010–2013. We find that the average level of early stage entrepreneurial activity (TEA) was 5.9 percent for the period 2006–2008, which increased to 10.7 percent for the period 2010–2013. Before the financial crisis, about 6 out of every 100 adults were entrepreneurs; after the crisis, this figure was 11 out of every 100 adults. When compared with the 2006–2008 period, the 2010–2013 period showed a more positive outlook for entrepreneurship in Turkey. The strong suggestion, nevertheless, is that this growth is predominantly a result of the growth of necessity-driven entrepreneurship.

Nascent entrepreneurship for 2006–2008 was engaged in by 2.4 percent of the population, but there was a noticeable expansion over the 2010–2013 period which recorded 5.7 percent of the population engaged in such entrepreneurial endeavor. On the other hand, the 3.6 percent of the adult population in Turkey who were owner-managers of 3–42 month-old (new) businesses in 2006–2008 increased to 5.3 percent in 2010–2013. The increase in the prevalence of new business may reflect an improvement in economic growth. Over this time period, therefore, nascent entrepreneurial activity showed a larger increase than did new business activity. This indicates a decrease in businesses that have survived beyond the startup phase. From a policy perceptive, therefore, the supporting and mentoring of entre- preneurs through the difficult process of firm birth are important for the sustainability of startups in Turkey.

Similar to entrepreneurial activity, entrepreneurial intention rates in Turkey have increased over the years. We find that there were more people who wanted to start businesses in 2013 compared with 2006. The entrepreneurial intention rate was 22 percent in 2006, meaning that 22 out of every 100 people had the intention to become involved in entrepre- neurial activity in the next three years. By 2013, this figure had increased to 34 percent, displaying that over one-third of the population had an entrepreneurial intention. Indeed, Turkey is ahead of many other developing economies in this respect, ranking 11th out of 30 comparison countries. This increase in the rate of entrepreneurial intention and the rate of entrepreneurship may well lead to an increase in the entrepreneurial activity in the coming years in Turkey.

However, not just the number of entrepreneurs and entrepreneurial intention have increased in Turkey; the proportion of entrepreneurs that are opportunity-driven has also increased and thus the quality of entrepreneurs has improved. The number of entrepreneurs who have turned to entrepreneurship in order to pursue a business opportunity has increased in Turkey from 3.4 percent during the period 2006–2008 to 6.8 percent in the period 2010–2013. Turkey had a more favorable ratio of opportunity- to necessity-driven early stage entrepreneurs in the period 2010–2013 compared with the period 2006–2008.

During the 2010–2013 period, the demographic portrait of early-stage entrepreneurs turns out to be very different from that of the 2006–2008 period. People who start business in Turkey are relatively older, of a higher income group and more educated. There is a slight increase in the share of women among early-stage entrepreneurs after 2009. After the crisis, therefore, early-stage entrepreneurs look like a more privileged group of people than before the crisis.

Several attitudinal factors may affect respondents' intentions to start a business. These include the perceptions of fear of failure, the status of entrepreneurs in society, having the skills to start a new business, and seeing opportunities for new enterprises (Özdemir and Karadeniz, 2011). Understanding these perceptions may provide deeper insights into entrepreneurial aspirations in Turkey. First, Turkish people are less risk averse than those from other developing countries. Only 33 percent of Turkish people indicated that a fear of failure would prevent them from starting a business. This figure was lower than 18 other countries (with Turkey ranking 12th of 30 comparison countries) in GEM 2013 and slightly lower than the average rate for developing countries of 42.30 percent. Another factor where Turkey ranked well against other developing countries was related to perceptions of entrepreneurs' societal status in Turkey. Seventy-four percent of Turkish people agreed that successful entrepreneurs enjoyed a good status in the country, and Turkey appeared to be ahead of other developing economies in this respect, ranking 8th out of 29 comparison countries.

Perceptions on entrepreneurs' career prospects were also analyzed. About 64 percent of Turkish people indicated that entrepreneurship is a good career choice. Turkey appeared to be lagging behind other developing economies in this respect, ranking 21st out of 29 comparison countries. Another factor where Turkey did not rank well against other developing countries was related to seeing good opportunities to start a business within the next six months; 39 percent of Turkish respondents reported that there would be good opportunities to start a business within the next six months; Turkey ranked 19th out of the 30 developing economies in this respect. Another factor where Turkey ranked close to the average against other developing countries was related to entrepreneurship education. Turkey ranked 16th out of 30 countries in terms of having the perceived skills to start a business. Some 52 percent of respondents felt they had the knowledge, skill, and experience to start a business, which was close to the average of developing countries of 54 percent.

The entrepreneurs' innovation aspiration in terms of product and business innovation and technology innovation increased during 2010–2013 in Turkey compared to the period 2006–2008. Those firms that use the latest technology expect less competition and introduce more new services or products to the market place. Entrepreneurs offering products seen as innovative are more than average in Turkey as compared to other GEM participating countries. The proportion of early-stage entrepreneurs with high growth aspirations in Turkey was 3.36 percent in 2013, which is higher than the average of efficiency-driven economies (1.35 percent), ranking Turkey in second place in the participating 30 efficiency-driven countries.

Networking in certain environments will enhance the performance of entrepreneurs. The kind of networking most used by Turkish entrepreneurs is their private environment for their business. Private networks are primarily family-oriented network structures. Women entrepreneurs generally tend to rely more on their private networks compared with men. In addition, the work environment is actually more prominent for women than for men. Thus, networks women create at work could also significantly influence their decision-making process. The more educated members are invariably likely to be exposed to a wider social structure which enables them to have access to a larger set of people within the social strata other than family members. The professional and international environment is especially noticeable for entrepreneurs who have higher income levels.

In sum, after seven years of participating in the GEM project, the Turkish entrepreneurial landscape has changed in many ways. The most pertinent finding has been that total early-stage entrepreneurial activity has increased. It must be noted that Turkey is still a long way from where it should be with regard to entrepreneurship when compared with similar economies. Entrepreneurial intention has risen significantly in recent years too, and is much higher than similar economies. Such national-level figures, however, mask significant intra-national or regional variations within Turkey so far as entrepreneurial activity and intention are concerned. To this, therefore, our attention now turns.

Regional entrepreneurial activities in Turkey

In the entrepreneurship literature, the study of regional variations is becoming increasingly important as a unit of analysis. Several studies have shown that regional differences in the level of entrepreneurship are extensive and persistent (Bosma, 2009; Tamásy, 2006). This study is the first attempt to investigate whether the level of entrepreneurial activity at the regional level in Turkey is similarly variable. In each region, the personal characteristics (gender, age, and education) of entrepreneurs, the motivation of entrepreneurs and people's attitudes towards entrepreneurship and entrepreneurial culture are examined in the following paragraphs.

In order to describe the regional variations in entrepreneurial activities in Turkey, the data from a standardized survey conducted with 33,287 individuals in 2013 in 26 regions is analyzed (see Table 5.1 for the regional classification used). Examining the data, the finding is that the Middle East Anatolian and South East Anatolian regions are found to have the highest rate of the entrepreneurial intention with 37.8 percent and 37.7 percent respectively. In sum, out of 100 individuals, approximately 38 of them have the intention to become an entrepreneur in the future. This is compared with an overall rate of 32 percent for Turkey as a whole. With respect to the sub-regions, the Van sub-region (with 44 percent) and Mardin sub-region (41 percent) have the highest values for the Potential Entrepreneurship Index.

According to the Potential Entrepreneurship Index, the West Marmara and East Black Sea regions have the lowest entrepreneurial level. The potential entrepreneur rate of West Marmara region is 24 percent, so out of 100 people only 24 have the intention to have an entrepreneurial activity or to become an entrepreneur within the next three years. Inside the region, consistent with the south part, the Balıkesir sub-region has a rate of 23.6 percent, while Tekirdag sub-region has 23.7 percent. The East Black Sea region, which consists of the Trabzon sub-region, has a potential entrepreneurial activity rate of 25.6 percent. The individuals living in this region have an intention level to become an entrepreneur or have an entrepreneurial activity that is much lower than the average intention rate of the whole country.

Turning away from entrepreneurial intention and towards actual entrepreneurial activity, there are again some marked regional variations within Turkey. To study this, we commence by examining "nascent entrepreneurs" who are just starting up a new business venture. The West Anatolian region has the highest rate of startup entrepreneurs (7.98 percent). The region that has the second highest number of startups is East Marmara (6.64 percent) and the third-placed region is found to be the Mediterranean region with a rate of 6.24 percent. The West Black Sea and East Black Sea regions are the ones with the lowest number of startup entrepreneurs with rates of 3.64 percent and 3.37 percent respectively. If we look at the sub-regional level startups, the Ankara, Aydin, and Bursa sub-regions have the highest number of startup entrepreneurs (8.4 percent, 7.6 percent and 7.5 percent respectively), whilst the Kastamonu and Trabzon sub-regions have the lowest rate of startups at 3.5 percent and 3.4 percent respectively. Again, therefore, there are significant regional and sub-regional

Table 5.1 Sub-Regions in Turkey – NUTS-1 and NUTS-2 Llevels

NUTS-1	NUTS-2
Istanbul Region (TR1)	Istanbul Subregion (TR10)
West Marmara Region (TR2)	Tekirdağ Subregion (TR21)
	Balıkesir Subregion (TR22)
Aegean Region (TR3)	Izmir Subregion (TR31)
	Aydın Subregion (TR32)
	Manisa Subregion (TR33)
East Marmara Region (TR4)	Bursa Subregion (TR41)
	Kocaeli Subregion (TR42)
West Anatolia Region (TR5)	Ankara Subregion (TR51)
	Konya Subregion (TR52)
Mediterranean Region (TR6)	Antalya Subregion (TR61)
	Adana Subregion (TR62)
	Hatay Subregion (TR63)
Central Anatolia Region (TR7)	Kırıkkale Subregion (TR71)
	Kayseri Subregion (TR72)
West Black Sea Region (TR8)	Zonguldak Subregion (TR81)
	Kastamonu Subregion (TR82)
	Samsun Subregion (TR83)
East Black Sea Region (TR9)	Trabzon Subregion (TR90)
Northeast Anatolia Region (TRA)	Erzurum Subregion (TRA1)
	Ağrı Subregion (TRA2)
Central East Anatolia Region (TRB)	Malatya Subregion (TRB1)
	Van Subregion (TRB2)
Southeast Anatolia Region (TRC)	Gaziantep Subregion (TRC1)
	Şanlıurfa Subregion (TRC2)
	Mardin Subregion (TRC3)

variations in startup rates in Turkey with some regions having twice the startup rate of other regions. Why this is the case will need to be investigated in future studies.

Similar regional variations are identified when examining the proportion of "new firm entrepreneurs". For this kind of entrepreneurship, the South East Anatolia region has the highest rate of 6.20 percent. Within this region, Sanlıurfa sub-region is the top region with the highest number of new firm entrepreneurs out of the 26 regions (6.5 percent), followed by Aegean and Middle Anatolia region (5.2 percent for both). In stark contrast, the West Marmara and West Black Sea regions have the lowest rates out of 12 regions, where Tekirdag sub-region (3.5 percent) and Kastamonu sub-region (2.5 percent) have the lowest rates out of all the 26 regions.

When the startup entrepreneurs and new firm entrepreneurs are combined, one has the "Early Stage Entrepreneurship Index" (TEA). Examining the regional variations in this index, the finding is that the West Anatolia region has the highest number of individuals (13 percent) that fits into the index definition. This number is 10 percent for the whole country, thus, out of 100 people, 10 of them have been planning or starting an entrepreneurial activity in Turkey. The index number is found to be 11 percent for South East Anatolia, 7 percent for West Black Sea, and 8 percent for East Black Sea regions. When we examine the TEA for the 26 sub-regions, we observe that the ones that have the higher index values are Aydın sub-region (13.33 percent), Ankara sub-region (13.24 percent), and Bursa sub-region (2.28 percent), whereas the ones with comparatively lower values are Trabzon sub-region (7.72 percent), Samsun sub-region (7.41 percent), and Kastamonu sub-region (5.84 percent). Figure 5.1 provides a summary map of the TEA Index for the 26 sub-regions.

When we seek to explain these regional variations in the level of entrepreneurship in Turkey, taking into account the differences in economic development in each region is crucial, which we believe determine whether an individual decides to become an entrepreneur for necessity-driven rationales (having no other option of earning money) or because of the opportunities (seeing entrepreneurship as a good option to earn money). For example, İstanbul, the city with the highest level of economic development, has the highest rate of opportunity-based entrepreneurial activities. In fact, 81 percent of the entrepreneurs in Istanbul have started their business because they have seen entrepreneurship as an opportunity. This rate is 67 percent for the whole country and 38 percent for the South East Anatolia region, which has the lowest income level. Figure 5.2 provides a summary map for the level of opportunity-driven entrepreneurship across the 26 sub-regions of Turkey. It is not solely the level of economic development in each region and sub-region however, that can influence the level and nature of entrepreneurship.

According to the entrepreneurship literature on the variations in the rate of entrepreneurial activities, the demographic characteristics of an individual are found to be one of the most important determinants of being an entrepreneur (Arennius and Minniti, 2005; Bosma and Harding, 2007; Parker, 2009; Kautonen et al, 2014). For example, on the issue of gender, most entrepreneurs are found to be men (Levesque and Minniti, 2006; Grilo and Irigoyen, 2005). In fact, 76.92 percent of entrepreneurs are male in the West Black Sea region which has the highest male entrepreneurs' rate, whereas this rate has its lowest value for the Aegean region (64.8 percent). Further, the rate of women entrepreneurs has the highest value for Aydın and Bursa sub-regions for the Early Stage Entrepreneurial Activities, while Kastamonu, Samsun, and Van sub-regions have the lowest number of women entrepreneurs. There are also variations by age. The North East Black Sea region, Middle East Anatolia, and South East Anatolia are the regions that have the highest young people population and for these regions, the rate of young entrepreneurs between the ages of 18 to 24 is the highest at 21 percent. This rate is 16 percent nationwide. Most of the entrepreneurs in the country (about 65 percent of them) are 25–44 years old.

There are variations at the education level as well. The university graduate entrepreneurs' rate is the highest in the Mediterranean region and İstanbul. In stark contrast, the lowest university graduate rate of entrepreneurship is seen in the Middle East Anatolia region. The Middle East and South East Anatolia regions, however, have entrepreneurs with the lowest education level overall. As we look at the different types of entrepreneurship based on the reason to start a business, the education level of opportunity-based entrepreneurship is found to be much higher than the necessity-based entrepreneurship overall, except in the Middle East Anatolia region. More specifically, for example, in İstanbul, 53 percent of university graduate entrepreneurs enter entrepreneurship for opportunity-driven rationales.

There are many other factors that influence the individuals' decisions to become an entrepreneur. Some people choose to be an entrepreneur because they know another person who is an entrepreneur. This kind of entrepreneurs' rate is 31.69 percent overall for Turkey and

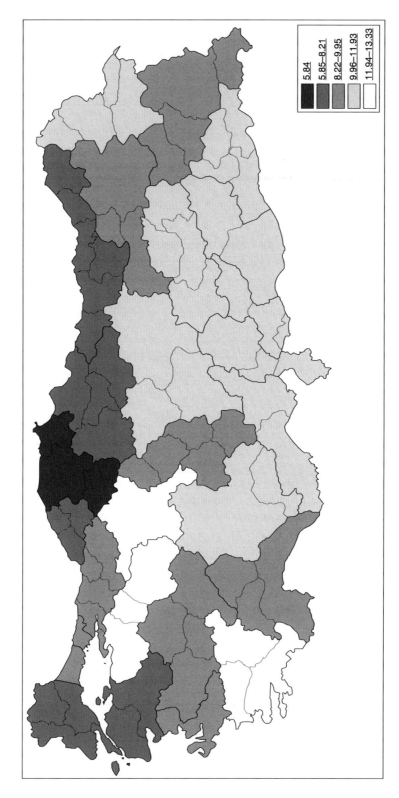

Figure 5.1 The Entrepreneurial Activities in 26 Sub-Regions of Turkey (NUTS-2)

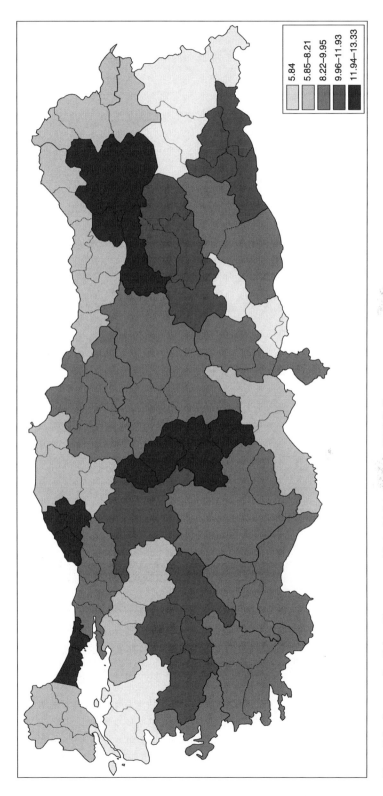

Figure 5.2 Opportunity-Driven Entrepreneurship in 26 Sub-Regions (NUTS-2)

Legend:
- 5.84
- 5.85–8.21
- 8.22–9.95
- 9.96–11.93
- 11.94–13.33

regionally highest for East Marmara (34.14 percent) and East Black Sea (34.25 percent), and lowest for West Anatolia region (30 percent). Another factor influencing people's decision to start their own business is fear of failure. Individuals in Turkey are found to be braver compared to other GEM project participating countries. In Turkey, people in the South East Anatolia region are the ones that have the least fear of failure (30.26 percent). However, in Middle Anatolia and İstanbul, the rate of individuals who have fear of failure is 37.2 percent and 35.55 percent respectively. Believing that new opportunities will appear to start a new business in the near future is another determinant of opening your own business and 46.29 percent of the individuals are found to think that way in the South East Anatolia region, which has the highest rate among all regions. In addition, thinking that one has enough knowledge and skill to be an entrepreneur provides courage to start their own business. Individuals who live in the North East and Middle East Anatolia regions perceive themselves to be most knowledgeable to be entrepreneurs, whereas people in West Black Sea region and İstanbul are the least confident about their knowledge and skill to start their own business. This could be due to the business environment for these areas, especially İstanbul, being extremely uncertain with respect to financial fluctuations and informal rules that a person needs to know if s/he wants to open a business.

Some people think that being an entrepreneur is a positive thing in one's career path and these kinds of individuals are mostly found in the South East (69.31 percent) and Middle East Anatolia (70.32 percent) regions. For the sub-regions, Van (72.17 percent), Mardin (71.40 percent), and Gaziantep (69.82 percent) are the cities that have people perceiving entrepreneurship as a positive career. Further, the more the individuals observe that being an entrepreneur is respected by society, the more likely they are to become an entrepreneur. Some 79.01 percent of the people who live in the South East Anatolia region think that entrepreneurs have a high status in society, where this percentage is 73.95 percent for the whole country and 80.25 percent for Gaziantep. Moreover, and related to this, only 49.41 percent of the people who live in İstanbul state that they see some news in the media about successful entrepreneurs. This value is lower than the nationwide percentage (52.66 percent) and is highest in the East Anatolia region (57.03 percent) and Van sub-region (58.31 percent).

Conclusions

This chapter has revealed that government support for entrepreneurship in Turkey is improving through the development of the formal institutional environment, such as the financial environment and government regulation policies and programs. This is reflected in the increase in entrepreneurial intention and entrepreneurial activity. However, these conditions still need to be improved. The gap between male and female entrepreneurship presents some concerns. The institutional environment in Turkey therefore needs to place more emphasis on supporting and encouraging female entrepreneurship in order to further increase female participation in entrepreneurial activity. Moreover, and more generally, more selective support measures and policies are needed for displaying an entrepreneurial intention so that it can be converted into entrepreneurial activity, as is more support required for opportunity-driven startups, which have the greatest impact on the economy.

Moreover, most Turkish entrepreneurs were found in the higher income levels of society. Clearly, starting a company if one's household income is relatively low is difficult. It reveals that banks and other lending institutions should develop more flexible lending policies for entrepreneurs, especially when collateral requirements are concerned. Special attention should be paid to these low- and middle-income earners. On the whole nevertheless, care must be taken in this regard. Support programs should be focusing on backing quality rather than quantity. It is clear, nevertheless, that there are significant national variations in entrepreneurial intention and activity and government support programs need to consider these variations and what might be done in order to support those populations with lower than average participation rates.

There are also significant regional variations in entrepreneurial intention and activity. Again, therefore, consideration for support of those regions with lower than average participation rates needs to be considered. The strong intimation, therefore, is that consideration of the institutional context is needed not only at a national but also the regional and local level. If this chapter encourages such a consideration, then it will have achieved its objective.

Acknowledgments

The authors are grateful to Republic of Turkey Small and Medium Enterprises Development Organization (KOSGEB), Turkish Economy Bank (TEB), and Yeditepe University for their support and contribution to the Global Entrepreneurship Monitor (GEM) project. The authors also thank PÄ±nar Eraslan for the construction of the maps.

References

Arennius, P. and Minniti, M. (2005). Perceptual variables and nascent entrepreneurship. *Small Business Economics*, 24(3), 233–247.

Bosma, N. (2009). *The geography of entrepreneurial activity and regional development: Multilevel analyses for Dutch and European regions*. Netherlands: A-D Druckb.b., Zeist.

Bosma, N. and Harding, R. (2007). *Global entrepreneurship: GEM 2006 summary results*, Babson College and London Business School, London, U.K., and Babson Park, MA.

Grilo, I. and Irigoyen, J. M. (2006). Entrepreneurship in the EU: to wish and not to be. *Small Business Economics*, 26(4), 305–318.

Kautonen, T., Down, S. and Minniti, M. (2014). Ageing and entrepreneurial preferences. *Small Business Economics*, 42(3), 579–594.

Levesque, M. and Minniti, M. (2006). The effect of aging on entrepreneurial behaviour. *Journal of Business Venturing*, 21(2), 177–194.

Özdemir, Ö. and Karadeniz, E. E. (2011). Investigating the factors affecting total entrepreneurial activities in Turkey. *METU Studies in Development*, 38(3), 275–290.

Parker, S. C. (2009). *The economics of entrepreneurship*. Cambridge, UK: Cambridge University Press.

Reynolds, P., Bosma, N., Autio, E., Hunt, S., Bono, N.D., Servais, I., Lopez-Garcia, P. and Chin, N. (2005). Global entrepreneurship monitor: data collection design and implementation 1998–2003. *Small Business Economics*, 24(3), 323–334.

Tamásy C. (2006). Determinants of regional entrepreneurship dynamics in contemporary Germany: a conceptual and empirical analysis. *Regional Studies*, 40(4), 365–384.

TUİK (2014). Turkish Statistical Institute, www.tukstat.gov.tr. Accessed June 6, 2015.

6

REGULATIVE ENVIRONMENT AND ENTREPRENEURIAL ACTIVITY

Insights from Sub-Saharan Africa

Eldrede Kahiya and Rebecca Kennedy

Introduction

The ever expanding prominence of entrepreneurship as a powerful driver of economic development and growth is undeniable. The entrepreneurship discipline has come a long way since Baumol, Kirzner, and Schumpeter among others, penned some of the influential articles on the subject matter.[1] As testament to its importance, entrepreneurship is now represented on a global scale through the Global Entrepreneurship Summit (GES). Starting in 2009, the GES has become one of the most vibrant fora where academics, entrepreneurs, researchers, and policymakers engage in an exchange of ideas, mentoring, and collaboration on various aspects pertinent to entrepreneurship. The sixth annual GES was held on July 25–26, 2015 in Nairobi where the US president gave the keynote speech outlining the drivers, barriers, and benefits of entrepreneurship. One excerpt of his address, which is pertinent to this chapter, was his description of entrepreneurship (The White House, Office of the Press Secretary, 2015, para. 4):

> Entrepreneurship creates new jobs and new businesses, new ways to deliver basic services, new ways of seeing the world—it's the spark of prosperity. It helps citizens stand up for their rights and push back against corruption. Entrepreneurship offers a positive alternative to the ideologies of violence and division that can all too often fill the void when young people don't see a future for themselves.

Worded carefully to align with the Sub-Saharan context, much of the keynote address highlighted not only the economic benefits but the social and geopolitical implications of entrepreneurial activities. In committing another US$1 billion toward funding projects around the world, the US president warned business leaders and policymakers to ensure that institutional reforms were in place to encourage entrepreneurs to take that first step. This connection between the regulative institutional environment and the capacity of entrepreneurs to "take that first step" forms the core of this chapter.

The purpose of this chapter is to examine the factors underlying entrepreneurial activity in Sub-Saharan Africa. The theoretical framework used derives from institutional theory.

Specifically, the chapter investigates the influence of the regulative institutional environment on entrepreneurial activity for a group of Sub-Saharan countries belonging to the Southern African Development Community (SADC). The selection of the SADC region as the context of this research is for two reasons. First, examining the SADC region is relevant for enhancing knowledge in entrepreneurship given that traditionally, and even in recent years, Africa's emerging markets have remained marginalized in mainstream research. Second, and from a practitioner's perspective, the SADC region is an integrated economic bloc with vast economic potential that remains largely untapped.

This chapter seeks to contribute to both knowledge and policy development at various levels. From a scholarly level the chapter investigates whether the relationship between institutional quality and entrepreneurial activities, developed predominantly from industrialized and non-African emerging markets, translates to the African context. This is fundamental for painting a more informative picture on the generalizability of theory to emerging market contexts. For business leaders and policymakers, the chapter identifies factors that impede or enable entrepreneurial activities and lays the platform from which institutional reforms can emanate. The chapter provides various indicators of regulative quality, drawing an empirical relationship between these factors and the level of entrepreneurial activities. The empirical results of this chapter are positioned to provide answers regarding the forms of institutional reform the SADC region requires to compete both regionally and globally. The subsequent section provides an overview of the literature on drivers of entrepreneurship which culminates in the construction of the theoretical framework linking the regulative institutional environment to entrepreneurial activity.

Drivers of entrepreneurship: an overview

This paraphrased literature review on the drivers of entrepreneurship is not designed to serve as an exhaustive discussion of the various facets of this multidimensional phenomenon; rather, it has been structured to outline some key themes and employ these as a prelude to the theoretical framework. The practice of entrepreneurship is considered to trace back to the beginning of time and the study of entrepreneurship goes back almost a century but attempts to create nomenclature on the drivers of entrepreneurial activities are fairly recent. Among some of the papers that have helped guide this substream of entrepreneurship literature are the studies by Gartner (1985), Covin and Slevin (1991), and Low and MacMillan (1988).

Gartner (1985) argued that new venture formation was a multifaceted phenomenon that involved individuals, the organization, process, and the environment.[2] A venture could be described in terms of the attributes of its founders, the type of entity it morphed into, the process from which it culminated, and also how the environment shaped or molded it. Gartner discussed individual characteristics as elements of an entrepreneur's personal and behavioral profiles. The organization was conceptualized as referring to the type or nature of the firm and how it fit into an entrepreneurial ecosystem. "Process" related mainly to how an entrepreneur set about to discover opportunities, mobilize resources, and create products necessary to exploit those opportunities. Similarly, in drawing a distinction between environmental determinism and strategic choice, Gartner defined the environment as a plethora of non-controllable exogenous elements that influence venture creation.

Covin and Slevin (1991) expanded Gartner's (1985) theorization and outlined a conceptual model of entrepreneurship comprising external variables, top management values and philosophies, business practices and competitive strategies, organizational structure, and entrepreneurial posture. There are parallels between Covin and Slevin's external variables and Gartner's description of the environment. Likewise, organizational structure in Covin and Slevin's model is conceptually similar to Gartner's perspective. However, Covin and Slevin sought to develop a deeper approach for encapsulating Gartner's individual and process variables, which they split into three elements in an effort to distinguish firm-wide competitive strategy from its entrepreneurial posture and also top management values and philosophies.

Another informative study published around the same time was Low and MacMillan's (1988) conceptual paper on the numerous theoretical perspectives from which entrepreneurship could be studied. In essence, Low and Macmillan proposed a way of organizing the myriad variables according to theory-based themes such as social–cultural, network, finance, economic, and population ecology perspectives. Gartner's (1985) individual factors align with the "trait approach" to entrepreneurship and the assertion that "entrepreneurs are born, not made" (Brockhaus, 1980, 1982; McClelland, 1961). This is also congruous with the social development model of venture creation wherein Gibb and Ritchie (1982) claim that multitudinous social factors (e.g. class structure, lifestyle, occupation choice and career development, work history, family origin, education) drive venture formation (Cooper and Dunkelberg, 1986; O'Farrell and Pickles, 1989). A myopic focus on theory-based themes driven by individual-level factors is deficient as it fails to address exogenous drivers of new venture formation.

Entrepreneurship and new venture creation comprises a bifurcation of phenomena; nascent exploitable opportunities and enterprising individuals (Venkataraman, 1997). This is supported by Cooper's (1981) assertion that the strategic drivers of venture formation are the entrepreneur (including their unique background influencing motivations, skills, knowledge, and perceptions) and the influence of environmental factors exogenous to the individual that influence the salience of the business environment and formation endeavors. Baumol (1996) has also articulated a relation between the institutional environment and enterprising individuals who are willing to create firms. Milne and Thompson (1982) claim that venture growth is not solely derivative of static personal traits extant at start-up; indeed, individual factors adapt in response to engaging with the dynamic external context within which the new venture operates. An example of this is firm restructuring and redundancy events which act as psychological "trigger" events, "pushing" individuals to form new ventures (Binks and Jennings, 1986; Birley and Westhead, 1994; Storey, 1982).

It must be stressed that no singular factor can articulate the complex drivers contributing toward nascent ventures (Westhead, 1990). Reciprocal interactions may exist between the institutional environment and individual characteristics; the environment likely influences individual, process, and organization factors, and entrepreneurs likely engage in behaviors that impact the external environment (Shane, Locke and Collins, 2003).

The specific focus of this chapter is on the population ecology perspective. This perspective aligns with the external variables/environment in that it suggests that the very existence or survival of a species is intertwined with the vagaries of the broader ecosystem (Aldrich, 1990). We adopt this perspective to examine if, and how, entrepreneurial activity is connected to the broader external environment.

Institutional environment and entrepreneurial activities

The theoretical framework for this chapter is constructed around Gartner's (1985, p. 700) description of the institutional environment as the "relatively fixed conditions imposed on a new venture from without." According to Shane and Kolvereid (1995), the institutional

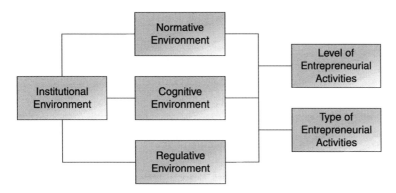

Figure 6.1   Institutional Environment and Entrepreneurial Activities

Source: Adapted from Scott (1995)

environment dictates the level of resource endowment in the market (munificence), the magnitude of dynamism (volatility), the intensity of competitive rivalry (hostility), and the assortment of issues the venture must face (complexity). As such, Aldrich and Wiedenmayer (1993) contend that the quality of the institutional environment has an effect on entrepreneurial activities.

Scott (1995) pointed out that a way to capture this relationship involves separating the institutional environment into three components, namely normative, cognitive, and regulative, as shown in Figure 6.1. Stenholm, Acs, and Wuebker (2013) describe the normative dimension in the context of beliefs, attitudes, and norms regarding entrepreneurial activities. According to Spencer and Gomez (2003), the normative perspective takes into account the general cultural values and individual traits that may be linked to entrepreneurial proclivity. The cognitive dimension is associated with the mental frameworks entrepreneurs use to process and interpret information on relevant phenomena (Stenholm, Acs and Wuebker, 2013). Elements of the cognitive dimension include knowledge, skills, and information entrepreneurs in a particular country possess or have access to (Kiss and Danis, 2008).

The regulative dimension is an amalgamation of formally sanctioned rules, regulations, and procedures that influence entrepreneurial activities (Scott, 1995), and constitutes the primary focus of this chapter. Not only does the regulative environment facilitate or constrain entrepreneurial activities, it creates institutional embeddedness which induces ventures to pursue strategies that align with such an environment. Likewise, Stenholm et al. (2013) explain that the institutional environment can impact both the level and the type of entrepreneurial activity, in particular the capacity to exploit international opportunities (Kiss and Danis, 2008). This chapter combines these perspectives and addresses the question of how the restraining or enabling role of the institutional environment may influence the level of entrepreneurial activity (Stenholm et al., 2013).

Building on North's (1990) work on institutional theory, a compelling line of enquiry arguing that the institutional environment can influence entrepreneurship has emerged (see Aldrich, 1990; Baumol, Litan and Schramm, 2009; Bruton, Ahlstrom and Li, 2010; Gnyawali and Fogel,1994; Hwang and Powell, 2005; Shane and Kolvereid, 1995; Scott, 1995; Stenholm et al., 2013). The remainder of this discussion is confined to an overview of some of the key factors limiting or expediting entrepreneurial activities. For a detailed discussion of the myriad regulative factors and their impacts on entrepreneurial activities, refer to Bruton et al.'s (2010) review.

The economic/political branch of the regulative dimension of institutional theory forms the basis of the conceptual framework (Baumol et al., 2009; Bruton et al., 2010; Scott, 1995). Entrepreneurs are discouraged from starting new ventures if formal rules and regulations are restrictive or non-existent, a situation which creates voids that are filled by informal regulations (Bruton et al., 2010). Conversely, entrepreneurs are encouraged by transparent regulations which are favorable to entrepreneurial activity (Campbell and Rogers, 2007). Thus the rules, regulations, procedures, documentation, cost, and time which set the parameters for ventures to operate, have an impact on entrepreneurial activity (Estrin, Aidis and Mickiewicz, 2007). The propensity to establish a new venture is heightened if entrepreneurs are confronted with fewer hurdles in the start-up phase, as dictated by the characteristics of the regulative regime, indicating that government policy can affect the development of an environment to support, or constrain, entrepreneurship (Dana, 1987, 1990; Young and Welsch, 1990). This need for a conducive regulative environment may be greater in emerging market economies and developing countries (El-Namaki, 1988; Segura, 1988). In line with past studies,[3] this chapter theorizes that:

H$_1$: The better the quality of the regulative institutional environment the higher the level of entrepreneurial activity

The Sub-Saharan context

Because one of the things that we have come to understand—and this is particularly relevant to Africa—is that in order to create successful entrepreneurs, the government also has a role in creating the transparency, and the rule of law, and the ease of doing business, and the anti-corruption agenda that creates a platform for people to succeed.
(The White House, Office of the Press Secretary, 2015, para. 8)

An interesting case in point is De Soto's (2000) observation on how registering a new firm in Sub-Saharan Africa can take two to three months as opposed to a day or two in countries such as Hong Kong. These disparities may explain differences in relative levels of entrepreneurial activities observed around the world (Spencer and Gomez, 2003). Keefer and Knack (1997) have gone as far as arguing that such discrepancies account for why some developing countries may never emerge, while De Soto has used the same premise to illustrate why western capitalism fails in countless jurisdictions around the world.

Against this backdrop, this chapter contributes to the body of knowledge on the relationship between the regulative institutional environment and levels of entrepreneurial activity by examining this in an African context. The general under-representation of studies focusing on African emerging markets is a reverberating theme in entrepreneurship research. For this reason, Kshetri and Dholakia (2011) have implored researchers to investigate more emerging markets beyond Brazil, Russia, India, China, and South Africa (BRICS). Not only do Bruton, Ahlstrom, and Obloj (2008) view the under-representation of emerging markets as disappointing, they consider the current situation untenable.

African economies have been commended by Ernst & Young (2015), the McKinsey Institute (see Roxburgh et al., 2010), and *The Economist* (2011) for making considerable strides over the last two decades. Among the highlights of the McKinsey report are, consumer spending of nearly $1 billion USD, 316 million mobile phone users since 2000, a collective GDP of $2.6 trillion USD by 2020, and a labor pool of over 1 billion employees by 2040 (Roxburgh et al., 2010). Despite these advances, major structural and regulative challenges persist. This reported growth comes against the milieu of significant trials including economic and social upheavals, unstable political environments, suppression of personal and economic freedoms, corruption, and unfavorable conditions for investment and entrepreneurship (*The Economist*, 2011). Given the impetus to investigate emerging markets beyond BRICS, the chapter focus is appropriately on the regulative dynamics of African economies, specifically, the Southern African Development Community (SADC).

SADC was formed in 1992 and comprises Angola, Botswana, Democratic Republic of Congo (DRC), Lesotho, Madagascar, Malawi, Mauritius, Mozambique, Namibia, Seychelles, South Africa, Swaziland, Tanzania, Zambia, and Zimbabwe. Its origins trace back to 1980, when members of the then Frontline States created the Southern African Development Coordination Conference (SADCC) following the Lusaka Declaration. The specific mandate of SADC is to foster regional integration, eradicate poverty, promote peace, and enhance economic development (SADC, n.d.).[4] Economic development is very much a headliner on SADC's agenda given that 10 of its 15 members have a per capita GDP of less than $5,000 USD (SADC, 2011), yet the entrepreneurial potential of this economic bloc is self-evident. Global Entrepreneurship Monitor's (GEM) work on Sub-Saharan Africa, a region which encompasses all SADC members, illustrates that there are high rates of total early-stage entrepreneurial activity (TEA), yet somewhere along the entrepreneurial pipeline this potential is lost, with only a small proportion of this capacity actually translating to established ventures (Herrington and Kelley, 2013, p. 8). In extending the pipeline metaphor, it is unclear as to whether the entrepreneurial pipeline is clogged or leaking. This chapter seeks to contribute to SADC's economic development goal by examining the institutional level factors that hinder or assist entrepreneurial activity.

Finally, although cross-national comparisons can be informative for the purposes of isolating country-level differences (Busenitz, Gomez and Spencer, 2000), treating countries within a particular region as a collective is valid and justifiable, especially where such countries share economic, political, and historical ties (Bruton et al., 2008). This study considers the 15-member SADC bloc as a collective and investigates governance-level indicators underpinning the level of entrepreneurial activities. The results of this study are vital for highlighting issues to SADC policymakers, in order to encourage entrepreneurial activity. This is imperative given that entrepreneurial activities, whether domestic or cross-border, are the lifeblood of economic growth (Herrington and Kelley, 2013).

Methods and measures

This chapter adopts North's (1990) perspective on how the regulative institutional environment "sets the rules of the game" for participants. As such, the formally sanctioned rules, regulations, and procedures that constrain or enable start-ups are conceptualized as antecedents of the level of entrepreneurial activities. Among the predictors used in past research are general policies affecting entrepreneurship, macroeconomic factors, and governance indicators (see Campbell and Rogers, 2007; Estrin et al., 2007; Spencer and Gomez, 2003). For this study, we employ the World Bank's *Ease of Doing Business Index (EDBI)* as proxy for the nature and types of rules, regulations, and procedures influencing new start-ups. Preference for the EDBI is based on its reliable and standardized governance indicator, and has been adopted in some recent studies including Morris and Aziz (2011) and Stenholm et al. (2013).

The EDBI comprises 10 primary categories—starting a business, dealing with construction permits, getting electricity connected, registering property, getting credit, protecting minority investors, paying taxes, trading across borders, enforcing contracts, and resolving insolvency.

Table 6.1 Antecedents of Entrepreneurial Activity

Category	Indicator	Included
Starting a business	Procedures (number)	Yes
	Time (days)	Yes
	Cost (% of income per capita)	Yes
	Capital (% of income per capita)	No
Dealing with construction permits	Procedures (number)	Yes
	Time (days)	Yes
	Cost (% of income per capita)	No
	Cost (% of warehouse value)	Yes
Getting electricity connected	Procedures (number)	Yes
	Time (days)	Yes
	Cost (% of income per capita)	No
Registering property	Procedures (number)	Yes
	Time (days)	Yes
	Cost (% of property value)	Yes
Getting credit	Strength of legal rights index (0–12)	Yes
	Depth of credit information (0–8)	Yes
	Credit registry coverage	No
	Credit bureau coverage	No
Paying taxes	Payments (number per year)	Yes
	Time (hours per year)	Yes
	Total tax rate (% of profit)	Yes
Enforcing contracts	Procedures (number)	Yes
	Time (days)	Yes
	Cost (% of claim)	Yes

Data source: Ease of Doing Business Index (EDBI).

"Included" denotes an instance where more than half the data were missing which led to the exclusion of that indicator from the final analysis.

Further, there are 31 individual indicators associated with these elements. The variables used in this study, and the categories from which they were selected, are listed in Table 6.1. The foremost primary factors that are relevant to the level of entrepreneurial activity comprise ease of starting a business, dealing with construction permits, registering property, getting electricity connected, obtaining credit information, paying taxes, and enforcing contracts. Protecting investors, trading across borders, and resolving insolvency were not considered for this research as they are applicable mainly in the post start-up phase as opposed to inception. From each of these seven primary categories, we drew specific indicators which were then modelled as antecedents of entrepreneurial activity.

The number of new start-ups was used as an indicator of entrepreneurial activity. Specifically, we adopted the World Bank Group's Entrepreneurship Survey which tracks the level of entrepreneurial activities using business entry density. The business entry density measures the number of newly formed limited liability firms per 1,000 individuals of working age (i.e. aged between 15 and 64). Overall, the methodology used in this chapter is consistent with Campbell and Rogers (2007), Estrin et al. (2007), and Stenholm et al. (2013).

Data and Analysis

The chapter focused on the entire period (2004–2015) covered by the EDBI. Over this 12-year period the 15 SADC countries generated 180 possible data points. Angola, Mozambique, Seychelles, Swaziland, Tanzania, and Zimbabwe do not have data on business entry density across the relevant period which eliminated 72 data points from the initial 180. Further, the data on business entry density cover the period 2004 to 2012, which meant the period 2013 to 2015 was omitted from the analysis. This resulted in the elimination of an additional 27 data points from the analysis. Thus, the effective sample size for this study comprised 81 data points covering nine SADC countries over a nine year period (2004–2012). Aside from a few missing cases for DRC, Madagascar, and Malawi, data were complete across all independent and dependent variables.

Data analysis was conducted using the linear modelling variant of linear regression, designating the 19 EDBI elements as predictor variables and business entry density as the outcome variable. Choice of this approach was motivated by the need to account for multi-collinearity, missing data, and outliers. The linear model also adopts a stepwise procedure which allows the resultant model to include only the variables considered "important." This approach was fundamental for improving the overall validity and reliability of the results.[5]

Results

The results section is organized as follows. First, we provide some descriptive statistics on the performance of the SADC countries across the selected variables. Second, we provide an overview of model fit for the linear technique chosen focusing on residuals and prediction accuracy. Finally, we identify the most important EDBI variables that predict business entry density while enlightening the reader vis-à-vis the relationship between each of these important variables and business entry density.

Botswana is the top performer regarding cost of construction, depth of credit information, and procedures for enforcing contracts while South Africa excels at cost of starting a business, time requirements for dealing with constructions permits, and number of tax payments per year. Similarly, Mauritius leads the group for the time required to start a business, time required to register property, and depth of credit information. However, this group of SADC countries appears to have regulative institutional environments that dissuade entrepreneurial activities. Averages that draw the readers' attention include time delays for starting a business (53 days), getting construction permits (244 days), getting electricity connected (145 days), and enforcing contracts (586 days). This extends to the number of procedures for starting a business (9) and dealing with construction permits (13), and the cost of enforcing contracts (39 percent of claim). The remainder of this results section focuses on how these elements of the regulative institutional environment influence entrepreneurial activity.

The linear model provided in this chapter appears to carry better than modest power in explaining the predictors of business entry density. The deviation between expected and observed cumulative probability appears negligible and the residuals plot is virtually identical to the approximation of best fit denoted by the dotted lines. Moreover, examining the overall strength of the linear modeling-based regression analysis, as a collective, the predictors improve our understanding of the aspects underlying business entry density to 71.8 percent. Stated differently, the model explains nearly 72 percent of the variability in business entry density within the SADC region.

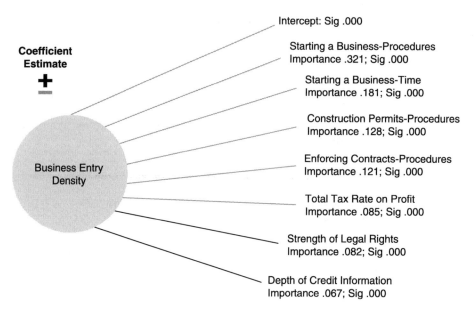

Figure 6.2   Strength of Relationship(s) between Predictors and Business Entry Density

The most important variables predicting business entry density within the SADC region are starting a business (procedures and time), procedures relating to securing construction permits and enforcing contracts, total tax on profit, strength of legal rights, and depth of credit information. To offer additional insights to the reader, we provide Figure 6.2, which depicts the significance tests and coefficients for each of the predictor variables.

Figure 6.2 shows that all seven variables designated as important by the linear model are statistically significant at the $p < 0.00$ level. The sign of each coefficient sheds light on the direction of relationship between each predictor and business entry density. A vast portion of the important variables included in our model are inversely related to business entry density. Procedures relating to starting a business, the time required to start the business, procedures pertaining to securing construction permits, procedures for enforcing contracts, and tax on total profit have an indirect relationship with entry density of ventures. From among these variables, procedures and time delays associated with starting a business exhibit the strongest relationships. These results suggest that the greater the costs, procedures, and time requirements concerning new venture formation, the less likely new ventures are to take root. Additionally, strength of legal rights and depth of credit information have a direct relationship with the entry density of firms. This means that new ventures are encouraged to sprout where the regulative institutional environment affords them legal protection while providing transparency around credit information. Overall, our results support our hypothesis and demonstrate both the enabling and impeding role the regulative institutional environment plays in motivating the level of entrepreneurial activity. This chapter corroborates past research (e.g. Campbell and Rogers, 2007; Estrin et al., 2007; Morris and Aziz, 2011; Spencer and Gomez, 2003; Stenholm et al., 2013) and contributes to knowledge development regarding drivers of entrepreneurial activities in an emerging market context. In the subsequent section, we discuss and draw conclusions from these results before outlining the implications, with a view to informing the reader how the findings of this chapter can drive entrepreneurial activities within SADC.

Discussion and conclusions

Regarding the performance of each country relative to the EDBI variables chosen for this chapter, some patterns begin to emerge. For example, Botswana, Mauritius, and South Africa appear among the top performers with respect to at least three indicators. On the opposite end of the spectrum are countries such as Angola, Madagascar, Mozambique, and Zimbabwe whose names are represented disproportionately among the worst performers. Angola and Zimbabwe in particular make the list of worst performers with respect to four or more indicators. Another noteworthy aspect is the inability of countries to effectively manage two elements (e.g. cost and procedures) simultaneously. For instance, in the category enforcing contracts, Zimbabwe is the top performer for enforcing claims speedily but it also carries the highest cost as a percentage of the value of those claims. Likewise, in the context of dealing with construction permits, Botswana is the least costly but the process itself requires 20 procedures, the most among SADC countries.

Thus, this chapter counsels researchers and policymakers to be wary of the pitfalls of making sweeping statements about African nations in general and SADC in particular. Even within the same regional or economic grouping, African countries may exhibit substantial differences. As this chapter illustrates, the regulative environments in these countries are nowhere near identical. For instance, it takes six days to start a business in Mauritius and three months in Zimbabwe. Enforcement of contracts takes three-and-a-half years in Angola suggesting the possible existence of a laborious and bureaucratic legal framework. Contrast that to Zimbabwe, where the process is significantly more efficient but at a much higher cost. In Namibia, a new venture can get power connected in little over a month whereas another venture in Madagascar may have to wait some 450 days before power can be connected. It is important to reflect on how the SADC region compares to markets elsewhere. When compared to frontier markets, defined by the World Bank as the markets epitomizing best practice, the weaknesses in the SADC region become apparent. For example, New Zealand is a frontier market for starting a business, with a process that involves one procedure which can be completed within one day, in contrast to an average of nine procedures over an average period of 53 days in SADC countries. In Hong Kong, a frontier market for number of tax payments per year, firms make only three payments, unlike in the DRC where firms are expected to make 50 such payments. Likewise, firms in the UAE (another frontier market) spend 12 hours per year handling tax-related matters while in Lesotho a full two weeks is used to process tax-related issues.

Recall that GEM's (2012) findings for Sub-Saharan Africa demonstrate that the entrepreneurial pipeline for this region appears chock-full at the start with high TEA rates, yet the actual number of nascent and new ventures that hit the market is a mere trickle. As shown in Figure 6.3, some of the widest net gaps noted between TEA rates and established business rates (EBR) are in Sub-Saharan Africa and involve SADC members Angola, Botswana, Malawi, and Zambia. In most parts of the world, the difference between TEA and EBR ranges between 0 to 9 percent, indicating higher conversion rates and an ability of these markets to generate a constant stream of new start-up ventures (Herrington and Kelley, 2013, pp. 24–27). The need to find ways to close this gap, thereby increasing throughput, becomes paramount. This chapter argues that sweeping changes to the regulative institutional environment constitute the most efficient plumbing tool to unclog the pipeline and let entrepreneurial activities flow within SADC.

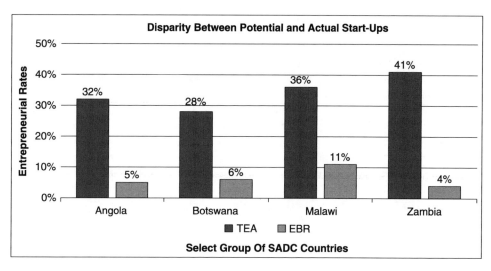

Figure 6.3　Comparison between Potential and Actual Start-Ups

See Herrington and Kelley (2013: 8).

Implications and recommendations

As discussed in the theoretical framework, much has been reported in mainstream research and other media concerning the ostensibly insurmountable political and socio-economic challenges that Africa faces. This chapter argues to the contrary that some of these seemingly indefatigable challenges require straightforward solutions. A case in point, covered in this chapter, is the concept of stimulating the level of entrepreneurial activity. Without seismic geopolitical shifts, foreign investment, or the need for pivoting policy toward the East or West, the SADC region has the power to alter the regulative institutional environment(s) among its member countries to motivate the emergence of new ventures. This evidently calls for changing the rules of the game to allow new ventures to form and thrive. The success of these fledgling ventures will help drive economic activities within each country and the region at large.

In seeking to alter the rules of the game, the SADC region could lean on (1) exemplars of recent successes involving emerging markets and (2) frontier markets that set the bar. The World Bank's (2014) Doing Business Report 2015 comprises copious examples of emerging markets that have made the deliberate choice to improve their regulative institutional environments as a way of motivating entrepreneurial activities. While embarking on the requisite changes requires resolute commitment, the gains can be immediate. As a matter of fact, emerging markets which have embraced change are starting to realize some gains. For example, the World Bank documents that Tajikistan, Benin, Togo, Cote d'Ivoire, Senegal, Trinidad and Tobago, DRC, Azerbaijan, and United Arab Emirates have adopted reforms which have led to an improvement in their regulative institutional environments over the period 2013/2014 (World Bank, 2014, p. 6).

Another option the SADC region can consider is benchmarking against frontier markets. Benchmarking against such high performing markets creates "aspirational goals" which can guide institutional reform within SADC.

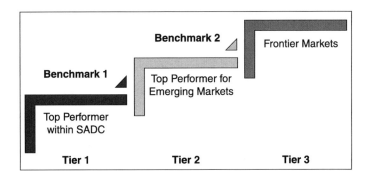

Figure 6.4   Benchmarking Regulative Institutional Environments

Given the region's commitment toward integration, it will be worthwhile working toward a "convergence criteria" for all 15 member states. Such criteria would seek to create uniform standards regarding procedures, documents, costs, and time across the entire region. Figure 6.4 shows a three-tiered approach for pursuing such a strategy. The first tier could focus on "home-grown solutions." For instance, other member states could benefit from South Africa's relative success with entrepreneurial activities. Other countries from whom the rest of the SADC region can learn are Botswana and Mauritius. The main priority at this tier is to motivate countries such as Angola, Mozambique, and Zimbabwe, among others, to elevate their standards to match the best performing country in the region. Once the region has made progress toward matching the best performer within SADC, the focus should shift to the second tier which looks at high-achievers in non-African emerging markets. This will probably constitute an incremental step since the best performing SADC countries closely match the top performing non-African emerging markets. The first benchmark (Benchmark 1) could be set at the level of the best performing emerging markets, with countries being tasked to meet that standard within two to three years. Alternatively, a more challenging regional benchmark (Benchmark 2) could be pegged above the best performing non-African emerging markets but below the frontier markets. Achieving this standard would probably require three to five years but, in working toward it, the SADC countries would be positioning themselves to have a competitive advantage in the global marketplace. Overall, the impact of fostering an enabling regulative institutional environment extends beyond the confines of this research. In bringing up their standards to world level, African countries stand to reap trickledown benefits including a greater capacity for domestic ventures to seek and exploit international opportunities and also the ability to attract foreign direct investment.

The limitations of this chapter emanate from the fact that we tested only a small portion of the model provided in Figure 6.1. First, the chapter examined just one element of institutional environment—the regulative component. The framework did not include the normative or cognitive dimensions of the institutional environment, let alone other drivers of entrepreneurial activities such as individual and organizational attributes. Second, our focus was restricted to the levels of entrepreneurial activities and did not incorporate the notion of types of entrepreneurial activities. Future research can pit rival groups of predictors and test these against both the levels and types of entrepreneurial activities. It may also be informative to extend this research to other emerging markets and assess the relationships in the context of both domestic and international entrepreneurial activities. Nonetheless, this chapter in its current form expands our understanding of the relationship between the quality of the regulative institutional environment and levels of entrepreneurial activities, thereby empowering policymakers to craft reforms to motivate entrepreneurship.

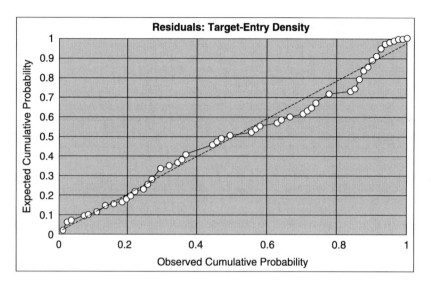

Appendix 6.1   Residuals for Linear Model

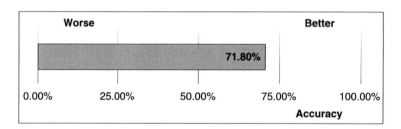

Appendix 6.2   Overall Model Fit

Notes

1 See Baumol's (1959) *Business behaviour, value and growth*, Kirzner's (1978) *Competition and entrepreneurship*, Schumpeter's (1934) *The theory of economic development*.
2 Refer to the complete model (Gartner, 1985: 702).
3 Estrin et al. (2007) {H1$_b$}, Spencer and Gomez (2003) {H$_{10}$}, Stenholm et al. (2013) {H1$_a$} posit there is a positive relationship between the regulative institutional environment and entrepreneurial activity as the number of new ventures increases with a better regulative environment.
4 See www.sadc.int. Accessed July 19, 2015.
5 Unlike other versions of linear regression, the linear modeling approach automatically adjusts for multi-collinearity, imputes missing data, and adjusts for outliers.

References

Aldrich, H.E. (1990). Using an ecological perspective to study organizational founding rates. *Entrepreneurship Theory and Practice*, 14(3), 7–24.

Aldrich, H.E., and Wiedenmayer, G. (1993). From traits to rates: An ecological perspective on organizational foundings. In J. Katz and R. Brockhaus (Eds.), *Advances in Entrepreneurship, Firm Emergence, and Growth* (pp. 145–195). Greenwich, CT: JAI Press.

Baumol, W. J. (1959). *Business behavior, value and growth.* New York: Macmillan.

Baumol, W.J. (1996). *Entrepreneurship, management, and the structure of payoffs.* Cambridge, MA: MIT Press.

Baumol, W.J., Litan, R.E., and Schramm, C.J. (2009). *Good capitalism, bad capitalism, and the economics of growth and prosperity.* New Haven, CT: Yale University Press.

Binks, M., and Jennings, A. (1986). New firms as a source of industrial regeneration. In M. Scott, A. Gibb, J. Lewis, and T. Faulkner (Eds.), *Small firms' growth and development* (pp. 3–11). Aldershot: Gower.

Birley, S. and Westhead, P. (1994). A taxonomy of business start-up reasons and their impact on firm growth and size. *Journal of Business Venturing,* 9(1), 7–31.

Brockhaus, R.H. (1980). Risk taking propensity of entrepreneurs. *Academy of Management Journal,* 23(3), 509–520.

Brockhaus, R.H. (1982). The psychology of the entrepreneur. In C.A. Kent, D.L. Sexton, and K.H. Vesper (Eds.), *Encyclopedia of Entrepreneurship* (pp. 39–57). Englewood Cliffs, NJ: Prentice Hall.

Bruton, G.D., Ahlstrom, D., and Obloj, K. (2008). Entrepreneurship in emerging economies: Where are we today and where should the research go in the future. *Entrepreneurship Theory and Practice,* 32(1), 1–14. doi: 10.1111/j.1540-6520.2007.00213.x.

Bruton, G.D., Ahlstrom, D., and Li, H.-L. (2010). Institutional theory and entrepreneurship: where are we now and where do we need to move in the future? *Entrepreneurship Theory and Practice,* 34(3), 421–440. doi: 10.1111/j.1540-6520.2010.00390.x.

Busenitz, L.W., Gomez, C., and Spencer, J.W. (2000). Country institutional profiles: Unlocking entrepreneurial phenomena. *The Academy of Management Journal,* 46(3), 994–1003. doi: 10.2307/1556423.

Campbell, N.D. and Rogers, T.M. (2007). Economic freedom and net business formation. *Cato Journal,* 27(1), 23–36. doi: 10.3846/16111699.2011.633348.

Cooper, A.C. (1981). Strategic management: New ventures and small business. *Long Range Planning,* 14(5), 39–45.

Cooper, A.C. and Dunkelberg, W.C. (1986). Entrepreneurship and paths to business ownership. *Strategic Management Journal,* 7(1), 53–68.

Covin, J. G., and Slevin, D.P. (1991). A conceptual model of entrepreneurship as firm behavior. *Entrepreneurship Theory and Practice,* 16(1), 7–25.

Dana, L.P. (1987). Entrepreneurship and venture creation – An international comparison of five commonwealth nations. In N.C. Churchill, J.A. Hornaday, B.A. Kirchoff, O.J. Krasner, and K.H. Vesper (Eds.), *Frontiers of entrepreneurship research* (pp. 573–583). Wellesley, MA: Babson College.

Dana, L.P. (1990). Saint Martin/Sint Maarten: A case study of the effects of culture on economic development. *Journal of Small Business Management,* 28(4), 91–98.

De Soto, H. (2000). *The mystery of capital: Why capitalism triumphs in the West and fails everywhere else.* New York: Basic Books.

El-Namaki, M.S.S. (1988). Encouraging entrepreneurship in developing countries. *Long Range Planning,* 21(4), 98–106.

Ernst & Young. (2015). EY's Attractiveness Survey-Africa 2015: Making choices. Retrieved from http://www.ey.com/Publication/vwLUAssets/EY-africa-attractiveness-survey-2015-making-choices/$FILE/EY-africa-attractiveness-survey-2015-making-choices.pdf. Accessed July 5, 2015.

Estrin, S., Aidis, R., and Mickiewicz, T. (2007, February). Institutions and entrepreneurship development in Russia: A comparative perspective (Working Paper No. 867). Retrieved from http://deepblue.lib.umich.edu/bitstream/handle/2027.42/57247/wp867?sequence=1. Accessed July 27, 2015.

Gartner, W.B. (1985). A conceptual framework for describing the phenomenon of new venture creation. *The Academy of Management Review,* 10(4), 696–706.

Gibb, A. and Ritchie, J. (1982). Understanding the process of starting a small business. *European Small Business Journal,* 1(1), 26–45.

Gnyawali, D., and Fogel, D. (1994). Environments for entrepreneurship development: Key dimensions and research implications. *Entrepreneurship Theory and Practice,* 18(4), 43–62.

Herrington, M. and Kelley, D. (2013). African entrepreneurship: The Sub-Saharan African Regional Report. *Global Entrepreneurship Monitor.* Retrieved from http://www.gemconsortium.org/

country-profile/108/1395325623GEM_2012_Sub-Saharan_Africa_Regional_Report.pdf. Accessed July 2, 2015.

Hwang, H., and Powell, W.W. (2005). Institutions and entrepreneurship. In S.A. Alvarez, R. Agarwal, and O. Sorenson (Eds.), *Handbook of entrepreneurship research: Disciplinary perspectives* (pp. 201–232). New York: Springer.

Keefer, P., and Knack, S. (1997). Why don't poor countries catch up? A cross-national test of an institutional explanation. *Economic Enquiry*, 35(3), 590–602.

Kirzner, I.M. (1978). *Competition and entrepreneurship*. Chicago: University of Chicago Press.

Kiss, A.N., and Danis, W.D. (2008). Country institutional context, social networks, and new venture internationalization speed. *European Management Journal*, 26(6), 388–399. doi: 10.1016/j.emj. 2008.09.001.

Kshetri, N., and Dholakia, N. (2011). Regulative institutions supporting entrepreneurship in emerging economies: A comparison of China and India. *Journal of International Entrepreneurship*, 9(2), 110–132. doi: 10.1007/s10843-010-0070-x.

Low, M.B., and MacMillan, I.C. (1988). Entrepreneurship: Past research and future challenges. *Journal of Management*, 14(2), 139–161.

McClelland, D.C. (1961). *The achieving society*. Princeton, NJ: Van Nostrand.

Milne, T., and Thompson, M. (1982) The infant business development process (Management Studies Working Paper No. 2). University of Glasgow.

Morris, R., and Aziz, A. (2011). Ease of doing business and FDI inflow to Sub-Saharan Africa and Asian countries. *Cross Cultural Management: An International Journal*, 18(4), 400–411. doi: 10.1108/13527601111179483.

North, D.C. (1990). *Institutions, institutional change and economic performance*. Cambridge: Cambridge University Press.

O'Farrell, P.N. and Pickles, A.R. (1989). Entrepreneurial behavior within male work histories: A sector-specific analysis. *Environment and Planning A*, 21(3), 249–263.

Roxburgh, C., Dörr, N., Leke, A., Tazi-Riffi, A., van Wamelen, A., Lund, S., Chironga, M., Alatovik, T., Atkins, C., Terfous, N., and Zeino-Mahmalat, T. (2010, June). Lions on the move: The progress and potential of African economies. Retrieved from http://www.mckinsey.com/~/media/McKinsey/dotcom/Insightspercent20andpercent20pubs/MGI/Research/Productivitypercent20Competitiveness percent20andpercent20Growth/Lionspercent20onpercent20thepercent20movepercent20Thepercent 20progresspercent20ofpercent20Africanpercent20economies/MGI_Lions_on_the_move_african_ economies_full_report.ashx. Accessed June 30, 2015.

Schumpeter, J. (1934) *The theory of economic development*, Cambridge, MA: Harvard University Press.

Scott, W.R. (1995). *Institutions and organizations: ideas and interests*. Thousand Oaks, CA: Sage Publications.

Shane, S., and Kolvereid, L. (1995). National environment, strategy, and new venture performance: A three country study. *Journal of Small Business Management*, 33(3) (April), 37–49.

Shane, S., Locke, E.A., and Collins, C.J. (2003). Entrepreneurial motivation. *Human Resource Management Review*, 13, 257–279. doi:10.1016/S1053-4822(03)00017-2.

Segura, E. (1988). Industrial, trade and financial sector policies to foster private enterprises in developing countries. *Columbia Journal of World Business*, 23(1), 19–27.

Southern African Development Community (SADC, 2011). Issues-Statistics. Retrieved from http://www.sadc.int/issues/statistics. Accessed June 19, 2015.

Southern African Development Community (SADC, n.d.) About SADC-SADC Overview. Retrieved from http://www.sadc.int/about-sadc/overview. Accessed June 19, 2015.

Spencer, W.J., and Gomez, C. (2003). The relationship among national institutional structures, economic factors, and domestic entrepreneurial activity: A multicountry study. *Journal of Business Research*, 57(10), 1098–1107. doi:10.1016/S0148-2963(03)00040-7.

Stenholm, P., Acs, Z.J, and Wuebker, R. (2013). Exploring country-level institutional arrangements on rate and type of entrepreneurial activities. *Journal of Business Venturing*, 28(1), 176–193. doi:10.1016/j.jbusvent.2011.11.002.

Storey, D. J. (1982). *Entrepreneurship and the new firm*. London: Croom Helm.

The Economist. (2011, January 6). A more hopeful continent: The lion kings? Retrieved from http://www.economist.com/node/17853324. Accessed July 7, 2015.

The White House, Office of the Press Secretary. (2015, July 25). Remarks by President Obama at the Global Entrepreneurship Summit [Press Release]. Retrieved from http://www.ges2015.org/

press-releases/2015/7/25/remarks-by-president-obama-at-the-global-entrepreneurship-summit. Accessed July 26, 2015.

Venkataraman, S. (1997). The distinctive domain of entrepreneurship research: An editor's perspective. In J. Katz, and R. Brockhaus (Eds.), *Advances in entrepreneurship, firm emergence, and growth* (Vol. 3, pp. 119–138). Greenwich, CT: JAI Press.

Westhead, P. (1990). A typology of new manufacturing firm founders in Wales: Performance measures and public policy implications. *Journal of Business Venturing*, 5(2), 103–122.

World Bank. (2014). *Doing business 2015: going beyond efficiency*. Washington, DC: World Bank. doi: 10.1596/978-1-4648-0351-2

Young, E.C., and Welsch, H.P. (1993). Major elements in entrepreneurial development in central Mexico. *Journal of Small Business Management*, 31(4), 80–85.

7

NASCENT ENTERPRISES AND GROWTH ASPIRATIONS IN A POST-CONFLICT ENVIRONMENT

The role of social capital

Anna Rebmann, Adnan Efendic and Tomascz Mickiewicz

Introduction

This chapter focuses on the effects of social capital on the growth aspirations of owners and managers of young businesses in a post-conflict country, namely Bosnia and Herzegovina (BiH). As post-conflict environments are fragile yet may also offer opportunities for economic turnaround, they call for special attention (Collier, 2008). Consistent with Penrose (1959), it is posited that firms' growth strategies are primarily due to managerial capital; moreover, it is in the early stage of business activity in young firms that growth dynamism is particularly constrained by management. Enterprise is as much about firm growth as about emergence of new firms (Penrose, 1959), with growth being the critical stage of their development (Wright and Marlow, 2012).

In a post-conflict environment young firms' growth aspirations can be easily damaged. In particular, where much of social capital was destroyed during wartime, it becomes the key factor limiting aspirations. It is in this context that social capital affecting the managerial growth aspirations of young firms in BiH is considered. The evidence from BiH should be of interest for other post-conflict environments in line with the views of Light and Dana (2013), that the general boundaries of social capital are likely to be stronger in non-conventional settings.

This study focuses on the social links seen from the entrepreneur's perspective. Considering social links at micro, meso and macro level, social capital is treated as a multi-dimensional and multi-level phenomenon. This approach follows Granovetter's (1985) call to avoid both 'oversocialized' and 'undersocialized' theories (see also Estrin et al., 2013b): the former put stress entirely on macro-level social structures (e.g. Marxist-type social class analysis), while the latter model considers individuals as atomized, abstracting from any social features. Trust in institutions and people, facets of macro-level social relations that support entrepreneurship, are studied. This focus is important, we argue, because a wider variation exists in these macro-level social relations for a country with weak institutions compared to countries with strong institutions, where the institutional environment is more homogenous. At the meso level, an additional consideration is that in a post-conflict, multi-ethnic country, such as BiH, the presence of ethnic pluralism in a locality is a likely indicator of local social norms of tolerance that facilitate experimentation, competition, enterprise and growth aspirations. At the micro level, the effect of entrepreneurs' discussion networks on growth aspirations is investigated.

With the exception of Kwon and Arenius (2010) and Estrin et al. (2013a), the social determinants of growth aspirations are not yet attracting the attention they deserve (e.g., Autio and Acs, 2010; Levie and Autio, 2011). This reflects a broader gap in the entrepreneurship literature. While 'increased appreciation for the importance of social relationships in entrepreneurship' exists (Gedajlovic et al., 2013: 455), the influence of these factors on enterprise development remains under-investigated (Thornton et al., 2011). Yet negative social and cultural influences may eradicate high growth aspirations entrepreneurship (van Stel and Storey, 2004) and thus affect entrepreneurial performance particularly in post-conflict contexts. Thus, investigating the links between entrepreneurship and social dimensions in a post-conflict context focuses attention on situations where social capital is both most fragile and most needed. The chapter is organized as follows. The introductory section briefly discusses the context: the ethnically complex post-conflict environment and current state of entrepreneurship in BiH. Next, the research framework and hypotheses are introduced, followed by discussion of the data and model specification respectively, before reporting the empirical findings. Finally, conclusions are offered.

Context: entrepreneurship in Bosnia and Herzegovina

In the late 1980s and early 1990s, the six constituent republics of former federal Yugoslavia, including BiH, were overwhelmed with unresolved internal political and economic issues. A series of inconsistent transition reforms started during this period were supposed to strengthen internal cohesion and bring economic improvement, but in practice contributed to the disintegration of Yugoslavia (Hadziahmetović, 2011). When BiH, the most ethnically mixed republic, obtained international recognition of independence in 1992, a four-year civil war brought massive destruction. When the war was ended by the Dayton Peace Accord (DPA) in 1995, BiH had lost around a quarter of its population and estimated GDP per capita had fallen from $1,900 in 1991 to around $500 by 1995 (World Bank,1997).

Today, BiH is a middle-income country where entrepreneurial growth aspirations are limited, as in other Central and East European (CEE) countries that have been transiting from a socialist to a market economy. Autio (2011: 259) defines 'high aspiration early stage entrepreneurs' as owners-mangers of businesses that are less than 42 months old, who 'expect to employ twenty or more individuals within five years' time'. The prevalence rate of high aspiration entrepreneurs in BiH amongst the adult population is a low 0.5 per cent, similar to neighbouring Croatia and Serbia which were also affected by conflicts in the 1990s. This contrasts with Latin American and South East Asian economies, where entrepreneurial dynamism is significantly higher (Kelley et al., 2010).

BiH as a part of ex-Yugoslavia (1945–1992) was a multi-ethnic republic with a high level of ethnic tolerance (Dyrstad, 2012; Hodson et al., 1994). Three major ethnic groups make up the population of BiH: Bosniaks, Serbs and Croats (these ethnicities largely correspond to Muslim, Orthodox and Catholic religious traditions respectively). Unfortunately, the Bosnian war caused a radical change from an ethnically tolerant to a quite intolerant society in just a few years (Dyrstad, 2012). It also caused large population movements leaving the population concentrated in more ethnically homogenous territories. The ethnic divisions created during the war period have largely been institutionalized by the post-war constitution (Bieber, 2006). Each of the three main ethnic groups has substantial autonomy and control over their own ethno-territorial units which predominate over the state-level institutions (Bieber, 2010). Consequently, and rather uniquely, for each ethnic group there is some part of BiH where it remains an ethnic minority and another part where it is the majority. Yet, ethnic minorities remain within areas dominated by Bosniak, Serb or Croat majority populations. Moreover, some areas avoided ethnic cleansing, preserving pluralism (Armakolas, 2011). Cultural differences are smaller than in other divided societies as the three groups speak virtually the same language, share similar traditions, and ways of thinking, which typically facilitate post-conflict reintegration (Collier, 2008). All these factors make BiH a highly suitable context for studying the impact of social capital and ethnic pluralism on entrepreneurial aspirations.

Theoretical framework

Entrepreneurial growth aspirations

This study follows Penrose in treating enterprise 'as a psychological predisposition on the part of [the] individual to take a chance in a hope of gain' (Penrose, 1959: 30). Moreover, 'the decision on the part of a firm to investigate the prospective profitability of expansion is an enterprising decision, in the sense that whenever expansion is neither pressing nor particularly obvious, a firm can choose between continuing in its existing course or of expanding and committing resources to the investigation of whether there are further opportunities of which it is not yet aware' (Penrose, 1959: 30). Penrose emphasizes that in such a decision, not resource constraints but managerial predispositions are the limiting factor. This perspective turns attention away from a production function approach that would investigate resource constraints, towards considering managerial attitudes.

In this theoretical perspective, the growth aspirations of those running the firm become important. Growth decisions play a special role in the stage of a firm's development when it has survived the initial period of incubation, and has next to decide whether and how fast to expand (Messersmith and Wales, 2011). A substantial body of research exists confirming the positive relationship between an entrepreneur's growth aspirations and subsequent firm the positive relationship between an entrepreneur's growth aspirations and subsequent firm performance (Baum et al., 1998, 2001; Delmar and and Wiklund, 2008; Kolvereid and Bullvag, 1996; Wiklund and Shepherd, 2003). Accordingly, this study is located within a recent strand in the entrepreneurship literature focusing on the individual and contextual determinants of growth aspirations (Autio and Acs, 2010; Bowen and De Clerq, 2008; Estrin et al., 2013a; Levie and Autio, 2011).

To the best of our knowledge, growth aspirations have not been analyzed with respect to a post-conflict environment. This matters for two reasons. From a theoretical perspective, non-standard contexts help in understanding whether some of the observed mechanisms are general or not (Light and Dana, 2013). From a policy perspective, post-conflict environments need particular attention, because they offer both opportunities for economic turnaround and also high risks of lapsing back into violence (Collier, 2008). The opportunities relate to breaking up specific social and political structures that inhibited economic dynamism in the past (Olson, 1982; Acemoglu and Robinson, 2012). The risks are that initial weak economic dynamism may lead to social frustration, which feeds extremism, and a consequent return to violence. In this context, understanding of the micro foundations of growth becomes important.

Social capital

This study utilizes the concept of social capital as referring to ties between people (Nooteboom, 2007). At the core of the concept is the idea that goodwill stemming from social relations is a resource for facilitating action (Adler and Kwon, 2002), and that social linkages formed in one social sphere may be appropriate and used in another sphere. The literature can be split into two major conceptualizations of social capital: one focusing on societal relations and the other on personal relations. The societal relations stream defines social capital as widely shared, cooperative social norms, such as trust and reciprocity (Fukuyama, 1995; Putnam, 2000; Rothstein and Stolle, 2008). The personal relations stream focuses on the micro structural element of social relations, such as the properties of social networks that the individuals can use to secure benefits (Bourdieu, 1986; Burt, 2000; Sobel, 2002).

Both personal relations and societal relations are important pillars of social capital: business appropriable social capital depends not only on the network structure of an individual's social relations but also on the general norms that enable people to act collectively (Woolcock and Narayan, 2000). The theoretical model tested in this study examines the multiple dimensions of social capital attributing them to different societal levels (see Figure 7.1). The dependent variable is entrepreneurs' growth aspirations. At the macro level institutional trust and generalized trust have positive influences on growth aspirations, as does ethnic pluralism at the meso level. At the personal level, the entrepreneur's business network composition (the use of strong and weak ties) also has an impact on growth aspirations. All these dimensions of social capital are discussed below.

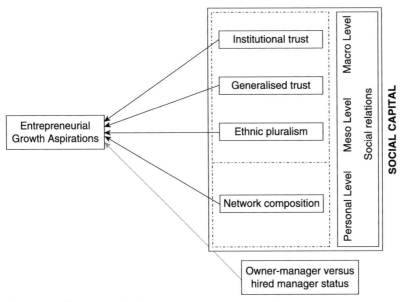

Figure 7.1 Theoretical Model

Trust

Trust is a key dimension of social capital (Kwon and Arenius, 2010; Westlund and Adam, 2010). It indicates the presence of cooperative norms in society that enable the use of social relations to access resources (Paldam, 2000). Furthermore, it is a crucial component in the institutional structure of a market economy facilitating transactions (Arrow, 1974). However, not all trust is considered equally beneficial. A key distinction in the literature is made between 'particularized trust' (Rothstein, 2003) and 'extended' trust (Raiser, 1999). Particularized trust is trust emerging between two or more individuals such as family members and friends (Rothstein, 2003) and is based on knowledge of the individual. Extended trust, in contrast, is more abstract, enabling transactions to take place with only limited information about the counterpart's specific attributes (Raiser, 1999).

There are two main forms of extended trust: institutional trust (trust in institutions) and generalized trust (trust in unknown individuals). Institutional trust is trust in the functioning of the institutional framework including formal rules, organizations and enforcement mechanisms (World Bank, 2002). It is theorized to enable transactions outside the circle of known individuals, extending the radius of trust, as institutions can provide formal mechanisms which give security that a transaction will take place as promised (Zucker, 1986). If institutional systems are strong, institutional trust will be high and supportive of entrepreneurship and business growth (Welter, 2012). Parallel to this, generalized trust is trust in unknown individuals (Rothstein and Stolle, 2008) and as such reflects confidence in wide social norms, i.e. the expectation of accepted behaviour of individuals in society in general.

Raiser (1999) and Fukuyama (1995) argue that 'extended trust' is crucial to a modern market economy as unlike particularized trust, it enables individuals to engage in transactions beyond closed circles of family or well-known business contacts, such links being necessary for any complex division of labour. In contrast, low trust environments are thought to hinder entrepreneurship, because businesses have to rely on particularized trust through personal networks, which increases transaction costs (Hohmann and Welter, 2002). This is seen as particularly damaging to entrepreneurial growth aspirations. Growth is associated with increased complexity of transactions, and increased risks; thus low trust and a poor institutional environment become binding constraints. Relying on particularized trust, individuals may successfully launch new businesses but expansion becomes more difficult (Aidis and Mickiewicz, 2006; Estrin et al., 2013a).

Transition economies are frequently characterized as low trust societies, due to their communist legacy (Fukuyama, 1995; Raiser, 1999; Estrin and Mickiewicz, 2011a) and extended trust in BiH has been further undermined by the recent war (UNDP, 2009).The conflict seriously damaged the rule of law, confidence in formal institutions, perceptions of equality under the law, and of due judicial process. However, both Armakolas (2011) and Welter and Smallbone (2006) point out that trust also differs across regions and sectors. Norms of trust and perceptions of formal institutions can be diversified and localized. The way the individuals relate to the macro environment via institutional and generalized trust may also vary due to their individual characteristics, experiences and social status. Entrepreneurs with fewer connections may in some countries feel less secure about their access to the legal system than those entrepreneurs who are better connected and wealthier (Glaeser et al., 2003; Aidis et al., 2008). Those entrepreneurs feeling less secure are likely to scale down their growth aspirations due to threat of expropriation either by corrupt agents representing formal institutions or by business partners coming from outside their radius of particularized trust as the growing size of the business venture would extend it beyond the radius of trust into the social space of distrust. Accordingly, it is hypothesized that the trust an individual expresses in relation to institutions (institutional trust) and to people (generalized trust) affects entrepreneurial growth aspirations positively. The above discussion generates two hypotheses for this study:

> *Hypothesis 1: The greater entrepreneurs' trust in institutions, the higher their growth aspirations.*

> *Hypothesis 2: The greater entrepreneurs' generalized trust, the higher their growth aspirations.*

Local ethnic pluralism

BiH is an ethnically diverse country but relations between ethnicities vary immensely not just at a regional level but at the individual level too. These ethnic relations structure interactions amongst individuals. Thus how individuals situate themselves in their ethnic environment is an important facet of social capital.

Currently, the limited existing literature on the relationship between ethnic structures and economic outcomes focuses on ethnic diversity. Ethnic diversity is typically measured in two ways. In studies analyzing diversity due to immigration in advanced economies, researchers tend to measure diversity by the proportion of foreign born individuals in an area (e.g. Lee et al., 2004; Smallbone et al., 2010). In contrast, studies focusing on developing countries measure diversity by ethnic fractionalisation – the probability that two randomly drawn individuals in a certain geographical area come from different ethnic groups (Alesina and La Ferrara, 2005). However, the concept of ethnic diversity only captures whether different ethnic groups are present in a geographical area not how they interact, which is crucial for how ethnic diversity may affect entrepreneurs' growth aspirations.

Ethnic diversity may have both positive and negative effects on economic outcomes (Ram et al., 2011). On the one hand, where ethnic diversity is associated with fragmentation and conflict, it is likely to impact negatively on economic performance leading to poor economic choices and policies (Easterly and Levine, 2001). On the other hand, a diverse ethnic mix may bring different experiences and ways of thinking, which may lead businesses towards innovation, creativity and better economic performance (Alesina and La Ferrara, 2005; Florida, 2004, 2005; Smallbone et al., 2010; Lee et al., 2004). Such conditions are conducive both to a larger and more diversified pool 'of underexploited knowledge useful for commercialisation of new ideas' (Marino et al., 2012). Growth aspirations are enhanced by wider access to resources that comes with ethnic heterogeneity. Both Aldrich and Kim (2007) and Light and Dana (2013) emphasize that start-up teams are typically formed relying on close ties to the social neighbourhood. Only in the expansion phase do entrepreneurs face a need to recruit, reaching out for competences that may be available only in wider and more mixed communities (Zain and Ng, 2006; Light and Dana, 2013). Thus, richer social links make scaling up entrepreneurial projects easier and therefore affect entrepreneurial aspirations positively.

Whilst the presence of ethnic heterogeneity increases the likelihood of a more diversified pool of knowledge being present, this does not mean that this knowledge is being exchanged. There need to be low communication barriers so that access to this knowledge is relatively easy, creating an environment for entrepreneurial dynamism (Lee et al., 2004; Marino et al., 2012; Audretsch et al., 2010; Smallbone et al., 2010). Different ethnic groups may live side by side but have little interaction and exchange of ideas.

In BiH, relations between the ethnic groups vary immensely not just between regions but also at the individual level. In some ethnically diverse towns, such as Mostar, ethnic groups live separately from one another, whereas in others, such as Tuzla, no such divide exists. Measuring ethnic fractionalization does not capture these differences in the environment. Thus, how individuals situate themselves in their ethnic environment is an important facet of social capital and we emphasize the importance of this individual experience for understanding local ethnic relations. Entrepreneurs in such areas are more likely to take advantage of the opportunities that come with the more heterogeneous, but at the same time not fragmented, environment. Here this is termed 'ethnic pluralism' on the grounds that this concept better captures the aspects of co-existence and of inter-ethnic cooperation for the individual than ethnic diversity.

In a post-conflict environment, more than anywhere else, local ethnic pluralism becomes an indicator of the relatively stronger local climate of tolerance. Hence, based on these opportunities to increase competence and knowledge, ethnic pluralism is expected to be positively related to entrepreneurs' aspirations to grow their businesses. In contrast, individuals belonging to a homogenous ethnic majority or minority neighbourhood, in an ethnically fragmented environment, face a narrower knowledge base, and this is likely to affect growth ambitions negatively.

Hypothesis 3: In an ethnically diverse country, entrepreneurs in an ethnically mixed neighbourhood (characterized by ethnic pluralism) have higher growth aspirations.

Business discussion networks as social capital

As mentioned above, a large stream of the social capital literature stresses that entrepreneurs are embedded in personal networks, which may facilitate their actions (Hansen, 1995; Casson and Della Giusta, 2007; Jack et al., 2010). Personal networks enable individuals to obtain knowledge and information, such as contacts for new customers, or new business opportunities (Greve and Salaff, 2003; Hoang and Antončič, 2003; Jack, 2010; Witt, 2004) which feeds into entrepreneurial growth aspirations. Networks also provide access to resources that would not otherwise be available or would be more expensive to obtain via the market. Relying on networks is a strategy to overcome constraints to growth such as accessing finance, finding qualified human resources, and dealing with regulatory obstacles such as customs regulations or obtaining commercial licences. This latter aspect suggests why business networks may work as a substitute for weak institutions (Estrin et al., 2013a).

The composition of entrepreneurs' networks affects their ability to obtain a variety of information and resources (Raiser et al., 2007; Jack et al., 2010; Watson, 2011; Zang, 2011). A central debate in the literature on network structure concerns whether strong or weak ties bring more benefits to individuals (Granovetter, 1973; Krackhardt, 1992; Greve and Salaff, 2003; Wang and Altinay, 2012). Strong ties are built on strong levels of particularized trust, and are often family based, which helps gain access to resources as well as providing the entrepreneur with emotional and motivational support which would help with growing a business. Yet, at the same time strong ties to family can have negative economic consequences and act as constraints on entrepreneurial activity (Alesina and Giuliano, 2013; Khavul et al., 2009). In kinship-based societies ties can impose obligations to share and support an extended family, reducing the ability and motivation of individuals to act entrepreneurially (di Falco and Bulte, 2011; Khavul et al., 2009). Bosnia and Herzegovina is a society where family ties are strong (UNDP, 2009; Alesina and Guiliano, 2013), thus family obligations may place more of a constraint on growth aspirations for individuals in BiH who include more family members in their business networks.

Weak ties may offer an advantage over strong ties in providing access to non-redundant knowledge and information. However, while more valuable knowledge may be found beyond the family circle, the extent to which it can be effectively acquired relies on the degree of trust between the individuals in the network. Obtaining valuable knowledge and resources from weak ties may be particularly difficult in the post-conflict environment, where the social tissue has been damaged and people are unwilling to share knowledge with strangers or mere acquaintances. In such environments, to be able to benefit from business contacts, strong personal links need to be built on top of networks. Thus to understand the impact of network structure on growth aspirations, a distinction between acquaintances and friends is necessary (e.g. Krackhardt and Stern, 1988; Greve and Salaff, 2003). Accordingly, the following is hypothesized:

> *Hypothesis 4: In a low-trust context, growth aspirations are enhanced by a larger proportion of ties that are family- or friends-based (in contrast with acquaintances).*

Methods

Data

In this research the data on young businesses were obtained from a specially designed cross-sectional survey implemented in the period June–August 2011. The data were gathered from the owners, owner-managers and hired managers from six different regions covering the two entities constituting the state of BiH – the Republic of Srpska and the Federation of Bosnia and Herzegovina with an average of 40 firms surveyed per region. The multi-ethnic division of BiH between three nationalities is represented in the choice of regions, as each of the three dominant nationalities (Bosniaks, Serbs and Croats) is in a majority in two out of these six regions. The survey was administered through face-to-face meetings. It was decided to survey firms formed between July 2005 and December 2008 in order to ensure a more homogenous sample, because the business environment changed dramatically when the economic crisis hit BiH in 2009. In addition, to achieve more homogeneity, the sample does not include small firms from the following sectors, namely, agriculture, forestry, fishing, and craft-workshops.

Initially, 734 companies that met the criteria were identified for the survey on the basis of public records. No firm size limit was applied. The final number of surveyed companies was 243. The response rate was 33 per cent. The list of the questions administered to obtain data for the key variables of interest is presented in Table 7.1 and summary statistics for all variables used in the econometric analysis are reported in Table 7.2.

The dependent variable *Employment aspirations* utilizes the two questions presented in the first row of Table 7.1, which are based on the Global Entrepreneurship Monitor methodology (Reynolds et al., 2005). Combining answers the study produces a continuous variable, capturing the expected percentage change in the number of employees five years into the future in comparison to the current situation. Following Estrin et al. (2013a) the dependent variable is created as the difference between the firm's employment aspirations in five years and its current number of employees divided by the current number of employees. The distribution of the dependent variable was left skewed with 12 observations identified as severe outliers (outside the outer fence, using the inter quartile range) which had unrealistic

Table 7.1 Survey Questions Used to Obtain Data for Key Variables

Variable name	Question
Employment aspirations	What is the total number of employees in your enterprise currently? What is the total number of employees in your enterprise expected in 5 years' time?
Area ethnically mixed	In the neighbourhood where you work now, is your ethnic group in the majority minority there is a balance between two or three major groups it is diverse
Generalized trust	Generally speaking, would you say that most people can be trusted or that you need to be very careful in dealing with people? Most people can be trusted Need to be very careful
Institutional trust	For each one, could you please tell me how much confidence you have in The state government Entity and cantonal government Municipal authority Tax administrations The Office of the High Representative The Courts (1) a great deal, (2) quite a lot, (3) average, (4) not very much, (5) none at all
percent external ties	Please can you think about the people from outside your firm with whom you regularly discuss aspects of running your own business? Write down the initials for up to 5 of them (Interviewer asked about each person). Is this contact a: Acquaintance Close friend Family member?

Table 7.2 Descriptive Statistics

	Mean	Median	SD	Min	Max
Employment aspirations (expected change in number of employees)	6.53	0.5	41.41	−1	498.5
Area ethnically mixed (mixed = 1, otherwise = 0)	0.14	0	0.34	0	1
Ethnic majority (majority = 1, otherwise = 0)	0.80	1	0.40	0	1
Ethnic minority (minority = 1, otherwise = 0)	0.06	0	0.24	0	1
Generalized trust (most people can be trusted: yes = 1, no = 0)	0.08	0	0.27	0	1
Institutional trust (confidence in institutions: none = 1, a great deal = 5)	2.46	2.5	0.72	1	4.3
% of external ties in network (no external ties = 0, all ties external = 1)	0.32	0.4	0.27	0	1

	Mean	Median	SD	Min	Max
Owner/manager status	0.42	0	0.49	0	1
(respondent owner-manager of firm = 1, otherwise = 0)					
Network size (continuous)	14.49	9	31.66	0	300
(no. of people in discussion network)					
Network size 0–3	0.30	0	0.46	0	1
(network size: 0–3 people = 1, otherwise = 0)					
Network size 4–9	0.20	0	0.40	0	1
(network size: 4–9 people = 1, otherwise =0)					
Network size 10	0.26	0	0.44	0	1
(network size: 10 people = 1, otherwise = 0)					
Network size over 10	0.23	0	0.42	0	1
(network size: 11+ = 1, otherwise = 0)					
Female	0.33	1	0.42	0	1
(male = 0, female = 1)					
Age	38.63	38	9.80	20	79
(Age of respondents in years)					
Business experience	9.98	7	7.66	1	40
(Business experience in years)					
No. of employees	11.01	4	28.99	1	400
(current number of employees)					
Manufacturing	0.09	0	0.29	0	1
(firm's main sector manufacturing = 1, otherwise = 0)					
Hotels	0.03	0	0.18	0	1
(firm's main sector hotels)					
Construction	0.06	0	0.24	0	1
(firm's main sector construction = 1, otherwise = 0)					
Transport	0.03	0	0.17	0	1
(firm's main sector transport = 1, otherwise = 0)					
Trade	0.45	0	0.50	0	1
(firm's main sector trade = 1, otherwise = 0)					
Business services	0.33	0	0.47	0	1
(firm's sector business services = 1, otherwise = 0)					

values in the range of 400 per cent–4980 per cent and consequently were excluded (following Autio and Acs, 2010; Estrin et al., 2013a).

The respondents' perception of ethnic pluralism in the neighbourhood where they work is measured by the variable *Area ethnically mixed*. Based on the question presented in Table 7.1, this variable takes:

- a value of 1 when the respondent perceives either (a) the area is ethnically diverse, or (b) the area contains a balance of two or three major ethnic groups;
- a value of 0 when the respondent perceives their ethnicity to either be (c) in the majority or (d) minority in their work neighbourhood.

The conceptualization that a perception of belonging to an ethnically mixed neighbourhood rather than being in a majority or minority indicates less polarized ethnic relationships is

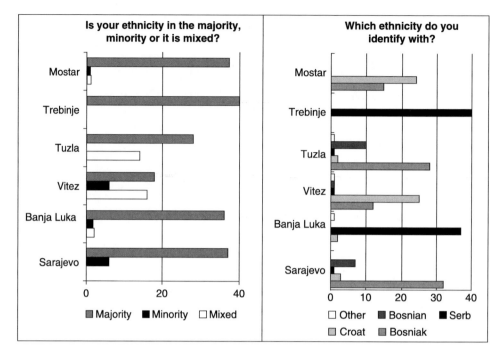

Figure 7.2 Bar Charts Showing Ethnicity and Perceptions of Neighbourhood Ethnic Diversity

Note: The question on ethnic self-identification was open ended. In addition to the three major ethnic groups, some respondents declared their ethnicity more broadly as 'Bosnian'.

supported by the correspondence between these data and what is known about the ethnic composition of BiH. For example, Mostar is a city where different ethnic groups (Croats and Bosniaks) live isolated from one another (in the Western and Eastern parts respectively). In the sample there is a reasonable balance between the two ethnicities. However, perceptions of the ethnic composition of their neighbourhood fall almost unanimously into the ethnic majority category. In contrast, in areas such as Tuzla, where there is also a mix of ethnicities, but not the stark spatial division of ethnicities, this mix is associated with individuals perceiving themselves to live in an ethnically mixed area rather than to be in the majority or minority, entirely consistent with Armakolas (2011). This is illustrated by Figure 7.2.

The measure for *Generalized trust* is based on the World Values Survey (WVS) question as presented in Table 7.1. The response is dichotomous with 0 representing the answer 'need to be very careful' in dealing with people, and 1 representing the response 'most people can be trusted'. Only 8.2 per cent of respondents in the sample indicated that they possess generalized trust, reflecting both the post-conflict and post-Communist legacy (Estrin and Mickiewicz, 2011a). *Institutional trust* is a scale formed from the respondents' answers to the questions on their confidence in key institutions in BiH (following Efendic et al., 2011), as listed in Table 7.1. These answers were measured on a scale of 1 (no confidence at all) to 5 (a great deal of confidence). Cronbach's Alpha (0.86) and factor analysis indicate that these items can be combined to form a scale. Accordingly, these individual scores were added together and divided by six to form a scale ranging from 1 to 5.

The strength (composition) of ties in the respondents' network is measured by asking for detail on the strength of the tie for five members of their business discussion network. This is composed of the 'people that entrepreneurs turn to when they discuss aspects of establishing and running a business' (Greve and Salaff, 2003: 3). It would be better to have information on all ties, but respondent fatigue makes such data collection challenging. In examining the role of kin relations in entrepreneurship, Greve and Salaff (2003) argue that restricting the survey to five ties should be adequate.

The tie is defined as strong if the network contact is indicated to be a family member or a close friend and as weak if the contact is classified as an acquaintance by the respondent. Following Greve and Salaff's (2003) measure for kin in network, the variable percentage of external ties in the network was created. This is formed from counting the number of acquaintances named in the five most important ties in the network and dividing this by five. Explicit distinctions are made between the share of ties with family (Family/Total ties), with close friends (Friends/Total ties), and with acquaintances (Acquaintances/Total ties). The remaining variables are controls. They include respondents' characteristics, firm characteristics and area fixed effects. For firms' characteristics the controls are the current number of employees as a proxy for the firm's size (No. of employees) and sector (six sectors reported in Table 7.2). For respondent characteristics the controls are for gender (Female), age (Age) and respondent's years of business experience (Business experience). Additionally, we control for owner-manager status (Owner-manager), a dichotomous variable where 1 indicates that the individual is both owner and manager of the firm and 0 indicates all other positions including owners not actively involved in management.

Discussion network size is another control variable. To establish network size, the respondents were asked to approximate the number of people from outside their firm with whom they discussed aspects of running their business. The size of the network does not have a continuous distribution above the value of eight. Accordingly, a categorical variable is constructed by partitioning the empirical distribution into four roughly equal parts.

Model specification

The benchmark specification which captures the factors affecting growth aspirations of BiH's young businesses has the following form (corresponding to Model 1 below):

$$Employment\ aspirations_i = \hat{\beta}_0 + \hat{\beta}_1\ Institutional\ trust_i + \hat{\beta}_2\ Generalized\ trust_i +$$
$$\hat{\beta}_3\ Area\ ethnically\ mixed_i + \hat{\beta}_4\ Network's\ external\ links +$$
$$\hat{\beta}_5\ (Controls)_i + \mathbf{X\beta} + \hat{\varepsilon}_i$$

Indices 'i' represent firms 1–243, $\hat{\beta}_0$ is the constant term, $\hat{\beta}_{1-4}$ the coefficients of variables to be estimated that correspond with hypotheses 1–4, $\hat{\beta}_5$ the controls, and $\mathbf{X\beta}$ area fixed effects. The error term is denoted with $\hat{\varepsilon}$. The hypotheses and variables used to test them as well as the expected signs are summarized in Table 7.3.

Control variables are network size, respondent's characteristics (gender, age, business experience, owner-manager), and firm's characteristics (firm size and sector). Owner-manager status is expected to have a positive relationship to growth ambitions as where institutional contexts are weak, such as in a post-conflict environment, separation of owner-ship and control may have a particularly negative influence on firm management. Network size is included to account for the possibility that the share of external ties masks the effect of larger size, when the latter is omitted from the model. Larger networks might be supportive in creating more ambitious business plans through the provision of information and resources (Jenssen and Greve, 2002; Witt, 2004; Witt et al., 2008). Larger size (No. of employees),

Table 7.3 Summary of Hypotheses

Hypothesis	Variable used to test hypothesis	Expected sign
H1: The greater managers' trust in institutions, the higher their growth aspirations.	Institutional trust	+
H2: The greater managers' generalized trust, the higher their growth aspirations.	Generalized trust	+
H3: Managers in an ethnically mixed neighbourhood have higher growth aspirations.	Area ethnically mixed	+
H4: Growth aspirations are enhanced by a larger proportion of ties that are strong (family and friends based).	External/Total ties	−

male gender (Male) and more business experience (Business experience) are expected to have a positive effect on growth aspirations, consistent with empirical evidence (Wagner, 1992; Estrin and Mickiewicz, 2011b). There is no clear prediction for the effect of age (Age) on growth aspirations, as the results in the literature are mixed (Parker, 2009). In addition, the model controls for different business sectors. Finally, the variables introduced to represent education were statistically insignificant and/or proved to be incompatible with model diagnostics and so are not included in the final model.

Results

The specifications are estimated by OLS regression in Stata 13 and reported in Table 7.5. Model 1 is estimated with 227 observations. However, the variables for network composition contain more missing values, consequently models 2 and 3 are estimated with 166 observations.

The econometric model was tested to ensure correct functional form, and robust standard errors were used to mitigate problems with heteroskedasticity. No indication of serious multi-collinearity was found in the specifications: the variance inflation factor (VIF) ranges between 2.52 and 3.92 for the variables. In taking both dependent and independent variables from a cross-sectional survey, endogeneity is always a concern. In this study, network variables and growth aspirations may be considered problematic as they may be simultaneously defined – individuals with higher growth aspirations may decide to grow their networks to meet their aspirations. However, the variables are constructed so that growth aspirations are forward-looking (respondents were asked about employment growth aspirations for the next five years) and network variables are backward-looking (the last six months). Furthermore, networks are developed slowly over time, particularly in a low-trust environment. On these grounds it is argued that simultaneity between network size and aspirations is not a serious problem for this study.

The results, presented in Table 7.4, are now discussed. Institutional trust, capturing (formal) institutional environment is statistically significant in all reported models, at 1 per cent level in Model 1a based on a larger sample and no area fixed effects, and between 10 per cent– 5 per cent level when area fixed effects are included (Model 1b) or based on smaller samples (Models 2–3). It correlates positively with growth aspirations in every model reported, supporting Hypothesis 1. Thus, those individuals who have greater confidence in formal

Table 7.4 OLS Regression – Dependent Variable: Employment Growth Aspirations

Models:	(1a)	(1b)	2(a)	(2b)	(3)
Institutional trust	0.191**	0.161*	0.152*	0.162†	0.167*
	(0.062)	(0.067)	(0.076)	(0.086)	(0.084)
Generalised trust	0.034	0.023	−0.057	−0.154	−0.165
	(0.137)	(0.142)	(0.142)	(0.156)	(0.159)
Area ethnically mixed	0.442***	0.288*	0.384**	0.290*	0.286*
	(0.121)	(0.140)	(0.122)	(0.137)	(0.136)
External/total ties			−0.681***	−0.416†	
			(0.178)	(0.229)	
1/5 external tie					
2/5 external ties					
3/5–5/5 external ties					
Family/total ties					0.183
					(0.377)
Friends/total ties					0.500*
					(0.249)
Owner–manager status	0.196*	0.222*	0.168†	0.185†	0.195†
	(0.081)	(0.087)	(0.097)	(0.099)	(0.102)
Network size 4–9	0.102	0.105	0.073	0.106	0.122
	(0.114)	(0.117)	(0.143)	(0.134)	(0.132)
Network size 10	0.069	0.072	0.030	0.012	0.010
	(0.113)	(0.129)	(0.155)	(0.173)	(0.174)
Network size over 10	0.275*	0.254+	0.304†	0.262	0.265
	(0.118)	(0.130)	(0.168)	(0.183)	(0.182)
Female	0.178†	0.167	0.286**	0.263*	0.294*
	(0.096)	(0.102)	(0.103)	(0.109)	(0.113)
Age	−0.003	−0.001	−0.000	0.002	0.002
	(0.005)	(0.005)	(0.006)	(0.006)	(0.006)
Business experience	0.002	−0.004	−0.005	−0.008	−0.006
	(0.006)	(0.007)	(0.008)	(0.008)	(0.009)
Number of employees	−0.001	−0.001	−0.001	−0.001	−0.001
	(0.001)	(0.001)	(0.001)	(0.001)	(0.001)
Manufacturing	0.067	0.051	0.125	0.083	0.080
	(0.135)	(0.141)	(0.156)	(0.169)	(0.170)
Hotels and restaurants	−0.301*	−0.203	−0.300*	−0.112	−0.063
	(0.149)	(0.154)	(0.143)	(0.165)	(0.162)
Construction	−0.073	−0.064	0.002	0.006	0.010
	(0.223)	(0.220)	(0.259)	(0.248)	(0.251)
Transport	0.327	0.157	0.285	0.213	0.260
	(0.334)	(0.325)	(0.353)	(0.367)	(0.359)
Professional and business services	−0.010	0.021	0.059	0.114	0.112
	(0.094)	(0.093)	(0.114)	(0.113)	(0.114)
Constant	−0.094	−0.126	0.138	−0.247	−0.718*
	(0.226)	(0.254)	(0.283)	(0.391)	(0.318)
Area fixed effects	NO	YES	NO	YES	YES
Observations	227	227	166	166	166
Adjusted R-squared	0.144	0.171	0.209	0.232	0.230
F	3.792	5.042	4.869	6.950	6.781

Notes: Robust standard errors in parentheses. ***$p<0.001$ **$p<0.01$, *$p<0.05$, †$p<0.10$

institutions report higher growth aspirations. In contrast, no evidence is found to support Hypothesis 2 – the degree of generalized trust is not statistically significant in any of the models. This may in part be due to the lack of variability in the measure of generalized trust.

Next, ethnically mixed areas are characterized by systematically greater growth aspirations in comparison to more homogenous areas, clearly supporting Hypothesis 3, at 0.1 per cent level in Model 1a (larger sample with no area fixed effects), at 1 per cent in Model 2a (smaller sample, no area fixed effects) and 5 per cent in Models 1b, 2b, and 3 (smaller sample and area fixed effects included). Given that the variable has a larger positive relationship with growth aspirations when area fixed effects are not included, it suggests that the variable is not just a reflection of the respondent's optimism, but does reflect the social environment in which they are situated. To verify if these results are indeed related to ethnic pluralism and not enforced by categorization, alternative specifications were applied (unreported but available on request) where majority and minority perceptions are distinguished using separate Ethnic majority and Ethnic minority variables. However, according to the Wald test, the difference between the coefficients for Ethnic majority and Ethnic minority is statistically insignificant.

To investigate the relationship between the composition of networks and aspirations (Hypothesis 4) the External/Total ties variable (Models 2a and 2b) is added. A higher proportion of external ties in the discussion network is found to be negatively related to growth aspirations, indicating that the proportion of strong ties rather than weak ties is positively related to business aspirations. The effect is larger and the variable has a higher significance level (1 per cent) without area fixed effects (Model 2a) than with fixed effects (Model 2b), suggesting a regional variation in network composition.

To further test the robustness of the result for network composition, Model 3 distinguishes between family-based strong ties (Family/Total ties), friends-based strong ties (Friends/Total ties) and weak ties with acquaintances. The proportion of friends-based strong ties is positively related to business aspirations and is statistically significant at the 5 per cent level. In contrast, the proportion of family-based strong ties is not statistically significant. Thus it is not the difference between family and others but the difference between friends versus others that matters.

With respect to the controls, we find that owner-managers are characterized by 20 per cent higher growth aspirations compared with hired managers. The result is significant at the conventional 5 per cent level, but weaker once the sample becomes smaller in Models 2–3 (significant at 10 per cent). A large network size (over 10 people in business discussion network) is significant at 5 per cent and positively associated with higher aspirations in Model 1, but again the significance level is at 10 per cent when fixed effects are included or the sample size becomes smaller. When area fixed effects and the network composition variables are added the size of networks becomes insignificant. Being female has a positive and significant effect in the model, suggesting that women have systematically higher growth aspirations than males. This result goes against conventional findings (see, for example, Estrin and Mickiewicz, 2011b) and is rather surprising, as BiH's society still might be considered as a rather patriarchal society in which women are less engaged in the social, political, and economic aspects of life compared to men (Somun-Krupalija, 2011). None of the other control variables are statistically significant, apart from the area fixed effects which are not reported.

Discussion and conclusions

This study contributes to the literature on entrepreneurship by bringing together different perspectives on social capital and analyzing the influence of multiple dimensions of social capital on entrepreneurial growth aspirations in a post-conflict context. The hypotheses tested relate to the aspirations of the owners and managers of young businesses. Following Penrose (1959) managers are seen as important agents: companies are not black boxes, where different input combinations produce alternative outcomes. Rather, firm growth and entrepreneurialism results from their ambitions. What makes this study particularly interesting is the non-standard context; the social capital dimensions of ethnic pluralism, institutional and generalized trust, and business network composition are considered in a post-conflict context, where social capital is fragile yet it also matters greatly.

We find that an entrepreneur's institutional trust is associated with stronger growth aspirations. This demonstrates that a micro perspective on formal institutions is valuable, particularly in a post-conflict, weak institutional context as one finds significant variance in individuals' experience of institutions, for example, with better experience associated with more entrepreneurial dynamism. Thus, from a policy perspective, these findings suggest that much can be achieved by identifying and emulating already existing best local practice. The latter policy approach will also come with lower risks related to 'institutional transplants' from far away (Mamadouh et al., 2002).

An especially interesting finding is that in a context where ethnic tensions are a salient issue, local ethnic pluralism is an important part of social capital affecting employment growth aspirations via norms of tolerance supporting experimentation, via a broader knowledge base and via wider access to resources – human capital in particular. To capture the potential benefits of living and working in a more diverse context, it is necessary for individuals from different groups to interact. Relations between the ethnic groups vary immensely not just between regions but also at the individual level: indices of fractionalization, which measure the ethnic composition on a regional or city level, are not able to capture this aspect of ethnic relations. This study offers a new measure, 'ethnic pluralism', to capture how individuals perceive ethnicity in their local neighbourhoods. It was found that entrepreneurs in local areas that are perceived to be ethnically mixed rather than fragmented and polarized into majority and minority groups, have higher growth aspirations. These results are important when seen in the context of the cross-country economic literature, as the latter suggests that ethnic diversity may be associated with negative economic outcomes. This conclusion may be correct to the extent that diversity is associated with likelihood of internal conflicts and divided communities, but not in the case of interaction between the different groups.

While the strength of business ties in the literature is recognized as a potential determinant of business aspirations, the empirical results are ambiguous (Greve and Salaff, 2003). This study offers an explanation of this ambiguity. Strong ties provide young businesses with limited amounts of new knowledge. Furthermore, family obligations may constrain entrepreneurial action, particularly in societies like BiH where kinship provides an important basis for social and economic support. In contrast, networks based on external weak ties may potentially offer more valuable resources, yet in a weak trust environment, these resources will not be utilized effectively, unless the external ties become considerably strengthened. This is captured by the difference between acquaintances and friends. In the latter case, trust, resulting from transforming external ties into stronger ones, better enables entrepreneurs of young businesses to access valuable knowledge.

Moreover, the findings on network composition and institutional trust contrast it with the insignificant results on generalized trust. This suggests that owners and managers of young companies may rely on their local discussion networks to compensate for lack of (generalized) trust in strangers. However, it is more difficult to compensate for obstacles created by formal institutions: it may be this difficulty in finding alternative managerial strategies explains why the local perception of formal institutions plays such a significant role.

The findings highlight the importance of different social determinants of business growth for policies aimed at supporting young business development and have particular resonance for post-conflict areas. Entrepreneurs' trust in institutions as well as stronger social ties beyond the family circle are both associated with higher business growth aspirations. Equally important, ethnic pluralism is an opportunity not a threat; in the regions where ethnic pluralism is preserved, business aspirations are stronger.

References

Acemoglu, D. and Robinson, J. (2012). *Why nations fail*. London, Profile Books.

Adler, P. and Kwon, S. (2002). Social capital, prospects for a new concept. *Academy of Management Review*, 27(1), 17–40.

Aidis, R. and Mickiewicz, T. (2006). Entrepreneurs, expectations and business expansion, lessons from Lithuania. *Europe-Asia Studies*, 58(6), 855–880.

Aidis, R., Estrin, S. and Mickiewicz, T. (2008). Institutions and entrepreneurship development in Russia. A comparative perspective. *Journal of Business Venturing*, 23(6), 656–672.

Aldrich, H. E. and Kim, P. H. (2007). Small worlds, infinite possibilities? How social networks affect entrepreneurial team formation and search. *Strategic Entrepreneurship Journal*, 1(1–2), 147–165.

Alesina, A. and La Ferrara, E. (2005). Ethnic diversity and economic performance. *Journal of Economic Literature*, 43(3), 762–800.

Alesina, A. and Giuliano, P. (2013). Family ties, National Economic Bureau Working Paper 18966, Cambridge, MA.

Armakolas, I. (2011). The paradox of Tuzla City, explaining non-nationalist local politics during the Bosnian war. *Europe-Asia Studies*, 63(2), 229–261.

Arrow, K. J. (1974). *The limits of organization*. New York, Norton.

Audretsch, D., Dohse, D. and Niebuhr, A. (2010). Cultural diversity and entrepreneurship, a regional analysis for Germany. *The Annals of Regional Science*, 45(1), 55–85.

Autio, E. (2011). High aspiration entrepreneurship. In, Minniti, M. (ed). *Dynamics of entrepreneurship*. Oxford, Oxford University Press, pp. 251–276.

Autio, E. and Acs, Z. (2010). Intellectual property protection and the formation of entrepreneurial growth aspirations. *Strategic Entrepreneurship Journal*, 4(3), 234–251.

Baum, J. R., Locke, E. A. and Kirkpatrick, S. A. (1998). A longitudinal study of the relation of vision and vision communication to venture growth in entrepreneurial firms. *Journal of Applied Psychology*, 83(1), 43–54.

Baum, J. R., Locke, E. A. and Smith, K. J. (2001). A multidimensional model of venture growth. *Academy of Management Journal*, 44(2), 292–303.

Bieber, F. (2006). *Post-war Bosnia, ethnicity, inequality and public sector governance*. Basingstoke, Palgrave Macmillan.

Bieber, F. (2010). Bosnia and Herzegovina since 1990. In, Ramet, S. P. (ed). *Central and Southeast European politics since 1989*. Cambridge, Cambridge University Press, pp. 311–328.

Bourdieu, P. (1986). The forms of capital. In, Richardson, J. (ed). *Handbook of theory and research for the sociology of education*. New York, Greenwood, pp. 241–258.

Bowen, H. P. and De Clercq, D. (2008). Institutional context and allocation of entrepreneurial effort. *Journal of International Business Studies*, 39(4), 747–767.

Burt, R. S. (2000). The network structure of social capital. *Research in Organisational Behaviour*, 22(6), 345–423.

Casson, M. and Della Giusta, M. (2007). Entrepreneurship and social capital. *International Small Business Journal*, 25(3), 220–244.

Collier, P. (2008). *The bottom billion*. Oxford, Oxford University Press.

Delmar, F. and Wiklund, J. (2008). The effect of small business managers' growth motivation on firm growth, a longitudinal study. *Entrepreneurship Theory and Practice*, 32(3), 437–457.

di Falco, S. and Bulte, E. (2011). A dark side of social capital? Kinship, consumption, and savings. *Journal of Development Studies*, 47(8), 1128–1151.

Dyrstad, K. (2012). After ethnic civil war, Ethno-nationalism in the Western Balkans. *Journal of Peace Research*, 49(6), 817–831.

Easterly, W. and Levine, R. (2001). Africa's growth tragedy, policies and ethnic divisions. *Quarterly Journal of Economics*, 112(4), 1203–1250.

Efendic, A., Pugh, G. and Adnett, N. (2011). Confidence in formal institutions and reliance on informal institutions in BiH, an empirical investigation using survey data. *Economics of Transition*, 19(3), 531–540.

Estrin, S. and Mickiewicz, T. (2011a). Entrepreneurship in transition economies, the role of institutions and generational change. In, Minniti, M. (ed). *Dynamics of entrepreneurship*. Oxford, Oxford University Press, pp. 181–208.

Estrin, S. and Mickiewicz, T. (2011b). Institutions and female entrepreneurship. *Small Business Economics*, 37(4), 397–415.

Estrin, S., Korosteleva, J. and Mickiewicz, T. (2013a). Which institutions encourage entrepreneurial growth aspirations? *Journal of Business Venturing*, 28(4), 564–580.

Estrin, S., Mickiewicz, T. and Stephan, U. (2013b). Entrepreneurship, social capital, and institutions. Social and commercial entrepreneurship across nations. *Entrepreneurship Theory and Practice*, 37(3), 479–504.

Florida, R. (2004). *The rise of the creative class*. New York, Basic Books.

Florida, R. (2005). *Cities and the creative class*. London, Routledge.

Fukuyama, F. (1995). *Trust, the social virtues and the creation of prosperity*. London, Penguin.

Gedajlovic, E., Honig, B., Moore, C., Payne, G. and Wright, M. (2013). Social capital and entrepreneurship, a schema and research agenda. *Entrepreneurship Theory and Practice*, 37(3), 455–478.

Glaeser, E., Scheinkman, J. and Shleifer, A. (2003). The injustice of inequality. *Journal of Monetary Economics*, 50(1), 199–222.

Granovetter, M. (1973). The strength of weak ties. *American Journal of Sociology*, 78(3), 1360–1380.

Granovetter, M. (1985). Economic action and social structure, the problem of embeddedness. *The American Journal of Sociology*, 91(3), 481–510.

Greve, A. and Salaff, J. W. (2003). Social networks and entrepreneurship. *Entrepreneurship Theory and Practice*, 28(1), 1–22.

Hadziahmetović, A. (2011). *Ekonomija Evropske Unije*. Sarajevo, University Press.

Hansen, E. L. (1995). Entrepreneurial networks and new organizational growth. *Entrepreneurship Theory and Practice*, 19(4), 7–19.

Hoang, H. and Antončič, B. (2003). Network-based research in entrepreneurship, a critical review. *Journal of Business Venturing*, 18(2), 165–187.

Hodson, R., Sekulić, D. and Massey, G. (1994). National tolerance in the former Yugoslavia. *American Journal of Sociology*, 99(6), 1534–1558.

Hohmann, H. H. and Welter, F. (2002). Entrepreneurial strategies and trust, structure and evolution of entrepreneurial behavioural patterns. In, Hohmann, H.H. and Welter, F. (eds). *East and West European environments – concepts and considerations*. Bremen, Forschungsstelle Osteuropa, Arbeitspapiere und Materialine, 37, Universitat Bremen, pp. 11–18.

Jack, S. (2010). Approaches to studying networks, implications and outcomes. *Journal of Business Venturing*, 25(1), 120–137.

Jack, S., Moult, S., Anderson A. R. and Dodd, S. (2010). An entrepreneurial network evolving: Patterns of change. *International Small Business Journal*, 28(4), 315–337.

Jenssen, J. I and Greve, A. (2002). Does the degree of network redundancy in social networks influence the success of business start-ups? *International Journal of Entrepreneurial Behavior and Research*, 8(5), 254–267.

Kelley, D. J., Bosma, N. and Amorós, J. E. (2010). *Global entrepreneurship monitor*, 2010 Global Report, Babson Park, MA, Babson College.

Khavul, S., Bruton, G. D. and Wood, E. (2009). Informal family business in Africa. *Entrepreneurship Theory and Practice*, 33(6), 1219–1238.

Kolvereid, L. and Bullvag, E. (1996). Growth intentions and actual growth, the impact of entrepreneurial choice. *Journal of Enterprising Culture*, 4(1), 1–17.

Krackhardt, D. (1992). The strength of strong ties, The importance of philos in organizations. In, Nohria, N. and Eccles, R.G. (eds). *Networks and organizations, structure, form, and action*, Boston, MA, Harvard Business School Press, pp. 216–239.

Krackhardt, D. and Stern, R. N. (1988). Informal networks and organizational crises: An experimental simulation. *Social Psychology Quarterly*, 51(2), 123–140.

Kwon, S. W. and Arenius, P. (2010). Nations of entrepreneurs, a social capital perspective. *Journal of Business Venturing*, 25(3), 315–330.

Lee, S. Y., Florida, R. and Acs, Z. (2004). Creativity and entrepreneurship, a regional analysis of new firm formation. *Regional Studies*, 38(8), 879–891.

Levie, J. and Autio, E. (2011). Regulatory burden, rule of law and entry of strategic entrepreneurs, an international panel study. *Journal of Management Studies*, 48(6), 1392–1419.

Light, I. and Dana, L. P. (2013). Boundaries of social capital in entrepreneurship. *Entrepreneurship Theory and Practice*, 37(3), 603–624.

Mamadouh, V., De Jong, M. and Lalenis, K. (2002). *The theory and practice of institutional transplantation*. Dordrecht, Springer Netherlands.

Marino, M., Parrotta, P. and Pozzoli, D. (2012). Does labour diversity promote entrepreneurship? *Economic Letters*, 116(1), 15–19.

Messersmith, J. G. and Wales, W. J. (2011). Entrepreneurial orientation and performance of young firms, The role of human resource management. *International Small Business Journal*, 31(2), 115–136.

Nooteboom, B. (2007). Social capital, institutions and trust. *Review of Social Economy*, 65(1), 29–53.

Olson, M. (1982). *The rise and decline of nations, economic growth, stagflation, and social rigidities*. Yale, Yale University Press.

Paldam, M. (2000). Social capital, one or many? Definition and measurement. *Journal of Economic Surveys*, 14(5), 629–653.

Parker, S. (2009). *The economics of entrepreneurship*. Cambridge, Cambridge University Press.

Penrose, E. (2009 [1959]). *The theory of the growth of the firm*. Oxford, Oxford University Press.

Putnam, R. D. (2000). *Bowling alone, the collapse and revival of American community*. New York, Simon and Schuster.

Raiser, M. (1999). Trust in transition. EBRD Working Paper No. 39.

Raiser, M., Rousso, A., Steves, F. and Teksoz, U. (2007). Trust in transition, cross–country and firm evidence. *The Journal of Law, Economics and Organization*, 24(2), 407–433.

Ram, M., Jones, T., Edwards, P., Kiselinchev, A., Muchenje, L. and Woldesenbet, K. (2011). Engaging with super-diversity: New migrant businesses and the research-policy nexus. *International Small Business Journal*, 31(4), 337–356.

Reynolds, P. D., Bosma, N., Autio, E., Hunt, S., De Bono, N., Servais, A., Lopez-Garcia, P. and Chin, N. (2005). Global entrepreneurship monitor, data collection design and implementation 1998–2003. *Small Business Economics*, 24(3), 205–231.

Rothstein, B. (2003). Social capital, economic growth and quality of government, the causal mechanism. *New Political Economy*, 8(1), 49–71.

Rothstein, B. and Stolle, D. (2008). The state and social capital, an institutional theory of generalized trust, *Comparative Politics*, 40(4), 441–459

Smallbone, D., Kitching, J. and Athayde, R. (2010). Ethnic diversity, entrepreneurship and competitiveness in a global city. *International Small Business Journal*, 28(2), 174–190.

Sobel, J. (2002). Can we trust social capital? *Journal of Economic Literature*, 40(1), 139–154.

Somun-Krupalija, L. (2011). Gender and employment in Bosnia and Herzegovina – A country study, International Labour Office Bureau for Gender Inequality. Geneva, ILO 2011 1 v.

Thornton, P. H., Riberio-Soriano, D. and Urbano, D. (2011). Socio-cultural factors and entrepreneurial activity, An overview. *International Small Business Journal*, 29(2), 105–118.

UNDP. (2009). The ties that bind – social capital in Bosnia and Herzegovina. The National Human Development Report. Sarajevo, UNDP.

Van Stel, A. and Storey, D. (2004). The link between firm births and job creation, is there an upas tree effect?. *Regional Studies*, 38(8), 893–909.

Wagner, J. (1992). Firm size, firm growth, and persistence of chance. *Small Business Economics*, 4(2), 125–131.

Wang, C. L. and Altinay, L. (2012). Social embeddedness, entrepreneurial orientation and firm growth in ethnic minority small business in the UK. *International Small Business Journal*, 30(1), 3–23.

Watson, J. (2011). Networking, gender differences and the association with firm performance. *International Small Business Journal*, 30(5), 536–558.

Welter, F. (2012). All you need is trust? A critical review of the trust and entrepreneurship literature. *International Small Business Journal*, 30(3), 193–212.

Welter, F. and Smallbone, D. (2006). Exploring the role of trust in entrepreneurial activity. *Entrepreneurship Theory and Practice*, 30(4), 465–475.

Westlund, H. and Adam, F. (2010). Social capital and economic performance, a meta-analysis of 65 studies. *European Planning Studies*, 18(6), 893–919.

Wiklund, J. and Shepherd, D. (2003). Aspiring for and achieving growth, the moderating role of resources and opportunities. *Journal of Management Studies*, 40(8), 1919–1941.

Witt, P. (2004). Entrepreneurs' network and success of start-ups. *Entrepreneurship and Regional Development*, 16(5), 391–412.

Witt, P., Schroeter, A. and Merz, C. (2008). Entrepreneurial resource acquisition via personal networks, an empirical study of German start-ups. *The Service Industries Journal*, 28(7), 953–971.

Woolcock, M. and Narayan, D. (2000). Social capital: Implications for development theory, research and policy. *The World Bank Research Observer*, 15(2), 225–249.

World Bank. (1997). *Bosnia and Herzegovina from recovery to sustainable growth*. Washington, DC, World Bank.

World Bank. (2002). *Building institutions for markets – World Development Report 2002*. New York, Oxford, Oxford University Press.

Wright, M. and Marlow, S. (2012). Entrepreneurial activity in the venture creation and development process. *International Small Business Journal*, 30(2), 107–114.

Zain, M. and Ng, S. I. (2006). The impacts of network relationships on SMEs' internationalization process. *Thunderbird International Business Review*, 48(2), 183–205.

Zang, J. (2011). The problems of using social networks in entrepreneurial resource acquisition. *International Small Business Journal*, 28(4), 338–361.

Zucker, L. G. (1986). The production of trust, institutional sources of economic structure, 1840–1920. *Research in Organization Behaviour*, 8, 53–111.

8

PLANNING AS A MEANS TO INNOVATION IN ENTREPRENEURIAL FIRMS IN INDIA

Safal Batra and Neharika Vohra

Introduction: innovation in Indian organizations

The state of innovation in India offers some positive and some alarming insights. India has witnessed high growth in the past which is predominantly driven by the development of technology infrastructure (Archibugi and Coco, 2004). However, in a ranking list of G45 nations based on various technology and innovation indices, India ranks 39 in the World Economic Forum's technological readiness index, 45 in the World Bank's knowledge index, and 45 on Archibugi Coco ArCo index (Archibugi et al., 2009). According to Mahroum and Al-Saleh's (2013) index of national innovation efficiency (IEI; based on the analysis of 133 countries), India has been recognized as a high capacity but low performance nation.

In an exhaustive innovation readiness survey conducted by the Ministry of Micro, Small and Medium Enterprises (MSME), it was found that small firms realized innovation as crucial for competitiveness in a global economy (FICCI-MSME Summit, 2012). However, due to a traditional emphasis on productivity rather than innovation, and lack of understanding of how firms can enhance their innovation capabilities, there was lesser attempt towards innovation compared with other Asian economies like Korea and Thailand. Since mere emphasis on efficiency and productivity are not enough for SMEs to compete amongst themselves and with large firms (Corso et al., 2003), it is imperative for SMEs to enhance their innovation attempts and outcomes (Radas and Bozié, 2009). Despite the realization that innovation is crucial for national growth and allocation of significant resources towards innovation, India has not been able to upscale its innovation performance, and needs to strive harder and faster in order to move up the innovation ladder.

According to Wan (2005), 'factor-driven high growth emerging economies' are essentially those which grow by investing in factors such as R&D and education, rather than by building strong institutions. Although it is not easy to bucket countries into this classification, we believe India can be considered as a factor-driven emerging economy, especially given its growth trajectory in software industry. In such economies, firms can survive either by creating close networks with political actors or by emphasizing innovation capabilities as opposed to production capabilities. If India has to take the latter route, there would be a persistent need and pressure on Indian organizations to innovate. While there could be multiple routes to successful innovation, our research on 123 Indian SMEs clearly reveals that strategic planning is one possible route to fostering various kinds and degrees of innovation.

In this chapter, we first introduce various kinds and degrees of innovations, and then explain how strategic planning could possibly help in fostering these innovations in SMEs. Subsequently, we present the analysis conducted on data collected from Indian SMEs. We conclude the chapter by discussing the implications of the findings in helping create more innovations in emerging economies.

Why do organizations innovate?

Innovation has been identified as a source of sustainable competitive advantage for organizations. Several empirical studies on the implications of organizational commitment to innovation on financial performance have yielded support for innovation. Organizations need to innovate and keep pace with the environment by persistently generating novel ideas (Amabile, 1997) and obstinately executing them by building an appropriate culture (Hurley and Hult, 1998). Organizations can win 'only by managing effectively for today while simultaneously creating innovation for tomorrow' (Tushman and Nadler, 1986, pp. 74–92).

The motivation for firms to innovate could be two-fold. The motivation could originate internally or as a response to the changing environment (Crossan and Apaydin, 2010; Damanpour and Evan, 1984). As an example, a firm might have access to slack resources and capabilities which can be put to use by trying novel recombination. Also, most organizations put their slack resources to explore a wide range of knowledge and incorporate that knowledge into new uses in order to remain competitive (Knight, 1967). However, innovation is not contingent only on internal factors. The external environment and the institutional context also play an instrumental role. If firms sense a potential market opportunity which could be capitalized through novelty, they may be inclined to seize that opportunity. When organizations operate in uncertain environments, i.e. environments characterized by quick unpredictable changes, firms need to respond quickly through persistent innovations (Tidd, 2001). Demand side expectations also exert pressure on organizations to compete through advanced products and services. When the market for a certain product is rising, organizations are bound to enhance their competitiveness and market shares using innovation as a means of differentiation (Utterback, 1971).

Innovation and its types

Innovations could be in the form of introducing new products and services, or incorporating new processes and methods to enhance productivity (Bantel and Jackson, 1989). Firms launching a new or significantly improved product stand a chance of occupying a new market space quickly (Andries and Faems, 2013). Firms emphasizing process innovations utilize their resources in a more efficient manner (Ar and Baki, 2011). While large firms have been reported to invest more in process innovations due to larger expected returns (Bommer and Jalajas, 2004), small businesses have been found to invest significantly more in product innovations (de Oliveira and Kaminski, 2012).

Alternatively, innovations could be in the form of building new relationships with suppliers, entering new markets which were earlier unexplored, and finding better ways of organizing (Naveh et al., 2006). When firms enter new markets, they get access to newer resources, giving possibilities of exploration as well as exploitation. While large firms often demonstrate commitment to incorporate new ways of organizing to reduce bureaucracy and rigidities, small firms are somewhat less inclined to try new ways of organizing (de Oliveira and Kaminski, 2012).

Product, service and process innovations originate in the central activities of the organization and belong to the technical system, while administrative innovations comprising new markets, new sources of supply and new ways of organizing originate at the periphery and belong to the social system of the organization (Damanpour and Evan, 1984; Bantel and Jackson, 1989). Administrative innovations involve promoting new rules and procedures to facilitate change (Naveh et al., 2006). All these innovations have different attributes and their initiation and implementation requires different expertise (Damanpour, 1987; Ibarra, 1993). When innovations are created to fulfil market needs, firms are more likely to apply newer technologies and introduce product innovations. However, when the firms create innovations to benefit from a technological opportunity or to create scale economies, they are more likely to undertake process innovations.

Innovation and its degrees

Radical innovations include products, services, processes or solutions which are altogether different from those that already exist (Damanpour, 1991; Pérez-Luño and Cambra, 2013). On the other hand, incremental innovations are significant improvements to already existing products and technologies (Damanpour, 1991; Pérez-Luño and Cambra, 2013). Future markers can be created and captured only when firms invest a proportion of their revenues towards creating radical innovations. Shifting the way marketers and strategists think about the viability of a certain market only comes through radical innovations (Kelley et al., 2013). Breakthroughs happen when existing knowledge is reutilized in unique ways, taking cues from existing technological developments (Kelley et al., 2013). Thus, for radical innovations to happen, it is crucial for firms to look for developments in diverse technologies.

Radical innovations provide substantial value enhancement to customers and incorporate substantial new technology (Chandy and Tellis, 1998; Sorescu et al., 2003). When a firm is willing to cannibalize its existing investments in older technologies and ready to adapt new ones, its likelihood of innovating radical products is higher (Chandy and Tellis, 1998). Radically new products require the creation of a large amount of new knowledge by the firm (Schoonhoven et al., 1990), which implies that firms should persistently look for ideas both within and outside their industry (Utterback, 1971). Higher levels of discontinuity entail higher risks, greater uncertainty, and more resources (Tushman and Nadler, 1986).

Several researchers have addressed the issue of the relative importance of radical and incremental innovations and have contradictory views. For example, Banbury and Mitchell (1995) argued that incumbent firms that persistently introduce incremental innovations acquire significant market shares, whereas Robinson (1990) concluded that incremental innovations in products don't lead to success. What is commonly agreed, however, is that a large majority of new products and services comprise small incremental improvements over the existing ones, by recombining existing ideas and resources of the organization (Damanpour, 1996; Tushman and Nadler, 1986). Incremental innovations either target a technology change or a market change (Garcia and Calantone, 2002). Accordingly, the resource requirements for incremental innovations are relatively lower. Despite some differences in the attributes and implications of each kind of innovation in the organization, researchers have found strong synergies between these different forms. Damanpour et al. (1989) pointed out that different kinds of innovation complement and assist each other and organizations which maintain a balance between these innovations stand a chance of a better performance.

Strategic planning and innovation

While numerous antecedents of innovation have been discussed in the innovation literature, this study explored the role of strategic planning in enhancing innovation outcomes in organizations. Utilizing the resource based view of the firm, it was argued that strategic planning positively assists innovation in SMEs. Innovation requires a persistent commitment of resources from the organization. However, firms have limitations in terms of the amount of resources which they can allocate to new projects. If a firm devotes excessive resources into an innovation, but fails to create equivalent value and appropriate sufficient return to justify the efforts, its performance stands to suffer. The ability to plan the resources in advance and utilize them among parallel innovation projects enables organizations to undertake multiple innovation projects. Accordingly, it can be argued that despite the resource scarcities that they face, SMEs that strategically plan their resources stand a better chance of success in their innovation attempts.

While managers at the middle and operational level are most equipped to propose individual product, process and service innovations, top management understands the administrative set-up better and hence is better suited to propose innovations in suppliers, markets and ways of organizing (Daft, 1978). Successful implementation of either innovation, however, involves both groups working together and gathering sufficient commitment from each other. Hence, it was expected that strategic planning would equally impact all kinds of innovation.

Innovations built through the existing stock of knowledge lead to incremental innovations (Malerba, 1992; Subramaniam and Youndt, 2005). It's easier for firms to learn and apply their knowledge in areas related to their existing practices (Kogut and Zander, 1992). However, when it comes to more radical innovations, organizations need to access unrelated and external knowledge and develop an ability to integrate and assimilate that knowledge with its existing knowledge (Phene et al., 2006). While transferring knowledge is difficult, what is most difficult is to aggregate and utilize such knowledge at one place (Grant, 1996). Hence, any organization that intends to create radical innovations cannot rely on emergent strategies, and needs to plan for persistent knowledge transfer and aggregation. Strategic planning for a radical innovation entails planning not only for the technological ingredients which go into the innovation but also for the new market dynamics which get created post the innovation launch (Garcia and Calantone, 2002). Organizations which don't have sufficient resources to plan frequently end up using improvisation (Zahra et al., 2006), which may not be suited for radical innovations. Last but not the least, radical innovation emanates in a cumulative fashion, involving efforts and stewardship of several leaders before taking its final shape (Makri et al., 2006). Based on these arguments, it was expected that strategic planning would more strongly impact radical than incremental innovations.

Method and Findings

Sample

In order to validate our proposed assumptions about the linkages of strategic planning and various degrees and kinds of innovation, data were collected by administering a quantitative instrument to founders of small and medium enterprises in India. In order to create a sampling plan, we first identified some dominant industrial bodies of the Punjab region in India working in the manufacturing space. A cut-off of 500 employees was chosen as the appropriate criterion to classify firms as SMEs, as this is one of the most common criteria employed in academic research. About 500 firms registered with these bodies and employing fewer than 500 people were initially approached with the questionnaires. Around 200 firms finally filled the survey questionnaire. In order to ensure that strategic planning in these small organizations is not a one-off activity but is persistent in the culture of the organization, all these 200 firms were once again approached after six months. Of these, 123 firms could finally confirm the continuity of business planning, and thus were considered as the final sample.

Questionnaire design

The questionnaire was designed and administered in English. Wherever required, our assistants, who were adequately trained on consistent and accurate translation of items, helped the respondents with the meaning of the item.

Measures

In order to ensure that the exhaustive scales chosen for this study are also relevant to the context of emerging economies, almost all possible scales on strategic planning and innovation were carefully analyzed, and expert opinions were considered. Finally, the 34-item scale of strategic planning designed by Ramanujan and Venkatraman (1987) was used to measure strategic planning, the six-item scale of Johannessen et al. (2001) was used to measure various kinds of innovation (new products, processes, services, suppliers, markets and new ways of organizing) and the six-item scale of Subramaniam and Youndt (2005) was chosen to measure various degrees of innovation (radical and incremental).

Analysis

Data thus collected underwent numerous stringent rounds of checks before hypothesis testing. First, the data was tested for normality, linearity and multi-collinearity, and seemed to fulfil all these assumptions of multivariate analysis. Subsequently, confirmatory factor analysis was conducted on the measures individually as well as collectively. Strategic planning was operationalized as a second-order multi-dimensional construct, made up of 15 items representing five sub-dimensions – namely external analysis, internal analysis, functional coverage, resources available to strategic planning, and commitment to strategic planning. The sub-dimension representing tools and techniques used for strategic planning did not load on the overall construct, since Indian SMEs did not utilize any formal techniques for strategic planning. Cronbach's alpha for this construct was 0.93 and average variance extracted (AVE) was 0.79, thus indicating acceptable reliability and validity. Collectively, the six-item scale of innovation had a Cronbach's alpha value of 0.88 and AVE of 0.54.

Results and discussion

To test the relationship between strategic planning and various kinds of innovations, six structural models were run with the dependent variable changed to new products, new services, new methods-of-production, new markets, new suppliers, and new ways of organizing. The findings clearly revealed that strategic planning was correlated to all dimensions of innovation. Next, a different measurement model was created which had two independent

Table 8.1 Strategic Planning and Various Kinds of Innovation

Dependent variable: New Products

IV – DV	B	SE B	β	R^2
SP – New Product	.46★★★	.11	.27	.27
SP – New Services	.54★★★	.12	.34	.28
SP – New Methods of Production	.82★★★	.11	.54	.35
SP – New Markets	.74★★★	.12	.46	.32
SP – New Suppliers	.67★★★	.12	.42	.32
SP – New ways of Organizing	.62★★★	.12	.38	.31
SP – Incremental Innovation	.03	.09	.03	.06
SP – Radical Innovation	.28★	.11	.23	.10

variables – incremental innovations and radical innovations. As the results indicated (see Table 8.1), strategic planning had higher correlation with radical as compared to incremental innovations.

Our findings clearly reveal that strategic planning is a possible route to facilitate innovations of all kinds including technological and administrative; and radical and incremental. These findings have implications for encouraging innovation in small and medium set-ups of emerging economies. More often than not, SMEs are unaware of the implications of pursuing an innovation strategy. Even if they are aware that innovation could be a route of sustainable competitive advantage, they face a bigger challenge of how to pursue innovation. Indeed by having a clear focus on internal resources and keeping an eye on the changing external environment, by making strategic planning a part of the organizational culture and allocating sufficient resources to this process, and finally by integrating strategic planning with all functional exercises in the organization, managers can see an enhanced interest among the employees in pursuing innovation.

Every firm requires significant resources to perform exploratory search activities to demonstrate commitment towards new projects (Amabile et al., 1996), and to exploit the innovations (Lawson and Samson, 2001). SMEs in emerging economies are characterized by resource scarcity (Wu, 2007). The emerging economy business environment is characterized by uncertainties and turmoil and a rapidly changing business environment (Zhou and Li, 2010). The environmental uncertainties of emerging economies make it imperative for firms to create new resources and capabilities (Wright et al., 2005). Firms that strategically plan and align their resources to exploit environmental opportunities perform better (Griffith et al., 2006).

Since SMEs in emerging economies have flexible organizational structures that are amenable to strategic planning, and entrepreneurs founding the SMEs exercise most of the strategic decision making powers, it is expected that an appropriate commitment to strategic planning on the part of SMEs can deliver excellent innovation results. Searching the environment for appropriate opportunities and generating limited resources that are valuable to organization are activities which SMEs can perform efficiently if they are committed to strategic planning.

While conducting this research, we came across numerous cases where strategic planning assisted various degrees and kinds of innovation. We point out a few examples to illustrate how some businesses are able to leverage strategic planning for enhanced innovation outcomes. One organization in our sample, though small, provided resources and time to its employees to keep themselves abreast with the latest technological know-how in their domain, and keep an eye on the actions of large competitors. This helped them to offer enhanced products to the customers despite the prevalence of large players in the industry. Another organization which started extremely small ten years ago, but became so large that we could not include in our large sample analysis, emphasized that the breakthrough innovation achieved by their organization was a result of persistent movement in one direction for ten years. They had to proactively understand the industry evolution, strategize to build long-term and short-term plans, and allocate resources to understand the market needs. Finally, an organization was able to innovate its business processes by incorporating everyone in the organization in strategic decision making and allocating substantial resources to this activity. These are just few of the numerous successful innovators in Indian SMEs that leveraged the positive implications of strategic planning in their favour.

In sum, entrepreneurs need to evaluate their new product aspirations vis-à-vis their current resources and capabilities, and plan to build the missing competencies. Without appropriate product planning, SMEs may undertake redundant tasks, misunderstand their deliverables and face coordination problems. Additionally, strategic planning can help SMEs allocate appropriate tasks to the right people and appropriate resources to the right tasks. Since innovations require persistent effort and commitment and take a lot of time to materialize, SMEs need to persist with their strategic planning efforts. According to Brews and Hunt (1999, p. 906), persistence in planning '. . . is key to the realization of any performance enhancements'.

We hope that studies such as these will provide insights for entrepreneurs to be successful and innovative in their businesses. This is also the area where we believe an urgent need for researchers and practitioners to work together can be foreseen in order to come up with innovative, inexpensive, and meaningful solutions for development and growth.

References

Amabile, T.M. (1997). Motivating creativity in organizations: On doing what you love and loving what you do. *California Management Review*, 40(1), 39–58.

Amabile, T.M., Conti, R., Coon, H., Lazenby, J. and Herron, M. (1996). Assessing the work environment for creativity. *Academy of Management Journal*, 39(5), 1154–1184.

Andries, P. and Faems, D. (2013). Patenting activities and firm performance: Does firm size matter. *Journal of Product Innovation Management*, 30(6), 1089–1098.

Ar, I.M. and Baki, B. (2011). Antecedents and performance impacts of product versus process innovation: empirical evidence from SMEs located in Turkish science and technology parks. *European Journal of Innovation Management*, 14(2), 172–206.

Archibugi, D. and Coco, A. (2004). A new indicator of technological capabilities for developed and developing countries. *World Development*, 32(4), 629–654.

Archibugi, D., Denni, M. and Filippetti, A. (2009). The technological capabilities of nations: The state of the art of synthetic indicators. *Technological Forecasting and Social Change*, 76(7), 917–931.

Banbury, C. M. and Mitchell, W. (1995). The effect of introducing important incremental innovations on market share and business survival. *Strategic Management Journal*, 16(1), 161–182.

Bantel, K. A. and Jackson, S. E. (1989). Top management and innovations in banking: Does the composition of the top team make a difference? *Strategic Management Journal*, 10(S1), 107–124.

Bommer, M. and Jalajas, D. (2004). Innovation sources of large and small technology based firms. *IEEE Transactions on Engineering Management*, 51(1), 13–18.

Brews, P.J. and Hunt, M.R. (1999). Learning to plan and planning to learn: resolving the planning school/learning school debate. *Strategic Management Journal*, 20(10), 889–913.

Chandy, R.K. and Tellis, G.J. (1998). Organizing for radical product innovation: The overlooked role of willingness to cannibalize. *Journal of Marketing Research*, 35(4), 474–487.

Corso, M., Martini, A., Paolucci, E. and Pellegrini, L. (2003). Knowledge management configurations in Italian small-to-medium enterprises. *Integrated Manufacturing Systems*, 14(1), 46–56.

Crossan, M.M. and Apaydin, M. (2010). A multidimensional framework of organizational innovation: A systematic review of the literature. *Journal of Management Studies*, 47(6), 1154–1191.

Daft, R.L. (1978). A dual-core model of organizational innovation. *Academy of Management Journal*, 21(2), 193–210.

Damanpour, F. and Evan, W.M. (1984). Organizational innovation and performance: The problem of 'organizational lag'. *Administrative Science Quarterly*, 29(3), 392–409.

Damanpour, F. (1987). The adoption of technological, administrative, and ancillary innovations: impact of organizational factors. *Journal of Management*, 13(4), 675–688.

Damanpour, F. (1991). Organizational innovation: a meta-analysis of effects of determinants and moderators. *Academy of Management Journal*, 34(3), 555–590.

Damanpour, F. (1996). Organizational complexity and innovation: developing and testing multiple contingency models. *Management Science*, 42(5), 693–716.

Damanpour, F., Szabat, K.A. and Evan, W.M. (1989). The relationship between types of innovation and organizational performance. *Journal of Management Studies*, 26(6), 587–601.

de Oliveira, A.C., and Kaminski, P.C. (2012). A reference model to determine the degree of maturity in the product development process of industrial SMEs. *Technovation*, 32(12), 671–680.

FICCI-MSME Summit (2012). Innovation readiness of Indian SMEs: issues and challenges. Retrieved from http://www.ficci.com/spdocument/20144/FICCI-MSME-Summit-2012-knowledge-paper-new.pdf. Accessed 1 December 2013.

Garcia, R. and Calantone, R. (2002). A critical look at technological innovation typology and innovativeness terminology: A literature review. *Journal of Product Innovation Management*, 19(2), 110–132.

Grant, R.M. (1996). Towards a knowledge-based theory of the firm. *Strategic Management Journal*, 17(S2), 109–122.

Griffith, D.A., Jacobs, L. and Richey, R. (2006). Fitting strategy derived from strategic orientation to international contexts. *Thunderbird International Business Review*, 48(2), 239–262.

Hurley, R.F. and Hult, G.M. (1998). Innovation, market orientation, and organizational learning: An integration and empirical examination. *Journal of Marketing*, 62(3), 42–54.

Ibarra, H. (1993). Network centrality, power, and innovation involvement: Determinants of technical and administrative roles. *Academy of Management Journal*, 36(3), 471–501.

Johannessen, J., Olson, B. and Lumpkin, G.T. (2001). Innovation as newness: what is new, how new, and new to whom? *European Journal of Innovation Management*, 4(1), 20–31.

Kelley, D.J., Ali, A. and Zahra, S.A. (2013). Where do breakthroughs come from? Characteristics of high-potential inventions. *Journal of Product Innovation Management*, 30(6), 1212–1226.

Knight, K.E. (1967). A descriptive model of the intra-firm innovation process. *Journal of Business*, 40(4), 478–496.

Kogut, B. and Zander, U. (1992). Knowledge of the firm, combinative capabilities, and the replication of technology. *Organization Science*, 3(3), 383–397.

Lawson, B. and Samson, D. (2001). Developing innovation capability in organizations: a dynamic capabilities approach. *International Journal of Innovation Management*, 5(3), 377–400.

Mahroum, S. and Al-Saleh, Y. (2013). Towards a functional framework for measuring national innovation efficacy. *Technovation*, 33(10), 320–332.

Makri, M. Lane, P. J. and Gomez-Mejia, L.R. (2006). CEO Incentives, innovation, and performance in technology-intensive firms: A reconciliation of outcome and behaviour based incentive scheme. *Strategic Management Journal*, 27(11), 1057–1080.

Malerba, F. (1992). Learning by firms and incremental technical change. *The Economic Journal*, 102(413), 845–859.

Naveh, E., Meilich, O. and Marcus, A. (2006). The effects of administrative innovation implementation on performance: an organizational learning approach. *Strategic Organization*, 4(3), 275–302.

Pérez-Luño, A. and Cambra, J. (2013). Listen to the market: ao its complexity and signals make companies more innovative? *Technovation*, 33(6), 180–192.

Phene, A. Fladmoe-Lindquist, K. and Marsh, L. (2006). Breakthrough innovations in the U.S. bio-technology industry: the effects of technological space and geographic origin. *Strategic Management Journal*, 27(4), 369–388.

Radas, S. and Bozié, L. (2009). The antecedents of SME innovativeness in an emerging transition economy. *Technovation*, 29, 438–450.

Ramanujam, V. and Venkatraman, N. (1987). Planning system characteristics and planning effectiveness. *Strategic Management Journal*, 8(5), 453–468.

Robinson, W.T. (1990). Product innovation and start-up business market share performance. *Management Science*, 36(10), 1279–1289.

Schoonhoven, C.B., Eisenhardt, K.M. and Lyman, K. (1990). Speeding products to market: Waiting time to first product introduction in new firms. *Administrative Science Quarterly*, 35(1), 177–208.

Sorescu, A.B., Chandy, R.K. and Prabhu, J.C. (2003). Sources and financial consequences of radical innovation: Insights from pharmaceuticals. *Journal of Marketing*, 67(4), 82–102.

Subramaniam, M. and Youndt, M.A. (2005). The influence of intellectual capital on the types of innovative capabilities. *Academy of Management Journal*, 48(3), 450–463.

Tidd, J. (2001). Innovation management in context: environment, organization and performance. *International Journal of Management Reviews*, 3(3), 169–183.

Tushman, M. and Nadler, D. (1986). Organizing for innovation. *California Management Review*, 28(3), 74–92.

Utterback, J.M. (1971). The process of technological innovation within the firm. *Academy of Management Journal*, 14(1), 75–88.

Wan, W.P. (2005). Country resource environments, firm capabilities, and corporate diversification strategies. *Journal of Management Studies*, 42(1), 161–182.

Wright, M., Filatotchev, I., Hoskisson, R.E. and Peng, M.W. (2005). Strategy research in emerging economies: challenging the conventional wisdom. *Journal of Management Studies*, 42(1), 1–33.

Wu, L.-Y. (2007). Entrepreneurial resources, dynamic capabilities and start-up performance of Taiwan's high-tech firms. *Journal of Business Research*, 60(5), 549–555.

Zahra, S.A., Sapienza, H.J. and Davidsson, P. (2006). Entrepreneurship and dynamic capabilities: a review, model and research agenda. *Journal of Management Studies*, 43(4), 917–955.

Zhou, K.Z. and Li, C.B. (2010). How strategic orientations influence the building of dynamic capability in emerging economies. *Journal of Business Research*, 63(3), 224–231.

9

THE FAILURE OF GOVERNMENT POLICIES TO DRIVE ENTREPRENEURIAL PERFORMANCE IN CROATIA

Will Bartlett

Introduction: transition and crisis

In the latter half of the twentieth century, the Socialist Republic of Croatia was a constituent republic of the former Yugoslavia. During this period, private enterprise played an important role in the economy. Unlike the countries of the former Soviet bloc, Croatia had a thriving private sector, composed of private agriculture organised in small farms, and private industrial and service sectors organised in small-scale 'craft' businesses. The latter were allowed to operate as family businesses with a limit of five full-time employees. This form of enterprise was common in the tourism sector on the Dalmatian coast, where over two-fifths of local businesses were of this type (Lydall, 1984).

In the non-private sector, a system of social, rather than state, ownership prevailed. This meant that most industrial companies were established as self-managed enterprises, within which managers had a high degree of autonomy to trade on the market, with strong involvement of employees in management through the institution of the Workers' Council. Within these constraints, managers were able to make all decisions relating to their business operations. Well before the collapse of the Yugoslav state, the process of economic transition had begun in the late 1980s under the so-called Marković reforms, which opened the socially owned enterprises to a process of privatisation (Bartlett, 2003).

Croatia emerged as an independent country from the former Socialist Federal Republic of Yugoslavia in 1991. In the first half of the 1990s, the new country was engaged in a period of armed conflict, first with the Yugoslav army in a short war of independence, and later with rebel forces within its own territory which culminated in the 'Oluja' Offensive of 1995 which led to the expulsion of more than 200,000 Croatian citizens of mainly Serb ethnicity from the rebel-held territories of the Krajina (Tanner, 1997; Goldstein, 1999). Complete cessation of hostilities did not come about until 1998 with the reunification of Eastern Slavonia into the Croatian state.

Following independence, new company laws permitted the creation of private businesses under various legal forms including private and publicly traded share ownership alongside the existing craft sector. Privatisation of the socially owned enterprises continued, resulting in the sale of a large portion of their assets during the 1990s to politically well-connected new owners as well as to incumbent managers and employees, with a residual portion taken under state ownership. In the late 1990s, the domestic banking sector experienced a dramatic crisis which led to the collapse of several regional banks on the back of unwise loans that had been made to the newly privatised enterprises. This paved the way for the takeover of most of the banking sector by foreign banks in the early 2000s, facilitating an inflow of credit that fuelled a consumer boom. The privatisation programme came under severe criticism from Croatian economists who characterised the new system as one of 'crony capitalism' (Bićanić, 1993). The Croatian Democratic Union (HDZ) had created a system in which the largest and most profitable companies had been transferred to a new elite of privileged owners with party connections. This strong connection between the political and managerial elites persists until the present day within the clientelistic form of capitalism that has been created in Croatia.

The political and institutional context within which entrepreneurship emerged in post-socialist Croatia was thus formed in part by the legacy of the past as well as by the policies pursued by various governments through a period of dramatic uncertainty. During this period, until the end of the 1990s, the dominant political force in the country was the nationalist Croatian Democratic Union, led by hard-line President Franjo Tudjman, who had over-seen the drive to independence. His death in 1999 ushered in a period of democratic reform under the Social Democratic Party which briefly held power in the early 2000s. The next government was led by a reformed and pro-EU HDZ under the leadership of Ivo Sanader, laying the groundwork for the country's eventual EU membership.[1] In 2011 the SDP has returned to power. The 2000s were characterised by a period of pre-accession institutional change leading to the country's eventual membership of the EU in July 2013 (Ott, 2004).

Since the onset of the Eurozone crisis in 2009, the economy has been subject to a deep recession with six years of negative GDP growth. The initial decline in GDP was due to the negative shock inflicted on the world economy by the crisis of the international financial system that began in 2007 and led to a global economic downturn in 2009, followed by the continuing crisis of the Eurozone. Croatia has languished in recession in each subsequent year. On joining the EU in 2013, the country's external debt was approaching 100 per cent of GDP. By mid-2015 this had increased to 115 per cent of GDP. This poor economic performance indicates deep structural problems and difficulties in adjusting the economy in the wake of the initial recession and reveals an underlying problem of weak competitiveness of the Croatian economy. Partly, this may be due to the weakness of entrepreneurial activity and corresponding policies.

Although entrepreneurship is deeply embedded in the historical legacy in Croatia, another element of the legacy of communism in Croatia has been that of the primacy of politics over economics, and the strong influence of the power of personal connections in business success. The former socialist system in Croatia has been characterised as one of 'political capitalism', and the system that emerged from it as 'clientelistic' capitalism (Cvijanović and Redžepagić, 2011) or 'crony' capitalism. This indicates the difficulties that new and aspiring entrepreneurs face in establishing their businesses. This weakness has hindered the ability of the economy to respond to economic shocks and has undermined economic competitiveness. It is hardly surprising, therefore, that the economy has been unable to escape from the long six-year recession that began in 2009.

Characteristics of the business sector

Despite the legacy of private enterprise within the former socialist system, today the culture of entrepreneurship appears to be relatively weak, as measured by the rate of entry of new

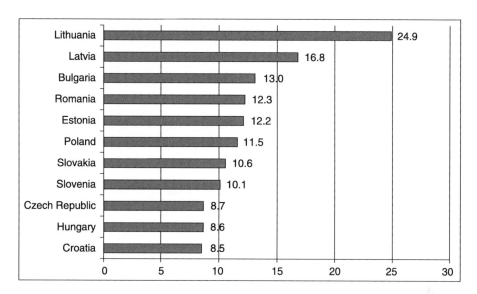

Figure 9.1 Birth Rate of Enterprises in EU New Member States and Croatia, 2012

Source: Eurostat online data.

business. In 2012, for example, the entry rate of new businesses in Croatia was just 8.5 per cent compared to an average of 13 per cent in the new member states of Central and Eastern Europe (see Figure 9.1). This rate of new firm formation is more similar to the average of the old member states of the EU. It is close to the entry rate in Hungary and the Czech Republic, but far below that in the Baltic States, and even below Bulgaria and Romania.

The Global Entrepreneurship Monitor has carried out regular surveys of the adult population of Croatia since 2002 to identify the proportion of adults who are engaged in early-stage business activity. The measured indicator is the rate of total early-stage entrepreneurial activity (TEA). The TEA rate in Croatia rose to a peak in of 8.5 per cent in 2006 and then fell back after the onset of the economic crisis to just 5.5 per cent in 2010 (see Figure 9.2). Since then it has recovered, and by 2014 had almost recovered to its earlier peak.

A strong gender difference is seen, with the rate of male TEA substantially higher than that of females. In 2014, the male TEA was 11.3 per cent compared to just 4.8 per cent for women (see Figure 9.2). The average TEA gender gap has been 5.7 per cent over the period from 2004 to 2014, with peaks coinciding with periods of maximum TEA, reaching as high as 7 per cent in 2006 and 2012 (and a minimum of 3.2 per cent in 2010), indicating that early-stage entrepreneurship is greater among Croatian males compared to females in both a static and dynamic sense, and that female TEA is more stable than male TEA.[2]

A weak positive statistical relationship exists between the male TEA and the lagged rate of economic growth (real GDP growth rate), with a Pearson correlation coefficient of 0.35. This suggests that the male rate of entrepreneurial entry is pro-cyclical, increasing with the economic upswing and declining during a slump. However, there is no correlation between the female TEA rate and lagged GDP growth, providing further evidence of the relative stability of the female TEA rate in Croatia.

Further evidence on the propensity for entrepreneurship in Croatia is provided by the data on the established business ownership rate from the GEM survey. This measures the percentage of 18–64-year-olds who own and manage an active business for more than 42 months.

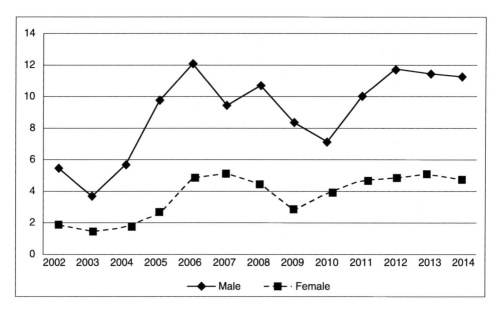

Figure 9.2 Total Early-Stage Entrepreneurial Activity by Gender (%) (TEA)

Source: GEM population survey data.

Between 2004 and 2014 this averaged 3.7 per cent, with a period in which it increased from 2 per cent in 2004 up to 5 per cent just before the onset of the economic crisis. This was followed by a period of decline to 3 per cent in 2012, from which point there has been only a shallow and gradual recovery.

By 2014 the rate of established business owners had recovered somewhat reaching 3.6 per cent. However, this was still far below other European countries. In the EU new member states the rate was almost twice as high, at 7.0 per cent (see Figure 9.3). Encouragingly, by 2014 the rate of total early-stage entrepreneurial activity (TEA) had recovered, reaching 8 per cent compared to 9.7 per cent in the new member states, and was slightly above that in both the old member states and the EU periphery countries. This suggests an upturn in relative entrepreneurial activity in Croatia in recent years.

The TEA rate itself is composed of two subcomponents. The first, the nascent entrepreneurship rate, measures the share of adults who are in the process of starting a business. This indicator was higher in 2014 than in any of the comparator country groups. In contrast, the new business ownership rate, which measures the share of newly established businesses that have been active for not more than 42 months, was lower than for any of the comparator groups (see Figure 9.3). The fact that nascent entrepreneurship seems to have rebounded in relative terms compared to comparators provides an early sign of economic recovery and pick-up from the long recession that Croatia has endured for the last six years.

It should be noted that there is a substantial informal sector in Croatia, although this seems to have diminished over time. Writing in the early 2000s, Katarina Ott (2002) reported on research carried out into the informal economy by the Institute of Public Finance in Zagreb between 1996 and 2002. This revealed that the size of the informal economy was around 25 per cent of GDP. More recently Schneider (2011) has estimated that the informal economy amounts to about 30 per cent of GDP. It is mainly located in agriculture, and less so in manufacturing and retailing. However, other estimates by Croatian economists find much

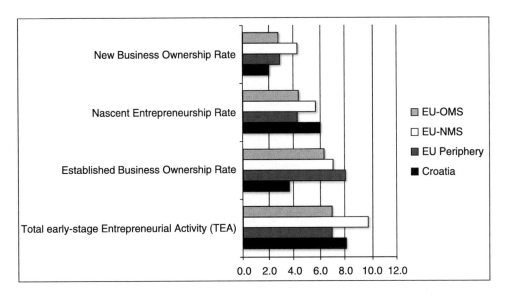

Figure 9.3   Entrepreneurship in Croatia Compared to Elsewhere in Europe

Source: GEM population survey data.

Note: *OMS = EU Old Member States, NMS = EU New Member States, EU Periphery consists of Greece, Italy, Portugal and Spain.*

lower levels of the informal economy at around 8 to 9 per cent of GDP (Lovrinčević et al., 2001; Madžarević-Šujster and Mikulić, 2001). Whatever its size, Baric and Williams (2013) note that policy towards the informal economy has been uncoordinated and mainly based upon attempts to suppress such activities rather than to provide sensible incentives for employers to avoid taking the drastic step of operating on an informal basis. The existence of an informal economy does not mean that one quarter or more of businesses are unregistered. It rather reflects the widespread practice of tax evasion, either through an employer failing to register workers for social security purposes, or else under-reporting the wages to avoid payment of labour taxes and social contributions.

Widespread tax avoidance reflects the difficulties that many entrepreneurs have in raising loan finance for their business activities, requiring them to maximise in every way possible the profit of the business so that this can be used to self-finance investment and growth. The GEM survey provides evidence on this point. The survey of expert opinion asks a question about the availability of financial resources for SMEs, which scores an average of just 2.4 on the 1–5 scale used, and which shows a decline from a peak of 2.7 in 2007 to 2.3 in 2014, indicating that the problem has worsened over the period of the recession. Commercial banks have often preferred to lend to larger companies with strong political connections, than to small innovative entrepreneurial businesses. Bank credit to small firms has typically been provided only on a short-term basis at relatively high cost (Kraft, 2002). Some evidence demonstrates that bank officials lacked effective loan assessment skills in making loans to risky small businesses (Cziraky et al., 2005). In the early 2000s many Croatian banks were taken over by large European banks and the flow of funds into the country increased and the skills of loan assessment officers were upgraded. However, foreign banks in transition countries have tended to focus on mortgage lending to households and on lending to subsidiaries of foreign companies, rather than to small domestic entrepreneurs (de Haas et al., 2007). The continuing and indeed increasing difficulties for small entrepreneurs to access bank loans can therefore hardly be explained by technical features of loan operations, but should rather be sought in the realm of political connections of large incumbent firms who have been able to attract the greater part of available loan finance.

According to a World Bank statement in 2015 'innovative SMEs [in Croatia] still need support in the Croatian entrepreneurial landscape in particular with accessing early stage financing, that is, helping companies move from idea to product or service'.[3] In response to this need, in July 2015 the World Bank approved a €20 million Loan Agreement for an Innovation and Entrepreneurship Venture Capital Project. The project aims to strengthen risk capital financing for innovative SMEs and start-ups.

Entrepreneurial motivations

Not surprisingly, given the severity of the recession in Croatia over the last six years, the proportion of 18–64-year-olds who were not already entrepreneurs who saw good opportunities to start a firm in the area in which they lived fell dramatically. From a peak of 45 per cent in 2008, the proportion fell to just 17.5 per cent by 2012 and has remained below 20 per cent since then (see Figure 9.4).

Despite the perceived lack of opportunities, there has been an almost equal and opposite pick-up in intentions to form a business. Intentions to form a business may be derived from either 'push' or 'pull' factors. Push factors arise when a person starts up a business in response to a lack of other alternatives to earn an income, often called 'necessity entrepreneurship'. Pull factors refer to a situation in which a person decides to start a business in response to a perceived opportunity, hence called 'opportunity entrepreneurship'. The data from the GEM survey show that the proportion of those who were not already active in business, but who intended to start a business within three years, increased from a low point of 7.4 per cent in 2010 to reach almost 20 per cent in each of the three years from 2012 to 2014, far exceeding

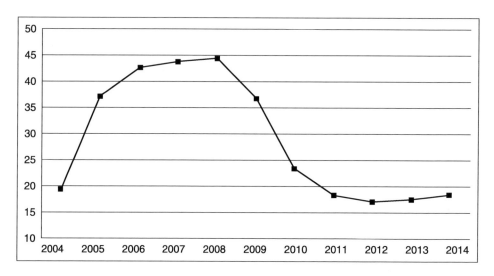

Figure 9.4 Perceived Opportunities (%)

Source: GEM population survey data.

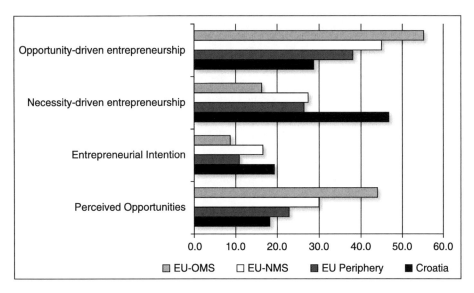

Figure 9.5   Entrepreneurial Motivations in Croatia and Elsewhere in Europe, 2014

Source: GEM population survey data.

pre-crisis levels which had peaked at 10 per cent in 2007. The main reason for this was reflected in an upturn in necessity-driven entrepreneurship. This is defined in the GEM survey as the share of those involved in early-stage business activity (TEA) that were in business because they had no other option for work. The share of this type of entrepreneur in early-stage activity increased from 28.4 per cent in 2008 to 46.5 per cent in 2014. Correspondingly there was a fall in opportunity-driven entrepreneurs (hardly surprisingly given the dramatic fall in opportunity perceptions). The share of opportunity entrepreneurs fell from a peak of 57 per cent in 2008 to a low of 28.7 per cent in 2014, with no signs of improvement.

The relative motivation of Croatian entrepreneurs compared to that in other parts of Europe (in 2014) is shown in Figure 9.5. The comparison reveals the depth of the economic crisis in Croatia. According to the results of the GEM survey, perceived opportunities were lower in 2014 than anywhere else in Europe, with just 23 per cent of the relevant age group not already in business identifying good opportunities to start a firm compared to 55.2 per cent in the EU old member states. Croatia had also fallen behind the new member states and the EU periphery countries as well in this respect. As could be expected from the discussion in the previous paragraph, necessity-driven entrepreneurship was higher in Croatia in 2014 than elsewhere in Europe (46.6 per cent of the relevant age group compared to just 16.4 per cent in the old member states) while opportunity-driven entrepreneurship was correspondingly at a lower level. Strikingly, entrepreneurial intentions were higher in 2014 than elsewhere; however, this was a reflection of the absence of any alternatives, and not inspired by a positive entrepreneurial response to opportunities, which as we have seen had become vanishingly small.

Entrepreneurial performance

The growth expectations of early-stage entrepreneurs are monitored annually by the GEM survey. This shows that between 2004 and 2013 there has been a gradual decline in the proportion of early-stage entrepreneurs who expect to employ an additional five workers five years after the survey. The proportion of respondents who held this expectation declined from 40 per cent in 2002 to 30 per cent in 2012. However, in 2014 there was a surprising pick-up, suggesting that early-stage entrepreneurial expectations have improved, and that the end of the recession may be within sight.

A positive finding from the GEM survey is the steady increase in the international orientation among Croatian entrepreneurs. This has increased fairly steadily since 2004 when the proportion of early-stage entrepreneurs who indicate that at least 25 per cent of their customers are from other countries was just 15 per cent. Since then, the proportion of inter-nationally oriented entrepreneurs has increased to around 40 per cent in each of the four years from 2011 to 2014 (see Figure 9.6). The gradual integration of the Croatian economy into the EU market, culminating in full EU membership in 2013, has no doubt been a strong factor influencing this development.

A comparison of the business strategies of Croatian entrepreneurs to those in other European regions for 2014 is shown in Figure 9.7. This reveals that by 2014 Croatian entrepreneurs had become relatively more internationally oriented and had relatively higher growth expectations for the future than their counterparts elsewhere in Europe. This is especially important for the future prospects of the competitiveness of the Croatian economy, since the main aim of the economic strategy of the government is to boost export performance. It appears that Croatian entrepreneurs are beginning to have some success in this respect. This is most likely a result of the effect that the long recession has had in reducing unit labour costs in Croatia through a combination of falling real wages and improved efficiency.

However, Croatian entrepreneurs are revealed to be far less innovative than entrepreneurs in the three regions to which they are compared. The GEM survey data show that only 27 per cent of early-stage entrepreneurs consider that their product or service is new to at least some customers compared to over one half of this group in the new member states. The rela-tively weak innovative performance may be a sign that the strengthening export orientation may be less sustainable than might be hoped, since international competitiveness is highly dependent on innovative performance, as well as simple reductions in unit labour costs.

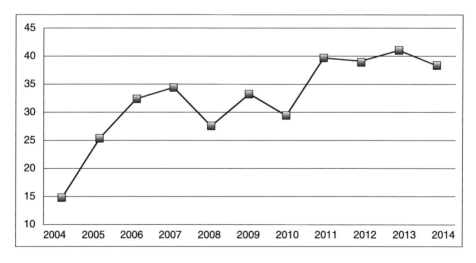

Figure 9.6   International Orientation among Early-Stage Entrepreneurs

Source: GEM population survey data.

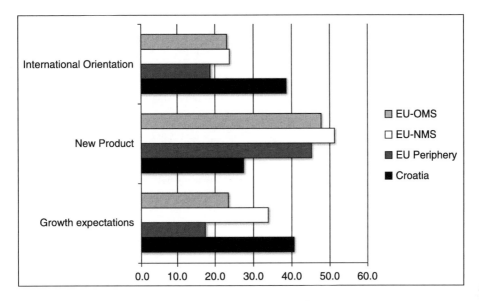

Figure 9.7   Performance of Entrepreneurs in Croatia and Elsewhere in Europe, 2014

Source: GEM population survey data.

Among the barriers to enterprise growth, corruption has been perceived as one of the most significant. On the eve of entering the EU, a report issued by Ernst & Young identified Croatia, along with Slovenia as the most corrupt country in Europe. In a survey of 3,400 people in Croatia, 90 per cent of respondents believed that bribery and corrupt practices among businesses are widespread.[4]

Entrepreneurship policy

One of the first institutions established to support entrepreneurship was the Croatian Guarantee Agency (HGA) while a nation-wide 'Programme to Encourage Small Business' was introduced in 1997. The main aims of the policy were to establish incubators and small business zones, to provide expert and financial assistance to encourage entrepreneurial activity, to assist the commercialization of innovation, to deliver support for start-ups and business development, and to train and educate professional advisors. The priority was the provision of low-cost finance to SMEs in order to overcome the difficulties such firms faced in accessing bank loans at the time. Franičević and Bartlett (2002) carried out research on the implementation and effects of the policy based on interviews with 25 key stakeholders in Zagreb, Osijek and Split in Autumn 1998 and Spring 2000. The authors concluded that the businesses that received subsidised loans would in any case have set up or expanded their business activity even in the absence of the programme. The programme, therefore, was biased by the rent-seeking behaviour of privileged entrepreneurs who were able to apply political pressure on the implementing institutions (banks and local authorities). The programme was also overly bureaucratic, raising transaction costs, while the subsidies were insufficiently backed up by the provision of business services, in the form of advice, counselling and training due to the limited scope and quality of consultancy services, themselves subject to rent-seeking and political bias in the selection of registered consultants.

Following the return to power of the HDZ under the reformist leader Ivo Sanader in 2003, a Croatian Agency for Small Business (HAMAG) was established to reinvigorate entrepreneurship policy. Its main aims were to increase the number of SMEs and craft firms, create new entrepreneurial zones, remove administrative obstacles to small businesses, increase the competitiveness of the economy and promote the export orientation of SMEs. An 'Incentive Program for SMEs' was adopted in May 2004 to promote production and exports by SMEs. The Agency also established a guarantee scheme, provided interest subsidies on commercial loans to SMEs and craft firms, and provided subsidised consultancy services for SME development. However, the Agency had little success in achieving its aims. Critics have identified numerous problems of design and implementation, among which the lack of transparency and the lack of coordination among the institutions in charge of the programme, the lack of long-term finance, and the quality of consultancy services have been highlighted (Čučković and Bartlett, 2007).

In 2006, a new policy aimed at cutting red tape facing entrepreneurs was initiated by establishing a one-stop shop for business registration known as hitro.hr, later becoming the Hitrorez programme. Its aim was to simplify the rules and regulations facing new small businesses, and removing administrative obstacles. The initiative was supposed to contribute significantly to improved entrepreneurship and a more helpful private sector climate (Banović, 2015). However, the programme was short lived, and it was closed down following the 2007 election that returned the HDZ to power. The reason seems to have been embedded resistance to reform from various sources including large business interests that did not wish to see the market opened up to new entrepreneurs, low-level government bureaucrats who feared for their jobs in a liberalised climate as well as lawyers and notaries who benefited from the persistence of complex administrative regulations (Banović, 2015).

In the absence of a real commitment to reduce bureaucracy and administrative obstacles to new entrepreneurial firms' entry and growth, the government policies have continued to stress the removal of financial barriers through the provision of subsidised loans and grants to favoured firms. The most recent programme, rolled out in 2015 by the Ministry of Entrepreneurship and Crafts, provided HRK 14 million (€2 million) through its Business Impulse Program, to co-finance projects intended to strengthen competitiveness in the manufacturing and service sectors and assist entrepreneurs and craftsmen to participate in trade fairs abroad. Through the programme, entrepreneurs in manufacturing can receive grants of between HRK 50,000 and HRK 400,000 (covering up to 75 per cent of the investment for micro businesses, and up to 50 per cent for small businesses) and in the service industry between HRK 30,000 and HRK 200,000 (up to 75 per cent of the value of the investment). The subsidies also enable entrepreneurs and craftsmen to participate in international trade fairs, with grants of between HRK 30,000 and HRK 80,000 (up to 80 per cent of the cost). The minister, Gordan Maras, stated that

> We want to help micro and small enterprises to be more competitive on the market, to create new value and to secure new markets and new customers, to export and finally to open new jobs. The measures the government has designed for our entrepreneurs and craftsmen have shown a positive effect. Croatia's economy is rising again and the forerunners of that growth are SMEs.[5]

As the above discussion shows, over the last 20 years, the Croatian government has consistently attempted to promote entrepreneurship through encouraging the entry and the development of new entrepreneurial private enterprises. Government policies have been mainly focused on providing subsidised loans and co-financed grants to SMEs. However, these policies have been subject to numerous drawbacks that are well known to apply to such programmes, including deadweight effects (subsidising entrepreneurs who in any case would have been successful even without the subsidy) and substitution effects (whereby the favoured firm is inefficient and crowds out the entry of an unsubsidised but potentially more efficient firm) (Santarelli and Vivarelli, 2007). Subsidy programmes for SMEs are likely to be even more ineffective in a system of clientelistic capitalism that predominates in the Croatian case, with its high probability that subsidies will be misdirected to politically well-connected and favoured businesses.

The weakness of the policy environment for entrepreneurship in Croatia can be confirmed from the GEM survey of expert opinion, which aggregates the responses of numerous experts to a set of statements measured on a scale of 1 = not true to 5 = very true. Most scores for the main policy indicators, over the period from 2007 to 2014, range from an average of 1.8 (taxes and bureaucracy) to an average of 2.7 (post-school entrepreneurial education and training). This is a clear indication of an unsupportive entrepreneurial environment, in which taxes and bureaucracy are neither size neutral nor encourage new firm entry, in which public policies fail to support entrepreneurship (2.2), and government programmes fail to directly assist SMEs (2.5). In addition, internal markets are relatively closed in terms of the extent to which new firms are free to enter existing markets (2.2). Finally, the extent to which training in creating or managing SMEs is provided by higher education institutions such as vocational, college, business schools is rather more encouraging to entrepreneurship but still only scores 2.7 on the 1–5 scale (see Figure 9.8).

Not only is the policy environment in support of entrepreneurship relatively weak, but also it appears to have deteriorated over time. Figure 9.8 compares the evolution of some key polices in the seven-year period from 2007 to 2014, covering the period leading up to

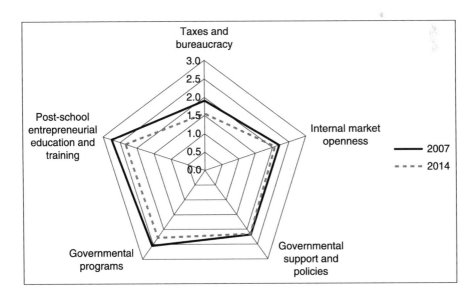

Figure 9.8   Change in Policy Environment for Entrepreneurship, 2007–2014

Source: GEM expert survey (statements were posed to a panel of experts on a 1–5 scale from 1= not true at all to 5= very true).

EU accession. On the measured scale all policies have deteriorated, especially in regard to the provision of post-school training, tax brackets according to firm size, bureaucracy and the quality of government programmes to assist SMEs. All of these deteriorated by around 0.3 points on the scale from 1 to 5.

The issue of post-school training for entrepreneurship is especially relevant in the context of the relative weakness of business education within the school system. A survey carried out by the Croatian Chamber of Commerce in 2011 revealed that small business owners lack organisation and management skills (CCE 2011). In 2010 the government adopted a Strategy for Entrepreneurial Learning to introduce business studies into the educational curriculum at all levels of formal and informal education and training (Čučković and Bartlett, 2012). However, the results of the GEM survey concerning this policy area suggest that the strategy has so far been rather ineffective.

Following Croatia's EU accession in 2013, a new dimension has been brought into play, namely the European perspective on support for entrepreneurial activity. A Strategy for Development of Entrepreneurship in Croatia 2013–2020, adopted in October 2013, aims to increase the competitiveness of small businesses with a target to increase gross value added per employee by 40 per cent by 2020. The three key strategic objectives are (i) to increase the share of SMEs in value added from 52 to 62 per cent, through greater investment in research and development, innovation and increasing exports and the development of business networks, (ii) to improve access to finance for small businesses by 40 per cent, (iii) promote entrepreneurship, enhance entrepreneurial skills and improve the business environment. The Strategy will receive funds from the ERDF from 2014 to 2020. The support of the ERDF may be crucial in overcoming the defects of Croatian policies towards entrepreneurship, although past experience and the embeddedness of policy failure suggest that the new policies may have no more success than previous ones.

Conclusions

Entrepreneurship in Croatia has deep roots in the former socialist system, which permitted private enterprise to flourish within limits set by a restriction on the number of employees, and in agriculture on the size of private farms. The subsequent privatisation of the formerly socially owned enterprises led to a system of clientelistic capitalism in which large enterprises developed close connections to the new political elite. Despite the removal of restrictions on small private enterprises and the development of a more liberal legal environment even before the collapse of the previous system, the entrepreneurial small firm sector has failed to flourish with negative consequences for the competitiveness of the Croatian economy.

The rate of entry of new businesses in Croatia is well below that in the other EU new member states. Total early-stage entrepreneurship (TEA) peaked in 2006 and subsequently fell as the recession hit the economy. There are significant gender differences, and the TEA rate for women is less than half that of men. Male entrepreneurship seems to be strongly pro-cyclical, while female entrepreneurship has a greater degree of stability. Within early-stage entrepreneurship, the rate of nascent entrepreneurship has been relatively high in recent years suggesting a pick-up in entrepreneurial intentions. Although established business ownership is also about half the rate in the EU new member states, it too has caught up in recent years.

Informal activity is present in the Croatian economy although its size is indeterminate with estimates varying between 10 per cent and 30 per cent of GDP. It reflects the widespread practice of tax evasion. Policies to suppress informal activity have been rather unsuccessful, while alternative policies of incentivising a shift away from informality have hardly been tried. With relatively high taxes and social contributions, entrepreneurial firms struggle to generate a surplus for reinvestment, while the availability of bank loans is limited and has been shrinking in recent years. Larger politically well-connected firms have been able to access the lion's share of available finance, leading to a low availability of financial resources for small entrepreneurial firms. This has undermined the innovative potential of the Croatian economy.

As a consequence of the recession and the barriers facing small entrepreneurial firms, the perceived opportunities for entrepreneurship have collapsed following the onset of the recession. The perceived opportunities are actually lower now than in any other European country. Not surprising, therefore, that the recent pick-up in nascent entrepreneurship has been driven far more by necessity motives than by opportunity motives.

With regard to performance, there has been a gradual decline in the expectations of entrepreneurs that they will employ more workers in the future, although expectations in this regard have picked up in the last year, suggesting perhaps that the end of the recession may be within sight. There has also been a steady improvement in the international orientation of Croatian entrepreneurs. This may reflect the gradual integration of the Croatian economy into that of the EU especially following Croatia's accession to the EU in 2013. By 2014, Croatian entrepreneurs had become relatively more internationally oriented and had relatively higher growth expectations than their counterparts in Europe. However, the Croatian entrepreneurs appear to be less innovative than counterparts elsewhere in Europe, casting doubt on the sustainability of the strengthening export orientation. The widely perceived high extent of corruption, endemic to the clientelistic form of capitalism that has emerged following the collapse of the socialist system, may be another factor that is likely to hold back the development of innovative entrepreneurship in Croatia in future years unless dealt with in an effective way.

Croatian governments of all hues have tried hard to promote the spirit of entrepreneurship through numerous legislative acts and the introduction of supportive polices, strategies and measures to promote entrepreneurial small firms. Since the 1990s, governments have promoted small business incubators and business zones, provided expert and financial assistance to encourage entrepreneurial activity, provided training programmes for entrepreneurs and developed a small army of trained business consultants and advisors. However, within the context of clientelistic capitalism, none of the measures has had the desired impact in kick-starting an entrepreneurial economy with a high innovative potential and improved competitiveness on international markets. The policy environment for entrepreneurship seems to have even worsened in the last six years since the start of the economic crisis. The entry of Croatia into the EU may bring about some improvement in this respect as EU entrepreneurship programmes begin to be adopted with the support of the European Regional Development Fund and other significant interventions to support entrepreneurship. It to be hoped that these programmes will find ways to overcome the inertia embedded in the clientelistic economy and support a stronger voice for entrepreneurs and a stronger political will within government to open the economy to new ideas and new entrants than in the past.

Notes

1 Ivo Sanader was subsequently jailed for corruption, an event indicative of the nature of the political elite in Croatia.

2 The coefficient of variation of male TEA is 6.9 compared to just 1.8 for female TEA.
3 World Bank Press Release, 'Croatia to Improve Financing Environment for Innovative SMEs and Startups with World Bank's Help', 8 July 2015.
4 Andrew Rettman, 'Survey: Croatia and Slovenia most corrupt in EU', *EU Observer*, 8 May 2013.
5 Reported in Dalje.com, 'SME Min: Three new tenders for govt subsidies for SMEs', 7 July 2015.

References

Banović, R. S. (2015). Cutting the red ribbon but not the red tape: the failure of business environment reform in Croatia. *Post-Communist Economies*, 27(1), 106–128.

Baric, M. and Williams, C. (2013). Tackling the undeclared economy in Croatia. *South-East Europe Journal of Economics*, 1, 7–36.

Bartlett, W. (2003). *Croatia: between Europe and the Balkans*, London: Routledge.

Bićanić, I. (1993). Privatisation in Croatia. *East European Politics and Societies*, 7(3), 422–439.

CCC. (2011). Training need analysis. Report on Regional Survey 2010. Zagreb: Croatian Chamber of Commerce.

Cvijanović, V. and Redžepagić, D. (2011). From political capitalism to clientelist capitalism? The case of Croatia, Proceedings of the Rijeka Faculty of Economics. *Journal of Business and Economics*, 29(2), 355–372.

Cziraky, D., Tisma, S. and Pisarović, A.(2005). Determinants of the low SME loan approval rate in Croatia. *Small Business Economics*, 25(4), 347–372.

Čučković, N. and Bartlett, W. (2007). Entrepreneurship and competitiveness: the Europeanization of SME policy in Croatia. *Journal of Southeast European and Black Sea Studies*, 7(1), 37–56.

Čučković, N. and Bartlett, W. (2012). Skill matching in the Croatian SME sector and competence based education and training: progress and prospects, in: M. Arandarenko and W. Bartlett (eds.), *Labour markets and skills in the Western Balkans*, Belgrade: FREN, pp. 155–175.

De Haas, R., Ferreira, D. and Taci, A. (2007). What determines banks' customer choice? Evidence from transition countries, Working Paper No. 104, London: European Bank for Reconstruction and Development.

Franičević, V. and Bartlett, W. (2002). Small business development policy in Croatia: design and implementation, in: W. Bartlett, M. Bateman and M. Vehovec (eds.), *Small enterprise development in South-East Europe: policies for sustainable growth*, Boston: Kluwer, pp. 267–294.

Goldstein, I. (1999). *Croatia: a History*, London: Hurst & Co.

Kraft, E. (2002). Bank lending to SMEs in Croatia: a few things we know, in: W. Bartlett and M. Bateman (eds.), *Small enterprise development in South-East Europe: policies for sustainable growth*, Dordrecht: Kluwer Academic publishers, pp. 127–144.

Lovrinčević, Ž., Mikulić, D. and Nikšić-Paulić, B. (2001). Pristup službene statistike procjeni neslužbenog gospodarstva. *Financijska teorija i praksa*, 26(1), 83–116.

Madžarević-Šujster, S. and Mikulić, D. (2001). Procjena neslužbenog gospodarstva sustavom nacionalnih računa. *Financijska teorija i praksa*, 26(1), 31–56.

Lydall, H. (1984). *Yugoslav socialism: theory and practice*, Oxford: Clarendon Press.

Ott, K. (2002). The unofficial economy and the state in transition, in: W. Bartlett, M. Bateman and M. Vehovec (eds.), *Small enterprise development in South-East Europe: policies for sustainable growth*, Boston: Kluwer, pp. 71–82

Ott, K. (ed.) (2004). *Croatian Accession to the European Union: Institutional Challenges*, Zagreb: Institute of Public Finance

Santarelli, E. and Vivarelli, M. (2007). Entrepreneurship and the process of firms' entry, survival and growth. *Industrial and Corporate Change*, 16(3), 455–488.

Schneider, F. (2011). Shadow economies all over the world: new estimates for 162 countries from 1999 to 2007, in: F. Schneider (ed.), *Handbook on the shadow economy*, Cheltenham: Edward Elgar.

Tanner, M. (1997). *Croatia: a nation forged in war*, New Haven, CT: Yale University Press.

10

ECONOMIC ASPECTS OF ENTREPRENEURSHIP

The case of Peru

Matthew Bird

Introduction

Peru occupies a critical place in the study of entrepreneurship policy in developing countries. In the early 1980s, Hernando de Soto and his team at the *Institute of Liberty and Democracy* (ILD) pioneered the institutional analysis of informality and offered new policy prescriptions based on it (de Soto 1986, 2001). In the 1990s, the International Fund for Agricultural Development (IFAD) and Chemonics International independently developed in the Andean highlands innovative demand-driven rural development projects, which leveraged the entrepreneurial proclivities of beneficiaries by allowing them to participate in the market creation process (IFAD 2002, Riordan 2011). Both models were later applied globally. Between 2008 and 2015, the Economist Intelligence Unit (EIU) named Peru, for eight consecutive years and counting, as home to the globe's most sophisticated and inclusive microfinance industry (EIU 2015). And between 2005 and 2014, the Global Entrepreneurship Monitor (GEM) consistently placed Peru among the top three entrepreneurial countries in the world, oscillating at the head of the rankings with fellow Andean nations, Bolivia and Ecuador (GEM 2014).

These achievements emerged in the context of a poor, crisis-riddled country. In 1990, at the height of acute economic and political instability, well over half the population lived in poverty. But after macroeconomic stabilization and free-market reforms in the early 1990s, Peru embarked on the longest period of sustained growth since independence from Spain in 1821 (PRODUCE 2014). Although the concomitant expansion of an emerging middle class spurred domestic demand, much of the economic growth occurred on the back of mineral exports to China – not uncommon for other emerging market countries benefiting from the commodities boom in the early 2000s. But in 2011, minerals prices began to drop, prompting Peruvian policymakers to reexamine the country's macroeconomic growth model – and with it, its approach to entrepreneurship.

Peru confronted a challenge shared by other countries caught in a middle-income trap (Gill & Kharas 2007): A nation's growth accelerates given a stock of natural resources or low-wage labor. Yet once becoming middle-income, the country struggles to enter the high-income category. Manufacturing nations relying on low wages may suffer from wage increases, making them less competitive. Those dependent on commodity exports must escape the "resource curse" by using proceeds from times of bonanza to diversify production, thus decreasing exposure to commodity cycles while generating more employment for the socially mobile population. Peru was a member of the latter group. But any plan for spurring productive diversification implies a new approach to entrepreneurship policy, one focused less on informal self-employment and more on higher value-added entrepreneurship.

This chapter examines the challenges Peru has faced transitioning from low-income to middle-income policy.[1] In doing so, it not only provides a critical overview of entrepreneurship policy in Peru, but also explores a neglected but emerging area of entrepreneurship research. The field often divides countries into a developing and developed dichotomy, yet the development process – like that of any economy – is ongoing. Although both low-income and middle-income countries are considered "developing," their entrepreneurial needs differ. What, then, does the transition in entrepreneurship policy in Peru tell us about the challenge of middle-income entrepreneurship policy in general?

To explore this issue, the second section of the chapter introduces a theoretical framework for understanding the relationship between entrepreneurship and economic development. The third section provides background for understanding the Peruvian case. The fourth section examines the unexpected consequences of unbundling institutional reforms targeting informality. The fifth section describes briefly Peru's middle-income transition before critically evaluating the proposed policy response. The final section explores briefly implications of the Peruvian case for middle-income entrepreneurship policy in the context of new production structures in the twenty-first century.

The entrepreneur's role in the economy

Although entrepreneurs were traditionally ignored in economic theory, without them economic markets would not function (Baumol 2010). Efficiency gains would not be made and innovations that change an economy, and with it a society, would not appear. Alongside land, labor, and capital, an economy's "stock" of entrepreneurship may even be considered as a fourth factor of production. But what is it that entrepreneurs do to "develop" economies – i.e., invent and expand markets, generate jobs and reduce poverty (Aghion & Howitt 1997)?

Although members of the founding Chicago, German, and Austrian schools of entrepreneurship tackled their subject from different perspectives, together they offer a multidimensional but coherent view of what makes the entrepreneur and the entrepreneurial act so critical to market functioning (Hebert & Link 1989). They must have the alertness or interest and knowledge to recognize an opportunity (Kirzner 1973), but they then must assess whether the opportunity is feasible for them personally and whether they want to pursue it (McMullen and Shepherd 2006). Pursuing these opportunities implies a higher degree of risk bearing (Knight 1921), while exploitation of them requires the innovative recombination of resources (Schumpeter 1934). Entrepreneurs are critical to market functioning because their actions lead to equilibrium when they fulfill an efficiency-generating role (à la Kirzner) or disequilibrium – creative destruction – when they result in disruptive innovation and market creation (à la Schumpeter).

But what is the specific relationship between entrepreneurship and economic development? One framework suggests that as economies develop, the entrepreneurial role shifts from one driven by factors to efficiency and, finally, innovation (Porter et al. 2002, Acs et al. 2008, Acs 2010).

Factor-driven entrepreneurship: informality and necessity

High levels of self-employment characterize the factor-driven stage. They produce low value-added goods, compete via low-cost efficiencies, and are largely driven by necessity or subsistence (Schoar 2010), as there is a high inverse statistical correlation between a country's per capita income and the rate of informality, own-account, and necessity-driven entrepreneurs (Wennekers et al. 2005, 2010). Although it may be reductive to conceptualize the entrepreneurial decision as one motivated by opportunity vs. necessity (Williams and Youssef 2011), this does not eliminate the empirical reality: when making occupational choices, low-income individuals often feel compelled to engage in production and trade, often informally, because they deem it as the best economic alternative available. Whether the self-employed perceive the decision as one of opportunity or necessity, the larger structural context of reduced wage-generating occupational opportunities remains. Interestingly, the two major interpretations of informality implicitly align with the question of whether the self-employment decision is one motivated by necessity or opportunity.

Appreciation of the informal sector began when Keith Hart coined the term "informality" in a 1970 article on small-scale entrepreneurs in Ghana. He and later Victor Tokman (2007) and the International Labour Organization (1970, 1972) argued that the survival strategies used by rural-urban migrants constituted not a marginal but an *integral* economic activity. Yet informality had its limits. The ILO asserted that it was caused by excess labor supply, undercapitalization, and a lack of skills and technology. Address these conditions by providing finance, technology, and education, they reasoned, and growth would ensue, causing unemployment to drop. In other words, people created informal employment out of necessity. Once conditions for formal wage work emerged, most informal entrepreneurs transitioned into it. Evidence suggests that this may be the case—that informal entrepreneurship, while admirable, is not in itself a path to growth (La Porta and Shleifer 2014).

The institutional analysis of informality offers an opportunity-framed interpretation. The problem is not so much the lack of resources as the legal system's inability to define and guarantee the assets the poor already possess. Hernando De Soto's reframing of this problem began with the publication of *El otro sendero* (1986)—"the other path"—a study of Peru's informal sector. He concluded that informality emerged from exorbitant transaction costs. The high costs of business formalization—of obtaining the proper operating licenses, for example—outweighed the costs of staying informal. Yet informality's short-term efficiencies generated longer-term costs. When you are not legal, the costs of detection lead you to disperse activities, shun publicity, and spend on sanction-dodging bribes. When you are not legal, you are forced to deal exclusively in cash, often in an inflationary environment and choose to save in tangible goods rather than in cash. When you are not legal, you may benefit from avoiding taxes and labor laws, but this forces you to hire less qualified workers and become more labor, rather than capital, intensive. When you are not legal, you have no guarantee of your ability to use an asset, appropriate returns from it, or change its form or substance. You thus lack the incentive to invest in your own property and cannot use it as collateral for credit. When you are not legal, you have trouble enforcing your contracts. Many of your exchanges rest on oral agreements, and when a dispute occurs you cannot easily resolve it through a judicial court mechanism. But reduce legal and institutional barriers and the entrepreneurs will formalize, which in turn will give them the tools and assets to grow and generate employment.

Following de Soto's prescription, the World Bank helped implement massive property rights reforms in Peru and later spread the intervention globally. The framework inspired the World Bank's Doing Business Report, an annual survey measuring the degree of formal regulatory barriers impeding business formation and operation (Djankov et al. 2002). In 2005, the United Nations Development Program announced the creation of the Commission for the Legal Empowerment of the Poor, co-chaired by de Soto and Madeleine Albright, former U.S. Secretary of State. The objective was to spur economic development by implementing legal structures that would help the poor better use and grow economic assets to the point that they could pull themselves out of poverty.

While the Tokman and de Soto approaches recognize positive aspects of self-employment, both implicitly acknowledge that the economy-wide goal was to transition out of it and into efficiency-driven entrepreneurship.

Efficiency-driven entrepreneurship

Self-employment tends to decrease as an economy's firms begin to exploit economies of scale. Historically, this may be due to an increased extension of the market via infrastructure, communication, technology, and manufacturing improvements, often accompanied by policy changes such as free-trade agreements and institutional reforms. In this context, the entrepreneurial role focuses on exploiting opportunities for scale and driving efficiencies, which in turn generates employment, thus pulling more of the self-employed into wage positions. In other words, entrepreneurs become more opportunity- as opposed to necessity-driven (Acs 2006, Ardagna & Lusardi 2010). The overall rate of entrepreneurship also falls below that in a factor-driven context (Carree et al. 2002, 2007; Wennekers et al. 2005, 2010).

Yet there are differences between two major classes of middle-income economies—manufacturing and commodities. Each provides distinct growth challenges, for example, the latter has the risk of falling into a resource curse (Sachs & Warner 2001).[2] Regardless, the challenge faced by middle-income countries is that of a middle-income trap. Increasing national returns from manufacturing or commodities contribute to employment creation and welfare gains, both of which raise per capita incomes. However, the accompanying rise in wages erodes the country's competitive position. Or in the case of commodity-dependent economies, internal demand may be stimulated but lack of higher value-added productive diversification, historically in the form of manufacturing industries, leaves the country vulnerable to international market shifts. The goal in either case is to stimulate higher value-added entrepreneurship.

But three elements complicate this linear transition in the wake of the emerging market boom in the early 2000s. First, countries that become middle-income on the back of manufacturing differ from those with high per capita income created by commodity exports, with the latter subject to a resource curse. Second, while poverty fell during the emerging market boom, the vast majority of the globe's poor still live in middle-income countries. The countries that struggle to pull out of their middle-income trap must also continue to contend with significant pockets of factor-driven self-employment. Third, a silver lining rests in the still unexplored consequences of knowledge-intensive information and communications technologies, which provide opportunities for opening up global niche value-added markets—if countries can develop the policies for identifying and exploiting them. Rules of the game appear to have changed but to what extent remains unclear. The case of India's IT industry and Kenya's Safaricom, arguably the global leader in mobile banking, are but two examples of the leap from factor-driven to innovation-driven entrepreneurship.

Innovation entrepreneurship

Historically, there was a tendency for the rate of entrepreneurship to fall with the rise of developed, scale economies. However, with the appearance of new technologies and knowledge-intensive industries, the trend may have reversed in high-income countries (Romer 1990, Audretsch and Thurik 2001). Evidence suggests that the relationship between the rate of entrepreneurship and economic development is U-shaped (Carree et al. 2002, Wennekers et al. 2005, 2010), although questions remain over whether the relationship is best characterized as an L (Caree et al. 2007).

One element contributing to the higher rate of entrepreneurship in high-income countries may be the degree to which technology enables capital to substitute for labor. Consider Instagram. In 2010, two people founded the mobile-based photo sharing and social networking site. In 2012, it was sold, with only 13 employees, for $1 billion to Facebook. Regardless of whether entrepreneurial rates rise in innovation-driven economies, few question that the quality of the entrepreneurship is driven more by opportunity and is more knowledge-intensive. Within this setting, creating environments conducive to knowledge spillovers and capital access are critical (Audrestch & Keilbach, 2007, Audrestch et al. 2008, Stenholm et al. 2013). Relative to the factor- and efficiency-driven contexts in which innovation may account for as little as 5 percent and 10 percent of activity, this contribution is estimated to rise to 30 percent in the innovation-driven stage (Sali-i-Martin 2007).

Whether in a factor-, efficiency-, or innovation-driven context, interventions fostering entrepreneurship may focus on a number of components: human capital, finance, technology, regulation, institutions, market access, information, and social capital. Policy decisions lie in identifying which components and what combinations are needed to foster the rate and quality of entrepreneurship desired, given the national context and development goals. For example, evidence suggests that a focus on regulation is more important in factor- and efficiency-driven economies compared to innovation-driven settings, while the latter calls more for the creation of enabling conditions to foster knowledge spillover (Acs 2006, Stenholm et al. 2013).

Since at least the 1980s, Peru's entrepreneurship policy focused on the factor-driven context. Only after accelerated growth in the early 2000s did it revisit its policy assumptions. Importantly, this transition took place within a specific historical context. The remainder of the chapter explores the dual challenges Peru – and by extension most middle-income countries – face seeking to articulate a middle-income entrepreneurship policy in the wake of the emerging market boom in the early 2000s.

The context of Peruvian entrepreneurship

Peru's transition from a low-income to middle-income country parallels those of other developing countries in the late-twentieth and early twenty-first centuries, especially in Latin America, where proxy ideological battles between the United States and Soviet Union played out. In the two decades following World War II, Peru officially entered the lower-middle-income country category (Aiyar et al. 2013). It relied on commodity exports for growth and, with the most liberal economic policies in the region, welcomed foreign investment, part of which built on low-wage competitiveness and helped form a nascent manufacturing industry in the 1950s and 1960s (Thorp and Bertram 1978). Politically, however, the transition was more difficult. Beginning in the 1930s, each time the leading left-wing party threatened to win the popular election, the military intervened, later democratizing when it was sure that a more moderate democratic force would win (Klarén 1973).

Growth in the post-war period did little to reduce the country's inequalities, stemming from deep colonial and geographical divides between the more Hispanic coast and the more indigenous Andean highlands. In fact, the reverse occurred. Massive rural-to-urban migration commenced between 1900 and 1950 and picked up speed thereafter (Matos Mar 1977, 1985). At mid-century, conflict over land—from squatter settlements in Lima to peasant protests in the Andes—created increasing support from new social democratic parties to relieve the social pressure (Collier 1976). One of these parties won the presidency in a 1963 election, following a brief military rule. But in 1968, a new kind of actor intervened in the political process.

Unlike in other Latin American countries, where right-wing military dictatorships intervened and aligned with the United States, Peru was "peculiar" in that a left-wing military dictatorship interceded and sought to restructure society via a series of education, land, and industrial reforms, involving large-scale appropriations and nationalizations. But by the mid-1970s, the military found it difficult to finance the reforms and, amid social protests, initiated a democratization process. But on Election Day in 1980s, the Shining Path (a Maoist guerrilla group) bombed a ballot box in a small Andean village, announcing its arrival on the political scene. As the 1980s progressed, the group's activities spread to the rest of Peru. Meanwhile, the economy worsened following implementation of unsustainable heterodox policies and subsequent macroeconomic mismanagement. Unable to make foreign debt payments, the country lost access to international credit. By the end of the decade, Peru suffered from crippling hyperinflation, economic contraction, and crushing guerrilla violence, taking 70,000 lives and displacing 600,000 people.

In 1990, the country elected an outsider candidate, Alberto Fujimori, who subsequently initiated a macroeconomic "shock" program, which eliminated price controls and subsidies overnight. Inflation rose 5 percent daily and prices doubled every 13 days (Hanke & Krus 2013). Peru's poverty rate rose from 42 to 70 percent between 1985 and 1990. Fujimori also cracked down militarily on what became two guerrilla groups. In 1992, the Shining Path's leader was captured, Fujimori closed Congress, the constitution was rewritten and a series of economic liberalization reforms began. From 1992 to 2001, an increasingly corrupt and authoritarian regime took hold, subverting Peruvian democracy (McMillan & Zoido 2004). The country rebounded in the mid-1990s, registering 13 percent growth in 1995 and cumulative average annual growth of 3.76 percent between 1992 and 2001. But these gains came at a high institutional cost.

Peru's globally renowned entrepreneurial spirit thus emerged within a specific context. Historically, the rural Andean population shared an ethic of economic self-sufficiency. Agricultural production rested on a household's reciprocal exchange of the labor needed to manage multiple plots of land at various altitudes (Murra 2002, Mayer 2002). One was not considered a full member of society until an independent household was formed. Andean migrants later extended this logic to small business creation in Lima (Bird 2010, 2013). With the worsening economic situation between the 1970s and early 1990s, formal wage employment opportunities decreased, further incentivizing self-employment. Many opted to stay informal, given the relative cost of formalization. Reforms inspired by Hernando de Soto in the 1980s and 1990s were intended to improve Peru's factor-driven entrepreneurship and open the way for the transition to an efficiency-driven phase.

Reforming informality in Peru: a cautionary tale

Peru holds a special place in the analysis and policy response to informality, giving birth to an institutional analysis and new policy prescriptions eventually advocated by the World Bank and United Nations. However, the unintended consequences of unbundling de Soto's institutional reforms highlight the challenges of entrepreneurial policy in the context of a low-income to middle-income transition (Bird 2013).

When de Soto and his colleagues took to the streets of Lima in the 1980s, they identified three institutional factors hindering economic activity:

- *Unregistered firms.* To avoid detection and the associated fines or bribes for operating unlicensed businesses, extra-legal firms dispersed production activities and refrained from publicity. This hindered economies of scale and increased sales via marketing.
- *Lack of property rights.* The high cost of obtaining formal property rights theoretically cut Lima's micro-entrepreneurs off from access to formal credit and created disincentives for investing in their own assets because of lack of guarantees.
- *Weak contract enforcement.* The inability to force parties to commit to an exchange agreement created obstacles to increased specialization because many businesses chose to do more activities in-house rather than through the market. To compensate, they sunk costs into limited informal contract enforcement mechanisms.

The ILD subsequently recommended business registration, property rights, and arbitration reforms targeting each issue. The first two were implemented, while contract enforcement was not. Regardless, results from the business registration and property rights reforms were notable.

Business registration In the 1980s, businesses took 289 days and $1,231 paid in either registration fees or bribes to formalize. Some other salient features are as follows:

- After reform in the 1990s, the World Bank estimated that it took 100 days and $510 to complete the process. In 2003, researchers discovered that Gamarra's formalization costs had fallen to 61 days and $163 (Jaramillo 2004).
- Later, a separate study of a pilot program in a Lima district found that the intervention lowered the cost from 40 to 16 days and from $212 to $124 (Mullainathan and Schnabl 2010). While the specific time needed and costs incurred differed depending upon the specific methodology used and district examined in Lima, the tendency of falling costs was clear.

Property rights In the early 1980s, the ILD estimated that it cost individuals $2,156 to secure a land title. Some other salient features are as follows:

- By the early 2000s, costs fell to less than $100, with over 1.3 million plots of land issued titles (Cantuarias and Delgado 2004). Roughly seven million people in Peru were purported to have benefited from the titling program, bringing over $4 billion in unrecognized assets into the formal economic system.
- According to the World Bank's Doing Business Report, between 2005 and 2012 titling costs further fell from five procedures, 33 days, and 3 percent cost of property value to four procedures and seven days, with the 3 percent cost remaining.

- In 2014, Peru ranked 26th globally in titling ease. Yet the individual impact of titling was less clear. Although individual investments in properties did rise by two-thirds and it freed up labor for more productive activities since it was hypothesized that less effort was given to protection, there was no evidence that titles increased credit access.
- Furthermore, evidence reveals that plots subsequently lost their formality due to unregistered transactions using the land, e.g., inheritance (Molina 2014).

Contract enforcement The only significant institutional area not addressed in Peru was contract enforcement. In 1992, the ILD presented draft legislation, which created a legal channel for parties to bypass the judicial system and resolve disputes via arbitration. The proposal led to the inclusion of certain provisions in an arbitration law passed that year and later in a 1996 property rights law to help resolve ownership conflicts. However, arbitration did not emerge as a viable option for the resolution of commercial disputes between small-scale entrepreneurs. Meanwhile, contract enforcement remained as costly in the 2000s as in the 1980s. In 2014, the World Bank's Doing Business Report estimated that it took 426 days to recover 36 percent of the claim. And even if courts do rule in one's favor, entrepreneurs still have difficulty enforcing the court's judgment.

Reform results were seen clearly in the country's global ranking in the Doing Business Report. It ranked 34th globally in 2014 for ease of doing business and was 10th in credit access, 26th in property registration, and 84th in business registration. However, its worst performing institutional indicator was contract enforcement, ranking 100th. Peru unbundled its institutional reforms, enabling a unique opportunity for understanding the role of contract enforcement.

The consequence was the creation of an unintended, pernicious SME-multiplier effect, which weakened the limited informal enforcement mechanisms already in place, which, in turn, prevented firms from specializing in order to capture gains from trade (Bird 2013). This process was seen most vividly in Gamarra, Latin America's largest garment cluster, which at one point employed 100,000 people working in 20,000 firms earning $1 billion in annual revenues.

When interviewed in 2006, owners did not identify property rights, business formalization, or credit access as major operational and growth barriers (Bird 2007). They had less of a fear of detection, though many worried about the state tax agency, and they had greater access to financing, though some complained of high interest rates. Instead, they spoke most about fierce competition, shrinking profit margins, underutilized capacity, and the lack of trust. What happened?

Reforms lowered entry barriers to such a point that they incentivized firm creation. A rising number of firms increased anonymity in the market, which in turn weakened existing informal contract enforcement mechanisms and hindered firms from specializing in order to capture gains from trade. Gamarra's firms were forced to "rationally" stay small because they were squeezed. On the one hand, they were pushed to integrate activities within the firm, yet ran up against internal agency costs. Employees were willing to steal designs, know-how, and clients to start a firm. On the other hand, the owners returned to the market to sub-contract but faced shirking. In the end, they opted to stay small and do the work themselves—and productivity suffered since they could not achieve gains from specialization (see Figure 10.1).

A representative cluster-wide survey, performed in 2012, quantifies the costs of contract enforcement for Gamarra's firms. Roughly 40 of the 70 questions focused on trust between

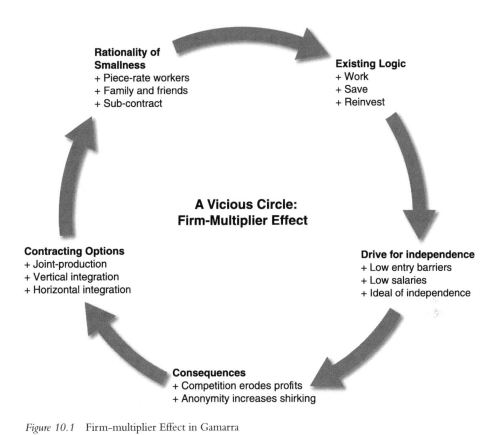

Figure 10.1   Firm-multiplier Effect in Gamarra

Source: Author's elaboration.

the firms and their internal and external counterparts, as well as attitudes and valued attributes of commercial relations.

Regression results suggest that the biggest predictors of firm size, as measured by the number of employees, were those related to contract enforcement (see Table 10.1). While access to human capital and formal property titles made a statistically significant contribution to the number of employees, business formalization and access to financial credit did not. Meanwhile, the impact of human capital and property titles was smaller compared to the combined returns from using contract enforcement mechanisms with customers, having trust in suppliers, and valuing certain attributes in partners. While a more sophisticated model of these relationships is possible, this simple regression highlights a basic finding: Firms that find a way informally to solve their contract enforcement challenges are bigger. They specialize more, increase productivity, and capture more gains from trade.

In sum, Peru improved its regulatory environment considerably following the 1980s. Within the context of macroeconomic reform in the 1990s, the self-employed formalized their business activities, which in turn contributed to growing internal demand, which micro- and small-sized businesses helped to fill. However, with macroeconomic stability, free-trade agreements, and a favorable international environment came foreign investment and competition from larger efficiency-driven firms and, in some cases, the arrival of lower-priced imported goods. The latter hurt Gamarra's garment manufacturers. One source

Table 10.1 Factors Explaining the Number of Employees in Gamarra Firms (n=483): Regression Coefficients and Interpretation

Firm Aspects	Variables	β	Interpretation
Customers	Offers Customers Credit	0.615★ (0.357)	Firms that offer credit to clients have 0.61 more employees
	Uses Written Contracts	0.648★★ (0.292)	Firms which use written contracts have 0.65 more employees
	Request Partial Payment	0.560★★ (0.227)	Firms which request partial upfront payment have 0.56 more employees
Suppliers	Number of Suppliers	0.222★★★ (0.051)	For every one–unit increase in suppliers, firms have 0.22 more employees
	Trust in Suppliers	0.242★★ (0.120)	For every one–unit increase in trust, firms have 0.24 more employees
	Sub–contracts Regularly	1.073★★★ (0.376)	Firms which sub–contract regularly have 1.07 more employees
Attitudes	Importance of Integrity	0.413★★★ (0.130)	Firms with a one–unit increase in the importance of integrity have 0.41 more employees
	Importance of Shared Identity	−0.146 (0.091)	Firms with a one–unit increase in the importance of shared identity have 0.15 *fewer* employees
	Difficulty with Stolen Designs	0.211★ (0.109)	Firms with a one–unit increase in the perceived difficulty with stolen designs have 0.21 more employees
	Difficulty with Contract Fulfillment	−0.398★★★ (0.129)	Firms with a one–unit increase in the perceived difficulty with contract fulfillment have 0.40 *fewer* employees
Firm Characteristics	Degree of Specialization	0.714★★★ (0.221)	Firms with a one–unit increase in the degree of specialization have 0.71 more employees
	Age of Business	0.044★★ (0.020)	Firms with one additional year of existence have 0.044 more employees, i.e., five years is equivalent to 0.22 more employees
Formalization	Number of Property Titles	0.990★★★ (0.340)	Firms with a one–unit increase in property titles have 0.99 more employees
	Formal Business Registration	−0.185 (0.281)	Whether a firm has a formal business license is not significant
Financing	Current Use of Financial Credit	−0.399 (0.310)	Whether a firm currently accesses formal credit is not significant
Human Capital	Educational Level	0.181★★★ (0.066)	Firms with a one–unit increase in educational attainment have 0.18 more employees
	Received Training in Past Year	1.106★★ (0.545)	Firms that received training in the past year have 1.11 more employees
Controls	Age	−0.026★★★ (0.009)	Firms owners with a one–unit increase in age have 0.026 *fewer* employees, i.e., five years of age difference equals 0.13 *fewer* employees

Firm Aspects	Variables	β	Interpretation
	Gender	0.477** (0.206)	Male owners have 0.48 more employees than female owners
	Lima Native vs. Migrant	−0.0757 (0.284)	Whether a firm owner is a migrant to Lima is not significant
	Constant	−1.019 (0.833)	–

Note: R^2=0.33 (p<.05), *** Significant at 1%, ** significant at 5%, * significant at 10%.

estimated that nearly half of the workshops may have closed between 2013 and 2015 due to textile dumping from China (Ninahuanca 2015).

Could Gamarra's firms have defended themselves better if they could have solved the contract enforcement issue? Would it have helped them to specialize, improve productivity, and increase competitiveness? To what extent were the impact of business registration and property rights reforms diluted due to the lack of contract enforcement? Would access to financial credit have a greater impact if contract enforcement issues were solved? It is unlikely that we will ever know definitively for the Peruvian case, but the lesson remains: Ignore contract enforcement at one's own peril, especially when articulating a middle-income entrepreneurship policy.

Becoming a middle-income country: the Peruvian case

From 2001 to 2013, Peru embarked on the longest sustained period of growth since independence. Between 2002 and 2012, annual expansion averaged 6.3 percent per year. The adjusted per capita income had risen from $1,890 in 2001 to $6,410 in 2014 (World Bank 2015). The poverty rate fell from 55 percent of the population in 2001 to 24 percent in 2013. But in 2011, mineral prices began to fall, negatively impacting growth. By 2014, growth slowed to 2.8 percent. Prudent fiscal management created a buffer against the deceleration, but the country reached a crossroads.

Peru was one of the globe's largest minerals producers, with annual production worth $27 billion in 2012, accounting for nearly 15 percent of the GDP (Pricewaterhouse Coopers 2013). Between 2013 and 2015, roughly half of all the country's private investment was in mining. However, social unrest also emerged in surrounding communities given environmental concerns and the fact that the mines operated at high altitudes near many of the country's poorest communities.

Peru remained among the globe's most entrepreneurial countries, according to the Global Entrepreneurship Monitor, but the entrepreneurial profile was slowly shifting, with a gradual fall in necessity entrepreneurship and slight rise in opportunity entrepreneurship as per capita income rose (GEM 2014) considerably as predicted (Wennekers et al. 2005, 2010). The country also developed new efficiency-driven entrepreneurial dynamism (see Box 10.1 for vignettes).

However, Peru's economy was still driven by mining and agricultural exports. Its comparative wages, as an upper-middle-income country, did not make it competitive as a source of mass manufacturing, and its internal market, with a population of only 30 million citizens, was not large enough to support manufacturing for domestic markets. Finally, it lacked an

---

Box 10.1   The emergence of new efficiency-driven entrepreneurs in Peru

Peru's economic expansion created opportunities for efficiency entrepreneurs of at least three types: Formalization, organic, and business groups.

The first was represented by TopiTop, founded by Alquilino Flores, a poor Andean migrant who eventually grew his company into the one of the country's largest garment producers, exporting 70 percent of production, while managing a chain of retail stores in three countries (Moffett 2011). In a sense, more firms were supposed to follow Flores's path in the wake of institutional reforms, as de Soto would predict.

The second type is that of Gastón Acurio, a middle-class chef who returned to Peru in the early 1990s, and borrowed money from friends and family members to open a small restaurant. Two decades later, he had led a culinary revolution. Not only did his firm, Acurio Restaurantes, manage scores of establishments in North America, South America, and Europe, but he also created a culinary movement. The vision is to export Peruvian food and its ingredients, which only grow in the country, to the rest of the world. This included a concerted marketing campaign with the government to rebrand the country. In Acurio's wake, other culinary entrepreneurs followed, making Peru home to several of the top 50 restaurants in the world, according to the esteemed San Pellegrino list. With international demand for Peruvian cuisine, agricultural and human capital linkage effects followed.

The third example is that of Intercorp Group. Founded in 1994 with the purchase of a fledgling state bank, its CEO, Carlos Rodriguez Pastor, exemplified the importance of corporate entrepreneurship in a developing economy (Robinson 2011). As Peru's economy expanded, the group's corporate strategy focused on serving the needs of the country's emerging middle class via financial, retail, education, and health services. In executing the strategy, it took risks before competitors, especially new foreign entrants, and scaled, for example, multiple chains of retail stores—malls, pharmacies, department stores, home centers, fast food restaurants—in regions where modern retail had never existed. In some cases, it purchased start-ups, such as a nascent system of private schools, and helped to scale them.

Yet Intercorp's education initiative highlights larger challenges. Despite a marked transition toward new species of efficiency-driven entrepreneurship—in the garment, retail, and even culinary space, though the latter had elements of Schumpeterian innovation—the economy remained resource-dependent.

---

existing human capital and high technology base from which it could transition into higher value-added production. It consistently ranked among the lowest on the OECD's international PISA basic educational performance test, the percentage of GDP dedicated to Research and Development (R&D) was among the lowest in Latin America (PRODUCE 2014), and the percentage of high technology exports (as a proportion of manufacturing exports) was only 4 percent in 2013 (World Bank 2015).

As Peru's Minister of Production recognized (PRODUCE 2014), the country does not have the option of following the path of Korea, Taiwan, or, later, China. In the wake of falling mineral prices, it was caught in the middle-income trap—and as it did during the crises in the 1980s and 1990s, it looked to the country's entrepreneurial spirit to escape it.

Policy response: a national plan for diversified production

In 2014, the Ministry of Production and its new minister—Piero Ghezzi, a senior economist and former head of emerging markets analysis at Deustche Bank and Barclays Capital—articulated a National Plan for Diversified Production. The policy framework rested on three axes, each of which relied on entrepreneurial action—i.e., on a critical mass of individuals leading existing or new organizations to assume risk and develop new efficiency- or innovation-driven solutions to expand or create new productive capacities. In parallel, other ministries sought to provide enabling conditions via education reform, inclusive social policies, and infrastructure investment.

The *first axis* sought to promote more diverse production for export, targeting existing or new firms who already do or would like to reach external markets. It included the creation of mechanisms through which the public and private sector would select sectorial foci, an institute dedicated to raising quality standards, entrepreneurship and innovation promotion via competitive funds, and regulatory reforms enabling private angel investment. The *second axis* tackled regulatory issues with the goal of lowering costs and improving competitiveness. Areas of focus included improving labor, health, and environmental regulation, as well as reduction of tax compliance barriers and offering transparent government information. The *third axis* targeted all industry sectors and sought to improve productivity through technology transfer. This would involve the creation of sector-specific "Technological Innovation Centers" (CITE, in Spanish acronym) throughout the country, dedicated to technology transfer. It would also include the building of industrial parks.

By mid-2015, four sector areas were identified and had set up private–public or public–public partnerships: forestry, aquaculture, creative industry, and textiles. A new tax law was passed incentivizing corporations for R&D. For R&D dollars spent by the corporations, they could get deductions for every $1.75 spent (from the earlier $1.50). Twelve CITEs had been created with a total of 47 scheduled to be in operation by 2016. Focus areas included aquaculture, biotechnology, forestry, agroindustry, leather, logistics, shoes, energy, food processing, and textiles and garment manufacturing among others. The Peruvian CITE model is arguably the first such technology transfer intervention of its kind. Plans for one national and six regional industrial parks were developed and in the implementation phase. The National Quality Institute was created. A new factoring financing law was passed for micro-, small-, and medium-sized enterprises. And finally, "Innóvate Peru"—the national innovation program—managed roughly $225 million in innovation funds to be dispersed through such channels as Start-Up Peru, an annual competitive venture-funding contest.

In other words, Peru was betting on its entrepreneurs by creating the best possible conditions to move into higher value-added production, whether via efficiency-driven entrepreneurship, seeking to exploit untapped assets and opportunities or innovation-driven entrepreneurship in more knowledge-intensive sectors that built off of natural strengths such as Peru's unique biological diversity. In many respects, the Ministry called into question the logic of a phased transition from efficiency- to innovation-driven entrepreneurship, seeking to exploit them both. On one axis, the policy sought to improve productivity, while on another it aimed to diversify production through more profound value-added innovations, enabled by knowledge spillovers and capital financing mechanisms.

The specter of contract enforcement

However, as with the country's previous institutional reforms targeting informality, the plan did not contemplate arguably the greatest barrier to firm growth—contract enforcement

(Greif 2005, Acemoglu and Johnson 2005).[3] A previous analysis of the Global Entrepreneurship Monitor, comparing opportunity entrepreneurs with necessity entrepreneurs, discovered that weak contract enforcement institutions hurt opportunity entrepreneurs more than necessity entrepreneurs (Ardagna and Lusardi 2010). Evidence also suggests a strong relationship between contract enforcement and firm size in other middle-income countries such as Brazil (Ponticelli 2014), India (Bloom et al. 2009), and Vietnam (McMillan and Woodruff 1999). The Gamarra case offers additional evidence (Bird 2013).

A firm is not just a production function—inputs in, products out—but a nexus of internal and external contracts. Owners must manage employees. They also must conduct transactions with suppliers, customers, sub-contractors, banks, and other service providers. If firms fail to find contract enforcement solutions, then specialization is greatly hindered. One must either exert time and resources to enforce a transaction, thus diverting resources for production, or one has to forego the market mechanism and incorporate the transaction within the firm where one has greater control (Williamson 1985), a strategy commonly exercised by business groups (Kali 1999, Khanna and Yafeh 2005), including those in Peru (Vazquez 2000). Yet without specialization one sacrifices productivity and gains from trade. "One cannot take enforcement for granted," Douglas North wrote. "It is (and always has been) the critical obstacle to increasing specialization and division of labor" (1990: 33)—and thus capturing returns from trade.

From all of Peru's Doing Business Indicators, it performs the worst on contract enforcement. However, at small scale it is not feasible without a public or private third-party mechanism which provides information about a party's reputations and behaviors and a credible cost or threat of punishment in case of breach (Dixit 2009). The issue is already crippling for Peru's still vast self-employed sector, despite notable institutional improvements in other areas. Evidently, the barrier will not disappear with implementation of the National Diversified Production Plan. Individuals and organizations must collaborate, share technology, innovate, and build value chains. They must fulfill their formal and informal contractual commitments many times over. At a small scale, solving contract enforcement issues may be possible, as some firms will develop alternative bi-lateral and even multi-lateral solutions. However it is not feasible without an efficient, scalable public or private third-party mechanism that provides information about a party's reputations and behaviors and a credible cost or threat of punishment in case of breach (Dixit 2009). Without this contract enforcement mechanism, commercial relationships will splinter and Peru's middle-income entrepreneurship policy experiment—the bet that its entrepreneurs can make an efficiency- and innovation-driven leap in the twenty-first-century economy—may struggle to fulfill its promise.

The middle-income policy challenge in Peru—and beyond

Peru's national production diversification plan is an experiment in middle-income entrepreneurship policy, as there are few examples of countries successfully escaping the middle-income trap. If the plan is consistently executed—a challenge given the risk of discontinuity with the impending democratic transition of power in 2016—success could be in the offing. The CITE framework is the first of its kind, globally, and is designed to encourage the "cost discovery" process critical for entrepreneurs to bear risk and explore the viability of specializing in new production options (Haussman et al. 2007). In other words, this is a massive portfolio approach in which losers are expected in the hope of identifying a handful of winners. The country possesses natural comparative advantages relating to its ecological and biological diversity – as it is home to over 90 percent of the world's microclimates. Yet unless the country solves its deep-rooted institutional challenges—chiefly weak contract enforcement—the middle-income entrepreneurship policy may struggle to gain traction.

Regardless of the policy's fate, Peru, at least in the near future, will continue to occupy a critical place in the study of entrepreneurship policy in developing countries, as it has historically. Successful or not, the policy experiment could teach the globe lessons about what to do—or not do—to escape the middle-income trap.

Notes

1 Technically, Peru was considered to have fallen in the lower-middle income category as early as the 1950s (Felipe et al. 2012). However, its policies were decidedly "low-income" in that they came to target the self-employed, largely own-account, informal sector.
2 It is also possible for a country to simultaneously exploit both types of scale economies, as in the case of Brazil.
3 One could also add the issue of the lack of a strong intellectual property rights regime in Peru.

References

Acemoglu, D. and S. Johnson. 2005. Unbundling Institutions. *Journal of Political Economy*, 113(5): 949–995.

Acs, Z.J. 2006. How is Entrepreneurship Good for Economic Growth? *Innovations: Technology, Governance, Globalization*, 1(1): 97–107.

———. 2010. Entrepreneurship and Economic Development: The Valley of Backwardness. *Annals of Innovation & Entrepreneurship*, 1(1): 1–18.

Acs, Zoltan J., Sameeksha Desai, and Leora F. Klapper. 2008. What Does "Entrepreneurship" Data Really Show? *Small Business Economics*, 31(3): 265–281.

Aghion, P. and P. Howitt. 1997. *Endogenous Growth Theory*. Cambridge, MA: MIT Press.

Aiyar, Shekhar, Romain Duval, Damien Puy, Yiqun Wu, and Longmei Zhang, 2013. Growth Slowdowns and the Middle-Income Trap. IMF Working Paper 71, Washington, DC.

Ardagna, S. and A. Lusardi. 2010. Heterogeneity in the Effect of Regulation on Entrepreneurship and Entry Size. *Journal of the European Economic Association*, 8(2–3): 594–605.

Audretsch, D.B. and A.R. Thurik. 2001. What is New about the New Economy: Sources of Growth in the Managed and Entrepreneurial Economies. *Industrial and Corporate Change*, 10(1), 267–315.

Audretsch, D.B., W. Bönte, and M. Keilbach. 2008. Entrepreneurship Capital and Its Impact on Knowledge Diffusion and Economic Performance. *Journal of Business Venturing*, 23(6): 687–698.

Audretsch, D.B. and M. Keilbach. 2007. The Theory of Knowledge Spillover Entrepreneurship. *Journal of Management Studies*, 44(7): 1242–1254.

Baumol. W. 2010. *The Microtheory of Innnovative Entrepreneurship*. Princeton, NJ: Princeton University Press.

Bird, Matthew. 2007. Traveling Down the Other Path: Learning to See Extra-legality as an Investment Opportunity, in Michael Klein, ed., *Business and Development: The Private Path to Prosperity* (Washington, D.C.: International Finance Corporation/Financial Times): 16–25.

———. 2010. Critique of Reciprocity: Shifting uses of *Ayni* among Andean groups, in Robert Marshall, ed., *Cooperation in Social and Economic Life* (Society for Economic Anthropology Monograph Series) (Lanham, MD: AltaMira Press): 55–79.

———. 2013. Unbundling Institutional Reform: The Case of a Garment Cluster in Lima, Peru, in Mai Thi Thanh Thai and Ekaterina Turkina, eds., *Entrepreneurship in the Informal Economy: Models, Approaches and Prospects for Economic Development* (New York: Routledge Press): 145–160.

Bloom, N., B. Eifert, T. Heller, E. Jenson, and A. Mahajan. 2009. Contract Enforcement and Firm Organization: Evidence from the Indian Textile Industry, CDDRL Working Papers, 104.

Cantuarias, F. and M. Delgado. 2004. Peru's Urban Land Titling Program. World Bank, mimeo.

Carree, M.A., A.J. van Stel, A.R. Thurik, and A.R.M. Wennekers 2002. Economic Development and Business Ownership: An Analysis Using Data of 23 OECD Countries in the Period 1976–1996. *Small Business Economics*, 19(3), 271–290.

————. 2007. The Relationship between Economic Development and Business Ownership Revisited. *Entrepreneurship and Regional Development*, 19(3): 281–291.

Collier, David. 1976. *Squatters and Oligarchs: Authoritarian Rule and Policy Change in Peru*. Baltimore, MD: Johns Hopkins University Press.

De Soto, H. 1986. *El otro sendero: la revolución informal*. Lima: Editorial El Barranco.

————. 2001.The mystery of capital. *Finance & Development*, March, 38(1), available at http://www. imf.org/external/pubs/ft/fandd/2001/03/desoto.htm.

Dixit, A. 2009. Governance Institutions and Economic Activity. *American Economic Review*, 99(1): 5–24.

Djankov, S., R. La Porta, F. Lopez-Salinas, and A. Scheifer. 2002. Regulation of Entry. *Quarterly Journal of Economics*, 117(1): 1–37.

Economist Intelligence Unit. 2015. *Global Microscope: The Enabling Environment for Financial Inclusion*. London: EIU.

Felipe, Jesus, Arnelyn Abdon, and Utsav Kumar (2012) Tracking the Middle-income Trap: What is it, Who is in it, and Why? Working Paper 715, Levy Economics Institute of Bard College, Asian Development Bank.

GEM (Global Entrepreneurship Research Association). 2014. *Global Entrepreneurship Monitor 2014 Global Report*. London: London Business School.

Gill, I. and H. Kharas. 2007. *An East Asia Renaissance: Ideas for Economic Growth*. Washington, DC: World Bank.

Greif, Avner. 2005. Commitment, Coercion, and Markets: The Nature and Dynamics of Institutions Supporting Exchange, in Claude Menard and Mary M. Shirley, eds., *The Handbook for New Institutional Economics* (Norwell, MA.: Kluwer Academic), 727–786.

Hanke, Steve and Nicholas Krus. 2013. World Hyperinflations, in Randall Parker and Robert Whaples, eds., *Handbook of Major Events in Economic History*. London: Routledge, 367–377.

Hart, Keith J. 1970. Small-Scale Entrepreneurs in Ghana and Development Planning. *Journal of Development Studies*, 6(4): 104–120.

Haussmann, Ricardo, Jaons Hwang, and Dani Rodrik. 2007. What You Export Matters. *Journal of Economic Growth*, 12(1): 1–25.

Hebert, R.F. and A.N. Link. 1989. *The Entrepreneur: Mainstream Views and Radical Critiques* (2nd ed.). New York: Praeger.

International Fund for Agricultural Development. 2002. Experiencias innovadoras en los proyectos del FIDA en la República del Perú, accessed at http://www.ifad.org/evaluation/public_html/eksyst/ doc/thematic/pl/peru_s.pdf on September 2, 2015.

International Labour Organization. 1970. *Towards Full Employment: A Programme for Colombia*. Geneva: ILO.

————. 1972. *Employment, Income and Equality: A Strategy for Increasing Productive Employment in Kenya*. Geneva: ILO.

Jaramillo, Miguel. 2004. Starting a Garment Manufacturing Firm in Peru: Background and Case Study. Research Report 1. Ronald Coase Institute, St. Louis, MO.

Kali, R. 1999. Endogenous Business Networks. *Journal of Law, Economics and Organization*, 15(3): 615–636.

Khanna, T. and Y. Yafeh. 2005. Business Groups in Emerging Markets: Paragons or Parasites? European Corporate Governance Institute, Working Paper 92.

Kirzner, I.M. 1973. *Competition and Entrepreneurship*. Chicago: University of Chicago Press.

Klarén, Peter. 1973. *Modernization, Dislocation, and Aprismo: Origins of the Peruvian Aprista Party, 1870–1932*. Austin: University of Texas Press.

Knight, F.H. 1921. *Risk, Uncertainty and Profit*. Washington, DC: Beard Books.

La Porta, Rafael and Andrei Shleifer. 2014. Informality and Development. NBER Working Paper 20205.

Matos Mar, José. 1977. *Las barriadas de Lima*. Lima: Instituto de Estudios Peruanos.

————. 1985. *Desborde Popular y Crisis del Estado*. Lima: IEP.

Mayer, Enrique. 2002. *The Articulated Peasant*. Boulder, CO: Westview Press.

McMillan, J. and C. Woodruff. 1999. Interfirm Relationships and Informal Credit in Vietnam. *Quarterly Journal of Economics*, 114(4): 1285–1320.

McMillan, J. and P. Zoido. 2004. How to Subvert Democracy: Montesinos in Peru. *Journal of Economic Perspectives*, 18(4): 69–92.

McMullen, J.S. and D.A. Shepherd. 2006. Entrepreneurial Action and the Role of Uncertainty in the Theory of the Entrepreneur. *Academy of Management Review*, 31(1), 132–152.

Ministry of Production of Peru (PRODUCE). 2014. Plan Nacional de Diversificación Productiva. Peruvian Ministry of Production.

Moffett, M. 2011. A Rags-to-Riches Career Highlights Latin Resurgence. November 15, *The Wall Street Journal*. Accessed at http://www.wsj.com/articles/SB10001424052970204422404576595211 776435404

Molina, Oswaldo. 2014. Loss of Plot Formality through Unregistered Transactions: Evidence from a Natural Experiment in Peru. Lincoln Institute of Land Policy Working Paper, WP14OM1.

Mullainathan, S. and P. Schnabl. 2010. Does less market entry regulation generate more entrepreneurs? Evidence from a regulatory reform in Peru, in J. Lerner and A. Schoar, eds., *International differences in entrepreneurship, National Bureau of Economic Research Conference Report*. Chicago, IL: University of Chicago Press, 159–177.

Murra, John. 2002. *El mundo andino: población, medio ambiente, y economía*. Lima: Instituto de Estudios Peruanos.

Ninahuanca, Christian. 2015. Gamarra en crisis, *La República*, July 5, 2015. Accessed at http://larepublica.pe/impresa/economia/12932-gamarra-en-crisis on September 2, 2015.

North, Douglas. 1990. *Institutions, Institutional Change, and Economic Performance*. Cambridge: Cambridge University Press.

Panaritis, E. (1999). *Peru – Urban Property Rights Program*. Washington, DC: World Bank.

Ponticelli, Jacopo. 2014. Court Enforcement and Firm Productivity: Evidence from a Bankruptcy Reform in Brazil. Mimeo.

Porter, M., J. Sachs, and J. McArthur. 2002. Executive Summary: Competitiveness and Stages of Economic Development, in M. Porter, J. Sachs, P. K. Cornelius, J. McArthur, and K. Schwab, eds., *The Global Competitiveness Report 2001–2002*. New York: Oxford University Press: 16–25.

PricewaterhouseCoopers. 2013. Mining Industry: Doing Business in Peru. PWC Report. Acccessed at http://www.pwc.de/de/internationale-maerkte/assets/doing-business-in-mining-peru.pdf on Septermber 2, 2015.

Riordan, J. 2011. *We Do Know How: A Buyer-led Approach to Creating Jobs for the Poor*. Washington, DC: New Academia Publishing.

Robinson, Edward. 2011. Publicity Shy Tycoon Forging Modern Peru Amid Expanding Economy. Accessed at http://www.bloomberg.com/news/articles/2011-08-03/publicity-shy-tycoon-forging-modern-peru-amid-expanding-economy on September 2, 2015.

Romer, P. 1990. Endogenous Technological Change. *Journal of Political Economy*, 98(5): S71–S102.

Sachs, J. and A. Warner. 2001. The Curse of Natural Resources. *European Economic Review*, 45(4-6): 827–838.

Sali-i-Martin, X. 2007. *The Global Competitiveness Report 2007–2008*. London: World Economic Forum, Palgrave/Macmillan.

Schoar, A. 2010. The Divide between Transformation and Subsistence Entrepreneurs, in J. Lerner and S. Stern, eds., *Innovation Policy and the Economy*. Chicago: University of Chicago Press, 57–81.

Schumpeter, J. A. 1934. *The Theory of Economic Development*. New Brunswick, NJ: Transaction.

Stenholm, Pekka, Zoltan J. Acs, and Robert Wuebker. 2013. Exploring Country-level Institutional Arrangements on the Rate and Type of Entrepreneurial Activity. *Journal of Business Venturing*, 28(1): 176–193.

Thorp, Rosemary and Geoffrey Bertram. 1978. *Peru, 1890–1977: Growth and Policy in an Open Economy*. New York: Columbia University Press.

Tokman, V. 2007. Modernizing the Informal Sector. UN/DESA Working Paper no. 42. United Nations, Department of Economic and Social Affairs.

Vazquez, Enrique. 2000. *Estrategias de Poder: Grupos económicos en el Perú*. Lima: Centro de Investigación, La Universidad del Pacifico.

Vera, M. and Y. Ching Wong. 2013. Peru: Latin America's Economic Performer, IMF Survey Magazine. Accessed at http://www.imf.org/external/pubs/ft/survey/so/2013/car022213d.htm on September 2, 2015.

Wennekers, S., A. van Stel, M. Carree, and R. Thurik. 2010. The Relationship between Entrepreneurship and Economic Development: Is it U-shaped? *Foundations and Trends in Entrepreneurship*, 6(3): 167–237.

Wennekers, S., A. van Stel, R. Thurik, and P. Reynolds. 2005. Nascent Entrepreneurship and the Level of Economic Development. *Small Business Economics*, 24(3): 293–309.

Williams, C. and Y. Youssef. 2011. Is Informal Sector Entrepreneurship Necessity- or Opportunity-driven? Some Lessons from Brazil. *Business and Management Research*, 3(1), 41–53.

Williamson, Oliver. 1985. *Economic Institutions of Capitalism*. New York: Free Press.

World Bank. 2015. Doing Business 2015. Going Beyond Efficiency. Comparing Business regulations for domestic firms in 189 economies. A World Bank Group Flagship Report. Washington, DC: World Bank.

11

DEVELOPING AN ENTREPRENEURSHIP CLIMATE IN INDONESIA

A case study of batik as a cultural heritage

Vanessa Ratten

Introduction

Indonesia is one of the newly emerging developing countries as it has a large population and potential for both economic and social growth. Despite its developing country status, it has had success with keeping traditional products and services as part of its cultural heritage in the international marketplace. This chapter will examine the role of batik entrepreneurs by focusing on the Solo region located in Central Java as an area promoting cultural-based entrepreneurship that links social and sustainability initiatives. The role of artisans in making the batik in combination with the business development of the batik industry on a global scale will be discussed in the chapter. In addition, the chapter will examine the attachment of the Javanese people to making batik in combination with the retaining of traditional weaving and batik techniques, which are passed on to future generations. Implications for developing country entrepreneurs interested in harnessing their cultural heritage as a way to grow businesses will be discussed in addition to theoretical implications for researchers interested in cultural entrepreneurship in developing countries.

Entrepreneurship is considered as opportunity–driven behavior that incorporates innovation with economic growth and development. Entrepreneurship is needed in developing countries to increase innovation and improve living conditions and a way to increase business opportunities is to focus on cultural aspects of developing countries (Williams and Lansky, 2013). In developing countries, economic development is typically characterized in terms of technological innovation that absorbs traditional sectors. However, some traditional sectors including rural, agricultural, and artisans can grow in an economy despite the increases in technology (Dahles and Prabawa, 2013). This means that modern economies still have traditional forms of economic production that include cultural heritage. The batik industry is one of the main cultural and economic growth areas for the Indonesian government because of its entrepreneurial ability to link culture, heritage, and business.

Enterprising individuals in developing countries can move out of poverty but are still constrained by environmental complexities that affect their ability to start new businesses (Wood et al., 2014). Some of these constraints involve behavioral conditions including

131

positive cognitive traits that can be encouraged by focusing on optimism instead of pessimism about adverse circumstances. Optimism is important for entrepreneurs in developing countries that have a limited belief about their own capabilities (Chakrabarty, 2009). This can include knowledge about future possibilities that affect the entrepreneur's beliefs systems (Wood et al., 2014).

The shape of entrepreneurship in developing countries is influenced by the informal institutional structure governing business activities (Manolova et al., 2008). Actions of entrepreneurs are constrained by cultural forces that influence business development (North, 1990). These cultural forces can be enabled by opportunities presenting themselves about the local market conditions (Bruton et al., 2008). Entrepreneurs from developing countries are embedded in markets affected by institutional structures that influence business activities but also shape their behavior. In developing countries, entrepreneurs sometimes use substitutes for the weaker institutional structure and financial capital market. This is due to entrepreneurs working within the existing structure to facilitate business development (Williams et al., 2015a).

Entrepreneurship includes the evaluation, exploitation, and identification of business opportunities which are made possible by creating, starting, or maintaining a business venture (Gupta et al., 2014). There has been a growing recognition of the importance of entrepreneurship to developing countries that is different from the developed country context. Developing countries have been associated with the lack of institutions needed for the growth of private business. This is due to entrepreneurship being influenced by the social and economic behavior of participants that are directed by beliefs, norms, and expectations existing in a country (Veciana and Urbano, 2009). Most entrepreneurship research has focused on developed countries with little attention paid to whether they translate to developing countries (Peng, 2002). Bruton et al. (2008) propose that developed economies may have different environments to developing countries, which affects business creation. The various histories, social norms, and cultural values embedded in a society means entrepreneurship is different in developing countries (Kiss et al., 2012).

In order to capture the entrepreneurship of the informal sector in a developing country, this chapter will analyze batik entrepreneurs in Indonesia. Tourism is a major industry in Indonesia especially businesses that relate to cultural heritage such as batik clothing. This chapter will discuss the role of batik entrepreneurship by focusing on cultural and subsistence entrepreneurship in the developing country context. This chapter is therefore structured as follows. In the next section the role of entrepreneurship in developing countries is discussed in order to lay the foundations for the role of cultural entrepreneurship. Next the social elements of entrepreneurship are examined in terms of how they are important in the transition process of developing countries. Next batik entrepreneurship is discussed in Indonesia as it is a developing country context. Following this, the findings for cultural and heritage entrepreneurs are discussed. The conclusion states the implications for social entrepreneurs and suggestions for future research in developing countries.

Developing countries and entrepreneurship

Developing countries are increasingly depending on entrepreneurship to transform society and increase living standards. A society's acceptance of entrepreneurship is associated with its intention to create new ventures (Cardon et al., 2011). Entrepreneurship is defined in different ways according to the type of activity (Spencer and Gomez, 2004). Developing countries are similar to developed countries in terms of their emphasis on entrepreneurship;

however, they lack understanding of the entrepreneurial process (Bruton et al., 2008). This means that entrepreneurship may be characterized in a different way in a developing country (Peng, 2002).

Developing countries are those with less economic development than developed economies (Bruton et al., 2008). Underdeveloped countries have different economic conditions which affect entrepreneurial behavior. In addition, the difference between developed and developing countries declines as globalization spreads improved information technology innovations. This means that the large variation in living conditions between developed and developing countries is the result of the economic and institutional environment (Bruton et al., 2008).

More firms from developing countries are going international because of the market potential. In the developing world context entrepreneurs are considered successful when they explore a new market, particularly in the international environment. In some developing countries, there has existed a monopoly which has favored particular entrepreneurs especially in low technology industries. Often developing countries have obsolete methods of economic participation, which might be a result of the cultural heritage of a country. This is partly due to developing countries being known for their often unpredictable and volatile institutional environment (Ahlstrom and Bruton, 2006). This means that there are uncodified or unregulated laws which change depending on political power in developing countries. There can be uncertain property rights which make it difficult to understand the legal environment in a developing country (Bruton and Ahlstrom, 2003). This uncertainty for firms domiciled in a developing country environment makes it unpredictable for enterprises. In addition, as the market for goods and services in a developing country is still changing it makes it risky for entrepreneurs (Ahlstrom and Bruton, 2006).

Network connections play a greater role in developing countries due to the challenging environment (Ahlstrom and Bruton, 2006). This is due to network connections substituting the weak former institutions which are hard to navigate and understand. Sometimes the institutions in developing countries can have less corporate control and legal power to protect business. In addition, network connections offer protection from government interference and bureaucracy. Networks are especially important for entrepreneurship in developing countries due to how they function and process business activities (Bruton et al., 2008).

Market-based solutions to poverty in developing countries are required to foster entrepreneurship. This is because developing economies have different types of business owners, some of whom are entrepreneurs depending on their ability to take risk and create value (Khavul et al., 2009). Entrepreneurship and new venture creation offers a solution to poverty particularly in developing countries. This is due to entrepreneurship encouraging economic growth and reducing poverty by maximizing job creation and capital investment. By focusing both on public sector and private enterprise job creation developing economies can spend efforts on solving problems through government initiatives.

Informal entrepreneurship and developing countries

In developing countries, there has been the emergence of the anti-economy that is located at the margins of legal business conditions (Williams and Horodnic, 2015). Enterprises in developing countries start informal firms for a variety of reasons including class, education, ethnicity, gender, ethnicity, income level, and religion (Babbitt et al., 2015). This anti-economy is part of the informal economy as it represents business activity that is perceived as being no longer useful in creating value for society (Dahles and Prabawa, 2013). In addition, the informal sector contributes a substantial part of the overall economy of developing countries (Dahles and Prabawa, 2013). The unpredictability inherent in developing countries restricts formal institutional governance of market systems by placing more importance on informal institutions (Ahlstrom and Bruton, 2006).

Informal business ventures are seen in developing countries as being survivalist and based on necessity rather than innovation (Williams, 2014). This has led to some informal businesses being considered as not entrepreneurial as they are low tech activities (Dahles and Prabawa, 2013). The informal sector has been adopted by the International Labor Organization in studies of developing countries to understand business opportunities (Williams et al., 2011). The informal economy has also been referred to as the unorganized sector as it includes family and household forms of economic activity and contrasts with the black, clandestine, shadow economy, also referred to as the underground economy, because it is usually unregulated and conducted in an unstructured manner (Williams, 2011). In addition, the informal economy is referred to as the bazaar economy as it often focuses on arts and cultural aspects popular with both locals and tourists (Williams, 2006).

Developing economies see the informal sector in a similar way to developed countries as it includes unlicensed enterprises and undeclared labor. The key characteristics of the informal sector are the unregulated enterprises which can be illegal depending on the type of business conducted (Gërxhani, 2004). The main difference between the informal sector in developing and developed countries is that in developing regions the businesses often evolve from the need to escape poverty conditions (Dahles and Prabawa, 2013). Developed countries can have informal businesses that are not always coming from poverty alleviation but from the flexibility of the businesses in this sector. The main feature of informal sector in developing countries is on creating a livelihood that may not include innovation or growth (Williams, 2004). There is growing recognition in the informal sector about the opportunity-driven motives that are based on choice instead of necessity. There are different kinds of entrepreneurial approaches in the informal economy and as a source of employment and income it is part of a developing countries' growth (Babbitt et al, 2015).

Informal sector entrepreneurship operates outside formal institutional boundaries but within informal institutional frameworks. Societies have formal institutions represented by rules and regulations. Some societies emphasize their informal institutions more because they are created and communicated outside official channels (Williams and Shahid, 2014). The informal institutions include socially shared rules that are seen as being a community together (Webb et al., 2009). The norms and values included within informal institutions are especially evident in a developing country that emphasizes trust and reciprocity in business dealings.

Entrepreneurs in the informal sector in developing countries are illegal in terms of formal institutions but legitimate from society's viewpoint (Webb et al., 2009). This dichotomy between formal and informal institutions in developing countries determines entrepreneurship levels (Williams and Shahid, 2014). The informal sector acts as a test pad for evaluating business opportunities. In developing countries such as Pakistan there are a larger proportion of businesses operating in the informal economy. This is caused by necessity-driven entrepreneurs in developing countries engaging in business as a means of survival (Williams and Shahid, 2014).

Entrepreneurs in developing countries are excluded often involuntarily from formal businesses and by necessity work in the informal sector. Although some research suggests that even in developing countries informal entrepreneurship is a choice depending on personal circumstances. This is due to entrepreneurs in developing countries lacking awareness of the regulations needed to formally register their businesses (Williams and Shahid, 2014).

Subsistence entrepreneurship

Subsistence entrepreneurship is defined as "entrepreneurial efforts that many individuals, non-profits and governments are actually seeking to encourage in centers of extreme poverty which create little value for the person and the society." In developing countries, ventures are entrepreneurial when risk is involved that creates value. Subsistence entrepreneurship offers hope for countries wanting to improve their standards of living and is important in developing countries as it involves new ventures that have little potential but offer monetary compensation to those involved. Subsistence entrepreneurship is entrepreneurship in settings of poverty that significantly improve lives of people operating the business. In developing countries, subsistence entrepreneurs improve standards of living by alleviating poverty conditions. Most subsistence entrepreneurs are small lifestyle businesses with little growth potential (Fischer, 2013).

Subsistence entrepreneurial ventures usually benefit the entrepreneur's family as family members are utilized as labor. This can mean that sometimes subsistence entrepreneurs operate under the cultural and political institutional framework that limit growth but does improve their living standards. Entrepreneurs need to form businesses that go beyond subsistence enterprises that offer minimum wages (Fischer, 2013). This is due to entrepreneurial firms having a bigger societal impact in developing economies when they create innovative products. By gathering both financial and non-financial capital subsistence entrepreneurs can transition to more value-added services that increase living standards.

More subsistence businesses are being launched by entrepreneurs in developing countries as they focus on the achievement of a reasonable standard of living. These subsistence business enterprises drive economic prosperity and help people in developing countries (Wood et al., 2014). Subsistence businesses are usually in local regions but spur economic growth through job creation. Subsistence businesses are linked to economic activities at the base of the pyramid as they provide income for many families in a local community. By offering a standard of living subsistence business entrepreneurs can pull themselves and their peers out of poverty (Wood et al., 2014).

Entrepreneurs in developing and subsistence economies face challenges in getting access to appropriate resources and infrastructure to build their businesses. Often entrepreneurs in developing regions face long delays and complicated forms to obtain business approval. This means that sometimes developing country entrepreneurs have to deal with government suspicion of small business activities (Wood et al., 2014). Generally corruption and bribery in developing countries complicate entrepreneurship. In addition, businesses in developing countries have a reputation for being inefficient operators due to high business expenses. This can lead to competitive pressure for entrepreneurs wanting to do business in developing countries. However, past research by Wood et al. (2014) suggests that entrepreneurs in subsistence economies have a positive attitude to overcoming poverty. The poor in developing countries have been creative in developing solutions for business problems with limited resources. This is due to the experimentation taking place as developing country entrepreneurs use available resources and come up with inventive solutions for business problems. The environmental context of poverty can influence people to take action in hard circumstances.

Necessity entrepreneurship involves the starting of a business as the last resort whilst opportunity entrepreneurship is about exploiting a business opportunity. Research examining subsistence and social entrepreneurship in developing countries is limited. The small business sector is the focus of international and national aid agencies because of its linkage with economic growth rates. Business solutions to poverty require the belief structure of a society to change (George et al., 2015). In developing economies, organizations can design the businesses to connect with opportunities that encourage experimentation with innovative solutions to pressing poverty concerns (Autio and Fu, 2015).

Institutions govern both formal and informal entrepreneurship in developing economies due to the linkage with potential and economic goals (Autio and Fu, 2015). Im and Sun (2015) address the role of microfinance institutions in developing countries to reach social goals that follow a social welfare approach. It can take some time for developing countries to industrialize and change their economic structure, which makes entrepreneurship important in poverty reduction (Si et al., 2015). Poverty alleviation emerges from new venture creation involving different stakeholders in a society (Hart and Christensen, 2002). Sometimes poverty reduction can involve behavioral change from business ventures focused on innovation as a way to change existing societal structures.

Developmental economics as a discipline has focused on the explanations and solutions to poverty. There is a criticism of some developing countries regarding the amount of government spending on business initiatives without solving the poverty problem. Innovation and new venture creation are crucial to the reduction of poverty (Ahlstrom, 2010). The challenge in developing countries is to encourage entrepreneurship as a way to improve living standards (Yu et al., 2014).

Cultural entrepreneurship and batik business in Indonesia

Cultural entrepreneurship is the process of storytelling and is often embedded within societies as part of the historical development of a country (Lounsbury and Glynn, 2001). The cultural component of a society shapes entrepreneurship as it enables cultural capital to be mobilized for enterprise endeavors. Cultural capital is acquired when stories help shape an opportunity for entrepreneurs in the marketplace. An entrepreneurial endeavor to integrate a story into a business venture can increase market potential. In developing countries, the cultural context of goods and services can create opportunities for entrepreneurs. This is especially the case in developing countries in which individuals operate under necessity entrepreneurship conditions and face daily hardships in their quest for survival (Dacin et al., 2010). Storytelling is a way entrepreneurs in developing countries differentiate their products with mass marketed consumer goods. This enables entrepreneurs to preserve and overcome resource and market access challenges in developing countries (Khoury and Prasad, 2015).

Cultural entrepreneurship is important in the developing world as it enables the safeguarding of cultural important places, events, and people with business opportunity. Cultural entrepreneurship enables entrepreneurs to share their background with others interested in the same themes. The cultural perspective is appreciated by individuals who share the same feelings and can be told through a story. Often storytelling is inherent in the marketing of products such as crafts, coffee, and chocolates from developing countries (Khoury and Prasad, 2015). Cultural products enable subsistence entrepreneurs to offer a competitive advantage by focusing on difficult-to-source products. The use of storytelling with developing country entrepreneurship is a means of fostering local enterprises. In this way, farmers, entrepreneurs, and markets in developing countries converge by offering a product to suit a certain cultural aspect of society (Khoury and Prasad, 2015).

By supplying stories with products, entrepreneurs can link the struggle and difficulty of living in a developing world environment. This is valuable when globalization is diminishing the cultural orientation of individuals and there is a desire to reconnect with society.

Some cultural entrepreneurship may be localized to a particular region that has special customs (Khoury and Prasad, 2015). Regional cultures and customs offer new ways entrepreneurs can offer distinct products. People who have an affinity with this culture can purchase the products based on their interest. Entrepreneurs can offer products that are sympathetic to certain stories that encourage like-minded consumers to purchase them (Khoury and Prasad, 2015).

The supportive values people have means the social context in which the entrepreneurship occurs is important (Dacin et al., 2010). This means that cultural entrepreneurship can be used to link stories to the creation and fostering of business opportunities (Khoury and Prasad, 2015). Entrepreneurs in developing countries can use the environmental conditions to leverage cultural traits to business opportunities. In addition, cultural entrepreneurship can be influenced by gender boundaries that entrepreneurs in developing countries face. An entrepreneur's personal or familial affiliation affects the constraints placed on building customer relationships (Chakrabarty, 2009). This social pressure limits an entrepreneur's ability to use social networks to increase market performance.

The transformation of developing countries has given rise to more opportunities for cultural entrepreneurs. A deeper understanding of informal and formal institutional structures in developing countries is required in order to represent a better approach to future entrepreneurs. Understanding the dynamics of culture as a form of entrepreneurship allows researchers to emphasize the role of society in business growth. Given the contemporary focus of developing countries it is important for scholars, practitioners, and policy makers to focus more on understanding how culture entrepreneurship progresses in developing countries, which is the reason for discussing the role of batik entrepreneurship.

Batik entrepreneurship

The word batik is used to describe painted cloth and the industry is a popular and growing sector of the Indonesian economy. Solo has the goal of being the Indonesian batik capital city because of the co-creation of creativity with entrepreneurship in helping business success. Becoming a batik hub has meant that tourism and creative economy combine to give a natural competitive advantage to Solo. The batik industrial cluster at Solo acts as an entrepreneurial system as there are firms, education and financial agencies working together around batik market needs. Batik is considered part of the cultural and artistic heritage of Indonesia and was acknowledged by UNESCO as an intangible world heritage product.

The batik industry has developed as a creative home industry driven by entrepreneurial initiatives. Batik as a cultural product is familiar due to its social value within Indonesian society. The main batik industrial areas in Indonesia, Yogyakarta and Solo, are on the island of Java. In these cities there are communities of batik entrepreneurs who use their craft ability to pursue business opportunities.

The batik industry has developed by diversifying their products to cater for international market needs. One way they have done this to compete globally is by developing specific batik designs based on local environments. This enables the batik to be unique, based on cultural arts endemic to specific areas. Batik entrepreneurs are increasing production by making handicrafts using batik material as the material is created by writing, drawing, or painting on a cloth using wax. The term membatik, which means to create batik, is the process of painting a motif on a piece of material. The whole process of creating batik starts from designing the pattern to waxing and dying the material.

Batik has traditionally been worn by nobility in Indonesia but has increasingly been worn by a diverse section of society as a shawl, long tunic, scarf, and sarong. Ornamental styles are often used on batik and arranged in a pattern. Ornaments, in the form of natural things, including plants, trees, and animals are often used on the batik. The ornamental style of batik can be in the form of stylization, distortion, or decorative. Stylization means transforming the patterns onto the batik whilst keeping the original characteristics of the design. Distortion involves accentuating certain parts of the pattern on the batik. Decorative involves simplifying a pattern to beautify the batik. Batik patterns can involve different motifs based on the designer's perspective. Batik is an important part of preserving the cultural identity of Indonesia. Popular batik designs include the cultural arts and natural environment of the Yogyakarta and Solo area. The cultural sites including the temples of Borobudur, Praubanan, and Sewu are popular batik designs whilst the natural environment of Merapi mountains, Parangtritis beach, and Menoreh hill are popular. New and creative batik designs are based on photos and computer pictures.

The firms in Solo include the traditional market and agencies that make and sell the batik. The educational institutions include Solo State University, which is close to the batik industrial area. The financial agencies include the bank of Central Java, which lends to batik entrepreneurs. The entrepreneurial system for supporting batik businesses is also linked to the local government and Ministry of Tourism and Creative Economy. In nearby Surakarta there is also the small and micro enterprise office that connects the batik Solo industrial cluster.

Indonesia can increase its exports by focusing on cultural heritage products made from batik. As it is hard for a developing country like Indonesia to compete based on price, the creative industry provides a way to increase the sale of batik fabrics. Batik clusters, particularly those in Java, are locally integrated and connected to global marketplaces. Enterprises in developing countries usually have less productivity because of the linkage to working standards. Businesses in developing countries can use added value as a way to enhance economic growth. Clusters are companies of a similar nature geographically connected because of their complementary nature. Batik clusters encourage entrepreneurs to compete and collaborate with each other. The commonality of firms, institutions, and individuals in batik clusters means that they can support business growth. The batik cluster comprises business associations and providers of services that support the development and production of batik-related products. This can involve developing new products and encouraging joint marketing efforts around batik.

Managerial relevance

In developing countries entrepreneurs have a higher level of new enterprise development than established firms (Bosma and Levie, 2009). Local entrepreneurs can utilize their knowledge of culture and markets to exploit gaps in the marketplace (Khoury et al., 2014). Local entrepreneurs in developing countries can be disadvantaged compared to other types of entrepreneurs as resource constraints limit their influence with government officials (Scherer and Palazzo, 2011). Large companies in developing countries are enabled to influence community leaders by focusing on their market power (Khoury and Prasad, 2015). Local entrepreneurs can enhance their competitiveness in developing countries by focusing on cultural entrepreneurship.

There has been less research in developing countries because of the difficulty in gaining access to firm and individual behavior (Seelos and Mair, 2007). This is due to the distinct challenges entrepreneurs in developing countries have due to market and research access.

This chapter's discussion about cultural entrepreneurship in a developing country provides a valuable approach to the issues confronted by local subsistence entrepreneurs. A focus on cultural entrepreneurship helps shapes local entrepreneurs' ability to focus on niche markets that can over the long term have international opportunities. The geographical context of developing countries provides a way to understand the dynamic process of competitiveness (Mair and Marti, 2009). More managers should explore the entrepreneurial processes for developing country entrepreneurs when they move to another country. Nongovernmental organizations (NGOs) and intergovernmental organizations (IGOs) such as the World Intellectual Property Organization offer help to entrepreneurs in developing countries (Khoury and Peng, 2011). These NGOs and IGOs act as catalysts for developing country entrepreneurs as they can be an intermediary between cultural products and available markets.

Discussion and conclusions

The goal of this chapter was to examine batik entrepreneurship in the developing world context. The Indonesian batik industry provides a success story of creative entrepreneurial initiatives. By focusing on cultural products such as batik, developing countries can create a positive environment for entrepreneurship. Developing countries like Indonesia are under pressure to develop their creative industries as a way to increase economic growth rates and decrease reliance on imports. Advanced economies are likely to learn from developing countries like Indonesia in terms of their batik entrepreneurs and linkage to cultural heritage. Batik entrepreneurs are exploring international markets to facilitate collaboration with foreign companies in order to increase their market share. Governments in developing countries can use informal entrepreneurship to encourage investment in batik clusters. This will help contribute to developing countries' entrepreneurial ecosystems and creative endeavors.

Developing countries have promoted technology development but should focus more on their creative and heritage industries such as their batik crafts. Future research can address differences in craft-based industries in developing countries and their policy agenda. For researchers, the recognition of the informal economy in the creative industry in developing countries is very important. As more developing countries focus on industries similar to the batik one it will be important to see how entrepreneurial ecosystems can be developed. Future research needs to look at longitudinal data to see how creative industries in developing countries are changing based on cultural and heritage reasons.

More research is required on tools for encouraging entrepreneurship in developing countries that recognize the different informal and formal activities within subsistence entrepreneurship. The ways to do this might be to examine different subsistence business models that can be grown into large entrepreneurial ventures that have a bigger economic impact. Young et al. (2014) propose that in emerging economies often informal or gray market actions are required as part of the entrepreneurial process. It would be interesting to see how informal firms interact with government policy to decrease poverty conditions. Scholars should research more into how subsistence entrepreneurship changes and is dynamic depending on the context of the developing economy.

The theoretical advances of this chapter include highlighting the way informal entrepreneurship is used in the developing country context using a creative industry. This chapter has advanced the informal and creative entrepreneurship literature by showing how culture and heritage are utilized by batik entrepreneurs. In terms of policy implications this chapter reveals the role of informal entrepreneurship in creating an entrepreneurial ecosystem for batik entrepreneurs in Indonesia. The lack of a supportive environment for entrepreneurship needs to be changed in order to foster business growth in developing countries. Government policy needs to endorse the teaching of entrepreneurial skills to help business start-ups and budding entrepreneurs. More emphasis on how governments can reduce bureaucracy and make it easier to establish and strengthen businesses is required. In conclusion, this chapter has examined the role of cultural entrepreneurship in Indonesia, which is a developing country. It is hoped that this chapter has contributed to a better understanding of entrepreneurship in developing countries with a focus on cultural initiatives.

References

Ahlstrom, D. (2010). Innovation and growth: How business contributes to society. *Academy of Management Perspectives*, 24(3), 10–24.

Ahlstrom, D. and Bruton, G.D. (2006). Venture capital in emerging economies, Networks and Institutional change. *Entrepreneurship Theory and Practice*, 30(2), 299–320.

Autio, E. and Fu, K. 2015 Economic and political institutions and entry into formal and informal entrepreneurship. *Asia Pacific Journal of Management*, 32(1), 67–94.

Babbitt, L.G., Brown, D. and Mazaheri, N. (2015). Gender, entrepreneurship, and the formal-informal dilemma, Evidence from Indonesia. World Development, 72, 163–174.

Bosma, N. and Levie, J. (2009). *Global Entrepreneurship Monitor, 2009*. Global Report. Global Entrepreneurship Research Association. London: London Business School.

Bruton, G.D. and Ahlstrom, D. (2003). An institutional view of China's venture capital industry, Explaining the differences between China and the West. *Journal of Business Venturing*, 18(2), 233–259.

Bruton, G.D., Ahlstrom, D. and Obloj, K. (2008). Entrepreneurship in emerging economies, Where are we today and where should the research go in the future. *Entrepreneurship Theory and Practice*, 32(1), 1–14.

Cardon, M., Stevens, C. and Potter, D. (2011). Misfortunes or mistakes, Cultural sensemaking of entrepreneurial failure. *Journal of Business Venturing*, 26(1), 79–92.

Chakrabarty, S. (2009). The influence of national culture and institutional voids on family ownership of large firms, A country level empirical study. *Journal of International Management*, 15(1), 32–45.

Dacin, P., Dacin, T. and Matear, M. (2010). Social entrepreneurship, Why we don't need a new theory and how we move forward from here. *Academy of Management Perspectives*, 24(3), 37–57.

Dahles, H. and Prabawa, T.S. (2013). Entrepreneurship in the informal sector, The case of the Pedicab drivers of Yogyakarta, Indonesia. *Journal of Small Business & Entrepreneurship*, 26(3), 241–259.

Fischer, G. (2013). Contract structure, risk sharing and investment choice. *Econometrica*, 81(3), 883–939.

George, G., Rao-Nicholson, R., Corbishley, C. and Bansal, R. (2015). Institutional entrepreneurship, governance and poverty: Insights from emergency medical response services in India. *Asia Pacific Journal of Management*, 32(1). 39–65.

Gërxhani, K. (2004). The informal sector in developed and less developed countries, A literature survey. *Public Choice*, 120(3–4), 267–300.

Gupta, V.K., Guo, C., Canever, M., Yim, H.R., Sraw, G.K. and Liu, M. (2014). Institutional environment for entrepreneurship in rapidly emerging major economies, The case of Brazil, China, India and Korea. *International Entrepreneurship and Management Journal*, 10(2), 367–384.

Hart, S.I. and Christensen, C.M. (2002). The great leap, Driving innovation from the base of the pyramid. *MIT Sloan Management Review*, 44(1), 51–56.

Im, J. and Sun, S.L. 2015. Profits and outreach to the poor: The institutional logics of microfinance institutions. *Asia Pacific Journal of Management*, 32(1), 95–117.

Khavul, S., Bruton, G.D. and Wood, E. (2009). Informal family business in Africa. *Entrepreneurship Theory and Practice*, 33(6), 1219–1238.

Khoury, T.A., Cuervo-Cazurra, A. and Dau, L.A. (2014). Institutional insiders and outsiders, The response of domestic and foreign investors to the quality of intellectual property rights protection. *Global Strategy Journal*, 4(3), 200–220.

Khoury, T.A. and Peng, M. (2011). Does institutional reform of intellectual property rights lead to more inbound FDI in developing countries? Evidence from Latin America and the Caribbean. *Journal of World Business*, 46(3), 337–345.

Khoury, T.A. and Prasad, A. (2015). Entrepreneurship amid concurrent institutional constraints in less developed countries. *Business & Society*, 54(1), 1–36.

Kiss, A.N., Danis, W.M. and Cavusgil, S.T. (2012). International entrepreneurship research in emerging economies, A critical review and research agenda. *Journal of Business Venturing*, 27(2), 266–290.

Lounsbury, M. and Glynn, M.A. (2001). Cultural entrepreneurship, Stories, legitimacy and the acquisition of resources. *Strategic Management Journal*, 22(6–7), 545–564.

Mair, J. and Marti, I. (2009). Entrepreneurship in and around institutional voids, A case study from Bangladesh. *Journal of Business Venturing*, 24(5), 419–435.

Manolova, T.S., Eunni, R.V. and Gyoshev, B.S. (2008). Institutional environments for entrepreneurship, Evidence from emerging economies in Eastern Europe. *Entrepreneurship Theory and Practice*, 32(1), 203–218.

North, D. (1990). *Institutions, institutional change and economic performance*, New York, Norton.

Peng, M.W. (2002). Towards an institutional view of business strategy. *Asia Pacific Journal of Management*, 19(2), 251–267.

Scherer, A.G. and Palazzo, G. (2011). The new political role of business in a globalized world, A review of a new perspective on CSR and its implications for the firm, governance and democracy. *Journal of Management Studies*, 48(4), 899–931.

Seelos, C. and Mair, J. (2007). Profitable business models and market creation in the context of deep poverty, A strategic view. *Academy of Management Perspectives*, 21(4), 49–63.

Si, S., Yu, X., Wu, A., Chen., S., Chen, S. and Su, Y. (2015). Entrepreneurship and poverty reduction: A case study of Yiwu, China. *Asia Pacific Journal of Management*, 32(1), 119–143.

Spencer, J.W. and Gomez, C. (2004). The relationship among national institutional structures, economic factors and domestic entrepreneurial activity, A multicountry study. *Journal of Business Research*, 57(10), 1098–1107.

Veciana, J.M. and Urbano, D. (2009). The institutional approach to entrepreneurship research. *International Entrepreneurship and Management Journal*, 4(4), 365–379.

Webb, J.W., Tihanyi, I., Ireland, R.D. and Sirmon, D.G. (2009). You say illegal, I say legitimate, Entrepreneurship in the informal economy. *Academy of Management Review*, 34(3), 492–510.

Williams, C.C. (2004). *Cash-in-Hand Work, The Underground Sector and the Hidden Economy of Favours*. Basingstoke, Palgrave Macmillan.

Williams, C.C. (2006). Beyond marketization, rethinking economic development trajectories in Eastern and Central Europe. *Journal of Contemporary European Studies*, 14(2), 241–254.

Williams, C.C. (2011). Reconceptualising men's and women's undeclared work, evidence from Europe. *Gender, Work and Organisation*, 18(4), 415–437.

Williams, C.C., Rodgers, P. and Round, J. (2011). Explaining the normality of informal employment in Ukraine, A product of exit or exclusion? *The American Journal of Economics and Sociology*, 70(3), 729–755.

Williams, C.C. (2014). *Confronting the shadow economy, evaluating tax compliance behaviour and policies*. Cheltenham, Edward Elgar.

Williams, C.C. and Horodnic, I. (2015). Marginalisation and participation in the informal economy in Central and Eastern European nations. *Post-Communist Economies*, 27(2), 153–169.

Williams, C.C. and Lansky, M. (2013). Informal employment in developed and developing economies, Perspectives and policy responses. *International Labour Review*, 152(3–4), 355–380.

Williams,C.C., Dzhekova, R., Franic, J. and Mishkov, L. (2015). Evaluating the policy approach towards the undeclared economy in FYR Macedonia. *International Journal of Entrepreneurship and Small Business*, 24(2), 268–286.

Williams, C.C., Horodnic, I.A. and Windebank, J. (2015). Explaining participation in the informal economy, An institutional incongruence perspective. *International Sociology*, 30(3), 294–313.

Williams, C.C. and Shahid, M.S. (2014). Informal entrepreneurship and institutional theory, Explaining the varying degrees of (in)formalization of entrepreneurs in Pakistan. *Entrepreneurship and Regional Development*, 1(1–2), 1–25.

Wood, M.S., Bradley, S.W. and Artz, K. (2014). Roots, reasons and resources, Situated optimism and firm growth in subsistence economies. *Journal of Business Research*, 68(1), 127–136.

Young, M.N., Tsai, T., Wang, X., Liu, S. and Ahlstrom, D. (2014). Strategy in emerging economies and the theory of the firm. *Asia Pacific Journal of Management*, 31(2), 331–354.

Yu, B., Hao, S., Ahlstrom, D., Si, S. and Liang, D. (2014). Entrepreneurial firms' network competence, technological capability, and new product development performance. *Asia Pacific Journal of Management*, 31(3), 687–704.

PART II

Entrepreneurs' motivations

12

MOTIVATIONS OF ENTREPRENEURS IN DEVELOPING COUNTRIES

An introductory overview

Colin C. Williams and Anjula Gurtoo

Introduction

For many years, a widely held belief was that entrepreneurship in developing countries was conducted by marginalized populations engaged in such endeavour out of necessity as a survival practice and last resort in the absence of alternatives (Castells and Portes, 1989; Lagos, 1995; Maldonado, 1995). In recent decades however, this has been recognized as an *a priori* assumption rather than an empirical finding. In Part II of this handbook, the aim is to begin to unpick this assumption that entrepreneurs operating in the global South are necessity-driven entrepreneurs. The result will be to advance understanding of the lived practices of entrepreneurship in developing countries.

To provide an introductory overview to this topic, this introductory chapter briefly reviews how the literature on entrepreneurs' motives has become increasingly dominated by the classificatory schema that represents entrepreneurs as either necessity- or opportunity-driven, along with how the literature focusing on entrepreneurship in developing countries has depicted entrepreneurs to be largely necessity-driven. Following this, it then reviews how this necessity-driven view is grounded in the notion that entrepreneurs engage in such endeavour purely for monetary gain. Akin to the developed world, this will again reveal that this view that entrepreneurship is always and everywhere a profit-driven endeavour is being challenged, as it is recognized that entrepreneurs in developing countries engage in not-for-profit activity as social entrepreneurs. This then sets the scene for a brief review of how each of the chapters in Part II of this handbook are seeking to advance understanding of the motivations underpinning entrepreneurship in developing countries.

Entrepreneurship in developing countries: necessity- or opportunity-driven?

Entrepreneurship scholarship has employed various analytical frameworks to explain the factors underpinning the decision to start up a business (Baty, 1990; Bolton and Thompson, 2000; Brockhaus and Horowitz, 1986; Burns, 2001; Chell et al., 1991; Cooper, 1981; Kanter, 1983). Over the past few decades however, a particular classificatory scheme has become increasingly dominant. Despite earlier warnings not to over-simplify the complex rationales of entrepreneurs (Rouse and Daellenbach, 1999), a classificatory schema has come to the fore which builds on the work of Bögenhold (1987) who differentiated between entrepreneurs motivated by economic needs and those driven by a desire for self-realization. It has become increasingly common to distinguish between 'necessity-driven' entrepreneurs pushed into entrepreneurship as a survival strategy in the absence of alternative means of livelihood, and 'opportunity-driven' entrepreneurs pulled into this endeavour more out of choice (Aidis et al., 2007; Benz, 2009; Harding et al., 2006; Maritz, 2004; Minniti et al., 2006; Perunović, 2005; Reynolds et al., 2001, 2002; Smallbone and Welter, 2004).

One prominent reason for the increasing dominance of this structure/agency binary is that it has been used in the Global Entrepreneurship Monitor (GEM), the predominant global survey of the degree and nature of entrepreneurship (Bosma and Harding, 2007; Bosma et al., 2008; Devins, 2009; Harding et al., 2006; Minniti et al., 2006; Reynolds et al., 2001, 2002). GEM aims to explore the link between entrepreneurship and economic development (Bosma and Harding, 2007; Bosma et al., 2008; Devins, 2009; Reynolds et al., 2001, 2002). To do this, it makes a distinction between 'necessity entrepreneurship', defined as people who view entrepreneurship as the best option available and not necessarily the preferred option, and 'opportunity entrepreneurship', defined as those who engage in entre-preneurship out of choice (Acs, 2006; Adom and Williams, 2012; Bosma et al., 2008; Williams, 2007, 2008, 2009, 2010; Williams et al., 2006, 2009, 2010, 2011, 2013a,b; Williams and Lansky, 2013; Williams and Youssef, 2014). As Minniti et al. (2006: 21) assert in relation to the GEM survey, 'In most countries . . . nearly all individuals can be sorted into one of the two categories'. As such, it has become common to analyze the ratio of 'opportunity-to-necessity' entrepreneurs. The finding is that developed countries have a higher ratio of opportunity-to-necessity entrepreneurs than developing countries (e.g., Minniti et al., 2006; Reynolds et al., 2001). This has provided support for the view that the vast majority of entrepreneurs in developing countries are marginalized populations participating in such endeavour out of necessity as a survival practice and last resort in the absence of alternative means of livelihood.

In recent decades, however, this view has started to be put under the spotlight and questions raised about whether this is indeed the case (Cross, 2000; Gerxhani, 2004; Maloney, 2004). It has been recognized that many entrepreneurs in developing countries act out of choice, not least due to the flexible hours, especially for women with caring responsibilities, but also due to the economic independence, better wages and avoidance of taxes and inefficient government regulation offered by this sphere, as well as the fact that some entre-preneurs are in formal jobs and engage in entrepreneurial endeavour as an additional income-earning opportunity (Maloney, 2004; Perry and Maloney, 2007; Williams and Gurtoo, 2013). As Cross (2000) found in one of the earliest studies, although street vendors have been conventionally represented as necessity-driven entrepreneurs, most he studied did so out of choice. Later studies in both Latin America (see Perry et al., 2007) and India (Gurtoo and Williams, 2009) similarly reveal the prevalence of opportunity-drivers in entrepreneurs' rationales, and call for the recognition of 'exit' (opportunity-driven entrepreneurship) as well as exclusion (necessity-driven entrepreneurship) when explaining entrepreneurship in developing countries.

The result is that studies of entrepreneurship in developing countries have started to gauge the ratio of necessity-to-opportunity entrepreneurship in different developing country con-texts, as well as who engages out of necessity and who does so voluntarily, and how the activities that they engage in differ. As the chapters in Part II will reveal, there appears to be a socio-spatial contingency of entrepreneurs' motives in terms of the ratio of necessity-to-opportunity entrepreneurship with greater proportions of necessity-driven entrepreneurship for example in deprived populations and opportunity entrepreneurship in more affluent populations. There has also been a recognition that necessity- and opportunity-drivers can often combine when considering the motives of individual entrepreneurs and an understanding that entrepreneurs' motives can change over time, such as from more necessity-oriented to opportunity-oriented rationales. It is not just the recognition that some entrepreneurs in developing countries voluntarily engage in entrepreneurial endeavour for opportunity-oriented rationales that is opening up entrepreneurship in developing countries to re-representation.

Entrepreneurship in developing countries: commercial or social entrepreneurs?

In recent decades, the view that entrepreneurship is always and everywhere a profit-driven endeavour has also begun to be challenged. A growing literature has displayed how entrepreneurship is not always a purely profit-driven endeavour and how many entrepreneurs engage in not-for-profit activity (Austin et al., 2006; Defourny and Nyssens, 2008; Galera and Borzega, 2009; Hynes, 2009; Lyon and Sepulveda, 2009; Nicholls and Cho, 2006; Thompson, 2008). In other words, besides 'commercial entrepreneurs' who engage in entrepreneurial endeavour for a primarily for-profit objective, there are also 'social entrepreneurs' who pursue primarily social and/or environmental objectives and reinvest the surpluses for that purpose in the business or community (e.g., Austin et al., 2006; Dees, 1998; Dees and Anderson, 2003; Defourny and Nyssens, 2008).

For many decades, the notion that entrepreneurship and enterprise culture might be other than a profit-driven endeavour conducted for monetary gain was seldom entertained in developing countries. Since the turn of the millennium however, there has been a rapidly growing literature that has documented how entrepreneurs are not always purely profit-driven and that social rationales often prevail (Austin et al., 2006; Defourny and Nyssens, 2008; Galera and Borzega, 2009; Hynes, 2009; Lyon and Sepulveda, 2009; Nicholls and Cho, 2006; Thompson, 2008). In this emergent social entrepreneurship literature, rather than view commercial and social entrepreneurship as separate, discrete and different, a spectrum has started to be conceptualized ranging from wholly commercial entrepreneurship at one end of the continuum to wholly social entrepreneurs at the other end, with many blends in-between (Austin et al., 2006; Moore et al., 2010). From this perspective, therefore, social and commercial objectives are commonly combined and intertwined in entrepreneurs' logics, with different entrepreneurs giving varying weights to each. As Mair and Marti (2006: 2) assert, 'Social entrepreneurship is seen as differing from other forms of entrepreneurship in the relatively higher priority given to promoting social value and development versus capturing economic value'.

Until now, nevertheless, this body of literature has largely focused on the developed world. Little attention has been paid to whether this is the case in developing countries, perhaps due to the dominance of the depiction that entrepreneurship is necessity-driven and thus conducted purely for monetary gain. Compared with the burgeoning social entrepreneurship literature in the developed world, therefore, relatively little has been written on the prevalence and nature of social entrepreneurship in the developing world. Nevertheless, and as the chapters in Part II reveal, a literature on social entrepreneurship in developing countries is emerging which reveals not only the need for, but also the existence of, social entrepreneurship in the developing world.

Contributions of the chapters

In chapter 13, 'Opportunity and necessity entrepreneurs in rural Vietnam: who performs better?', Jürgen Brünjes and Javier Revilla Diez highlight how rural entrepreneurship in developing countries has been continuously portrayed as being necessity-driven or as a survival strategy in the absence of alternatives. In this chapter, they discuss whether the opportunity/necessity concept derived in the developed world is applicable in the rural context of developing countries and whether opportunity entrepreneurs perform better than necessity entrepreneurs in this setting. Interviewing 346 non-farm entrepreneurs in rural Vietnam, the finding is that many of these entrepreneurs are opportunity-driven but that necessity-driven entrepreneurs are only significantly more likely to make lower profits if they are purely necessity-driven, and also that they do not significantly differ from opportunity entrepreneurs in their capacity to generate employment for other households.

To begin to escape the dominance of the necessity/opportunity dichotomy, the next two chapters influence some of the wider factors influencing participation in entrepreneurship in developing countries. Esra Karadeniz and Ahmet Özçam, in chapter 14, examine 'Being an entrepreneur of the Vicenarian and Tricenarian generation: the case of Turkish entrepreneurs, 2006–2012'. Using a logistic cumulative distribution function to evaluate the probability of being an entrepreneur with respect to demographic, economic and perceptual determinants, the finding is that in the case of Turkey from 2006 to 2012, the probability of being an entrepreneur is 0.11 for men and 0.05 for women. Moreover, the age after which the probability of being an entrepreneur becomes negative was about 33 and the gender gap less important in older entrepreneurs. The fearless factor contributes more to being an entrepreneur at the early stages of working life, while the subjective belief of having adequate skills and knowing other entrepreneurs contributed most to the probability of being an entrepreneur at 33 years old.

Meanwhile, in chapter 15, 'Factors enterprises perceive to influence their success: a case study of agribusiness in Laos', Sutana Boonlua investigates the factors influencing the success of agribusiness enterprises in Laos. Reporting in-depth interviews with 80 Lao owners of agribusiness, and analyzing 24 independent variables grouped into five categories (government, business, technology, social, and international factors), the correlation matrix reveals that all the factors influence the success of enterprises at the 1 per cent level of significance, albeit to varying degrees.

Turning attention to the existence of social entrepreneurship in the developing world, in chapter 16 entitled 'Social entrepreneurship and the nonprofit sector in developing countries', Michelle J. Stecker, Tonia L. Warnecke and Carol M. Bresnahan focus upon the impact of social entrepreneurship on the non-profit sector in developing nations. First, they review the diverse landscape of non-profit organizations (NPOs), non-governmental organizations (NGOs), and international non-governmental organizations (INGOs), noting the diverse challenges faced by these institutions in the developing world. They then discusses social entrepreneurship's influence on non-profit management, scaling, replicability, impact assessment, sustainable business model development, and the trends in philanthropy and social impact finance. Reviewing best practices for cross-sector partnerships, the chapter concludes by examining the reach and maturation of non-profit organizations specializing in social entrepreneurship and opportunities in social entrepreneurial education.

Contributing further to the identification of the multifarious varieties of entrepreneurship beyond the developed world, Tanya Chavdarova in chapter 17, entitled 'Types of small-scale entrepreneurship: some lessons from Bulgaria', examines the developments in small-scale entrepreneurship in Bulgaria after 1989 and discusses the applicability of different theoretical approaches to entrepreneurship in a post-socialist context. Three basic ideal types of entrepreneurs are empirically verified: entrepreneurs vs. autonomous workers, formal vs. informal entrepreneurs and market vs. network entrepreneurs. Their reflection in the self-perceptions of small entrepreneurs is revealed. It is argued that hybridization is the main trait of small-scale entrepreneurship. The mixture of types concerns not only transitions within each type but also combinations between the different types.

In chapter 18, 'Social entrepreneurship, international development, and the environment', Tonia Warnecke discusses social enterprise and situates social entrepreneurship in the context of international development, with a special focus on the environment. Reviewing the various conceptualizations of social entrepreneurship in the literature, followed by the changing role of business in international development, the argument is that the ways that businesses contribute to development goals have evolved, resulting in 'inclusive business' models and a movement for social enterprises in the developing world. Highlighting the challenges facing social enterprises, ways to move forward are then discussed.

Making a further contribution to the understanding of social entrepreneurship, Chapter 19 by Vanessa Ratten, Joao Ferreira, Cristina Fernandes examines 'Social entrepreneurship and fashion innovation in Brazil: a case study of Crafty Women (Mulheres Arteiras) and Rede Asta'. This chapter discusses the role of social and cultural entrepreneurship in developing countries from the perspective of craft entrepreneurs in Brazil. Crafty Women (Mulheres Arteiras) is a social enterprise on the outskirts of Rio de Janeiro which works with artisans from poor local communities to help them build their skills and sell their products in Rede Asta stores, which operates as a cooperative social enterprise, and partners with other social enterprises around Brazil. It provides a study of the importance of creative and social entrepreneurship in the developing world and an example of a way forward for other developing countries.

References

Acs, Z. J. (2006). How is entrepreneurship good for economic growth? *Innovations*, 1(1), 97–107.

Adom, K. and Williams, C.C. (2012). Evaluating the motives of informal entrepreneurs in Koforidua, Ghana. *Journal of Developmental Entrepreneurship*, 17(1), 1–18.

Aidis, R., Welter, F., Smallbone, D. and Isakova, N. (2007). Female entrepreneurship in transition economies: the case of Lithuania and Ukraine. *Feminist Economics*, 13(2), 157–183.

Austin, J., Stevenson, H. and Wei-Skillern, J. (2006). Social and commercial entrepreneurship: same, different or both? *Entrepreneurship Theory and Practice*, 31(1), 1–22.

Baty, G. (1990). *Entrepreneurship in the nineties*. London: Prentice Hall.

Benz, M. (2009). Entrepreneurship as a non-profit seeking activity. *International Entrepreneurship and Management Journal*, 5(1), 23–44.

Bögenhold, D. (1987). *De Gründerboom: Realität und Mythos de neuen Selbständigkeit*. Frankfurt: Campus.

Bolton, B. and Thompson, J. (2000). *Entrepreneurs: talent, temperament, technique*. Oxford: Butterworth-Heinemann.

Bosma, N. and Harding, R. (2007). *Global entrepreneurship monitor: GEM 2006 results*. London: London Business School.

Bosma, N., Jones, K., Autio, K. and Levie, J. (2008). *Global entrepreneurship monitor: 2007 executive report*. London: Global Entrepreneurship Monitor Consortium.

Brockhaus, R.H. and Horowitz, P.S. (1986). The psychology of the entrepreneur. *Entrepreneurship Theory and Practice*, 23(1), 29–45.

Burns, P. (2001). *Entrepreneurship and small business*. Basingstoke: Palgrave.

Castells, M. and Portes, A. (1989). World underneath: the origins, dynamics and effects of the informal economy. In A. Portes, M. Castells and L. A. Benton (eds.), *The Informal Economy: studies in advanced and less developing countries* (pp. 19–42). Baltimore, MD: John Hopkins University Press.

Chell, E., Haworth, J. and Brearly, S. (1991). *The entrepreneurial personality: concepts, cases and categories.* London: Routledge.

Cooper, A.C. (1981). Strategic management: new ventures and small businesses. *Long Range Planning,* 14(5), 39–45.

Cross, J.C. (2000). Street vendors, modernity and postmodernity: conflict and compromise in the global economy. *International Journal of Sociology and Social Policy,* 20(1), 29–51.

Dees, J.G. (1998). *The meaning of social entrepreneurship.* Durham, NC: Duke University Press.

Dees, J.G. and Anderson, B.B. (2003). For-profit social ventures. *International Journal of Entrepreneurship Education,* 2(1), 1–26.

Defourny, J. and Nyssens, M. (2008). Social enterprise in Europe: recent trends and developments. *Social Enterprise Journal,* 4(3), 202–228.

Devins, D. (2009). Enterprise in deprived areas: what role for start-ups? *International Journal of Entrepreneurship and Small Business,* 8(4), 486–498.

Galera, G. and Borzega, C. (2009). Social enterprise: an international overview of its conceptual evolution and legal implementation. *Social Enterprise Journal,* 5(3), 210–228.

Gerxhani, K. (2004). The informal sector in developed and less developed countries: a literature survey. *Public Choice,* 120(3–4), 267–300.

Gurtoo, A. and Williams, C.C. (2009). Entrepreneurship and the informal sector: some lessons from India. *International Journal of Entrepreneurship and Innovation,* 10(1), 55–62.

Harding, R., Brooksbank, D., Hart, M., Jones-Evans, D., Levie, J., O'Reilly, J. and Walker, J. (2006). *Global Entrepreneurship Monitor United Kingdom 2005.* London: London Business School.

Hynes, B. (2009). Growing the social enterprise: issues and challenges. *Social Enterprise Journal,* 5(2), 114–125.

Kanter, R.M. (1983). *The change masters.* New York: Simon and Schuster.

Lagos, R.A. (1995). Formalising the informal sector: barriers and costs. *Development and Change,* 26(1), 110–131.

Lyon, F. and Sepulveda, L. (2009). Mapping social enterprises: past approaches, challenges and future directions. *Social Enterprise Journal,* 5(1), 83–94.

Mair, J. and Marti, I. (2006). Social entrepreneurship research: a source of explanation, prediction and delight. *Journal of World Business,* 41(1), 36–44.

Maldonado, C. (1995). The informal sector: legalization or laissez-faire? *International Labour Review,* 134(6), 705–728.

Maloney, W. F. (2004). Informality revisited. *World Development,* 32(7), 1159–1178.

Maritz, A. (2004). New Zealand necessity entrepreneurs. *International Journal of Entrepreneurship and Small Business,* 1(3–4), 255–264.

Minniti, M., Bygrave, W. and Autio, E. (2006). *Global Entrepreneurship Monitor: 2005 executive report.* London: London Business School.

Moore, C.W., Petty, J.W., Palich, L.E. and Longnecker, J.G. (2010). *Managing small business: an entrepreneurial emphasis.* London: South-Western Cengage Learning.

Nicholls, A. and Cho, A. (2006). Social entrepreneurship: the structuration of a field. In A. Nicholls, (ed.), *Social entrepreneurship: new models of sustainable social change,* Oxford: Oxford University Press, pp. 99–118.

Perry, G.E., Maloney, W.F., Arias, O.S., Fajnzylber, P., Mason, A.D. and Saavedra-Chanduvi, J. (eds.). (2007). *Informality: exit and exclusion.* Washington DC: World Bank.

Perry, G.E. and Maloney, W.F. (2007). Overview: informality – exit and exclusion. In G.E. Perry, W.F. Maloney, O.S. Arias, P. Fajnzylber, A.D. Mason and J. Saavedra-Chanduvi. (eds.), *Informality: exit and exclusion* (pp. 1–20). Washington DC: World Bank.

Perunović, Z. (2005). Introducing opportunity-based entrepreneurship in a transition economy. Michigan: Policy Brief 39, William Davidson Institute, University of Michigan.

Reynolds, P., Bygrave, W.D., Autio, E. and Hay, M. (2002). *Global Entrepreneurship Monitor: 2002 executive monitor.* London: London Business School.

Reynolds, P., Camp, S.M., Bygrave, W.D., Autio, E. and Hay, M. (2001). *Global Entrepreneurship Monitor: 2001 executive monitor.* London: London Business School.

Rouse, M. and Dallenbach, U. (1999). Rethinking research methods for the resource-based perspective: isolating sources of sustainable competitive advantage. *Strategic Management Journal,* 20(5), 487–494.

Smallbone, D. and Welter, F. (2004).Entrepreneurship in transition economies: necessity or opportunity driven? www.babson.edu/entrep/fer/BABSON2003/XXV/XXV-S8/xxv-s8.htm (last accessed 9 April 2013).

Thompson, J.L. (2008). Social enterprise and social entrepreneurship: where have we reached? A summary of issues and discussion points. *Social Enterprise Journal*, 4(2), 149–61.

Williams, C.C. (2007). Entrepreneurs operating in the informal economy: necessity or opportunity driven? *Journal of Small Business and Entrepreneurship*, 20(3), 309–320.

Williams, C.C. (2008). Beyond necessity-driven versus opportunity-driven entrepreneurship: a study of informal entrepreneurs in England, Russia and Ukraine. *International Journal of Entrepreneurship and Innovation*, 9(3), 157–166.

Williams, C.C. (2009). The motives of off-the-books entrepreneurs: necessity- or opportunity-driven? *International Journal of Entrepreneurship and Management*, 5(2), 203–217.

Williams, C.C. (2010). Spatial variations in the hidden enterprise culture: some lessons from England. *Entrepreneurship and Regional Development*, 22(5), 403–423.

Williams, C.C. and Gurtoo, A. (2013a). Beyond entrepreneurs as heroic icons of capitalism: a case study of street entrepreneurs in India. *International Journal of Entrepreneurship and Small Business*, 19(4), 421–437.

Williams, C.C. and Lansky, M. (2013b). Informal employment in developed and emerging economies: perspectives and policy responses. *International Labour Review*, 152(3–4), 355–380.

Williams, C.C. and Youssef, Y.A. (2014) Is informal sector entrepreneurship necessity- or opportunity-driven? Some lessons from urban Brazil. *Business and Management Research*, 3(1), 41–53.

Williams, C.C., Round, J. and Rodgers, P. (2006). Beyond necessity- and opportunity-driven entrepreneurship: some case study evidence from Ukraine. *Journal of Business and Entrepreneurship*, 18(2), 22–34.

Williams, C.C., Round, J. and Rodgers, P. (2009). Evaluating the motives of informal entrepreneurs: some lessons from Ukraine. *Journal of Developmental Entrepreneurship*, 14(1), 59–71.

Williams, C.C., Round, J. and Rodgers, P. (2010). Explaining the off-the-books enterprise culture of Ukraine: reluctant or willing entrepreneurship? *International Journal of Entrepreneurship and Small Business*, 10(2), 65–80.

Williams, C.C., Nadin, S. and Rodgers, P. (2011). Evaluating competing theories of informal entrepreneurship: some lessons from Ukraine. *International Journal of Entrepreneurial Behaviour and Research*, 18(5), 528–543.

Williams, C.C., Nadin, S., Newton, S., Rodgers, P. and Windebank, J. (2013a). Explaining off-the-books entrepreneurship: a critical evaluation of competing perspectives. *International Entrepreneurship and Management Journal*, 9(3), 447–463.

Williams, C.C., Round, J. and Rodgers, P. (2013b). *The role of informal economies in the post-Soviet world: the end of transition?* London: Routledge.

13

OPPORTUNITY AND NECESSITY ENTREPRENEURS IN RURAL VIETNAM

Who performs better?[1]

Jürgen Brünjes and Javier Revilla Diez

Introduction

Over the last decades the opportunity/necessity concept has become very popular in the entrepreneurship literature. Trying to explain entrepreneurial activities, the necessity/opportunity concept acknowledges that some individuals are pulled into entrepreneurship by opportunity recognition while others are pushed into entrepreneurship because they have no other choice to earn a living (Reynolds et al., 2002). In the context of developed countries, we see two types of entrepreneurs, not only determined by different factors but also differing in their socio-economic characteristics, in business management and in performance (Williams, 2007, 2009, 2010; Williams et al., 2013). In addition, opportunity entrepreneurs are more likely to lead the business cycle (Verheul et al., 2010). Scholars of developing economies also suggest opportunity entrepreneurs can be drivers of structural change as they have a greater potential to innovate, push specialisation in manufacturing and increase employment and productivity (Gries and Naudé, 2010; Naudé, 2010). This is supported by data from the Global Entrepreneurship Monitor. The data indicates opportunity entrepreneurship increases when countries progress in economic development, while necessity entrepreneurship first decreases very rapidly in an early stage of development and then declines in a more moderate way (Kelley et al., 2011).[2]

Similarly, in rural areas in developing countries, where the economy is dominated by agricultural production, differently motivated non-farm entrepreneurs are likely to exist. Haggblade et al. (2007) outline a push scenario in which increases in agricultural incomes and a growing demand for non-farm goods and services can lead to increasing investments into non-farm businesses in rural areas and a pull scenario in which low farm productivity and landlessness pushes households to engage in non-farm activities due to low opportunity costs and a lack of alternatives. The few existing studies on differently motivated entrepreneurs in such contexts support these ideas and show that rural non-farm entrepreneurs can also be motivated by necessity and by opportunity (exemptions are Rosa et al., 2007; Gurtoo and Williams, 2009; Brünjes and Diez, 2013a, 2013b). However, the effect of different motivations on business performance has not been studied in a rural developing context.

Yet, if they perform better, non-farm opportunity entrepreneurs could be regarded as a revitalising element of the rural economy.

This chapter starts with a discussion on whether the opportunity/necessity concept is applicable in the rural context of a developing country like Vietnam. We then test whether opportunity entrepreneurs perform better than necessity entrepreneurs in this setting. For the rural areas in Vietnam this is a crucial question. If opportunity entrepreneurs perform better, they may be the long-sought-after drivers of change that contribute to the development of rural areas. Since the introduction of the reform process towards a multi-sector, market-oriented economy in 1986, the country has achieved high rates of economic growth, including a dramatic reduction of poverty. The reform process triggered a process of increasing concentration of industrial production and economic growth in Ho Chi Minh City and its surrounding areas as well as in Hanoi and Haiphong (Garschagen et al., 2012; Mausch et al., 2012; Revilla Diez, 1999). This was accompanied by increasing migration to these areas and continuing urbanisation. However, despite impressive developments in urban areas, more than 70 per cent of the Vietnamese population still lives in rural areas (World Bank, 2011). These people often have to deal with the strong omnipresence of necessities related to agricultural activities. Households are strongly affected by covariate natural shocks, including storms, the flooding of agricultural land, crop pests and livestock diseases (Völker and Waibel, 2010). Extreme weather events may even increase as the process of climate change continues (Chaudhry and Ruysschaert, 2007). The non-farm economy in rural areas traditionally relies on small family-based enterprises with low capital investments and low productivity because foreign investment and industrial growth remains scarce in these settings (Beresford, 2008). Structural change is advancing slowly. On the one hand, between 2002 and 2008, the share of people engaged in non-farm wage jobs as their main form of employment has increased considerably from 15.2 per cent to 22.2 per cent (General Statistics Office, 2009). On the other hand, the share of people primarily engaged in non-farm self-employment remained relatively stable at around 14.0 per cent (General Statistics Office, 2009). However, the sector has recently shown some tendencies of increasing professionalisation and specialisation (Oostendorp et al., 2009). Identification and support for those businesses that could revitalise the rural economy in the future, is therefore critical.

The remaining parts of this chapter are structured as follows. First, we provide a conceptual discussion on opportunity and necessity entrepreneurship and performance in general. Then we discuss the application of the concept in a rural developing context; after which we present the data and the methodology used to study Vietnam. In the following section, empirical results are presented and discussed. Finally, conclusions for research and policy are drawn.

Opportunity and necessity entrepreneurship and performance

The concept of opportunity and necessity entrepreneurship has been developed in the context of developed economies. Exemplifying this is Smith (1967) who distinguishes the craftsman-entrepreneur and the opportunistic-entrepreneur in the United States. For him, the craftsman-entrepreneur is oriented towards the past and the present and less confident. The opportunistic-entrepreneur is oriented towards the future, highly flexible and well educated. Later, researchers more generally distinguished push and pull entrepreneurship (Amit and Muller, 1995). Accordingly, the past-oriented craftsman-entrepreneur with lower levels of education represents push entrepreneurship while the future-oriented and better-educated opportunistic entrepreneur represents a form of pull entrepreneurship. Building on these conceptualisations, the necessity/opportunity concept was further elaborated in the context the Global Entrepreneurship Monitor (GEM). Since 2001, respondents of the GEM are asked whether they started a business because they wanted to exploit an opportunity or because they had no better options for work (Reynolds et al., 2002). In the first case, the owner would be an opportunity entrepreneur; in the second case, the owner would be a necessity entrepreneur.

Recently, the widely used necessity/opportunity dichotomy was also criticised for being too limited as the boundary between the two types of entrepreneurs is not as clear as most empirical studies pretend. Very often, business activities are motivated by necessity as well as by opportunity (Giacomin et al., 2011; Hughes, 2003; Solymossy, 1997; Williams and Nadin, 2010; Williams and Round, 2009; Williams and Williams, 2014). Given this, some recent studies reveal how entrepreneurs have started the business out of opportunity and necessity at the same time (Bhola et al., 2006; Giacomin et al., 2011; Verheul et al., 2010).

But how do differently motivated entrepreneurs differ in terms of performance? Up to now a lack of more fine-grained theory on the issue of success factors of necessity compared to opportunity entrepreneurship exists (Block and Wagner, 2010). However, the literature on necessity and opportunity entrepreneurship has shown opportunity entrepreneurs in developed countries are more likely to be successful than necessity entrepreneurs (Amit and Muller, 1995; Arias and Pena, 2010; Block and Wagner, 2010). This could be explained by an indirect and a direct effect of necessity and opportunity motivations on business performance. The indirect effect is human capital and personal risk attitude. Regardless of the human capital, every household is likely to recognise an urgent personal necessity sooner or later regardless of its human capital. However, the recognition of an opportunity is not inevitable, and rather a complicated task requiring a certain level of knowledge and expertise that the opportunity entrepreneurs are more likely to have. While running the business, the same human capital also improves their capability in management, innovation and specialisation. This can eventually result in businesses with better performance. Similarly, the personal risk attitude could also differ between opportunity and necessity entrepreneurs and also influence performance. Opportunity entrepreneurs may be rather prone to risk because they are highly attracted by the potential of the business opportunity while necessity entrepreneurs may be more risk averse given the negative experiences they have had in the past. At the same time this risk attitude could have a positive or a negative effect on the performance of the business.

The direct way in which entrepreneurial motivation can influence performance is through the opportunity itself. If an entrepreneur is motivated by a perceived business opportunity, then it is more likely that such an opportunity actually exists and translates into real outcomes later on. In turn, if an entrepreneur is solely motivated by a perceived necessity, it is very likely that the necessity exists but no business opportunity is prevalent at the same time. As a result, perceiving a business opportunity may be correlated with running a more successful business, for example in terms of growth rates in sales and employment.

Application to a rural developing context

Can we assume that rural entrepreneurs motivated by opportunity are also performing better in a rural developing context? This may only be assumed if the necessity/opportunity concept is applicable in rural settings where a large proportion of the population living in rural areas depend on agriculture as a main source of income. Yet, existing concepts and indicators for necessity and opportunity entrepreneurs were mainly derived in the context of industrialised developed countries and have rarely been tested in a rural developing setting.[3] The few existing studies indicate that the necessity/opportunity concept should only be applied carefully in developing countries because poorly educated individuals in rural areas often do not understand the concepts of opportunity and necessity used in the existing questionnaires (Rosa et al., 2007). However, the general distinction of differently motivated entrepreneurs can be very helpful for deriving policy conclusions. For example, Gurtoo and Williams (2009) find informal entrepreneurs in India are not always motivated purely by necessity and conclude that governments should therefore not ignore this source of entrepreneurship. Rosa et al. (2007) also find most new businesses in Uganda and Sri Lanka are actually opportunity-driven. In turn, the very poor are trapped in a state of routine where they are unable to earn surplus income which could be invested in a necessity-driven business.

From a conceptual point of view, therefore, the application to rural areas in developed countries is reasonable. Livelihoods researchers do not focus on entrepreneurship. Rather the discussion is on the form of income diversification outside the agricultural sector, for example as a means to reduce natural risks in the agricultural sector. Similar to entrepreneurship scholars, livelihoods researchers contrast necessity (involuntary) and choice (voluntary and proactive) as reasons for income diversification into non-farm activities (Ellis, 1998, 2000). Frequently, necessity and choice factors are referred to as 'push and pull' factors driving non-farm engagement (Reardon, 1997). The literature on rural livelihoods shows that, instead, people have to deal with periodical underemployment and insufficient incomes due to shocks, risks and seasonality related to agricultural production on their own farm (Reardon et al., 2007). Pull factors include higher payoffs or lower risks from non-farm engagement. Push factors, in contrast to industrialised countries, do not primarily relate to unemployment, which is predominantly an urban phenomenon.

The push factors can be classified into five different types, as shown by Reardon et al. (2007). First, a drop in seasonal income from farming can push households into non-farm activities to smooth income and consumption in the low season. Second, a transitory drop in income resulting from a shock, such as drought, could force households to cope ex-post with such events and take up additional occupation. Third, permanent insufficiency of farming income due to physical reasons such as environmental degradation or due to market or policy changes could result in a need for income diversification. Fourth, strong variations in farm incomes can lead to high risks. For example, due to rainfall instability, households could be forced to engage in non-farm activities that are less prone to natural risks. Fifth, an idiosyncratic failure in the credit market or insurance failures could force households to get extra income from non-farm sources in order to fund input purchases or insure against risks.

In summary, although the precise nature of necessities and opportunities may differ in rural areas of developing countries, the general conceptual overlapping between the concept of necessity and opportunity entrepreneurship and the push and pull factors in the rural livelihoods literature justifies an application of the necessity and opportunity concept in a rural developing country setting. Thus, necessity and opportunity entrepreneurs in a rural developing country setting may differ in similar ways as in developed countries. Given this, we assume opportunity entrepreneurs are better educated and have a higher level of skills:

> H1: Opportunity entrepreneurs are better educated and skilled compared to necessity entrepreneurs.

Such greater skills could be used to specialise, to innovate and to run a successful business. Opportunity entrepreneurs may also thus have a greater potential to be successful in a rural developing country setting. However, what success actually means in a rural developing country setting and how performance can be measured should be discussed first. Success of a business should ideally be evaluated by the goals of the entrepreneurs and the personal or household motivation. The discussion on motivations for starting non-farm businesses in the livelihoods literature discussed above indicates businesses in rural developing settings do not aspire to become a highly innovative company. Instead, very often the aim of non-farm activities is to generate a stable income for the family (Reardon et al., 2007). The most important measures for success are therefore profits and survival. The profits generated by the business usually directly benefit the wealth of the household. Survival in turn influences the stability of the income generated by the firm in the long run. From a regional policy perspective, evaluation of the ability of firms to generate non-farm income opportunities for other people is important as well. From that viewpoint, employment is the central output generated by the non-farm businesses. Other indicators, for example sales or productivity, are not as appropriate. They predominantly measure firm size and directly indicate neither the output for the entrepreneur nor the impact on rural labour markets. Keeping these ideas about business performance in a rural developing setting in mind, we can assume that, like their counterparts in developed countries, opportunity entrepreneurs in rural Vietnam are more successful than necessity entrepreneurs:

> H2: Entrepreneurs motivated by opportunity are more successful in terms of performance than entrepreneurs motivated by necessity.

If these two hypotheses were valid, policy makers may be best advised to identify and support opportunity entrepreneurs even in rural remote settings in developing countries in order to stimulate structural change and economic development in these settings.

Data and methods

We use a dataset of 346 non-farm businesses in rural Vietnam collected between April and May 2010 in the context of an interdisciplinary research group funded by the German Research Foundation (DFG) which deals with analysing vulnerability to poverty in South East Asia. The research group interviewed more than 2,000 households in three Vietnamese provinces (Ha Tinh, ThuaThien-Hue and Dak Lak). The sampling of households was arranged in a three-stage procedure in which communes and villages were selected with respect to size, and households were selected randomly with equal probability from household lists. The first stage additionally had to be designed with respect to different agro-ecological zones (coastal, mountain and rice plain area) in order to evade insufficient sample sizes in some of these zones (Hardeweg et al., 2007). The research group had already interviewed the same households in 2006 and 2008.[4] However, the household questionnaire contained very little information on entrepreneurial activities. For the 2010 survey, we added an additional questionnaire module for owners of non-farm businesses to every second household questionnaire in order to gain detailed insights into the entrepreneurial activities of the households.[5] If self-employment or small business activities existed in the household, the owners of these businesses were questioned with this additional questionnaire module. As a result, we obtained detailed data on 346 non-farm household businesses and their households (excluding non-local businesses and farming businesses).

The data collection benefited from four major factors. First, the research group consisted of development economists, agricultural economists and economic geographers experienced in collecting data in a rural developing country context. Second, the research group co-operated with Vietnamese research institutes and universities as well as with local governments. Third, the team had already optimised the process of data collection in the first two surveys. Fourth, the households themselves were already familiar with being interviewed. As a result of these factors, non-response was very limited.

Given the problems related to previous definitions of necessity and opportunity entrepreneurship outlined in the second and third sections, we use our own method to understand motivations for starting businesses in rural Vietnam. In this way the realities in a rural developing country context are more easily addressed. We directly asked the entrepreneurs for the most important reason and the second most important reason for starting the business. Besides nine previously designed answer categories, it was also possible to specify any other reason in case the proposed answers would not apply. Most reasons can be assigned to necessity or opportunity without problems. For example, if the owner started the business because s/he figured this kind of business could be successful, this is a future-oriented motivation related to opportunity. Contrarily, if the business was started because of insufficient income in another activity, this is a motivation related to necessity. Some respondents used the opportunity to specify their own reasons. In these cases the stated reasons have to be observed one by one and then assigned to either of the two broader categories.[6] In addition, some people inherited the business or major equipment and thus simply continued a family tradition. In such cases, we cannot clearly state whether this is a reason related to opportunity or necessity.[7]

As the question of definition is so critical, opportunity and necessity entrepreneurs are distinguished in two ways. The first classification only uses the primary reasons for starting the businesses, similar to the GEM definition. If the primary reason is a necessity motivation, these entrepreneurs are classified as necessity entrepreneurs. In turn, if the primary reason is an opportunity motivation, the entrepreneur is an opportunity entrepreneur.[7] The second classification uses both reasons for classifying businesses, thereby responding to the criticised dualism of necessity and opportunity entrepreneurship (Williams and Williams, 2014; Giacomin et al., 2011). As a result three categories emerge instead of two: those who are driven only by necessity, those who are driven only by opportunity, and those who are driven by a combination of both.

Performance here is measured in terms of profits and employment. These indicators primarily reflect the output for the entrepreneur and for the rural labour market. Unfortunately, business survival cannot be taken into account due to a lack of longitudinal data.[8]

Results and discussion

The stated primary and secondary reasons for starting the businesses are displayed in Table 13.1. The table shows the most common reasons are the speculation that the planned business can be successful in the specific location, insufficient income from agricultural jobs, and insufficient income from farming. The least common reason for starting a business is unemployment, underlining the insignificance of this phenomenon in rural areas.

The results of the classification exercise are shown in Table 13.2. When using the first classification of necessity and opportunity entrepreneurship, 169 of 346 entrepreneurs are classified as opportunity entrepreneurs and 168 are classified as necessity entrepreneurs. Only nine entrepreneurs cannot be assigned to either of the two categories because of insufficient information. Using the second classification, we find that 93 businesses were driven only by opportunity, 112 were driven only by necessity and 132 were driven by both (again nine businesses cannot be assigned to either category).

Table 13.1 Reasons for Starting the Business

	Type of reason	Primary reason (%)	Secondary reason (%)
Previous experience in this kind of business	opportunity	6.4	2.6
Saw other successful business of that kind	opportunity	10.1	7.2
Figure that this kind of business can be successful	opportunity	27.5	17.1
Unemployment	necessity	4.9	2.0
Insufficient income from farming	necessity	13.0	11.3
Insufficient income from agricultural job	necessity	17.9	12.7
Insufficient income from non-agricultural job	necessity	5.5	4.3
Inherited the business	unclear	6.4	0.9
Other reasons	mixed[a]	7.5	3.2
No answer/not applicable	not used	0.9	38.7
N (100%)		346	346

Source: Authors' own calculations based on DFG-FOR 756 Household Survey 2010.

Notes: [a]*Specified reasons were observed manually and assigned to one of the two categories.*

Table 13.2 Classifications of Opportunity and Necessity Entrepreneurs

	Classification 1 using primary reason		Classification 2 using primary and secondary reason	
	N	%	N	%
Opportunity only	169	48.8%	–	–
Necessity only	168	48.6%	–	–
Primarily opportunity	–	–	93	26.9%
Primarily necessity	–	–	112	32.4%
Mixed	–	–	132	38.2%
Inconclusive	9	2.6%	9	2.6%
	346	100.0%	346	100.0%
Chi² –Test	0.00		6.78**	

Source: Authors' own calculations based on DFG-FOR 756 Household Survey 2010.

Notes: The Chi² -Test for classification 1 and 2 tests whether the distribution is different from a theoretical uniform distribution.

Clearly, entrepreneurship in rural Vietnam does not mainly consist of necessity entrepreneurs. About half are primarily driven by opportunity and half are primarily driven by necessity. A chi squared test shows the distribution not significantly different from a uniform distribution ($p = 0.96$). Necessity and opportunity are thus equally important as primary reasons. However, including information on the secondary reasons reveals 65 per cent of entrepreneurs driven by an opportunity as a primary or secondary motivation while about 70 per cent mention necessity as a primary or secondary reason. This difference is statistically significant. Necessities are thus slightly more important when considering secondary motivations in rural Vietnam. Overall, neither necessity nor opportunity motivations clearly dominate. This supports findings from other developing countries where entrepreneurship in the informal sector is not always dominated by necessity (Adom and Williams, 2012; Gurtoo and Williams, 2009; Günther and Launov, 2011; Williams and Gurtoo, 2011, 2012; Williams and Youssef, 2014).

Table 13.3 shows some selected general characteristics of necessity and opportunity entrepreneurs. We see that opportunity and necessity entrepreneurs only differ slightly in terms of their sectoral composition. The majority of rural entrepreneurs engage in traditional non-farm activities with little innovative capacity. Generally speaking, the majority of

Table 13.3 General Characteristics

	Classification 1			Classification 2			
	Primarily opportunity	Primarily necessity		Only opportunity	Only necessity	Mixed	
	Mean/ Share	Mean/ Share	t-test/ chi²-test	Mean/ Share	Mean/ Share	Mean/ Share	F-test/ chi²-test
Sectoral distribution:							
Rice Mills	4.7%	2.4%	1.4	3.2%	2.7%	4.6%	0.7
Handicrafts	11.8%	10.7%	0.1	15.1%	9.8%	9.9%	1.8
Repair shops	5.3%	3.0%	1.2	4.3%	4.5%	3.8%	0.1
Construction	5.3%	1.8%	3.1★	3.2%	0.0%	6.8%	8.2★★
Food processing and selling	10.7%	16.1%	2.1	11.8%	16.1%	12.1%	1.1
Restaurant/café/hotel	6.5%	3.0%	2.3	6.5%	4.5%	3.8%	0.9
Retail-Shop (sales store)	27.8%	25.0%	0.3	28.0%	26.8%	25.0%	0.3
Petty trader (sales on street)	7.1%	8.3%	0.2	8.6%	7.1%	7.6%	0.2
Wholesale	10.1%	20.2%	6.8★★★	7.5%	17.9%	18.2%	5.8★
Taxi and transport	2.4%	6.6%	3.5★	2.2%	8.0%	3.0%	5.2★
Others	8.3%	3.0%	4.5★★	9.7%	2.7%	5.3%	4.7★
Total	100%	100%		100%	100%	100%	
Characteristics							
Age of owner	43.3	44.3	-0.7	43.1	44.1	44.0	0.2
Female	59.8%	67.9%	2.4	61.3%	67.9%	62.1%	1.2
Ethnic minority	3.0%	6.6%	2.4	2.2%	6.3%	5.3%	2.0
Bad health status	9.5%	17.9%	5.0★★	8.6%	17.0%	14.4%	3.1
Age of business	9.6	8.2	1.7★	9.7	7.9	9.2	1.8
Registration	50.3%	38.7%	4.6★★	51.6%	39.3%	43.9%	3.2
Is primary occupation of the owner	67.5%	56.6%	4.3★★	72.0%	56.3%	59.9%	5.8★
Days worked in business per month	24.6	23.4	1.7★	23.8	23.2	24.8	1.57
N	169	168		93	112	132	

Source: Authors' own calculations based on DFG-FOR 756 Household Survey 2010.

Notes: *T-Test or F-Test was calculated for comparing group means, Pearson Chi² test was calculated for comparing shares.* *significant at the 10% level.* ★★ *significant at the 5% level.* ★★★ *significant at the 1% level.*

entrepreneurs are in the service and retail sectors. In addition, repair shops, handicrafts and rice mills are also typical enterprises in the rural environment. Necessity entrepreneurs are more often engaged in wholesale and in taxi and transport. Opportunity entrepreneurs more often engage in the construction sector and are more often in the very heterogeneous 'others' section, indicating their engagement in particular activities.[9]

Regarding other characteristics, no significant differences are found in terms of age of the owner, gender and ethnicity of the entrepreneurs. Most business owners are in their early forties, and the vast majority of entrepreneurs belong to the Kinh (ethnic Vietnamese). In addition, as opposed to many developed countries (Williams and Horodnic, 2015), entrepreneurship in Vietnam is not an activity dominated by men. About two-thirds of both types of entrepreneurs are women. However, we find that entrepreneurs who are primarily motivated by necessity state they have health problems significantly more often, reflecting old and sick people who are unable to continue their regular work and thus start a small business at home in order to maintain a certain level of income. Businesses primarily motivated by opportunity are also significantly older, which reflects the better survival prospects of opportunity entrepreneurs. Not surprisingly, they are also more often registered as household businesses or according to the enterprise law. Furthermore, opportunity entrepreneurs show higher commitment. The businesses are clearly more often the primary employment of the owner, which is evident in both classifications, and the owners work more days per month – a sign of professional entrepreneurship among the opportunity entrepreneurs.

Education and skills

Our first hypothesis says opportunity entrepreneurs are better educated and skilled compared with necessity entrepreneurs. In such a case, opportunity entrepreneurs might have a greater potential because a higher level of skills is needed to specialise, to innovate and to run a successful business. We measure skills in two ways. First, we look at the employment and migration background. Previous activities indicate what kind of skills a person might have acquired. If these activities have been acquired in some other location of the country, they might be more valuable that the ones acquired within the same location. Migrant entrepreneurs can bring in important know-how, new production technologies and contacts which may provide them with a competitive advantage and can help revitalise the rural economy (Démurger and Xu, 2011). In a second step we look at the educational attainment and use a self-assessment of the skills of the entrepreneur.

The primary employment statuses before starting the businesses in Table 13.4 reveal one of the major differences between necessity and opportunity entrepreneurs in rural Vietnam. Necessity entrepreneurs were more often previously engaged in agriculture. About three-quarters of necessity entrepreneurs but only about half of the opportunity entrepreneurs were self-employed farmers before becoming engaged in the business. These results reflect that necessities which lead to business formation in rural areas may primarily be related to agricultural production. In contrast to urban areas and developed countries, unemployment does not play an important role in rural business formation. Less than 1 per cent of the entrepreneurs started a business out of unemployment and less than 6 per cent started a non-farm business out of casual wage employment. In turn, opportunity entrepreneurs were more often engaged in another non-farm business or were students at a school or university. This already indicates opportunity entrepreneurs having acquired more skills in the non-farm sector or in schools or universities.

Regarding the location of the previous activity, we cannot find any clear differences. The majority of businesses are started by people from the same commune or province, supporting

Table 13.4 Primary Employment Status and Location Before Starting the Business

	Classification 1			Classification 2			
	Primarily opportunity	Primarily necessity	Chi²-test	Only opportunity	Only necessity	Mixed	Chi²-test
Type of activity							
Own Agriculture	53.0%	73.7%	15.4★★★	44.6%	73.0%	68.2%	19.7★★★
Non-farm Business	18.5%	11.4%	3.3★	21.7%	11.7%	12.9%	4.7★
Wage Labour	14.3%	10.8%	0.9	12.0%	11.7%	13.6%	0.2
Student/Pupil	8.3%	1.8%	7.4★★★	14.1%	0.9%	2.3%	21.8★★★
Housewife	4.8%	1.2%	3.7★	5.4%	1.8%	2.3%	2.7
Unemployed	0.0%	0.6%	1.0	0.0%	0.9%	0.0%	2.0
Other	1.2%	0.6%	0.3	2.2%	0.0%	0.8%	2.7
Total	100%	100%		100%	100%	100%	
Location of activity							
Same commune	81.0%	86.2%	1.7	73.9%	86.5%	87.9%	8.7★★
Same province rural	4.8%	4.8%	0.0	6.5%	4.5%	3.8%	0.9
Same province urban	3.6%	1.8%	1.0	4.4%	1.8%	2.3%	1.4
Other province	10.7%	7.2%	1.3	15.2%	7.2%	6.1%	6.2★★
Total	100%	100%		100%	100%	100%	
N	169	168		93	112	132	

Source: Authors' own calculations based on DFG–FOR 756 Household Survey 2010.

Notes: T-Test or F-Test was calculated for comparing group means, Pearson Chi² test was calculated for comparing shares. ★ significant at the 10% level. ★★ significant at the 5% level. ★★★ significant at the 1% level.

the idea that entrepreneurship is a local or regional event (Feldman, 2001) and thus constitutes a development potential also in rural developing regions. However, the share of return migrants who were previously employed or studying in another province appears to be higher among the opportunity entrepreneurs. In this group, the share of return migrants is 15.5 per cent. In contrast, only 7.2 per cent of the necessity-only entrepreneurs are return migrants according to classification 2. A recent study from rural China also found urban to rural return migrants to be more likely to become entrepreneurs than non-migrants (Démurger and Xu, 2011). These return migrants have acquired skills in the urban centres of the country that might help them to set up more successful and innovative companies.

In terms of formal education, opportunity entrepreneurs are also better equipped with human capital. As is shown in Table 13.5, entrepreneurs primarily motivated by opportunity have acquired more than eight years of schooling on average – about 1.5 years more than entrepreneurs primarily motivated by necessity. We also asked the entrepreneurs directly to self-assess where they have acquired the skills they use for running the current business (Table 13.5). Therefore, clearly, most entrepreneurs have learned the majority of their skills from other family members while formal education is not perceived to be important. Yet again we see opportunity entrepreneurs as better skilled. They acquired skills more often in a previous business or in vocational training.

Overall, the results support our first hypothesis. Opportunity entrepreneurs are better skilled on average. This is confirmed by the business and non-farm experience the entrepreneurs have

Table 13.5 Education and Skills

	Classification 1			Classification 2			
	Primarily opportunity	Primarily necessity		Only opportunity	Only necessity	Mixed	
	Mean/ Share	Mean/ Share	t-test/ chi²-test	Mean/ Share	Mean/ Share	Mean/ Share	F-test/ chi²-test
Education of entrepreneur (years)	8.1	6.6	4.2★★★	8.3	6.6	7.3	6.5★★★
Acquired skills in school	3.0%	1.2%	1.3	3.2%	0.9%	2.3%	1.4
Acquired skills in vocational training	13.6%	6.6%	4.6★★	12.9%	8.9%	9.1%	1.1
Acquired skills in farming	9.5%	11.9%	0.5	8.6%	8.9%	13.6%	2.0
Acquired skills in previous business	14.2%	4.8%	8.7★★★	9.7%	3.6%	14.4%	8.3★★
Acquired skills in wage labour	4.1%	3.6%	0.1	5.4%	2.7%	3.8%	1.0
Acquired skills in family	60.4%	62.5%	0.2	54.8%	62.5%	65.2%	2.5
N	169	168		93	112	132	

Source: Authors' own calculations based on DFG-FOR 756 Household Survey 2010.

Notes: T-Test or F-Test was calculated for comparing group means, Pearson Chi² test was calculated for comparing shares. ★significant at the 10% level. ★★significant at the 5% level. ★★★significant at the 1% level.

acquired in previous activities, by the years spent in formal education, and by the self-assessment of skills used in the business which are more often derived from previous businesses or from vocational training. These results may also reflect that opportunity recognition requires a certain level of education or experience from other businesses. In addition, better educated people might only start a business if they have recognised an opportunity which can be explained with higher opportunity costs. Educated people also have the option to engage in better-paid wage employment. Nonetheless, opportunity entrepreneurs appear to be better skilled. These skills could help them to develop innovative business strategies.

Performance

We now test whether opportunity entrepreneurs are actually more successful compared to necessity entrepreneurs, our second hypothesis. We use two indicators for performance: profits, converted to USD purchasing power parities, and the number of employees. Comparing means shows opportunity entrepreneurs on average as achieving higher profits than necessity entrepreneurs. According to classification 1, entrepreneurs driven primarily by opportunity reach 345.8 USD of profits per month and have 0.6 employees while entrepreneurs driven primarily by necessity only reach 235.5 USD of profits and have 0.2 employees. According to classification 2, entrepreneurs driven only by opportunity reach 338.6 USD of profits per month and have 0.6 employees, entrepreneurs driven only by necessity reach 207.0 USD and have 0.1 employees, while entrepreneurs driven by both necessity and opportunity reach 328.7 USD and have 0.5 employees. Although the differences are consistently statistically significant (p<0.01), this may be a result of differences in general and location characteristics.

Consequently, we test whether the relationship remains significant in multivariate regression models while controlling for a set of other factors that may determine business success. We estimate standard ordinary least squared (OLS) regressions to separately explain profits and employment. Independent variables indicate business motivations. In the first model, classification 1 is represented by including a dummy indicating business was primarily started out of opportunity (primarily opportunity). The reference group is having started primarily out of necessity. In the second model, classification 2 is represented by one dummy for having started the business only out of opportunity (opportunity only) and one dummy for having started the business out of opportunity and necessity (mixed). Here, the reference group has started the business out of necessity only.

Further independent variables are added to control for other factors that can influence profits and employment. Primarily these are general characteristics of the entrepreneur and his/her business which influence business growth according to previous theoretical and empirical work (Storey, 1994). The years spent in formal education (education) and a dummy for having acquired skills in vocational training (vocational skills) represent the human capital of the entrepreneur that can lead to higher returns in the business. A dummy for being female (female) and a dummy for not being part of the Kinh majority (minority) reflect important socio-demographic characteristics and possible social marginality. Women entrepreneurs in Vietnam are still constrained by gender stereotypes, values and norms (Vietnam Women Entrepreneurs Council, 2007). As a result, female entrepreneurs, who are in the majority in Vietnam, could be less successful than their male counterparts. Similarly, ethnic minorities are socially disadvantaged as they often face lower returns to productive characteristics (van de Walle and Gunewardena, 2001). The largest minority groups in the research provinces are the Ede people in Dak Lak and the Taoi and Cotu people in Thua Thien-Hue. Also, the age of the business (business age) is an important control as older businesses managed to survive, had more time to grow, to learn from mistakes and to improve the business routines and are thus much more likely to be prosperous. Initial investment (initial investment) may also be an important determinant of future returns in informal activities (Grimm et al., 2011), and is also included as an independent variable (in USD purchasing power parities). Finally, sectoral affiliation is crucial. Thus, 10 dummies representing the sectors shown in Table 13.6 are added. The reference sector is retail.

Besides the general characteristics of the entrepreneurs, we control for a set of location characteristics. First of all, sales and profits could be stimulated by local demand which can be expected to be higher in communes with better access to non-farm wage employment. We measure this by calculating the share of nucleus household members of working age in other households in the same commune that are engaged in non-farm wage employment (non-farm wage rate). The distance to the next market in minutes (distance to market) could influence business profits because longer distances to markets can mean extra transportation costs and distance may lead to limited business opportunities as well. Theoretically, not only the distance to a local market but rather access to larger input and output markets are crucial. In the three research provinces, these markets can be more easily accessed in proximity to the provincial capital. Hence, the natural logarithm of the distance to these intermediate cities (distance to intermediate city) is also controlled for. Finally, many rural businesses in Vietnam are situated next to larger streets and highways such as the national highway number one. Close to such major infrastructure, businesses may be more successful due to larger sales

Table 13.6 Motivation as a Determinant of Business Success (OLS)

	Profits classification 1	Profits classification 2	Employees classification 1	Employees classification 2
Motivation:				
Primarily opportunity	0.14★★★		0.05	
(vs. primarily necessity)	(2.7)		(0.9)	
Opportunity only		0.12★★		0.07
(vs. necessity only)		(2.0)		(1.2)
Mixed (vs. necessity only)		0.22★★★		−0.00
		(4.0)		(−0.1)
General characteristics:				
10 sectoral dummies included	yes	yes	yes	yes
Business age	0.17★★★	0.17★★★	0.09★	0.09★
	(3.5)	(3.4)	(1.8)	(1.8)
Initial investment (ln)	0.45★★★	0.44★★★	0.32★★★	0.32★★★
	(7.6)	(7.5)	(5.6)	(5.7)
Education	−0.01	0.00	−0.04	−0.05
	(−0.2)	(0.1)	(−0.9)	(−0.9)
Vocational skills	0.01	0.02	−0.08	−0.07
	(0.2)	(0.3)	(−1.5)	(−1.4)
Female	−0.09	−0.09	−0.10	−0.10
	(−1.4)	(−1.3)	(−1.6)	(−1.6)
Minority	−0.05	−0.06	0.02	0.03
	(−0.9)	(−1.1)	(0.5)	(0.5)
Natural shocks	−0.12★★	−0.13★★	−0.01	−0.01
	(−2.4)	(−2.5)	(−0.3)	(−0.2)
Locational characteristics:				
Non-farm wage rate	0.16★★★	0.18★★★	0.02	0.02
	(2.7)	(3.0)	(0.4)	(0.4)
Distance to market	−0.09	−0.06	−0.00	−0.00
	(−1.6)	(−1.3)	(−0.0)	(−0.0)
Distance to intermediate city (ln)	0.02	0.03	−0.08	−0.08
	(0.4)	(0.5)	(−1.5)	(−1.4)
Two lane road	0.03	0.01	−0.09	−0.10
	(0.3)	(0.1)	(−1.1)	(−1.2)
ThuaThien Hue	−0.13★	−0.12★	−0.05	−0.05
	(−1.9)	(−1.8)	(−0.8)	(−0.8)
Dak Lak	0.08	0.07	−0.06	−0.07
	(0.8)	(0.8)	(−0.7)	(−0.8)
N	318	318	326	326
F statistic	7.71	7.94	9.19	8.88
R²	0.39	0.40	0.42	0.43
adjusted R²	0.34	0.35	0.38	0.38
LR test Motivation	7.20★★★	8.01★★★	0.89	1.10
LR test Individual characteristics	3.83★★★	3.64★★★	9.66★★★	9.71★★★
LR test Locational characteristics	2.40★★	2.50★★	0.87	0.87

Source: Authors' own calculations based on DFG-FOR 756 Household Survey 2010.

Notes: For profits, the natural logarithm was used and cases with negative or zero profits/sales had to be excluded. Displayed are standardised coefficients. t statistics in parentheses ★ $p < 0.10$, ★★ $p < 0.05$, ★★★ $p < 0.01$

markets. Consequently, we also include a dummy for being located in a village connected with a two-lane road. Finally, regional dummies are included to indicate whether the business is located in Thua Thien Hue, Dak Lak, or Ha Tinh (reference category). Thua Thien Hue is the province with the largest number of entrepreneurs and the most viable non-farm economy – particularly in Hue city – opening up new business opportunities. However, strong urban competition could also hamper businesses in rural areas due to leakage effects that occur in a later stage of non-farm development (Start, 2001).

The results of the OLS regressions are displayed in Table 13.6. We see profits as significantly influenced by entrepreneurial motivation, even after including the control variables. The results are robust for both types of classifications. Classification 1 shows entrepreneurs primarily driven by opportunity generate more profits than entrepreneurs primarily motivated by necessities. These results thus clearly support our first hypothesis. However, our second classification shows this relation as more complex. The results do reveal entrepreneurs driven only by opportunity generating significantly more profits than entrepreneurs driven only by necessities, in support of our first hypothesis. However, those businesses driven by both necessity and opportunity are also more successful than entrepreneurs driven only by necessity which also supports the first hypothesis. However, the coefficient for the mixed category is even higher than for the opportunity only category, indicating entrepreneurs motivated by both opportunity and necessity might be the most successful ones. The dichotomy of necessity versus opportunity entrepreneurship, therefore, does not hold. Opportunities predominantly determine profits while necessities only have negative implications in the absence of such opportunities. If they simultaneously appear with opportunities, they might even function as an additional motivation to engage in the business that improves the performance of the business in terms of profits.

Furthermore, the general characteristics show some interesting results. Sectoral affiliation determines business success, with construction being the most profitable non-farm sector. Construction businesses are easy to implement in a rural environment and appear to be the major beneficiaries of the economic growth that has occurred in the three research provinces in the last decade. At the same time the sector is traditionally highly sensitive to economic fluctuation. In addition, the age of the business is crucial. As expected, older businesses have been able to generate more sales and to become more successful over time than younger businesses. The strongest effect of all independent variables is the initial investment, which is also hardly surprising. Entrepreneurs, who invest more in the beginning, may be more serious and more committed throughout and may thus realise larger returns later on. Education and vocational training, in turn, seem not to be very important determinants of profits. This may be surprising at first sight. However, given the low technological level of the majority of non-farm businesses in rural areas, we see education not playing a strong role in determining business success. Also, gender and ethnicity do not play strong roles as determinants of business success in the specification as the effects are statistically insignificant. Females and ethnic minorities do generate lower profits than males and ethnic Vietnamese, which can mainly be attributed to differences in initial investments which are controlled for in the regressions. Females and ethnic minorities initially invest less money in their businesses. Small businesses thus do not help to ease the generally problematic situation of Vietnamese ethnic minorities in terms of living standards (Dang, 2010). The role of the location characteristics is limited to the local non-farm wage rate. Profits are significantly higher when more people are working in non-agricultural wage employment in other households in the same commune. This could be explained by higher incomes and greater demand for products and services in regions with better access to non-farm wage employment. The other location factors do not show any significant effects on profits when controlling for general business characteristics and motivation.

In contrast to profits, the results for employment do not confirm our second hypothesis. When controlling for general and location characteristics, the effect of business motivation does not remain a significant determinant of employment figures regardless of the classification, and can be explained by the fact that a large number of businesses fall in the category of single employee self-employed.. Non-farm businesses in rural Vietnam often hesitate to grow in terms of employment. We found 91 per cent of all entrepreneurs not planning to hire additional non-family employees in the next year. Again 91 per cent of these entrepreneurs state lack of work as the main reason. Opportunity entrepreneurs are slightly more willing to hire non-family employees (11.3 per cent vs. 4.9 per cent; $p < 0.01$). Yet, as is shown in the multivariate analyses, their overall capability to create employment for other rural households is limited.

Conclusions

In this chapter we evaluate whether opportunity entrepreneurs in rural Vietnam have a greater potential to perform well than necessity entrepreneurs by applying the concept of necessity and opportunity entrepreneurship. We show that, although the concept has so far been primarily applied to developed countries, distinguishing necessity and opportunity entrepreneurs is very suitable in a rural developing country context if some contextual specifics of the rural environment are taken into account. First, many entrepreneurs in the rural environment are motivated by a combination of both necessity and opportunity (Solymossy, 1997; Hughes, 2003; Giacomin et al., 2011; Brünjes, 2012). Second, unemployment should not be regarded as the primary necessity faced by rural people in developing countries. Instead, underemployment, risks, and shocks, often related to agricultural production, can lead to low incomes and poverty. Rural necessity entrepreneurs then start informal businesses in order to supplement and increase their incomes and to avoid poverty. Third, opportunity entrepreneurs in rural areas of developing countries are also not comparable to those of developed countries. Perceived opportunities predominantly relate to local market potentials or to business new to an area rather than technological upgrading and innovation.

Nonetheless, opportunity entrepreneurs have greater entrepreneurial skills than necessity entrepreneurs. They have a farming background less often but instead have been involved in non-farm businesses before or started their business directly after school or university more often. As a consequence they are better educated and more experienced in doing business. In terms of output, entrepreneurs motivated by opportunity generate higher profits even after controlling for general business characteristics and location characteristics. This is even the case for businesses that are motivated by both necessity and opportunity. Starting a business out of necessity is thus not automatically a hopeless endeavour. Necessity entrepreneurs are only less successful if they do not perceive an opportunity at the same time.

However, like necessity entrepreneurs, opportunity entrepreneurs have only a relatively limited capacity to generate non-farm employment for other households. At this point, we can only speculate about the reasons. One might conclude this is because perceived opportunities in the rural environment rarely relate to innovative business ideas and businesses are often not oriented towards employment growth. But in the case of Vietnam, institutional bottlenecks as a consequence of the transition process are also plausible. A lack of policies providing support for households and individuals in early phases of the entrepreneurship process still remains (Ha, 2007). The missing willingness is probably the most difficult challenge. There are widespread negative and indifferent attitudes towards small and medium enterprises among policy makers at different levels of the administration. So far, business development programmes have been largely driven by the central administration. Yet, the majority of programmes need to be understood, supported and implemented by local policy makers, often at the provincial and district level. This is often not the case. For example, the enterprise reform of 2000 was generally positively evaluated by foreign donors. However, implementation was hindered by government bodies at different levels that were not aware of a need for reform (GTZ and CIEM, 2006). The SME Development plan 2006–2010 recognises inefficient and ineffective administration as one of the key challenges in the future. Accordingly, civil servants often do not have a professional working attitude and lack working ethics. Possibly as a result, 'SMEs are still considered to be a complementary sector of the economy, which often violates the laws and their key role in economic structural shift has not been widely recognized' (Agency for SME Development, 2006). Vietnamese scholars note traders and entrepreneurs as ranked low in the society, partly due to traditional cultural values in Vietnam rooted in Chinese-originated Confucianism (Hoang and Dung, 2009; Huy, 1998). However, negative attitudes regarding entrepreneurship may be among the most critical challenges in the support of entrepreneurship in rural Vietnam.

Entrepreneurs motivated by opportunity appear to have a greater potential to become drivers of future endogenous development in the rural non-farm economy due to their generally greater entrepreneurial ability. Opportunity entrepreneurs in rural areas in developing countries may not be as innovative as their counterparts in urban areas or in developing countries. Yet they constitute one of the very few valuable and scarce resources at the 'bottom of the pyramid' (Prahalad, 2005) that could result in future endogenous non-farm growth in rural areas. In order to achieve a spatially balanced and endogenous growth in rural Vietnam, future research needs to focus on how to exploit the 'hidden' entrepreneurial potential.

Notes

1 A previous version of this chapter has been published as chapter 6 in Brünjes (2012).
2 Since the incorporation in the Global Entrepreneurship Monitor (GEM) in 2001, national levels of opportunity and necessity entrepreneurship are observable in a number of developed and developing countries (Reynolds et al., 2002).
3 A limited number of studies analyse motivations for entrepreneurship in urban areas. Swierczek and Thai (2003) find that business owners in Hanoi, Hue city and Ho Chi Minh City are often motivated by challenge and achievement while necessity is less important. In turn, Benzing et al. (2005) note that businesses in Hanoi and Ho Chi Minh City have also started to increase income and to create jobs for family members.
4 The household sample reduced from 2,195 households in 2007 to 2,136 in 2008 and 2,099 in 2010 because of attrition.
5 We added this module only to every second household questionnaire in order to save time and costs. The households that were interviewed with the extended questionnaire were selected randomly before the survey.
6 Other reasons often mentioned were that the household member was too old to pursue any other occupation (necessity reasons), or intrinsic motives like simply enjoying doing this kind of business (opportunity reason).
7 If the manual observation of the primary reason is inconclusive, the secondary reason for starting the business is used in this classification.
8 Survival analysis requires longitudinal data.
9 Such activities are, for example traditional healers, mobile tents, or veterinary services.

References

Adom, K. and Williams, C.C. (2012). Evaluating the motives of informal entrepreneurs in Koforidua. Ghana. *Journal of Developmental Entrepreneurship*, 17(1), 1–19.

Agency for SME Development (2006). *Small and medium enterprise development 5 year plan 2006–2010.* Hanoi: ASMED.

Amit R. and Muller E. (1995). 'Push' and 'pull' entrepreneurship. *Journal of Small Business and Entrepreneurship*, 12(4), 64–80.

Arias A. and Pena I. (2010). The effect of entrepreneurs' motivation and the local economic environment on young venture performance. *International Journal of Business Environment*, 3(1), 38–56.

Benzing, C., Chu, H.M. and Callanan, G. (2005). A regional comparison of the motivation and problems of Vietnamese entrepreneurs. *Journal of Developmental Entrepreneurship*, 10(1), 3–25.

Beresford, M. (2008). Doi Moi in review: The challenges of building market socialism in Vietnam. *Journal of Contemporary Asia*, 38(2), 221–243.

Bhola, R., Verheul, I., Thurik, R. and Grilo I. (2006). Explaining engagement levels of opportunity and necessity entrepreneurs. EIM Working Paper Series. Research report H200610. Retrieved from http://hdl.handle.net/1765/9705

Block, J.H. and Wagner, M. (2010). Necessity and opportunity entrepreneurs in Germany: characteristics and earnings differentials. *Schmalenbach Business Review*, 62(4), 154–174.

Brünjes, J. (2012). *Non-farm wage labour and entrepreneurship in rural Vietnam.* Göttingen: Optimus Verlag.

Brünjes, J. and Diez, J.R. (2013a). 'Recession push' and 'prosperity pull' entrepreneurship in a rural developing context. *Entrepreneurship and Regional Development*, 25(3–4), 251–271.

Brünjes, J. and Diez, J.R. (2013b). Non-farm businesses in rural Vietnam – response to crisis or exploiting opportunities? In: Tamásy, C. and Diez, J.R. (eds), *Regional resilience, economy and society – globalising rural places.* Washington, DC: Ashgate, 115–130.

Chambers, R. (1995). Poverty and livelihoods: whose reality counts? *Environment and Urbanization*, 7(1), 173–204.

Chaudhry, P. and Ruysschaert, G. (2007). Climate change and human development in Viet Nam: a case study. *Human Development Occasional Papers*, 46, 1–17.

Dang, H.-A. (2010). A widening poverty gap for ethnic minorities. In: Hall, G. and Patrinos H. (eds), *Indigenous peoples, poverty and development.* Washington, DC: Cambridge University Press, 304–343.

Démurger, S. and Xu H. (2011). Return migrants: the rise of new entrepreneurs in rural China. *World Development*, 39(10), 1847–1861.

Ellis, F. (1998). Household strategies and rural livelihood diversification. *Journal of Development Studies*, 35(1), 1–38.

Ellis, F. (2000). *Rural livelihoods and diversity in developing countries.* New York: Oxford University Press.

Feldman, M.P. (2001). The entrepreneurial event revisited: firm formation in a regional context. *Industrial and Corporate Change*, 10(4), 861–891.

Garschagen, M., RevillaDiez, J., Nhan, D.K. and Kraas, F. (2012). Socio-economic development in the Mekong Delta: between the prospects for progress and the realms of reality. In: Renaud, F. and Künzer, C. (eds), *The Mekong Delta system – interdisciplinary analyses of a river delta.* The Netherlands: Springer, 83–132.

General Statistics Office (2009). *Results of the survey on household living standards 2008.* Hanoi: Statistical Publishing House.

Giacomin, O., Janssen, F., Guyot, J.-l. and Lohest, O. (2011). Opportunity and/or necessity entrepreneurship? The impact of the socio-economic characteristics of entrepreneurs. Unpublished working paper.

Gries, T. and Naudé, W. (2010). Entrepreneurship and structural economic transformation. *Small Business Economics*, 34(1), 13–29.

Grimm, M., Krüger, J. and Lay, J. (2011). Barriers to entry and returns to capital in informal activities: Evidence from Sub-Saharan Africa. *Review of Income and Wealth*, 57(Supplement s1), 27–53.

GTZ, CIEM(2006). *Six years of implementing the enterprise law – issues and lessons learnt.* Hanoi: GTZ Office Hanoi.

Gurtoo, A. and Williams, C.C. (2009). Entrepreneurship and the informal sector: Some lessons from India. *The International Journal of Entrepreneurship and Innovation*, 10(1), 55–62.

Günther, I. and Launov, A. (2011). Informal employment in developing countries: Opportunity or last resort? *Journal of Development Economics*, 97(1), 88–98.

Ha, L.V. (2007). *Start-up in Dak Lak Province.* Hanoi: GTZ Office Hanoi.

Haggblade, S., Hazell, P.B.R. and Dorosh, P.A. (2007). Sectoral growth linkages between agriculture and the rural nonfarm economy. In: Haggblade, S., Hazell, P.B.R. and Reardon, T. (eds), *Transforming the rural nonfarm economy.* Baltimore, MD: Johns Hopkins University Press, 141–182.

Hardeweg, B., Praneetvatakul, S., Duc, T.P. and Waibel, H. (2007). Sampling for vulnerability to poverty: cost effectiveness versus precision. *Proceedings of Tropentag 2007 – Conference on international agricultural research for development*, University of Kassel-Witzenhausen.

Hoang, V.Q. and Dung, T.T. (2009). The Cultural Dimensions of the Vietnamese Private Entrepreneurship. *The IUP Journal of Entrepreneurship Development*, 6(3–4), 54–78.

Hughes, K.D. (2003). Pushed or pulled? Women's entry into self-employment and small business ownership. *Gender, Work and Organization*, 10(4), 433–454.

Huy, N.N. (1998). The Confucian incursion into Vietnam. In: Slote, W.H. and d. Vos, G.A. (eds), *Confucianism and the family.* New York: State University of New York, 91–103.

Kelley, D., Bosma, N. and Amorós, J.E. (2011). *Global Entrepreneurship Monitor 2010 – global report.* Babson Park, Santiago, London: Global Entrepreneurship Research Association.

Mausch, K., Revilla Diez, J. and Klump, R. (2012). Rural-rural differences in Vietnames pro-poor growth: does households' income composition make a difference? In: Klasen, S. and Waibel, H. (eds), *Vulnerability to poverty: Theory, measurement and determinants.* Basingstoke, UK: Palgrave Macmillan, 136–162.

Naudé, W. (2010). Entrepreneurship, developing countries, and development economics: new approaches and insights. *Small Business Economics*, 34(1), 1–12.

Oostendorp, R.H., Trung, T.Q. and Tung, N.T. (2009). The changing role of non-farm household enterprises in Vietnam. *World Development*, 37(3), 632–644.

Prahalad, C.K. (2005). *The fortune at the bottom of the pyramid.* Upper Saddle River, NJ: Pearson Education, Inc.

Reardon, T. (1997). Using evidence of household income diversification to inform study of the rural nonfarm labor market in Africa. *World Development*, 25(5), 735–747.

Reardon, T., Berdegué, J., Barrett, C.B. and Stamoulis, K. (2007). Household income diversification into rural nonfarm activities. In: Haggblade, S., Hazell, P.B.R. and Reardon, T. (eds), *Transforming the rural nonfarm economy.* Baltimore, MD: Johns Hopkins University Press, 115–140.

Revilla Diez, J., (1999). Vietnam: addressing profound regional disparities. In: Yue, C. S. (ed), *Southeast Asian Affairs.* Singapore: Institute of Southeast Asian Studies Press, 358–374.

Reynolds, P.D., Camp, S.M., Bygrave, W.D., Autio, E. and Hay, M. (2002). *Global Entrepreneurship Monitor 2001 – summary report.* Babson Park, London: London Business School and Babson College.

Rosa, P., Kodithuwakku, S. and Balunywa, W. (2007). Entrepreneurial motivation in developing countries: what does 'necessity' and 'opportunity' entrepreneurship really mean? *Frontiers of Entrepreneurship Research*, 26(20), 531–542.

Smith, N. (1967). The entrepreneur and his firm: The relationship between type of man and type of company. Occasional Papers, Bureau of Business and Economic Research, Michigan State University, 109.

Solymossy, E. (1997). Push/pull motivation: does it matter in venture performance? *Frontiers of Entrepreneurship Research*, 17(5), 204–217.

Start, D. (2001). The rise and fall of the rural non-farm economy: poverty impacts and policy options. *Development Policy Review*, 19(4), 491–505.

Storey, D.J. (1994). *Understanding the small business sector.* Thomson Learning Emea.UK: Cengage Learning EMEA.

Swierczek, F.W. and Thai, T.H. (2003). Motivation, entrepreneurship and the performance of SMEs in Vietnam. *Journal of Enterprising Culture*, 11(1), 47–68.

van de Walle, D. and Gunewardena, D. (2001). Sources of ethnic inequality in Viet Nam. *Journal of Development Economics*, 65(1), 177–207.

Verheul, I., Thurik, R., Hessels, J. and van der Zwan, P. (2010). Factors influencing the entrepreneurial engagement of opportunity and necessity entrepreneurs. EIM Research Reports, H,2010/11, 1–24.

Vietnam Women Entrepreneurs Council (2007). *Women's entrepreneurship development in Vietnam.* Hanoi: ILO Office Vietnam.

Völker, M. and Waibel, H. (2010). Do rural households extract more forest products in times of crisis? Evidence from the mountainous uplands of Vietnam. *Forest Policy and Economics*, 12(6), 407–414.

Williams, C.C. (2007). The nature of entrepreneurship in the informal sector: evidence from England. *Journal of Developmental Entrepreneurship*, 12(2), 239–254.

Williams, C.C. (2009). Entrepreneurship and the off-the-books economy: some lessons from England. *International Journal of Management and Enterprise Development*, 7(4), 429–444.

Williams, C.C. (2010). Spatial variations in the hidden enterprise culture: some lessons from England. *Entrepreneurship and Regional Development*, 22(5), 403–423.

Williams, C.C. and Gurtoo, A. (2011). Evaluating competing explanations for street entrepreneurship: some evidence from India. *Journal of Global Entrepreneurship Research*, 1(2), 3–19.

Williams, C.C. and Gurtoo, A. (2012). Evaluating competing theories of street entrepreneurship: some lessons from Bangalore, India. *International Entrepreneurship and Management Journal*, 8(4), 391–409.

Williams, C.C. and Horodnic, I. (2015). Self-employment, the informal economy and the marginalisation thesis: some evidence from the European Union. *International Journal of Entrepreneurial Behaviour and Research*, 21(2), 224–242.

Williams, C.C. and Nadin, S. (2010). Entrepreneurship and the informal economy: an overview. *Journal of Developmental Entrepreneurship*, 15(4), 361–378.

Williams, C.C. and Round, J. (2009). Evaluating informal entrepreneurs' motives: some lessons from Moscow. *International Journal of Entrepreneurial Behaviour and Research*, 15(1), 94–107.

Williams, C.C.and Youssef, Y.A. (2014). Is informal sector entrepreneurship necessity- or opportunity-driven? Some lessons from urban Brazil. *Business and Management Research*, 3(1), 41–53.

Williams, C.C., Nadin, S., Newton, S., Rodgers, P. and Windebank, J. (2013). Explaining off-the-books entrepreneurship: a critical evaluation of competing perspectives. *International Entrepreneurship and Management Journal*, 9(3), 447–463.

Williams, N. and Williams, C.C. (2014). Beyond necessity versus opportunity entrepreneurship: some lessons from English deprived urban neighbourhoods. *International Entrepreneurship and Management Journal*, 10(1), 23–40.

World Bank (2011). *World development indicators and global development finance*. Washington, DC: World Bank.

14

BEING AN ENTREPRENEUR OF THE VICENARIAN AND TRICENARIAN GENERATION

The case of Turkish entrepreneurs, 2006–2012[1]

Esra Karadeniz and Ahmet Özçam

Introduction

In the last two decades, many developing countries have faced considerable population growth (Levesque and Minniti, 2011). Turkey is one such developing country with a population of 76.7 million and a growth rate of almost 1.2 percent. Turkey has a fairly young population with almost 42.3 percent under 24 years of age, while only around 6.7 percent are over 65 years old. One-third of young people in Turkey are unemployed. This is important so far as entrepreneurship is concerned because age has been identified as one of the most important determinants of the level of entrepreneurship (Kautonen et al., 2014), even if several other factors are also known as triggering factors, including household income, education, gender, networking, perception of opportunity, trust in own skills, fear of failure, and so forth (Arenius and Minniti, 2005; Koellinger et al., 2005; Özdemir and Karadeniz, 2011).

In this chapter, therefore, we explore the determinants of entrepreneurship in Turkey using data covering the 2006–2012 period. Moreover, our intention is that the methodology we use contributes to the existing literature. Commonly, the Logistic or Probit models are used in the case where the dependent variable is a binary variable (0 or 1) representing the entrepreneurship status of the person. So far, there have been voluminous studies in the literature investigating the factors that affect entrepreneurship.

The interpretations of the parameters in these studies have been done so far in two ways as follows:

i) The estimated parameter values have been discussed only in terms of their signs (+ or −) and therefore only a pure directional result was extracted.
ii) The interpretations of Odds Ratios (OR) have been given.

For example, according to the Odds Ratio one may assert that men are 50 percent more likely to be entrepreneurs compared to their women counterparts and therefore one can

171

obtain only a relative measure. Even though this piece of information is important, it brings forth only a comparative conclusion. For example, although men are said to be twice as likely to be entrepreneurs compared to women, the exact probability of being entrepreneurs for men and women (like 10 percent and 15 percent or 20 percent and 30 percent) has not been discussed. Although there exists another method which uses the Cumulative Distribution Function (CDF) directly in interpreting the Logistic and Probit models in the econometric literature (Greene, 2012; Wooldridge, 2003), this approach has not been used in the literature on entrepreneurship so far according to the authors' best knowledge. As such, this chapter makes a methodological contribution.

In this chapter we aim at calculating precisely the probability of being an entrepreneur under different scenarios of characteristics of persons. We will stress the importance of the age factor in particular (Storey, 1994; Grilo and Thurink, 2004; Bosma and Harding, 2007; Delmar and Davidson, 2000; Parker, 2009; Kautonen et al, 2011). Moreover, the age variable will be combined together with other factors like gender, income, network, fear, skill, and opportunity. In this respect, we will seek answers to the following questions:

i) Does the probability of being an entrepreneur increase up to a certain age level and decrease afterwards? If so, what is this age level in Turkey? Is it at the age of 20s (Vicenarian) or at 30s (Tricenarian) of the person or perhaps at an age level in a later period in the person's life?

ii) Does the maximum probability of being an entrepreneur change when the age factor is considered along with the other variables like gender, income, fear, skill, opportunity . . .?

iii) How do the different categorizations of the other factors, for example gender (female or male) affect the probability of being an entrepreneur as the age variable increases?

Theoretical background

Entrepreneurship studies have generally been analyzed at three levels, micro, meso, and macro (Verheul et al., 2003). In this chapter, we will research on a micro level which focuses on the decision-making process by individuals and people's motives to become business owners and self-employed. Therefore, we examine personal factors, such as personality traits, education levels, family background, and previous work experience. At the micro level, researchers analyze why some people become entrepreneurs and others do not. There are certain economic, demographic, and perceptual factors that determine entrepreneurship.

Demographic and economic characteristics

In general, and across all countries, entrepreneurs are mostly men. Several studies demonstrate that there is significant difference in the rate of entrepreneurship between men and women (Grilo and Irigoyen, 2006). According to Reynolds et al. (2002), men are about twice as likely to be involved in entrepreneurship activity as women.

The variable of age has been widely reported in every study of a representative sample of nascent entrepreneurs. The likelihood of becoming self-employed varies with age. Many business owners are within the age category of 25 to 45 years old (Storey, 1994; Uhlaner and Thurik, 2004). Nascent entrepreneurship rates are highest in the age category of 25–34 years old and least prevalent in the 55–64 year old group (Bosma and Harding, 2007). Delmar and Davidson (2000), Arenius and Minniti (2005), and Levesque and Minniti (2006) suggest that people increasingly start a business at a younger age.

The importance of education on entrepreneurship has been extensively covered in the literature; however, the impact of education on entrepreneurship and entrepreneurial success is tentative (Storey, 1994). Delmar and Davidson (2000) and Arenius and Minniti (2005) show clearly the positive effect of education on nascent entrepreneurs. However, Uhlaner and Thurik (2004) show that a higher level of education in a country is accompanied by a lower self-employment rate. Blanchflower (2004) reports education being positively correlated with self-employment in the US, but negatively in Europe. Grilo and Irigoyen (2005) report a U-shape relationship between education and entrepreneurship.

The entrepreneurial decision is positively related to individual's incomes. Moreover, the availability of income weakens financial constraints. The assumption here is that in economics only those with sufficient available financial resources are able to get involved in creating a new firm.

Perceptual variables

It is apparent that perceptual variables have a major influence on the likelihood that a particular individual may become involved in early-stage entrepreneurial activity. These relate in particular to their perception of opportunities within their environment, belief in their skills to be able to successfully start a new enterprise, their having recent entrepreneurs as role models within their personal network and a reduced reluctance to become involved in entrepreneurial activity through fear of failure (Arenius and Minniti, 2005; Koellinger et al., 2005).

Knowing other entrepreneurs may influence an individual's propensity to start a business. Formal and informal networks (Aldrich and Martinez, 2001) and importance of role models (Wagner and Sternberg, 2004) are significant factors for entrepreneurial decisions. Networks are a rich source for entrepreneurs to get information and other resources about the opportunities they will pursue. Social networks provide information about opportunities.

Opportunity recognition represents the most distinctive and fundamental entrepreneurial behavior (Eckhardt and Shane, 2003; Shane and Venkataraman, 2000). This confirms the entrepreneurship definition of Kirzner that entrepreneurs are individuals who are more likely than others to be *alert* to identification and exploitation of profit opportunities.

Another factor that may influence an individual's propensity to start a business is the fear of failure. In America, the fear of failure is less of a deterrent factor because failure is considered to be part of the learning process (Saxenian, 1994). On the contrary, entrepreneurial failure is highly dishonored in Europe (European Commission, 2003) and those who go bankrupt tend to be considered as "losers." In cultures where a relatively greater tolerance and/or acceptance of entrepreneurial failure exists, a far larger proportion of the adult population tend to engage and become involved in entrepreneurial activities.

Confidence in one's own skill, knowledge, and ability to start a new business increases entrepreneurial alertness and, therefore, leads to the creation of more business (Verheul et al., 2003). Individual self-confidence, defined as individuals' belief in their capability to perform a task, influences the development of both entrepreneurial intentions and actions or behaviors (Boyd and Vozikis, 1994).

Data and definitions of variables

Data

The data used in this chapter were collected by means of the national adult population survey (APS) from the Global Entrepreneurship Monitor (GEM) project conducted in Turkey covering the years 2006–2012. The dataset consisted of 14,600 interviews with a representative sample of adults (18–64 years old). Random Sampling Method was used and CATI (Computer Assisted Telephone Interview) was conducted by the vendor company.[2]

The Turkish population was 76,667,864 in 2013 according to the Population Survey conducted by the Turkish Statistical Institute (TurkStat). The percentages of males and females were found to be 50.2 percent and 49.8 percent respectively. In our sample of 14,600 persons, we found these percentages to be 52.4 percent and 47.6 percent respectively. Therefore we can assert that our sample is quite representative of the whole population with respect to gender.

Definitions of variables

Dependent Variable:

Being a TEA Entrepreneur (TEA=1) or Not a TEA Entrepreneur (TEA= 0)

Independent variables:

1   Age (AGE): between 18 and 64 years,
2   Household income (INC): Lower 33 percent = 1, Middle 33 percent = 2 and Upper 33 percent = 3,
3   Education (EDUCATION): 1 = up to Second degree, 2 = Second degree, 3 = Post Second, 4 = Graduate,
4   Gender (GENDER): Male = 1 and Female = 2,
5   Knowing entrepreneurs (NETWORK): Respondents were asked whether they knew someone personally who had started a business in the 24 months preceding the survey: (NO = 0, YES = 1),
6   Opportunity perception (OPPORT): Respondents were asked if they believed that, in the six months following the survey, good business opportunities would exist in the area where they lived: (NO = 0, YES = 1),
7   Self-confidence (SKILL): Respondents were asked whether they believed that they had the knowledge, skill, and experience required to start a business: (NO = 0, YES = 1),
8   Fear of Failure (FF): Respondents were asked whether the fear of failure would prevent them from starting a business: (NO = 0, YES = 1).

Econometric specification

The logistic and linear probability models

In Table 14.1, the Model-1 (column 2) is the *Logistic Regression Model* (LRM) and is obtained starting from a full model including all possible interactions of the independent variables. See Appendix 14.A at the end for details. Among the independent variables only EDUC is insignificant and is therefore discarded. Then we have a total of seven remaining independent variables (Age, Inc, Gender, Network, Opport, Skill, and FF). The Age variable enters the regression in a quadratic fashion. Additionally two Interactive Terms are kept: AGE*FF and INC*NETWORK.[3]

Table 14.1 Estimation of Being a TEA Entrepreneur

INDEPENDENT VARIABLES	LOGISTIC REGRESSION MODEL (MODEL-1)	LINEAR PROBABILITY MODEL (MODEL-2)
Constant	−5.2885 (0.00★★)	−0.015 (0.68)
AGE	0.1195 (0.00★★)	0.0064 (0.00★★)
AGE^2	−0.0019 (0.00★★)	−9.92E−05 (0.00★★)
INC	0.6255 (0.00★★)	0.0252 (0.00★★)
GENDER	−0.856 (0.00★★)	−0.0616 (0.00★★)
NETWORK	1.6982 (0.00★★)	0.0506 (0.03★★)
OPPORT	0.4748 (0.00★★)	0.042 (0.00★★)
SKILL	1.027 (0.00★★)	0.06605 (0.00★★)
FF	−0.7533 (0.051★)	−0.0604 (0.013★★)
AGE★FF	0.0171 (0.097★★)	0.012 (0.038★★)
INC★NETWORK	−0.4597 (0.00★★)	0.003 (0.76)
McFaddedR²	0.154	−
Akaike criterion	0.5355	0.2986
Schwarz criterion	0.5471	0.3102
No of Correctly Predicted	90.48%	−
No of Obs.	6,460	6,460

Note: The numbers in parentheses are the p-values. (★★) indicates 5% significance level and (★) indicates 10% significance level.

Then the Logistic Regression Model (LRM) is given as:

$$\Pr(TEA = 1) = G(\beta_0 + \beta_1 AGE + \beta_2 AGE^2 + \beta_3 INC + \\ \beta_4 GENDER + \beta_5 NETWORK + \beta_6 OPPORT + \\ \beta_7 SKILL + \beta_8 FF + \beta_9 AGE \star FF + \\ \beta_{10} INC \star NETWORK) = G(B'X) \tag{1}$$

where G(.) is the Cumulative Logistic Distribution Function, B is a(11 × 1) vector of coefficients, and X is a (11 × 1) vector in which we have a constant term, seven independent variables (Age and Age squared are separate variables) and the two Interaction Terms.

Arenius and Minniti (2005) find that the EDUCATION variable is not significant and that the perceptual variables do not depend on GENDER. In our chapter, we reach similar results in that EDUCATION is not significant either and GENDER does not enter either of the two interaction terms which are AGE★FF and INC★NETWORK. Therefore, the perceptual variables do not seem to differ with respect to gender.

In the third column of Table 14.1 (Model-2), we present the Linear Probability Model (LM). The derivatives of the independent variables in LM are simply the estimated coefficients but their magnitudes are not directly comparable with those of LRM which are presented in the second column of the same table (Model-1). They can be compared with those of the Logistic Regression Model (LRM) only after we calculate the derivatives of the independent variables from the estimated coefficients in LRM.[4]

To accomplish this, we write the derivatives of independent variables in LRM in general as:

$$\frac{\partial \Pr(TEA = 1)}{\partial x_j} = g(B'X) \frac{\partial (B'X)}{\partial x_j} \tag{2}$$

where the (11×1) vectors of X and B are as defined above, $g(B'X)$ is a Scaling Factor (SF) and $g(.)$ is the Probability Density Logistic Function. The x_j s are the independent variables $j = 1, 2, \ldots 7$ (Age, Inc, Gender, Network, Opport, Skill, and FF).

For our GENDER, OPPORT, and SKILL variables (those which do *not* appear in the interaction terms), Eq. (2) implies (for $j = 3, 5$, and 6):

$$\frac{\partial \Pr(TEA = 1)}{\partial x_j} = g(B'X) \star \beta_{j+1} \tag{3}$$

whereas for INC, NETWORK, and FF variables (those which also appear in the interaction terms), Eq. (2) implies (for $j = 2, 4$ and 7):

$$\frac{\partial \Pr(TEA = 1)}{\partial x_j} = g(B'X) \star (\beta_{j+1} + \beta_i \star OTHER) \tag{4}$$

where β_i is the coefficient of the Interaction Term, $i = 9$ or 10, and *OTHER* is the other independent variable rather than x_j in the Interaction Terms.

In Table 14.2, we are now able to compare the derivatives (or marginal effects) of the Logistic Regression Model (LRM) with those of the Linear Probability Model (LM) using Eq. (3) and (4) above. The derivatives of the independent variables in both models are evaluated at the sample means of all independent variables in order to represent the typical characteristics of entrepreneurs in the sample. We observe that the derivatives obtained from these two models are extremely close to each other for each of the independent variables, except the FF variable, since perhaps this variable was interacted with a quadratic variable such as AGE.[5] The closeness of estimated derivatives confirms that our calculations are correct.

These derivatives (marginal effects) in Table 14.2 (second column), imply that when the person is a male (GENDER), then the probability of being an entrepreneur increases by 6 percent holding all other variables at their sample means. Similarly, the probabilities of being an entrepreneur increase by 3.3, 5.2, 3.3, 7.2, and 0.75 percent when the person's income increases and she belongs to the next upper class (INC), knows an entrepreneur personally (NETWORK), believes good business opportunities exist in the area (OPPORT), believes she has knowledge, skill and experience (SKILL), and has no fear of failure (FF) respectively. We observe that SKILL has the highest effect (7.2 percent) and FF has the lowest effect (0.75 percent).

Here, we believe that there are three additional important issues to be discussed. First, in the literature of entrepreneurship, we frequently observe that *only the signs* of the estimated coefficients or some Odds Ratios are interpreted in Logistic Regression Models (LRM) rather than the exact calculations of probabilities (the probability of being an entrepreneur) as we are trying to show explicitly in this chapter. Second, in the Linear Probability Model (LM), the coefficients refer to the change in the probability of being an entrepreneur given a unit change in the independent variable and this constant marginal effect is the same irrespective of the levels at which the other variables are held constant, whereas in the LRM,

Table 14.2 Comparison of Derivatives from the Logistic Regression Model (LRM) with Those of the Linear Probability Model (LM)

INDEPENDENT VARIABLES	DERIVATIVES OF LOGISTIC REGRESSION MODEL (MODEL-1)	DERIVATIVES OF LINEAR PROBABILITY MODEL (MODEL-2)
GENDER	−0.06	−0.0616
INC	0.0329	0.0252
NETWORK	0.0515	0.0506
OPPORT	0.033	0.042
SKILL	0.072	0.06605
FF	−0.0075	−0.0604

being a nonlinear model, changing magnitudes of the partial effects are introduced since the derivative now depends on the specific values of the independent variables, for example on B'X as given by Eq. (2).[6] In other words, the simple constant marginal effect (coefficient) in LM can be obtained approximately by LPM by fixing the values of the independent variables at their sample means as we tried to show in Table 14.2. Third, when we are concerned about calculating the exact probabilities of being an entrepreneur for persons with different economic/social/personal characteristics combined (as in this chapter), the combined levels at which these characteristics are fixed matter substantially.

To show this important dimension, we now turn to the estimation of probability of being an entrepreneur by allowing the AGE variable to change together with the other characteristics of the persons in turn using our Eq. (1).

The probability of being a TEA entrepreneur of the Vicenarian and Tricenarian generation

Levesque and Minniti (2006) discuss the potential implications of age for individuals' employment status. Building on the theory of time allocation in which individuals distribute their time between income-producing activities and leisure and particularly on time allocations with newly formed ventures (Levesque and Minniti, 2011), they additionally introduce the effect of age and show the individuals' preferences with respect to occupational choices (to be an entrepreneur or not) to be a function of age using a theoretical optimization model in which the individuals maximize their utility by deciding how many hours to allocate to working and how to distribute those hours between waged labor and entrepreneurship at each time period. They confirm the empirical fact that new firm creation is a young man's game and therefore find that the age variable is an inherent factor triggering entrepreneurship. In their theoretical model, they argue that, for any individual a threshold age exists which is critical for the allocation of that individual's working time between waged labor and trying to start a new firm. This theoretical inverse U-shaped relationship between age and the entrepreneurial activities is also supported by many empirical studies (Blanchflower, 2004; Grilo and Irigoyen, 2006).

In this chapter we are also particularly interested in the probability of the *Vicenarian* and *Tricenarian* generation to be an entrepreneur (Wikipedia). These terms refer to the part of the population aged 20s and 30s respectively (the term *Early Adulthood* refers to people of age 20–39). It seems very reasonable to think that as the individual gets older, leisure becomes more important as displayed by the total amount of remaining working activities declining over time along with the total discounted income (from a stream of expected future incomes) from entrepreneurship diminishing as well. Clearly, the model by Levesque and Minniti (2006) refers to TEA entrepreneurs and not established entrepreneurs, since they mention that in their model, wage labor and starting a new business are not mutually exclusive and the individual can carry out a certain amount of both. Similar to their mathematical work, our aim in this chapter is to investigate empirically whether there really exists an inverse U-shaped relationship between the probability of being a TEA entrepreneur and age, and if so, what is this threshold age level, using the Turkish GEM data, 2006–2012. Moreover, we would like to examine the other demo-economic and perceptual variables together with age. We believe that the best way to do this is by using the cumulative distribution function of the Logistic Regression Model (LRM) and measuring the age variable on the horizontal axis as in Figure 14.1. Then, the probabilities of being an entrepreneur with respect to the other characteristics of the individual over her working life span can be represented by various functions.

In Figure 14.1 we show the probabilities of being a TEA entrepreneur with respect to AGE and GENDER together in the case of Turkey. The upper function displays the chances of being a MALE entrepreneur as AGE that varies from 18 to 64 whereas the lower function shows the chances for a FEMALE one (using Eq. (1)). In the middle function the GENDER variable is fixed at the sample mean which is 1.476 (47.6 percent female and 52.4 percent male persons). All three functions are concave, displaying increasing but diminishing returns up to the age of 33.2 at which they are maximum. After this age, the returns become negative.[7] The maximum probabilities for men, sample mean, and female are 0.11, 0.078 and 0.05 respectively. This is at the age of 33.2. The difference in probability between male and female 0.06 (0.11–0.5) corresponds to the *derivative* of the GENDER variable obtained from LRM shown in the second column of Table 14.2 which was − 0.06.[8] Conducting a comprehensive study covering 28 countries about the effects of demo-economic and perceptual variables on nascent entrepreneurs, Arenius and Minniti (2005) found that women

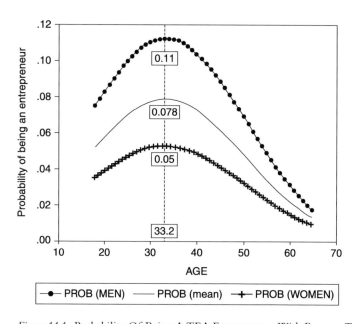

Figure 14.1 Probability Of Being A TEA Entrepreneur With Respect To Gender And Age

are only half as likely to start a new business as men and that this was consistent with previous empirical findings (Reynolds et al., 2002). In Figure 14.1 we found a similar result (0.11 is about twice as big as 0.05) and therefore Turkey does not seem to be an exception in this respect. However, using Eq. (1) (the cumulative distribution function of the Logistic Regression Model (LRM)) additionally allowed us to calculate the precise (exact) levels of the probabilities of being an entrepreneur.

Therefore we have two important results. First, because in those 28 countries, even though the men might be twice as likely to be entrepreneurs as women, the probability levels could be 12 percent versus 6 percent, 16 percent versus 8 percent or 20 percent versus 10 percent and so on . . . and therefore be quite different when the exact levels of probabilities are calculated in each of those countries. Second, Levesque and Minniti (2006) argue that, consistent with the empirical and theoretical literature, the relationship between age and the likelihood of starting a new business picks up at a relatively early age and decreases thereafter. This is precisely what we have checked in Figure 14.1 by allowing the AGE variable to be quadratic in Eq. (1). The probability of being a TEA entrepreneur increases up to the age of 33.2 (threshold age) and decreases afterwards. However, a traditional approach of LRM often used in the entrepreneurship literature which aims at interpreting the estimated coefficients in terms of Odds Ratios does not allow one to reach such a general result; for example, what are the exact probabilities with respect to age or precisely after which age the returns to age start effectively decreasing?

This threshold age level (33.2) can be found mathematically as follows:

$$\frac{\partial \Pr(TEA = 1)}{\partial AGE} = g(B'\bar{X}) \star (\beta_1 + 2\beta_2 AGE + \beta_9 \bar{FF})$$

$$= \exp(B'\bar{X}) \star (\beta_1 + 2\beta_2 AGE + \beta_9 \bar{FF}) / (1 + \exp(B'\bar{X}))^2 = 0 \qquad (5)$$

where $\bar{X}$ is the vector in which all independent variables except for AGE are held constant at their sample means. The solution to Eq. (5) is:

$$AGE = (-\beta_1 - \beta_9 \bar{FF})/(2\beta_2) = (-0.1195 - 0.0171 \star 0.313)/(2 \star - 0.0019) = 33.2 \qquad (6)$$

since exp(.) is strictly positive for all values in its domain.

Moreover, the *difference* in the probability of being an entrepreneur between men and women is shown in Figure 14.2. As expected, this difference has a maximum of 0.06 precisely at the age of 33.2. However, more interestingly we observe that this differential also has a concave shape. This leads us to our important result that the *Gender Difference* is increasingly important up to the age of 33.2, covering all of the ages of the 20s and part of the 30s (up to 33.2) and decreasing steadily afterwards. Therefore, we conclude that the gender differential does depend on age. For example at the ages of 45, 50, 55, 60, and 65 the difference is equal to 0.05, 0.04, 0.028, 0.02, and 0.01 respectively. This is an important result because it indicates that the gender difference is more important for younger entrepreneurs than for older entrepreneurs.

Results

We present our conclusions with respect to gender in the following corollary. Corollary 1: Men seem to be *twice* as likely to be entrepreneurs compared to women and the relationship

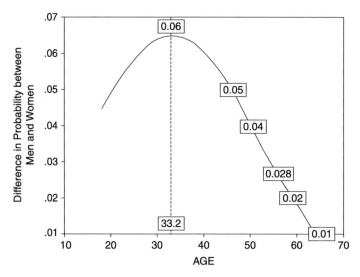

Figure 14.2   Gender Difference In Probability Of Being A TEA Entrepreneur With Respect To Age

between age and the likelihood of starting a new business peaks at a *relatively early age* as found empirically in 28 countries. First, we can assert additionally that in the case of Turkey using data from 2006–2012, the *exact* probability of being an entrepreneur is 0.11 for men and 0.05 for women and therefore we are able to give a measure of levels of probabilities of being entrepreneurs for men and women rather than a simple relative measure (a ratio like 2 to 1). Second, we found that the early age after which the returns to age of being an entrepreneur become negative discussed in the literature was about 33.2 for Turkey (in the 30s or tricenarian generation). Third, this threshold age level (33.2) corresponds precisely to the peak (maximum) difference in probability of being entrepreneurs between men and women. Therefore, not only does this threshold age level represent a maximum for both men and women, but it is also the age level at which the discrepancy in entrepreneurial activity is highest for these two categories. Put differently, it is the age level at which gender is most important. Moreover, the gender gap becomes much less important as entrepreneurs get older; for example after the age of 50, the gender gap is less than 4 percent.

We may interpret perhaps the fear of failure (FF) variable as representing the risk propensity (risk aversion). In Figure 14.3, we compare the probabilities of being a TEA entrepreneur with respect to fear of failure (FF) over the working age of the individual. Note that the FF variable was used in the Interaction Term with AGE and therefore we find that the highest probabilities for the two categories (No Fear = 0 and Yes Fear = 1) differ with respect to age. The maximum probabilities of being a TEA entrepreneur are 8.3 percent and 7 percent at the ages of 32 and 36 respectively for these two categories as shown in Figure 14.3. At the age of 44, there is no difference. Moreover at ages greater than 44, the difference becomes quite small, implying that FF is not a significant factor for older TEA entrepreneurs. Being able to graph the non-linear cumulative logistic function allowed us to draw such results.

Therefore we conclude that the fear factor contributes more to being an entrepreneur at early stages of working life than later. For young people seeking entrepreneurship, the probability of starting a firm seems to be much higher for risk lover individuals (FF=0), since the expected reward of the stream of future incomes from entrepreneurship might be higher. Given the fact that younger individuals have less experience and less knowledge about the

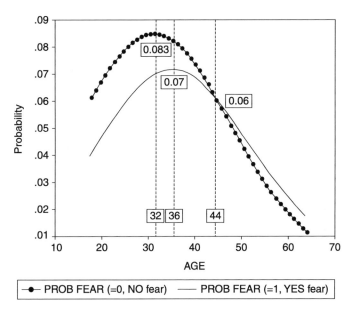

Figure 14.3 Probability Of Being A TEA Entrepreneur With Respect To Fear Of Failure And Age

difficulties to be encountered once they enter the entrepreneurial profession, it seems like they may fear less and may be more confident due to their inexperience.

Corollary 2: For young people seeking entrepreneurship, the probability of starting a firm seems to be much higher for risk lover individuals (FF = 0). However, the fear factor becomes much less important, and the degree of risk taking practically makes no difference as the person becomes older. In this sub-section we would like to compare the highest possible probabilities of SKILL (=1), NETWORK (=1), GENDER (=1, Male), INCOME (=3), and OPPORT (=1) when these variables are set at their highest categories in turn, while the other variables are set at their sample means as before. In Figure 14.4, first we see that the highest probabilities occur for the variables of SKILL and NETWORK with the probabilities of being a TEA entrepreneur equaling 12.4 percent and 12.2 percent respectively. Second, being a MALE entrepreneur and having the highest level of INCOME (=3) affect the probability somewhat less. They are 11.5 percent and 11.4 percent respectively. Finally, someone who believes that good business opprtunities exist in the area they live in (OPPORT) has the lowest probability. This probability is only 10.3 percent.

When we compare Graph-3 with Graph-4 above we observe that FF has a lower impact than SKILL, NETWORKING, GENDER, INCOME, or OPPORT.

In Figure 14.5, we observe that when a man is self-confident (Skill) and knows an entrepreneur (Networking), his probability of being a TEA entrepreneur can rise up to 25.8 percent at the age of 33.2.

Conclusions

In this chapter we have calculated the *exact* probability of being an entrepreneur with respect to its demographic, economic, and perceptual determinants like age, gender, education, knowing an entrepreneur, fear of failure, and so forth. Moreover, we looked at the probability of being an entrepreneur when the age variable was considered together with the other

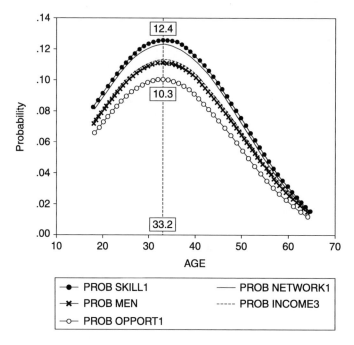

Figure 14.4   Probability of Being A TEA Entrepreneur When Skill, Network, Gender, Income And Opportunity Are At Their Highest Categories

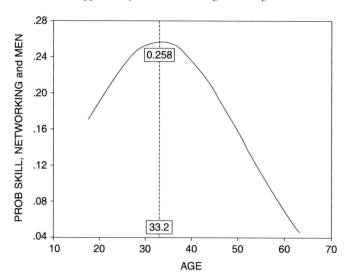

Figure 14.5   Probability Of Being A TEA Entrepreneur When Skill, Networking And Gender Are Together At Their Highest Categories

characteristics of the persons. An important contribution of our work is the rather long span of time (2006–2012) that it covers. Moreover, we hope that our methodology contributes to entrepreneurship scholarship. Commonly, the Logistic or Probit models are used in the case where the dependent variable is a binary variable (0 or 1) representing the entrepreneurship status of the person. Even though the Odds Ratio interpretation is common in the literature, we preferred to use the Cumulative Distribution Function (CDF) in interpreting the estimated parameters of the Logistic Regression Model.

We found men to be *twice* as likely to be entrepreneurs compared with women and the relationship between age and the likelihood of starting a new business peaks at a *relatively early age* as found empirically in some 28 countries. First, we could assert additionally that in the case of Turkey, using data from 2006–2012, the *exact* probability of being an entrepreneur is 0.11 for men and 0.05 for women and therefore we were able to give a measure of the probability of being an entrepreneur for men and women rather than a simple relative measure (a ratio like 2 to 1). Second, we found that the early age after which the returns to age of being an entrepreneur become negative discussed in the literature was about 33.2 for Turkey (in the thirties). Thirdly, we also found this threshold age level (33.2) to correspond precisely to the peak (maximum) difference in probability of entrepreneurship between men and women. Therefore, not only did this threshold age level represent a maximum for both men and women, but it was also the level of age at which the discrepancy in entrepreneurial activity was highest for these two categories. Consequently, the gender gap was found to be much less important in the case of older entrepreneurs; for example at age after 50, it was found to be less than 4 percent. Fourthly, we found the fearless factor to contribute more to being an entrepreneur at early stages of working life than later, which agrees with our common sense. Fifthly, we found that the subjective belief of having adequate skills and knowing other entrepreneurs contributed the most to the probability of being an entrepreneur, equaling 12.4 percent and 12.2 percent respectively at the age of 33.2 when these two variables were considered separately. Finally, when skills and networking are considered jointly, the probability of being an entrepreneur increased up to 25.8 percent.

Acknowledgments

The authors are grateful to Republic of Turkey Small and Medium Enterprises Development Organization (KOSGEB), Turkish Economy Bank (TEB), and Yeditepe University for their support and contribution to Global Entrepreneurship Monitor (GEM) project.

Notes

1 The authors thank the GEM Project team for their initiative contribution, KOSGEBS (Small and Medium Enterprises Development Organization), Siemens and Technological Development Association of Turkey, Ak Bank and Endeavour in Turkey for their financial support.

2 The vendor company, Akademetre is a member of the European Society of Opinion, Marketing Researchers (ESOMAR), and the Turkish Association of Marketing, and Opinion Researchers. It has an honour agreement with Association of Researchers and possesses ISO 9000-2001 quality certification.

3 The sample averages of variables are as follows: TEA (0.095), AGE (37.87), INC (2.095), GENDER (1.476), NETWORK (0.339), OPPORT (0.365), SKILL (0.506), FF (0.313). Due to individual-level missing data and the exclusion of established entrepreneurs, our final sample included 6,460 observations out of 14,600 interviews.

4 Since six of our seven independent variables (except Age) are binary or discrete variables, an alternative calculation of the marginal effects is to take the *difference* in cumulative probabilities when these binary or discrete (discontinuous) values are plugged in Eq. (1) above, using the sample means of all other independent variables. Our formulation in Eq. (3) and (4) above is an approximation that is often surprisingly accurate (Greene, 2012).

5 The small discrepancies arise from the fact that LRM is a nonlinear model. An alternative approach to calculate the derivatives in LRM is taking the average of squared of AGE rather than plugging the average value of AGE which is 37.87 into the quadratic function in AGE in B'X. The difference is rarely large (Wooldridge, 2003).

6 In LM, except for AGE which is thought to be quadratic and exhibiting diminishing and later negative effects. This reflects a concave-shaped behavior which agrees with the literature and our intuition.

7 Empirical studies have shown the critical peak of entrepreneurial activity to be around 25 to 34 years of age, even though the exact number varies across countries and is linked to the level of development of each country (Levesque and Minniti, 2011).

8 Since Male=1 and Female=2, the estimated derivative of GENDER is negative.

References

Aldrich, H. E. and Martinez, M. A. (2001). Many are called, but few are chosen, an evolutionary perspective for the study of entrepreneurship. *Entrepreneurship Theory and Practice*, 25(4), 41–56.

Arenius, P. and Minniti, M. (2005). Perceptual variables and nascent entrepreneurship. *Small Business Economics*, 24(3), 233–247.

Blanchflower, D. G. (2004). Self-employment, More may not be better, NEBE. Working Paper 10286.

Bosma, N. and Harding, R. (2007). Global entrepreneurship, GEM 2006 summary results. Babson College and London Business School, London and Babson Park, MA.

Boyd, N. G. and Vozikis, G. S. (1994). The influence of self-efficacy on the development of entrepreneurial intentions and actions. *Entrepreneurship Theory and Practice*, 18(4), 63–77.

Delmar, F. and Davidson, P. (2000). Where do they come from? Prevalence and characteristics of nascent entrepreneurs. *Entrepreneurship and Regional Development*, 12(1), 1–23.

Eckhardt, J. T. and Shane, S. A. (2003). Opportunities and entrepreneurship. *Journal of Management*, 29(3), 333–349.

European Commission (2003). Green Paper Entrepreneurship in Europe. Report no. COM(2003) 27, Brussels: Commission of the European Communities.

Greene, W. H. (2012). *Econometric analysis*. Prentice Hall, 7th Edition.

Grili, I. and Irigoyen, J. M. (2006). Entrepreneurship in the EU, to wish and not to be. *Small Business Economics*, 26(4), 305–318.

Grilo, I. and Thurink, R. (2004). Determinants of entrepreneurship in Europe, Max Planck Institute Discussion Paper on Entrepreneurship Growth and Public Policy, 3004, Jena, Germany, Max Planck Institute of Economics.

Kautonen, T., Tornikoski, E. T. and Kibler, E. (2011). Entrepreneurial intentions in the third age, the impact of perceived age norms. *Small Business Economics*, 37(2), 219–234.

Kautonen, T., Simon, D. and Minniti, M. (2014). Ageing and entrepreneurial preferences. *Small Business Economics*, 42(3), 579–594.

Koellinger, P., Minniti, M. and Schade, C. (2005). I think I can, I think I can, overconfidence and entrepreneurial behavior, DIW, Discussion Papers No.501, Berlin, Germany.

Levesque, M. and Minniti, M. (2006). The effect of aging on entrepreneurial behavior. *Journal of Business Venturing*, 21(2), 177–194.

Lévesque, M. and Minniti, M. (2011). Age matters, how demographics influence aggregate entrepreneurship. *Strategic Entrepreneurship Journal*, 5(3), 269–284.

Özdemir, Ö. and Karadeniz, E. E. (2011). Investigating the factors affecting total entrepreneurial activities in Turkey. *METU Studies in Development*, 38 (December), 275–290.

Parker, S. C. (2009). *The economics of entrepreneurship*. Cambridge: Cambridge University Press.

Reynolds, P., Bygrave, W. D., Autio, E. and Hay, M. (2002). *Global Entrepreneurship Monitor, 2002 executive monitor*. London, London Business School.

Saxenian, A. (1994). *Regional advantage*. Cambridge, MA, Harvard University Press.

Sepúlvedaa, J. P. and Bonillab, J. A. (2014). The factors affecting the risk attitude in entrepreneurship, evidence from Latin America. *Applied Economics Letters*, 21(8), 573–581.

Shane, S. and Venkataraman, S. (2000). The promise of entrepreneurship as a field of research. *Academy of Management Review*, 25(1), 217–226.

Storey, D.J. (1994). *Understanding the small business sector*. London, New York, Routledge.

Uhlaner, L. M. and Thurik, A.R. (2004). Post materialism influencing total entrepreneurial activity across nations. Discussion papers on Entrepreneurship, Growth and Public Policy, No 07-2004. Jena: Max Planck Institute for Research into Economic Systems.

Verheul, I., Uhlaner, L. M., and Thurik, A. R. (2003). Business accomplishments, gender and entrepreneurial self-image, Scales Paper; N2003 12. Zoetermeer, EIM.

Wagner, J. and Sternberg, R. (2004). Start-up activities, individual characteristics, and the regional milieu, Lessons for entrepreneurship sort policies from German micro data. *Annals of Regional Science*, 38(2), 219–240.

Wooldridge, J. M. (2003). *Introductory econometrics, a modern approach*. Mason, OH Michigan: South-Western.

DEPENDENT VARIABLE: *Being an Entrepreneur TEA=1 and Not an Entrepreneur TEA=0*

INDEPENDENT VARIABLES	INITIAL LOGISTIC REGRESSION MODEL (LRM) USING ALL INTERACTIONS	LOGISTIC REGRESSION MODEL (LRM) (MODEL-1)
Constant	−4.587 (0.0001**)	−5.2885 (0.00**)
AGE	0.1096 (0.0027**)	0.1195 (0.00**)
AGE^2	−0.001936 (0.0**)	−0.0019 (0.00**)
INC	0.6757 (0.041**)	0.6255 (0.00**)
EDUC	−0.0002 (0.96)	−
GENDER	−1.4451 (0.01**)	−0.856 (0.00**)
NETWORK	1.8849 (0.001**)	1.6982 (0.00**)
OPPORT	0.1885 (0.75)	0.4748 (0.00**)
SKILL	0.3972 (0.55)	1.027 (0.00**)
FF	−0.376 (0.58)	−0.7533 (0.051*)
AGE*INC	0.00089 (0.88)	−
AGE*GENDER	0.0099 (0.33)	−
AGE*NETWORK	−0.0074 (0.42)	−
AGE*OPPORT	−0.0067 (0.46)	−
AGE*SKILL	0.0096 (0.37)	−
AGE*FF	0.0165 (0.12)	0.0171 (0.097**)
INC*GENDER	−0.0439 (0.76)	−
INC*NETWORK	−0.486 (0.00**)	−0.4597 (0.00**)
INC*OPPORT	0.0549 (0.68)	−
INC*SKILL	−0.016 (0.92)	−
INC*FF	−0.121 (0.42)	−
GENDER*NETWORK	0.0317 (0.88)	−
GENDER*OPPORT	0.2242 (0.30)	−
GENDER*SKILL	0.2819 (0.27)	−
GENDER*FF	−0.0219 (0.93)	−
NETWORK*OPPORT	0.2161 (0.26)	−
NETWORK*SKILL	0.0244 (0.92)	−
NETWORK*FF	−0.1682 (0.46)	−
OPPORT*SKILL	−0.0611 (0.80)	−
OPPORT*FF	0.1523 (0.49)	−
SKILL*FF	−0.0401 (0.87)	−
McFadden R²	0.156	0.154
Akaike criterion	0.5404	0.5355
Schwarz criterion	0.5729	0.5471
No of Correctly Predicted	90.48%	90.48%
No of Obs.	6,460	6,460

Note: *The numbers in parentheses are the p-values.* (**)*indicates 5% significance level and* (*) *indicates 10% significance level.*

In Table-A above, the Logistic Regression Model (LRM) with Interactions (second column) is the initial model where the independent variables EDUC, OPPORT, SKILL and FF are insignificant individually. Moreover, all interaction terms except INC*NETWORK are insignificant. To reduce the dimensionality of the initial model we used a stepwise elimination of independent variables starting with the ones which had the highest p-values down to lower ones. The final form of Logistic Regression Model (Model-1) is given in column 3. Both Akaike and Schwarz criteria improved to some extent. In both models, 90.48% of the observations of the dependent variable are correctly predicted using a value of 0.5. In the final model (Model-1) the EDUCATION variable is not significant. Perhaps this is not surprising, since the extant literature on growth and entrepreneurship has not explained yet why certain countries exhibit higher rates of innovation and competitiveness despite low R&D expenditures and educational attainments (Levesque and Minniti, 2011).

15

FACTORS ENTERPRISES PERCEIVE TO INFLUENCE THEIR SUCCESS

A case study of agribusiness in Laos

Sutana Boonlua

Introduction

Lao People's Democratic Republic (PDR) or Laos is a market-orientated economy and has experienced high rates of economic growth prior to the global economic crisis. The country has been able to attract foreign investment and increase exports to both regional and international markets. While other countries have focused more on developed countries as trading partners and overlooked regional and emerging markets, Laos has realized it is well placed to take advantage of its geographical proximity to emerging markets and therefore has adopted this alternative trading strategy (Vorachith, 2010). On the whole, however, Laos suffers from low labor productivity and subcontracting has been heavily used in production processes (Kimura, 2002; Kongmanila and Takahashi, 2010).

As a member of the Association of Southeast Asian Nations (ASEAN) and the ASEAN Free Trade Area (AFTA) since 1995, and World Trade Organization (WTO) since 2013, Laos has sought to integrate itself into the regional and world trading system. To do so, it believes that it is necessary to develop the private sector to encourage domestic and international investment and increase exports. Its focus in order to achieve this is to take advantage of its geographical position as a "land-linked country" and to pursue a regional integration strategy. However, Laos needs to create a production base that is favorable to member countries in order to create a long-term sustainable economy (Boonlua and Aditto, 2013).

In the context of the Millennium Development Goals and the Laotian strategic imperative to graduate from its least developed country status by 2020 (Vorachith, 2010), the strategy has sought to promote exports, foreign direct investment (FDI), official development assistance, private sector development, and tourism. Nevertheless, the Laos economy is currently in a weak position with a domestic gross product (GDP) of US\$ 11,771,725,798, a 7 percent GDP growth rate, and a population of 6.9 million in 2014 (World Bank, 2015) compared to its neighbors such as Vietnam. The impact of the financial crises around the world, trade barriers increasing, and a higher number of international competitors are among the difficulties faced. The weakening of the US dollar and the relative strengthening of the local currency have also meant greater financial risks for exporters, especially small and medium enterprises (SMEs).

Given this macro-economic perspective, this chapter examines SME agribusinesses in Laos and their perceptions of the factors that influence the success of their enterprises. In Laos, raw materials, particularly mineral ore, timber, and other natural resources, are exported to supply processing industries in neighboring countries. In the case of timber, the nature of the problem is complicated because countries such as China, Thailand, and Vietnam are large importers of timber to supply their advanced wood-processing industries. Local efforts to ban the export of timber from Laos is a controversial topic fuelled by the conflicting argument over whether it is better to adopt bans in order to force the development of a local wood-processing industry or to take advantage of the revenue gained from exports, particularly in the initial phase of the country's capital accumulation (Vorachith, 2010). The continued export of timber with little value creation has disadvantaged the local wood-processing industry, which suffers from inadequate inputs of raw material and a sawmill capacity exceeding timber supply in the country. The wood-processing industry in Laos is also disadvantaged by the lack of funding, skilled labor, and markets for processed wood products. The intention in this chapter, therefore, is to examine the factors perceived to influence the success of enterprises operating SME agribusinesses in Laos.

Entrepreneurship and Laos culture

One argument is that entrepreneurship is heavily related to the existence of the "spirit of capitalism" and "protestant work ethic" (Weber, 1930; Dana, 1993). This means that the existence of entrepreneurship can be traced to the existence of the values of frugality, deferred gratification, and asceticism. Dana (1993) argues that the existence of such cultural attributes disposes people toward entrepreneurial activity, similar to Weber (1930) who argues that entrepreneurial behavior is influenced by values, beliefs, and disbeliefs. In Japan, similarly, entrepreneurship results from the existence of cultural attributes associated with hard work, diligence, and frugality inspired by Confucianism from Chinese culture. Indeed, Wu (1983) identified these Chinese cultural values as 1) a high propensity to save and re-invest business earnings; 2) a universal strong desire to secure a better education for their children who would then be expected to carry on the business; and 3) a strong sense of loyalty and mutual obligation within the extended Chinese family.

The Lao culture, meanwhile, is heavily influenced by Theravada Buddhism. It is common for boats cruising the Mekong river to dock for the crew to jump ashore to light incense and pray. Modern Laos was created as a result of a series of Siamese-French treaties signed between 1893 and 1907. Subsequently, France united the Lao principalities into one political entity, a French protectorate. The French were not particularly interested in Laos, except as a buffer zone between economically important French Vietnam and the British colonies further west, particularly Burma or Myanmar. In 1949, Laos was recognized as an independent associate within the French union after Japan occupied Laos in 1941 and eventually forced King Srisavang Vong to declare independence from France (Dana, 1993). In 1953, Laos became a constitutional monarchy. The United States, to encourage loyalty to the democratic cause and to counter expanding North Vietnamese power, between 1968 and 1973, gave US$ 0.5 billion to Laos, making it one of the highest per capita recipients of foreign aid in the world (Dana, 1993). Following the 1975 withdrawal of the United States from Vietnam, the communist Lao People's Revolutionary Party took control of Laos and renamed it the Lao People's Democratic Republic. The hammer and sickle was adopted as the national symbol, and strict economic policies immediately reduced private enterprise in the new state. Agriculture collectivized and businesses were nationalized. From 1975 to

1986, the closed economy operated at a subsistence level. In 1986, the Fourth National Congress of Laos decided to embark on a program of reform. In 1987, Laos restored diplomatic and economic relations with China. The first legal code was enacted in 1988. The first official constitution was drafted in 1990. The collapse of Soviet-style communism resulted in the introduction of free enterprise in Laos. The emergence of entrepreneurship, therefore, needs to be understood in this historical context.

Hypotheses

Scrimgeour et al. (2006) argue that the success of agribusiness depends not only on the choices of agribusiness firms and organizations, but also on the environment in which they operate. It is appropriate to carefully identify and characterize the trends and shocks which have therefore impacted on agribusiness. Five key contextual foci have been identified as follows:

1) Government Factor: Economic and political change has substantial impacts. Changes in international economic conditions: incomes, exchange rates, energy price, as well as political changes (e.g., trade rules, terrorism and counter-terrorism policies, monetary and fiscal policies) are all significant to firm performance. Agribusiness entrepreneurs must be aware of the changing views on competition policy, tax policy, government expenditure priorities, environmental, health and employment regulations as they all impact on the success of agribusiness.

2) Business Factor: The evolution of agribusiness and its success is part of the wider evolution of business. Individual firms and organizations are adapting on the back of increased wealth, changing market and political conditions, and the evolution of marketing and sector organizations. Commercial change in other sectors impacts on how agribusinesses evolve.

3) Technology Factor: Technological change is a significant element of agribusiness success. This is partly a matter of introducing new technologies as a result of scientific research or technical innovation, and partly a result of organizational response to market conditions. For example, technological change associated with large lambs in New Zealand has primarily been led by price signals. Technology can influence either agribusiness in general, or merely sectors within it. New generic technologies such as ICT have substantially impacted almost all agribusiness activities while specific advances in precise activities (e.g., vacuum-packing technologies) have had a major impact on particular activities and products.

4) Social Factor: Social change is important for agribusiness. Changing social expectations impact the choices of SMEs' entrepreneurs, customers, and regulators. Likewise, businesses are increasingly realizing the importance of understanding changes in consumer values and beliefs as a critical determinant of long-term demand patterns. These sociometric measures of changing social values are important for agribusiness in all their neighboring markets, which are the major markets for Laos.

5) International Factor: The principals of businesses with more resources, denser information and business networks, and considerable management experience are more likely to be successful in doing business in the international market (Westhead, 2001). However, Terstriep (2009) confirms that networks can successfully support the SMEs in their efforts to reach out to the international market. Businesses with more resources, denser information and business networks, and considerable management experience are more likely to be successful in doing business in the international markets (Westhead, 2001). That requires certain prerequisites in an organization, the ability to work in teams, and openness toward other cultures. Also, the small companies are limited in their efforts in

the global market by low managerial and financial knowledge, and resource restrictions (Brouthers et al., 2009). Therefore, concentrating on a small number could be a success factor for importing and exporting small companies.

Accordingly, five hypotheses are developed as follows:

H_1:   *Government factors positively affect the Laos enterprises*
H_2:   *Business factors positively affect the Laos enterprises*
H_3:   *Technology factors positively affect the Laos enterprises*
H_4:   *Social factors positively affect the Laos enterprises*
H_5:   *International factors positively affect the Laos enterprises*

Methodology

The sample size in this research is calculated through the Yamane (1967) formula. The formula is applied to the population considering 95 percent confidence level and 5 percent sampling error. Calculation sample size is estimated as follows:

$$n = \frac{P(1-P)^2}{e^2} \tag{1}$$

Where: n = the sample size
          P = component of sample proportion variance estimate (maximized at 0.5)
          e = the tolerable error level for estimation (5 percent or 0.05)

Thus

$$n = \frac{0.5(1-0.05)^2}{(0.05)^2}$$
$$n = 180.5$$

Therefore, a sample of 181 is sufficient (Aaker, Kumar, and Day, 2001). Aaker, Kumar, and Day (2001) state that a 20 percent response rate is deemed sufficient to analyze the data. In this study, the response rate was 44 percent.

To collect data, a questionnaire was used because a representative sample can be collected from the chosen population in a variety of locations at a low cost (Greene, 2003; Hair et al., 2006). The questionnaire in this research consists of two parts. Part one asks for general information about the key informant such as gender, age, level of education, experience in SMEs in agribusiness, initial capital, type of agribusiness, number of laborers, location, government support programs, loan, input sources, and main markets. Part two, meanwhile, contains 24 questions about the factors influencing the success of the entrepreneurs. These items are adapted from literature and are designed on a five-point Likert scale, rating from 1 (Irrelevant) to 5 (Critical).

A weighted Likert scale was used to measure Laos enterprises' perceptions on success factors. Each scale indicates the respondent's level of agreement with a statement measured on a five-point scale, with "1" irrelevant, "5" critical and "3," some importance. The success of an SME's agribusiness owner is calculated as a function of the five categories of variables (measured on a 5-point Likert-type scale) and characteristics of the firm, the owner and the financial situation. Implicitly, the empirical model can be written as follows:

$$TTT = f(TG, TB, TT, TS, TI, \varepsilon) \tag{2}$$

Where:

TTT = The success factors among enterprises in Laos
TG = Government factor
TB = Business factor
TT = Technology factor
TS = Social factors
TI = International factor
ε = Error term

Findings

The Likert scale was used to measure the levels of significance for factors influencing the success of enterprises in Laos. The higher the score, the more important are the variables as evaluative criteria. Five-point scales were used to measure the importance of factors in such a way that the mean score could be calculated to examine the importance of factors to the perceptions of success factors among SME agribusiness firms in Laos. With five-point scales, it means that the scores falling between the following ranges could be considered as (Boonlua, 2011):

4.51 – 5.00   Critical
3.51 – 4.50   Important
2.51 – 3.50   Some importance
1.51 – 2.50   Minimal importance
1.00 – 1.50   Irrelevant

In this research, the respondents are the enterprises in Laos. The 80 respondent characteristics are described by the demographic characteristics of gender, level of education, and experiences in agribusiness (see Table 15.1).

The results show that 56 percent of respondents are female and most of the respondents have a secondary level of education (34 percent). The majority (75 percent) of respondents has less or equal to 10 years of experience in agribusiness.

The characteristics of the agribusiness firms are presented by type of agribusiness, location, skill of labor, funds (LAK), source of funds, inputs, distribution, and supportive programs (see Table 15.2). The results indicate that most firms are located outside the industrial estate (80 percent), have both skilled and unskilled labor (50 percent each), have about 5,000,001 –10,000,000 LAK of funds (25 percent), do not borrow for the short term from any sources (89 percent), possess funds other than internally generated (31 percent), have inputs of production proceeding from domestic sources (91 percent), serve the domestic market (95 percent), and support training on improving business skill (41 percent).

Descriptive findings

Table 15.3 shows the mean and standard deviations for the variables under the perceptions of factors influencing the success of Laos enterprises in the government factor. All factors are rated in terms of their level of importance (mean = 3.01, S.D. = 1.05). It can be seen that

Table 15.1 Respondent Characteristics

	Frequency	Percentage
Gender		
Male	35	43.75
Female	45	56.25
Total	**80**	**100.00**
Level of Education		
Did not go to school	0	0.00
Elementary	12	15.00
Secondary	27	33.75
Lower/higher vocational	8	10.00
Undergraduate	24	30.00
Post graduate	9	11.25
Total	**80**	**100.00**
Experiences in Agribusiness (Years)		
Less or equal 10	62	77.50
11 – 20	12	15.00
21 – 30	3	3.75
31 – 40	3	3.75
Higher than 40	0	0.00
Total	**80**	**100.00**

Table 15.2 Laos Agribusiness Firms' Characteristics

	Frequency	Percentage
Type of Agribusiness		
Delicatessen	28	35.00
Beauty products and health	4	5.00
Agricultural and chemical	8	10.00
Others	40	50.00
Total	**80**	**100.00**
Location		
In the industrial estate	16	20.00
Outside the industrial estate	64	80.00
Total	**80**	**100.00**
Skill of labor (Answer more than 1)		
Skilled	80	50.00
Unskilled	80	50.00
Total	**160**	**100.00**
Funds (LAK)		
Less or equal 5,000,000	19	23.75
5,000,001 – 10,000,000	20	25.00
10,000,001 – 50,000,000	19	23.75
50,000,001 – 100,000,000	9	11.25
Higher than 100,000,000	13	16.25
Total	**80**	**100.00**

Loan status	Short-term loan		Long-term loan	
	Frequency	*Percentage*	*Frequency*	*Percentage*
Borrow	9	11.25	13	16.25
Not borrow	71	88.75	67	83.75
Total	**80**	**100.00**	**80**	**100.00**
Source of Funds				
Family or relatives		8		25.00
Commercial banks		6		18.75
Government or state banks		6		18.75
Loan sharks		2		6.25
Others		10		31.25
Total		**32**		**100.00**
Inputs				
Domestic		73		91.25
Import		7		8.75
Total		**80**		**100.00**
Distribution				
Domestic markets (at least 60%)		76		95.00
International markets		4		5.00
Total		**80**		**100.00**
Supportive Programs				
Knowledge to improve business skill		13		40.63
Special interest rate for funds		5		15.62
Lower price for production inputs		5		15.62
Distribution supportiveness		9		28.13
Others		0		0.00
Total		**32**		**100.00**

under these four variables, namely national political changes in the country (mean = 2.88, S.D. = 1.44), government policy to support and encourage investment in the country (mean = 3.46, S.D. = 1.28), exchange rate (mean = 3.09, S.D. = 1.33), and changes in interest rate policy (mean = 2.63, S.D. = 1.32) are rated of minor importance by respondents indicating that these factors are not really important for the SMEs in Laos. The obstacles from the government policy are not rated as critical success factors by Laos enterprises.

Table 15.4 shows the mean and standard deviations for variables under the business factor influencing the success of Laos enterprises. It can be seen that under these six variables, operational experiences of the enterprises (mean = 3.83, S.D. = 1.05), amount of the investment or working capital in the enterprises (mean = 4.15, S.D. = 0.87), the plans/targets of the enterprises are clarified (mean = 3.84, S.D. = 1.02), good financial management within the enterprises (mean = 3.95, S.D. = 0.91), and executive/entrepreneur with abilities to take advantages from competitiveness (mean = 3.78, S.D. = 1.27), are rated important by respondents indicating that these factors are perceived as quite important by SMEs in Laos for their success. Being well organized in dividing functions within enterprises (mean = 3.33,

Table 15.3 Perceptions of Government Factors in Influencing the Success of Laos Enterprises

	Mean	S.D.	Level of Importance
1. National political changes in the country	2.88	1.44	Some importance
2. Government policy to support and encourage investment in the country	3.46	1.28	Some importance
3. Exchange rate	3.09	1.33	Some importance
4. Changes in interest rate policy	2.63	1.32	Some importance
Total	3.01	1.05	Some importance

Table 15.4 Perceptions of Business Factors in Influencing the Success of Laos Enterprises

	Mean	S.D.	Level of Importance
1. Operational experiences of the enterprises	3.83	1.05	Important
2. Amount of the investment or working capital in the enterprises	4.15	0.87	Important
3. The plans/targets of the enterprises are clarified	3.84	1.02	Important
4. Good financial management within the enterprises	3.95	0.91	Important
5. Executive/entrepreneur with abilities to take advantages from competitiveness	3.78	1.27	Important
6. Well organized in dividing functions within enterprises	3.33	1.35	Some importance
Total	3.81	0.78	Important

S.D. = 1.35) is considered of only minor importance. The SMEs in Laos consider business factors, especially setting goals, controlling the cash flow and working experience in doing business as more important in determining success than setting up the internal functions within enterprises.

Table 15.5 shows that the mean and standard deviations for variables under the technology factor for Laos enterprises (mean = 3.63, S.D. = 0.77). The quality management and product quality control system (mean = 4.21, S.D. = 0.91) and modern technology changes in production process (mean = 3.96, S.D. = 1.18) are considered to be important while the invention and creation of new products (mean = 3.46, S.D. = 1.17) and the appropriated proportion of skilled labors in the enterprises (mean = 2.88, S.D. = 1.27) are considered to be of less importance. This indicates that the SMEs in Laos regard quality management and technological changes in the production process as more important than product innovation and skilled laborers in the enterprises in determining the success of enterprises.

Table 15.6 shows the mean and standard deviations for variables under the social factors for Laos enterprises (mean = 3.38, S.D. = 0.75). Awareness of information, investment, market, economic and other (mean = 3.09, S.D. = 1.35), value and attitude changes of the customers (mean = 3.35, S.D. = 1.02), and competitors' changes in the competitive environment (mean = 3.29, S.D. = 1.08) are considered of some importance while ability to produce goods to meet market demands (mean = 3.78, S.D. = 0.97) is considered important. This indicates that the SMEs in Laos regard producing goods to meet market demands as important in determining their success.

Table 15.5 Perceptions of Technology Factors in Influencing the Success of Laos Enterprises

	Mean	S.D.	Level of Importance
1. The quality management and product quality control system	4.21	0.91	Important
2. The invention and creation of new products	3.46	1.17	Some importance
3. The appropriated proportion of skilled labors in the enterprises	2.88	1.27	Some importance
4. Modern technology changes in production process	3.96	1.18	Important
Total	3.63	0.77	Important

Table 15.6 Perceptions of Social Factors in Influencing the Success of Laos Enterprises

	Mean	S.D.	Level of Importance
1. Awareness of information, investment, market, economic and other	3.09	1.35	Some importance
2. Ability to produce goods to meet market demands	3.78	0.97	Important
3. Value and attitude changes of the customers	3.35	1.02	Some importance
4. Competitors' changes in the competitive environment	3.29	1.08	Some importance
Total	3.38	0.75	Some importance

Table 15.7 shows the respondents' opinions about the importance of international factors in influencing their success. The higher mean score indicates higher level of importance while lower mean score indicates lower importance level. The standard deviation (SD) score indicates the degree of deviation from the mean. The international factor considered six variables which are changes in the global economy, the policy to promote relations between the neighboring countries, such as the establishment of the ASEAN Economic Community (AEC), the modernization of transport and logistic system, the abundance of natural resources in the country, the increasing of the production costs such as energy costs, petroleum prices,

Table 15.7 Perceptions of International Factors in Influencing the Success of Laos Enterprises

	Mean	S.D.	Level of Importance
1. Changes in the global economy	2.87	1.33	Some importance
2. The policy to promote relations between the neighboring countries, such as the establishment of the ASEAN Economic Community (AEC)	3.73	1.21	Important
3. The modernization of transport and logistic system	3.99	1.10	Important
4. The abundance of natural resources in the country	4.03	1.11	Important
5. The increasing of the production costs such as energy costs, petroleum prices, etc.	4.14	0.92	Important
6. The impacts of climate changes on agricultural products	3.89	1.28	Important
Total	3.77	0.65	Important

etc., and the impacts of climate changes on agricultural products are important with a mean score of 3.77 and SD of 0.65. However, the only factor of some importance is changes in the global economy (mean = 2.87, SD = 1.33). This may be because the SMEs focus more on the neighboring economies which are trading partners and thus pay less attention to the global economy.

Among the five factors, business, international, and technology factors are ranked the most important with the mean scores of 3.81, 3.77 and 3.63 respectively. It seems the SME enterprises in Laos focus more on the production process and how to deal with business overseas more than the domestic market. Since the social and government factors are considered of some importance with the mean scores of 3.38 and 3.01 respectively, it may be because the social environment and government regulations in Laos do not affect the SME enterprises.

Regression analysis

The correlation matrix shows that total factors (TTT) has a positive correlation with total government factor (TG) at .791, total business factor (TB) at .843, total technology factor (TT) at .787, total social factor (TS) at .754, and total international factor (TI) at .567 indicating that TG, TB, TT, TS, and TI relate to the factors influencing the formality of enterprises in Laos (see Table 15.8).

TG (government factor) indicates that factors such as national political changes in the country, government policy to support and encourage investment in the country, exchange rate, and changes in interest rate are rated as highly important in terms of perceptions of success. The success of enterprises in Laos is most strongly related to the business factors (TB) indicating that operational experiences of the enterprises, amount of the investment or working capital in the enterprises, the plans/targets of the enterprises being clarified, good financial management within the enterprises, executive/entrepreneur with abilities to take advantage of competitiveness, and being well organized in separating functional areas within enterprises. Similarly, high positive correlation is indicated between the factors influencing the formality of enterprises in Laos and the technology factor (TT) such as quality management, product quality control system, invention and creation of new products, and appropriated proportion of skilled laborers. The international factor (TI) is found to be the least important factor for success. These are factors like changes in the global economy, policy to promote relations between the neighboring countries, modernization of transport and logistics system, increase in production costs, and the impacts

Table 15.8 Descriptive Statistics and Correlations Matrix for Laos Enterprises

Variables	Mean	S.D.	TTT	TG	TB	TT	TS	TI	VIF
TTT	3.51	0.61	1						–
TG	3.01	1.05	.791**	1					1.642
TB	3.81	0.78	.843**	.584**	1				2.272
TT	3.63	0.77	.787**	.405**	.620**	1			2.035
TS	3.38	0.75	.754**	.456**	.610**	.611**	1		1.958
TI	3.77	0.65	.567**	.362**	.344**	.377**	.169	1	1.289

N = 80
**Correlation is significant at the 0.01 level (2-tailed).*
VIF refers to Variance Inflation Factor

Table 15.9 Determinants Influencing the Success of Enterprises in Laos

Independent Variables	Coefficients
Constant	2.185★★
Government Factor (TG)	.257★
Business Factor (TB)	.347★
Technology Factor (TT)	.255★
Social Factor (TS)	.248★
International Factor (TI)	.215★
No. of respondents	80
R^2	93%
R^2Adjusted	92%
F-Statistic	43.84
Durbin-Watson	0.819

★ *represents statistical significance at 1% level*

of climate changes on agricultural products. The international factor (TI) indicates that factors such as changes in the global economy, the policy to promote relations between the neighboring countries, the modernization of the transport and logistics system, the abundance of natural resources in the country, the increasing of production costs, and the impacts of climate changes on agricultural products becomes the least important factor for success.

The next step is to test the hypotheses and interpret the results. The coefficients of all variables are estimated in Table 15.9.

Table 15.9 shows the factors perceived to influence the success of enterprises in Laos performed satisfactorily; there was a very high adjusted R^2 (92 percent) for all estimates. The Durbin-Watson test shows no presence of autocorrelation (Greene, 2003). All independent and dependent variables have relatively high explanatory power (R^2 and adjusted R^2). The F-test failed to accept the null hypothesis that the estimated parameters are equal to zero. All factors (24 variables) are positive and significant at the 1 percent level of significance. This shows that the enterprises in Laos are significant and positively affected by government, business, technology, social, and international factors. Hence, an increase in all factors encourages the success of enterprises in Laos.

The results also show that the business factor is the most significant one affecting the success of enterprises in Laos. Holding other factors constant, a 1 percent increase in the business factor will increase the success factors among enterprises in Laos by 0.347 percent. The international factor has the least influence on the success of enterprises in Laos, even though it is also positive and statistically significant at the 1 percent level of significance. These data thus support all Hypotheses ($H_1 - H_5$).

Conclusions

The descriptive results found that the political and government factor was rated as the most important factor on average with the mean score of 4.03. Following that the geographical/location factors, economic and market factors, social and cultural factors, and financial factors have average mean scores of importance of 3.77, 3.63, 3.44, and 3.28 respectively. There are 24 independent variables grouped into five groups named TG (government factor),

TB (business factor), TT (technology factor), TS (social factor), and TI (international factor). The correlation matrix shows that the perceptions of success factors among small and medium size (SMEs) agribusiness enterprises in Laos (dependent variable) have positive correlation to all independent variables at the 1 percent level of significance. The most important of the five factors for agribusiness enterprises in Laos is the business factor followed by the government factor, technology factor, social factor, and international factor respectively. The strong intimation, therefore, is that this provides some indication of the critical factors that agribusiness enterprises deem important for the success of their enterprises and perhaps indicates the form of interventions required by the state in order to facilitate the development of this sector. Importantly, it reveals that what enterprises deem important to their success and what governments and macro-economic indicators deem important may well not be the same and more careful consideration is required of where the focus of intervention should lie. To rely solely on macro-economic variables or solely the perceptions of entrepreneurs about what is required does not appear to be the way forward. Instead, greater consideration is required both when taking decisions on the changes required in the wider business environment and beyond.

References

Aaker, D.A., Kumar, V. and Day, G.S. (2001). *Marketing Research*. New York, John Wiley and Sons.

Boonlua, S. (2011). A Comparative Analysis of the US and Japan FDI in Thailand. *Journal of Academy of Business and Economics*, 11(3), 71–83.

Boonlua, S. and Aditto, S. (2013). Factors Influencing among the Small and Medium Enterprises (SMEs) in Laos. *Journal of International Business and Economic*, 13(3), 33–47.

Brouthers, L.E., Naoks, G., Hadjimarcou, J. and Brouthers, K.D. (2009). Key Factors for Successful Export Performance for Small Firms. *Journal of International Marketing*, 17(13), 21–38.

Dana, L.P. (1993). An Inquiry on Culture and Entrepreneurship, Case Studies of Business Creation Among Immigrants in Montreal. *Journal of Small Business and Entrepreneurship*, 10(4), 16–31.

Greene, W.H. (2003). *Econometric Analysis* (5th ed.). Upper Saddle River, NJ: Prentice Hall.

Hair, J.F., Black, W.C., Babin, B.J. and Anderson, R.E. (2006). *Multivariate Data Analysis*. Upper Saddle River, NJ: Pearson Prentice Hall.

Kimura, F. (2002). Subcontracting and the Performance of Small and Medium Firms in Japan. *Small Business Economics*, 18(1–3), 163–175.

Kongmanila, X. and Takahashi, Y. (2010). Determinants of Subcontracting and Firm Performance in Lao PDR, Evidence from a Garment Industry Cluster. *Asia Pacific Management Review*, 15(1), 97–112.

Scrimgeour, F., McDermott, A., Saunders, C., Shadbolt, N. and Sheath, G. (2006). New Zealand Agribusiness Success, An Approach to Exploring the Role of Strategy, Structure and Conduct on Firm Performance. Paper Presented at the New Zealand Agricultural and Resource Economics Society Conference, August 25–27, 2006.

Terstriep, J. (2009). *Innovations- und Wettbewerbsfahigkeit von KMU sichern-Internationalisierung durch Vernetzung*, Institut Arbeit und Technik. Gelsenkirchen.

Vorachith, S. (2010). Laos from Land-Locked to Land-Linked, A Case Study in the Benefits of South-South Trade for Least Developed Countries. *International Trade Forum*, 4(18), 1.

Weber, M. (1930). *The Protestant Ethic and the Spirit of Capitalism*. Translated by Talcott Parsons. London: Allen and Unwin.

Westhead, P. (2001). The Internationalization of New and Small Firms, A Resource-Based View. *Journal of Business Venturing*, 16(4), 333–358.

World Bank. (2015). The Data Statistics, Factbook. Retrieved June 25, 2015, from the Central Intelligence Agency, http,//www.cia.gov/cia/publications/factbook.

Wu, Y.L. (1983). The Role of Alien Entrepreneurs in Economic Development, An Entrepreneurial Problem. *American Economic Review*, 73(2), 112–117.

Yamane, T. (1967). *Solutions to Problems to Accompany Statistics – An Introductory Analysis*. New York: Prentice-Hall.

16

SOCIAL ENTREPRENEURSHIP AND THE NONPROFIT SECTOR IN DEVELOPING COUNTRIES

Michelle J. Stecker, Tonia L. Warnecke and Carol M. Bresnahan

Social entrepreneurs are not content just to give a fish or teach how to fish. They will not rest until they have revolutionized the fishing industry.

– *Bill Drayton, Founder and CEO of Ashoka*

Introduction

In the last 30 years, the increase in the number of nonprofit organizations is astounding; in all corners of the globe, nonprofits are present and active (Salamon, 2010). Despite this upsurge, nevertheless, caution is required about asking too much of this sector. The nonprofit sector does not have the capacity to solve the complex social and environmental problems of the twenty-first century, and its reliance on philanthropic and government funding is increasingly unsustainable, especially in the wake of economic downturns and global financial instability.

Globalization has increased our sense of mutual dependence and interconnection. Chimiak (2014) argues that "we have the moral responsibility but also the self-interest to engage in activities aiming at leveling the disparities between the more advanced and less developed regions in the world." The remarkable advances in technology, travel, transportation, communication, finance, and "global consciousness" or "internationalism" have contributed to the growth of social entrepreneurship and the reach of global civil society. Many opportunities exist for effective cross-sector collaborations of the nonprofit, public, and private sectors for solving the most pressing social problems of our time.

This chapter focuses on the impact of social entrepreneurship on the nonprofit sector in developing nations. First, we review the diverse landscape of nonprofit organizations (NPOs), non-governmental organizations (NGOs), and international non-governmental organizations (INGOs), noting the diverse challenges faced by these institutions in the developing world. Next, we discuss social entrepreneurship's influence on nonprofit management, scaling, replicability, impact assessment, sustainable business model development, and the trends in philanthropy and social impact finance. After presenting best practices for cross-sector partnerships, we conclude by examining the reach and maturation of nonprofit organizations specializing in social entrepreneurship and opportunities in social entrepreneurial education.

Definition, role, and scope of the nonprofit sector

The nonprofit sector plays a vital role in the global economy (United Nations, 2003). Salamon (2010) estimates that, in 40 diverse countries, the operating expenditures of non-profit institutions represent $2.2 trillion USD, larger than the gross domestic product of all but six countries; an employment survey of 42 countries documented the equivalent of over 56 million full-time nonprofit volunteers. Private philanthropy is a small percentage of the revenues of the nonprofit sector, accounting for only 14 percent, while earned income and fees represent 50 percent, and public support 36 percent. Nonprofit institutions are a "dynamic presence," outpacing the employment increase in the public and private sectors (Salamon, 2010).

Before 1993, data on nonprofit institutions in the international System of National Accounts (SNA) was not systematically collected (UN 2003, 2). The "two-sector" economy of business and government swallowed up nonprofits that either received most of their income from sales or the government. Entities that were technically nonprofit, like hospitals, but earned fees for services were classified as for-profit enterprises. Nonprofits heavily subsidized by governments were counted as public sector entities. Lester Salamon (2010), director of the Johns Hopkins Comparative Nonprofit Sector Project (CNP), argues that despite the global increase in "philanthropy, volunteering, and civil society organizations," nonprofits "have long been the lost continent on the social landscape of our world."

Nonprofit institutions, nevertheless, are now being counted and analyzed. The United Nations 2003 Handbook, committed to identifying all nonprofits, drafted a definition and recorded a value of their volunteer labor and the focus of their activities (UN, 2003). Nonprofit institutions include nonprofit organizations (NPOs), non-governmental organizations (NGOs), international non-governmental organizations (INGOs), charities, and private community, religious, and associational organizations. The nonprofit sector provides goods and services that neither for-profit entities nor the public sector provide due to lack of ability, capacity or desire (Stecker, 2014).

The nonprofit sector is variously known as the third sector, civil society, or the voluntary or charitable sector (Smith et al., 2006). It is best defined by the structure and operations of the nonprofit institutions. The CNP, launched in May 1990, identified and categorized five features of nonprofits: they are organized, private, non-profit-distributing, self-governing, and voluntary. Under this framework, entities must be structured and conduct meetings or gatherings over a period of time (that is, they cannot be temporary); must be separate from and not controlled by public sector actors, but can be funded by the government; cannot distribute revenues to the governing board; cannot be controlled by external entities; and must allocate responsibility for some aspect of governance to volunteers (Salamon, 1997).

The types of organizations that meet UN criteria are (a) nonprofit service providers, (b) "non-governmental organizations promoting economic development or poverty reduction in less developed areas"; (c) arts and cultural organizations; (d) sports clubs; (e) advocacy groups; (f) foundations; (g) community-based or grassroots associations; (h) political parties; (i) social clubs; (j) unions, business and professional associations; and (k) religious congregations. Organizations that straddle the business or public sector include cooperatives, self-help groups, social ventures, quasi-non-governmental organizations, universities, hospitals, and indigenous or territorial groups (UN, 2003).

Evolution and impact of INGOs

International non-governmental organizations (INGOs) are massive nonprofit organizations with "extensive global programmatic reach as a result of their membership of global con-federations," consortia, and affiliations (Morton, 2013). INGOs should not be confused with IGOs—intergovernmental organizations that are nonprofit government coalitions—such as the North Atlantic Treaty Organization (NATO), the United Nations, and the European Union (Smith et al., 2006). "General-purpose" IGOs set policy at a macro level, while the INGOs send on-the-ground personnel to, and fund aid efforts in, developing countries (Chimiak, 2014).

The first of three phases in the history of INGOs was a generation of organizations that provided relief during and after World War II. In the 1960s, the second generation promoted self-reliance and economic growth. The third, starting in the 1990s, focused on sustainable development (Chimiak, 2014). With globalization, decolonization, and technological progress, the number of INGOs increased from 832 to 27,472 between 1950 and 2006, with 75 percent of 2005's estimated 27,472 INGOs created since 1975 (Turner 2010, 82, 84). Today, there are more than 40,000 INGOs, many of which are evolving into "single-issue organizations" (Arment, 2012; Chimiak, 2014).

The size, reach, and scale of INGOs, and their access to financial resources, make them "a powerful force in the delivery of aid, and important actors within the international devel-opment architecture" (Morton, 2013). They are funded through donations from individuals, public sector entities, businesses, foundations, and trusts. The largest INGOs are complex "multi-billion dollar organizations" (Turner, 2010). World Vision, the world's largest INGO, operated with a budget of $2.79 billion USD, employed 40,000 staff, and reached 100 million people in 120 countries in 2011 (Morton, 2013).

INGOs may serve as the main international presence in remote regions affected by conflict or lack of economic or political stature (Morton, 2013). Such institutions, because of their neutrality, recognition, and ethical standards (e.g., the International Red Cross), are admitted within borders in times of crisis. INGOs play an important role as first responders in times of emergency. Their headquarters are based in a variety of developed and, lately, developing countries, with operations in multiple global sites. Save the Children, based in London, UK, serves 80 million children in 120 countries; Action Aid, headquartered in Johannesburg, South Africa, provides aid to 25 million people in 45 countries; and Oxfam International, based in Oxford, UK, has a presence in more than 90 countries (Morton, 2013; Save the Children, 2015; Action Aid, 2015; Oxfam, 2015). Other well-known INGOs include Doctors Without Borders/Médecins Sans Frontières, the International Federation for Human Rights, Amnesty International CARE, Lutheran World Relief, the Red Cross, Adventist Development and Relief Agency, Caritas, SOS Children's Villages, Plan International, Action Aid, Greenpeace, and the World Wide Fund for Nature.

Efficient in providing relief and developmental aid, INGOs are increasingly focused on research and assessment, and collaborate with academic centers. Despite their size, many INGOs are nimble, adapting rapidly to global change and focusing on "the reduction of poverty and inequality, the realization of rights, the promotion of gender equality and social justice, protection of the environment and strengthening of civil society and democratic governance" (Morton, 2013).

INGOs support indigenous NGOs, and influence the policies of global companies, governing organizations, and countries (Turner, 2010). Over 3,000 INGOs have earned "consultative status" at the United Nation's Economic and Social Council (ECOSOC)

(Turner, 2010). Besides being present on the ground, INGOs have large budgets, and well-paid, expert staff who work in partnership or oversee subcontracting work with NGOs. At the same time, conflicts can arise between INGOs and local development organizations over grants and contracts. INGOs may contribute to "brain drain" from developing countries because they pay higher salaries and benefits than indigenous NGOs and governments (Pfeiffer et al., 2008; Morton, 2013).

Challenges facing NPOs and INGOs in developing countries

While the growth of the nonprofit sector has been robust because of the "expanding communications technologies, frustrations with state-centered approaches to development, and new efforts to empower the rural poor," the nonprofit sector faces many challenges in developing countries (Salamon et al., 2004). Financing NPOs and INGOs remains an obstacle. Compared to nonprofits in the developed world, nonprofits in developing countries receive less funding from governments (34 percent v. 22 percent), have fewer paid staff, and are more dependent on fees or earned income and private philanthropy, largely from international sources (Salamon et al., 2004). Recent cutbacks in government funding have led to office consolidations, employee layoffs, and transfers to the southern hemisphere to better compete for donor dollars and serve needs (Smedley, 2014). Countries ruled by authoritarian regimes experience even lower levels of government spending for public welfare, and rely on higher rates of volunteerism (Anheier and Salamon, 1998). Many developing-country nonprofits lack financial sustainability, which makes pursuit of their mission more difficult.

The institutional environment affects organizational sustainability. Cultural beliefs and norms shape local perceptions of nonprofit activity, and these norms vary across countries and regions. Rural inhabitants, less familiar with nonprofits, are accustomed to "social assistance relying on clan and family relationships" (Salamon et al., 2004). In some developing countries, the expansion of nonprofit organizations has occurred through a "top-down approach," with governments controlling how those institutions relate to public sector bodies (Hoque and Parker, 2015). In addition, INGOs of Western origin may not understand local context, projecting a set of needs that reflect inaccurate Western assumptions (Warnecke, 2013). Strategies for managing change diverge; Western approaches "may be entirely inappropriate in cultures that are more hierarchical" and risk averse (Jackson and Claeye, 2011). A culture of corruption, and lack of penalties for corrupt activities, may also affect nonprofits. Poor pay compared to similar public or private sector positions can exacerbate corruption while making it harder for NPOs to attract qualified leaders and board members.

The legal environment for nonprofits is like shifting sand, especially in countries newer to democratic rule and post 9/11 (Simon, 2007). In several sub-Saharan African nations, governmental instability has led to restrictions on NPOs; examples include the enactment of laws limiting associational freedoms and foreign donations (International Center for Not-for-Profit Law, 2011). Some laws force informal groups to register and forbid them from activity if they fail to do so. Others promote a burdensome registration process that prevents indigenous NPOs from receiving official status. Still others require a large number of founders before an NPO can be formed; Angola sets a minimum of 15, while Sudan requires 30 (International Center for Not-for-Profit Law, 2011).

Some countries give broad latitude for government officials to reject NPO registrations, and once organizations are registered, governments may be intrusive, interfering with operations and restricting or banning activities and foreign aid (International Center for Not-for-Profit Law, 2011; Altman, 2013; Chimiak, 2014). After independence in 1947, Pakistan restricted the advocacy role of nonprofits (Salamon et al., 2004). Similarly, most advocacy groups cannot register as NPOs in China. Recognized NPOs provide basic social services, such as health care, education, and aid to the poor and disabled. As many as 1.5 million grassroots organizations are not registered by China and are operating illegally, but some are tolerated and even encouraged at the local level (Heisman, 2013; *The Economist*, 2014). Such examples demonstrate the complexities facing the nonprofit sector.

Social entrepreneurship as an agent of change

Social entrepreneurial principles can be applied to nonprofit institutions. Practitioners work for systems-wide change through nonprofits, for-profits, and hybrid organizations. Social entrepreneurs disrupt inequality and suffering; they identify problems at a systemic level, and build innovative, sustainable solutions that bring about "a new, stable equilibrium" with more promising outcomes for both the group at which improvement is aimed and the whole society (Martin and Osberg, 2007; Stecker, 2014).

Academicians in the nascent field of social entrepreneurship debate frameworks, typologies, and even the definition of social entrepreneurship (Dacin et al., 2010; Brouard and Larivet, 2010). Some definitions are overbroad; others are too narrow. Social entrepreneurship cannot be divorced from entrepreneurship. As Dees et al. (2002) conclude "Entrepreneurs are innovative, opportunity-oriented, resourceful, value-creating change agents." Like entrepreneurs, social entrepreneurs create something new. The social aspect of the innovation is the measurable "mission-related impact" (Martin and Osberg, 2007). Although "a business entrepreneur might create entirely new industries, a social entrepreneur comes up with new solutions to social problems and then implements them on a large scale" (Ashoka, 2015). The issue of scalability is contentious. Dees et al. (2002) argue that it should be left up to the individual to decide if scaling up is the right direction for the enterprise; scaling deep may be a better decision.

Martin and Osberg (2007) call for a narrow definition of social entrepreneurship:

(1) identifying a stable but inherently unjust equilibrium that causes the exclusion, marginalization, or suffering of a segment of humanity that lacks the financial means or political clout to achieve any transformative benefit on its own;
(2) identifying an opportunity in this unjust equilibrium, developing a social value proposition, and bringing to bear inspiration, creativity, direct action, courage, and fortitude, thereby challenging the stable state's hegemony;
(3) forging a new, stable equilibrium that releases trapped potential or alleviates the suffering of the targeted group, and through imitation and the creation of a stable ecosystem around the new equilibrium ensuring a better future for the targeted group and even society at large.

This system's approach to solving social problems focuses on discovering the root, not the symptom, of suffering, and finding a scalable solution to fix the problem, creating a new equilibrium.

A broader definition of social entrepreneurship "encompasses the activities and processes undertaken to discover, define, and exploit opportunities in order to enhance social wealth by creating new ventures or managing existing organizations in an innovative manner" (Zahra et al., 2009). This definition includes nonprofits that utilize social enterprise for earned income and embrace traditional management practices.

The social entrepreneurship literature and the definitions being used by organizations supporting social entrepreneurs reveal four "pillars." Social entrepreneurship is (1) an innovative entrepreneurial venture (2) with measurable social impact (3) that is sustainable and (4) scalable and/or replicable. If one pillar is missing, it is not social entrepreneurship. Social entrepreneurs start enterprises that are for-profit, nonprofit, or hybrid, and select whatever entity is best for making social change in keeping with the laws of the particular jurisdiction. Entrepreneurs who work in existing organizations and lead innovative, high-impact social change with their organizations are considered *intrapreneurs*.

A classic example of a social entrepreneur who meets the four-pillar requirement is Muhammad Yunus, the founder and CEO of the Grameen Bank and the father of microcredit. Born in Bangladesh and educated in the United States, he returned home, where he was moved by the suffering of women in the village of Jobra, who lived in poverty and did not have collateral for traditional bank loans. Yunus loaned 42 village women $27 USD, which they repaid. In 1976, he founded the Grameen Bank, which provides microloans to the poor (Bornstein, 2007). Yunus displayed innovation (loaning to people banks would refuse), created an enterprise with measurable social impact like empowering women, made it sustainable by charging a nominal rate of interest, and scaled it by reaching millions in Bangladesh (Yunus, 2010).

There are a variety of pathways for tackling problems through social entrepreneurship. Zahra et al. (2009) propose a useful typology that describes three types of social entrepreneurs: social bricoleur, social constructionist, and social engineer. Social bricoleurs are industrious, indigenous "handymen" or "handywomen," who make good use of limited resources and local knowledge to address "small-scale local social needs"; they vary in how they find opportunities, "determine their impact on the broader social system, and assemble the resources needed to pursue these opportunities" (Zahra et al., 2009).

Social bricoleurs exploit their context, environment, and resources to innovate social change, and are more concerned about fixing a local problem than scaling their idea. Bunker Roy, an Indian social bricoleur who founded Barefoot College in 1972 in Tilonia, Rajasthan, believes that the rural poor must be self-reliant and not depend on outside experts for development. Barefoot College equips illiterate or semiliterate people to solve local problems, and learn how to provide safe drinking water, basic health care, and education for their communities. Ordinary people, often illiterate women educated as solar engineers, electrified the college and thousands of homes. Barefoot-trained engineers figured out how to build hand water pumps in the Himalayas, which experts said could not be done. Barefoot College is likely the only rural college built and operated by the poor (Elkington and Hartigan, 2008).

The social constructionist does not need local knowledge or resources, but is open to opportunities for social change. Social constructionists exploit "market failures by filling gaps to underserved clients in order to introduce reforms and innovations to the broader social system" (Zahra et al., 2009). One social constructionist is Jacqueline Novogratz, who in 2001 founded the nonprofit Acumen Fund which provides venture capital to entrepreneurial organizations working to solve global poverty. Based on her expertise in international banking and on-the-ground experience with microfinance in Rwanda, she sensed a gap in the needs of organizations that could benefit from "business 'acumen' from the industrialized world" (Zahra et al., 2009).

Social engineers achieve large-scale systemic or revolutionary change. They are disrupters of the status quo and usher in a new equilibrium for social change. Muhammad Yunus disrupted the traditional banking industry on two fronts: by developing the microloan industry granting loans to individuals without collateral, and giving the vast majority of loans to women, who before Yunus's intervention comprised only 1 percent of bank loan recipients in Bangladesh (*Harvard Business Review*, 2012).The scale of the Grameen Bank is astonishing. Yunus leveraged the resources of the public and private sector to launch more than 1,000 branches of the Grameen Bank in the 1980s and 1990s (Bornstein, 2007). By 2005, there were 2,422 branches which lent $6.25 billion USD to 7.06 million borrowers, 97 percent of whom were women. By June 2015, a total of $17.3 billion USD had been disbursed to 8,681,302 borrowers (8,345,610 women and 335,692 men) in 2,568 branches, with a recovery rate of 98.3 percent (Grameen Bank, 2015).

How social entrepreneurship is transforming the nonprofit sector

This section examines how social entrepreneurship affects the nonprofit sector and offers best practices for nonprofits.

Innovation

Innovation is fundamental to social entrepreneurship, and innovative methodologies can be integrated into INGOs, NPOs, and NGOs. Human-centered design thinking is a process in which interdisciplinary teams use a circular, iterative process to solve problems. The steps include gathering empathy, defining the problem, ideating, prototyping, and testing. Gathering empathy through talking to end users and discerning their spoken and unspoken needs is critical. Ideation is brainstorming that improves creativity—every idea, no matter how crazy, deserves a minute of life. Through a thoughtful, open process, the team formulates and prototypes a solution, then solicits feedback from end-users in a testing phase, and the process starts all over again (Kelley and Kelley, 2013).

An innovation that started as a class project at the school at Stanford University in 2007 is now saving thousands of premature and low-birth-weight babies in the developing world; this journey of innovation shows the critical nature of empathy. Using human design thinking methodology, the students were challenged to design an extremely low-cost infant incubator that would prevent neonatal hypothermia. Each year, out of 15 million premature and low-weight newborns, almost one million die within 24 hours of birth. After visiting a modern urban hospital in Nepal and finding $20,000 USD incubators empty, the students discovered that the real problem was reaching babies born in remote areas (Kelley and Kelley, 2013). After many prototypes were examined and discarded following consultation with mothers, medical workers, and business people, the Embrace Warmer pouch was developed (Embrace, 2015). Embrace Warmers cost less than 1 percent of a traditional incubator and are now distributed in 11 countries through the efforts of NGO partners, local governments, and for-profit health care companies (Embrace, 2015).

The effectuation model of innovation is highlighted in a recent study analyzing the impact of innovation on the operations and effectiveness of NGOs and INGOs in poverty alleviation in Vietnam. Luke and Chu (2013) found that micro-enterprise development programs (MEPs) that incorporated innovative and entrepreneurial approaches were more effective than those using more traditional approaches. High-performing MEPs were more likely to use strategic operational management techniques to focus on "customer needs and market opportunities," rather than resources that were simply at hand (Luke and Chu, 2013). Understanding the "actual needs of poor communities and existing market demands" is critical to innovation (Luke and Chu, 2013). Innovative organizations formed indigenous groups comprised of mixed poor and non-poor households. The poor and the non-poor learned from each other, developed valuable relationships, pooled skills and capabilities, and were more successful in their project outcomes. The group was able to learn "from past challenges and failures . . . similar to effectuation processes within entrepreneurship" (Luke and Chu, 2013).

High-performing MEPs built cross-sector relationships with local government leaders. The MEPs provided in-kind credit of livestock, with repayment in the form of the return of the livestock or offspring to other poor households; equipped indigenous farmers to become trainers tailored to local needs rather than using standardized "one-size-fits-all" training approaches; helped indigenous farmers learn how to manage market constraints; and built collectives that efficiently managed supply chains. Innovative approaches can provide more effective outcomes "to better address complex social problems" (Luke and Chu, 2013). Since entrepreneurs found many nonprofits, it makes sense to adapt a posture of continuous innovation throughout the lifecycle of NPOs (Glaeser and Shleifer, 2001).

Measurable social impact

Without an appropriate metric to measure social impact in the nonprofit sector, it is impossible to hold organizations and leaders accountable (Zahra et al., 2009). It is necessary to share assessment data with donors and foundations, and to examine the effectiveness of the operations in order to improve services and products. Some nonprofit impact is easy to assess, while other outcomes, particularly those seeking social justice, environmental, restoration, or subjective, non-quantifiable goals, present a challenge. Despite the difficulties, assessment is key to social entrepreneurship.

Zahra et al. (2009) advocate a "total wealth" standard of measuring social impact that takes into consideration both economic and social wealth. Social wealth is the sum of "tangible (i.e. products, clients served, or funds generated) and intangible outcomes such as wealth, happiness and general well-being." The equation is "Total Wealth (TW) = Economic Wealth (EW) + Social Wealth (SW)" with "TW = EW + SW, where EW = Economic Value (EV) − Economic Costs (EC) − Opportunity Costs (OC); SW Social Wealth = Social Value (SV) − Social Costs (SC). The bottom-line metric is TW = EV + SV − (EC + OC + SC)" (Zahra et al., 2009).

Comparative studies of nonprofits undertaken by the Johns Hopkins Comparative Nonprofit Sector Project (CNP) required the creation of a new Global Civil Society Index to measure scale or capacity, sustainability, and impact. Salamon admitted that trying to find "a common metric in which to express the contribution of civil society organizations engaged in community organizing, health care delivery, education, human rights advocacy, artistic expression, and protection from homelessness is almost impossible," but necessary. CNP developed four proxy indicators—value added, nonprofit service share, workforce in expressive field, and organizational membership—to measure the impact of the service functions and expressive and representational roles of nonprofits, and a separate standard measuring five social roles of nonprofits, including economic contribution, human service contribution, contribution to advocacy and expression, popular commitment, and performance of key roles (Salamon et al., 2004).

In the microfinance industry, several assessment tools have been developed to provide environmental and social audits. For example, "the Green Index monitors 11 indicators across 3 categories: (1) formal environmental strategy (having an environmental policy, reporting strategy, and dedicated personnel to this area); (2) environmental risk management . . . and (3) leverage of green opportunities" (Warnecke, 2015; Allet, 2014). The Green

Index can be used alongside Social Performance Indicators (SPI), a social audit tool that contains gender, poverty, and rural extension modules (Warnecke, 2015). SPI offers both self-assessment and external certification models, supporting a learning curve for appropriate assessment practices (Cerise, 2015).

Sustainable business model

Social entrepreneurship uses the best of for-profit business practices to build sustainable business plans and models. Given the lack of robust public sector support in many developing nations, and dependency on private philanthropy, nonprofit leaders must develop earned income streams to support their efforts. Nonprofits can gauge their sustainability through the Comparative Nonprofit Sector Project, which measures self-generated income, government support, popular support as reflected in the number of people volunteering, and the legal environment (Salamon et al., 2004).

Organizations may add a commercial for-profit social enterprise to subsidize the nonprofit. Embrace is a nonprofit company advancing "maternal and child health," and its Embrace Innovations arm is a separate for-profit social enterprise (Embrace, 2015). Nonprofits can charge fees for services or sell goods that are not even related to the mission of the nonprofit in order to achieve financial sustainability.

One famous case is the Aravind Eye Care System in Madurai, India. Dr. Govindappa Venkataswamy, the entrepreneurial founder, wanted his hospitals to be the McDonald's of eye care—low-cost, good quality, and with the capacity to serve millions of poor clients. In 1976, Aravind started with an 11-bed hospital and four doctors, using a business model that charged paying patients enough to cover the costs of treating poorer clients, who comprise 75 percent of those receiving free or low-cost care (Ee, 2010). The system works. Aravind has treated over 32 million patients, and performed over four million surgeries using "assembly-line efficiency, strict quality norms, brand recognition, standardization, consistency, ruthless cost control and above all, volume" (Rosenberg, 2013).

In developing countries like India, health organizations rely on public sector assistance and private philanthropy, but "Aravind's core services are sustainable: patient care and the construction of new hospitals are funded by fees from paying customers" (Rosenberg, 2013). When the use of the intraocular lens became the standard for cataract surgeries in the 1980s, the price of the lens was $100 and manufacturers would not lower the prices enough to make their use financially feasible. Aravind countered by founding Aurolab, which makes the lens for $2 each and is a major supplier to the world (Rosenberg, 2013).

Scaling and replicability

There is no one-size-fits-all prescription for scalability. Scaling can occur through replication of a service, product, or business model; replication of the social impact; or scaling and diffusing ideas (Harris, 2010). Frumkin (2010) argues that the ability of a nonprofit organization to effectively scale depends on "financial strength, program expansion, comprehensiveness, multisite replication, and accepted doctrine." In their SCALERS model, Bloom and Chatterji focus on "staffing, communicating, alliance building, lobbying, earnings generation, replicating, and stimulating market forces" (Bloom and Chatterji, 2010). The Comparative Nonprofit Sector Project gauges scale and capacity by measuring the extent of paid employment and volunteer employment, the amount of charitable contributions, and the degree of diversification of the civil society sector (Salamon et al., 2004).

The financial sustainability of Aravind's Eye Care System is related to its scale. Aravind invests in enrolling non-paying clients; its philosophy is not to restrict demand, but to build capacity to meet the demand (Rosenberg, 2013). The large volume of free clients improves the service to the paying clients by advancing the capabilities of the physicians (who can develop specialties), and by improving cost efficiencies and service. Each doctor completes more than 2,000 eye surgeries per year at Aravind, almost seven times the average rate of doctors in other Indian hospitals. The cost per client has also plummeted through scale. For example, Aravind completes almost 60 percent "as many eye surgeries as the United Kingdom's National Health System, at one one-thousandth of the cost" (Rosenberg, 2013). The efficiency protocols of Aravind are now included in the World Health Organization's guidelines for scaling up male circumcision in the prevention of AIDS, and are being replicated in Africa (Rosenberg, 2013).

Bandhan (relationship), a microfinance institution in India, shows innovation in scaling and sustainability. Begun as a single branch with four employees in 2001 and registered as an Indian Non-Banking Financial Company (NBCF), it had, by 2015, 2,022 branches across 22 Indian states and territories with 13,101 employees and over 6.6 million female clients (Dasgupta, 2015; Gupta, 2014; Bandhan, 2015). Established by Chandra Shekhar Ghosh, a Senior Ashoka Fellow who learned about microfinance in Bangladesh, it sought to empower women, who are "poorer and more disadvantaged than men" (Bandhan, 2013).

Committed to the "triple bottom line," Bandhan enjoys a repayment rate over 99 percent and offers services that include insurance (Bandhan, 2013). Among its most successful programs is Targeting the Hard Core Poor (THP). "The idea," Bandhan notes, "is to help [the hard core poor] . . . uplift themselves to mainstream society" (Bandhan, 2013). Program assessment shows that basic literacy increased by nearly 80 percent and knowledge of healthy habits increased by 89 percent; a large majority reported improved relations with relatives and neighbors (Bandhan, 2013). In addition to traditional micro lending, Bandhan became a commercial bank in August 2015, offering a full range of financial services to the poor—a groundbreaking achievement. It also unveiled the use of innovative technology in the form of handheld "human teller machines," allowing customers to make transactions from home, which transforms lives by providing better access to banking services (Dasgupta, 2015).

Trends in philanthropy and social impact finance

Salamon (2014) contends that "a significant revolution appears to be underway on the frontiers of philanthropy and social investment" that will affect nonprofit funding and work around the world. These dramatic changes are coming at a time when public sector and private philanthropy rates are stagnant, and worldwide needs are increasing. Although in its infancy, the leveraging of financial resources promises to change the nonprofit landscape.

The revolution is being waged on multiple fronts, with an expansion in the types of new instruments and institutions used to finance social enterprise, as well as new ways of thinking about aid. Philanthropy is moving beyond the simple giving of grants, and is offering in-kind assistance in addition to "loans, loan guarantees, equity-type investments, securitization, fixed-income instruments, and, most recently, social impact bonds" (Salamon, 2014). For social impact bonds, "philanthropic funders and impact investors—not governments—take on the financial risk of expanding proven social programs" (Bensoussan et al., 2013). This is a results-based approach, where government payment is made only upon successful achievement of measured social impact (Glennie, 2011).

Foundations are creating new ways to finance social enterprise through "capital aggregators, secondary markets, social stock exchanges, social enterprise brokers, [and] internet portals." Philanthropy is moving beyond raising capital through bequests from the wealthy, and is instead looking at "the privatization of formerly public or quasi-public assets or the establishment of specialized social-purpose investment funds" (Salamon, 2014). Matching programs combining contributions from governments, private corporations, and citizens are another option (Bensoussan et al., 2013).

Modern philanthropy is becoming more global, more diverse in its institutions and instruments, more entrepreneurial, and more collaborative. "Traditional" philanthropy focuses most of its aid on nonprofit organizations, while modern philanthropy assists cross-sector approaches and "a wide assortment of social enterprises, cooperatives, and other hybrid organizations" (Salamon, 2014). Bugg-Levine et al. (2012) argue for financial engineering— unbundling the social and financial returns of social enterprises to attract more diverse sets of donors and investors. A very different approach to financing can be found in crowd-funding. Although it cannot compete in dollar figures with the budgets of major INGOs, crowdfunding plays a democratizing role in the landscape of social finance, with platforms such as Kickstarter and Indiego making it possible for anyone to support development projects (Millner, 2013). These trends in philanthropy will transform the training and education of nonprofit leaders and social entrepreneurs as they learn best business practices to scale up, measure impact, and build sustainable organizations.

Best practices for cross-sector partnerships and key trends

Moving from isolated to partnering and collective impact approaches

Development issues are often too big for any single nonprofit to tackle. For development problems that are narrow in scope, with a known solution, a partnership between two organizations can be a good strategy if each organization contributes a different set of skills and resources. Often, NPOs lack management expertise, technological resources, or the funds and know-how required to scale solutions. Corporations, on the other hand, can offer these resources but often lack understanding of the local context. Governments may have funds to devote to development projects, but lack on-the-ground means of applying those funds effectively. Given their social mission but emphasis on financial sustainability, social entrepreneurship can be a good bridge between NPOs and corporations. To establish a partnership, it is important to choose the right partner, empower collaboration leaders, define the partnership, clarify the shared mission and goals, divide responsibilities, and develop a memorandum of understanding; to sustain a partnership, mutual trust and evaluating the partnership are necessary (Hanover Research, 2013).

For complex and cross-cutting development problems, a simple partnership will likely be insufficient. In order to make large-scale social impact, NPOs should combine forces with public, private, and other nonprofit organizations to implement systemic solutions (Kania and Kramer, 2011). Collective impact initiatives are "long-term commitments by a group of important actors from different sectors to a common agenda for solving a specific social problem . . . supported by a shared measurement system, mutually reinforcing activities and ongoing communication, and . . . staffed by an independent backbone organization" (Kania and Kramer, 2011; Hanleybrown et al., 2012). It is a systemic approach focusing on lasting— not project-delimited—inter-organization relationships (Kania and Kramer, 2011), and engagement with the "civic culture" of the surrounding community that is crucial to its success (Harwood, 2015). Philanthropic organizations can stimulate this collective approach by funding long-term, collaborative solutions rather than funding isolated and competing organizations (Kania and Kramer, 2011). The collaborative approach helps organizations scale and replicate solutions. In the process, organizations can learn from mistakes, experiment, communicate, and establish best practices. The influence of social entrepreneurs on the work of NPOs promises to move the needle from an isolated impact to collaborative impact model.

Networked NGO model

Given the recent reductions in government aid to INGOs and the emerging efforts to work in cross-sector partnership, this model involves "a network of multiparty stakeholders or partners from civil society, government departments, indigenous communities, even the media, mostly located within the country where the development work is taking place" (Smedley, 2014). The role of the INGOs and NGOs changes from designing and implementing programs to "supporting capacity building and knowledge sharing" within the diverse network of stakeholders (Smedley, 2014). For instance, INGOs that are headquartered in the north may need to move operations and the headquarters to the south where the work is coordinated. In the future, INGOs may be doing less on-the-ground service delivery and more coordinating and networking with local stakeholders.

International NGO networks can suffer from collaborative ineffectiveness, limiting the extent to which the network actually builds capacity for any single member (Oostergard and Nielsen, 2005). Knowledge sharing at the inter-organizational level also remains a challenge. Executing a network-wide policy document on knowledge management, assigning personnel specifically to this area, mapping information flows and gaps, facilitating staff exchange programs, and assessing current technology platforms to determine how they best leverage knowledge management can improve network efficacy (Smith and Lumba, 2008).

Public sector involvement

Collaboration with the public sector, though desirable, may not always be possible. The Aspen Institute (2002) notes that "governments and the nonprofit sector are involved in a wide array of relationships—some cooperative, others adversarial, and still others complementary" (see also Boris, 2006). In many developing countries, governments rely on civil society to provide public goods—an unsustainable trend. The proliferation of social enterprise can be viewed as a critique of governmental failure to provide public goods and relevant services to the poor or to under-served areas (Leadbeater, 2007).

Governments are learning from social entrepreneurs, and can (1) create social enterprises aligned with strategic priorities; (2) support social enterprises through funding or training; and (3) partner with social enterprises, other businesses, and NPOs to save money and increase efficiencies (Duniam and Eversole, 2013). Through public procurement, social enterprises can also deliver government-commissioned goods or services (Leadbeater, 2007). For any type of collaboration with the public sector, having "bridge" employees—individuals with the skill set to "work between distinct organizations and speak credibly to both parties"—is critical (Sweiker, 2015). Working with the government also provides entry points for discussions on public policy issues relevant to the other organizations' work.

Key traits for cross-sector success

In an illuminating study of over 100 social entrepreneurs from 91 organizations that received a coveted Skoll Award for Social Entrepreneurship (SASE) over the last 15 years, leaders at the Skoll Foundation discovered two features that entrepreneurs focused on changing to achieve financial sustainability: "the actors involved and the enabling technologies applied" (Martin and Osberg, 2015). Successful entrepreneurs, who were awarded a three-year $1.25 million SASE grant to scale their enterprises, were able to leverage the power of consumers, government actors or NPOs (cross-sector partnerships). Educating or mobilizing customers can also be "a potent and sustainable means of altering a suboptimal social equilibrium" (Martin and Osberg, 2015). Social entrepreneurs in a wide range of industries can build certification systems to educate consumers, who then "vote with their wallets" to eradicate child labor, environmental degradation, etc. Focusing on new actors to promote change promotes sustainability for the organization.

The nonprofit organization Amazon Conservation Team (ACT) is leveraging the resources of the Brazilian government and using emerging technology to protect the Amazon basin from illegal deforestation. In the past, the government was not able to react quickly enough to stop loggers, ranchers, or miners from destroying the rain forests; now, indigenous peoples, who live in the basin, are equipped with handheld GPS devices that can pinpoint illegal activity. ACT helped indigenous peoples map more than 70 million acres of ancestral tribal lands in Central America with GPS technology (Amazon Conservation Team, 2015). The partnership with new actors and the use of enabling technology have been transformational.

Burt Weetjens, founder of the non-profit APOPO, has replaced expensive technology with a less expensive way to detect and deactivate landmines in more than 50 nations, including Tanzania, Mozambique, Thailand, Angola, Cambodia, and Vietnam. Weetjens trains giant pouched rats to detect landmines and the presence of tuberculosis through their sophisticated sense of smell. Hero RATs are lightweight enough not to detonate landmines and ordnance, 14 times faster than human mine clearers, and cost-effective. They are now the "preferred landmine countermeasure technology" in Africa, responsible for detecting almost 50,000 pieces of ordnance, clearing over 18 million square meters of land for sustainable farming enterprise, and freeing over 900,000 people from the threat of explosives (Skoll Foundation, 2015). Hero RATs also quickly and accurately detect tuberculosis, potentially saving the lives of thousands of patients, and reducing the rate of infection. In Africa, Hero RATs are reported to increase the detection of TB by up to 40 percent; in 10 minutes, they can evaluate more sputum samples than a lab technician in a day (Skoll Foundation, 2015).

Weetjens has used the SASE grant to scale up his operations, train more rat handlers, develop best practices, and generate more earned income. He works closely with the Sokoine University of Agriculture (NPO) in Morogoro, Tanzania, and multiple governments. APOPO is a great example of how NPOs and the public sector can scale impact and create a sustainable enterprise by identifying new actors and enabling technologies.

Conclusions

Although the globalization of finance, trade, and technology has been a catalyst for nonprofit growth in developing countries, globalization also contributes to social and environmental challenges and institutional instability. Funding shortages, in addition to cultural, legal, and political barriers, continue to test nonprofit organizations' capacity for change making. At the same time, governments are increasingly relying on nonprofit institutions to help provide social welfare and institute development strategies. Tackling these challenges is complicated given the diversity of the nonprofit sector. Strategies for increased, sustainable social impact must be developed with local input, through human-centered design or other methodologies. For the sector to be more effective in its work, international law must continue to evolve in its support, cross-sector approaches to development need to be more robust, and nonprofit institutions must become more nimble, transparent, and business-like.

The intersection of the nonprofit sector and social entrepreneurship promises to lead to an era in development work that will be more entrepreneurial, innovative, and sustainable and have more impact in meeting the needs of the world. Social entrepreneurial principles such as innovation, measurable social impact, sustainable business models, scalability and replicability have the potential to transform the way nonprofits operate. Although significant funding obstacles remain for social mission-based organizations, many philanthropic organizations are moving beyond the traditional grant-based model and exploring loans, loan guarantees, in-kind assistance, equity investments, or the establishment of social investment funds. Social enterprise has benefited from and exposed the nonprofit sector to new tools and approaches for funding, including social impact bonds, matching programs, financial engineering, and crowdfunding.

Social entrepreneurship is not a panacea for the problems faced by the nonprofit sector. Cross-sector partnerships (including public–private partnerships, collective impact approaches, and networked NGOs), as well as capable, supportive, institutional environments at the macro and micro levels, are essential. The continued maturation and reach of nonprofit sector organizations specializing in social entrepreneurship must be a high priority for funders. Nonprofit organizations such as Ashoka (founded in 1980), the Skoll Foundation (founded in 1998), the Schwab Foundation (founded in 1999), and Dasra (founded in 1999) support thousands of social entrepreneurs across six continents, and demonstrate the importance of investing for long-term social returns.

The demand for social entrepreneurship education is exploding. Ashoka boasts a network of about 150 schools, colleges, and other institutions across the globe, all of which prize "the cultivation of empathy, teamwork, leadership, and change making" (Ashoka, 2015). In Mexico, the Universidad de Monterrey has adopted social responsibility and sensitivity, including empathy, among its 14 core values (Universidad de Monterrey, 2015). In India, Karnataka University offers a Master of Social Entrepreneurship. Several nonprofit organizations offer free human-design thinking tutorials online; applicable to any discipline, this methodology has already led to innovations ranging from sanitation to irrigation and employment in the developing world.

With the proliferation of nonprofit organizations in all corners of the globe and the maturation of social entrepreneurship, complex problems are being addressed and solved by a committed generation of change makers. The further integration of social entrepreneurial principles, intentional cross-sector partnerships, and strategic philanthropy promises to accelerate profound, positive change in our world.

References

Action Aid (2015). Accessed July 12, 2015: http://www.actionaid.org.

Allet, M. (2014). The Green Index, an Innovative Tool to Assess the Environmental Performance of MFIs. E-MFP Brief No. 5. European Microfinance Platform. Luxembourg.

Altman, L. (2013). In South Africa, Nonprofits Seek Answers from Government. Nonprofit Quarterly, January 25. Accessed July 15, 2015: http://nonprofitquarterly.org/2013/01/25/in-south-africa-nonprofits-seek-answers-from-government.

Anheier, H. K. and Salamon, L. M. (1998). *The Nonprofit Sector in the Developing World: A Comparative Analysis.* Manchester and New York: Manchester University Press.

Amazon Conservation Team (ACT) (2015). Accessed July 8, 2015: http://www.amazonteam. orgAPOPO (2015); accessed July 8, 2015: https://www.apopo.org

Arment, J. F. (2012). *The Elements of Peace: How Nonviolence Works.* Jefferson, NC: McFarland & Company, Inc.

Ashoka (2015). Accessed July 13, 2015: https://www.ashoka.org.

Bandhan (2013). *Annual Report 2012–13.* Salt Lake City, Kolkata, India.

Bandhan (2015). Accessed July 28, 2015: http://www.bandhanmf.com/bn_default.aspx.

Bensoussan, E., Ruparell, R. and Taliento, L. (2013). *Innovative Development Financing.* McKinsey Global Institute, August. Retrieved from http://www.mckinsey.com/insights/social_sector/innovative_development_financing.

Bloom, P. N. and Chatterji, A. K. (2010). Scaling Social Entrepreneurial Impact: The SCALERS Model. *The Evaluation Project,* 15(1), 8.

Boris, E. T. (2006). Nonprofit Organizations in a Democracy: Varied Roles and Responsibilities. In Elizabeth T. Boris and C. Eugene Steuerle (eds.), *Nonprofits and Government* (2nd ed). Washington, DC: The Urban Institute Press, 1–36.

Bornstein, David (2007). *How to Change the World: Social Entrepreneurs and the Power of New Ideas.* Oxford: Oxford University Press.

Brouard, F. and Larivet, S. (2010). Essay of Clarifications and Definitions of the Related Concepts of Social Enterprise, Social Entrepreneur and Social Entrepreneurship. In Alain Fayolle and Harry Matlay (eds.), *Handbook of Research on Social Entrepreneurship.* Cheltenham, UK: Edward Elgar Publishing, 34–42.

Bugg-Levine, A., Kogut, B. and Kulatilaka, N. (2012). A New Approach to Funding Social Enterprises. *Harvard Business Review,* 90 (January–February), 118–123.

Cerise (2015). Impact and Social Performance. Accessed July 25, 2015: http://www.cerise-microfinance. org/-impact-and-social-perfomance.

Chimiak, G. (2014). The Rise and Stall of Non-Governmental Organizations in Development. *Polish Sociological Review,* 18(5), 25–44.

Dacin, P. A., Dacin, T. M. and Matear, M. (2010). Social Entrepreneurship: Why We Don't Need a New Theory and How We Move Forward From Here. *Academy of Management Perspectives,* 24(3), 37–57.

Dasgupta, M. (2015). Bandhans Human Teller Machines to Bring Bank to Doorstep. The Financial Express, June 20. Accessed July 26, 2015: http://www.financialexpress.com/article/industry/banking-finance/bandhans-human-teller-machines-to-bring-bank-to-doorstep-2/87506.

Dasra (2015). Accessed July 9, 2015: http://www.dasra.org/pdf/eg-educate-girls-measurement-journey.pdf.

Dees, G. J., Emerson, J. and Economy, P. (2002). *Strategic Tools for Social Entrepreneurs: Enhancing the Performance of Your Enterprising Nonprofit.* New York: John Wiley & Sons, Inc.

Duniam, M. and Eversole, R. (2013). *Social Enterprises and Local Government: A Scoping Study.* Sydney: Australian Centre of Excellence for Local Government.

Ee, G. (2010). No Charity for Charities. In Willie Cheng and Sharifah Mohamaed (eds.), *The World that Changes the World: How Philanthropy, Innovation, and Entrepreneurship are Transforming the Social Ecosystem.* New York: John Wiley & Sons.

Elkington, J. and Hartigan, P. (2008). *The Power of Unreasonable People: How Social Entrepreneurs Create Markets That Change the World.* Boston: Harvard Business Review Press.

Embrace (2015). Accessed July 19, 2015:http://embraceglobal.org.

Frumkin, P. (2010). The Five Meanings of Scale in Philanthropy. *The Evaluation Project,* 15(1), 7.

Glaeser, E. L. and Shleifer, A. (2001).Not-for-profit Entrepreneurs. *Journal of Public Economics,* 81(1), 99–115.

Glennie, J. (2011). Is Cash on Delivery the Future of Aid? *The Guardian,* May 13.

Grameen Bank (2015). Accessed July 20, 2015: http://www.grameen-info.org/monthly-reports-06-2015.

Gupta, S. (2014). Bandhan Founder Chandra Shekhar Ghosh: From Sweet Shop to Bank Owner. *The Economic Times,* April 4. Accessed July 25, 2015: http://articles.economictimes.indiatimes.com/2014-04-04/news/48867133_1_chandra-shekhar-ghosh-bandhan-bank-licence.

Hanleybrown, F., Kania, J. and Kramer, M. (2012). Channeling Change: Making Collective Impact Work. Stanford Social Innovation Review online. Accessed July 24, 2015: http://www.ssireview. org/blog/entry/channeling_change_making_collective_impact_work.

Hanover Research (2013). *Best Practices in University-Nonprofit Partnerships*. Washington, DC: Hanover Research.

Harris, E. (2010). Six Steps to Successfully Scale Impact in the Nonprofit Sector. *The Evaluation Project*, 15(1), 4–6.

Harvard Business Review (2012). Muhammad Yunus, (December). Accessed July 28, 2015: https://hbr. org/2012/12/muhammad-yunus.

Harwood, R. C. (2015). Putting Community in Collective Impact. Collective Impact Forum. Accessed July 25, 2015: http://collectiveimpactforum.org/resources/putting-community-collective-impact.

Heisman, E. (2013). Philanthropic Leapfrog: Giving in China. Nonprofit Quarterly. Accessed July 16, 2015: http://nonprofitquarterly.org/2013/09/06/philanthropic-leapfrog-giving-in-china.

Hoque, Z. and Parker, L. (2015). Accountability, Governance, and Performance Management in Nonprofit Organizations: An Overview. In Hoque and Parker (eds.), *Government Performance Management in Global Organizations*. New York: Routledge, 1–9..

International Center for Not-for-Profit Law (2011). NGO Laws in Sub-Saharan Africa. Global Trends in NGO Law 3(3), June. Accessed July 7, 2015: http://www.icnl.org/research/trends/trends3-3. pdf.

Jackson, T. and Claeye, F. (2011). Cross-Cultural management and NGO Capacity Building. In Kathryn A. Agard (ed.), *Leadership in Nonprofit Organizations*. London: Sage, 859–870.

Kania, J. and Kramer, M. (2011). Collective Impact. *Stanford Social Innovation Review*, (Winter), 9(1), 36–41.

Kelley, T. and Kelley, D. (2013). *Creative Confidence: Unleashing the Creative Potential Within Us All*. New York: HarperCollins.

Leadbeater, C. (2007). *Social Enterprise and Social Innovation: Strategies for the Next Ten Years*. London: Office of the Third Sector.

Luke, B. and Chu, V. (2013). Social Enterprise Versus Social Entrepreneurship: AnExamination of the Why and How in Pursuing Social Change. *International Small Business Journal*, 31(7): 764–784.

Martin, R. L. and Osberg, S. (2007). Social Entrepreneurship: The Case for Definition. *Stanford Social Innovation Review* (Spring): 5(2), 28–39.

Martin, R. L. and Osberg, S. R. (2015).Two Keys to Sustainable Social Enterprise. *Harvard Business Review* (May): 93(5), 86–94.

Millner, J. (2013). How Crowdfunding Drives Development. *The Guardian*, September 3.

Morton, B. (2013).An Overview of International NGOs in Development Cooperation, Case Study 7 in Working with Civil Society in Foreign Aid: Possibilities for South-South Cooperation? United Nations Development Plan. Accessed July 11, 2015: http://www.cn. undp.org/content/dam/ china/docs/Publications/UNDP-CH11%20An%20Overview%20of%20International%20NGOs%20 in%20Development%20Cooperation.pdf.

Oostergard, L. R. and Nielsen, J. (2005). To Network or Not to Network: NGO Experiences with Technical Networks. Accessed July 25, 2015: http://cercle.lu/download/partenariats/AIDSNET networkornotnetwork.pdf.

Oxfam (2015). Accessed July 12, 2015: https://www.oxfam.org/en/worldwide.

Pfeiffer, J., Johnson, W., Fort, M., Shakow, A., Hagopian, A., Gloyd, S. and Gimbel-Sherr, K. (2008). Strengthening Health Systems in Poor Countries: A Code of Conduct of Nongovernmental Organizations. *American Journal of Public Health*, 98(12): 2134–2140.

Rosenberg, T. (2013). Fixes: A Hospital Network with a Vision. New York Times. Accessed July 20, 2015: http://opinionator.blogs.nytimes.com/2013/01/16/in-india-leading-a-hospital-franchise-with-vision/?_r=0.

Salamon, L. (1997). *The International Guide to Nonprofit Law*. New York: John Wiley & Sons.

Salamon, L. (2010). Putting the Civil Society Sector on the Economic Map of the World. *Annals of Public and Cooperative Economics*, 82(2): 167–210.

Salamon, L., Wojciech Sokolowski, and Associates (2004). *Global Civil Society: Dimensions of the Nonprofit Sector* (Vol. Two). Bloomfield, CT: Kumarian Press.

Salamon, L. (2014). *Leverage for Good: An Introduction to the New Frontiers of Philanthropy and Social Investment*. New York: Oxford University Press

Save the Children (2015). Accessed July 12, 2015: http://www.savethechildren.org.

Schwab Foundation (2015).Accessed July 8, 2015: http://www.schwabfound.org.

Simon, K. W. (2007). International Non-Governmental Organizations. *The International Lawyer*, 41(2), 525–539.

Skoll Foundation (2015). Accessed July 8, 2015: http://www.skollfoundation.org/entrepreneur/bart-weetjens.

Smedley, T. (2014). Shifting Sands: The Changing Landscape for International NGOS. *The Guardian*. Accessed July 20, 2015: http://www.theguardian.com/global-development-professionals-network/2014/mar/28/internaitonal-ngos-funding-network.

Smith, D. H., Stebbins, R. A. and Dover, M. A. (2006). *A Dictionary of Nonprofit Terms and Concepts*. Bloomington & Indianapolis: Indiana University Press.

Smith, J. G. and Lumba, P. M. (2008). Knowledge Management Practices and Challenges in International Networked NGOs: The Case of One World International. *The Electronic Journal of Knowledge Management*, 6(2), 167–176.

Stecker, M. J. (2014). Revolutionizing the Nonprofit Sector Through Social Entrepreneurship. *Journal of Economic Issues*, 48(2), 349–357.

Sweikar, M. (2015). Pooling Public-Private Partnership Best Practices. Accessed July 25, 2015: http://www.devex.com/news/pooling-public-private-partnership-best-practices-85276.

The Aspen Institute (2002). *The Nonprofit Sector and Government: Clarifying the Relationship*. *Nonprofit Sector Strategy Group*. Washington, DC: The Aspen Institute.

The Economist (2014). Enter the Chinese NGO: The Communist Party is Giving MoreFreedom to a Revolutionary Idea. *The Economist*. Accessed July 20, 2015: http://www.economist.com/news/leaders/21600683-communist-party-giving-more-freedom-revolutionary-idea-enter-chinese-ngo.

Turner, E. A. L. (2010). Why Has the Number of International Non-GovernmentalOrganizations Exploded since 1960? *Cliodynamics*, 1: 81–91.

United Nations (2003). Handbook on Non-Profit Institutions in the System of National Accounts, Statistical Papers, Series F, No. 91, United Nations Publication, Sales No. E.03.XVII.9. Accessed July 11, 2015: http://unstats.un.org/unsd/publication/seriesf/seriesf_91e.pdf.

Universidad de Monterrey (2015). Accessed July 21, 2015: http://www.udem.edu.mx/Eng/Somos-UDEM/Pages/valores2.aspx.

Warnecke, T. (2013). Entrepreneurship and Gender: An Institutional Perspective. *Journal of Economic Issues*, 47(2): 455–463.

Warnecke, T. (2015). Greening Gender Equity: Microfinance and the Sustainable Development Agenda. *Journal of Economic Issues*, 49(2): 553–562.

Yunus, M. (2010). *Building Social Business: The New Kind of Capitalism that Serves Humanity's Most Pressing Needs*. New York: Public Affairs.

Zahra, S. A., Gedajlovic, E., Neubaum, D. O. and Shulman, J. M. (2009). A Typology of Social Entrepreneurs: Motives, Search Processes and Ethical Challenges. *Journal of Business Venturing*, 24(5): 519–532.

17

TYPES OF SMALL-SCALE ENTREPRENEURSHIP

Some lessons from Bulgaria

Tanya Chavdarova

Introduction

The collapse of socialism has intensified the interest of the social sciences in small-scale entrepreneurship[1] in transition economies such as Central and Eastern Europe (CEE). On a theoretical level, the debate mirrors a tension at the core of theories of entrepreneurship, emphasising either supply-side or demand-side perspectives (Thornton, 1999). Supply-side perspectives argue that special types of people are entrepreneurs and thus emphasise the psychological characteristics of individuals. Alternatively, demand-side perspectives focusing on the institutional environment argue that people are drawn into entrepreneurship by a culture that supports it and stems from a number of infra-structural factors (Davidsson, 1995). The focus of entrepreneurship studies in transition economies has switched over the last 25 years from the supply-side to the demand-side viewpoint (Smallbone and Welter, 2009). Accumulated knowledge about various traits of post-socialist entrepreneurship raised the issue of its proper conceptualisation. In particular, a highly relevant question is whether concepts of entrepreneurship developed in a market economy context can provide an appropriate interpretative framework for the CEE context. This chapter aims to contribute to the debate by analysing the types of small-scale entrepreneurship in existence in Bulgaria.

This chapter makes use of data from a number of national and cross-national representative surveys of the Bulgarian population and Bulgarian business. It is underpinned empirically by a number of qualitative studies in which the author has been involved. These include a study of the patterns in which sole proprietors emerge and become established[2] (Chavdarova, 2005, 2007); a study of cultural encounters in business based on 25 in-depth interviews with Bulgarian and foreign entrepreneurs and managers (Chavdarova, 2004); a study of informal self-employment based on 24 semi-structured interviews with informally self-employed workers (Chavdarova, 2010, 2014a); and a study of contracts with hidden clauses based on 12 semi-structured interviews with young workers who have concluded fake labour contracts with companies operating in Sofia (Chavdarova, 2015). Qualitative sampling makes the findings valid only for the group of respondents studied. The chapter begins with an introduction of the theoretical framework. The second section briefly outlines the structure of small businesses in Bulgaria and their institutional context. The final section comprises a discussion of the main findings from the research related to the different types of small-scale entrepreneurship.

Theoretical notes

Historically, entrepreneurship has at least two meanings (Sternberg and Wennekers, 2005). The *occupational* notion of entrepreneurship refers to owning and managing a business (Hebert and Link, 1982). Its dynamic aspect focuses on the creation of new businesses, while a static aspect relates to the number of business owners. The *behavioural* notion of entrepreneurship refers to the specific behaviour of occupational entrepreneurs and emphasises them as individuals (Acs and Armington, 2006).

Starting from the assumption that all small business owners are occupational entrepreneurs, this work goes further to explore their types of behaviour. They are interpreted here first through their entrepreneurial functions in two opposing ideal types: *judging possibilities* and *calculating certainties*.[3] From the behavioural viewpoint, an entrepreneur is only conceptualised as 'someone who specialises in making judgmental decisions about the coordination of scarce resources' (Casson, 1982). The term *judgmental* implies that the decision cannot be simply a routine application of a standard rule (Acs, 2006). In the behavioural sense, the entrepreneur is the Schumpeterian type whose primary function is to innovate by seizing an opportunity[4] (Schumpeter, 1961). The entrepreneur follows the logic of profit maximisation and accumulation. The opposite pool in the continuum is shaped by those occupational entrepreneurs whose primary function is to calculate certainties, the first of which is their own working capacity. I interpret this ideal type as an *autonomous worker* who is an occupational entrepreneur by necessity. The genesis of small enterprises is driven by push factors: people set up enterprises because they have few other choices. Their calculations are guided by the desire to maximise consumption. Accordingly, in a behavioural sense, the distinction between an entrepreneur and an autonomous worker is closely linked to their motivation and business aims.

The types of entrepreneur described are at the core of the discussion of entrepreneurship in CEE, although they may be named differently. Thus, Scase (1997, 2003) distinguishes between *entrepreneurship* and *proprietorship*. Entrepreneurship refers to a person's commitment to capital accumulation and business growth, whereas proprietorship describes the ownership of property and other assets which may be used for trading purposes to realise profits, but which are not used for the longer term purposes of capital accumulation. According to Scase (2003), an entrepreneur may forego personal consumption and may actively search out market opportunities, which involves taking risks and coping with uncertainty. A proprietor does not reinvest surpluses for the purposes of future long-term capital accumulation but rather consumes and uses them to sustain a particular standard of living.

In a similar vein, a distinction is made between *Schumpeterians* and '*shopkeepers*' (Wennekers and Thurik, 1999) or between *entrepreneurs* and *self-employed people* (Róna-Tas, 2001). By following the Weberian distinction, Róna-Tasunder underscores the difference between an enterprise and a household. In the case of entrepreneurship, the main unit is the enterprise, which is separated from the household and follows its own logic. In the case of self-employment, the natural limits are set by the household. Whatever extra money is needed is borrowed from family and friends. When small enterprises hire new workers, they hire from a limited pool of relatives and friends.

In terms of development, the entrepreneurial approach sees economic units on a continuum from the smallest single-person business to the largest company. Each size is a station in the process of entrepreneurial expansion. Hence the fusing of small- and mid-sized enterprises into the single concept of SMEs. The alternative approach perceives small (or rather micro-) enterprises as unwilling and unable to grow. A large segment is not even self-employed full-time, using self-employment to supplement their incomes as traditional employees. Thus, the second approach sees the economy not as continuous, but as segmented by size, which explains the necessity to study small businesses as separate units (Reynolds et al., 2002).

Both Scase and Róna-Tas claim that the point of departure in CEE is not the entrepreneur, but rather the proprietor or self-employed person, who can choose between various options to deploy their labour. Clearly, few business owners are purely either one or another type in practice. The learning experience and some external conditions are proven to be important factors for mingling the two types (e.g. Smallbone and Welter, 2006). In this perspective, the first objective of this chapter is to verify the presence of the types of entrepreneurship outlined and to describe the interplay between them. Its second objective is to identify the typical self-perceptions of small-scale entrepreneurs concerning the character of their activities and to juxtapose their 'subjective classifications' with 'objectively' derived types based on research data. Consequently, the third objective is to evaluate the need for other typologies to characterise entrepreneurship that might be relevant not only to Bulgaria but also to other CEE countries. This chapter argues that different types of small-scale entrepreneurship coexist in the post-socialist context of Bulgaria. They appear as hybrid forms within a continuum between opposing types: entrepreneurs vs. autonomous workers, formal vs. informal and market vs. network entrepreneurs. In the course of their business development, small entrepreneurs can and often do undergo a transition from one type to another. Studying these *transitions* is equally, if not even more, important than a static description of the distinguishing features of small-scale entrepreneurship. Their analysis could help in formulating a more adequate theory of entrepreneurship in CEE.

Small businesses in Bulgaria: structure and institutional constraints

Small-scale entrepreneurship began to gain ground in Bulgaria in the last couple of years before 1989. Private activities were typically part-time or 'on-the-side', with people keeping one foot firmly in the state sector (Chavdarova, 1994). Since 1990, an explosion of small business start-ups has been observed in CEE.[5] The vast majority of this expansion was due to self-employment and tiny new start-ups, often consisting of no more than a single entrepreneur or a few partners and/or employees. Entrepreneurial activity is steadily increasing. Data from the Euro Barometer Survey on Entrepreneurship reveals that over a third of Bulgarians (36 percent as compared with 23 percent in the EU) reported in 2012 that they had previously started a business or were taking steps to do so, while in 2009 the figure was only 15 percent (EC, 2014b). Yet the proportion of entrepreneurs who have started their own business to exploit a market opportunity is lower than average (42 percent as compared with 49 percent in the EU) (ibid.).

The distribution of types of enterprise in Bulgaria is similar to that in the EU: the largest proportion are micro enterprises at 92.2 percent of the total number,[6] followed by small (6.5 percent), medium (1.2 percent) and large enterprises (0.2 percent) (BSMEPA, 2013). However, the contribution of SMEs in creating added value (62.6 percent vs. 57.6 percent in the EU) and especially in providing jobs (75.5 percent vs. 66.5 percent in the EU) exceeds the EU average in almost all sectors. Their labour productivity, however, is below the EU average because of the lower capacity to benefit from economies of scale, especially in low-value sectors: almost half of Bulgarian SMEs are active in the wholesale and retail trade sector (EC, 2014b; BSMEPA, 2013).

So far Bulgarian business has undergone three stages in its development. The first stage (1989–1997) involved a huge degree of uncertainty leading to substantial year-to-year variations in all economic and social indicators. The years 1996 and 1997 were crucial both economically (with the bankruptcy of 16 banks, hyperinflation and introduction of a currency board) and politically (with the beginning of intensive social protests which brought down the government). The second period (1998–2008) was more settled in terms of conditions for business. The third stage began with the unfolding of the global economic crisis. It has seriously affected the small businesses sector by putting strong pressure on them to improve productivity and diversify their markets. From 2008 to 2013, the value added by SMEs in Bulgaria declined by 4 percent, whereas in large companies it increased by about 8 percent (EC, 2014b). The fourth stage began with the first signs of economic recovery after 2013.

In Bulgaria, as in all ex-socialist societies, the period after 1989 saw a deliberate process of transferring and imposing the market institutions inherent to capitalism. This transfer is still facing three major types of difficulty. The first obstacle relates to the institutional instability and unpredictability inherent in the frequent changes in market legislation in Bulgaria. Basic tax laws, for instance, were amended 66 times between 1991 and 1998, while the regulations for their implementation underwent 43 amendments. The *Centre for Legal Initiatives* has noted that the amount of legislative amendments increased over the period from 2005 to 2010 (Valtchev et al., 2011).

The second major problem relates to the need to guarantee effective enforcement of market rules. Corruption, cronyism, red tape and administrative inefficiency became significant obstacles to business in Bulgaria. The means for effectively enforcing market legislation have consolidated over time, especially during the 2000s. Despite improved business conditions (World Bank, 2011) and improved security in terms of property rights, the most critical threats to the protection of property rights are still the low level of independence of the judicial authorities and the unreliability of legal structures (Heritage Foundation, 2011).

The third main problem concerns the almost total absence of public confidence in the reliable functioning of market institutions. This is abundantly documented in the Bulgarian case (for a review see Chavdarova, 2014b). In some societies including Bulgaria, systemic distrust has profound historical roots. In such societies, conflicts arise between legality and legitimacy; the official economic order may be legal but is not legitimate, whereas socio-economic practices and conventions, even when (partly) illegal, gain legitimacy (Giordano, 2003). If trust in the system is low, it must be substituted by clearly delineated interpersonal trust. As a result, activities become more deeply embedded in networks, which may compensate for the lack of institutional linkages. Networking thus becomes of vital importance for entrepreneurship and may constitute another criterion to distinguish between the ideal types of 'market' and 'network' players.

Institutional constraints to a large extent explain the sharp rise of the informal economy in CEE over the last 25 years (Williams et al., 2013). The socialist informal economy in Bulgaria has been transformed both in qualitative and quantitative terms. Qualitatively, one of the main changes is the increasing number of informally self-employed people and undeclared work in small businesses (Chavdarova, 2014a). Quantitatively, while in 1988 the informal economy accounted for between 20 percent and 25 percent of GDP (Chavdarova 2014b), by 2012 Bulgaria had the largest share of informal economy across the EU27, accounting for 31.9 percent of GDP (Schneider, 2012). According to data from the Special Euro Barometer Survey on undeclared work, the estimated share of people who perform undeclared work[7] in the EU27 member states ranges between 15 percent and 30 percent and is notably higher only in Bulgaria and Latvia (EC, 2007). These data clearly reveal the need to consider two other types of entrepreneurial behaviour: formal entrepreneurs abiding with market regulations and informal entrepreneurs who circumvent them.

Weak institutions and unfair competition from the informal sector offer incentives to destructive entrepreneurship (Baumol, 1990), which is related to corruption in its various forms. In these conditions, successful entrepreneurs are not always admired or accorded a high social status. A representative sociological study of the public image of the Bulgarian entrepreneurs reveals that the public have little confidence in entrepreneurs, declining in the 2007–2012 period (Luleva et al., 2013). Although on an individual level entrepreneurs are more associated with positive characteristics (hard-working, visionary, etc.), their wealth is often perceived as acquired in violation of moral principles. Two out of every three believe that large gains are a result of such violations. Between 40 and 60 percent of the entrepreneurs surveyed also share the view that entrepreneurship in Bulgaria is not sufficiently fair (ibid.: 12). Data from earlier representative surveys show that there is a stable group of entrepreneurs (33 percent in 1997; 33 percent in 2004; 34 percent in 2011), who cannot or who do not wish to be emancipated from the view that business is a zero-sum game, i.e. people only gain wealth at the expense of other people (BSMEPA, 2013). The wealth dilemma in Bulgarian society is a complex result of ideological schemes, ongoing practices and historical legacy.

Types of small-scale entrepreneurship

Entrepreneur vs. autonomous worker

Three distinctive types of small-scale entrepreneurs can be empirically verified. The first type mirrors the criterion of the entrepreneurial paradigm. It consists of entrepreneurs who have not been forced to set up their businesses by external factors and who set capital accumulation and business expansion as their goal. They become accustomed to risks and uncertainty and increase their economic effectiveness *by managing risk and by fighting*.[8] Risk is assessed as mostly related to the problem of scarce capital, trust in business partners or unfair competition and bribes. Schumpeterian entrepreneurs have a long-term vision of business development: they are those who say to themselves: *Let's try to make a rocket: If we eventually produce a bicycle or even a wheelbarrow, it will be much better than if we plan a wheelbarrow from the very beginning.*

The autonomous worker type was also clearly identified by the research and consisted of those who were forced to set up their business because of potential or actual unemployment. Typically, these individuals run their business on a day-to-day basis and lack any elaborated vision. Unpredictable changes in market regulations are not conducive to the development of long-term orientation. This is why very few Bulgarian companies have a strategy, vision or goal.

The studies also identify a third type which I refer to as a *hybrid entrepreneur,* characterised by a number of specific combinations. First in relation to motivation, the research shows that some of those forced into business in order to make ends meet have gradually developed internal drive and entrepreneurial qualities and vice versa: for some respondents there were no push factors when they started their business. In the course of time, therefore, they relinquished their ambitions but continued running their business just as a way of getting by. Some of the individuals studied were also subject to a combination of pull and push factors at the very beginning of their business activities. Second, hybridisation occurs between survival and expansion and between short- and long-term thinking. In the highly insecure Bulgarian business environment, one of the strategies that can ensure business survival is expansion. One group of respondents started with great ambitions and long-term planning and, after experiencing much insecurity and ups and downs, ended up with a sense of resignation and living day by day.

The three types of small-scale occupational entrepreneurship outlined above are closely reflected in the self-perceptions of the individuals studied. Those who define themselves as entrepreneurs consider creativity and vision as the benchmark of their entrepreneurialism. Profit is only seen as a symbolic manifestation of the social status they have achieved.

In contrast, there are many more shades of self-perception among autonomous workers. In some cases, those who define themselves as such view the running of an enterprise just like any other job. Their distinctive quality is to be a *worker without a boss*.

> [I am] a common worker without a boss. You have the advantage of fixing your own working hours, your coffee breaks, you have a bit more spare time, a bit more freedom. This is an advantage. But there are disadvantages: you take responsibility for everything. (. . .) I see myself rather as a worker in business. Nothing else. How can I be an entrepreneur when I can invest in nothing but that small shop? That's all I have strength for.
>
> *(male, aged 33, coffee shop)*

Business is primarily viewed from the point of view of investment opportunities and entrepreneurial qualities are only ascribed to big investors. For the same reason, in some other cases autonomous workers perceive themselves either as *artisans* or as *traders*.

> The thing is that we offer quite small services. Resources are limited, we can't make any investments and we can't even hire workers. (. . .) I would definitely apply the word 'entrepreneur' to other spheres, not to my line of business. I'm just an artisan, not an entrepreneur.
>
> *(female, aged 35, cosmetics studio)*

> I wouldn't call myself an entrepreneur, [but] a trader with a small business. To me a trader is not an entrepreneur.
>
> *(male, aged 45, production of calendars)*

Another nuance in the self-perception of autonomous workers stems from their focus on *professionalism*. This is typical among those who were brought up during the socialist period and who offer highly qualified services.

> I and my fellow colleagues do not define ourselves as businessmen. We represent a generation brought up in an entirely different tradition. (. . .) We see business rather as a profession: we have acquired some knowledge, some background, which is remote from what we see in the actual work process, but we just treat the business as a profession which we need to perfect and develop.
>
> *(female, aged 49, software development)*

The hybrid entrepreneur type is reflected first in an indeterminate self-perception of being both an employer and a worker. Here a specific understanding emerges: in order to be a good employer you have to be a good worker. This category also includes those who are unable or do not wish to define their status in any way. Rather, they perceive themselves in terms of negation. Their negative definitions result from their self-perception as being still unaccomplished entrepreneurs. More often, however, they reflect the prevailing negative connotations of the term entrepreneur/businessman in Bulgaria as being associated with some kind of illegal economic behaviour.

> In terms of revenue, employees and the scope of my activities, my business is probably medium-sized, but in terms of the resources I personally use, in terms of lifestyle, many small business people can afford more things than I can. In terms of personal attitude, I am not a businessman, not at all . . . I don't fit the common image of the Bulgarian businessman.
>
> *(male, aged 40, furniture production)*

Another rather extreme self-perception is linked to the idea that nobody can be an entrepreneur in Bulgaria.

> At present you cannot be an entrepreneur in this country, because everything is very difficult, very difficult and there is nothing to motivate you to be an entrepreneur. (. . .) There would not be any problem for me to be an entrepreneur if I was somewhere else and not in Bulgaria. That is because Western entrepreneurs, as far as I know, can get credit to buy equipment, to do everything necessary and only after that he/she pays everything back, [after] he/she starts making money. While in this country all you can do is only to keep body and soul together.
>
> *(female, aged 44, hairdressing)*

This view is an emanation of social pessimism backed by an idealistic view of the Western markets. It confirms a perception that the socioe-conomic environment in Bulgaria is hostile to the entrepreneurial spirit and people are entrepreneurs *despite* and not *because* of the environment.

This research reveals correlation between the three objectified types of small-scale entrepreneurship and subjective self-perceptions. Although the non–representative data do not allow any conclusions to be drawn about how widespread the three types are, empirical findings confirm that the area of small businesses abounds in various transitions from one type to another one.

Formal vs. informal entrepreneur

Informal entrepreneurship is a substantial part of the informal economy all over the world (Williams, 2006). Three groups are considered by the general public in the EU27 member states as most likely to be involved in undeclared work: unemployed people, self-employed people and illegal immigrants (EC, 2007). Small businesses, including self-employment,[9] are a major source of informality in Bulgaria. The main reasons are that legislation and credit practices do not favour micro and small enterprises and market institutions are not effective. Companies spare no criticism about the frequent changes in legislation and especially about municipal administrations. They consistently complain about the tax burden, social security payments, official charges and difficult access to finance (e.g. BSMEPA, 2013; Chavdarova, 2014b).

Centeno and Portes (2003) argue that the character of informality is dependent on the relationship between the state and civil society. The results of two qualitative studies of young informally self-employed workers and of contracts with hidden clauses concluded by wage workers in the capital city of Sofia corroborate this line of argumentation. Tax evasion and avoidance are typically justified with the argument that there is a reciprocal relationship between the citizen and the state: if the state fails to perform its obligations, citizens should likewise have no obligations. The individuals interviewed share the view that going informal is not a matter for discussion; it is just *a fact* in the country's economic landscape.

> No, I am doing nothing wrong, so I have an easy conscience. (. . .) I think that [undeclared activity] goes on all over the place and most people do not give a second thought to whether it is right or not. It is an established fact.
>
> *(female, aged 24, foreign language teacher)*

In principle informal self-employment raises at least three types of risk. The first concerns possible legal and social sanctions, and is protected by the legitimacy of illegality and weak institutional control. The second risk is related to the lack of social security protection for entirely self-employed people. This is not perceived to be a serious risk as, in any case, the health and social services provided by the state are considered scanty and of poor quality. The third risk is connected to the lack of contract enforcement guarantees, for which networking largely compensates. Its core is the need to replace the vacuum of trust in the system with personal trust. The particular way economic activities are embedded in the constellation of institutions, networks and culture can solve the problem of opportunism and create a perception that the risks faced by informally self-employed people are not significantly greater than those incurred by registered self-employed workers.

In the perspective of small entrepreneurs as employers, two forms of informality have gained ground: first, the use of hired labour without a signed employment contract; and second, the practice of concealing remuneration by paying remuneration in part in cash, known as 'envelope wages' (Williams, 2008). Here, paying cash 'on the black' involves signing an employment contract with hidden clauses either concerning pay or working hours or both. The practice of concealing actual remuneration and paying salaries partly in cash is based on mutual verbal agreement: The employer pays the lowest possible social security contributions for the worker, while the latter also benefits by not paying the full amount of income tax, although remaining socially under-insured.

Envelope wages involve between 14 percent and 21 percent (according to different surveys) of employed persons in Bulgaria (Dzhekova and Williams, 2014). Employers believe that this phenomenon has been increasing since 2010, while they also reported higher levels of involvement in such practices (ibid., 47–48). A nationwide representative survey carried out in 2014 identifies four types of practices that result in payment of envelope wages (MLSP, 2014). The most widespread is signing fake part-time contracts instead of full-time ones: employees were officially appointed to work 4 or even only 2 hours per day, while they actually worked 8 or more hours per day. The second practice is to deliberately reappoint persons from positions with a higher *Minimum Social Insurance Threshold*[10] to positions with a lower threshold. The third practice identified is the appointment of people on contracts with low wages, supplemented by cash 'on the black'. The fourth practice of hiring people without any contract is less common. A qualitative study of contracts with hidden clauses conducted in 2012 fully confirms these findings (Chavdarova, 2015). The respondents were employees in different-sized companies, predominantly small businesses. Differences between their practices in concluding employment contracts with hidden clauses are only noticeable with regard to the amount of wages fixed in the contract: larger companies can afford to pay higher labour charges.

Data from the research support the assumption that the distinction between formal and informal entrepreneurship is highly relevant in the typology of entrepreneurship. Unlike in the first typology, here the pure types appear to carry less weight. Their hybridisation is what matters. The particular way small entrepreneurs combine formal and informal practices in their economic activities alters in accordance with legislative changes.

Market vs. network entrepreneur

Economic action is always socially embedded. Its structural embeddedness (also called *network embeddedness*, see Granovetter 1985) is defined as 'the contextualization of economic exchange in patterns of ongoing interpersonal relations' (Zukin and DiMaggio, 1990). Network resources embedded in both inter-organisational ties and interpersonal connections benefit entrepreneurs through the transmission of valuable information resources. These in turn help to consolidate the reliability and reputation of companies. Embedding economic action in networks may, however, also lead to negative entrepreneurial selection where those who survive may be the ones who are good at networking and know whom and how to bribe.

While traditional resources exist 'within a firm's boundaries', the network resources exist 'outside a firm's boundaries and within its social networks' (Gulati, 2007). Whereas prior research on small business focused on the functions of intra-company resources, socio-economic conditions in CEE require explicit emphasis on the company's ties with key external constituents including, but not limited to, partners, suppliers and customers. The creation and accumulation of social capital from networks becomes *a key* resource for small entrepreneurship in CEE. In the Bulgarian case, networks appear to be of such vital importance that they may shape the very definition of being entrepreneur. The ability to create and rationally use network resources might turn into a core function of a new entrepreneurial type – the *network entrepreneur* (Burt, 2000).[11] The network function of entrepreneurs creates a new demarcation that could be used in another typology of entrepreneurship. Market players who conduct transactions at arm's length and have no relations with each other are neither supported by structural conditions nor by the cultural legacy of the informal institution referred to in Bulgaria as *vruzki* (*connections*) (Chavdarova, 2013).

Research also confirms the importance of networking in distinguishing a specific type of entrepreneurship. Representative data about entrepreneurs' attitudes to work reveal that during the last 20 years about 87 percent of entrepreneurs consider hard work as a main factor for success. Nevertheless, the share of entrepreneurs who believe that success also requires luck and 'connections' has more than doubled, reaching 86 percent in 2011 (BSMEPA, 2013).

In the qualitative studies, respondents also underscore the network type of entrepreneurship. While revealing their ideas about the set of qualities and achievements that identify someone as an entrepreneur, they outline three subgroups: creativity and ambition; profit making; contacts and ties. Creativity is perceived primarily as the ability to be innovative, something which goes hand-in hand with the Schumpeterian type. Although profit is always mentioned when it comes to entrepreneurship, some of the individuals interviewed indicate profit maximisation as an exclusive entrepreneurial feature. They connect it to investment opportunities. Third, entrepreneurship is seen as a networking activity. The individuals who share this opinion pay considerable attention to the particular nature of the Bulgarian market.

> As an entrepreneur you have to have particular qualities depending on the area of activity. If you find an unworked niche and, crucially, if you have good connections,

the state system might help you. However, if you are in another area, e.g. in the consultancy business, and you are a very good consultant, if you do not have any ties and connections the state will place a lot of obstacles in your way such as taxes, licenses, and anything related to money which you can hardly make up for unless you know the right people who can help you in your business and orders. The state helps only if you have a strong support.

(female, aged 31, HR consultancy)

The decisive point here is that networking is seen as a way to work in the shadows and to avoid taxation, licences and other state requirements. Networking and informal types of entrepreneurship presuppose one another but do not overlap.

This research about registered small entrepreneurs and young informal self-employed workers provides some hints about the way their economic activities are structurally embedded. The most widespread informal networks are family networks which are traditional in Bulgarian society, friends, (friends of friends) and colleagues. The manner and extent to which their activities are embedded in networks differ depending on their stage of business development. For registered small entrepreneurs, the role of the family is of crucial importance. Family business makes up 42.1 percent of the total number of enterprises and accounts for 28.3 percent of total employment (NSI and AFB, 2011). Stabilisation and expansion increase the importance of networks of friends and colleagues. For young informal entrepreneurs, the role of friends is central in the initial phase but diminishes as the business stabilises, while the role of 'friends of friends' advances due to their importance for strengthening the reputation of the enterprise. Almost all of those interviewed said that the most intensive way of expanding their customer network is recommendation by word of mouth, which highlights the effectiveness of transitive trust.

The research data also show that networks are able to cope with opportunism. This is especially visible with the example of riskier informal entrepreneurship. One-quarter of the respondents said that they had never been confronted with any kind of unfair behaviour. The remainder reported unfavourable experiences but most said that they were uncommon and entailed limited losses. Network players differ substantially from those who mostly conduct transactions at arm's length in terms of how they assess the risk of opportunism. The 'network' group emphasises the enormous importance of trust which diminishes risks. The 'market' players group, in contrast, highlights the irrelevance of opportunism since in their line of business personal trust is irrelevant. They are able to take preventive measures (e.g. not delivering the product before receiving payment), thus minimising the risk. This explains why they are frequently involved in transactions at arm's length for which no personal trust is required.

Concluding remarks

The post-socialist transformation offers a fruitful setting for investigating the various types of small-scale entrepreneurship. Starting from a situation in which private initiative was severely repressed, business and capital accumulation appeared abruptly and unexpectedly at the beginning of the 1990s. Many individuals considered entrepreneurship either as their only opportunity or as a new opportunity. Market forces have highlighted distinctions between entrepreneurs, not only by establishing different types of entrepreneurship but also by shaping typical transitions from one type to another. At least three demarcation lines can be drawn in this regard: entrepreneurs vs. autonomous workers, formal vs. informal entrepreneurs and market vs. network players. These ideal types are shaped by the specific institutional, structural and cultural context in Bulgaria but may be relevant for the CEE region in general. What is mostly observed in practice is the hybridisation of small-scale entrepreneurship. Combinations involve not only the continuum within each type but combinations between the different types.

A quarter of a century after the collapse of the centrally planned economy, the socio-economic landscape is still unsettled and dynamic. It mostly favours informal networking among both entrepreneurs and autonomous workers. This is reflected in the contradictory image of all business strata in Bulgarian society and mixed self-perceptions among small entrepreneurs. The heterogeneity of small-scale entrepreneurship emphasises the need to reconsider the usefulness of theories and concepts based on the principles of market economy. Their applicability should be questioned in a context where market rules are accommodated by institutions in a manner strongly dependent on informal practices.

Notes

1　The term *small-scale entrepreneurship* is used here for the owners of formal and informal micro- and small-sized enterprises, including self-employed workers. *Micro*-enterprises are those with fewer than 10 people employed and an annual turnover not exceeding €2 million; *Small* enterprises employ fewer than 50 persons and their annual turnover does not exceed €10 million as defined by EU criteria (see EC, 2009).
2　In 2002, 181 small businessmen located in Sofia were interviewed via a standardised interview. A six-branch quota sampling was applied with the following branches: craft and construction services; small industries and handicrafts; catering; transport; trade; and highly qualified services. Out of the quota sample, 30 small entrepreneurs were interviewed via semi-structured interviews in 2003.
3　'The entrepreneur is a maker of history, but his guide in making it is his judgment of possibilities and not a calculation of certainties'. (Shackle, 1982)
4　The difference between *opportunity* and *necessity* entrepreneurship indicates whether individuals started and grew their business in order to 'take advantage of a business opportunity (opportunity entrepreneurship) or because you have no better choices for work (necessity entrepreneurship)' (Reynolds et al. 2002: 12).
5　The average annual number of new enterprises per 1000 people in the 1995–2000 period for Bulgaria is 7.9, while the average for all CEE-EU member states (not including Croatia) is 4.9 (Ovaska and Sobel 2005:13).
6　Among them, those registered as self-employed represented 8 percent of all employed persons in 2014 (NSI, 2015).
7　Undeclared work is defined as: "Any paid activities that are lawful as regards their nature but not declared to public authorities, taking into account differences in the regulatory system of Member States" (EC, 2014a).
8　The phrases and sentences in italics here and below are excerpts from interviews with small entrepreneurs.
9　The opinion that self-employed people are the group most likely to be involved in undeclared work is shared by 16 percent of Bulgarian respondents as compared to 13 percent for the EU27 member states on average (EC 2007: 37).
10　*Minimum Social Insurance Thresholds* are determined on an annual basis for different business sectors and depend on the company's principal activity.
11　Unlike Burt (2000), this conceptualisation is not reduced to the act of brokerage.

References

Acs, Z. (2006). How is Entrepreneurship Good for Economic Growth? *Innovations, Technology, Governance, Globalization*, 1(1), 97–107.

Acs, Z. and Armington, C. (2006). *Entrepreneurship, Geography and American Economic Growth*. Cambridge, Cambridge University Press.

Baumol, W. (1990). Entrepreneurship, Productive, Unproductive and Destructive. *Journal of Political Economy*, 98(5), 893–921.

BSMEPA (Bulgarian Small and Medium Enterprises Promotion Agency). (2013). A Study of Entrepreneurship and the Prospects for Innovations Development in SMEs (2012–2013). Sofia, BSMEPA. http://www.sme.government.bg/en/uploads/2013/06/SMEs_2013_en.pdf [accessed 10 June 2015].

Burt, R. (2000). The Network Entrepreneur. In, Swedberg, R. (ed.). *Entrepreneurship – The Social Science View*. Oxford, Oxford University Press, pp. 281–307.

Casson, M.C. (1982). *The Entrepreneur, An Economic Theory*. Oxford, Martin Robertson.

Centeno, M.A. and Portes, A. (2003). The Informal Economy in the Shadow of the State. In, Fernandez-Kelly, P. and J. Sheffner (eds.) *Out of the Shadows, Political Action and the Informal Economy in Latin America*. Princeton, NJ, Princeton University Press, pp. 25–48.

Chavdarova, T. (1994). Irregular Economic Activity, The Case of Bulgarian Privatization. In, Ringen, S. and C. Wallace (eds.) *Societies in Transition, East-Central Europe Today*. Vol. 1, Aldershot, Avebury, pp. 163–74.

Chavdarova, T. (2004). Cultural Encounters in Business, Between the Bulgarian and Western Economic Culture. In, Kabakchieva, P. and R. Avramov (eds.) *East–West Cultural Encounters. Entrepreneurship, Governance, Economic Knowledge*. Sofia, Lik, pp. 25–130.

Chavdarova, T. (2005). The Bulgarian Small Business Owners, Entrepreneurs or Workers without Boss? *Sociological Problems*, 32(1), pp. 5–22.

Chavdarova, T. (2007). Business Relations as Trusting Relations, The Case of Bulgarian Small Business. In, Roth, K. (ed.) *Soziale Netzwerke und soziales Vertrauen in den Transformationslandern*. [Social Networks and Social Trust in the Transformation Countries]. Münster, Berlin, LIT Verlag, pp. 277–302.

Chavdarova, T. (2010). Informally Self-employed Young Bulgarians, Social Networks and Market Anonymity. In, Chavdarova, T., P. Slavova and S. Stoeva (eds.) *Markets as Networks*. Sofia, St. Kliment Ohridski University Press, pp. 49–61.

Chavdarova, T. (2013). Institutionalisation of Market Order and Re-institutionalisation of Vruzki (Connections) in Bulgaria. In, Giordano, C. and N. Hayoz (eds.) *Informality in Eastern Europe. Structures, Political Cultures and Social Practices*. Bern, Peter Lang, pp. 179–96.

Chavdarova, T. (2014a). Risky Businesses? Young People in Informal Self-Employment in Sofia. *International Journal of Urban and Regional Research*, 38(6), 2060–77.

Chavdarova, T. (2014b). *Sozialna vgradenost na drebnoto predpriemachestvo*. [The Social Embeddedness of Small-Scale Entrepreneurship]. Sofia, St. KlimentOhridski University Press.

Chavdarova, T. (2015). Towards a Private Market Ordering, Envelope wages in Bulgaria. In, Balla, B., W. Dahmen and A. Sterbling (eds.) *Demokratische Entwicklungen in der Krise? Politische und gesellschaftliche Verwerfungen in Rumänien, Ungarn und Bulgarien*. Hamburg, Krämer Verlag, pp. 221–48.

Davidsson, P. (1995). Culture, Structure and Regional Levels of Entrepreneurship. *Entrepreneurship and Regional Development*, 7(1), 41–62.

Dzhekova, R. and Williams, C. C. (2014). Tackling the Undeclared Economy in Bulgaria. A Baseline report. GREY Working Paper 1.University of Sheffield. http://papers.ssrn.com/sol3/papers.cfm?abstract_id=2430876 [accessed 30 November 2014].

EC (European Commission). (2007). Special Eurobarometer. October. Undeclared Work in the European Union. Brussels, EC. http://ec.europa.eu/public_opinion/archives/ebs/ebs_284_en.pdf [accessed 10 June 2015].

EC. (2009). The New SME Definition. User Guide and Model Declaration. Brussels, Enterprise and Industry Publications. http://ec.europa.eu/enterprise/policies/sme/files/sme_definition/sme_user_guide_en.pdf [accessed 10 June 2015].

EC. (2014a). Special Eurobarometer 402. Undeclared Work in the European Union. Brussels, EC. http://ec.europa.eu/public_opinion/archives/ebs/ebs_402_en.pdf [accessed 10 June 2015].

EC. (2014b). Enterprise and Industry. SBA Fact Sheet—Bulgaria. Brussels, EC. http://ec.europa.eu/enterprise/policies/sme/facts-figures-analysis/performance-review/files/countries-sheets/2014/bulgaria_en.pdf [accessed 10 June 2015].

Giordano, C. (2003). Beziehungspflege und Schmiermittel. Die Grauzone zwischen Freundschaft, Klientelismus und Korruption in Gesellschaften des öffentlichen Misstrauens. In, Hettlage, R. (ed.)

Verleugnen, Vertuschen, Verdrehen, Leben in der Lügengesellschaft. Konstanz, UVK Verlagsgesellschaft, pp. 97–119.

Granovetter, M. (1985). Economic Action and Social Structure, The Problem of Embeddedness. *American Journal of Sociology*, 91(3), 481–510.

Gulati, R. (2007). *Managing Network Resources, Alliances, Affiliations and other Relational Assets.* Oxford, Oxford University Press.

Hebert R.F. and Link, A.N. (1982). *The Entrepreneur, Mainstream Views and Radical Critiques.* New York, Praeger.

Heritage Foundation. (2011). 2011 Index of Economic Freedom. http://www.heritage.org/Index/Visualize?countries=Bulgaria&type=9 [accessed 6 October 2011].

Luleva, A., Dimitrova, B., Kolev, I., Janakiev, K., Ivanov, M. and Ganev, P. (2013). *Proizvoditeljatnavus mozhnosti. Obrasutnapredpriemacha v Bulgaria* [Producer of Opportunities. The Image of Entrepreneur in Bulgaria]. Sofia, IME.

MLSP (Ministry of Labour and Social Policy). (2014). Measuring the Impact of the Minimum Social Insurance Income on Employment. Survey Report Résumé. Sofia, MLSP. http://www.mlsp.government.bg/bg/docs/Rezume_MTSP-MOD.pdf [accessed 30 November 2014].

NSI and AFB (National Statistical Institute and Association of Family Business). (2011). *Familenbisnes v predprijatijata, Danni sa 2010* [Family Business in Enterprises, 2010 Data]. Sofia, AFB.

NSI (National Statistical Institute). (2015). Pazarnatruda. Saetiliza I koefizientinasaetost [Labour Market. Employed and Employment rates]. http://www.nsi.bg/en/content/6500/employed-and-employment-rates-national-level-statistical-regions-districts [accessed 13 June 2015].

Ovaska, T. and Sobel, R. (2005). Entrepreneurship in Post-Socialist Economies. *Journal of Private Enterprise*, 21(1), Fall, 8–28.

Reynolds, P., Hay, M., Bygrave, W., Camp, M. and Autio, E. (2002). *Global Entrepreneurship Monitor, Global Executive Report.* Kansas City, MO, Kauffman Center for Entrepreneurial Leadership.

Róna-Tas, A. (2001). The Worm and the Caterpillar, The Small Private Sector in the Czech Republic, Hungary and Slovakia. In, Bonnell, V. and T. Gold (eds.) *The New Entrepreneurs of Europe and Asia, Patterns of Business Development in Russia, Eastern Europe, and China.* Armonk, N.Y., M.E. Sharpe, pp. 39–65.

Scase, R. (1997). The Role of Small Businesses in the Economic Transformation of Eastern Europe, Real but Relatively Unimportant. *International Small Business Journal*, 16(1), 113–21.

Scase, R. (2003). Entrepreneurship and Proprietorship in Transition, Policy Implications for the SME Sector. In, McIntyre, R. and B. Dallago (eds.) *Small and Medium Enterprises in Transitional Economies.* Basingstoke, Palgrave, pp. 64–77.

Schneider, F. (2012). Size and Development of the Shadow Economy of 31 European and 5 other OECD Countries from 2003 to 2012, Some New Facts. http://www.econ.jku.at/members/Schneider/files/publications/2012/ShadEcEurope31_March%202012.pdf [accessed 13 June 2015].

Schumpeter, J. (1961). *The Theory of Economic Development. An Inquiry into Profits, Capital, Credit, Interest, and the Business Cycle.* New York, Oxford University Press.

Shackle, G.L.S. (1982). Foreword to Hebert, R.F. and A.N. Link, *The Entrepreneur, Mainstream Views and Radical Critiques.* New York, Praeger.

Smallbone, D. and Welter, F. (2006). Conceptualising Entrepreneurship in a Transition Context. *International Journal of Entrepreneurship and Small Business*, 3(2), 190–206.

Smallbone, D. and Welter, F. (2009). *Entrepreneurship and Small Business Development in Post-Socialist Economies.* New York, Routledge.

Sternberg R. and Wennekers, S. (2005). The Determinants and Effects of Using New Business Creation Using Global Entrepreneurship Monitor Data. *Small Business Economics*, 24(3), 193–203.

Thornton, P. (1999). The Sociology of Entrepreneurship. *Annual Review of Sociology*, 25, 19–46.

Valtchev et al. (2011). *YuridicheskiBarometar, 3* [Legal Barometer, 3]. Sofia, CLI. http:((cli-bg.org(Legal_barometer_BG_3.pdf [accessed 16 October 2011].

Wennekers, S. and Thurik, R. (1999). Linking Entrepreneurship and Economic Growth. *Small Business Economics*, 13(1), 27–55.

Williams, C.C. (2006). *The Hidden Enterprise Culture, Entrepreneurship in the Underground Economy.* Cheltenham, Edward Elgar.

Williams, C.C. (2008). Envelope Wages in Central and Eastern Europe and the EU. *Post-Communist Economies*, 20(3), 363–76.

Williams, C.C., Round, J. and Rodgers, P. (2013). *The Role of Informal Economies in the Post-Soviet World, The End of Transition?* London, Routledge.

World Bank. (2011). Doing Business. Measuring Business Regulations. http://www.doingbusiness.org/data/exploreeconomies/bulgaria [accessed 16 October 2011].

Zukin, S. and DiMaggio, P. (1990). Introduction. In, Zukin, S. and P. DiMaggio (eds.) *Structures of Capital, The Social Organization of the Economy*. Cambridge, Cambridge University Press, pp. 1–36.

18

SOCIAL ENTREPRENEURSHIP, INTERNATIONAL DEVELOPMENT, AND THE ENVIRONMENT

Tonia Warnecke

Sustainable development is possible only when people have the means to become agents of change.

(United Nations Development Group, 2013)

Introduction

As we navigate the twenty-first century, having experienced the promise and perils of globalization, the persistence of pressing social issues calls for new ways of thinking, learning, and doing. Global inequality is deepening; social, political, and environmental concerns range from societal tensions, jobless growth, and weakened representative democracy to increased severe weather events, corruption, and insufficient infrastructure (World Economic Forum, 2015). The interrelatedness of these concerns makes them harder to address using traditional public, private, and third sector methods.[1]

This chapter discusses an alternative approach—social enterprise—and situates social entrepreneurship in the context of international development, with a special focus on the environment. First, a discussion on the various conceptualizations of social entrepreneurship in the literature is initiated. Next, the changing role of business in international development is reviewed. Major world events including the Great Depression, World War II, and the OPEC oil embargo heavily influenced development thinking, particularly with regard to the state's role in economic planning. As development thinking evolved, the ways that businesses contribute to development goals evolved as well, from development project implementation, equipment/materials supply, delivery of social services, and advocacy for business-friendly development policies to philanthropy, corporate social responsibility, public–private partnerships, and the base-of-the-pyramid approach.

Increasing interest in "inclusive business" models has catalyzed the movement for social enterprises in the developing world. Although the institutional environment can be challenging, the widening gap between private and public sector provision of many goods and services has created many opportunities for social enterprise. I illustrate how social enterprises address environmental issues such as water access, clean energy, sustainable agriculture, and waste management, increasing synergy among economic, social, and environmental dimensions of sustainable development. Finally, I discuss challenges facing social enterprises, consider ways to move forward, and note the limitations of this approach to development problem-solving.

What is social entrepreneurship?

Social entrepreneurship has been an increasingly popular, but nebulous concept over the last couple of decades. A social enterprise utilizes business tools and skills to tackle pressing social problems in innovative and sustainable ways. Social enterprises focus on a wide array of social problems ranging from poverty, hunger, unemployment, and inequity to political exclusion, lack of financial access, poor education, and environmental degradation; no matter the social issue in mind, social value creation—not wealth creation—lies at the core of the organization's mission. Social enterprises may be organized as non-profit or for-profit businesses, or may incorporate a hybrid model combining both non-profit and for-profit, and in that, blurring sector boundaries (Dees, 2001).

While this is liberating on the one hand, on the other it has led social entrepreneurship to lack proper definition (Newbert and Hill, 2014). Where is the boundary line? Which enterprises are social enterprises and which are not? After all, many for-profit companies have corporate social responsibility platforms, and non-profit organizations often focus on social issues. Researchers have increasingly worked to answer this question, focusing on definitions of "social" and "entrepreneurship" to do so.

Entrepreneurship has been defined in terms of outcomes (e.g. self-employment rates), ways of thinking (e.g. creativity, innovation), or process (e.g. creative destruction) (Warnecke, 2013). In the late nineteenth century, French economist Jean Baptiste Say focused on the creation of value through entrepreneurship—shifting resources to higher productivity uses and/or greater yield (Dees, 2001). In 1934, Austrian-American economist Joseph Schumpeter emphasized entrepreneurship as a catalyst for change in available products and services (Warnecke, 2013). In 1985, Austrian-American management consultant Peter Drucker noted that entrepreneurship is not limited to the creation of new businesses, and not all new businesses are entrepreneurial (Dees, 2001). Instead, he concentrated on systematic, purposeful innovation within and outside the business or industry (Drucker, 1985). Within the business/industry, sources of innovation include unexpected success/failure, divergence between assumed and actual reality, process need, and unexpected change in industry/market structure; outside the business/industry, sources of innovation include demographics, changes in perception, and new knowledge (Drucker, 1985). This preoccupation with finding opportunity persists in more recent entrepreneurship literature (Timmons and Spinelli, 2011). The Global Entrepreneurship Monitor regularly conducts country studies to gauge the level of 'opportunity entrepreneurship'—entrepreneurship entered into by choice after discovering an opportunity and possessing the resources and skills needed to exploit it (Shane and Venkataraman, 2000).

Since social entrepreneurship is based around social value creation, we need to understand what that entails, and we still face the problem of measuring that value. Since "markets do not do a good job of valuing social improvements" it is difficult to measure social impact and compare that to the cost of the resources used to achieve that impact (Dees, 2001; see Ormiston and Seymour (2011) for a brief overview of impact measurement strategies). There are many forms of non-economic value such as social, cultural, and natural value, any of which can be cultivated through social entrepreneurship (Ormiston and Seymour, 2011). Social entrepreneurs are not a homogenous group. Zahra et al. (2009) classify three types of social entrepreneurs: social bricoleurs discover and address "small-scale local social needs"; social constructionists capitalize on market failures "by filling gaps to underserved clients in order to introduce reforms and innovations to the broader social system"; and social engineers "recognize systemic problems within existing social structures and address them by introducing revolutionary change."

Newbert and Hill (2014) suggest that for an enterprise to be social, benefits cannot be limited to the buyer and seller; the public should benefit. Social enterprises could create positive social benefit (for example, better education improves productivity) or reduce social harm (for example, reduced pollution improves health). Santos (2012) emphasizes the enterprise's creation of localized positive externalities that can be reaped by disadvantaged groups. He argues that social enterprises seek sustainable system-level solutions rather than organizational firm-level advantages, and emphasize empowerment rather than control. However, Agafonow (2014) argues that this conceptualization could refer to non-profits relying entirely on donations or to businesses with a social mission who emphasize value creation and reinvest proceeds back into the business, enabling growth and ideally increased social impact.

We can take away several insights from these definitional debates. Like traditional entrepreneurs, social entrepreneurs are committed leaders, innovative, and focused on opportunity recognition (Abu-Saifan, 2012). We can see this in Zahra et al. (2009): "Social entrepreneurship encompasses the activities and processes undertaken to discover, define, and exploit opportunities to enhance social wealth by creating new ventures or managing existing organizations in an innovative manner." Therefore, social enterprises are "not limited to business start-ups" (Dees, 2001). The distinguishing factor for social enterprise is the overriding focus on social impact. Most social enterprises fit into two categories— non-profit organizations which are financially self-sufficient, or on the path to being so (selling products/services), and for-profit organizations focusing first and foremost on social impact (Abu-Saifan, 2012; see also Tan and Yoo, 2015). Arguably, non-profits in a state of dependency are not entrepreneurial enough, and for-profit companies with social impact as a by-product, not the core of their mission, are not social enough. In the for-profit space, this helps to differentiate corporate social responsibility endeavors from social entrepreneurship, and in the non-profit space, it illustrates that social enterprises are a subset of socially focused organizations.

Business in international development

Changing tides of development thinking

Since approaches to international development have evolved significantly over the last century, a brief review helps to situate social entrepreneurship within the development landscape. In the wake of the Great Depression, the desire for strong governments to build stability and tackle pressing problems such as unemployment led to development efforts focused on large-scale, top-down planning processes. This approach was heavily shaped by John Maynard Keynes and his focus on using public policy to address market failures and reach full employment. Emphases on state-led development continued after World War II, given the economic boom facilitating full employment in the United States and high growth in several other industrialized countries, combined with geopolitical interests commanding the allocation of large amounts of foreign aid. During this time (the 1950s and 1960s), state-led development for a variety of developing nations (particularly in Latin America) included import substitution industrialization—funding the development of new national product markets to reduce dependence on industrial countries. However, in the early 1970s the breakdown of the Bretton Woods international monetary regime, followed by the OPEC oil embargo, contributed to a change in economic thinking that impacted countries at all stages of development. Rising unemployment rates and high inflation rates required re-prioritization of public sector resources, and neoliberal characterizations of "big government" led to increasing focus on private sector-led growth.

In the 1970s and 1980s, the resurgence of the private sector and growing skepticism about public sector efficiency shaped development approaches by prioritizing export-led growth and setting the stage for the proliferation of structural adjustment programs. In Latin America and Asia, and more recently in other regions including Africa, export processing zones (EPZs) became a "popular policy tool for development and export-oriented growth" (OECD, 2011). In exchange for private investment in export operations, EPZs provide business incentives including reduced taxation and (often) exemption from many labor and environmental laws. Structural adjustment programs (SAPs), on the other hand, represented a new way to allocate foreign aid. In order to receive aid disbursements from the 1980s onward, countries needed to follow a set of policy prescriptions supported by the International Monetary Fund and the World Bank. These policy prescriptions generally included streamlining public sector budgets, reducing social spending on education and health, liberalizing trade and finance, devaluing the currency, freezing prices and/or wages, privatizing state-owned business, and altering taxation structures. Although in some countries SAPs led to favorable macroeconomic outcomes, critiques of the approach intensified in the 1990s, particularly given the adverse impact on health, education, and gender inequality (Warnecke, 2006).

Many critics of EPZs, SAPs, and the neoliberal approach to development the programs symbolized, found refuge in human development theory. Human development theory (HDT), a response to the development approaches of the 1980s, is a people-centered theory based on four pillars of development: equality, sustainability, productivity, and empowerment (ul Haq, 2008). It is concerned with the "quality and distribution of economic growth, not only the quantity of such growth" (ul Haq, 2008), and the expansion of human freedoms through the maximization of individual capabilities (Sen, 1999). Proponents of HDT tend to support bottom-up, participatory approaches to development to ensure that people's expressed needs (not other people's assumptions about their needs) are being met. The Human Development Index, a quantitative measurement of socio-economic development based on education, income, and life expectancy, emerged from HDT in 1990 (Padgett and Warnecke, 2011); we can also see the influence of HDT in the Millennium Development Goals, eight development goals created in 2000 to address extreme poverty and hunger; primary education; gender equality; child mortality; maternal health; HIV/AIDS, malaria, and other diseases; environmental sustainability; and a global partnership for development (United Nations, 2014). Given the expiration of the 2015 deadline for the Millennium Development Goals, and concerns about lack of progress in some social and environmental aspects of development (Warnecke, 2015), implementing a new set of goals—this time called the Sustainable Development Goals—will be the next priority for international development institutions.

The role of business in international development

Business has always played a role in generating employment and wealth in developing countries, but was not considered a bona fide partner in development until recently (Razeq, 2014). The profit-maximizing, self-interested objectives of business contrasted with the public sector and intergovernmental organization focus on public welfare, and there were "many structural failures on record involving the private sector and development cooperation" (Razeq, 2014), with private sector-friendly SAPs representing one notable example. By the late 1990s, however, the push for human development increased emphasis on business regulations, a global code of conduct for multinational corporations, and the responsibilities of the private sector in the development sphere (Razeq, 2014).

Meanwhile, several factors including ongoing skepticism about the efficacy and transparency of large-scale planning and the foreign aid system contributed to the search for alternative agents of development (McWade, 2012). NGOs were increasingly motivated to seek private sector partners due to the need for funding, greater awareness of the influence of multinational corporations in the era of globalization, desire for credibility (particularly in regard to their own business models); outreach to new constituencies; and "the desire to change corporate behavior" (Molina-Gallart, 2014). The 2008 global financial crisis and continued turmoil in the euro-zone limited capacity for some sources of program funding and official development assistance, but also sparked discussions on new forms of economic cooperation between countries of the Global South (UNDP, 2011; Molina-Gallart, 2014). Concerns about the proliferation of vulnerable employment as well as spiking food prices renewed calls for development that is economically, socially, and environmentally sustainable (Heltberg et al., 2012).

We can see several distinct pathways for business involvement in international development. Traditionally, private companies have been hired for development project implementation, equipment/materials supply, or—in the era of privatization—delivery of social services; alternatives include advocacy for business-friendly development policies, philanthropy, and corporate social responsibility (CSR) initiatives (Ohno, 2013). By 2001 the United Nations (UN) had launched its Global Compact to support CSR efforts through a voluntary "strategic policy initiative for businesses that are committed to aligning their operations and strategies with ten universally accepted principles in the areas of human rights, labour, environment and anti-corruption" (United Nations, 2012). Given widely publicized scandals including Enron, the early years of the UN Global Compact coincided with increased focus on implementation, assessment, and better integration of CSR into strategic frameworks (United Nations, 2013).

Still, CSR "has been principally built on the 'business case', by which the inclusion of economic, social and environmental aspects is subordinated to their contribution to protecting or widening the business opportunity of the enterprises that promote them" (Perez de Mendiguren and Carlos, 2013). Though CSR may contribute to development objectives, its voluntary nature and associated lack of external accountability call into question its actual impact (Perez de Mendiguren and Carlos, 2013; United Nations, 2004).

The twenty-first century has also witnessed a dramatic rise in the number of public–private partnerships (PPP) for development, particularly for large infrastructure projects. Public–private partnerships encompass a variety of actors, with some not actually part of the public or private sector. One partnership model involves an international NGO, a private company or foundation, and a bilateral donor (e.g. a government, via its aid-dispensing agency), but many other actors are involved in PPP in various combinations, including "consulting firms, universities, the World Bank Group, and the United Nations system" (Runde and Zargarian, 2013).

One key incentive for public–private partnerships is to leverage expertise and resources. Non-governmental organizations typically have "on the ground" local knowledge; corporations often have financial resources, infrastructure assets, and technical expertise; and public sector institutions possess crucial connections and experience, as well as a longstanding strategic role in development funding. Financial partnerships match funders with implementers, expertise partnerships leverage competencies to increase program efficiency or effectiveness, and market partnerships "align with core business strategies of local and international companies to find market-based solutions to development problems" (Runde, 2011). Clear channels of central communication, partnership management, and monitoring are needed, and this remains a challenge for all engaging in PPP.

"Inclusive" business approaches

Given the increasingly competitive market in many upper- and middle-income economies, the desire to gain market share in future middle-income households, expand the consumer base, and capitalize on new innovation opportunities intensified private sector interest in development activities (Ohno, 2013). This translated to a new private sector approach called "Base of the Pyramid" (BoP)—focusing on people living at below 1,500 USD PPP a year. With more than four billion people in this income range, this represented a profitable opportunity (Prahalad and Hart, 2002). Conceptualizations of BoP have evolved significantly since the introduction of the phrase in 1998 and the first related publication in 2002 (Prahalad and Hart, 2002; Simanis and Hart, 2008).

In the beginning (BoP version 1.0), the focus was on reimagining the role of the poor— from aid recipients to consumers. The idea was for companies to develop low-cost products and services that the poor needed (and which cost less than existing alternatives), and profits would be made not through a high mark-up on each sale but rather through volume selling. Operationalizing this required a series of four steps: creating buying power (largely through microcredit), shaping aspirations through education and marketing, shaping local solutions, and improving access through communications and distribution (Prahalad and Hart, 2002). Useful products and services representing BoP 1.0 include the sale of medicines at a cheaper price in low-income countries, or improving access to sanitation products by developing new distribution centers in rural areas; product adaptation may also be required to meet consumer needs (Moulin, 2013). However, Perez de Mendiguren Castresana and Carlos (2013) review a number of criticisms of BoP 1.0, including questions about the size of the potential market, lack of participatory processes involving the poor, concerns about exploitation given the focus on credit as a means for consumption, and "the simplistic conception of poverty," since consumption alone is insufficient for increasing living standards and attaining "the structural changes and transformations needed for putting an end to poverty."

BoP version 2.0, more in line with conceptualizations of inclusive business today, calls for a more participatory "bottom up" strategy where the poor are considered co-creators, consumers, *and* producers. BoP 2.0 projects can entail selling products to the poor and purchasing products created by the poor. The poor should be directly involved in "deep dialogue" (not merely communicating their needs); they become business partners and co-venturers, so the relationship between external and local people becomes much more direct than in BoP 1.0 (Simanis and Hart, 2008). BoP 2.0 products are developed and often sold using BoP resources, including labor power; one example is Fundooz (by Danone), a nutritional product tailored for the needs of Indian children using milk from local producers and sold by local distributors (Moulin, 2013). The characteristics of informal markets and the need for local capacity building require "patient capital" and incremental investment (London, 2008); business operations, strategy and profitability take a markedly different pattern from other investment opportunities. This differentiates BoP 2.0 from other approaches which take already-existing technologies and methods to new markets with similar characteristics (London, 2008).

Social entrepreneurship is not synonymous with BoP, for a few reasons. First, the main characteristic of BoP (1.0 and 2.0) is the focus on people earning less than 1,500 USD PPP per year. Though social enterprises often operate in or serve that segment of the population and may be partners in BoP projects, social enterprises do not all target this group. Second, as mentioned above, the main characteristic of social enterprise is the situation of social impact at the core of the enterprise mission; this is not the case for all BoP projects, which often have profits at the core of their mission. For multinationals, social marketing related to BoP has the potential to generate sales for entirely different products from developed country consumers. With many challenges facing multinationals operating in the BoP space, some consider BoP a philanthropic endeavor or part of the company's CSR platform (Moulin, 2013).

Social enterprises involve "different ways of structuring or creating productive and communal relations between people, better enabling democracy and complex negotiation through new forms of engagement, or re-thinking or re-working market and economic behavior" (Westall, 2007). Although creating businesses to address social problems is perhaps the most discussed variant of social enterprise, Babu and Pinstrup-Andersen (2009) highlight two others: policy entrepreneurs and program entrepreneurs. Policy entrepreneurs typically operate at the macro level, connecting with national, regional, and multilateral agencies and working to create a policy environment conducive to creating and scaling successful social enterprises. Program entrepreneurs develop and implement state-of-the-art development programs funded by NGOs, agencies, and governments (Babu and Pinstrup-Andersen, 2009). All three variants need deep understanding of the social issues to be tackled.

The need for breadth of social enterprise activity—from the micro to the meso and macro levels—makes sense when we consider that today's social problems are multidisciplinary and often cross geographical and political borders, making them challenging to address for traditional public and private sector actors. As the OECD explains, "innovation to address social challenges has a public good nature. Market processes and the 'invisible hand' are . . . inefficient to co-ordinate these innovation activities that aim directly to address social challenges" (OECD, 2011).

For developing countries, lack of a sufficient risk management system and inadequate tax revenues mean that limited public sector funds are often used to handle immediate emergencies such as food, fuel, or financial crises, or civil unrest. Bureaucracy can also stifle attempts to tackle problems in new or creative ways. At the same time, relatively weak institutional and legal environments lead to corruption and uncertainty of profitability, which dissuade corporations from playing a large role, particularly in new endeavors with longer payback horizons. In many developing countries, immature labor markets, strict business regulations, and exclusionary banking practices have led a significant proportion of the working-age population to work in informal jobs situated outside the legal system (UNDP, 2004). All of these factors contribute to gaps between public and private provision of goods and services, exacerbating pre-existing inequalities and impinging on sustainable development efforts.

Tackling environmental challenges through social enterprise

Environmental issues and the "green economy"

Although the Millennium Development Goals made significant progress in reducing extreme poverty and attaining certain health and education outcomes, geographical disparities and the shortfall of progress in other outcomes led policymakers and practitioners to recognize that "growth and prosperity are being achieved at the expense of the planet's life-support systems" (UNEP, 2013). According to the 2014 Intergovernmental Panel on Climate Change (IPCC) Report, developing countries will be hit particularly hard by climate change, with prolonged monsoon seasons, intensified flooding and drought, reduced crop production, loss of coastal settlements, and reduced biodiversity. Less than 14 percent of land and marine areas are protected in low-income countries; in those countries alone, more than 1,000 fish species and more than 1,800 plant species are currently threatened (World Bank, 2015).

Environmental issues impact many aspects of daily life. Only 37 percent of the population in low-income countries has access to improved sanitation facilities; 31.2 percent has access to electricity (World Bank, 2015). Today, more than 30 percent of the low-income country population lacks access to an improved water source (World Bank, 2015). Pollution is also a major problem. Given the widespread usage of wood burning indoor stoves, agricultural burning, and high-emission vehicles, nearly 80 percent of low-income countries' population is exposed to fine particle pollution levels exceeding World Health Organization guidelines (World Bank, 2015; World Health Organization, 2014a).

In the developing world, these environmental issues are exacerbated by a host of factors including industrialization; population growth; urbanization; weak regulatory, monitoring, and enforcement mechanisms; proximity to extreme weather events; reduced technology capabilities; gender inequality; limited "green" jobs; patterns of international trade; and dependence on natural resources for basic needs (UNEP, 2007). The underdevelopment of infrastructure from roads and bridges to electricity and water systems limits access to goods, services, and employment and influences the resource intensity of daily activities. However, large-scale infrastructure projects are expensive and maintenance and upkeep costs are also costly. This leads to significant urban–rural gaps and worsening of existing inequalities.

As policymakers increasingly recognized the complex relationship between economic, social, and environmental dimensions of sustainability, the concept of an inclusive green economy emerged.[2] An inclusive green economy fosters growth which is not only environmentally sustainable, but also socially inclusive (UNDP, 2012). It "supports resource-efficient, low-carbon and climate-resilient growth; creates and sustains decent jobs . . . stimulates innovation and adoption of green technologies that can benefit the poor . . . improves health and well-being, especially among the poor . . . promotes equity, including gender equality . . . [and] reduces pollution" (Poverty-Environment Partnership, 2013). This is challenging to achieve.

In practice, many environmental sustainability efforts do not heighten access or rights of the poor to environmental products and services, consider the disproportionate impacts of climate change on the poor, or "safeguard them from adverse impacts" including the potential loss of resource-intensive employment (Poverty-Environment Partnership, 2013). On the other hand, many "pro-poor" environmental goods and services offered by development agencies have not been successful or financially sustainable due to lack of expertise, low commercial viability, lack of fit to local needs, poor quality, and insufficient maintenance systems (Molteni and Masi, 2009). These shortfalls provide several opportunities for social enterprises, given that they often focus on specific local communities and reach out to disadvantaged population groups.

"Green" social enterprises

Green social enterprises are consistent with the concept of an inclusive green economy. They "are led by an environmental mission or deliver environmental outcomes in the process of pursuing community benefits, which may include poverty reduction, gender equity, and social inclusion" (Social Traders and Sustainability Victoria, 2012). Like other social enterprises, they generate a substantial portion of their income from the sale of goods or services, reducing operational reliance on donations and grants; invest profits into activities supporting the enterprise mission, rather than distribute profits to owners; and may be organized in a variety of ways, including cooperatives (Social Traders and Sustainability Victoria, 2012). Green social enterprises address a wide range of issues including waste retrieval and recycling, water management, sustainable housing and transport, sustainable farming, renewable energy, clean production technologies, conservation and protection of nature and wildlife, environmental education, awareness and capacity-building (Vickers, 2010; Sustainability Victoria, 2011). In less developed nations, green social enterprises tend to focus on "basic issues and pressing needs . . . such as access to water and sanitation . . . or agricultural activities in rural areas" (Vickers, 2010). They may also create new employment opportunities in green social enterprises, introduce environmentally friendly techniques into existing occupations, and examine their own environmental footprint.

Water access

Access to safe, clean water is critically important for drinking, cooking, hygiene, sanitation, and overall health, however this has a significant gender equity dimension. Due to the traditional gender division of labor, women and girls in the developing world generally are responsible for the bulk of unpaid household work such as cleaning, cooking, caretaking tasks, and collection of water and firewood. In many rural areas, water is not located near the home, and a large portion of the day is spent going back and forth to the water source to carry sufficient water to supply the entire household's needs. In India, for example, women spend an estimated "150m work days every year fetching and carrying water" (Smedley, 2015). This creates time poverty, a situation where women and girls are so busy taking care of household maintenance that their available time for engaging in productive activities such as paid work or education is reduced.

By improving access to clean water, social enterprises improve environmental and social sustainability. A range of approaches exist—from rainwater collection/management systems and locally produced water filters to sewage treatment systems and toilets. Sarvajal, a for-profit Indian social enterprise founded in 2008, provides clean water access to underserved populations in both rural and urban areas. In small villages, rural schools, and urban slums, water is accessed through water ATMs—solar-powered, cashless "machines which use prepaid (or pay-as-you-go) smartcards that can be topped up just like a mobile phone" (*The Economist*, 2013). Water costs around 0.06 USD per liter at most of the water ATMs, though prices differ depending on whether delivery direct to the consumer is desired, whether chilled water is desired, etc. (Sevea, 2013). The machines provide instantaneous information about water quality, usage, and operations through a cloud-based system (Kumar, 2014).

Sarvajal utilizes a franchise system. The franchisee purchases a water purification system, four water ATMs, one delivery vehicle, one chiller, and bottles; Sarvajal provides maintenance and marketing support (Sevea, 2013). This reduces overall transportation costs and heightens the sense of community ownership. In urban schools and hospitals, Sarvajal installs a purification system as well as dispensary units on site; the government has been involved in pilot programs in these areas. So far, more than 150 plants have been established in India, serving more than 100,000 people (Sevea, 2013). As a green social enterprise, Sarvajal also has positive environmental impact. The solar powered ATM significantly reduces fuel usage and transport requirements; the system requires people to bring their own containers for dispensing water, thus reducing disposable plastic bottles; and all old mechanical parts are repurposed (Sevea, 2013).

Clean energy

Energy poverty—the lack of electricity and clean cooking technologies—significantly impacts productivity, health, and household energy costs. Without electricity, households and communities face many challenges with regard to business output, health care provision, educational needs, and required time for household chores. Burning kerosene, a popular alternative method of lighting, contributes to climate change through black carbon emissions; kerosene lamps also pose serious health hazards due to flammability and indoor air pollution (Tedsen, 2013). These health hazards multiply when cooking over open fires or using inefficient stoves fueled by wood, dung, charcoal, coal, and crop wastes; three billion people still cook and heat their homes this way, contributing to more than four million premature deaths a year (World Health Organization, 2014b). In developing countries, women and children face disproportionate health risks since they spend more time at home and have greater exposure to the pollutant-laden smoke (World Health Organization, 2014b).

Many social enterprises have tackled these problems with the aim of producing energy in more environmentally sustainable ways. Examples include micro hydropower plants for rural villages, solar lamps, solar panels, and clean cook stoves.[3] Solar Sister, a non-profit social enterprise operating in Uganda, Tanzania, and Nigeria, improves women's income-earning opportunities while supplying a range of clean energy products to rural villages. Founded in 2010, Solar Sister utilizes a distribution system similar to Avon, for which women sell products door-to-door. In contrast to Avon, however, Solar Sister does not produce any of the products sold; a range of existing brands are offered to reduce risk if one brand loses popularity (Petersen, 2012).

While devices combining solar power with mobile phone charging capability are most popular, basic solar lamps, clean cook stoves, and more comprehensive household lighting systems are also sold (Petersen, 2012). Rural entrepreneurs do not have sufficient pre-existing income to purchase inventory, so a micro-consignment model is used, where a small amount of inventory is loaned to each woman; the women pay for the inventory after selling it, upon which they receive more inventory on loan (ArcFinance, 2012). After they build up to about 300 USD worth of inventory, they transition to acquiring loans from a microfinance institution (ArcFinance, 2012).[4]

Like the entrepreneurs, consumers find it difficult to afford clean energy products. Although no direct consumer financing mechanisms are provided (MIT, 2015), Solar Sister facilitates the formation of "informal savings groups where members make weekly contributions toward the purchase of a single lamp" (ArcFinance, 2012). So far, 200,000 people have been served by more than 1,200 Solar Sister female entrepreneurs (Solar Sister, 2015). By increasing access to more efficient systems for lighting and cooking, Solar Sister improves health and environmental outcomes while also bolstering local economies through women's self-employment. This impacts economic, social, and environmental dimensions of sustainability, consistent with an inclusive green economy.

Sustainable agriculture

According to the Food and Agriculture Organization, nearly 800 million people in developing countries were undernourished in 2012–2014; about half reside in Sub-Saharan Africa or

South Asia (FAO, IFAD and WFP, 2014). While many factors contribute to food insecurity, agricultural practices shape the quantity, quality, and diversity of available food as well as risks from overreliance on certain crops or lack of irrigation (FAO, IFAD and WFP, 2014). Unsustainable practices including slash-and-burn, inappropriate use of chemical fertilizers, inefficient irrigation, overgrazing, monotonous planting, and reduced fallow periods have eroded land and soil quality (Professional Alliance for Conservation Agriculture, 2010). Climate change exacerbates this by reducing developing country yields (Nelson et al., 2009).

Green social enterprises have addressed this in a variety of ways, from establishing organic or fair-trade farms to supplying environmentally friendly fertilizers and pesticides, repurposing agricultural waste, and offering training in sustainable agriculture methods. International Development Enterprises – India (IDEI), a hybrid non-profit social enterprise founded in 1991, develops and sells low-cost irrigation drip technology to smallholder farmers. With more than four-fifths of farms in India less than 2 hectares in size, and nearly half less than 0.5 hectares, most agricultural plots are smallholder farms (FAO, 2014). Smallholders are not served well by modern irrigation technologies, which focus on plots of four or more acres and waste water on smaller farms (Acumen, 2015). Due to cost considerations, many smallholder farms rely on monsoon rains to water crops, but this reduces yields to one crop per year (Bhardwaj and Dutta, 2014). IDEI's technology "is designed to be one-fifth the cost of its competitors, scaled down to fit one-tenth hectare plots, and is able to generate sales at an unsubsidized market price" (IDEI, 2014). Farmers using IDEI's irrigation technology can break even on their investment within one cropping season; the systems—treadle pump and drip irrigation—are also infinitely expandable, simple, and inexpensive to maintain (IDEI, 2014).

IDEI pays for research and development, quality management, and marketing, but contracts out other portions of the business to manufacturers and village-based distributors, dealers, and mechanics—all IDEI-licensed and -trained (Sadangi, 2009; IDEI, 2014). To effectively reach villagers, IDEI takes an innovative approach, performing skits, showing movies, and holding live training demonstrations to illustrate the value of agricultural technology and sustainable agricultural practices (IDEI, 2014). So far, more than 1.25 million smallholder farm households in 15 Indian states have utilized IDEI products, either paying up front or purchasing on credit and paying after the harvest (Sadangi, 2009; IDEI, 2014). Farmers using the drip irrigation system have increased yields by 30–70 percent and their cash income has increased on average by 400 USD a year (Solomon, 2015). Given that approximately 77 million farmers in India are women (van Vark, 2014), there are also gender implications for making agricultural technology more accessible. Studies show that the treadle pumps are easy for both men and women to use, reducing the time spent on crop irrigation; as a result, some households have been able to send children back to school, no longer needing as much of their time helping on the farm (Sweetman, 1999; The Energy and Resources Institute, 2007). As a green social enterprise, IDEI also generates environmental benefits. Compared to diesel pumps, treadle pumps reduce carbon dioxide emissions, fertilizer and pesticide usage, and erosion (The Energy and Resources Institute, 2007; Sadangi, 2009). On average, farmers using IDEI's irrigation products have reduced electricity usage by 50 percent and water usage by 30–50 percent (Solomon, 2015).

Waste management

Solid waste management is a major issue for countries around the globe, but low income countries are most likely to experience sporadic, inefficient, costly waste collection and open dumping of waste (Hoornweg and Bhada-Tata, 2012). The health and environmental impacts of poor waste management are dangerous. Uncollected waste, unsafe burning of trash, and unsanitary landfills pollute the air, soil, and water, and contribute to the spread of disease (United Nations Environment Programme, 2015). Waste also contributes to climate change; post-consumer waste accounts for about 5 percent of global greenhouse gas emissions, and methane from landfills comprises 12 percent of global methane emissions (Hoornweg and Bhada-Tata, 2012).

Green social enterprises have addressed waste management in a variety of ways, from creating waste picking collectives, waste and recycling collection services to recycling agricultural waste, feed bags, and other items into useful products for sale. All Women Recycling, a for-profit social enterprise located in Cape Town, South Africa, collects discarded 2-liter plastic bottles and upcycles them into trendy gift boxes. Each gift box, called a kliketyklikbox™ is "designed, manufactured, and marketed entirely by women, most of whom are from disadvantaged backgrounds" and have been out of work for at least two years (Ressel, 2011; see also All Women Recycling, 2015). The women are taught how to make the boxes in addition to receiving business management and sales training (All Women Recycling, 2015). Few inputs are required to make the boxes: a 2-liter plastic bottle, scissors, paper, a pen, and glue (Haw, 2011). Through a printing system, the boxes can be customized for corporate gifts, wedding gifts, or any occasion.

Founded in 2008, All Women Recycling now produces about 350 boxes per day and employs 11 full-time workers (All Women Recycling, 2015). In addition to their signature gift box, the enterprise makes smaller gift boxes from 1-liter plastic bottles as well as greeting cards made from plastic bottles. The plastic bottles are "sourced from landfills, street waste collectors, and collection points located in schools" as well as a local recycling contractor, so All Women Recycling augments broader waste-related job opportunities and earnings in the community (SEED, 2014). Membership in Fairtrade International and a partnership with Contigo Fair Trade have bolstered All Women Recycling's ability to sell abroad; 60 percent of the product is exported to developed countries while the remainder is sold locally (Haw, 2011).

As a green social enterprise, All Women Recycling recycles waste, reducing trash levels in the landfill, reducing carbon emissions, and contributing to cleaner streets; the enterprise also elevates environmental awareness and supports principles of sustainable consumption for end users (SEED, 2014). By providing employment and skills training to women from disadvantaged backgrounds, All Women Recycling also fosters economic and social inclusion.

Recognizing challenges and moving forward

As we have seen, the combination of pressing needs, dissatisfaction with status quo approaches, and holistic conceptualizations of development paved the way for social enterprise in the developing world. Green social enterprise, in particular, has benefited from increased recognition of the relationship between social inclusion and environmental sustainability. Many possible entry points exist, and business models range from franchise and micro-consignment to base-of-the-pyramid with manufacturing or distribution by disadvantaged groups, among others.

There have been many successes, but failures as well. Social enterprises face several challenges in the complex landscape of international development. Key issues include the incorporation of local perspectives into the process of problem identification; acquiring appropriate, sufficient resources and operational systems to address the targeted problem; and implementation of information and communications technologies to facilitate solutions

(Katzenstein and Chrispin, 2011). Design thinking strategies can assist here. Through a process of empathizing, ideating, and implementing, design thinking enables social enterprises to obtain local input before deciding on a solution or operationalizing their idea; the process also ensures adequate prototyping; intentional development of partnerships to fill in resource gaps; adaptation of technologies for local needs and abilities; and development of monitoring and assessment protocols (IDEO, 2014; Allio, 2014).

Many challenges are ongoing. Balancing an environmental or social mission with financial sustainability can be difficult, particularly given increased competition between social enterprises and traditional for-profit business (Vickers, 2010). Social enterprises often find it difficult to scale the size of their operations. Although private investments targeting social enterprises are growing, the needs are significant. In addition, politics play a major role:

> To scale up, a social entrepreneur must invariably secure the support of the very institutions—NGOs, the private sector, and the state—that have failed to solve the problems he/she is trying to address. This requires compromises on the part of the social entrepreneur . . . none of these institutions are likely to relinquish control to a social entrepreneur unless they see the project as serving their interests.
>
> *(Nega and Schneider, 2014)*

Working with government officials to find common ground can help to erode opposition (Katzenstein and Chrispin, 2011). In situations where state and social enterprise interests overlap, partnerships can scale social entrepreneurial activity much more quickly than would otherwise be the case. To maintain strong links to local roots, many social enterprises scale by replication of their organization in a different location, rather than scaling themselves to a larger size (Howard, 2014).

However, many questions remain about legal status of social enterprise, its role in government procurement and subcontracting, and the way to form a "broad network of actors that are supportive of [social enterprise], including producers, users, regulators, standards institutes, investors and policy makers" (Vickers, 2010). In some cultures, entrepreneurship as an activity is not highly valued, so additional support—including new financing sources for social enterprise—is needed (Hernandez et al., 2012; Bugg-Levine et al., 2012; Urban, 2013). The social and environmental impacts generated by social enterprises, and their contributions to economic development may also be undervalued (Creech et al., 2014). To create an institutional environment more conducive to social enterprise, innovative strategies are needed in organizations dealing with education, law, research and development, finance, and politics.

Nega and Schneider (2014) highlight a broader concern: will social enterprises be used as a substitute for state-led development? Does the popularity of social enterprise give governments an excuse for abdicating their responsibilities for supporting infrastructure and providing public goods? We must recognize the limitations of social entrepreneurship: it can significantly impact peoples' lives, improve environmental benefits, and reduce environmental harms, but it is not a stand-alone solution to development problems. Human development, social welfare, and environmental sustainability are shaped by a complex array of institutions including government, private, and third sector actors, and partnerships among them.

Notes

1 Third sector encompasses non-governmental and non-profit organizations.
2 A leader in this movement was the United Nations Environment Program, which launched a Green Economy initiative in 2008.

3 Clean cook stoves use cleaner fuels (e.g. solar, ethanol) or use traditional fuels but reduce fuel consumption and cook time, along with maintaining or improving functionality (Differ Group 2012).
4 If the women cannot sell their inventory, they return it to Solar Sister (ArcFinance 2012).

References

Abu-Saifan, S. (2012). Social Entrepreneurship, Definition and Boundaries. *Technology Innovation Management Review*, 2(2), February, 22–27.

Acumen (2015). Global Easy Water Products. Accessed May 13, 2015, http://acumen.org/investment/global-easy-water-products-gewp.

Agafonow, A. (2014). Toward a Positive Theory of Social Entrepreneurship. On Maximizing Versus Satisficing Value Capture. *Journal of Business Ethics*, 12(5), 709–713.

All Women Recycling (2015). All Women Recycling. Accessed May 14, 2015, http://www.allwomenrecycling.com/index.php,

Allio, L. (2014). *Design Thinking for Public Service Excellence*. Singapore, UNDP Global Centre for Public Service Excellence.

ArcFinance (2012). *Solar Sister's Energy Consignment Model*. New York, ArcFinance.

Babu, S. and Pinstrup-Andersen, P. (2009). Social Innovation and Entrepreneurship, Developing Capacity to Reduce Poverty and Hunger. In J. von Braun, R. Hill and R. Pandya-Lorch (Eds.), *The Poorest and Hungry, Assessments, Analyses, and Actions*, pp. 541–548. Washington, DC, IFPRI.

Bhardwaj, M. and Dutta, R. (2014). India to Expand Irrigation to Cut Reliance on Monsoon. Reuters, April 14.

Bugg-Levine, A., Kogut, B. and Kulatilaka, N. (2012). A New Approach to Funding Social Enterprises. *Harvard Business Review*, 90(1–2), January-February, 3–7.

Creech, H., Paas, L., Huppé G., Voora, V., Hybsier, C. and Marquard, H. (2014). Small-scale Social-environmental Enterprises in the Green Economy, Supporting Grassroots innovation. *Development in Practice*, 24(3), 366–378.

Dees, G (2001). The Meaning of 'Social Entrepreneurship'. Accessed April 28, 2015, https://centers.fuqua.duke.edu/case/wp-content/uploads/sites/7/2015/03/Article_Dees_MeaningofSocial Entrepreneurship_2001.pdf.

Differ Group (2012). *A Rough Guide to Clean Cookstoves*. Differ Analysis Series. Oslo, Differ Group.

Drucker, P. (1985). *Innovation and Entrepreneurship*. New York, Harper Collins.

FAO (2014). *The State of Food and Agriculture 2014*. Rome, FAO.

FAO, IFAD and WFP (2014). *The State of Food Insecurity in the World 2014*. Rome, FAO.

Haw, P. (2011). From Actress to Entrepreneur. *Business Day*, April 18, 11.

Heltberg, R., Hossain, N. and Reva, A. (2012). *Living through Crises, How the Food, Fuel, and Financial Shocks Affect the Poor. New Frontiers of Social Policy*, Washington, DC, World Bank.

Hernandez, L., Nunn, N. and Warnecke, T. (2012). Female Entrepreneurship in China, Opportunity- or Necessity-Based? *International Journal of Entrepreneurship and Small Business*, 15(4), 411–434.

Hoornweg, D. and Bhada-Tata, P. (2012). *What a Waste, A Global Review of Solid Waste Management*. Urban Development Series, No. 15. Washington, DC, World Bank.

Howard, E. (2014). 10 Things We Learned About Scaling Social Enterprise, *The Guardian*, 20 November.

IDEI (2014). About Us. Accessed May 13, 2015, http://www.ide-india.org.

IDEO (2014), IDEO's Human Centered Design Toolkit, accessed May 7, 2015, https//pathways.epicenterusa.org/resources/168.

Katzenstein, J. and Chrispin, B. (2011). Social Entrepreneurship and a New Model for International Development in the 21st Century. *Journal of Developmental Entrepreneurship*, 16(1), 87–102.

Kumar, S. (2014). The Watercard. *Hindustan Times*, LiveMint, May 9.

London, T. (2008). The Base-of-the-Pyramid Perspective, A New Approach to Poverty Alleviation. *Academy of Management Proceedings*, 1(1), 1–6.

McWade, W. (2012). The Role for Social Enterprises and Social Investors in the Development Struggle. *Journal of Social Entrepreneurship*, 3(1), 96–112.

MIT (2015). *Experimentation in Product Evaluation, The Case of Solar Lanterns in Uganda, Africa. Comprehensive Initiative on Technology Evaluation (CITE)*. Cambridge, Mass., Massachusetts Institute of Technology.

Molina-Gallart, N. (2014). Strange Bedfellows? NGO–Corporate Relations in International Development, an NGO Perspective, *Development Studies Research*, 1(1), 42–53.

Molteni, M. and Masi, A. G. (2009). Social Entrepreneurship in Developing Countries, Green Technology Implementation to Push Local Social and Economic Innovation. Paper presented at 2nd EMES International Conference on Social Enterprise, Trento, Italy, July 1–4.

Moulin, M. (2013). Bottom of the Pyramid Strategies, Philanthropy or Profitable Business? *ESG Matters*, 5, 4–7.

Nega, B. and Schneider, G. (2014). Social Entrepreneurship, Microfinance, and Economic Development in Africa. *Journal of Economic Issues*, 48(2), 367–376.

Nelson, G. C., Rosegrant, M. W., Koo, J., Robertson, R., Sulser, T., Zhu, T., Ringler, C., Msangi, S., Palazzo, A., Batka, M., Magalhaes, M., Valmonte-Santos, R., Ewing, M. and Lee, D. (2009). *Climate Change, Impact on Agriculture and Cost of Adaptation*. Washington, DC, International Food Policy Research Institute.

Newbert, S. L. and Hill, R. P. (2014). Setting the Stage for Paradigm Development, A 'Small-Tent' Approach to Social Entrepreneurship. *Journal of Social Entrepreneurship*, 5(3), 243–269.

OECD (2011). *Fostering Innovation to Address Social Challenges*. Paris, OECD.

Ohno, I. (2013). Inclusive Business, New Partnership between Development and Business. National Graduate Institute in Policy Studies, Tokyo, Japan. Accessed May 1, 2015, http://www.grips.ac.jp/forum-e/IzumiOhno_E/lectures/2013_New_Lecture_texts/Inclusive_business_Lec4.pdf.

Ormiston, J. and Seymour, R. (2011). Understanding Value Creation in Social Entrepreneurship, The Importance of Aligning Mission, Strategy and Impact Measurement. *Journal of Social Entrepreneurship*, 2(2), 125–150.

Padgett, A. and Warnecke, T. (2011). Diamonds in the Rubble, The Women of Haiti—Institutions, Gender Equity, and Human Development in Haiti. *Journal of Economic Issues*, 45(3), 527–555.

Perez de Mendiguren, C. and Carlos, J. (2013). Social enterprise in the development agenda. Opening a new road map or just a new vehicle to travel the same route? *Journal of Social Enterprise*, 9(3), 247–268.

Petersen, K. (2012). *Social Entrepreneurship and the Solar Revolution. Global Social Benefit Fellowship Report*. Santa Clara, California, Global Social Benefit Institute.

Poverty-Environment Partnership (2013). *Building an Inclusive Green Economy for All*. Manila, Poverty-Environment Partnership.

Prahalad, C. K. and Hart, S. (2002). The Fortune at the Bottom of the Pyramid. *Strategy+Business*, 26(1), 54–67.

Professional Alliance for Conservation Agriculture [PACA] (2010). *Agricultural Practices that Cause Degradation*. PACA Education Series #3. New Delhi, PACA.

Razeq, Z. M. (2014). *UNDP's Engagement with the Private Sector, 1994–2011*. New York, Palgrave Macmillan.

Ressel, A. (2011). All Woman Recycling. *Sawubona*, April, 82–86.

Runde, D. (2011). *Seizing the Opportunity in Public-Private Partnerships*. Washington, DC, Center for Strategic & International Studies.

Runde, D. and Zargarian, A. (2013). The Future of Public-Private Partnerships, Strengthening a Powerful Instrument for Global Development. Center for Strategic & International Studies. Accessed May 1, 2015, http://csis.org/publication/future-public-private-partnerships-strengthening-powerful-instrument-global-development.

Sadangi, A. (2009). 2009 *Ashden Awards Case Study, International Development Enterprises – India*. New Delhi, IDEI.

Santos, F. (2012). A Positive Theory of Social Entrepreneurship. *Journal of Business Ethics*, 1(11), 335–351.

SEED (2014). All Women Recycling. SEED Initiative. Accessed May 14, 2015, http://www.seed.uno/awards/all/all-womenrecycling.html.

Sen, A. (1999). *Development as Freedom*. Oxford, Oxford University Press.

Sevea (2013). *Case Study-Sarvajal-India*. Les marches, France, Sevea.

Shane, S. and Venkataraman, S. (2000). The Promise of Entrepreneurship as a Field of Research. *Academy of Management Review*, 25(1), 217–226.

Simanis, E. and Hart, S. (2008). *The Base of the Pyramid Protocol, Toward Next Generation BoP Strategy*. 2nd edition. Center for Sustainable Global Enterprise, Cornell University.

Smedley, T. (2015). Can Social Enterprise Help 700m Without Access to Clean Water? *The Guardian*, March 22.

Social Traders and Sustainability Victoria (2012). *The Green Social Enterprise Case Study Series*. Victoria, Australia, Social Traders and Sustainability Victoria.

Solar Sister (2015). Impact. Accessed May 13, 2015, http://www.solarsister.org/impact.

Solomon, L. D. (2015). *Alleviating Global Poverty, The Role of Private Enterprise*. Bloomington, Ind., XLibris.

Sustainability Victoria (2011). *Support and Strengthen Green Social Enterprise*. Victoria, Australia, Sustainability Victoria.

Sweetman, Caroline (1999). *Gender and Technology*. London, Oxfam.

Tan, W. L. and Yoo, S. J. (2015). Social Entrepreneurship Intentions of Nonprofit Organizations. *Journal of Social Entrepreneurship*, 6(1), 103–125.

Tedsen, E. (2013). *Black Carbon Emissions from Kerosene Lamps*. Berlin, Ecologic Institute.

The Economist (2013). Social Entrepreneurs in India, Water for All. March 20.

The Energy and Resource Institute (2007). Socio-economic-techno-environmental Assessment of IDEI Products, Treadle Pump. Project Report No. 2006RR24. Bangalore, TERI.

Timmons, J. and Spinelli, S. (2011). *New Venture Creation, Entrepreneurship for the 21st Century*, 9th ed. New York, McGraw-Hill.

ul Haq, H. (2008). The Human Development Paradigm. In Georgio Secondi (Ed.), *The Economic Development Reader*, pp. 28–33. New York, Routledge.

United Nations (2004). Managing Corporate Social Responsibility for Rural Development in Least Developed Nations. Conference Room Paper. New York, United Nations.

United Nations (2012). The UN Global Compact and the OECD Guidelines for Multinational Enterprises, Complementarity and Distinctions. Accessed April 30, 2015, http://www.unglobal compact.org/docs/about_the_gc/UNGC_OECDGuidelines.pdf.

United Nations (2013). From corporate social responsibility to corporate sustainability, Moving the agenda forward in Asia and the Pacific. Studies in Trade and Investment No. 77, Economic and Social Commission for Asia and the Pacific. Bangkok.

United Nations (2014). *Millennium Development Goals Report 2014*. New York.

United Nations Development Group (2013). *A Million Voices, The World We Want*. New York, UNDG.

United Nations Development Programme (2004). *Unleashing Entrepreneurship, Making Business Work for the Poor*. New York, UNDP.

United Nations Development Programme (2011). *Towards Human Resilience, Sustaining MDG Progress in a Time of Economic Uncertainty*. New York, UNDP.

UNDP (2012). *Triple Wins for Sustainable Development*. New York, UN.

United Nations Environment Programme (2007). *Global Environment Outlook Geo4, Environment for Development*. Malta, UNEP.

United Nations Environment Program (2013). Integrating the Three Dimensions of Sustainable Development. UNEP Post 2015 Note No. 1. Nairobi, Kenya, UNEP.

United Nations Environment Program (2015). Solid Waste Management. Accessed April 14, 2015, http://www.unep.org/resourceefficiency/Home/Policy/SustainableCities/FocusAreas/SolidWaste Management/tabid/101668/Default.aspx.

Urban, B. (2013). Social Entrepreneurship in an Emerging Economy, A Focus on the Institutional Environment and Social Entrepreneurial Self-Efficacy. *Managing Global Transitions*, 11(1), 3–25.

Van Vark, C. (2014). Left to Tend Farm and Family, Reaching Female Farmers in Rural India. *The Guardian*, November 17.

Vickers, I. (2010). Social Enterprise and the Environment, a Review of the Literature. Working Paper No. 22. Birmingham, UK, Third Sector Reseach Centre.

Warnecke, T. (2006). A Gender-Aware Approach to International Finance, in *Ethics and the Market – Social Economic Contributions*, Routledge, pp. 175–90.

Warnecke, T. (2013). Entrepreneurship and Gender: An Institutional Perspective. *Journal of Economic Issues*, 47(2), 455–463.

Warnecke. T. (2015). 'Greening' Gender Equity, Microfinance and the Sustainable Development Agenda. *Journal of Economic Issues*, 49(2), 1–10.

Westall, A. (2007). *How can Innovation in Social Enterprise be Understood, Encouraged, and Enabled? Think Piece*, Office of the Third Sector, UK.

World Bank (2015). *World Development Indicators 2015*. Washington, DC, World Bank.

World Economic Forum (2015). *Outlook on the Global Agenda 2015*. Geneva, World Economic Forum.

World Health Organization (2014a). Ambient (outdoor) Air Quality and Health. Fact Sheet No. 313. Geneva, WHO.

World Health Organization (2014b). Household Air Pollution and Health. Fact Sheet No. 292. Geneva, WHO.

Zahra, S. A., Gedajlovic, E., Neubaum, D. O. and Shulman, J. M. (2009). A Typology of Social Entrepreneurs, Motives, Search Processes and Ethical Challenges. *Journal of Business Venturing*, 24(5), 519–532.

19

SOCIAL ENTREPRENEURSHIP AND FASHION INNOVATION IN BRAZIL

A case study of Crafty Women (Mulheres Arteiras) and Rede Asta

Vanessa Ratten, Joao Ferreira and Cristina Fernandes

Introduction

Crafty Women (Mulheres Arteiras) is a social enterprise located in the outskirts of Rio de Janeiro, Brazil. It was established to work with artisans from poor local communities to help them build their skills and sell their products in Rede Asta stores, which operates as a cooperative social enterprise. The aim of this chapter is to discuss the collaborative partnership between Crafty Women and Rede Asta, which also partners with other social enterprises around Brazil. The role of the cooperative as an incubator for design innovation whilst maintaining regional identities and usage of local materials in Brazil is discussed. This will include an analysis of social and community-based entrepreneurship in Brazil, which is amongst the world's largest developing countries. The increase in social businesses based on artisan products in Brazil will be examined, which aims at establishing a more sustainable commercial model in a geographic area that is in the process of moving towards higher income and wage levels. This chapter will also discuss the role of emerging social entrepreneurship in developing countries from the perspective of craft entrepreneurs in Brazil. The role of the entrepreneurial ecosystem for social and community-based entrepreneurship in Brazil for facilitating fashion innovation and development will be stated in order to form policy initiatives that apply to other transition economies.

Developing countries are characterized by the government policies towards economic growth and business development (Washington and Chapman, 2014). Past research has focused on developed countries and entrepreneurship in general. The aim of this chapter is to address a specific literature gap by focusing on social entrepreneurship in Brazil. The small and medium-sized enterprises employ the majority of the labour force in Brazil and are important components of the social economy (Cravo et al., 2012). In developing countries, the changes in the progression of an economy are dependent on the entrepreneur, human capital and institutional structure. A large portion of entrepreneurial activity in Latin America comes from necessity as individuals search for a source of income and employment. Many developing countries within Latin America including Brazil are reforming their economies to increase the number of market-based transactions. This has led to individuals in developing countries like Brazil relying on networks and alliances to negotiate business contracts especially when artisan businesses are involved. Latin American countries including Brazil implemented market-orientated structural reforms to improve economic growth rates (Arruda et al., 2013). This is due to the business environment having few enforceable business standards but there being a need to integrate culture with artisan products.

Brazil has a large population and market which draws policy attention because of its economic growth potential. Part of this attention is due to Brazil being considered as having the highest national reputation of emerging economies and is the largest country in South America that is close to other growing economies. The history of Brazil is that it once was a colony of Portugal and gained its independence in 1822. Brazil has a democratically elected government but previously had a monarchy and military dictatorship. The Brazilian government has championed an internationalization policy in order to increase its economic growth rates but at the same time there has been an increasing social inequality gap between rich and poor in the country. Brazil with its large population is increasing in prominence globally especially since hosting large sporting events including the Olympics.

Entrepreneurship is an important part of Brazil as it is a developing country but has a different significance in terms of its application in the social context. The word for entrepreneur in some languages tends to have negative meanings and is not favoured as an endearing term, and this is the case in Brazil. Research by Gupta et al. (2014: 378) highlights the translational differences in the word 'entrepreneur' by stating 'entrepreneurs are generally admired in the US and the label "entrepreneur" is typically used as a compliment to refer to a bold and creative individual pursuing a legally acceptable and socially endorsed activity, this may not be true in other countries'. The word entrepreneur is 'empresario' in Brazilian Portuguese and has a negative connotation (Gupta et al., 2014).

The economic climate of Brazil is considered as being less conducive to entrepreneurship and this means that more institutional change is required to help encourage start-up activity (Gupta et al., 2014). Policy makers in Brazil need to examine best practices in other developing countries to promote entrepreneurship and a way to do this is by focusing on cultural and social entrepreneurship engaged in by local artisans. There are 27 states in Brazil with most income and population being located in the southern states (Cravo et al., 2012). The World Bank's Doing Business index suggests that Brazil ranks poorly in terms of institutional conditions and paying taxes. Brazil is a developing country that has institutional constraints due to monetary and investor restrictions (Cravo et al., 2012). This chapter will focus on cultural and social entrepreneurship in Rio de Janeiro, which is Brazil's second largest city and is known for its geographical setting combining the ocean with mountainous surroundings (Acioly, 2001). The city has a wide range of cultural and tourist services that gives it an international flavour but at the same time there is a growing need for more social enterprises that link the culture to economic success. There is a high level of poverty in Rio de Janeiro due to the inequalities between the metropolitan and regional locations. The peripheral municipalities have a high level of low-income and unskilled labour that makes it hard to break the poverty cycle (Acioly, 2001). This means that more entrepreneurship is needed in Rio de Janeiro, which is associated with economic development by creating business opportunities and supporting social innovation.

This chapter seeks to understand social, cultural and gender entrepreneurship with reference to a developing country context. Understanding the way artistic endeavours are utilized in developing countries has important social and economic implications. This chapter thereby contributes to existing literature on developing economies and entrepreneurship by promoting an understanding of a social enterprise, Crafty Women in Rio de Janeiro.

The chapter begins by considering the literature on social entrepreneurship by highlighting the cultural nature of the concept. We then move to a discussion of cultural entrepreneurship and the artistic nature of some social enterprises. Following this, we present a case study of Crafty Women which incorporates social and cultural aspects of entrepreneurship. We conclude by suggesting the growing importance of cultural pursuits to business and the importance of ability to open more social businesses around artistic endeavours. The next section will focus on the role of social entrepreneurship in developing countries, which is important for understanding the role inequality provides for entrepreneurship.

Social entrepreneurship

Social enterprises are important in developing countries because of their ability to provide business training and to increase social mobility, particularly for women. This is important due to a large wealth gap between low- and middle-class incomes in developing economies, which makes it hard for people to gain employment. Social enterprises enable the growth of local economies that can help employ individuals in developing countries. A trend in developing countries has been to utilize social entrepreneurship to promote employment, economic growth and to address gender differences in the workforce. This has led to municipal community entrepreneurship as a form of social entrepreneurship developing to encourage participation of disadvantaged members of society, who in many cases are women. The partnership between communities involves both explicit and leadership support (Dupuis et al., 2003). This helps women learn business skills whilst at the same time integrating their culture in social enterprise development.

Social entrepreneurship is a key area of practice and research for developing countries because of its linkage with economic growth and social change (Choi and Majumdar, 2014). The term social entrepreneurship is a contested concept due to the competing definitions and complex framework. Some researchers refer to social entrepreneurship as not-for-profit organizations who find new business funding opportunities whilst others use the term to describe business creation for the poor that focuses on the developing world or disadvantaged parts of society in developed countries. A broad definition of social entrepreneurship adopted in this chapter is the use of social innovations to bring about change by solving problems within a society.

Social innovations can include financial and non-financial activities within a domestic or global application to the business world. A key aspect of social entrepreneurship is the value created by having a distinct mission that helps address issues in a society in an innovative manner. These issues can deal with social needs and behaviour that promote altruistic objectives including equality, tolerance and acceptance of disadvantaged members of society. This means that social entrepreneurship is a value laden concept as it involves virtuous behaviour that includes social interests that are sometimes hard to deal with by commercial bodies. Social entrepreneurs are integral to the value creation process as they initiate the project and manage the innovation's progression. By acting as the innovator, social entrepreneurs create ideas which involve social change and are crucial in carrying projects to completion (Swedberg, 1991).

The role of a social entrepreneur differs depending on the tasks involved and may include a person initiating, operating and managing a social business (Choi and Majumdar, 2014). The tasks can be complex with some social entrepreneurs beginning an organization that has a social purpose but then giving it to others to grow and develop. Therefore, social entrepreneurship is a business-like discipline as it involves determination, perseverance and innovation. This means that social entrepreneurs are social change agents but they also go beyond this concept as they include a business element with their organizational vision.

Social entrepreneurship is more defined than general entrepreneurship and has a key mission compared to more loosely structured initiatives such as activist movements that also involve social change. The main difference from activism is that social entrepreneurship occurs within both profit and non-profit organizations as it can happen between private, public and third sectors. Social entrepreneurship takes a dynamic and hybrid form as different types of organizational structures develop based on societal need. This societal focus is based on market orientation which links financial sustainability with social goals and is the main reason why social entrepreneurship has increased in popularity due to its effective use of limited resources with efficient organizational forms. The resource effectiveness has given rise to the disruptive approach of many social entrepreneurs being driven by the continuous innovation made possible by technology change. The next section will further discuss social entrepreneurship by looking at the role of culture in entrepreneurial business ventures that is relevant to developing countries including Brazil.

Creative entrepreneurship

The nature of entrepreneurship in the creative industries is complicated as there are varying definitions of entrepreneurship within the literature (De Bruin, 2005). It is difficult to describe entrepreneurship in the creative industries as it is dynamic and organized in a complex way based on project activity (De Bruin, 2005). Howkins (2002) defines creative entrepreneurs as individuals who unlock wealth that they have within themselves as human beings. This means that creative entrepreneurs utilize their environment to combine their behaviour in a way that involves both extrinsic and intrinsic factors (Henry et al., 2004). The extrinsic involves context-ual and business-orientated behavior that may have tangible outcomes in the global business world. The intrinsic involves the internal desire to contribute something of a personal nature and is within the soul of individuals depending on their personality. This chapter defines creative entrepreneurship as the use of artistic mindsets for business activities.

Sometimes the word 'artist' is used instead of 'creative' in the context of entrepreneurship (De Bruin, 2005). Welsch and Kickul (2001) describe artist entrepreneurs as having similar behaviour to traditional entrepreneurs but being more orientated towards invention and idea generation. Artists use their inspiration to make creative projects that involve their ideas and original thoughts (De Bruin, 2005). Creativity is part of the artistic process as it involves an entrepreneur seizing an opportunity in making something that involves discovery, invention and production (De Bruin, 2003).

Creative entrepreneurs can take a number of forms including authors, musicians, painters, artists and singers (De Bruin, 2005). The inherent artistic part of creative entrepreneurship is the way ideas are incorporated into creative pieces (Caves, 2003). Artistic inputs need to combine with business acumen in order to produce creative entrepreneurship (Caves, 2003). The entrepreneurial value chain is part of the creative process as it involves linking the ideas to inputs and outputs (De Bruin, 2003). Innovation is an important part of creative entrepreneurship as it enables the continued success of business endeavours, which is part of the social progress of a society in developing countries.

Creative behaviour is important to the art industry particularly when linked to entrepreneurship (Fillis, 2000). Literature about creativity has mostly been developed from social psychology as it links social environments to personality traits (Fillis, 2000). Something is creative when the process involves a different path to how things are usually conducted (Rampley, 1998). Part of the creative process is imagination and originality, which when used in a business setting becomes entrepreneurial. Creativity is important in business as it involves problem solving by responding in an original way (Bohm, 1998). Creative entrepreneurs are able to produce solutions as they are more prepared to consider alternative approaches to existing knowledge (Bridge et al., 1998). This means that creative entrepreneurs use originality more than others to challenge the status quo (Fillis, 2000). Creativity involves differentiating ideas based on change and the degree of effort involved (Collings, 1999). The process of creativity means using self-expression from instinct and spontaneity to develop an idea (Fillis, 2000). This enables individuals to use their artistic freedom to combine an aspect of change to their designs that are differentiated by their country of residence.

Entrepreneurship is the foundation of change in developing countries due to the changes it creates in the business world (Rao, 2014). These changes include new and sustainable forms of employment which leverage economic efficiences (Fiet, 2000). Creative entrepreneurship involves business start-up activity or growth in existing firms but can involve business ownership (Galloway et al., 2015). This means that creative entrepreneurship is considered as a potential way to foster better social equality given structural inequalities in developing countries. The difference between cultural entrepreneurship and other types of entrepreneurship is that most general entrepreneurship conceptualizations consider financial growth as being the core rationale despite the emergence of social aspects of entrepreneurial behaviour (Galloway et al., 2015). The diversity of creative entrepreneurs in the business world means that many are not growth-orientated but happy with the current state of their business activities. In developing countries, creative entrepreneurship is not always individual and growth-orientated as it may be a social or community activity involving different types of people. Most artistic businesses are not started by individuals but rather by teams of people that offer unique areas of expertise within their craft industry. The next section will further discuss the role of creative entrepreneurship by focusing on the development of women's entrepreneurship in developing countries.

Women's entrepreneurship

The role of women in developing countries is at the heart of economic development especially for those in metropolitan cities (Rao, 2004). Women make a contribution to the venture success of entrepreneurial projects due to their involvment in the businesses development process (Fischer et al., 1993). Female entrepreneurs differ from male entrepreneurs because of the way they pursue business goals and structure their activities (Carter et al., 1997). Some of these differences revolve around the various sectors and products that women are involved in (Verheul, 2003). In addition, women are playing a greater role in the economic development of countries because of their business ownership and role in the start-up environment (Nicholas and Victoria, 2010).

Often semi-literate women in developing countries start more businesses than males (Allen et al., 2007). This may be due to the social inequalities some women face in devleoping countries and their access to other job opportunities. Prior research in the developed world environment has found women entrepreneurs to be more educated than the general population. Women in developing countries often pursue entrepreneurship due to their desire to break out of their current social structure and achieve a better living standard for their families. Moreover, the challenge of balancing work and family life means that the self-regulated role of being an entrepreneur is atractive to women (Buttner et al., 1997).

Entrepreneurship offers females self-determination in that they can be their own boss and control the life they want to achieve. In developing countries, the number of family workers in a household affects the ability of a female to be an entrepreneur (Rao, 2014). Minniti and Arenius (2003) liken this association to the linkage between women literacy and entrepreneurship. Part of this linkage has been related to there being limited studies undertaken on women's entrepreneurship in developing countries particularly in micro-level enterprises (Rao, 2014). Moreover, there are few studies of cultural entrepreneurship in developing countries, particularly in the Brazilian context.

Economic reforms sometimes stimulate entrepreneurship as it provides a more favourable environment for business activity (Sharma, 2003). In developing countries, women have traditionally been confined to 'kitchen–enterprises' related to food and cooking or 'feminine enterprises' such as beauty products that are associated with their gender (Rao, 2014). However, with economic growth in developing countries this has shifted with more females involved in cultural enterprises. This is partly due to women focusing on low capital and less technologically intensive areas of business managmeent (Swarajya, 1998). The next section will discuss the role of Crafty Women in Rio de Janeiro, which is a group of female entrepreneurs who are engaged in cultural and social entrepreneurship.

Crafty Women: cooperative crafts

Crafty Women is a cooperative crafts-based entrepreneurial business which utilizes recycled products to make toys, predominately for the Brazilian market. The focus of the cooperative is social as it enables women to use their Brazilian culture to sell products they make in the marketplace, thereby earning an income. The aim of Crafty Women is to include local activism with creative pursuits that are supported by a business model. Crafty Women originally began in mid-2006 when the Work and Income Generation Project of the Brazil Habitar-BID Program was started. Part of this program was developed by the Municipal Social Assistance Niterói City Hall to fund social projects that linked with the cultural heritage of Brazilian people. In conjunction with this program a variety of courses focused on women's business was developed, especially for the women of the Morro da Cocada region and surrounding areas. This led to a group of artisans from Crafty Women forming a cooperative in 2007 so they could sell the products they made based on materials available in the Rio de Janeiro geographic area. Part of the educational development was to make ottomans from plastic bottles for domestic use in houses, offices and parties as a way to link culture with sustainable forms of entrepreneurship. This use of education to make ottomans was the origination of the cooperative called 'Women Arteiras' or in English, Crafty Women.

Initially Crafty Women was a group of 25 housewives who formed a social enterprise due to the need to address social concerns about the local community they resided in. The social business started because this group of women was not satisfied with the social inequality seen in the *Morro da Cocada* region. In this region approximately 380 families were located and the women decided to fight for social inclusion of disadvantaged groups of their community. This meant that the residents of the surrounding geographic area of Uba Uba started the action group called 'Community Action V'. This community action group in 2006 then became involved in a partnership with the Income Generation Project Program of Brazil, which was developed by the Municipal Social Assistance Niterói City Hall. As part of the education of this community action group the women completed several courses, some of which were about social entrepreneurship and the way to link culture to business pursuits.

After receiving education from these courses the group of women artisans started to form a cooperative to sell products they had created. Their business prospects further increased after they started making puffs with pet bottles structures—32–40 bottles for each puff. The group 'Women Arteiras' or Crafty Women has since produced more than a hundred puffs, which also means they are contributing to the recycling and sustainability of Rio de Janeiro. By making the puffs the group has participated in several forms of community integration especially in regard to social innovation of waste products. Currently they produce the puffs to be rented for parties at people's houses and also to be sold at various stores, and in the future they would like to export their products.

The work of Crafty Women aroused the interest of Emabrinq company because of their unique products but also the use of social innovation. This company is a manufacturer of craft educational toys and made orders for some that refer to folklore and this relates to Brazilian culture. The toys are produced manually and are hand sewn and glued by local Brazilians. The Community Action Uba V and the Social Service Program of Brazil support the Crafty Womens group in logistics and delivery of the material to this company. The material for making the products is bought with the money from sales and so it is essentially a self-funded social enterprise. As Crafty Women does not own headquarters the meetings to produce the products are held at the home of one of the cooperative members. Crafty Women receives orders through word-of-mouth dissemination and knowledge of the Brazilian economy.

The cooperative became a legalized social business in August 2008 and has since become known in the region for the quality of its products and link to social innovation. Crafty Women has participated in several exhibitions and fairs both in Rio de Janeiro as in Niterói and is able to provide its products at retail to larger department stores. The Community Action Uba V, Social Condominium Project Uba V, through its partnership with the City Department of Social Welfare of the Niterói City Hall (Brazil Habitar-BID Program and currently PAC/Cocada), has supported this initiative by helping them with the logistics and distribution of their work.

The work of Crafty Women has also aroused the interest of the Emabrinq company, an educational toys manufacturer. Emabrinq manually produced a sewing base and collage of products that refer to Brazilian folklore. This partnership resulted in the permanent training of artisans and initiated a new strand of their work. In June 2008, Crafty Women was chosen to receive the support of the Federal Savings Bank, through the Committee CASH ODM – VITEC – Rio de Janeiro, which is supported by the budget of the Organization of the United Nations Millennium Development Goals. As part of this support there is a relationship strategy with low-income communities, to promote the social, economic and environmental development in an integrated manner with the business objectives of CAIXA and public policy of the Brazilian Federal Government. The connection also helps Crafty Women as a strategy to encourage voluntary action of employees from local communities of Rio de Janeiro.

Limitations and future research

This chapter has focused on women's entrepreneurship in Rio de Janeiro, which is one of the biggest cities in Brazil with a high socio-economic divide between the poor, middle-class and high-income earners. This chapter focused on one city in Brazil; similar studies could be conducted in other cities to see the development of women's entrepreneurship from a cultural perspective. In addition, studies in other developing countries such as India could be conducted for comparison purposes to see if there are similar Crafty Women entrepreneurs in these regions and how they connect with culture.

This chapter focused on artistic endeavours in the form of cultural entrepreneurship and other entrepreneurial aspects such as family background were not covered. This means that future research might address the role of the family in women's entrepreneurship to see if there are impacts on cultural enterprises in their development process. This chapter offers an exploratory contribution to entrepreneurship in developing countries by focusing on social, women and cultural entrepreneurs in Brazil. Future research could analyze how Brazilian social enterprises invest in social business and whether this differs in developed economies. Other studies could examine the economic results of social enterprises in Brazil and their impact on regional growth and poverty alleviation.

Future studies might also focus on the social part of the enterprise development to see the different stages women entrepreneurs go through in their quest to link culture with business practices. More research is also needed on women entrepreneurial leaders to see the factors that might impact cultural applications of business success. A significant area of future research is entrepreneurial leadership and the role women in developing countries play in increasing living standards and translating the cultural heritage begun by their ancestors into business enterprises as well.

Conclusions

This chapter has discussed the role of creative entrepreneurs in the developing world context by focusing on Crafty Women in Brazil. The chapter discussed the role of social entrepreneurship as part of the creative process and the link between the artist and entrepreneur. The historical background and linkage to cultural pursuits in Rio de Janeiro was examined to focus on the importance of creative entrepreneurship in the developing world. The partnerships Crafty Women were involved with were discussed, which espoused the linkage between public and private enterprises for creative entrepreneurs. Hopefully this chapter has discussed the contribution of social and creative entrepreneurs to the economic, social and political development of Brazil. Creative industries are necessary for the development of the Brazilian economy, but also for maintaining its linkage to cultural history.

References

Acioly, C. (2001). Reviewing urban revitalization strategies in Rio de Janeiro, From urban project to urban management approaches. *Geoforum*, 32(4), 509–520.

Allen, E., Langowitz, N. and Minniti, M. (2007). *The 2006 Global Entrepreneurship Monitor special topic report, women in entrepreneurship*, Center for Women Leadership, Babson College, Babson Park, MA.

Arruda, C., Cozzi, A., Souza, G. and Penido, E. (2013). Towards an understanding of corporate venturing practices in Brazil. *Venture Capital*, 15(2), 135–149.

Bohm, D. (1998). *On Creativity*. London, Routledge.

Bridge, S., O'Neill, K. and Cromie, S. (1998). *Understanding Enterprise, Entrepreneurship and Small Business*, Basingstoke, Macmillan Press.

Buttner, E., Moore, H. and Dorothy, P. (1997). Women's organizational exodus to entrepreneurship, self-reported motivations and correlates with success. *Journal of Small Business Management*, 35(1), 34–46.

Carter, N.M., Williams, M. and Reynolds, P.D. (1997). Discontinuance among new firms in retail, the influence of initial resources, strategy and gender. *Journal of Business Venturing*, 12(2), 125–145.

Caves, R. (2003). Contracts between art and commerce. *Journal of Economic Perspectives*, 17(2), 73–83.

Choi, N. and Majumdar, S. (2014). Social entrepreneurship as an essentially contested concept, Opening a new avenue for systematic future research. *Journal of Business Venturing*, 29(3), 363–376.

Collings, M. (1999). *This is Modern Art*, UK, Weidenfeld & Nicolson General.

Cravo, T.A., Gourlay, A. and Becker, B. (2012). SMEs and regional economic growth in Brazil. *Small Business Economics*, 38(2), 217–230.

De Bruin, A. (2003). Electronic entrepreneurship, in de Bruin, A. and Dupuis, A., eds, *Entrepreneurship, New Perspectives in a Global Age*, Aldershot, Ashgate, pp. 76–91.

De Bruin, A. (2005). Multi-level entrepreneurship in the creative industries, New Zealand's screen production industry, *Entrepreneurship and Innovation*, 6(3), August, 143–150.

Dupuis, A., de Bruin, A., and Cremer, R. (2003). Municipal community entrepreneurship, in de Bruin, A. and Dupuis, A., eds, *Entrepreneurship, New Perspectives in a Global Age*, Ashgate, Aldershot, pp. 128–147.

Fiet, J. O. (2000). The pedagogical side of entrepreneurship theory. *Journal of Business Venturing*, 16(2), 101–117.

Fillis, I. (2000). Being creative at the marketing/entrepreneurship interface, Lessons from the art industry. *Journal of Research in Marketing and Entrepreneurship*, 2(2), 125–137.

Fischer, E.M., Reuber, A.R. and Dyke, L.S. (1993). A theoretical overview and extension of research on sex, gender and entrepreneurship. *Journal of Business Venturing*, 8(2), 151–168.

Galloway, L., Kapasi, I. and Sang, K. (2015). Entrepreneurship, leadership and the value of feminist approaches to understanding them. *Journal of Small Business Management*, 53(3), 683–692.

Gupta, V.K., Guo, C., Canever, M., Yim, H.R., Sraw, G.K. and Liu, M. (2014). Institutional environment for entrepreneurship in rapidly emerging major economies, the case of Brazil, China, India, and Korea. *The International Entrepreneurship and Management Journal*, 10(2), 367–384.

Henry, C., Johnston, K., Ó Cinnéide, B. and Aggestam, M. (2004). Where art meets the science of entrepreneurship, a study of the creative industries sector and the case of the music industry, paper presented at the Irish Academy of Management Conference, September.

Howkins, J. (2002). *The Creative Economy: How People Make Money From Ideas*. London: Penguin.

Minniti, M. and Arenius, P. (2003). Women in entrepreneurship, the entrepreneurial advantage of nations. *First Annual Global Entrepreneurship Symposium*, 18(4).

Nicholas, A. and Victoria, P.E. (2010). Incentives and female entrepreneurial activity, evidence from panel firm level data. *International Advances in Economic Research*, 16(4), 371–387.

Rampley, M. (1998). Creativity. *British Journal of Aesthetics*, July, 38(3), 265–278.

Rao, S. (2014). Nurturing entrepreneurial women. *Journal of Entrepreneurship in Emerging Economies*, 6(3), 268–297.

Sharma, S.D. (2003). India's economic liberalization, a progress report. *Current History*, 10(2), 176.

Swarajya, L .C. (1998). *Development of Women Entrepreneurship in India, Problems and Prospects*, New Delhi, Discovery Publishing House.

Swedberg, R. (1991). *Joseph A. Schumpeter, His Life and Work*, Cambridge, Polity Press.

Verheul, I. (2003). Commitment or control? Human resource management in female- and male-led businesses, Strategic Study B200206, Zoetermeer, EIM Business and Policy Research, London, Routledge.

Washington, M.L. and Chapman, Z. (2014). Entrepreneurial activity as an externality of inward foreign direct investment in emerging economies, Panel data from Argentina, Brazil, Colombia and South Africa. *Journal of Developmental Entrepreneurship*, 19(1), 145–152.

Welsch, H.P. and Kickul, J.R. (2001). Training for successful entrepreneurship careers in the creative arts, in Brockhaus, R., Hills, G., Klandt, H. and Welsch, H., eds, *Entrepreneurship Education, A Global View*, Aldershot, Ashgate, 167–183.

http//www.mulheresarteiras.com.br, last visited 30 June 2015.

http//www.bbc.com/news/business-27884803, last visited 30 June 2015.

PART III

Gender and entrepreneurship

20

GENDER AND ENTREPRENEURSHIP IN DEVELOPING COUNTRIES

An introductory overview

Colin C. Williams and Anjula Gurtoo

Part III of this handbook turns its attention to the issue of the gendering of entrepreneurship in developing countries. Until now, scholarship and discourse on entrepreneurship in developing countries has sometimes 'written out' women. Even when it has included them, however, women have been commonly portrayed as necessity-driven and engaging in entrepreneurial endeavour simply in order to earn some extra income for their families (ILO, 2006; Bhatt, 2006; Carr and Chen, 2002; Mehrotra and Biggeri, 2002).

Examining the lived practices of entrepreneurship in developing countries through a gender lens, however, the chapters in Part III start to provide an evidence-based analysis of not only the prevalence of entrepreneurship among women in the developing world but also how the gender disparities in the wider labour market are often mirrored and reinforced when studying the gendering of entrepreneurship. Women commonly receive lower incomes from their entrepreneurial endeavour than men despite being better educated, and often face additional barriers to engagement in entrepreneurship and developing their new ventures not suffered by many men. In the introductory overview, therefore, we first briefly review this literature on the gendering of entrepreneurship and then describe how the various chapters in Part III of this handbook advance understanding of the differences in women's and men's participation in entrepreneurship.

Until now, evidence-based evaluations of the gender dimension when examining the prevalence and nature of entrepreneurship have been relatively lacking. Instead, most of the studies have made assumptions about the gendering of entrepreneurship. A major assumption, and following on from Part II, has been that women entrepreneurs are more likely to be necessity-driven than men (ILO, 2006; Bhatt, 2006; Carr and Chen, 2002; Mehrotra and Biggeri, 2002). Based on this assumption, they have then focused on discussing their lack of access to credit, welfare funds, insurance and so forth. These studies consequently first argue that reliance on day-to-day profits for survival is high because they have little or no access to institutional credit (Schneider and Bajada, 2005), second, that they have to protect themselves from harassment by local authorities (ILO, 2002, 2006; Bhatt, 2006; Carr and Chen, 2002; Charmes, 1998; Nelson, 1997), third, that often their entrepreneurial endeavour is not constituted as a separate legal entity independent from the household

(Chen et al., 1999, 2004; Fawzi, 2003) and finally, that their activities tend to get locked into traditional roles such as selling flowers at the temple and keeping a basket of fruits (Bhatt, 2006; Charmes, 1998). On the whole, in consequence, the starting point is to assume women entrepreneurs are marginalized low-paid populations engaged in necessity-based entrepreneurship.

Whether the nature of, and rationales for, women's and men's entrepreneurship differ in this manner across the developing world has been seldom evaluated. Therefore, in a bid to further advance understanding of the gender variations in entrepreneurship, each of the chapters in Part III examine various facets of the gendering of entrepreneurship.

In chapter 21 entitled 'Barriers to women's entrepreneurship: evidence from Indonesia', Tulus Tambunan examines entrepreneurship in Indonesia with a focus on the determinants of women's entrepreneurship. Examining the nature of women's entrepreneurship in Indonesia, along with the main constraints preventing women becoming entrepreneurs, it then discusses the government interventions required to tackle these constraints and facilitate greater levels of entrepreneurship among women.

Mehrangiz Najafizadeh in chapter 22, 'Social entrepreneurship, social change, and gender roles in Azerbaijan', then provides a detailed analysis of gender issues in the Republic of Azerbaijan from the 1800s through to contemporary post-Soviet Azerbaijan. Adopting a social constructionist theoretical perspective as a framework for gender analysis and focusing upon social entrepreneurship in Azerbaijan as it pertains to gender, this chapter highlights a series of pivotal events dating from the 1800s through Sovietization and the social construction of the 'Soviet Azerbaijani woman' to the current re-emergence of independent Azerbaijan from 1991 to the present which has influenced the gendering of entrepreneurship, thus providing a rich detail context-bound understanding of the issue.

In chapter 23, 'Women entrepreneurs in the informal economy: is formalisation the only solution for business sustainability?', Shyama Ramani, Ajay Thutupalli, Tamas Medovarszki, Sutapa Chattopadhyay and Veena Ravichandran then argue that contrary to the current dominant discourses that seek to bring the informal economy into the fold of the formal economy, the business sustainability of women entrepreneurs in the informal economy depends upon their engagements or business partnerships with other women (and men) and women-focussed intermediaries. More than formalization, women entrepreneurs need 'spaces' for dialogue to build business capabilities. These results are formulated through an analysis of the existing literature and case studies of women entrepreneurs from developing countries. This chapter thus questions whether the currently dominant policy discourse is appropriate when it comes to fostering women's entrepreneurship in this particular context.

Leyla Sarfaraz and Nezameddin Faghih then examine in chapter 24 'The dynamics of women's entrepreneurship in Iran'. This chapter examines the state of women's entrepreneurship in Iran from a gender perspective. Examining the economic participation and opportunity of women (as a component of the Global Gender Gap Index) for Iran in the period of 2006 to 2014, along with Global Entrepreneurship Monitor data to investigate different stages of women's entrepreneurial journey in Iran, this chapter maps women's entrepreneurial motivation (necessity versus opportunity), and the entrepreneurial activity and business sustainability for women and men in Iran over the period 2008–2014. Indeed, the data and methods they use represent an exemplar of how the gendering of entrepreneurship could be analyzed in the many other developing countries included in the Global Entrepreneurship Monitor.

It is to be hoped, therefore, that the current emergent literature on the gendering of entrepreneurship, not least by the editors of this handbook (Gurtoo and Williams, 2011;

Williams, 2009a,b, Williams and Gurtoo, 2011a,b; Williams and Youssef, 2013; Williams et al., 2012), will in future years be added to in order to develop a firmer grasp of the gendering of entrepreneurship in developing countries. Indeed, the existence of campaign groups such as Women in Informal Employment: Global and Organizing (WIEGO) who are promoting the importance of this topic, and the advent of new academic outlets for research on this topic, such as the *International Journal of Gender and Entrepreneurship*, will hopefully encourage more researchers to conduct studies on this important facet of entrepreneurship in developing countries.

References

Bhatt, E. (2006). *We are Poor but so Many: The Story of Self-employed Women in India*. Oxford: Oxford University Press.

Carr, M. and Chen, M. (2002).Globalization and the informal economy: How global trade and investment impact on the working poor. Geneva: The Informal Economy Working Paper No. 1, Policy Integration Department, International Labor Office.

Charmes, J. (1998) *Street Vendors in Africa: Data and Methods*, United Nations Statistical Division, New York.

Chen, M., Sebstad, J. and Connell, L. (1999). Counting the invisible workforce: The case of home based workers. *World Development*, 27(3), 603–610.

Chen, M., Carr, M. and Vanek, J. (2004). *Mainstreaming Informal Employment and Gender in Poverty Reduction: A Handbook for Policymakers and Other Stakeholders*. London: Commonwealth Secretariat.

Fawzi, C. (2003). Gender, poverty and employment in the Arab region. Geneva: Capacity-Building Program on Gender, Poverty and Employment, Discussion Paper, International Labor Office.

Gurtoo, A. and Williams, C.C. (2011). Women entrepreneurs in the Indian informal sector: Marginalization dynamics or institutional rational choice? *International Journal of Gender and Entrepreneurship*, 3(1), 6–22.

ILO (2002). *Women and Men in the Informal Economy: A Statistical Picture*. Geneva: International Labor Office.

ILO (2006). *Decent Work for Women and Men in the Informal Economy: Profile and Good Practices in Cambodia*. Geneva: International Labor Office.

Mehrotra, S. and Biggeri, M. (2002). Social protection in the informal economy: Home-based women workers and outsourced manufacturing in Asia. Florence: Innocenti Working Paper no. 97, UNICEF Innocenti Research Unit.

Nelson, N. (1997). How women and men got by and still get by, only not so well: The sexual division of labor in the informal sector of a Nairobi squatter settlement. In *Cities in the Developing World: Issues, Theory, Policy*. J Gugler (ed.), 141–165. Oxford: Oxford University Press.

Schneider, F. and Bajada, C. (2005). An international comparison of underground economic activity. In *Size, Causes and Consequences of the Underground Economy: An International Perspective*, C. Bajada and F. Schneider (eds.), 73–106. Aldershot: Ashgate.

Williams, C.C. (2009a). Informal entrepreneurs and their motives: a gender perspective. *International Journal of Gender and Entrepreneurship*, 1(3), 219–225.

Williams, C.C. (2009b). Explaining participation in off-the-books entrepreneurship in Ukraine: a gendered evaluation. *International Entrepreneurship and Management Journal*, 5(4), 497–513.

Williams, C.C. and Gurtoo, A. (2011a). Women entrepreneurs in the Indian informal sector: marginalisation dynamics or institutional rational choice? *International Journal of Gender and Entrepreneurship*, 3(1), 6–22.

Williams, C.C. and Gurtoo, A. (2011b). Evaluating women entrepreneurs in the informal sector: some evidence from India. *Journal of Developmental Entrepreneurship*, 16(3), 351–369.

Williams, C.C. and Youssef, Y. (2013). Evaluating the gender variations in informal sector entrepreneurship: some lessons from Brazil. *Journal of Developmental Entrepreneurship*, 18(1), 1–16.

Williams, C.C., Adom, K., Nadin, S. and Youssef, Y. (2012). Gender variations in the reasons for engaging in informal sector entrepreneurship: some lessons from urban Brazil. *International Journal of Entrepreneurship and Small Business*, 17(4), 478–494.

21

BARRIERS TO WOMEN'S ENTREPRENEURSHIP

Evidence from Indonesia

Tulus T. H. Tambunan

Introduction

Only after the Asian financial crisis in 1997/98 did public (policy makers, academics, and practitioners) interest in the fostering of entrepreneurship in Indonesia start to emerge, for at least two main reasons. First, it was realized that entrepreneurship was a main driver of national economic growth. After having a bad experience with the 1997/98 crisis, the government of Indonesia came to realize that with capital, technology, and highly skilled workers alone, without having individuals with a high spirit of entrepreneurship, the country would not fully recover from the crisis and could never move to a higher level of economic development. Second, as poverty is still a serious social and political issue, the active involvement of local people in income-generating economic activities, not only as wage-paid workers, but also as business owners or entrepreneurs, was recognized to have a significant impact on poverty reduction. In particular, the engagement of women either as paid employees or as entrepreneurs is regarded as very important by the Indonesian government as an effective way to reduce poverty. A strong tradition of women's entrepreneurship in Indonesia, particularly in micro and small enterprises (MSEs), is found in all rural areas in the country. In medium and large enterprises, however, women are less likely than men to be owners. Therefore, the Indonesian government has been trying to encourage entrepreneurship development, especially among women, by supporting the development of micro, small, and medium enterprises (MSMEs) in the country through various programs, since these enterprises provide an avenue for the testing and development of entrepreneurial ability.

The purpose of this chapter is to examine entrepreneurship development in Indonesia with a focus on women entrepreneurs and to identify their key determinants. It has two research questions. First, what is the extent and nature of the development of women's entrepreneurship in Indonesia? Second, what are the main constraints on women becoming entrepreneurs in Indonesia? To answer these questions, it first conducts an analysis of secondary data from various sources including the Indonesian National Statistics Agency (BPS) on the number of women entrepreneurs, and second, reviews key literature on women's entrepreneurship in developing countries and Indonesia.

Development of MSMEs in Indonesia

Definition and key characteristics

In Indonesia there are several definitions of MSMEs, depending on which agency provides the definition. However, Indonesia also has a national law on MSMEs. The initial law was issued in 1995 by the State Ministry for Cooperatives and SME, namely the Law on Small Enterprises Number 9 of 1995. It defines a small enterprise (SE) as a business unit with total initial assets of up to Rp 200 million, not including land and buildings, or with annual sales of a maximum of Rp 1 billion, and a medium enterprise (ME) as a business unit with annual sales of more than Rp 1 billion but less than Rp 50 billion. Although the law does not explicitly define microenterprises (MIEs), data from the State Ministry for Cooperatives and SME on SEs also include MIEs. In 2008, the ministry issued the new law on MSMEs Number 20, replacing the 1995 Law. According to this new law, MSMEs are those companies that have annual sales/turnovers up to Rp 50 billion and fixed investment (excluding land and building) less than Rp 10 billion. Besides the law on MSMEs, the National Agency of Statistics (BPS) defines MSMEs based on the total number of workers: MIEs, SEs, and MEs are defined as units with 1–4, 5–20, 20–50 workers, respectively.

In reality, however, these subcategories of MSMEs in Indonesia (as in other developing countries) are not only different in total number of employees, annual revenues, or value of invested capital/assets as criteria to define them, they can also be distinguished easily from each other by referring to their different characteristics. Such characteristics include formality or ways of doing business, market orientation, social-economic profiles of their owners/producers, nature of employment, organization and management system, degree of mechanization (nature of production process), sources of main raw materials and capital, location, external relationships, motivation, level of entrepreneurship, and degree of women's involvement as entrepreneurs (Table 21.1). It is important to take these different characteristics into consideration when talking about market competition or when assessing the impact of the Competition Law No.5 1999 on MSMEs. For instance, as can be seen in Table 21.1, with respect to market orientation, MIEs serve the local market only, which is by nature not affected by modern firms or LEs. In other words, the level of market distortions or unfair competition practices by LEs in local markets or market segment of MIEs is or can be assumed to be zero. Thus, this means that the implementation of the Competition Law No.5 1999 has no effect at all on the marketing process of MIEs. Although, unfair competition can still be found in this market segment, not between MIEs and larger enterprises but among MIEs themselves. But this is beyond the Law because, as explained before, in article 50h of the Law No.5, 1999 small-scale enterprises which includes MIEs, are exempted from the provisions of the Law.

Current development

Most businesses in Indonesia are from MSMEs and their number steadily increases every year (Table 21.2). In 2012, their share of total enterprises (including LEs) was around 99 percent. The majority are scattered widely throughout rural areas, and therefore likely to play an important role in helping develop the skills of villagers, not only technical skills but also entrepreneurial, particularly for women. However, most of them, mainly micro and small enterprises (MSEs) are undertaken or set up by poor households or individuals who could not find a better job elsewhere, either as their primary or secondary (supplementary)

Table 21.1 Main Characteristics of MIEs, SEs, and MEs in Indonesia

Aspect	MIEs	SEs	MEs
Formality	operate in informal sector, unregistered & pay no taxes	some operate in formal sector, registered & pay taxes	all operate in formal sector, registered & pay taxes
Location	Majority in rural areas/villages	Many in urban areas/cities	Mostly in urban areas/cities
Organization & management	– run by the owner – no internal labor division – no formal management & accounting system (bookkeeping)	– run by the owner – no labor division (majority), – majority no formal management and accounting system (bookkeeping)	– many hire professional managers, – many have labor division, formal organizational structure & formal accounting system (bookkeeping)
Nature of employment	majority use unpaid family members	some hired wage laborers	– all hired wage laborers – some have formal recruitment system
Nature of production process	– degree of mechanization very low/mostly manual – level of technology very low	some use up-to-date machines	many have high degree of mechanization/access to modern technology
Market orientation	majority sell to local market and for low-income consumers	– many sell to national market and export – many serve also middle to high-income group	– all sell to national market and many also export – all serve middle and high-income consumers
Social & economic profiles of owners	– low or uneducated – from poor households	– some have good education, and from non-poor households	– majority have good education – many are from wealthy families – motivation: profit
Sources of inputs	– majority use local raw materials and use own money	– some import raw materials – some have access to bank and other formal credit institutions	– many use imported raw materials – majority have access to formal credit sources
External networks	– majority have no access to government programs and no business linkages with LEs	– many have good relations with government and have business linkages (such as subcontracting) with LEs.	– majority have good access to government programs – many have business linkages with LEs.
Motivation	to survive	– some for profit, some for survival	Profit maximization
Level of entrepreneurship	Low	Medium	High
Women entrepreneurs	ratio of female to male as entrepreneurs is high	ratio of female to male as entrepreneurs is high	ratio of female to male as entrepreneurs is low

Table 21.2 Total Enterprises by Size Category in All Economic Sectors in Indonesia, 2000–2012 (in thousand units)

Size category	2000	2003	2005	2007	2009	2010	2011	2012
MSEs	39,705	43,372.9	47,006.9	47,720.3	52,723.5	53,781.1	55,162.2	56,485.6
MEs	78.8	87.4	95.9	120.3	41.1	42.6	44.2	48.997
LEs	5.7	6.5	6.8	4.5	4.7	4.8	4.95	4.97
Total	39,789.7	43,466.8	47,109.6	49,845.0	52,769.3	53,828.5	55,211.4	56,539.6

Sources: processed data from Menegkop & UKM (www.depkop.go.id) and BPS (www.bps.go.id).

source of income. Therefore, the presence of MSEs in Indonesia is often considered a result of unemployment or poverty problems, not a reflection of entrepreneurial spirit (Tambunan, 2014).

The majority of MSMEs in Indonesia are engaged in the agricultural sector, including animal husbandry, forestry, and fisheries (51.5 percent). In 2008 there were about 42.7 million laborers in that sector, of which almost 99.5 percent worked in these enterprises. While there were about 26.4 million units in that sector, almost 100 percent were MSMEs. The MSMEs and MSEs are mostly agriculture-based compared to MEs. The second important sector for MSMEs is trade, hotels, and restaurants (28.8 percent). In the manufacturing industry, Indonesian MSMEs are traditionally not as strong compared to LEs or to MSMEs in Asian developed economies like Japan, Taiwan, and South Korea (where traditionally they are well presented in production linkages with LEs as suppliers or vendors, especially in the automotive, electronics, and machineries industries). This Indonesian structure of MSMEs by sector is, however, not unique to Indonesia. It is a key feature of this category of enterprises in developing countries, especially in countries where the level of industrialization and income per capita are relatively low.

According to the estimation of the Ministry of Industry in 2014, there were 4,324,190 MSMEs in the manufacturing sector, more commonly known as small and medium industries (SMIs) (Table 21.3). SMIs in Indonesia have some characteristics that make them different than LEs (or large industries/LIs), and also because of these characteristics they weathered

Table 21.3 Growth of SMEs in Indonesia, 2010–2014

No	Description	Year					Growth (%)
		2010	2011	2012	2013	2014*	
1	Total number of SMIs	3,806,566	3,909,343	4,026,624	4,159,502	4,324,190	3.24
2	Total workers	8,755,102	9,147,863	9,462,565	9,816,425	10,378,056	4.34
3	Investment (Rp trillion)	219	244	261	284	313	8.14
4	Production (Rp trillion)	521	561	609	671	753	9.63
5	Raw materials (Rp trillion)	156	163	174	188	207	7.27
6	Value added (Rp trillion)	265	398	435	483	546	10.60
7	Export (US$ million)	13,503	15,022	16,541	18,060	19,579	9.73

Source: MoI (2013).

Note: * projection

the 1997/98 Asian financial crisis far better than LIs (MoI, 2013). First, they were not as dependent as LIs on the financial and banking sectors (where the crisis initially erupted) and therefore they were able to survive and adapt to the sudden shock more quickly and flexibly. Second, SMIs generally are not as involved in the global market. In 2010, for example, SMIs contributed less than 20 percent to the country's manufacturing exports. Therefore, weakened export demand has not significantly affected the performance of SMIs in the current global slowing. Third, most SMIs produced basic goods, not luxury goods. Even when economic straits pushed purchasing power down, demand for their goods remained relatively high. For many types of goods they have their own market segments which generate a natural protection from competition from LIs or even from imported products. Within the manufacturing industry, food industry is the biggest group from the point of view of total number of SMIs operating in it. The second and third largest industry groups for SMIs are industries producing, respectively, various goods with wood, rattan, and bamboo as the main raw materials, and textiles and garments. As with many other developing countries, the Indonesian SMIs are also generally engaged in simple, traditional production activities, which is especially so for the small industries (SIs). Only very few of them, mostly medium industries (MIs), are involved in the production of medium to high technology-based goods like industrial machinery, production tools, and automotive components. In the automotive industry, for instance, most enterprises operate mainly as subcontractors producing certain components and spare parts for LIs, involving several multinational car companies in Indonesia, mainly from Japan, such as Toyota and Honda.

With respect to their contributions to the formation of gross domestic product (GDP), overall, MSMEs' share is always higher than that of LEs. In 2006 it was around 58 to 59 percent (at constant market prices), and in 2011, at current market prices, MSMEs' total output value reached Rp 4,303,571.5 billion or about 57.94 percent of Indonesia's GDP in that year, and increased to Rp 4,869,568.1 or 59.08 percent in 2012. As shown in Figure 21.1, within MSMEs, the GDP shares of MSEs are higher than those of MEs and LEs. This is not, however, because MSEs' productivity is higher than that of MEs or LEs, but rather due to the fact that the number of MSEs is much higher than that of MEs and LEs. In terms of growth, during the period 2011–2012, for instance, Indonesia's GDP

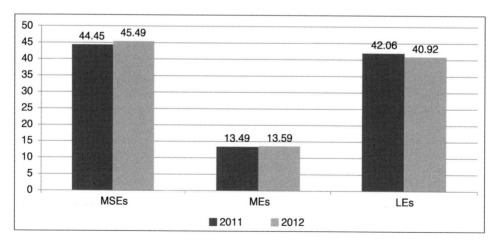

Figure 21.1   GDP Shares of MSEs, MEs and LEs in Indonesia, 2011 and 2012 (%)

Sources: processed data from Menegkop & UKM (www.depkop.go.id) and BPS (www.bps.go.id).

increased by 10.97 percent. In the same period, total output value of MSEs increased almost 13.6 percent, and MEs experienced a slightly lower growth rate at 11.79 percent. As a comparison, total output value of LEs increased at 7.96 percent. With respect to GDP share by economic sector, the GDP share of MSMEs varies by sector. In agriculture and trade, GDP shares of MSMEs are always high than in other sectors.

Main constraints facing MSMEs

Indonesian MSMEs (especially MSEs) are often hampered by many constraints, including institutional constraints to grow in size and become viable/efficient larger enterprises. The constraints may differ from region to region, between rural and urban areas, between sectors and subsectors, or between individual enterprises within a sector or subsector or a region. However, there are a number of constraints common to all MSMEs in the country, including the lack of funds to finance working, as well as investment, capital, human resources with high skills, advanced technology and up-to-date, comprehensive information; difficulties in procuring raw materials and other required inputs; marketing and distribution; high trans-portation costs; problems caused by cumbersome and costly bureaucratic procedures, espe-cially getting required licenses; and policies and regulations that generate market distortions. These are often described in the literature as external constraints to MSME growth.[1]

Based on BPS data, 2010 and 2013, Table 21.4 highlights the main constraints faced by MSEs in the manufacturing industry. Surprisingly, the data presented in this table indicate that not all surveyed producers consider lack of capital as their most serious business constraint; although lack of capital is ranked first among the types of difficulty. The proportion of those facing serious problems varies (in total as well as by type of constraint), however, by group of industry as well as by province, and even by district within a province. By group of industry, the variety may be related to differences in aspects such as the complexity of

Table 21.4 Number of MSEs in the Manufacturing Industry by Main Constraints in Indonesia, 2010 and 2013

Status	2010		2013	
	Total units	%	Total units	%
Have no serious obstacles	599,591	21.94	839,903	24.57
Have serious obstacles	2,133,133	78.06	2,578,463	75.43
Total respondents	2,732,724	100.00	3,418,366	100.00
Serious obstacles	Total units	%	Total units	%
Lack of capital	806,538	37.81	957,339	37.13
Marketing difficulties	495,100	23.21	535,176	20.76
Lack or high prices of raw materials	483,581	22.67	629,542	24.42
Other main constraints	184,516	8.65	267,612	10.38
High labor cost or lack of skilled workers	88,952	4.17	102,611	3.98
Transportation/distribution obstacles	39,676	1.86	39,255	1.52
High price or short supply of energy	34,770	1.63	46,928	1.82
Respondent total	2,133,133	100.00	2,578,463	100.00

Source: BPS (www.bps.go.id).

production process, market conditions for both output and inputs (especially raw materials, components, capital and human resources) and specific industry-related policies. Meanwhile, the variety by province or district may be related to differences in various characteristics of individual provinces such as infrastructure condition, geographical location, regional government policies and local market condition.

Entrepreneurship development in Indonesia

Level of entrepreneurship from an international perspective

As the flagships of entrepreneurship are MSMEs, the total number of MSMEs can be used as an indicator of entrepreneurship development. In Indonesia, as shown before, the total number of these enterprises keeps growing every year, which may suggest that the total number of entrepreneurs in the country increases every year. However, data from other various sources on the number of entrepreneurs collected by the research institute of Kompas Newspaper show that as a percentage of total population, Indonesia is the smallest country with respect to total entrepreneurs in comparison with many other countries such as the United States (US), Singapore, Thailand, South Korea, and Malaysia. As can be seen in Figure 21.2, by 2012 it was estimated that the total number of entrepreneurs in Indonesia was less than 1 percent of the country's total population, compared to, for instance, around 11.5 percent in the US.

Assuming that the figure reflects the facts, it may suggest that the level of entrepreneurship in a country is positively related to the level of economic development or industrialization in the country. Of course, there are many other factors that may contribute to the level of entrepreneurship development or opportunities for individuals to become entrepreneurs, such as current market structure, access to capital, and local constraints.

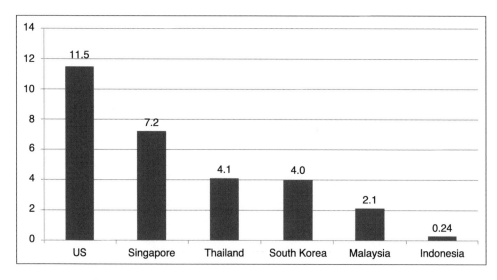

Figure 21.2   Total Entrepreneurs as Percentage of Total Population in Indonesia and Some Other Selected Countries, 2012

Source: Kompas (Ekonomi, Wednesday, 15 January 2014, p. 19).

Women entrepreneurs

Key characteristics and current development

At least five main characteristics of women entrepreneurship can be observed in Indonesia. First, the intensity of women being entrepreneurs or owning their own businesses is still low, though the rate varies by country due to differences in local factors such as employment and education opportunities, institution, culture or even religion. Second, MSMEs are more important than LEs for women entrepreneurs, as women face more constraints to enter LEs, such as lack of education and shortage of capital. Third, within MSMEs, the female–male entrepreneur ratio is generally higher in MIEs than in larger sized and modern enterprises. This is due to the fact that women in Indonesia, as in many developing countries, are more likely than men to be involved in informal activities which consist predominantly of MIEs, either as self-employed or employers or paid/unpaid workers. Fourth, many women conduct entrepreneurial endeavor as a means to survive; they are pushed to do so because all other options for them to get better jobs outside the home are either absent or unsatisfactory.

Information on the total number of women entrepreneurs in Indonesia is rather limited and it is fragmented across various sources. For instance, data on MSMEs shown in Figures 21.3 and 21.4 show ownership of the enterprises by gender, i.e. about 77 percent of MSMEs' owners are male and about 23 percent are female. As Figure 21.3 shows, women entrepreneurs dominate MIEs and SEs. This structure of business ownership by gender in Indonesia indicates that women entrepreneurs or women as business owners in the LE category are very few, and this may suggest that becoming an entrepreneur in Indonesia is still dominated by men, especially in modern companies. Another important source is the National Labor Force Survey which provides data on total population aged 15 years old and beyond by status of main work and gender. It shows that the total number of women not as employees but working alone (self-employment) or running their own businesses with paid workers is still lower than their male counterparts. In May 2013 there were only 0.85 million women with their own business compared with 3.41 million men, and in February 2014 (the most recent data) there were 0.77 million women against 3.38 million men (Figure 21.4). In percentage of total working population (aged 15 and beyond) by

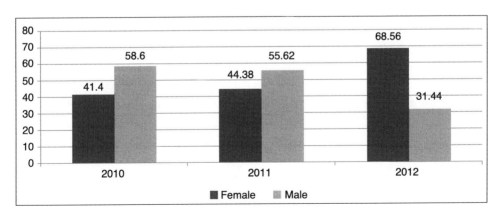

Figure 21.3 Percentage Distribution of MIEs and SEs by Gender of the Owner, 2010–2012

Sources: Menegkop & UKM (www.depkop.go.id) and BPS (www.bps.go.id).

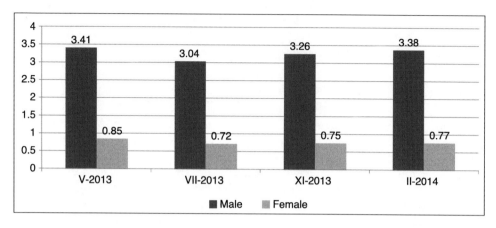

Figure 21.4   Number of Entrepreneurs/Business Owners by Gender, 2013 (May, July, November) and 2014 (February) (Million Persons)

Source: BPS (www.bps.go.id).

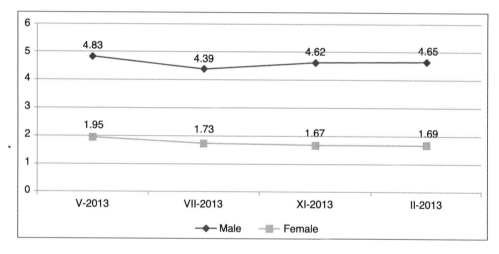

Figure 21.5   Percentage of Entrepreneurs/Business Owners by Gender, 2013 (May, July, November) and 2014 (February)

Source: BPS (www.bps.go.id).

gender, indeed the share of women entrepreneurs in Indonesia is much lower than that of male entrepreneurs (Figure 21.5).

Indonesia in global perspective

There are various international organizations which regularly produce reports on women's entrepreneurship or selected aspects related to women's empowerment in the world which may also give insight on the Indonesian position from a global perspective with respect to the development of women's entrepreneurship. One of the organizations is the World Economic Forum (WEF) in Geneva. Its annual report, entitled The Global Gender Gap

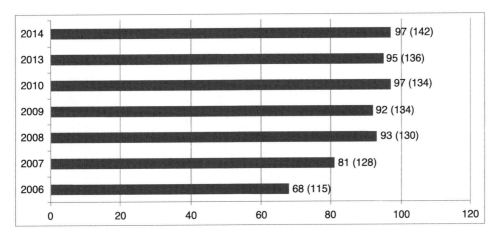

Figure 21.6 The Gender Gap Index of Indonesia, 2006–2014

Source: WEF (2006, 2007, 2008, 2009, 2010, 2013, 2014)

Note: in brackets are total surveyed countries

Report, measures the gender gap in individual countries with its own developed index, i.e. the Global Gender Index. The Index is designed to measure gender-based gaps in access to resources and opportunities in individual countries rather than the actual levels of the available resources and opportunities in those countries. So, the Index is independent from countries' levels of development. In other words, the Index is constructed to rank countries on their gender gaps, not on their development level. The Index examines the gap between men and women in four fundamental categories: economic participation and opportunity, educational attainment, health and survival, and political empowerment. If countries have a higher score (closer to one) it means that the condition of women in those countries is better than in those with a lower score (lower rank).[2] In *The Global Gender Gap 2014,* Indonesia's rank is 97 out of 142 countries surveyed.

The second index that can also be used to measure the level of women entrepreneurship development in Indonesia is the Gender Equity Index (GEI) developed by Social Watch.[3] The main aim of this index is to contribute to the understanding of gender-based inequities, and to monitor its situation and evolution in the different countries and regions of the world, according to a selection of indicators relevant to gender inequity in three dimensions, namely education, economic participation, and empowerment. The index's range of values is from 0 to 100, with the lower values indicating greater inequity and higher values greater equity. In its recent report, the Social Watch Report 2014 (Social Watch, 2014), Table 21.5 shows the ranks of ASEAN and other selected non-ASEAN countries and the values of the three dimensions of the index. As can be seen, within ASEAN, it is not Indonesia but the Philippines that reveals the greatest gender equity.

Other relevant indexes are those developed by UNDP, i.e. the Gender Inequality Index (GII) and the Gender Development Index (GDI). The first index which measures the gap between male and female is constructed based on three dimensions: labor market, empowerment, and reproductive health. The value of the first dimension is based on the percentage of women participation in the labor force. The value of the second dimension is calculated from two indicators, namely educational attainment (secondary level and above)

Table 21.5 The Ranks of ASEAN Countries for the Gender Equity Index (GEI) and its Dimensions

Country	GEI 2014	Education	Economic Activity	Empowerment
Bangladesh	55	80	65	18
Brunei Darussalam	72	99	78	39
China	64	95	76	21
Philippines	76	100	67	61
India	37	66	33	12
Indonesia	62	93	57	36
Cambodia	55	71	73	21
South Korea.	59	84	68	26
Malaysia	56	98	40	31
Nepal	47	65	56	21
Pakistan	29	55	19	14
Singapore	69	94	71	41
Sri Lanka	62	97	58	31
Thailand	71	97	77	39
Viet Nam	70	95	75	41

Source: Social Watch (2014).

and parliamentary representation. The value of the third dimension is based on two indicators, namely adolescent fertility and maternal mortality.[4] In presenting the Index, countries covered are divided into three groups: very high, high, medium. The second index is simply the well-known Human Development Index (HDI), as it measures achievements in the same basic dimensions as those of the HDI. However, the second index also covers inequalities between male and female. Table 21.6 shows the ranks for these two indexes for Indonesia and a number of other selected countries as a comparison.

Factors driving women to become entrepreneurs

Although the development of women's entrepreneurship in Indonesia is considered very important, especially by politicians and development policy makers as a means to reduce poverty, particularly in rural areas, studies on this particular issue are still limited. More studies are available on MSMEs but not focusing on gender aspects. Among the existing few studies on women's entrepreneurship development in Indonesia is the study by Maemunah (1996) who studied women entrepreneurs in home-based industries in Batanghari District in Sumatera island. The aim of the research was to identify the key characteristics of women's leadership in the home-based industry and to understand strategic constraints in the development of women's businesses. The method used for the research was interviews. Most of her interviewed women entrepreneurs are wives and mothers aged between 21 and 40 years old, and only about 8.33 percent of them had finished college. One important finding of the study is that from a business development perspective, most of the respondents cannot be considered as successful entrepreneurs. But in fact they are still in business mainly because of the need of the family for additional income. In other words, for many of them, the main motivation behind their engagement as entrepreneurs is mainly dominated by necessity. The second important finding is that the main constraint faced by the respondents

Table 21.6 The Ranks of Indonesia and Some Other Selected Countries for the Gender Inequality Index (GII) and the Gender Development Index from UNDP, 2014

Country*	Rank GII	Rank GDI
Very High and High HDI		
– Japan	25	79
– Singapore	15	52
– South Korea	17	85
– Brunei Darussalam	–	31
– Malaysia	39	91
– Thailand	70	14
– China	37	88
– Sri Lanka	75	66
Medium HDI		
– Philippines	78	17
– Vietnam	58	–
– Indonesia	103	98
– India	127	132
– Timor-Leste	–	122
– Lao PDR	118	112
– Kambodia	105	105
– Bangladesh	115	107
Low HDI		
– Pakistan	127	145
– Nepal	98	102

Source: UNDP (2014).

to develop their business is the lack of capital. Most respondents used their own capital or family capital for financing their business. They are unable to get loans from banks due to lack of collateral and as they said, the interest rate is also too high for them. However, despite this capital constraint, the number of women running their own businesses in Batanghari District has increased, which has improved the motivation of local women in managing and organizing their own businesses.

Manning (1998) and Oey (1998) tried to examine factors behind the rapid increase in the number of micro and small enterprises (MSEs) owned by women in Indonesia during the 1980s and early 1990s, when the country achieved rapid economic growth. According to them, the main reasons for that rapid increase are partly due to the increase of women's educational level, and to the economic or financial pressures the women faced in their households. In other words, they suggest that in Indonesia there are "pull" as well as "push" factors playing roles in determining the involvement of women as entrepreneurs. "Pull" factors are those which attract women to open their own businesses, while "push" factors are conditions that push women to work or to open their own businesses.

Sarwestri et al. (2001) studied women entrepreneurs and women workers in the home-based mattress-making industry in Mekar Mukti village in Bandung in the West Java province. The mattress industry is also among the so-called "women's industries," which means that the intensity of women's involvement in this industry, either as owners/entrepreneurs or paid workers is high. They found that most of their respondents have been involved in this industry when they were single, mainly because of two intertwined reasons: they lacked funds to continue their education, and also wanted to have their own income. They kept working in this industry when married, especially when their spouse's income was not enough to support the family. Only about 23.3 percent of the respondents have a bank account/or savings in the bank, and about 80 percent do this work because there are no other income-generating opportunities, mainly due to only an elementary level of education. Many respondents who run their own businesses learned the skill of making mattresses from learning by doing when they were paid workers in other people's firms.

Purwandari (2002) did a study of the handmade bags craft industry in Kulon Progo District in the Province of Yogyakarta. Her main objective in doing that research was not to investigate women entrepreneurs, but to understand the roles of the handmade bag industry in women's working opportunity and household income, and what social factors influence its role. Nevertheless, the study does give some important information about women entrepreneurs, as it shows that the handmade bag industry is among the most popular industries for women entrepreneurs in Indonesia for many reasons, which include that manufacturing handmade bags is relatively simple work that can be done by uneducated women and married women with children who cannot leave their houses. The study shows that about 60 percent of women entrepreneurs and workers in her sample enterprises have only elementary school (finished and unfinished) education; and those who have finished high school number only 7.5 percent. Although it depends on production volume, type of product (with respect to quality), and market orientation, this type of industry also does not need much capital. The industry is female labour intensive, and therefore, from Indonesian cultural values, traditions, and Islamic religious point of views, it is then easier for married women to do this job than in other more male labor-intensive industries like furniture, footwear, building materials, and many others.

From his study with a sample of 45 women running their own micro or small-sized businesses together with and without their husbands in the city of Blitar (the province of East Java), Widagdo (2003) gives an important, though not really unexpected, picture showing that the position of women in running their own businesses together with or without their husbands is still mainly dominated by their husbands in many business decision-making processes. This, based on Indonesian cultural values, creates a "given image" of women as housewives and men as the head of the family. The fact that women also work to contribute to the family income does not get considered as a "bread earning" activity. In many cases, when women and men have equal or almost equal income, conflicts normally arise, although the conflicts usually do not have serious impacts on their marriage and family life.

More interesting is a study by Arifin (2004) who analyzed the obstacles faced by women in MIEs and SEs, which include general problems derived not only from their business's marginality and informality, but also from gender stereotyping. The author proposes a systematic way of understanding women entrepreneurs' vulnerability for effective empowerment and organizing activity. His important findings include the following: (1) general problems usually faced by women entrepreneurs are risks in economic activity outside the law which include (a) discrimination, which includes removal of their stalls, (b) exploitation such as illegal charge by *preman* or even by authoritative agents such as the police or security officers, and (c) vulnerability to price rises, especially the prices of raw materials; (2) exploitation and discrimination based on gender, mainly because women are generally seen as weak economic players, operating outside the law; (3) most of the women have only limited resources to be used to prevent the negative impacts of these risks; and (4) sources of vulnerability of women entrepreneurs in MIEs and SEs are: (a) gender related patterns observed in the family and in the economic activities, for example differences in social status, interactions, and work division; and (b) intervention of external agents into their economic activities, communities and family life.

Dewayanti and Chotim (2004) attempted to investigate women's marginalization and exploitation in MIEs and SEs in rural Java. The objectives of the study were to highlight two things, namely structural problems in relation to business and gender, and empowerment efforts conducted by various non-government organizations to overcome the women's marginalization problem and exploitation. The concepts used to analyze household economic problems and business problems are marginalization and women's double burden. This study covers rural MIEs and SEs in two industries, namely the coconut processing industry in Banyumas in the Central Java province and the tile industry in Klaten, also in the same province. These are among low technology-based industries dominated by MIEs and SEs and with a high intensity of women's engagement not only as workers but also as business owners. Based on their findings, they argue that women's marginalization and exploitation are causal factors of underdevelopment of micro/small business which have implications of adding to women's load. This marginalization process generates poverty because most women survive within rural micro/small business scenarios. They find the marginalization issue as more urgent for women than men because the division of labor pattern in Indonesian households traditionally has women taking a larger share of the domestic duties. The women's selection of work and efforts cannot be separated from the family need patterns. Economically, work division can be explained by poverty. Facing this difficult condition, women play an important role with their additional work, like opening a stall, looking after cattle and garden.

More recently Tambunan (2014) conducted a survey on 139 women business owners in various sectors in locations such as Jakarta (the capital city of Indonesia), Tangerang (Banten Province), Bekasi and Depok (West Java Province), and Bukit Tinggi and Bandar Lampung in West Sumatra Province. The aim of the survey was to identify their main motivation for operating their own businesses. The findings show that many of the respondents had their own businesses on account of family or household economic hardship. In other words, the findings may suggest that not all women entrepreneurs in Indonesia are "pulled" by market opportunities or by high entrepreneurship spirit.

Based on its survey in 41 countries (including developing countries in Asia and Latin America), the Global Entrepreneurship Monitor in its 2007 report (GEM, 2007, 2013) labels this type of women entrepreneurs as necessity entrepreneurs (Table 21.7). When women conduct their own business because there are available market opportunities, they are labeled as opportunity entrepreneurs. As generally expected, the report shows that in low-income/poor countries, the ratio of necessity to opportunity entrepreneurship is significantly higher than in the high-income countries. Fifth, age, work status, education, income, social ties, culture and customs or tradition, family background, marriage status, family obligations, discrimination against women in many aspects of life (which is often the result of gender beliefs inherent in a culture or society), disproportionate bargaining power against men, and public/community perceptions are all significant social, economic, and institutional factors in a woman's decision to start a business.

Government policies to support entrepreneurship development

The Indonesian government realized this current situation with respect to entrepreneurship development in the country and therefore it has been trying to encourage entrepreneurship

Table 21.7 Total New Entrepreneurs in Selected Countries in Asia by Gender and Motivation, 2013*

Country	Opportunity		Necessity	
	Male (%)	Female (%)	Male (%)	Female (%)
China	70	58	28	41
India	58	58	40	37
Indonesia	76	73	24	27
Japan	73	63	20	34
South Korea	60	63	37	34
Malaysia	78	87	22	13
Philippines	60	52	40	48
Singapore	89	91	9	8
Taiwan	72	71	28	29
Thailand	83	74	14	24
Vietnam	75	75	25	25
Average	72	69	26	29

Source: (GEM, 2013).

Note: * *percentage of total entrepreneurs from related gender category who just opened new businesses*

development by a variety of measures/programs, especially after the 1997/98 Asian financial crisis. Only after the country's economy was severely hit by the crisis that led to the largest economic recession the country has ever experienced with a negative economic growth by 13.5 percent, and almost all big companies collapsed, did the government realize that Indonesia can never fully recover and become a highly competitive economy in the world without having a large pool of highly competitive entrepreneurs.

The programs include entrepreneurship and vocational trainings and various programs to support MSMEs, since these enterprises provide an avenue for the testing and development of entrepreneurial ability. MSMEs are considered very important especially for the development of women's entrepreneurship, given the fact that women in Indonesia still face many constraints in becoming entrepreneurs such as less education than their male counterparts and other social-cultural constraints.

Another important reason for the government to promote entrepreneurship development in Indonesia is unemployment, especially among the youth. For the past few years, the Indonesian government with the full support of the ILO Office for Indonesia has been promoting youth employment though various initiatives focusing on access to decent jobs, vocational and entrepreneurship training, skills training, and promotion of workers' rights. The government has been implementing a four-track development strategy which is pro-growth, pro-job, pro-poor, and pro-environment, which along with its commitment to the Millennium Development Goals (MDGs), aims to achieve full and productive employment and decent work for all, including youth. As part of this strategy, the government has requested universities to produce more potential young entrepreneurs.

Indonesia has an interesting experience with efforts to promote entrepreneurship, commencing with the so-called "Old Order" period (1945–1966). After independence from Dutch colonialism, President Sukarno chose and promulgated economic nationalism and that period was devoted mainly to offset the imbalance of economic power that was held mainly by Dutch and Chinese businesses, in favor of the indigenous Indonesians who had been left far behind. Nationalism became the order of the day and all businesses including banks, public utilities, railways, owned by Dutch and Chinese were turned over to state-owned companies (SOCs). However, in the end, attempts to foster ethnic Indonesian entrepreneurs were not very successful due to the lack of entrepreneurial capability of indigenous people (Bhasin and Venkataramany, 2010).

During the "New Order" period (1966–1998), Indonesia became more liberal including with regard to business–government relations: state dominance in the economy was abandoned, controls on private enterprises were removed, and local as well as foreign direct investment was encouraged. However, instead of fostering a healthy development of the private sector, through patronage, the New Order nurtured the growth of a dependent c apitalist class of client businessmen. The culture of cronyism and nepotism based on preferential treatment of the presidential family and friends, Chinese, and other selected businessmen based on the "reciprocity principle" became prevalent (Bhasin and Venkataramany, 2010).

After the 1997/98 Asian financial crisis until today (the era of *reformasi*), with the introduction of democracy and regional empowerment through the implementation of regional autonomy, entrepreneurship development through MSMEs development has been given much greater attention. Since then many studies have been conducted to examine the current development of entrepreneurship or MSMEs and to investigate the main factors affecting it. Almost all existing studies have found that entrepreneurship development in Indonesia is constrained by many factors, including lack of funding, high interest rates, high taxation, burdensome government requirements, lack of government understanding/supports, lack of education, lack of experience especially in managing a business, and also cultural factors such as high power distance, uncertainty avoidance and collectivism, lack of confidence, and lack of innovative behavior (lack of personality traits), all hinder entrepreneurship development (e.g. Riyanti and Dwi, 2004; Susanto, 2005; Cole, 2007; Bhasin and Venkataramany, 2010).

Conclusions

Entrepreneurship development in Indonesia has attracted serious attention from the government and has become a popular and important issue within the academic community after the Asian financial crisis in 1997–1998. After the crisis the Indonesian government has at last realized that to have a good and sustained economic development performance, not only are technology, capital, natural resources, and skilled workers needed but good entrepreneurs with bright ideas and creativity are also required. The increasing government attention on women's entrepreneurship development was initially based on the strong belief that it may contribute to gender equality and poverty reduction.

In sum, the degree of entrepreneurship in Indonesia has been rising, especially since the crisis, as the private sector has been given freedom with increasing global pressures to strengthen its role and reduce state dominance in economic development. However, there are still many constraints that hinder the speed of entrepreneurship development in Indonesia. Especially with respect to women's entrepreneurship, the current constraints to a certain extent are related to limited access to education and vocational training, responsibility for domestic work, tradition, customs, cultural and religious constraints, lack of access to necessary facilities to support business development such as capital. Unless these are overcome, women's ability to engage in entrepreneurial endeavor will remain unequal compared with men's ability to do so.

Notes

1 See for instance, Tambunan (2009a, b) for a survey of literature on this particular issue.
2 For more information about the methodology, see further WEF (2013), or its reports for previous years.
3 Social Watch, a network that today has members in over 60 countries around the world, was created in 1995 as a "meeting place for nongovernmental organizations concerned with social development and gender discrimination." This network was created to respond to the need to promote the political will required for making the United Nations promises come true. Social Watch, which is continually growing both qualitatively and quantitatively, has published 15 yearly reports on progress and setbacks in the struggle against poverty and for gender equality. These reports have been used as tools for advocacy on a local, regional, and international level (Social Watch, 2014).
4 See UNDP (2014), or Human Development Report from previous years for further information on the methodology.

References

Arifin, H. (2004). Cara memahami kerentanan perempuan pengusaha kecil (a way to understand the vulnerability of women-entrepreneurs). *Jurnal Analisis Sosial*, 9(2), 157–170.

Bhasin, B. B. and Venkataramany, S. (2010). Globalization of Entrepreneurship, Policy Considerations for SME Development in Indonesia. *International Business & Economics Research Journal*, 9(4), 95–104.

Cole, S. (2007). Entrepreneurship and Empowerment, Considering the Barriers – A Case Study from Indonesia. *Tourism Review*, 55(4), 461–473.

Dewayanti, R. and Chotim, E. E. (2004). *Marginalisasi dan Eksploitasi Perempuan Usaha Mikro di Perdesaan Jawa* (Women's marginalization and exploitation in micro business in rural Jawa). Bandung, Yayasan Akatiga.

GEM (2007). 2007 *Report on Women and Entrepreneurship, Global Entrepreneurship Monitor*, The Center for Women's Leadership at Babson College (http://www.gemconsortium.org). Accessed: 14 October 2009.

GEM (2013). 2013 *Global Report, Global Entrepreneurship Monitor*, The Center for Women's Leadership at Babson College (http://www.gemconsortium.org). Accessed: 8 August 2015.

Maemunah, M. (1996). *Studi tentang kepemimpinan wanita dalam industri rumah tangga di Kabupaten Batanghari* (Study on women leadership in home-based industry at Batanghari District). mimeo, March, Jambi, Faculty of Education Universitas Jambi.

Manning, C. (1998). *Indonesian Labour in Transition, An East Asian Success Story*, Cambridge University Press, Cambridge and New York.

MoI (2013). *Industry Facts and Figures*, Jakarta, Public Communication Center, the Ministry of Industry Republic of Indonesia (www.kemenperin.go.id). Accessed: 2 May 2014.

Oey, M. (1998). The Impact of the Financial Crisis on Indonesian Women, Some Survival Strategy. *The Indonesian Quarterly*, 26(2), 81–90.

Purwandari, I. (2002). *Peranan Industri terhadap kesempatan kerja wanita dan pendapatan rumah tangga* (The role of industry on women employment household income opportunities), internal research paper, January, Fakultas Pertanian STIPER, D.I. Yogyakarta

Riyanti, B. and Dwi, P. (2004). Factors influencing the success of small-scale entrepreneurs in Indonesia, in B. N. Setiadi, A. Supratiknya, W. J. Lonner, and Y. H. Poortinga (eds.), *Ongoing Themes in Psychology and Culture*, International Association for Cross-Cultural Psychology. Selected Papers from the Sixteenth International Congress of the International Association for Cross-Cultural Psychology, D.I. Yogyakarta, Kanisius.

Sarwestri, A., Sekarningsih, R. and Darwis, R. S. (2001). Laporan Penelitian, Faktor-Faktor yang Mempengaruhi Pendapatan Perempuan Pekerja pada Industri Rumah Tangga Pembuatan Kasur di Desa Mekar Mukti, Kecamatan Cililin, Kabupaten Bandung (Research Report, Factors which influence income of female workers in home-based industries producing mattress in Mekar Mukti Village, Cililin subdistrict, Bandung District), research report, February, Pusat Penelitian Peranan Wanita-Universitas Padjajaran, Bandung.

Social Watch (2014). *Social Watch Report 2014. Means and End*, http//www.socialwatch.org/report 2014. Accessed: 1 January 2015.

Susanto, J. (2005). Creative Entrepreneurship in Indonesia, Problems, Strategies and Challenges – A Case Study, Study Meeting on Creative Entrepreneurship, The Employers" Association of Indonesia and Asian Productivity Organization, Jakarta.

Tambunan, T. T. H. (2009a). *SME in Asian Developing Countries*, London, Palgrave Macmillan.

Tambunan, T. T. H. (2009b). *Development of SMEs in ASEAN Countries*, Readworthy Publications, Ltd, New Delhi

Tambunan, T. T. H. (2014). *UMKM Indonesia (Indonesian MSMEs)*. Jakarta, Triakti University Press.

UNDP (2014). *Human Development Report 2014*, Vienna and New York, United Nations Development Programs.

WEF (2006). *The Global Gender Gap Report 2006*, Geneva, World Economic Forum

WEF (2007). *The Global Gender Gap Report 2007*, Geneva, World Economic Forum.

WEF (2008). *The Global Gender Gap Report 2008*, Geneva, World Economic Forum.

WEF (2009). *The Global Gender Gap Report 2009*, Geneva, World Economic Forum.

WEF (2010). *The Global Gender Gap Report 2010*, Geneva, World Economic Forum.

WEF (2013). *The Global Gender Gap Report 2013*, Geneva, World Economic Forum.

WEF (2014). *The Global Gender Gap Report 2014*, Geneva, World Economic Forum.

Widagdo, B. (2003). Pola relasi gender dalam keluarga, Studi pada pekera perempuan sector industri rumah tangga di Kota Blitar (Family's gender relation patterns, Study on women working in the home-based industry in the city of Blitar), discussion paper, February, The study centre for women and society, Universitas Muhammadiyah, Malang.

22

SOCIAL ENTREPRENEURSHIP, SOCIAL CHANGE, AND GENDER ROLES IN AZERBAIJAN

Mehrangiz Najafizadeh

The concept of social entrepreneur has gained increased usage in recent years by scholars, the mass media, and practitioners. In my own research, I first utilized the concept of social entrepreneur over 25 years ago in my comparative historical analysis of the social construction of education as a social problem in the Third World. In that research, I focused on social and moral entrepreneurs within the broader rubric of education entrepreneurs as social actors who played critical roles in defining education as a social problem, and in advocating socially constructed appropriate solutions to that problem (Najafizadeh, 1989; Najafizadeh and Mennerick, 1989). More recently, I employed the concept of "social entrepreneur" in examining social transition and changing gender roles in the Republic of Azerbaijan (Najafizadeh, 2003a, 2003b).

In this chapter, I provide a detailed analysis of gender issues in the Republic of Azerbaijan from the 1800s when Azerbaijanis were governed by Czarist Russia, to contemporary post-Soviet Azerbaijan. In doing so, I provide a conceptualization of social entrepreneurship and of the social constructionist theoretical perspective as a framework for gender analysis. Then, to examine social entrepreneurship in Azerbaijan, as it pertains to gender, I focus on a series of pivotal events dating from the 1800s to the present. Specifically, first, I explore social entrepreneurship, social change, and related gender issues in the context of the emergence of the Azerbaijani Enlightenment Movement and the rise of Azerbaijani philanthropy from the mid-1800s to the early 1900s. Second, I examine the social construction of Azerbaijanism and the establishment of the Azerbaijan Democratic Republic in 1918. Third, I focus on Sovietization and the social construction of the "Soviet Azerbaijani woman" from 1920 to 1991, and fourth, I extend my analysis of social entrepreneurship and gender to the re-emergence of independent Azerbaijan from 1991 to the present.

The social constructionist theoretical perspective and the concept of social entrepreneurship

In framing my analysis of gender issues in Azerbaijan, I utilize a social constructionist perspective to focus on differing ways in which social actors perceive and define gender issues. Indeed, whereas some social actors view particular gender issues as problematic, other social actors dismiss these same issues as being of little or no relevance. Therefore, central to this perspective is the point that social actors may perceive and define the same gender issues in very different ways and that their perceptions and definitions may differ at distinct points in time or during distinct historical periods. As one example, some social actors may perceive the issue of equal access to educational opportunities among women and men to be of utmost societal importance, whereas other social actors may regard the same issue as insignificant (see, e.g., Burr, 2015; Harris, 2010; Haslanger, 2012; Hjelm, 2014; Holstein and Gubrium, 2008; Holstein and Miller, 2003; Kimmel, 2013; Lorber and Farrell, 1991; Najafizadeh, 2003a).

My attention to the social construction of gender raises important questions, such as which social actors attend to gender issues? Which particular issues do they define as most salient? How do these definitions vary over time? These social actors, whom I refer to as social entrepreneurs, engage in gender-related activities for diverse reasons ranging from moral concerns about what they perceive as right and wrong or as just and unjust, to other perspectives that are underpinned by their own sociopolitical beliefs and values interrelated with broader social and political ideologies. In the end, just as business entrepreneurs seek to convert their ideas and efforts into successful commercial or economic ventures, social entrepreneurs seek to convert their ideas and efforts into social change and into the resolution or amelioration of what they perceive as gender-related social problems. Furthermore, the concept of social entrepreneur encompasses a broad range of social actors including individual women and men, social and political leaders and groups, religious leaders and organizations, philanthropic groups, non-governmental organizations, government agencies, and government officials (Najafizadeh, 2003a, 2003b). (For discussions of varied definitions and perspectives pertaining to social entrepreneurship, see, e.g., Abu-Saifan, 2012; Dacin et al., 2011; Groot and Dankbaar, 2014; Howaldt et al., 2015; Mair et al., 2012; Mair et al., 2006; Martin and Osberg, 2007; McKenny, 2014; Rahim and Mohtar, 2015; Robinson et al., 2009; Roper and Cheney, 2005; Shaw and Carter, 2007; Zahra et al., 2009.)

Paramount among relevant gender issues is gender roles and power relations between women and men as these two elements are central to our understanding of the well-being of women in society. As I demonstrate in my analysis, various social entrepreneurs are instrumental in prescribing and advocating particular types of roles for women and for men. Further, I argue that gender-related cultural norms, values, and beliefs as well as sociopolitical ideologies are key elements that are influential in determining whether specific gender roles are defined as "appropriate" or as "problematic." Indeed, an enhanced understanding of who decides which gender roles are advocated and enforced and how these roles may vary from one social setting to another and from one historical period to another is critical to our broader knowledge of gender issues (also see Najafizadeh, 2003a, 2003b, 2015a).

The Azerbaijani enlightenment movement and philanthropy: social entrepreneurs and the social construction of a new vision of Azerbaijani society and women's place

The geopolitical region now known as the Republic of Azerbaijan is characterized by a dynamic social history. During the 1800s, Azerbaijan was incorporated into the Russian Empire as a result of the Russo-Persian Wars of 1804–1813 and 1826–1828. Due to the limited availability of schools and the need to engage in manual labor for economic survival, the majority of Azerbaijanis during the 1800s were illiterate or semi-literate and their daily lives continued to be heavily influenced by the longstanding traditions of Islam and of patriarchy. This was particularly the case for girls and women for whom education typically was not considered necessary and for whom women's roles primarily emphasized household and family caregiving activities, thereby excluding them from participation in the public realm which was reserved for men. In short, Islamic religious ideology dating back to the seventh century had longstanding patriarchal cultural norms as core elements in Azerbaijani society, and both strongly shaped women's roles and identity. Men typically served as heads of their families and as decision makers, both at home and in public life, whereas women were defined as wives, mothers, and family caregivers and had only limited access to formal education and limited participation in the public realm (see Alstadt, 1996: 199–209; Bolukbasi, 2011: 22–25; Swietochowski, 1995: 1–16, 1996: 211–234).

During the 1800s, moreover, Azerbaijan witnessed the emergence and expansion of an Azerbaijani intelligentsia and Azerbaijani Enlightenment Movement. Foremost among the intelligentsia, and foremost as a leader of the Azerbaijani Enlightenment Movement, was Mirza Fatali Akhundov. Born in 1812, Akhundov was highly educated (fluent in Russian, the official language, Azerbaijani, Persian, and Arabic) and worked as a translator for Russian government officials. As a major Azerbaijani social entrepreneur of the nineteenth century, Akhundov was a literary figure and a philosopher who began his activities in the 1830s aimed at a wide range of social reforms: expanding the training of Azerbaijani teachers, increasing access of common people to modern education, replacing the Arabic alphabet with a simplified Latin alphabet that would help expand literacy, and eliminating religious fanaticism and intolerance. Of special significance in Akhundov's social thought was his opposition to the social oppression of women and his advocacy for the rights of women. In turn, the Azerbaijani Enlightenment Movement continued to expand during the 1800s through the increased contact of Azerbaijanis with Russian and European scholars and increased exposure to the ideologies of modernism and secularism and to new ideas and ways of conceptualizing women's roles. This expansion of the Enlightenment Movement and of social entrepreneurship included mostly Azerbaijani men who typically had studied at Russian universities or transcaucasian teachers' institutions. As such, they had experienced secular-style education rather than traditional Islamic education, and quite often they were employed as government civil servants or as teachers in secular schools for Azerbaijani boys (Alstadt, 1996: 199–209: Cornell, 2011: 12–13; Najafov, 2008; Swietochowski, 1995: 25–36).

In the late 1800s and early 1900s, Azerbaijan also experienced an oil boom that made Azerbaijan a site for major international investments and a global leader in oil production. Various oil companies from Europe became major participants, and Azerbaijan produced more than half of the world's oil in 1900. As one consequence, not only European capital but also highly skilled European oil company personnel were imported into Azerbaijan, bringing with them significant elements of European culture. Yet, as a second consequence, major class divisions developed in Azerbaijan as the Russian government and international companies gained significant profits while most Azerbaijanis toiled as poor unskilled laborers in the oil industry or in agriculture. Nonetheless, the oil boom did promote the emergence of a relatively small Azerbaijani elite, referred to as the "Azerbaijani Oil Barons," whose newly gained wealth allowed them to travel to and from Europe and to become exposed to new world-views, new ideologies of secularism and modernism, and new definitions and social constructions of women's roles (Alakbarov, 2002; Aliyev, 1994; Cornell, 2011: 9–12; Gokay, 1999; Mir-Babayev, 2002; Swietochowski, 1985, 1995: 17–24; Tolf, 1976).

Ultimately, the Azerbaijani Enlightenment Movement and the emergence of this small, but quite wealthy, Azerbaijani oil-baron elite provided both the ideological and the economic base that set the stage for Azerbaijani philanthropy and social activism during the early 1900s and for the development of significant social entrepreneurial activities. In short, the development of the oil industry in Azerbaijan brought not only European technology but also European cultural influences that intertwined with the Azerbaijani Enlightenment Movement, resulting in increased social, cultural, and political consciousness and in new social constructions and ways of conceptualizing Azerbaijani women's roles and place in Azerbaijani society in the early 1900s.

One of the most prominent Azerbaijani social entrepreneurs to address women's issues was Haji Zeynalabadin Taghiyev, whose father was a shoemaker and who grew up in poverty. Starting work in his youth as a stonemason, Taghiyev later bought a small parcel of land, eventually struck oil, and ultimately became an extremely wealthy Azerbaijani oil baron. Although he had no formal schooling himself, he became an advocate for women's rights as he viewed education to be essential for women. Indeed, at the end of the 1800s, only a small number of Azerbaijani girls had access to formal secular education. In founding the first secular European-style boarding school for Azerbaijani Muslim girls in 1901, Taghiyev clearly established his position in Azerbaijani history. Taghiyev not only provided monetary funds for establishing and operating the school but also negotiated the fine lines between Russian politics and Islamic ideology. Hence, to gain Russian government approval, he named the school after the Russian Empress Alexandra (wife of the Russian Czar), and he countered objections from highly conservative Muslim opponents by obtaining statements of support for education for women from major Muslim theologians (Akhundov, 1994, 2007; Amrahov and Gafarova, 2012; Azerbaijan International, 1998; Suleymanov, 2002).

In addition, several educated and influential Azerbaijani women—such as Sakina Akhundzadeh, Khadija Alibeyova, Shafiga Efendizadeh, Hanifa Melikova, Sona Taghiyeva, and Hamida Javanshir—also served as social entrepreneurs during this period. For example, Taghiyev's wife, Sona Taghiyeva, managed the girls' school while also participating with other women of the elite class in forming and implementing charitable programs and organizations. In turn, Hamida Javanshir, wife of journalist and editor, Jalil Mammadguluzade, was a philanthropist and women's rights advocate who engaged in numerous charitable activities. Of major significance, Javanshir advocated education for Azerbaijani girls, and, in 1908, founded (in her home village of Kahrizli) the first coeducational school in Azerbaijan where boys and girls studied in the same classroom. Javanshir also advocated women's participation in cultural and civic affairs, and she founded, together with other women of Baku's elite, the Muslim Women's Caucasian Benevolent Society in 1910. The establishment of schooling where boys and girls attended school in the same classroom was quite a dramatic change given the cultural norms at that time. Likewise, the participation of these prominent Azerbaijani women in educational and philanthropic social entrepreneurial activities in the public realm challenged longstanding patriarchal and conservative religious norms of Azerbaijani society regarding the roles of women (Aliyeva, 2015; Altstadt, 1992: 50–73, 1996: 199–209; Hacilar, 2012).

Furthermore, the establishment of Azerbaijani language newspapers and periodicals also was of extreme importance during this era as they disseminated ideas and perspectives of the intelligentsia regarding various issues, including women's issues and the need for education for women. One publication of special significance was the social, cultural, and political satirical magazine, *Molla Nasreddin* [*Molla Nəsrəddin*]. Published from 1906 to 1931, *Molla Nasreddin* waged social and moral campaigns and was highly influential in raising consciousness about issues and problems including corruption and the political elite, extremist Islamic clergy and religious fanaticism, colonialism, illiteracy, and the oppression of women. Indeed, its editor, Jalil Mammadguluzade, and his contributing authors consisted of a wide array of

Azerbaijani literary figures including Omar Faig Nemanzadeh, Mirzəli Möcüz Şəbüstəri, Abdurrahim bey Hagverdiyev, Ali Nazmi, Aligulu Gamkusar, Mammed Said Ordubadi, and Mirza Alakbar Sabir, as well as illustrators Oskar Schmerling, Josif Rotter, and Azim Azimzade all of whom played major social entrepreneurial roles as they sought social change including respect for women's rights in an otherwise male-dominated society. Mammadguluzade was able to acquire permission from the government to publish in the Azerbaijani language, rather than in Russian, which was a bold venture given that Azerbaijanis were governed by Czarist Russia, and indeed the number of publications per year of this weekly, eight- to twelve-page magazine varied due to censorship and disruptions by government officials. In addition, authors often wrote using pseudonyms to avoid harassment by those with opposing viewpoints and/or arrest by government authorities. To appeal to a broad audience, roughly half of each issue was devoted to political drawings and illustrations so as to make the satirical content accessible to literate, semi-literate, and illiterate Azerbaijanis (*Azerbaijan International*, 1996; Garibova, 1996; Minkel, 2011; Paksoy, 2008; Slavs and Tatars, 2011).

In my own research on *Molla Nasreddin*, I utilized my fluency in the Azerbaijani language to examine and categorize political drawings and illustrations published between the first issue in 1906 and the establishment of the Azerbaijan Democratic Republic in 1918 (Najafizadeh, 2015a). Through this process, I conceptualized eight distinct themes reflecting the effects of patriarchal elements on Azerbaijani women. For example, one theme, which I refer to as forced marriage and domestic violence, is reflected in a two-panel drawing in which the first panel depicts the groom as being extremely respectful toward the bride at the time of the wedding, whereas the second panel—one month after the wedding—shows the new husband chasing his new wife attempting to beat her with a large stick (*Molla Nasreddin*, 1908, February 3:8). In turn, a second theme, which I refer to as Azerbaijani patriarchy and male child preference, is conveyed in another two-panel drawing wherein the first panel depicts family members, and especially the father, as being joyous at the birth of a son, but the second panel shows family members, and especially the father, sulking and distraught at the birth of a daughter (*Molla Nasreddin*, 1909, August 2:12). Still another theme, releasing Azerbaijani women from the constraints of patriarchy and conservative religious ideology, is depicted in an illustration in which an Azerbaijani Muslim woman wearing traditional clothing and bound in chains (symbolizing the constraints of patriarchy and conservative religion) is being released from the chains by several Azerbaijani Muslim women attired in "modern" clothing (*Molla Nasreddin*, 1913, December 21:1). Still other themes, that I developed in my analysis of drawings include the socialization of young Azerbaijani males into Azerbaijani patriarchal roles (see, e.g., *Molla Nasreddin*, 1909, November 1:11), patriarchy and the double-standard in marital relations (see, e.g., *Molla Nasreddin*, 1913, August 14 1:4), the exclusion of women from the public realm (see, e.g., *Molla Nasreddin*, 1909, August 9:12), the gender cultural divide contrasting "modern" Azerbaijani Muslim women and traditional Azerbaijani Muslim women (see, e.g., *Molla Nasreddin*, 1911, October 8:5), and the burdens of Azerbaijani patriarchal society on Azerbaijani women (see, e.g., *Molla Nasreddin*, 1906, July 14:4).

In the end, *Molla Nasreddin* played a powerful social entrepreneurial role in giving voice to Azerbaijani women and greater public visibility to the plight of women in early twentieth-century Azerbaijan. *Molla Nasreddin*, along with the social and political activities of various male and female social entrepreneurs, including members of the Azerbaijani intelligentsia, social activists, and political activists, paved the way for the eventual establishment of an independent Azerbaijan in 1918.

Social entrepreneurship, the social construction of *Azerbaijanism*, and the founding of the Azerbaijan Democratic Republic

During the early 1900s, intellectual and political sentiments regarding Azerbaijani nationalism greatly increased. Indeed, the activities of Azerbaijani social entrepreneurs such as Ali bey Huseynzade, Ahmed Agaoglu, Ali Mardan-bek Topchubashov, and especially Mammad Amin Rasulzade were crucial in converting cultural notions of Azerbaijani identity and nationalism into a political movement. During this era, while some Azerbaijanis advocated pan-Islamism and the unification of all Muslims regardless of their ethnic or national origins, Rasulzade argued that pan-Islamism impeded Azerbaijani national identity. In turn, others supported the ideology of pan-Turkism which sought to unify the Turkic peoples (including Azerbaijanis) of the world based on ethnicity, culture, and language. Ultimately, Azerbaijani intellectuals advocated a new national political ideology—Azerbaijanism—which emphasized the social, cultural, and political uniqueness of the Azerbaijani people but which also included the importance of Turkic heritage, Islam, and modernization. Indeed, the concept of Azerbaijanism—first proposed in 1905 by social entrepreneur, Ali bey Huseynzade, an intellectual and publisher of newspapers, including the newspaper, *Hayat*—ultimately became a key doctrine of the Azerbaijan Democratic Republic. Furthermore, in 1905, Azerbaijani intellectuals, as well as members of the Azerbaijani economic elite, also were instrumental in beginning to press the Russian government with initiatives that would include local self-governance, freedom and full political rights for Muslim Azerbaijanis, and the distribution of land to Azerbaijani peasants, as reflected in the meeting held at Haji Zeynalabadin Taghiyev's mansion in Baku on March 15, 1905, and that culminated in the first official document ever submitted from an Azerbaijani delegation to the Czar (Azerbaijan University of Languages, 2014; Cornell, 2011: 12–16; Najafov, 2008; Seyid-zade, 2011).

Following the October 1917 Revolution and the collapse of the Russian Empire, Azerbaijan together with Armenia and Georgia were united in April 1918 as part of the independent Transcaucasian Democratic Federative Republic. However, it soon became apparent that this Federative Republic would not be viable, and Azerbaijan, Armenia, and Georgia each declared their own independence, Azerbaijan doing so in May 1918. With the founding of the Azerbaijan Democratic Republic came the establishment of the first secular parliamentary republic in the Muslim world under the ideological leadership of social entrepreneur, Mammad Amin Rasulzade. Although Rasulzade never held political office, he was chairman of the Musavat National Party and in May 1918 became head of the 26-member National Council of Azerbaijan, which signed the "Act of Independence of Azerbaijan" thereby establishing the Azerbaijan Democratic Republic on May 28, 1918. The formulation of key principals in the establishment of the Azerbaijan Democratic Republic entailed the social construction of new and dynamic ways of defining and viewing the relationship between the state and the citizenry. Central to Rasulzade's social thought and to the Azerbaijan Democratic Republic was the notion of political rights and citizenship, regardless of religion, ethnicity, social class, or gender. And under Rasulzade's leadership, Azerbaijanism, as a new political ideology, was implemented thereby giving prominence to the Azerbaijani language and Turkic and Islamic heritage, as well as the values of modernization. As such, the Azerbaijan Democratic Republic incorporated European democratic values into the Azerbaijani cultural context, including the establishment of Azerbaijani as the national language. Furthermore, Azerbaijanism was crucial to the social construction of the "new" Azerbaijani woman and of new ways of bringing Azerbaijani women from the "shadows" of the home and private realm into new roles in the public realm. As such, the Azerbaijan Democratic Republic was at the forefront in establishing

Azerbaijani women's right to vote in political elections even before such rights were granted to women in numerous other countries worldwide.

The Azerbaijan Democratic Republic also is notable in Azerbaijani history as it marked the founding of the Ministry of Public Enlightenment (now referred to as Ministry of Education), the founding of the Azerbaijani military, and the establishment of the first national university (with funding from Haji Zeynalabadin Taghiyev) now known as Baku State University. Indeed, the first meeting of the Parliament was convened on December 7, 1918, in the building housing the first secular European-style boarding school for Azerbaijani Muslim girls built by Haji Zeynalabadin Taghiyev, and the concepts of Turkic heritage, Islam, and modernization were incorporated into the colors of the flag of the Azerbaijan Democratic Republic with blue representing Azerbaijan's Turkic heritage, white representing its Islamic heritage, and red representing the movement toward modernization (Akhundov, 1998; Alstadt, 1992: 89–107; Bolukbasi, 2011: 25–38; Cornell, 2011: 17–30; Karimova, 2015; Rasulzade, 1999; Seyid-zade, 2011; Swietochowski, 1985, 1995: 68–103).

The state as social entrepreneur: Sovietization and the social construction of the Soviet Azerbaijani woman

The Red Army invaded Azerbaijan on April 28, 1920, the Azerbaijan Democratic Republic, only 23 months after declaring independence, was forced to concede power to the Bolsheviks, and many Azerbaijani government officials had to flee into exile. Mammad Amin Rasulzade was imprisoned in Baku, but then as a long-time friend of Joseph Stalin he was taken to Moscow where Stalin offered him a position in the government. However, despite their friendship, Rasulzade and Stalin's ideological differences were too great, and Rasulzade found it necessary to seek sanctuary in Finland and ultimately in Turkey. By March 1922, Azerbaijan was incorporated into the Transcaucasian Socialist Federative Soviet Republic, together with Armenia and Georgia, until 1936 when it again gained independence, as the Azerbaijan Soviet Socialist Republic (see Cornell, 2011: 28–45; Rasulzade, 1999).

The Bolshevik invasion and the Sovietization of Azerbaijan brought dramatic changes as the Soviet state advocated socialist ideology and as the influence of previous Azerbaijani social entrepreneurs, whether intellectual or political, was greatly diminished or totally eliminated. The following 70 years of Sovietization suppressed not only democratic ideology in Azerbaijan but also Islamic religious ideology (Najafizadeh, 2012, 2014). Soviet social and political ideology dominated as the state, as social entrepreneur, implemented both ideological change and also structural change through the collectivization of agriculture and the nationalization of industry, education, medical care, and other social services. Of critical importance was the state's role—as social entrepreneur—in the social construction (and re-construction) of definitions of women's roles (see Najafizadeh, 2003a, 2014).

Despite initial assurances to protect Azerbaijani religious beliefs, culture, language, and national identity, the increasing entrenchment of Soviet ideology and social structures over time brought drastic changes, including changes brought by the Soviet "cultural revolution" which sought to lessen the importance of Islam and to promote new social constructions of Azerbaijani women's roles. As one example, Mustafa Kuliev, Commissar of Education of Soviet Azerbaijan, argued in his report, *The Cultural Revolution and Islam*, in 1928 that Islam was the "enemy of women" and that Muslim women must rid themselves of the veil and become educated and liberated. Another example pertains to Azerbaijani intellectuals who ultimately were silenced even though they shared certain goals with the Soviets, such as that of increasing women's access to education. Similarly, the satirical magazine *Molla Nasreddin*, was allowed to continue publishing in the 1920s on account of its critical stance on issues, such as fanatic clergy and oppression of women, which were consistent with Soviet ideology. Yet, increasing Soviet censorship ultimately led *Molla Nasreddin* to publish its final edition in early 1931. Clearly, Soviet literacy campaigns and de-veiling campaigns, in which Azerbaijani women were encouraged to participate in education and to discard the traditional Islamic veil, were significant forces in the social construction of the new Soviet Azerbaijani woman who through her "liberation" would embrace Soviet ideology and become integrated into the Soviet social and political system and Soviet workforce (Alstadt, 1992: 108–129; Cornell, 2011: 31–37; Hadjibeyli, 1957, 1958; Kuliev, 1958; Lester, 1997; Dilbazi, 1999; Najafizadeh, 2003a, 2003b, 2012, 2014; Talibzade, 2000; Suny, 1996).

The 1930s brought additional dramatic changes in two different forms. First was Stalin's "great purge" during which those perceived as opponents or critics of the Soviet system were imprisoned, exiled, or executed. During 1936–1938, many Azerbaijani intellectuals—as social entrepreneurs—were essentially eliminated. These included both men and women and ranged from teachers and doctors in rural areas to literary figures and journalists in Baku. Although numbers vary, well over 120,000 Azerbaijanis—including intellectuals, Communist Party members, and government and military officials—were executed or deported to Siberia or to Central Asia (Najafizadeh, 2003a: 38). Even members of Mammad Amin Rasulzade's family—including his stepmother, wife, and daughter and son—were exiled to a prison camp in Kazakhstan, while his oldest son was executed (Rasulzade, 1999). Continuing until Stalin's death in 1953, women constituted between 15 to 25 percent of those Azerbaijanis whom the Soviet government viewed as "enemies of the people" and punished accordingly. These included both Azerbaijani women who personally opposed the government as well as women who were wives, sisters, or daughters of men who opposed the government. In other instances, the wives—of men accused by the government—who had three or more children were sometimes given the option of divorcing their husbands or suffering the consequences of exile to a prison camp (Najafizadeh, 2014; also see Alstadt, 1992: 131–150; Bala, 1957; Cornell, 2011: 37–39; Rahimov, 1999; Sadikhli, 1999, 2006.)

The second major change directly affecting women was the adoption of the new Constitution of Azerbaijan in 1937 that formally gave "women equal rights with men in every sphere of economic, public, cultural, social, and political activity" (Novosti Press, 1967: 20). Yet, such formal declarations of gender equality did not always translate into reality. Family laws enacted in the 1930s and 1940s provide an example. Although the purported intent of these laws was to promote family stability, such laws banned abortion and made it more difficult and costly to obtain a divorce thereby limiting women's control over their own well-being. Through such laws, the state socially re-constructed women's roles so as to emphasize women's family caregiving roles, while simultaneously urging women to participate in the workforce, and in the 1940s to temporarily take on many "male jobs" in industry and agriculture as part of the war-effort during World War II. Nonetheless, despite some exceptions, Azerbaijani women continued to be concentrated mainly in lower-paying and caregiving jobs, such as teaching, medical, and social service jobs, typically defined as "women's work" (Najafizadeh, 2003a: 38–39; also see Buckley, 1989: 108–138; Clements, 1991). In the end, Sovietization during the 1920s, 1930s, and 1940s established the framework for subsequent decades. Most certainly, Azerbaijani women did gain significant access to formal education and to the public realm of economy and polity. Yet, despite the official emphasis on gender egalitarianism, the Soviet social re-construction of Azerbaijani women's roles often simply translated into women retaining many of the traditional caregiving and domestic responsibilities within the family and extended family while concurrently assuming additional work roles in the Soviet workforce. Similarly, politically, the Soviet system socially constructed the "illusion of equality" in that women occupied various positions in the Communist Party while the "key positions" remained reserved exclusively for men (Heyat, 2002; Ibrahimbekova, 2000a, 2000b; Najafizadeh, 2003a, 2003b; Sabi, 1999; Tohidi, 1998.)

In sum, Azerbaijani women's access to formal education and to occupations in the public realm did increase quite significantly during the Soviet era. Nonetheless, gender egalitarianism—as defined by the Soviet state social entrepreneur—never fully materialized. To the contrary, Azerbaijani women's roles typically merely increased so that women continued to occupy traditional roles in the private realm of the family while adding new roles in the political realm and the workplace with little real increase in their personal control of their own well-being.

Independence and the establishment of the Republic of Azerbaijan: social entrepreneurship and women's issues

On October 18, 1991, the Soviet Socialist Republic of Azerbaijan declared its independence from the Soviet Union and therein began a sometimes tumultuous journey of political and economic transition from the Soviet era to the building of the modern independent Republic of Azerbaijan. During this process, Abulfaz Elchibey replaced the first president, Ayaz N. Mutalibov, in June 1992, and Elchibey in turn was removed from the presidency in 1993. This ultimately led to Heydar Aliyev, a highly respected government official in Soviet Azerbaijan, being elected as president in August 1993, a position that he held until shortly before his death in 2003. As a political leader and as a social entrepreneur, President Heydar Aliyev—often referred to as the father of modern Azerbaijan—provided leadership that was crucial to the young Republic's ability to weather the sociopolitical and economic strains accompanying Azerbaijan's withdrawal from the Soviet Union.

Political leaders as social entrepreneurs

The initial years of transition from the Soviet system to one of independence, privatization, and free market economy were quite difficult and impacted both Azerbaijani men and women. With the collapse of much of the former Soviet social and economic infrastructure within Azerbaijan, men and women confronted unemployment rates as high as 38 percent while over half the population lived on the poverty level. Furthermore, with the "Soviet safety-net" of social services and assured employment gone, the situation for women was exacerbated because the education and medical systems, where a large percentage of Soviet-era Azerbaijani women had been employed, also faced severe deterioration. Indeed, the economic crisis especially impacted women as this often led to the "double burden" wherein women had to seek income, most often through the informal economy, to help provide for their families while simultaneously having to fulfill the traditional responsibilities of caregiver within their families. Furthermore, the Nagorno-Karabakh War with Armenia (1988–1994), which resulted in the loss of the lives of thousands of Azerbaijanis and nearly one million refugees and internally displaced persons, added to the economic crisis that the country was confronting. Refugee/IDP (Internally Displaced Person) women were severely affected by the war and shouldered both the burden of the economic crisis as well as the burden of forced displacement in caring for their families (Cornell, 2011; Heyat, 2002; Ibrahimbekova, 2000a, 2000b; Kamrava, 2001, Mikailova, 1999; Najafizadeh, 2006, 2013; Sabi, 1999; Samedova, 2000; SCFWCA, 2009, 2014; SPPRED, 2003, 2005; Tohidi, 1998; and UNDP, 1999.)

Following the demise of the Soviet Union, Azerbaijani women gained new forms of freedom, including religious freedom, but they also lost particular legal protections as well as employment opportunities and stability. As a social entrepreneur, President Heydar Aliyev was particularly instrumental in enacting several significant political projects that addressed women's issues. For example, in 1994, in anticipation of the Fourth World Conference on Women to be held in Beijing in 1995, he issued a decree establishing the National Preparatory Committee which included women both from government agencies and from NGOs. Clearly, the participation of Azerbaijani women in the Beijing Conference and their cooperative efforts following the Conference were of immense importance in giving visibility to salient issues and problems confronting Azerbaijani women. Furthermore, following the Beijing Conference, two presidential decrees were particularly significant. First was President Heydar Aliyev's 1998 decree that established the Republic of Azerbaijan State Committee on Women's Affairs. Second was the president's signing of the United Nations Millennium Development Goals in 2000, which included the goal of promoting gender equality and women's empowerment. These were significant social entrepreneurial actions that provided social and political legitimacy and formal governmental recognition of women's issues.

The year 1994 also was of immense importance to Azerbaijan economically as it marked the signing of the "Contract of the Century" by President Heydar Aliyev and a consortium of international oil companies. This agreement, together with subsequent economic developments, led the way to Azerbaijan becoming a major international supplier of oil and gas and established the economic foundation that has brought Azerbaijan out of the economic crisis of the early 1990s, the initial years of independence, to financial prosperity, particularly during the past decade. Following Heydar Aliyev's death in 2003, his son, Ilham Aliyev, was elected president of Azerbaijan, and he has continued, as a social entrepreneur, to engage in various government projects to further enhance public well-being and to address women's issues. Indeed, Azerbaijan has witnessed major improvements in the standard of living and overall public well-being. For women, this is reflected in Azerbaijan's improved ranking of 62nd out of 149 nations on the UNDP Gender Inequality Index, with 94 percent of women having completed at least the secondary level of schooling and 63 percent of women being employed in the workforce (Gureyeva, 2011, 2012; Najafizadeh, 2015b; Sarfarov, 2012; SCFWCA, 2009, 2014; UNDP, 1999, 2012a, 2012b, 2014: 173).

Government agencies as social entrepreneurs

The Republic of Azerbaijan State Committee for Family, Women and Children Affairs (Azərbaycan Respublikası Ailə, Qadın və Uşaq Problemləri üzrə Dövlət Komitəsi) is a high-level government agency that serves as a salient social entrepreneur in identifying and addressing gender issues. This agency, as mentioned earlier, was originally established in 1998 as the State Committee on Women's Affairs and subsequently reorganized and renamed by President Ilham Aliyev's decree in 2006 as the State Committee for Family, Women and Children Affairs within the Azerbaijan Cabinet of Ministers. As a major government unit, the State Committee—headed by Chairwoman Hijran Huseynova—structurally includes two deputy chairs and a head of the Apparatus of the State Committee, as well as ten sub-units. Charged with implementing relevant government policies, the State Committee focuses not only on women's issues and gender equality but also on the needs of families and children in Azerbaijan (Najafizadeh, 2015b).

More specifically, State Committee programs seek to improve women's well-being and to ensure protection of women's rights—based on the principles of gender equality—within various sectors of the economy, and it oversees policies on numerous other issues including domestic violence, early marriages, and human trafficking. The Committee also works closely with women's NGOs in conducting workshops and training sessions in both urban and rural communities regarding women's reproductive health and gender-based violence within the family. Furthermore, the Committee focuses on a range of issues pertaining to the child's well-being: for example, a safe home environment and adequate medical care as well as the prevention of child-labor and provision of assistance to at-risk children and children with special needs. The Committee also provides a wide variety of informational publications such as *Gender Bərabərliyi* [Gender Equality], *İnsan Alverinin Qurbanı Olma!* [Don't Become a Victim of Human Trafficking!], *Reproduktiv Sağlamlıq* [Reproductive Health], and *Uşaqları Qoruyaq!* [Let Us Protect Children!], as well as official reports including *Gender Balance and the Role of Women in Azerbaijan* (Manafova, 2013) and the 20th Anniversary of the Beijing Declaration and the Platform for Action National Report (SCFWCA, 2014). Thus, central to the State Committee for Family, Women and Children Affairs is the task of ensuring the rights of women and children, by preventing gender discrimination both within the family and in the broader society (also see Najafizadeh, 2015b; Sarfarov, 2012; SCFWCA, 2009). Ultimately, the State Committee's social entrepreneurial role is instrumental in raising consciousness about women's issues and children's issues within Azerbaijani society and in striving to resolve those issues.

Women's non-governmental organizations as social entrepreneurs

In addition, various women's non-governmental organizations (NGOs) in Azerbaijan also function as social entrepreneurs in addressing women's issues. One such significant NGO is the Azerbaijan Women and Development Center (AWDC) [Azərbaycan Qadın va İnkişaf Mərkəzi (AQİM)], which was established in 1994 by Elmira Suleymanova. AWDC was deeply involved in the preparations for the Beijing World Conference on Women in 1995 and continued to engage in Azerbaijani women's development activities following the Conference. Over the years, AWDC has worked with Azerbaijani government entities—including the Ministry of Education and Ministry of Health—and also with international units such as UNICEF, the UN Population Fund, and UNDP to empower Azerbaijani women and to improve women's place in Azerbaijani society. Based in the capital city of Baku, AWDC was established on the central principle of enhancing the well-being of Azerbaijani women and has assisted women from various segments of the population, including disabled women, women refugees/IDPs, rural women, low-income women, and elderly women, as well as attending to the needs of children and youth. As such, AWDC has reached out to women by conducting gender-related workshops for women from different backgrounds on matters including women's reproductive health and mother–child health issues, domestic violence and women's rights, children's rights, the rights of elderly women. The Center also has engaged in gender-education activities to sensitize youth to issues pertaining to gender roles and gender equality, as well as engaging in various activities to assist with the psychological and physical needs of elderly women and of women impacted by the trauma of the Nagorno-Karabakh War. Furthermore, AWDC has been instrumental in disseminating information on women's issues, including publications such as *Ailə Planlanmasında İctimai Xidmətin Təşkili Üzrə Vəsait* [Manual for Family Planning] (Suleymanova, 2008) and *Məhəbbətin İnsanlarda əks-Sədası* [Reflections of Kindness in People] (Xanmammadova, 2011). (Also see AQİM, 2011; Najafizadeh, 2003c, 2006, 2015b.)

AWDC's founder, Elmira Suleymanova, is an internationally recognized advocate for women and for human rights. She served as vice-president of the Woman's Organization of Azerbaijan between 1990 and 1994 and founded the Azerbaijan Women and Development Center (AWDC) in 1994. She was honored with the 100 Heroines Award in 1998 for her contributions in fostering the rights of women. In 2002, she was elected by the Republic of Azerbaijan Parliament to the position of Republic of Azerbaijan Commissioner for Human Rights (Ombudsman), and she continues to serve in that capacity where she oversees the resolution of citizenry problems including issues pertaining specifically to women. As but one example is Suleymanova's recent proposal to the Azerbaijan Parliament for the creation, by the government, of an "Alimony Fund" to provide financial assistance to divorced women and their children who do not have any means of support and whose husbands are unwilling to provide financial support (News.Az, 2015). Elmira Suleymanova, as founder of the Azerbaijan Women and Development Center and as Ombudsman, exemplifies a social entrepreneur who has had an important impact in bringing Azerbaijani women's issues to the forefront and in addressing such issues.

Scholars, academic institutions, and gender research centers as social entrepreneurs

Finally, Azerbaijani scholars and academic institutions and research centers also have served as important social entrepreneurs in conducting and disseminating gender-related research. For example, the Republic of Azerbaijan National Academy of Sciences [Azərbaycan Milli Elmlər Akademiyası] is one such institution that includes, among its numerous research units, a Gender Studies Center that focuses on research and dissemination of knowledge pertaining to gender issues in Azerbaijan. Of particular note are scholars such as Ali Abasov and Rena Mirzazade in the Azerbaijan National Academy of Sciences, who have published on a diversity of gender-related topics (see, e.g., Abasov and Mirzazade, 2004a, 2004b, 2009). Other important scholars include Mominat Omarova, a faculty member at Baku State University [Bakı Dövlət Universiteti] who was the National Project Coordinator for the UNDP Azerbaijan Human Development Report 2007, Gender Attitudes in Azerbaijan: Trends and Challenges (see UNDP, 2007), and Kifayat Aghayeva a scholar of gender studies (see, e.g., Aghayeva, 2007), who also has served as director of the Gender Research Center at Western University [Qərb Universiteti] in Baku, a center which has fulfilled significant social entrepreneurial functions as it promotes gender-related research through collaboration of researchers from other institutions in Azerbaijan and also through the hosting of gender-related professional conferences.

Concluding comments

Social entrepreneurs have played critical roles in shaping social change in Azerbaijan since the 1800s. In so doing, they have been instrumental in the social construction of women's issues as social problems in need of societal attention and in the social construction of new and dynamic roles for women in Azerbaijani society.

The Azerbaijan Enlightenment Movement in the 1800s, as well as the rise of social philanthropy at the beginning of the twentieth century, were crucial in incorporating new conceptions of secularism and modernism into Azerbaijani society and in the social construction of new roles for women that increasingly enabled women to move beyond the private realm of the home and the family and to participate more fully in education and in various public activities. In turn, Azerbaijani social entrepreneurs, through intellectual and political activism, established the foundation of an independent Azerbaijan upon the collapse of the Russian Empire. Such social entrepreneurs engaged in the social construction of an Azerbaijani national identity—Azerbaijanism—and they established a framework for new social constructions of the relationship between the state and the citizenry that assured Azerbaijanis social and political rights that previously had been limited. As such, the formation of the Azerbaijan Democratic Republic in 1918 included the social construction of the role of Azerbaijani women as full-fledged citizens with the formally declared rights to vote in political elections and to participate fully in public life.

In turn, the state, as social entrepreneur during 70 years of Sovietization, imposed a new ideology that included the social construction of dramatically different roles for Azerbaijani women. This process entailed women shedding the veil of Islam and expanding women's roles beyond the private realm of the home so as to embrace roles in the public realm of the Soviet social and political structure and the Soviet workforce.

Finally, the declaration of independence in 1991 and the founding of the contemporary Republic of Azerbaijan has included an array of other social entrepreneurs who have been of immense significance in establishing new socially constructed conceptions of the roles and rights of women. Azerbaijani political leaders, government agencies, women's NGOs, and scholars and research centers—as social entrepreneurs—have been instrumental not only in defining problematic issues pertaining to Azerbaijani women but in seeking solutions that would benefit women and enhance their position and their well-being both in the present and in the future.

References

Abasov, A. and Mirzazade, R. (2004a). *Təhsil və Gender* [Education and Gender]. Baku, Azerbaijan: Adiloğlu Nəşriyyati.

Abasov, A. and Mirzazade, R. (2004b). *Genderə Giriş* [Introduction to Gender]. Baku, Azerbaijan: Adiloğlu.

Abasov, A. and Mirzazade, R. (2009). *Gender, Demokratiya, Sülh Mədəniyyəti* [Gender, Democracy, Culture of Peace]. Baku, Azerbaijan: Təknur

Abu-Saifan, Samer. 2012. Social Entrepreneurship: Definition and Boundaries. *Technology Innovation Management Review*, 2(2), 22–27.

Aghayeva, K. (2007). *Etika və Gender: Sosial-Əxlaqi Davranışın Təhlili* [Ethics and Gender: Analysis of Social and Moral Behavior]. Baku, Azerbaijan.

Akhundov, F. (1994). Legacy of the Oil Barons. *Azerbaijan International*, 2(2), 43–45.

Akhundov, F. (1998). Democratic Republic of Azerbaijan Leaders (1918–1920). *Azerbaijan International*, 6(1), 26–30.

Akhundov, F. (2007). *Educating Women to Educate a Nation*. Baku, Azerbaijan: UNDP and UNFPA.

Alakbarov, F. (2002). Baku: City that Oil Built. *Azerbaijan International*, 10(2), 28–33.

Aliyev, N. (1994). The History of Oil in Azerbaijan. *Azerbaijan International*, 2(2), 22–23.

Aliyeva, J. (2015). Review of Anthology of Poetry by Women in Azerbaijan. *Journal of Balkan Libraries Union*, 3(1), 7–8.

Alstadt, A. L. (1992). *The Azerbaijani Turks: Power and Identity under Russian Rule*. Stanford, CA: Hoover Institution Press, Stanford University.

Alstadt, A. L. (1996). The Azerbaijani Bourgeoisie and the Cultural Enlightenment Movement in Baku: First Steps toward Nationalism (pp. 199–209). In *Transcaucasia, Nationalism, and Social Change*, edited by Ronald Grigor Suny, Ann Arbor, MI: University of Michigan Press.

Amrahov, M. I. and Gafarova, G. (2012). Haji Zeynalabdin Taghiyevs School for Girls – An Educated Girl Means an Educated Family, Visions of Azerbaijan, March–June: 64–68. Retrieved June 3, 2015 (http://www.visions.az/environmental,388).

Azerbaijan International (1996). Molla Nasreddin: Comic Sage of the Ages. *Azerbaijan International*, 4(3), 18–21.

Azerbaijan International. (1998). Education for Girls–Essential for Humankind. *Azerbaijan International* (6), 4–17.

Azerbaijan University of Languages. (2014). Ali bey Huseynzadas Role of the Formation of National Ideology, AUL, April 25. Retrieved June 20, 2015 (http://adu.edu.az/index.php?option= com_content&view=article&id=532:an-event-on-the-theme-ali-bey-huseynzada-s-role-in-the-formation-of-national-ideology-was-held-at-aul&catid=80&Itemid=586&lang=en).

AQİM. (2011). *Azərbaycan Qadın və İnkişaf Mərkəzi* [Azerbaijan Women and Development Center]. Bakı, Azərbaycan: YEK.

Bala, M. (1957). Soviet Nationality Policy in Azerbeidzhan [Azerbaijan]. *Caucasian Review*, 4, 23–46.

Bolukbasi, S. (2011). *Azerbaijan: A Political History*. New York: I.B. Tauris & Co.

Buckley, M. (1989). *Women and Ideology in the Soviet Union*. Ann Arbor, MI: The University of Michigan Press.

Burr, V. (2015). *Social Constructionism*. New York: Routledge.

Clements, B. E. (1991). Later Developments: Trends in Soviet Women's History, 1939 to the Present (pp. 267–278). In *Russia's Women: Accommodation, Resistance, Transformation*, edited by Barbara Evans Clements, Barbara Alpern Engel, and Christine D. Worobec. Berkeley: University of California Press.

Cornell, S. E. (2011). *Azerbaijan since Independence*. Armonk, NY: M.E. Sharpe.

Dacin, M. T., Dacin, P. A. and Tracey, P. (2011). Social Entrepreneurship: A Critique and Future Directions. *Organization Science*, 22(5), 1203–1213.

Dilbazi, M. (1999). A Century of Tears. *Azerbaijan International*, 7(3), 18–19.

Garibova, J. (1996). Molla Nasreddin – The Magazine: Laughter that Pricked the Conscience of a Nation. *Azerbaijan International*, 4(3), 22–23.

Gokay, B. (1999). History of Oil Development in the Caspian Basin. In *Oil and Geopolitics in the Caspian Sea Region*, edited by Michael Croissant and Bulent Aras, pp. 3–19. Westport, CT: Praeger.

Groot, A. and Dankbaar, B. (2014). Does Social Innovation Require Social Entrepreneurship? *Technology Innovation Management Review*, 4(12), 17–26.

Gurbansoy, F. (2001). Monument Reincarnated into Bronze: Khurshid Banu Natavan. *The Azeri Times–Baku Edition*, June 8–14, 7.

Gureyeva, Y. A. (2011). Policy Attitudes towards Women in Azerbaijan. Is Equality Part of the Agenda? Gunda Werner Institute for Feminism and Democracy. February 7. Retrieved December 20, 2014 (http://www.gwi-boell.de/en/2011/02/07/policy-attitudes-towards-women-azerbaijan-equality-part-agenda).

Gureyeva, Y. A. (2012). The Dynamics of the Adoption of the Law on Domestic Violence in Azerbaijan: Gender Policy-Making in a Patriarchal Context. Retrieved March 1, 2015 (http://www.academia.edu/5533568/The_Dynamics_of_Adoption_of_the_Law_on_Domestic_Violence_in_Azerbaijan).

Hacilar, A. M. (2012). General View on Education of Muslim Women in the Beginning of XX Century in Tiflis. *International Journal of Turkish Literature Culture Education*, 1(2), 83–89.

Hadjibeyli, D. (1957). The Campaign against the Clergy in Azerbaidzhan [Azerbaijan]. *Caucasian Review*, 4, 78–85.

Hadjibeyli, D. (1958). Anti-Islamic Propaganda in Azerbaidzhan [Azerbaijan]. *Caucasian Review*, 7, 20–65.

Harris, S. R. (2010). *What is Constructionism?* Boulder, CO: Lynne Rienner Publishers.

Haslanger, S. (2012). *Resisting Reality: Social Construction and Social Critique*. New York: Oxford University Press.

Heyat, F. (2002). *Azeri Women in Transition: Women in Soviet and Post-Soviet Azerbaijan*. London: Routledge.

Hjelm, T. (2014). *Social Constructionisms: Approaches to the Study of the Human World*. New York: Palgrave Macmillan.

Holstein, J. A. and Gubrium, J. F. (2008). *Handbook of Constructionist Research*. New York: The Guilford Press.

Holstein, J. A. and Miller, G. (2003). *Challenges and Choices: Constructivist Perspectives on Social Problems*. Hawthorne, NY: Aldine de Gruyter.

Howaldt, J., Domanski, D. and Schwarz, M. (2015). Rethinking Social Entrepreneurship: The Concept of Social Entrepreneurship under the Perspective of Socio-scientific Innovation Research. *Journal of Creativity and Business Innovation*, 1, 88–98.

Ibrahimbekova, R. (2000a). Gender Problems during the Transition Period in Azerbaijan. *Genderşünaslıq: Azərbaycan Beynəlxalq Elmi-Kütləvi Jurnal* [Genderology: Azerbaijan International Scientific Journal], 1, 13–15.

Ibrahimbekova, R. (2000b). Gender Aspects of Economy. *Genderşünaslıq: Azərbaycan Beynəlxalq Elmi-Kütləvi Jurnal* [Genderology: Azerbaijan International Scientific Journal], 2, 6–8.

Kamrava, M. (2001). State-Building in Azerbaijan: The Search for Consolidation. *Middle East Journal*, 55(2), 216–236.

Karimova, A. (2015). Azerbaijan Democratic Republic – a glorious page in Azerbaijan's history. Azernews, May 28, Retrieved June 1, 2015 (http://www.azernews.az/azerbaijan/82637.html).

Kimmel, M. (2013). *The Gendered Society*. New York: Oxford University Press.

Kuliev, M. (1958). The Cultural Revolution and Islam (1928), quoted in Djeihun Hadjibeyli, Anti-Islamic Propaganda in Azerbaidzhan [Azerbaijan]. *Caucasian Review*, 7, 60–61.

Lester, T. (1997). Foreign Affairs: New Alphabet. *The Atlantic Monthly*, July, 20–27.

Lorber, J. and Farrell, S. A. (1991). *The Social Construction of Gender*. Newbury Park, CA: Sage Publications.

Mair, J., Battilana, J. and Cardenas, J. (2012). Organizing for Society: A Typology of Social Entrepreneuring Models. *Journal of Business Ethics*, 11(3), 353–373.

Mair, J., Robinson, J. and Hockerts, K. (2006). *Social Entrepreneurship*. New York: Palgrave Macmillan.

Manafova, S. (2013). *Gender Balance and the Role of Women in Azerbaijan*. Baku, Azerbaijan: State Committee for Family, Women and Children Affairs of the Republic of Azerbaijan.

Martin, R. L., and Osberg, S. (2007). Social Entrepreneurship: The Case for Definition. *Stanford Social Innovation Review*, 5(2), 28–39.

McKenny, A. F. (2014). Research in Social Entrepreneurship: An Annotated Bibliography. Social Entrepreneurship and Research Methods, *Research Methodology in Strategy and Management*, 265–293.

Mikailova, U. T. (1999). Feminism in Azerbaijan: Women in Azerbaijan. Retrieved April 6, 2015 (http://www.cddc.vt.edu/feminism/aze.html).

Minkel, E. (2011). The Magazine that Almost Changed the World. *The New Yorker*. May 26. Retrieved March 27, 2015 (http://www.newyorker.com/books/page-turner/the-magazine-that-almost-changed-the-world).

Mir-Babayev, M. Y. (2002). Azerbaijan's Oil History: A Chronology Leading Up to the Soviet Era. *Azerbaijan International*, 10(2), 34–40.

Molla Nasreddin (1906). Reprinted in 1996: Azərbaycan Respublikasıı Elmlər Akademiyası, Molla Nəsrəddin, I Cild, Bakı: Azərbaycan Dövlət Nəşriyyatı, No. 15:4.

Molla Nasreddin (1908). Reprinted in 2002: Azərbaycan Respublikasıı Elmlər Akademiyası, Molla Nəsrəddin, II Cild, Bakı: Azərbaycan Dövlət Nəşriyyatı, No. 5:8.

Molla Nasreddin (1909).. Reprinted in 2005: Azərbaycan Respublikasıı Elmlər Akademiyası, Molla Nəsrəddin, III Cild, Bakı: Çinar-Çap Nəşriyyatı, No. 31:12.

Molla Nasreddin (1909). Reprinted in 2005:Azərbaycan Respublikasıı Elmlər Akademiyası, Molla Nəsrəddin, III Cild, Bakı: Çinar-Çap Nəşriyyatı, No. 32:12.

Molla Nasreddin (1909). Reprinted in 2005: Azərbaycan Respublikasıı Elmlər Akademiyası, Molla Nəsrəddin, III Cild, Bakı: Çinar-Çap Nəşriyyatı, No. 44:11.

Molla Nasreddin (1911). Reprinted in 2008: Azərbaycan Respublikasıı Elmlər Akademiyası, Molla Nəsrəddin, IV Cild, Bakı: Çinar-Çap Nəşriyyatı, No. 35:52.

Molla Nasreddin (1913). Reprinted in 2008: Azərbaycan Respublikasıı Elmlər Akademiyası, Molla Nəsrəddin, IV Cild, Bakı: Çinar-Çap Nəşriyyatı, No. 21:4.

Molla Nasreddin (1913). Reprinted in 2008: Azərbaycan Respublikasıı Elmlər Akademiyası, Molla Nəsrəddin, IV Cild, Bakı: Çinar-Çap Nəşriyyatı, No. 28:1.

Najafizadeh, M. (1989). Ideology, Education, and Social Change in the Third World. Paper presented at the Eighty-Fourth Annual Meeting of the American Sociological Association, August, San Francisco, CA.

Najafizadeh, M. (2003a). Gender and Social Entrepreneurship in Societies in Transition: The Case of Azerbaijan. *The Journal of Third World Studies*, 20(2), 31–48.

Najafizadeh, M. (2003b). Women Social Entrepreneurs as Social Change Leaders in Transitional Nation-States. Paper presented at the Twelfth Annual Conference of The Global Awareness Society International, May, Washington, DC.

Najafizadeh, M. (2003c). Women's Empowering Carework in Azerbaijan. *Gender & Society*, 17(2), 293–304.

Najafizadeh, M. (2006). Women's Empowering Carework in Azerbaijan. Reprinted in abridged form, in *Global Dimensions of Carework and Gender*, edited by Mary K. Zimmerman, Jacquelyn S. Litt, and Christine E. Bose, pp. 351–361. Stanford, CA: Stanford University Press.

Najafizadeh, M. (2012). Gender and Ideology: Social Change and Islam in Post-Soviet Azerbaijan. *The Journal of Third World Studies*, 29(1), 81–101.

Najafizadeh, M. (2013). Ethnic Conflict and Forced Displacement: Narratives of Azeri IDP and Refugee Women from the Nagorno-Karabakh War. *Journal of International Women's Studies*, 14(1), 161–183.

Najafizadeh, M. (2014). Gender and Religion in Soviet Azerbaijan. Paper presented at the Thirty-Second Annual Meeting of the Association of Third World Studies, October, Denver, CO.

Najafizadeh, M. (2015a). Ideology, Women's Roles, and the Portrayal of Women in Pre-Soviet Azerbaijan. Paper presented at the Twenty-Fourth Annual Conference of the Global Awareness Society International, May, Philadelphia, PA.

Najafizadeh, M. (2015b). Sources and Methods: Azerbaijan, Post-Soviet Period. In *Encyclopedia of Women and Islamic Cultures*, edited by Suad Joseph. Leiden, The Netherlands, and Boston, MA: Brill. forthcoming.

Najafizadeh, M. and Mennerick, L. A. (1989). Defining Third World Education as a Social Problem: Education Ideologies and Education Entrepreneurship. *Perspectives on Social Problems: A Research Annual*, 1, 283–315.

Najafov, E. (2008). Evolution of Azerbaijan Nationalism: Enlightenment, ADR, and Azerbaijanism. *Azerbaijan in the World*, 1(12), 101–104.

News.Az. (2015). Elmira Suleymanova: Azerbaijan Needs to Establish Alimony Fund. News.Az. March 6. Retrieved March 17, 2015 (http://www.news.az/articles/society/96215).

Novosti Press. (1967). *Azerbaijan Soviet Socialist Republic*. Moscow: Novosti Press Agency Publishing House.

Paksoy, H. B. (2008). Elements of Humor in Central Asia: The Example of the Journal Molla Nasreddin in Azerbaijan. Uysal-Walker Archive of Turkish Oral Narrative, Texas Tech University. Retrieved May 25, 2015 (http://aton.ttu.edu/NASREDDIN_IN_AZARBAIJAN.asp). (First published pp. 164–180 in *Turkestan als historischer Faktor und politische Idee*. Baymirza Hayit Festschrift, edited by Erling von Mende. Köln: Studienverlag, 1988.

Rahim, H. L. and Mohtar, S. (2015). Social Entrepreneurship: A Different Perspective. *International Academic Research Journal of Business and Technology*, 1(1), 9–15.

Rahimov, I. (1999). To Siberia and Back: Life as Political Prisoner SH-971. *Azerbaijan International*, 7(3), 33–35.

Rasulzade, R. (1999). Mammad Amin Rasulzade: Founding Father of the First Republic. *Azerbaijan International*, 7(3), 22–24.

Robinson, J., Mair, J. and Hockerts, K. (2009). *International Perspectives on Social Entrepreneurship*. New York: Palgrave Macmillan.

Roper, J. and Cheney, G. (2005). The Meanings of Social Entrepreneurship Today. *Corporate Governance: The International Journal of Business in Society*, 5(3), 95–104.

Sabi, M. (1999). The Impact of Economic and Political Transformation on Women: The Case of Azerbaijan. *Central Asian Survey*, 18(1), 111–120.

Sadikhli, M. (1999). Exile to Kazakhstan: Stalins Repression of 1937. *Azerbaijan International*, 7(3), 30–32.

Sadikhli, M. (2006). Mass Deportation to Siberia: No More Tears Left to Cry. *Azerbaijan International*, 14(1), 18–19.

Samedova, M. (2000). Some Aspects of Azeris Women's Employment. *Genderşünaslıq: Azərbaycan Beynəlxalq Elmi-Kütləvi Jurnal* [Genderology: Azerbaijan International Scientific Journal], 4, 6–8.

Sarfarov, E. (2012). *Prevention of the Domestic Violence in Azerbaijan*. Baku, Azerbaijan: State Committee for Family, Women and Children of Azerbaijan Republic.

SCFWCA – State Committee for Family, Women and Children Affairs of the Republic of Azerbaijan. (2009). 4th Periodic Report of the Republic of Azerbaijan to the United Nations Convention on Elimination of All Forms of Discrimination against Women. Baku, Azerbaijan: State Committee for Family, Women and Children Affairs of the Republic of Azerbaijan.

SCFWCA – State Committee for Family, Women and Children Affairs of the Republic of Azerbaijan. (2014). 20th Anniversary of the Beijing Declaration and the Platform for Action National Report,

Republic of Azerbaijan. Baku, Azerbaijan: State Committee for Family, Women and Children Affairs of the Republic of Azerbaijan.

Seyid-zade, D. (2011). *Azerbaijan in the Beginning of XX Century: Roads Leading to Independence*, second edition. Baku, Azerbaijan: Bizim Kitab.

Shaw, E. and Carter, S. (2007). Social Entrepreneurship: Theoretical Antecedents and Empirical Analysis of Entrepreneurial Processes and Outcomes. *Journal of Small Business and Enterprise Development*, 14(3), 418–434.

Slavs and Tatars (2011). Molla Nasreddin: The Magazine that Would've, Could've, Should've. Zurich, Switzerland: Christoph Keller Editions, JRP Ringier. Retrieved May 1, 2015 (http://www.slavsandtatars.com/MOLLA.pdf).

SPPRED – Republic of Azerbaijan State Programme on Poverty Reduction and Economic Development. (2003). *State Programme on Poverty Reduction and Economic Development 2003–2005*. Baku, Azerbaijan: SPPRED.

SPPRED – Republic of Azerbaijan State Programme on Poverty Reduction and Economic Development. (2005). *Progress Report 2003–2004*. Azerbaijan Progresses toward the Achievement of the Millennium Development Goals. Baku, Azerbaijan: SPPRED.

Suleymanov, M. (2002). Stories of Taghiyev: Baku's Most Renowned Oil Baron. *Azerbaijan International*, 10(2), 42–49.

Suleymanova, E. (2008). *Ailə Planlanmasında İctimai Xidmətin Təşkili üzrə Vəsait* [Manual for Family Planning]. Baku, Azerbaijan: YEK.

Suny, R. G. (1996). On the Road to Independence: Cultural Cohesion and Ethnic Revival in a Multinational Society, in *Transcaucasia, Nationalism, and Social Change*, edited by Ronald Grigor Suny, pp. 377–400. Ann Arbor, MI: University of Michigan Press.

Swietochowski, T. (1985). *Russian Azerbaijan: 1905–1920*. New York: Cambridge University Press.

Swietochowski, T. (1995). *Russia and Azerbaijan: A Borderland in Transition*. New York: Columbia University Press.

Swietochowski, T. (1996). National Consciousness and Political Orientations in Azerbaijan, 1905–1920, in *Transcaucasia, Nationalism, and Social Change*, edited by Ronald Grigor Suny, pp. 211–234. Ann Arbor, MI: University of Michigan Press.

Talibzade, K. (2000). Learning to Read All Over Again: Alphabet Changes in Azerbaijan Throughout the [Twentieth] Century. *Azerbaijan International*, 8(1), 64–66.

Tohidi, N. (1998). Guardians of the Nation: Women, Islam, and the Soviet Legacy of Modernization in Azerbaijan, in *Women in Muslim Societies*, edited by Herbert L. Bodman and Nayereh Tohidi, pp. 137–161. Boulder, CO: Lynne Rienner Publishers.

Tolf, R. W. (1976). *The Russian Rockefellers: The Saga of the Nobel Family and the Russian Oil Industry*. Stanford, CA: Hoover Institution Press.

UNDP. (1999). *Azərbaycan Qadınları. Azərbaycan Respublikasında Qadınların Vəziyyəti Haqqında Hesabat* [Women of Azerbaijan. The Report on the Status of Women of Azerbaijan Republic]. Baku, Azerbaijan: United Nations Development Program.

UNDP. (2007). *Azerbaijan Human Development Report 2007, Gender Attitudes in Azerbaijan: Trends and Challenges*. Baku, Azerbaijan: UNDP.

UNDP. (2012a). *Gender (Kişi və Qadınların) Bərabərliyinin Təminatları Haqqında Azərbaycan Respublikasının Qanunu* [The Law of the Republic of Azerbaijan Regarding Gender Equality]. Baku, Azerbaijan: United Nations Development Program.

UNDP. (2012b). *Economic and Social Rights of Women in Azerbaijan*. Baku, Azerbaijan: United Nations Development Program.

UNDP. (2014). *Human Development Report 2014*. New York: United Nations Development Program.

Xanmammadova, S. (2011). *Məhəbbətin İnsanlarda Əks-Sədası* [Reflections of Kindness in People]. Baku, Azerbaijan: Mars Print Nəşriyyat.

Zahra, S. A., Gedajlovic, E., Neubaum, D. O. and Shulman, J. M. (2009). A Typology of Social Entrepreneurs: Motives, Search Processes and Ethical Challenges. *Journal of Business Venturing*, 24(5), 519–532.

23

WOMEN ENTREPRENEURS IN THE INFORMAL ECONOMY

Is formalisation the only solution for business sustainability?

Shyama V. Ramani, Ajay Thutupalli, Tamas Medovarszki,
Sutapa Chattopadhyay and Veena Ravichandran

Introduction

The informal economy refers to organisations in the informal sector (i.e., those not registered with an authority and not paying taxes) and the activities of firms in the formal sector that employ informal workers, (i.e., workers without a formal work contract and without any formal safety net).[1] Western donor agencies and international organisations, including the World Bank,[2] the OECD,[3] and USAID[4] have been advocating the formalisation of such informal niches, for they view them as segments where marginalised populations are working simply because of the lack of a better alternative – and they assume that being incorporated into a formal organisation would improve the lives of such informal workers. Though extremely appealing, however, this premise remains to be proved. Addressing this issue is particularly important for women's welfare, as women are over-represented in the informal economy (Chen, 2001) and there are concerns that the business sustainability of their entrepreneurial ventures could be adversely affected by formalisation. Therefore, this chapter provides some insight on this debate by exploring answers to the central question: What would be the impact of formalisation on the business sustainability of women's ventures in the informal economy?

According to the World Bank (2013),[5] 'The informal sector covers a wide range of labour market activities that combine two groups of different nature. On the one hand, the informal sector is formed by the coping behaviour of individuals and families in economic environments where earning opportunities are scarce. On the other hand, the informal sector is a product of rational behaviour of entrepreneurs that desire to escape state regulations.' Since the informal sector is viewed as comprising people shirking regulations, or eking out an existence, it is supposed to be welfare enhancing for society as a whole to bring it into the fold of the formal sector. 'The fundamental challenge posed by the informal economy is how to integrate it into the formal economy, as a matter of equity and social solidarity. Policies must encourage movement away from the informal economy. Support for exposed groups in the informal economy should be financed by society as a whole' (Becker, 2004; p.4).

This view is also adopted by management science scholars calling upon firms to explore ways to better serve the poor at the 'Bottom/Base Of the income Pyramid' (or BoP) communities[6] living on a few dollars a day in the global income pyramid (Prahalad and Hart, 2002). Firms are exhorted to contribute to poverty alleviation and in the process also capture profits (estimated at \$5 trillion), by rising to the challenge of serving the BoP communities (Prahalad, 2005). Since BoP communities typically operate in the informal economy, such a strategy implies further penetration of the informal economy by formal sector organisations, and it is assumed that such inroads will generate positive externalities and increase social welfare. 'This market is currently served by the unorganised sector that is often inefficient and controlled by local monopolies such as money lenders and middlemen. The challenge is to convert the unorganised and fragmented markets to an organised private sector market' (Prahalad, 2012: 2). These arguments tend to be driven by the perception that BoP communities present potential business opportunities to the formal and private sector as customers, employees, distributors and intermediaries.[7]

At the same time, curiously contradicting themselves, Western donor agencies also voice the opinion that the informal economy is useful and therefore must not be hurt, even while attempting to transform it into a formal realm. 'Over the last decades, it has become clear that the informal economy has a significant job and income generation potential. Therefore, appropriate policy frameworks and strategies aimed at the informal economy must be developed, without hampering the potential of the informal economy for job creation and economic growth. The main challenge is thus to develop innovative and supportive policies that recognise the contributions of the informal economy and its workforce' (Becker, 2004; p.3).

In the meantime, some of the scholars point out that state regulation or any attempt to recreate the informal economy as a 'mirror reflection' of the formal economy risks the extermination of the synergy and stifling the creativity of the informal sector and bringing the growth of the informal sector to 'a grinding halt'. Hence, they assert that attempts to formalise the informal sector should be eased as the exercise would be cumbersome and fraught with uncertainties (Maiti and Sen, 2010; p.2). Such a lack of consensus raises two important questions: Is it always necessary to transform an activity of the informal economy into a formal one? Does formalisation always improve equity and the welfare of all stakeholders?

These questions are particularly important with respect to women, because contrary to the formal sector, women are over-represented (i.e., make up more than 50 per cent) in the informal sector in developing countries (Chen, 2001). Moreover, they are also important with respect to the formal economy, as the formal and informal economies are linked in complex and intimate ways. Branded products are retailed and consumed in the informal economy. Informal workers are the labour in the supply chain networks of registered firms and contribute to increasing profit through their supply of cheap labour. Intermediary organisations like banks, non-governmental organisations (NGOs), welfare organisations, researchers and students from universities and public laboratories, interact regularly with informal economy entrepreneurs and workers. Finally, informal economy entrepreneurs help both the formal economy and the informal economy through creating employment buffers to absorb unemployed labour in times of economic stress and crises.

In the above context, the present chapter aims to make a contribution to two streams of literature, namely on 'business sustainability and BoP markets' and 'gender and entrepreneurship'.

First, it has been proposed by scholars that the informal economy, which houses most of the BoP markets, can yield fortunes (estimated at \$5 trillion) to large firms if penetrated successfully (Prahalad, 2005; Prahalad and Hart, 2002). Such new perspectives are gaining in importance as the markets, especially in consumer durables, get saturated in the North. Indeed, following these seminal works, firms have been made aware that in order to tap new opportunities in the informal economy in terms of customer base and business partnerships, firms must explore and develop new strategies for informal economy penetration. Here 'sustainability' has been evoked as a core value that their business model must satisfy to manage a triple bottom line of social, environmental and financial objectives and risks (Elkington, 1999). However, 'business sustainability' in the formal and informal economies is very distinct, for in the latter, even business survival involves a daily struggle in over-crowded markets and neither environmental nor social risks form the core of their concerns. In the above context, this chapter proposes a model of linkages between informal and formal economy organisations to promote the business sustainability of both. Furthermore, we show that the creation of a continuum of informal spaces for conversations is a necessary pathway to carve out such cooperation.

Second, until about the new millennium, most of the gender literature on the economic participation of women consisted of feminist critiques of patriarchy and capitalism. It described how women are victimised and exploited by men, markets and the forces of inter-national capitalism. While this literature is still growing and continuing to provide fresh insights, a new stream of literature is also emerging. The latter takes 'patriarchy' and 'capital-ism' as societal parameters that cannot be wished away in the short run and focuses on exploring new strategies for women's empowerment given local constraints which may be diverse and of differing magnitudes (Scott et al., 2012; Hughes et al., 2012). Our chapter may be considered as an addition to this latter stream of literature.

The issues raised in the present work have been addressed using multiple data sources. First, standard databases of management and economics literature were examined. Second, all the intermediate and final reports of a set of research grantees of the International Development Research Centre (IDRC) who had worked on projects related to women in the informal economy were thoroughly analysed. This led to an in-depth understanding of the policy and institutional experiments in these countries that aimed to help women entrepreneurs and workers in the informal economy. Third, our findings were validated through in-depth interviews with the concerned IDRC grantees. Via such an iterated confrontation process involving literature survey, our conceptual framework and the interviews with the grantees, a grounded theory was built on the ways that the state and other intermediaries can help women in the informal economy (Glaser and Strauss, 1967; Eisenhardt, 1989).

The remainder of this chapter is organised as follows. The second section introduces the background and framework of our analysis. The third section contains our results from the meta-analysis of the literature. The fourth section presents the results of the analysis of IDRC reports and the interviews with the IDRC grantees. The fifth section discusses the results and presents the closed loop model of linkages between formal and informal economies. The final section concludes the discussion.

Background: framework of analysis and compilation of corpus

On women entrepreneurs in the informal economy

The informal economy is very large in developing countries because their formal economies are less well developed and unable to absorb their available working population. For instance, in India the informal economy accounts for 93 percent of total employment, in Mexico about 62 percent and in South Africa about 34 percent (Chen, 2005) and it has been increasing faster than the formal economy worldwide (Bacchetta, Ernst, and Bustamante, 2009). Given the sluggish employment generation by the formal economy, informal petty entrepreneurship is the easiest and sometimes the only way for households to generate revenues for themselves.

Despite women being over-represented in the informal sector, gender disparities are rampant. Chen (2001) infers from existing data that: (i) fewer women than men 'hire' labour; i.e. women are employees rather than employers; (ii) wages are lower in the informal sector compared with the formal sector; and within the informal sector, women earn a lower wage than men on average, with the gender-wage-gap being greater than in the formal sector; (iii) women are more present in the 'lower-value-added' activities of the informal economy; (iv) the most invisible informal workers, namely the home-based producers contribute the most to global trade as they form a significant share of the workforce in key export industries involving manual tasks or labour-intensive operations; and (v) the outsourcing of goods and services of the formal sector to the informal economy is increasing.

We define an entrepreneur as anyone who is working for themselves and retains profits or anyone who owns an enterprise with workers. In an exhaustive literature survey of entrepreneurship by women, Carter, Marlow and Bennet (2012) highlight that as in their developed country counterparts, in developing countries, women's ventures tend to be younger, smaller and created with fewer resources. However, unlike in developed countries, women entrepreneurs are more likely to be in the informal economy in developing countries. They usually operate from their homes, have low earnings and compete in overcrowded sectors. Production is based on very scarce financial, human and physical resources. They are also low-skilled and isolated from professional networks that characterise firms in the formal economy. More often than not, women are present as entrepreneurs in the informal economy, not out of a personal ambition to generate wealth, but rather out of a lack of choice given the poverty level of the household. Innovation and entrepreneurship usually go hand in hand as new market creation requires novelty in terms of a product, process or business model, but our knowledge and understanding of innovation processes in the informal economy, especially by women remains extremely limited.

Why is it that even though the informal sector offers a lower wage than the formal sector, without any of the typical advantages of the formal sector such as a regular labour contract, health insurance, workers' benefits, pension schemes, etc., that women are more attracted to it? According to Chen (2001) it is mainly because, '. . . women are less able than men to compete in labour, capital and product markets because they have relatively low levels of education and skills or are less likely to own property or have market know-how' and '. . . women's time and mobility are constrained by social and cultural norms that assign the responsibility for social reproduction to women and discourage investment in women's education and training' (p.7). Women might also be over-represented as entrepreneurs because of the disincentives associated with the formal sector as already highlighted by De Soto (1989) in the 1980s. Excessive government regulation, government corruption, costly and time-taking bureaucracy, high tax rates and lack of time flexibility in the formal sector might just be pushing women into the informal economy.

Given that women in developing countries seem to be involved in informal entrepreneurial ventures by default rather than anything else, the question is whether they would still prefer to do so if they had the opportunity to have formal employment. To answer this question and possibly refine the above result, we carried out a meta-analysis of the literature on women entrepreneurs in the informal economy followed by an analysis of the IDRC grantee reports ending with in-depth interviews with the report authors.

Meta-analysis of the literature

Compilation of the corpus

Two databases were consulted: Scopus, the 'largest abstract and citation database of peer-reviewed literature';[8] and Econlit – the standard database of economics and related social sciences and management literature. Our first search used the research equation: ('women' OR 'woman' OR 'gender' OR 'female') AND ('informal' AND 'economy') OR ('informal' AND 'sector') in the title, abstract or keywords in the two databases. As per the criteria described above, our search yielded 155 results in Scopus; the evolution of publications over time is illustrated in Figure 23.1.

As can be noted, there seem to be three phases of interest on the topic. A 'low interest' phase of academic work until the mid-1980s, followed by a 'medium or higher interest' phase from 1990 to 2000 with a clear take-off in the new millennium. This heightened interest can be explained by the adoption of liberalisation and increasing globalisation from the 1990s. As Western multinationals enter developing and emerging countries, they increasingly outsource their production and distribution activities to local firms, who also partner with informal organisations. As the number of business partners from the informal economy increases in the supply and distribution chains, and consumer bases are built in Base of Pyramid markets, market networks between formal and informal economies increase, and this phenomenon has been closely followed by academics. Since the last phase marks a context so distinct from the earlier ones, both in terms of academic production and growth of the informal economy, we shifted our focus to the years 2000–2012. The results of the second round of filtering are presented in Table 23.1.

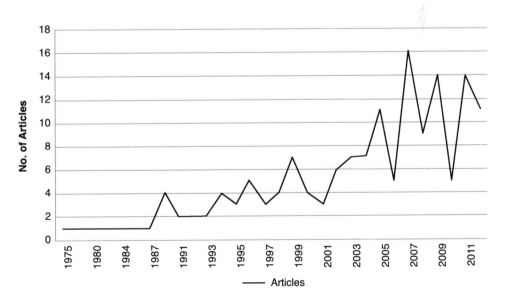

Figure 23.1 Publication Count in Scopus on Women and Informal Economy★

★*Note that the number for 2011 might be incomplete as registration in databases take time.*

Table 23.1 Number of Articles between 2000 and 2012*

Database	Just on informal economy	On women in the informal economy	On women in informal economy who are either involved in innovation or entrepreneurship	Share (percentage) of third and fourth column in the first; peer-reviewed literature on the informal economy
Scopus** (All fields)	6371	1818	648	28.54%; 10.17%
Scopus (title, abstract, key words)	1051	112	13	10.66%; 1.24%
Econlit (All fields)	8361	530	32	6.34%; 0.38%

*Percentages in fifth column are the number of articles in third column as a percentage of articles in second; the number of articles in fourth column as a percentage of articles in second column respectively.
**Search applied to articles in "Business, Economics and Management" streams

The numbers in Table 23.1 speak for themselves and clearly show that within the subject area of the informal economy, the study of the role of gender and women's involvement with innovation and entrepreneurship is extremely limited. However, the above figures are particularly disturbing because women are over-represented compared with men in the informal economy.

Further refinement of the corpus yielded 41 articles on women involved in innovation/ entrepreneurship in the informal economy. However none of these articles provided specific answers to our questions viz. Is it in the interest of all stakeholders, especially women entrepreneurs to formalise the informal economy? If so, how should such change be brought about? Finally we retained 28 articles which were at least informative on the above questions.

Even though the research focus intended to target women entrepreneurs working in the informal economy, only nine articles discussed women's entrepreneurship and that too outside of the informal economy context.[9] Nonetheless, the rest discussed case studies where women were mostly involved in informal work as self-employed entrepreneurs (16), working for a firm that is not registered with local authorities (5) and in one instance working for a firm that had no formal wage contract with some of its employees. A majority of authors are of the view that, as opposed to men, women are above all engaged in the informal economy out of necessity rather than opportunism.

In terms of innovation generation by women, despite the fact that we intentionally selected all articles that could potentially present cases of innovation generation by women, only three articles mentioned this and all three were in terms of 'service provision innovations' rather than new products. They described how women entrepreneurs identified unmet market demands and created new informal ventures to serve their customers, such as supplying to flower shops in addition to pedestrians in Ukraine (Williams and Round, 2009), opening up a temporary food stand at campuses during examination periods in Ghana (Adom and Williams, 2012) and setting up mobile 'call centres' by the road in Nigeria (Anugwom, 2011).

None of the articles bring up the debate about formalisation of the informal economy explicitly. However, about a third of the articles (i.e., 11 articles) seem to endorse the view that without changing social norms, policies, regulations (e.g., hereditary law reform to enable women to have property that may serve as collateral; access to credit schemes) and without providing inclusive education for women, formalisation may lower the income generation capacity of women's ventures (Williams and Round, 2009; Boyd, 2005; Amine and Staub, 2009). Chen (2002) adds that with formalisation women in the informal economy risk losing an important competitive advantage in a world characterised by global assembly lines where firms engage in a ruthless gamble of competitiveness through cost reduction – namely cheap labour. By being in the informal economy, as distinct from the formal one, women are able to leverage their own labour to bring down the final price of the product and be competitive with respect to the formal enterprise products. However, if the informal sector organisations were formalised, unless compliance to minimum wage laws was strictly monitored and enforced, which is not the case at the moment, women might be in a worse off exploited situation. Thus, the authors seem to be of the view that under existing patriarchal societal norms coupled with competitive markets, the formalisation of the informal economy is more likely to lower the profitability of informal economy ventures through increasing their fixed costs and eliminating some of their comparative advantages.

In order to delve further we then turned to the complementary question: why are women attracted to the informal economy in the first place? A detailed meta-analysis yielded Table 23.2 summarising the answers offered by the articles in our corpus.

The results of Table 23.2 and the prior discussions on what the literature has to say on the issue lead to our first result.

Result 1: Women are pushed to be workers or entrepreneurs in the informal economy on account of:

- Patriarchal social customs and norms;
- The high entry barriers and disincentives posed by participation in the formal economy;
- Resource constraints (lack of education, skills, finance, social networks) of women themselves.

Table 23.2 Why are Women More Present in the Informal Economy?

Factors	Examples	Frequency of citations	% of total citations
Societal norms that constrain women	– Constraints on when, where and how far a female can move outside of home; – Norms on when and how long a female should be educated; – With whom of the opposite gender females can interact with and under what circumstances; – What social networks a female can have outside of family network	15	31.25%
Disadvantage of women themselves	– Lack of financial literacy; – Lack of education and skills; – Lack of confidence; – Lack of or limited ownership of land and access to raw materials	14	29.17%

(Continued)

Table 23.2 (Continued)

Factors	Examples	Frequency of citations	% of total citations
Factors that make the formal economy less attractive to women	– High cost of new firm creation; – Efforts to comply with bureaucracy – Inflexible working conditions and hours incompatible with fulfilling family duties – High costs of administration and compliance to regulation	11	22.92%
Factors that make entry into the formal economy more difficult for women entrepreneurs	– General absence or scarcity of venture capital and business angels (in addition to women's general barrier to access credit because of social discrimination or lack of collateral) – Lack of knowledge and information about the nature of demand to be satisfied – Need for permanent office sites to expand sales and distribution – Lack of legal protection or counselling for micro-enterprises – Negative discrimination practised against women	8	16.67%
Total number of citations		48	100.00%

As Table 23.2 reveals, the first and foremost set of constraining factors for women workers and entrepreneurs are inherited social norms that are unfavourable to women. These norms give rise not only to disadvantages to women themselves, but also to discrimination against women in the market.

The traditional role of women as caretakers of children restricts the time they can invest in income generation. Norms (societal, religious or other) also determine the mobility of women and with whom they may interact. This places women entrepreneurs at a disadvantage because interaction within social networks is crucial for the success of entrepreneurial ventures. Social networks enable entrepreneurs to build up their market and expand their businesses and open new doors for gaining access to funding. Yueh's (2009) study on 9,000 entrepreneurs (not exclusively women) in urban China finds, for example, that one of the most determinant factors of a successful entrepreneurial venture is the existence of a social network that not only eases credit constraints but provides access to supply and distribution channels or even a channel to obtain the necessary licences to operate.

Second, social norms might stultify the functioning of standard institutions as Bushell (2008) illustrates through a case study in Nepal. Following the adoption of reforms in inheritance law that enabled women to own land, a Nepalese woman who wished to launch a start-up went to a bank to take out a loan but was refused. The bank agent agreed to make a loan only if her husband came to sign the necessary documents. Indeed, women's access to resources need not be sufficient for entrepreneurship if patriarchal sanctions block the way.

Third, women entrepreneurs may find it difficult to set up businesses in the formal economy as they are typically involved in break-even petty enterprises and often do not generate sufficient income to cover the typical costs of administration that the functioning of a formal enterprise requires. However, if barriers to education and qualification are removed and other problems related to women's restricted mobility are solved, then the rate of entry of women's ventures into the formal economy might increase (Chen, 2002).

Two case studies discussed in our corpus of articles are particularly interesting. The first concerns an informal economy organisation that is partially operating in the formal economy. The second is about an established multinational that is facilitating the creation of entrepreneurial ventures by women.

Datta and Gailey (2012) analyse the evolution of Lijjat, a unique social entrepreneurial venture created in 1959 to provide self-employment opportunities for poor urban women in India to produce and sell 'papad', a savory snack. It currently employs 42,000 women in 17 states of India. Lijjat is a cooperative whose membership is restricted to women, irrespective of religion or caste, and decision-making within Lijjat is based on consensus.

What made Lijjat's unique success happen? First, Lijjat provided job opportunities for unskilled women. Second, the production model was compatible with the social norms of the prevailing patriarchal society. The snacks were produced in women's homes or close to them (thanks to rapid branch expansion). Therefore, women did not need to leave their homes to work. Women could attend to their daily family responsibilities without any problem, making papads in their spare time. Women were paid the day after they supplied a batch of papads thereby receiving near-immediate compensation for their efforts. Third, Lijjat provided socio-compatible spaces of dialogue. Experienced women acted as inspectors and mentors engaging in visual inspection and dialogue to ensure continuous product quality as well as exchange of ideas on the production process and beyond work. Thus, with these three elements, Lijjat managed to empower women – without protests issuing from the men. Indeed, many women reported that their husbands did not raise objections to this kind of employment because the job involved work from home and exclusively with other women.

Some Western multinationals have also developed remarkable new business models to penetrate emerging markets using women, and at the same time, empowering them through creating spaces for learning – providing refreshing counter-examples to the often held view that large firms, capitalism and globalisation all serve to lower women's welfare. For instance, Scott et al. (2012) explain how Avon uses women in South Africa to sell their beauty products, through providing training that builds their capabilities, which in turn empowers them. A woman becomes an Avon team member with a modest registration fee. She is then made part of a 'team', a network with other women supervised and guided by 'mentors' who are also women. Thereafter, she is trained and provided with Avon beauty goods to sell, for which she gets a commission on the basis of the volume of sales. Mentors also ensure that women vendors constantly set targets for themselves and help them to improve and gain self-esteem. In the process, women learn to be entrepreneurs – and many branch off to create their own ventures.

The Avon case is very noteworthy because it reveals how a large company can promote formalisation of the informal economy. By drawing upon former informal workers and transforming at least some of them into women entrepreneurs in the formal economy, it promotes formalisation. Avon succeeded due to replication of some of the advantages offered by the informal economy to women. For instance, women could join Avon without needing much formal education or financial resources. They were assured that their household duties would not suffer and their participation in Avon would not conflict with social norms through the creation of spaces of dialogue that assured them. This leads us to note that with respect to women, large firms can best promote formalisation by including in their penetration strategies, schemes for the capacity building of women and women's ventures.

IDRC Grantee Reports and Interview Results

In 2008, the International Development Research Centre (IDRC) initiated a project on entrepreneurship and innovation by and for women in the informal economy.[10] Eight projects dealing with the situation of women from low-income communities working in the informal economy in developing countries were selected, on the basis of the clarity and pertinence of questions addressed, and the viability of the methodology. Table 23.3 summarises their main findings.

Thus, there seem to be essentially three types of governance designs that help women's empowerment and livelihoods in the informal economy (which can also be used in the formal economy), namely: (i) regulation (e.g. maternity leave, paid vacation, severance leave, minimum wage); (ii) facilitating participation in societal decision making (e.g. fixing quotas for women in governing councils and ensuring that the selection process is fair in terms of reaching women who are not positioned in power or dictated by male members); and (iii) creating new intermediary organisations (e.g., incubators).

What about the effectiveness of these governance initiatives on women in the informal economy? What are the determinants of their impact? We posed these queries to the IDRC grantees and had further in-depth discussions on the observations recorded in their reports. The analysis of the transcripts of the extensive interviews combined with the findings of their reports led us to formulate four results on the determinants of impact of policy initiatives as follows.

What's good for all, is good for women

Result 2: Policies that promote economic development with respect to both men and women, such as compulsory education and income-guaranteeing programmes, may have as much or even a greater impact on innovation and entrepreneurship by and for women in the informal economy than 'women-focused' policy initiatives.

We illustrate this result with the case of Vietnam, where some women-focused policy measures have been introduced. For instance, there is regulation responding to the gender-specific constraint of having monthly periods, whereby menstruating women can take half a day off when they are tired. And women raising new families or new mothers can work one hour less until the newborn is a year old without any change in the salary.[11] But, women do not want to 'declare' having periods in order to have half a day off and many women do not make use of the one less hour option. Another example is provided by firms. In Vietnam, firms are incentivised to employ women by availing of lower corporate taxes according to the proportion of women employed. Organisations which have a greater percentage of women workers pay lower corporate taxes and can avail of bank loans at lower interest rates (to implement 'The Law on Gender Equality' of Vietnam passed in 2001). However, most firms are not responding to this incentive system. They prefer to employ fewer women rather than avail of attractive bank loans.

The provision of universal education, on the other hand, has been noted to have empowered women greatly. Education has increased the confidence of Vietnamese women working in both the formal and informal 'parts' of the agribusiness sector. They can and do influence innovation generation and policy – though not in formal recognised ways but in

Table 23.3 Salient Results of Selected IDRC Grantee Projects

Country	Informal economy niche/processes in which the role of women is examined	How the challenges of women in this niche can be addressed	Helpful policy initiatives evoked
India	Habitat sector in India.	(i) Intermediaries can play a very crucial role in creating awareness and by making the information reach women workers. (ii) If awareness is created appropriation of value by informal workers can increase	– Compulsory education – Rural Employment Guarantee Scheme
Palestine	Innovation processes within integrated water resources management.	(i) women's needs, priorities, and capabilities have to be taken into consideration in the policy design and implementation of water projects (as water projects are important in a country where agriculture occupies the primary sector); (ii) Innovation by women with regard to water awareness, use, re–uses, treatment, and transport techniques must be identified and scaled up.	– Fixing quotas for women in governance councils
Uganda	Innovations from traditional knowledge	(i) Through facilitating the creation of innovation that empowers women. (ii) Through diffusion of innovations using women.	– Incubators for women's ventures – Public institutions that work to create innovation to improve women's welfare
Vietnam	Technology governance and policy processes in agro–based industries	(i) Women must have opportunities to express their opinions within organizations (ii) Women must be supported to work and raise families	– Guaranteeing maternity leave – Supporting time taken out for child care – Fixing quotas for women in governance councils – State sponsored councils for women's welfare
Zambia	Diffusion of a simple manual irrigation scheduling tool being tailored specifically for female farmers	(i) Through facilitating the creation of innovation that empowers women while increasing the income generation capacity of the household. (ii) Through generating data at household level that demonstrates how an innovation can increase the income generation capacity of a household.	Public institutions that work to create innovation to improve women's welfare and status

informal ways at all levels. This can be through taking initiatives, by proposing ideas, by creating awareness or by discussing. Through conversations women continuously bring about a change in the technology process and working conditions.

Make policies effective by enabling conversations on how to make them effective

Result 3: Whatever the policy (generic or gender specific), initiatives that create or support a continuum of spaces for conversations (rather than formal dialogues or discourses) from concept to market, help innovation and entrepreneurship by and for women in the formal or informal economy.

In many developing countries, spaces for conversation between women are absent. In this case, women may be isolated and their ideas may have no conduit for impact. Then the state is called upon as the actor to fill this vacuum. For example, in water-scarce Palestine, it has been observed that women are not less innovative than their male counterparts when it comes to integrated water resource management but their innovations relate to awareness and water conservation practices rather than technical solutions. However, most of these innovations go unnoticed because of two reasons: namely, lack of immediate financial impact and application in an informal economy context where agricultural activities carried out by women remain as a family business. In short, there are no spaces for the flow of conversations from the family level to the community level to finally reach the higher echelons of policy makers. Our interviewees in Palestine suggest that gendered spaces for conversations or women's discursive spaces can be created through organized training to solve this problem. Workshops can create a platform for women and a common pool of information at the community level on best practices. Currently, women's views on good water management practises have mainly been compiled in response to foreign donor request – for instance, when donors insist on the inclusion of women in a project as a condition for receiving a grant. In order to make that a mainstream routine a national action plan that provides both appropriate legal framework and incentives are necessary.

Sometimes state initiatives can create spaces for conversation unintentionally. In a radical break from the past, in India, the 'Mahatma Gandhi National Rural Employment Guarantee Act' of 2005 heralded the introduction of India's first national social security scheme targeting the rural poor. Adult members, both women and men, of every rural household are ensured one hundred days of employment in every financial year as unskilled manual labour in public works at minimum wages fixed by the government. An unexpected outcome of this act is that it is helping social welfare enhancing intermediaries like non-governmental organisations (NGO) and social entrepreneurs change outdated beliefs and behaviours that restrain and constrain the efforts of women as entrepreneurs or workers in the informal economy. For instance, when women come in groups to the Panchayats or village councils under the 100-days work schemes, social workers are able to interact with them. Starting with questions on how the women are faring with working outside of the home, social workers expose them to other opportunities by which they can become self-reliant through learning skills without putting at risk attendance of their household duties. Successful women from other villages, recruited as 'change makers' by the NGOs, explain to their peers that by learning skills and developing a livelihood, they have been able to contribute to household savings, pay for their children's education, earn respect from the husband and in-laws, and over time enjoy a definite increase in bargaining power in the family. Thus, though the debate on the efficiency of the implementation of these laws continues, it has definitely had a positive impact in terms of triggering conversations.

But pro-women innovations are best diffused only if they are also useful for households

Result 4: Pro-women innovations are more successfully adopted if the returns from innovation adoption are positive with respect to the entire household, including the men, rather than being useful only to the women.

In Zambia, 76 percent of the working women are engaged in agriculture. The 'Drip Planner Chart' is a micro-irrigation tool that was developed through collaboration with Wageningen University (Netherlands) and benefitted from a wide range of complementary skills. It requires households to gather data on water and take measurements in order to ensure efficient micro-irrigation. It is a tool that provides an easy, simple and cheap way to assess crop water requirements and irrigation scheduling, to enable farmers to produce year round, take advantage of the higher off-season prices and substantially increase their income. Moreover, it was developed as an 'innovation' that could lower the daily drudgery of women and thereby enhance women's empowerment.

The chart was introduced in rural Zambia in 'patriarchal' zones where women's autonomy or decision-making power was least, and by agricultural extension service teams that mainly consisted of men. Conversations occurred only between the men of the extension service and the men of the beneficiary households – women were not included. Now, the men of the household mainly saw it as investment that could reduce 'women's drudgery' without substantially increasing household income, for while the IDRC grantee had data on increased production at the laboratory scale, there had been no experimentation on household farms. Therefore, the innovation was adopted only by a few households where men felt that the lowering of drudgery of their womenfolk was worth the money spent. The lesson offered is that if the entire diffusion process of an innovation occurs through conversations between men and if the decision to adopt (or not adopt) the concerned innovation is also by men, then any innovation with the potential to help women is likely to be adopted only if it is beneficial to the entire household (rather than only to women).

More than policies, real life success stories work

Result 5: More than good policies, successful role models in the form of 'local heroines' who create employment and bring economic prosperity and rejuvenation into their communities catalyse change through emulation.

While in Zambia, the innovation to lower the drudgery of women was poorly adopted, the moves in India to give a voice to women in village councils through a quota system still function only in name in many places (e.g., husbands participate in meetings in the place of their elected wives) and the impact of women's welfare organisations in Vietnam vary greatly depending upon the commitment of their leaders, 'successful role models' and 'successful business models' need little state support for emulation or imitation. This premise is amply illustrated by the emergence of the oyster mushroom cottage industry in south-west Uganda.

In 1990, the Ugandan Ministry of Agriculture, Animal Industry and Fisheries (MAAIF) introduced oyster mushroom production in south-west Uganda where the weather is cool and most conducive to mushroom farming. The Mushroom Training and Resource Centre (MTRC) is a registered community-based organisation in south-west Uganda that has been very active in diffusing this technology in Kabale. With the help of the MTRC, local producers realised that mushroom could be grown on composted heaps of cattle manure and other agricultural wastes such as sorghum, millet, beans, peas and wheat. This allowed for the domestication of mushroom farming and made producers less dependent on seasonal and spontaneous spawning in the wild, making the business a lucrative one. Thus, from zero producers, there are now more than 400 mushroom producers in the Kabale district with most of them being women selling directly to consumers and supermarkets. Indeed, the success of oyster mushrooms has triggered the search for other home-based income-generating activities for women, which will permit women to attend to their household chores and domestic care activities while earning a livelihood. Finally, this case well illustrates how modern knowledge systems and local research centres can provide solutions to pressing local social needs while creating livelihoods and new markets.

Discussion of results and organisational implications

Large firms in the formal economy, and especially international firms, which are striving to increase their market presence in developing countries, are encroaching upon the informal economy more and more. They are trying to build a consumer base in BoP markets, employ informal workers and have business relationships with informal economy organisations. Women are predominant in all three niches.

We propose that the debate about whether or not to formalise the informal economy organisations stems from a linear view of the inter-linkages between the formal and informal economy as shown in Figure 23.2.

In contrast, the preceding sections showed that in restrictive societies opening up spaces for dialogue creates a closed-loop flow of knowledge and skills transfer as shown in Figure 23.3. Under the closed loop model, there is capability building through iterative cycles that ultimately leads to business success. Learning and knowledge are central to business sustainability of women entrepreneurs. The knowledge of women is often tacit and experiential being disseminated through 'peer-to-peer learning and doing' as women prefer democratic and consultative working processes. Therefore, entrepreneurship and innovation by and for women can be boosted by providing a continuum of spaces for useful conversations in informal, non-intimidating, non-hierarchical settings that permit women to explore, experiment, and discuss their way to business success. The construction of a unique

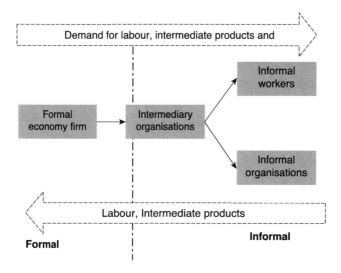

Figure 23.2 Linear Model of Linkages between Formal and Informal Economies

environment adapted to local women's needs provides spaces wherein women can gain access to resources, engage in dialogue, develop confidence and learn about successful women role models. Furthermore, accompaniment of participants through mentorship and training programmes can ensure that these initiatives are compatible with local patriarchal social norms.

Large firms wishing to use women's informal labour or have business relations with women entrepreneurs can take particular note of the above. Members of the informal economy are a living proof of the existence of an extraordinary entrepreneurial energy fuelled by desire to improve living conditions. It is this energy that governments and firms have to tap by finding ways to collaborate. Firms and public agencies that invest to create structured social spaces for women in the informal economy designed to fit local needs will gain more than access to labour or intermediate goods and services. They will earn a brand loyalty and if the branded products of the large firm are affordable, large firms will be able to create a consumer base. This may in turn induce the firms to go beyond being a purchaser of labour and commodities, towards making impact investments that improve the quality of lives of their informal economy stakeholders.

The corridors of conversation can be created through partnerships with intermediate organisations, such as NGOs and women's groups, via training workshops and educational support. Moreover, providing an informal work environment suited to the local social norms with the help of existing or newly created women self-help groups will help deal with situations that constrain many women employees. Thus, more than formalisation, business sustainability of both formal and informal economy organisations can be promoted through increasing inclusion of women via accompaniment in conversation corridors. Then, all stakeholders are likely to gain. Companies will get access to a cheap labour force and access to new distribution channels, women will gain access to a protected and regulated working environment, training and employment, and governments will save time and money and

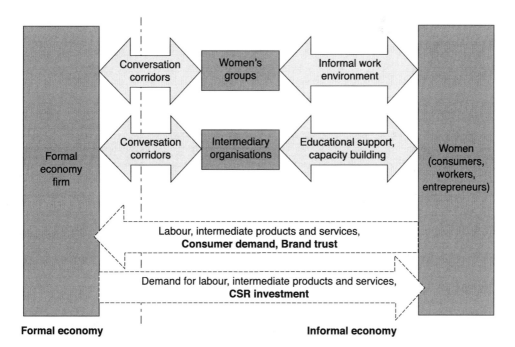

Figure 23.3   Closed-Loop Model of Linkages between Formal and Informal Economies

restrict themselves to their primary function, namely, ensuring an appropriate and favourable regulatory framework for these ventures to take off. A new perspective of business-to-business relationship formation in BoP settings will be gained from such initiatives.

Concluding remarks

The informal economy is largely represented by people excluded from formal economic systems. Current international policy and much of mainstream management literature advocates 'formalisation' through a variety of strategies in order to promote inclusive growth. The objective of this chapter has been to examine whether the promotion of growth via formalisation was compatible with the preservation of the business sustainability of entrepreneurial ventures in the informal economy and women's welfare in it as workers and entrepreneurs. Recognition of the important role that women play, the differences with respect to men and the distinct needs of women that are not necessarily translated into planning practice, motivated the search for the answers.

A meta-analysis of literature and an examination of transcripts of women's experiences in five emerging countries, namely India, Palestine, Uganda, Vietnam and Zambia, revealed that women were over-represented in the informal economy, with the informal economy being more compatible with women's needs and existing patriarchal social norms, even though women create entrepreneurial ventures in the informal economy more out of necessity than to seize opportunities. However, the literature offered little in terms of arguments *for* or *against* formalisation of the informal economy, because for the most part they were based on a linear view of the linkages between the formal and informal economy.

Then extensive interviews with the authors of country studies highlighted the role and impact of new regulation, policies and public investment that are being tried out to give women voices in decision making, facilitate life-work balance and access resources to start new businesses. All these different actions had one common goal in addition to a variety of specific ones, namely, to change the historically inherited social norms and societal expectations about women that constrain their economic lives as consumers, workers and producers.

Moreover, the interview findings led to a major revision of the linear model of linkages. The interviews indicated that many of the above top-down actions for women's empowerment are either less effective than desired or more effective when they are encapsulated in gender-neutral economic development programmes, perhaps because then they clash less with prevailing patriarchy. On the other hand, bottom-up initiatives for gender empowerment are more effective only when a continuum of gendered spaces (or women-only spaces) facilitates discussion and exchange of ideas and experiences to bring about transformative change. Contrary to top-down policies, bottom-up initiatives need gendered spaces in order to ensure the security of informal and non-intimidating spaces of dialogue to women bound and isolated by patriarchal traditional norms. Even well-intentioned interventions are neither necessary nor sufficient for change – for successful women role models made visible in conversation spaces provoke emulation and imitation and are often the best agents of sweeping change. Thus, rather than a linear model of linkages, companies and policy makers would do well to recognise the advantages of constructing a closed-loop model of interactions with women in the informal economy. Indeed, its application has a greater potential to offer solutions to tackle the environment-specific and gender-specific constraints of all stakeholders. As a consequence the closed-loop model has novel organisational implications for firms competing to catch up in the BoP markets of developing countries.

Notes

1 Definition proposed by the International Labour Organization (ILO) http://wiego.org/sites/wiego.org/files/resources/files/ILO_Statistical%20Update_Employment_Informal_Economy.pdfMarch 19,2013.
2 http://lnweb90.worldbank.org/eca/eca.nsf/Sectors/ECSPE/2E4EDE543787A0C085256A940073F4 E4?OpenDocument March 19,2013.
3 http://www.oecd.org/dac/povertyreduction/36563594.pdf March 19, 2013.
4 http://www.oecd.org/dac/povertyreduction/38452590.pdf March 19, 2013.
5 The term 'bottom/base of the income pyramid' or BoP is often used referring to households whose working members earn less than $3,000 USD per year, in PPP terms. The BoP is not a single homogeneous segment but a set of distinct socio-economic segments sharing the common feature of low household income. The nature of the BoP as a market is also likely to be specific to the sector concerned (see UNDP 2008 for examples).
6 http://www.accenture.com/SiteCollectionDocuments/PDF/AccentureIndiasQuestforInclusive Growth.pdf March 10, 2013.
7 http://www.info.sciverse.com/scopus/about March 19, 2013.
8 http://www.info.sciverse.com/scopus/about March 19, 2013.
9 This could have been the case because though the terms like 'informal' or 'formal' appeared in the abstract leading to its selection in our database, a careful reading revealed that the article did not treat our research questions.
10 To generate knowledge at the grass-roots level, it initiated a research competition on Gender and Innovation to understand (i) the involvement and influence of women in innovation processes; and (ii) the impacts (real or perceived) of specific innovations is on the lives of women – in the context of socio-economic development.
11 Also in Palestine.

Bibliography

Adom, K. And Williams, C.C. (2012). Evaluating the motives of informal entrepreneurs in Koforidua, Ghana. *Journal of Developmental Entrepreneurship*, 17(1), 1–17.

Alter C. M. (2005). Rethinking the informal economy: Linkages with the formal economy and the formal regulatory environment, Research Paper, UNU-WIDER, United Nations University (UNU).

Amine, L. S. and Staub, K. M. (2009). Women entrepreneurs in sub-Saharan Africa: An institutional theory analysis from a social marketing point of view. *Entrepreneurship and Regional Development*, 21(2), 183–211.

Anugwom, E. E. (2011). 'Wet in we for do?' Women entrepreneurs and the Niger Delta conflict. *Journal of Small Business and Entrepreneurship*, 24(2), 243–252.

Apro. (2011). Value chain governance and gender: saffron production in Afghanistan. IDRC Program on 'Gender and Innovation – Understanding their mutual influence and impacts'. Canada: IDRC.

Arocena, R. and Sutz, J. (2000). Looking at national systems of innovation from the South. *Industry and Innovation*, 7(1), 55–75.

Bacchetta, M., Ernst, E. and Bustamante, J. P. (2009). *Globalization and informal jobs in developing countries*. Geneva: International Labour Organization.

Basu, P. and Srivastava, P. (2005). Scaling-up microfinance for India's rural poor. World Bank Policy Research Working Paper 3646. Washington, DC: The World Bank.

Becker, C. F. (2004). *The informal economy*. Helsinki: SIDA.

Biggs, S. D., Gurung, S. M. and Messerschmidt, D. (2004). An exploratory study of gender, social inclusion and empowerment through development goups and group-based organizations in Nepal: Building on the positive. Report to the Gender and Social Exclusion Assessment (GSEA) Study, National Planning Commission. Katmandu: The World Bank and DFID.

Blofield, M. (2012). *Care Work and Class: Domestic Workers' Struggle for Equal Rights in Latin America*, University Park, PA: Penn State University Press.

Boyd, R. L. (2005). Race, gender, and survivalist entrepreneurship in large northern cities during the Great Depression. *Journal of Socio-economics*, 34(3), 331–339.

Brugmann, J. and Prahalad, C. K. (2007). Cocreating Business's New Social Compact. *Harvard Business Review*, 85(2), 80–90.

Bure, C. (2007). Gender in/and science, technology and innovation policy: an overview of current literature and findings. Commissioned paper for IDRC.

Bushell, B. (2008). Women entrepreneurs in Nepal: what prevents them from leading the sector? *Gender and Development*, 16(3), 549–564.

Byravan, S. (2008). Gender in/and innovation in South Asia. Commissioned paper for IDRC. Canada: IDRC.

Carter, S. and Jones-Evans, D. (2006). *Enterprise and small business: principles, practice and policy*. London: FT Prentice Hall.

Carter, S., Marlow, S. and Bennett, D. (2012). Gender and entrepreneurship. In Carter, S. and Jones Evans, D. (Eds.), *Enterprise and Small Business*. Financial Times (3rd). Upper Saddle River, NJ: Pearson Education, 218-231.

Chen, M. (2005). Rethinking the Informal Economy: Linkages with the Formal Economy and the Formal Regulatory Environment. WIDER Working Paper 10/2005. Helsingfors: UNU-WIDER.

Chen, M. A. (2002). Globalization and the informal economy. How global trade and investment impact on the working poor. ILO Employment Sector – Working paper on Informal economy, 2002/1.

Chen, M. A. (2001). Women and informality: a global picture, the global movement. *SAIS Review*, 21(1), 71–82.

Datta, P. B. and Gailey, R. (2012). Empowering women through social entrepreneurship: case study of a women's cooperative in India. *Entrepreneurship Theory and Practice*, 36(3), 569–587.

De Soto, H. (1989). *The other path: The invisible revolution in the third world*. New York: Harper and Row.

Della-Giusta, M. and Phillips, C. (2006). Women entrepreneurs in the Gambia: challenges and opportunities. *Journal of International Development*, 18(8), 1051–1064.

Development-Alternatives (2011).Women in the Habitat Services. IDRC Program on 'Gender and Innovation – Understanding their mutual influence and impacts'.

Dion, P. A., Easterling, D. and Javalgi, R. (1997). Women in the business-to-business salesforce: Some differences in performance factors. *Industrial Marketing Management*, 26(6), 447–457.

Eisenhardt, K. M. (1989). Building theories from case study research. *Academy of Management Review*, 14(4), 532–550.

Eklund, P. A., Felloni, F. and Imai, K. (2003). Women's organisations, maternal knowledge, and social capital to reduce prevalence of stunted children – evidence from rural Nepal. Economics Series Working Papers, 144.

El Harbi, S., Anderson, A. and Mansour, N. (2009).The attractiveness of entrepreneurship for females and males in a developing Arab Muslim country; entrepreneurial intentions in Tunisia. *International Business Research*, 2(3), 47–53.

Elkington, J. (1999). Triple bottom line: Implications for the oil industry. *Oil and Gas Journal*, 97(50), 139–141.

Field, E., Jayachandran, S. and Pande, R. (2010). Do traditional institutions constrain female entrepreneurship? A field experiment on business training in India, Papers and Proceedings, Available at http://faculty.wcas.northwestern.edu/~sjv340/entrepreneurs.pdf (accessed on 12 February 2013).

Franceys, R. and Weitz, A. (2003). Public-private community partnerships in infrastructure for the poor. *Journal of International Development*, 15(8), 1083–1098.

Gatewood, E. J., Brush, C. G., Carter, N. M., Greene, P. G. and Hart, M. M. (2009). Diana: a symbol of women entrepreneurs' hunt for knowledge, money, and the rewards of entrepreneurship. *Small Business Economics*, 32(2), 129–144.

Glaser, B. G. and Strauss, A. L. (1967). *The discovery of grounded theory: Strategies for qualitative research*. New Brunswick and London: Aldine Publications.

Hall, A. (2005). Capacity development for agricultural biotechnology in developing countries: an innovation systems view of what it is and how to develop it. *Journal of International Development*, 17(5), 611–630.

Hart, S. L. and London, T. (2005). Developing native capability. *Stanford Social Innovation*, 3(2), 28–33.

Heffernan, C., Thomson, K. and Nielsen, L. (2011). Caste, livelihoods and livestock: An exploration of the uptake of livestock vaccination adoption among poor farmers in India. *Journal of International Development*, 23(1), 103–118.

Hughes, K. D., Jennings, J. E., Brush, C., Carter, S. and Welter, F. (2012). Extending women's entrepreneurship research in new directions. *Entrepreneurship Theory and Practice*, 36(3), 429–442.

IDE and Wageningen-University (2011). Gender differentiated impact of low cost irrigation technologies. IDRC Program on 'Gender and Innovation – Understanding their mutual influence and impacts'. Canada: IDRC.

IEWS and BZU (2011). Gender, innovation and water. IDRC Program on 'Gender and Innovation – Understanding their mutual influence and impacts'. Canada: IDRC.

ILO (2002). Women and men in the informal economy: a statistical picture. Geneva: ILO.

International-Potato-Centre-(CIP). (2011). Improving innovation promoting methodologies by including gender perspective to foster women's participation in decision making processes. IDRC Program on 'Gender and Innovation – Understanding their mutual influence and impacts'. Canada: IDRC.

Kabir, M., Hou, X., Akther, R., Wang, J. and Wang, L. (2012). Impact of small entrepreneurship on sustainable livelihood assets of rural poor women in Bangladesh. *International Journal of Economics and Finance*, 4(3), 265–280.

Kotler, P., Roberto, N. and Leisner, T. (2006). Alleviating poverty: a macro/micro marketing perspective. *Journal of Macromarketing*, 26(2), 233–239.

LEAD. (2011). Entrepreneurship and skills development through school based enterprises: has it worked for women? IDRC Program on 'Gender and Innovation – Understanding their mutual influence and impacts'. Canada: IDRC.

Maiti, D. and Sen, K. (2010). The informal sector in India: a means of exploitation or accumulation? *Journal of South Asian Development*, 5(1), 1–13.

Mayoux, L. and Chambers, R. (2005). Reversing the paradigm: quantification, participatory methods and pro-poor impact assessment. *Journal of International Development*, 17(2), 271–298.

McDade, B. E. and Spring, A. (2005). The 'new generation of African entrepreneurs': networking to change the climate for business and private sector-led development. *Entrepreneurship and Regional Development*, 17(1), 17–42.

Mungai, E. N. and Ogot, M. (2012). Gender, culture and entrepreneurship in Kenya. *International Business Research*, 5(5), 175–183.

National Council for Science and Technology Policy Vietnam (2011). The involvement and the role of women in technology governance and policy process in Vietnam. IDRC Program on 'Gender and Innovation – Understanding their mutual influence and impacts'.

Ndhlovu, T. P. and Spring, A. (2009). South African women in business and management: transformation in progress. *Journal of African Business*, 10(1), 31–49.

OECD. (2012). Gender equality in education, employment and entrepreneurship: final report on the Meeting of the OECD Council at Ministerial Level, Paris.

Otoo, M., Fulton, J., Germaine, I. and Lowenberg-Deboer, J. (2011). Women's entrepreneurship in West Africa: the Cowpea Street food sector in Niger and Ghana. *Journal of Developmental Entrepreneurship*, 16(1), 37–63.

Prahalad, C. K. (2012). Bottom of the pyramid as a source of breakthrough innovations. *Journal of Product Innovation Management*, 29(1), 6–12.

Prahalad, C. K. (2005). *The Fortune at the bottom of the pyramid: A mirage*. London: Pearson Education.

Prahalad, C. K. and Hart, S. (2002). The fortune at the bottom of the pyramid, *strategy+business*, 26(1), 54–67.

Raina, R. S. (2006). Development and diffusion of energy efficient devices – lessons for pro-poor innovation from TIDE. Innovation systems for Competitiveness and Shared Prosperity in Developing Countries. Trivandrum, Kerala: Centre for Development Studies.

Rashid, A. T. (2010). Development through social entrepreneurship: Perspectives and evidence from Bangladesh. *Canadian Journal of Development Studies/Revue canadienne d'études du développement*, 30(3), 441–455.

Ray, D. (1998). *Development economics*. Princeton, NJ: Princeton University Press.

Rolfe, R., Woodward, D., Ligthelm, A. and Guimarães, P. (2010). The viability of informal micro-enterprise in South Africa. Conference on Entrepreneurship in Africa: Whitman School of Management, Syracuse University, Syracuse, New York, available at http://whitman.syr.edu/ABP/Conference/Papers/The%20Viability%20of%20Informal%20Micro-Enterprise%20in%20South%20Africa.pdf (accessed on 17 March 2011).

Roomi, M. A. and Harrison, P. (2008). Training needs for women-owned SMEs in England. *Education+Training*, 50(8–9), 687–696.

Rutashobya, L. K., Allan, I. S. and Nilsson, K. (2009). Gender, social networks, and entrepreneurial outcomes in Tanzania. *Journal of African Business*, 10(1), 67–83.

Sadreghazi, S. and Duysters, G. 2009. Serving low-income markets: rethinking multinational corporations' strategies. In: Dolfsma, W., Duysters, G. and Costa, I. (eds.) *Multinationals and emerging economies*. Cheltenham: Edward Elgar Publishing House.

Safa, H. I. (1995). *The myth of the male breadwinner: women and industrialization in the Caribbean*. Boulder, CO: Westview Press.

Samson, A. E. S. (2006). Gender and science, technology and innovation. Commissioned Paper for IDRC. Canada: IDRC.

Schneider, N. (2002). Size and measurement of the informal economy in 110 countries around the world. Doing Business Project. Washington, DC: World Bank.

Scott, L., Dolan, C., Johnstone-Louis, M., Sugden, K. and Wu, M. (2012). Enterprise and inequality: a study of Avon in South Africa. *Entrepreneurship Theory and Practice*, 36(3), 543–568.

Spring, A. (2009). African women in the entrepreneurial landscape: reconsidering the formal and informal sectors. *Journal of African Business*, 10(1), 11–30.

Srinivas, S. and Sutz, J. (2008). Developing countries and innovation: searching for a new analytical approach. *Technology in Society*, 30(2), 129–140.

Sullivan, D. M. and Meek, W. R. (2012). Gender and entrepreneurship: a review and process model. *Journal of Managerial Psychology*, 27(5), 428–458.

Szerb, L., Rappai, G., Makra, Z. and Terjesen, S. (2007). Informal investment in transition economies: individual characteristics and clusters. *Small Business Economics*, 28(2–3), 257–271.

Todaro, M. P. (1994). *Economic development* (fifth edition), White Plains, NY: Longman.

UIRI. (2011). Traditional science, technology and innovation systems in the context of a modern incubator research and development agency. IDRC Program on Gender and Innovation – Understanding their mutual influence and impacts. Canada: IDRC.

UNDP. (2008). Creating value for all: strategies for doing business with the poor. New York: United Nations Development Programme.

Van Birgelen, M., De Ruyter, K. and Wetzels, M. (2001). Conceptualizing and isolating cultural differences in performance data in international high-tech industrial markets. *Industrial Marketing Management*, 30(1), 23–35.

Vijayshree, P. and Hema, B. (2011). A study on problems and prospects of women entrepreneurs in informal market in Chennai. *International Journal of Business Economics and Management Research*, 2(5), 182–192.

Westermann, O., Ashby, J. and Pretty, J. (2005). Gender and social capital: the importance of gender differences for the maturity and effectiveness of natural resource management groups. *World Development*, 33(11), 1783–1799.

Williams, C. C. and Gurtoo, A. (2011). Evaluating women entrepreneurs in the informal sector: some evidence from India. *Journal of Developmental Entrepreneurship*, 16(3), 351–369.

Williams, C. C. and Round, J. (2009). Explaining participation in off-the-books entrepreneurship in Ukraine: a gendered evaluation. *International Entrepreneurship and Management Journal*, 5(4), 497–513.

World Bank (2013). Concept of Informal Sector. Informal Labour Markets in Transition Economies, available at http://lnweb90.worldbank.org/eca/eca.nsf/Sectors/ECSPE/2E4EDE543787A0C085256A940073F4E4? (accessed on 19 March 2013).

Yueh, L. (2009). China's entrepreneurs. *World Development*, 37, 778–786.

24

THE DYNAMICS OF WOMEN'S ENTREPRENEURSHIP IN IRAN

Leyla Sarfaraz and Nezameddin Faghih

Introduction

Entrepreneurship has received particular attention across many nations because of the role it can play in improving economic development and growth of countries. Besides the positive macro-economic impact of entrepreneurship, including job creation and its contributions to economic development and growth, the effect of entrepreneurship on the quality of life of individuals and so, on the well-being of the society, is also an important subject to be addressed. Hence, it seems that the importance of entrepreneurship is already clear to the world both in developed and developing economies. Entrepreneurs can play a major role in economic growth by being dynamic and innovative, identifying opportunities and putting useful ideas into practice. Entrepreneurs enjoy the ability to use resources more efficiently and more effectively. Fostering entrepreneurship and creating a friendly business environment in developing economies can encourage many potential individuals, such as the huge youth population, to be involved in entrepreneurship and reduce the possible social tension caused by poverty and unemployment.

The promotion of female entrepreneurship in these countries may also lower the unemployment rate among young women and young educated women in particular. The socio-economic participation of women at the international, regional, national and local levels means using significant potential resources more effectively. Women as potential untapped resources can turn into entrepreneurs in a friendly business environment. Indeed, entrepreneurship may be considered as one of the key vehicles of economic development that can involve women. More women entrepreneurs increase economic diversity (Verheul et al., 2004). While the number of women entrepreneurs is increasing rapidly in many developed and developing economies, female entrepreneurship in the Middle East and North Africa (MENA) region is lower than in any other regions across the world (Kelley et al., 2011). Within this region, women's entrepreneurship rate in Iran is ranked the lowest in 2010 (Zali and Razavi, 2010), although in recent years it has increased from 4.1 per cent in 2010 to 9.9 per cent in 2014.

Developing women's entrepreneurship can not only empower women but also prevent the transmission of poverty from one generation to the next in the long run. For women in less developed countries, especially those who are faced with poverty, entrepreneurship could be a practical solution to survive. To achieve this, the effective cooperation among the government, NGOs and the private sector is essential. Hence, providing an appropriate entrepreneurial ecosystem for women's economic and social participation in entrepreneurship is a crucial issue. Moreover, economic development cannot be achieved without the active participation of women. Scholars agree that women can play a key role in fostering entrepreneurship. The share of women's contribution to economic and social development depends on the promotion of gender equality and the level of support from institutions. Although women constitute about 50 per cent of the world population, compared with men, they have less opportunity to control their lives and make decisions (Revenga and Sudhir, 2012).

All countries consider entrepreneurial promotion as a crucial policy for sustained employ-ment creation, as well as innovation in products, production processes and organizations (OECD, 2012). According to Schumpeter (1959), the entrepreneurial process is a major factor in economic development and entrepreneurs are a key to economic growth. Countries with high total entrepreneurial activity rates are also associated with high female entrepre-neurial activity rates (Verheul et al., 2004). The number of female entrepreneurs across the world has been gradually growing in the recent years; researchers and policy makers have been paying more attention to female entrepreneurship (Nedelcheva, 2012). Despite the efforts made by some international organizations, such as the United Nations and the World Bank, to bridge the gender gap in access to opportunities, gender inequalities are still widely prevalent and women are deprived of having equal rights with men (Sarfaraz and Faghih, 2011). Treating women as a second-rate gender means ignoring and underestimating huge potential human resources. In spite of the growing number of female entrepreneurs, the share of female entrepreneurship is still significantly low (Minniti and Arenius, 2003). In less developed countries with a high female unemployment rate and for those women who are members of female-headed households and need to work at home, entrepreneurship can be a practical solution to earn income and alleviate poverty (Sarfaraz et al., 2013). Entrepreneurship often gives women the flexibility to handle their domestic responsibilities at home, while also providing financial support for their family (Bertaux and Crable, 2007). Women's involvement in entrepreneurial activity varies greatly across the nations and regions. While in MENA only about one-third of the entrepreneurs who start and own new enterprises are members of women, in general, early-stage women entrepreneurs constitute nearly half of the entrepreneurs (Kelley et al., 2013). Although gender inequality exists in entrepreneurship in general, there are some economies at different levels of economic development like Brazil, Indonesia, Philippines, Thailand, Russia and Switzerland where women and men have a similar proportion of entrepreneurship (Kelley et al., 2013). The highest gender inequality and the highest gender equality in early-stage entrepreneurial activity are observed in devel-oping regions. The Middle East and Mid-Asia show the highest gender inequality while Sub-Saharan Africa and Developing Asia exhibit the highest gender equality in entrepre-neurial activity (Kelley et al., 2013). Gender equality is expected to increase the support for female entrepreneurship (Baughn et al., 2006).

Women's entrepreneurship has been recognized as an important unexploited source of economic growth in the last decade (Georgeta, 2012). According to the Global Entrepreneurship Monitor (GEM) Women's Report 2012, an estimated 126 million women were starting or running new businesses and an estimated 98 million were running established businesses. Recognizing the factors affecting female entrepreneurship requires knowl-edge and understanding of women's entrepreneurship and its relationship with economic development. 'Although it is widely acknowledged that entrepreneurship is an important force shaping the changes in the economic landscape, our understanding of the relation-ship between entrepreneurship and development is still far from complete' (Bosma et al., 2009: 2). Some consistent cross-national measurements of entrepreneurial activity, provided separately for men and women by GEM, have paved the way for research and compar-ative studies across countries. This can help scholars and policy makers gain knowledge on entrepreneurship by gender and can provide a framework for the study of women's entrepreneurship.

Literature review

There have been relatively few studies focusing upon the determinants of female and male entrepreneurial activity at the country level (Verheul et al., 2004). Women entrepreneurs make an important contribution to the development of the world economy (Allen et al., 2007). According to the GEM Report on Women and Entrepreneurship, 'regardless of the country, men are more likely to be involved in entrepreneurial activity than women' (ibid.). Women own 13 per cent of 5,169 firms surveyed by the World Bank in MENA. Women in Iran are also less likely to become entrepreneurs than men. There are limited studies on the reasons behind the high gender gap and the low level of women's entrepreneurship in Iran. Saber (2002), Javaheri and Ghozati (2005), and Mirghafoori et al. (2010) have highlighted family barriers, educational factors, financial and socio-cultural problems as the main barriers and components affecting women entrepreneurs in Iran.

Arasti (2006) studied 105 Iranian women entrepreneurs with higher education degrees to find out the barriers to entrepreneurship in Iran. The respondents considered the follow-ing issues as the main entrepreneurial barriers to entrepreneurship: laws and regulations (83 per cent), administrative bureaucracy (81 per cent), obtaining licences (79 per cent), financing (71 per cent), gender discrimination (69 per cent), market inaccessibility (65 per cent), management and cost control (58 per cent), human resource recruitment (55 per cent), searching for suppliers (54 per cent), role conflicts (52 per cent), finding an appropriate partner (40 per cent) and managing the business (31 per cent). The author did not find the socio-cultural factor to be an important barrier for Iranian women entrepreneurs with higher education degrees while Saber (2002) considers the socio-cultural element as a con-straint to women entrepreneurial activity in the country. This may indicate that women entrepreneurs with higher education can deal more easily with the socio-cultural constraints than women in general.

Since the establishment of the School of Entrepreneurship at the University of Tehran in 2007, some graduate projects and theses have been undertaken on the area of entre-preneurship. Joining GEM in 2007 provided Iran with an opportunity to participate in a global entrepreneurship research and development programme to explore data on female and male entrepreneurial rates. The degree at which entrepreneurship affects the economy depends on numerous factors, including the motivation to start a business, gender composition, and type of entrepreneurial activity.

Gender, economic development and entrepreneurship

The concept of gender describes the socially created roles, norms, behaviour, expectations and activities attributed to women and men (Sarfaraz et al., 2013). Women's empowerment and gender equality issues have received increasing attention from international organ-izations such as the United Nations, World Bank, World Economic Forum and OECD in the last decades. The gender gap demonstrates varying dimensions of gender inequality in terms of education, economic participation and opportunity, work status, health and survival, and political participation. While the world has come a long way to close the gender gap in education, the attempt to narrow and remove gender inequality in other aspects has not been successful at least in many developing countries. Since the establishment of the Global Entrepreneurship Monitor (GEM) in 1999, and conducting the survey on both men's and women's entrepreneurship at the macro level (cross-country level), the gender gap in entrepreneurship has also been surveyed. The GEM study of 18 economies from 2002 to 2010 suggests that women's entrepreneurial activity is lower than that of their male counterparts at different stages of development (Kelley et al., 2011). However, interestingly the likelihood of women engaging in entrepreneurial activity is lower in the developed areas compared to the developing countries (ibid.). There are numerous factors that affect women's entrepreneurship. According to the GEM Survey, the highest and the lowest rate of female early-stage entrepreneurship is observed in developing countries. This result questions the relationship between the rate of entrepreneurship and the level of economic development. While the low rate of female entrepreneurs in some less-developed countries may be attributed to a significant gender gap in educational attainment and the lack of women's economic participation and opportunity, the low rate of female entrepreneurs in high-income economies may be attributed to the availability of job opportunities (Sarfaraz et al., 2013). Hence, we need to learn more about women's entrepreneurship and development. In other words, the rate of women's entrepreneurship *per se* does not indicate the degree to which entrepreneurship can improve women's well-being and prosperity and their share in the economic growth.

It seems that the motivation to start a business is a better index to measure the quality of entrepreneurship. Women in developing countries are more likely to start their business out of necessity when they have no better choice to earn income; whereas women in developed economies are more likely to start a venture because they identify an opportunity in the market. The size and the growth orientation of enterprises are also important factors in the contribution of entrepreneurs to the economic development and job creation in a country. Therefore, fostering women entrepreneurship in an economy needs to be guided towards creating high growth enterprises led by women entrepreneurs. However, this does not imply that necessity entrepreneurship in developing areas cannot improve and change the life of many women. The point is to pay enough attention to productive entrepreneurship and hence motivate women, in particular, young educated and highly skilled ones, to be engaged in high growth, innovative and knowledge-based entrepreneurship. In other words, to have a better understanding of women's entrepreneurship, we need to learn about women's entrepreneurial activity, their motivation to start a business, the scope of their business activity, and the durability and sustainability of their business.

Different aspects of gender equality improve as per capita income increases (Dollar and Gatti, 1999). The GEM survey over the years demonstrates that some countries display a widening entrepreneurial gender gap while others show a decreasing gender gap in entrepreneurship (Kelley et al., 2013). However, in general, the entrepreneurial gap between women and men decreases with the level of economic development (Kelley et al., 2011). As the economies move from the actor-driven stage to the efficiency-driven stage and to the innovation-driven stage, the gap between men and women entrepreneurs decreased from 5.2 percentage points to 4 points and to 3.4 respectively (ibid.). Overall, as economies move to a higher level of development, the rate of entrepreneurial activity decreases, regardless of gender (ibid.). 'In general, female TEA rates track similarly to that of males, albeit at lower levels' (Kelley et al., 2013, page 8). This can be explained through more availability of employment opportunities and job security in more developed economies.

There is no general prescription for female entrepreneurship across the globe. While female entrepreneurship across the world might share some common features, every country needs to be studied through its formal and informal institutions and its demographic and socio-economic context. Entrepreneurship is a complex phenomenon that requires multiple theoretical lenses to be understood (Landstrom and Lohrke, 2010). While gender equality itself does not predict the proportion of female entrepreneurs (Baughn et al., 2006), women's equal access to resources would provide them with a better chance to start ventures. Gender equality implies equal access to opportunities and rights. Hence, in a gender-neutral society, gender would be expected not to be an issue for the women who have the tendency to become an entrepreneur. In most developing countries where gender disparity is an issue, developing female entrepreneurship can be a solution to the high rate of female unemployment. The high unemployment rate among women and educated women with a higher degree is widely observed in Iran and the MENA region. The unemployment rate among university-educated women in Iran and the United Arab Emirates is nearly three times higher than that of university-educated men, and is eight times higher in Saudi Arabia and more than three times higher in Turkey (Roudi, 2011).

Gender gap in Iran

Iran ranked 137th out of 142 countries in the 2014 Gender Gap Index, calculated by the World Economic Forum (WEF). Iran's scores on the four sub-indexes measured by the WEF Gender Gap Index including economic participation and opportunity, educational attainment, health and survival, and political empowerment in 2014 were 0.359, 0.957, 0.971 and 0.037 respectively (Hausmann, 2014). The figures imply that while Iran has successfully bridged the gender gap in educational attainment, as well as in health and survival, it has a long way to go to remove the gender disparity in economic participation and political empowerment. Our main concern here is equality in economic participation.

Table 24.1 shows Iran's gender gap in economic participation for the period 2006 to 2014. This reveals that the trend of the gender disparity score in economic participation for 2006–2014 in Iran decreased sharply in 2008 and 2011. It also displays that the score of economic participation in 2014 has almost been the same as its score in 2006, whereas the country's ranking has decreased from 108 (out of 115 countries) in 2006 to 137 (out of 142 countries) in 2014. The decrease in the ranking of a country can be attributed to the

Table 24.1 Gender Gap Scores and Ranks in Iran in the Period 2006 to 2014

	2006	*2007*	*2008*	*2009*	*2010*	*2011*	*2012*	*2013*	*2014*
Overall Score	0.580	0.590	0.602	0.584	0.593	0.589	0.593	0.584	0.581
Economic Participation Score	0.359	0.395	0.449	0.377	0.426	0.444	0.412	0.365	0.359
Rank	108	118	116	128	123	125	127	130	137
	(115)★	(128)	(130)	(134)	(134)	(135)	(135)	(136)	(142)

Data extracted from the Global Gender Gap Report (Haussmann, 2014).
★The numbers in parentheses show the number of countries that participated in the Gender Gap Survey.

stronger performance of other comparator countries or the weaker performance of the country under consideration.

Women's entrepreneurial activity

GEM measures entrepreneurial activity in terms of early-stage entrepreneurial activity (TEA) and established business owners. The TEA rate is the central measure of the GEM survey (Xavier et al., 2013). TEA displays the participation rate of the population aged 18–64 who have started a new business or been running an enterprise for less than 42 months, whereas those entrepreneurs who have run businesses for more than 42 months are recognized as established business owners.

TEA rates represent the presence of new and recent enterprises. Figure 24.1 shows the activity results of women's and men's entrepreneurship in Iran since the time Iran first participated in the GEM Survey in 2008. The lowest rate of female TEA in Iran was in 2010 and the highest rate was observed in 2014. Even though the gender gap among entrepreneurs in Iran is still significant, the gap started narrowing in 2013. Figure 24.2 displays that the

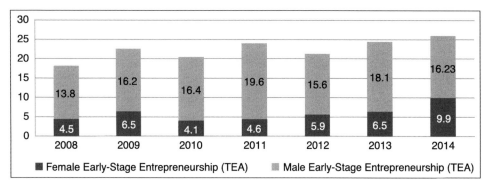

Figure 24.1   Female and Male Early-Stage Entrepreneurship (TEA) in Iran, 2008–2014

Data extracted from GEM Iran (Zali and Razavi, 2014).

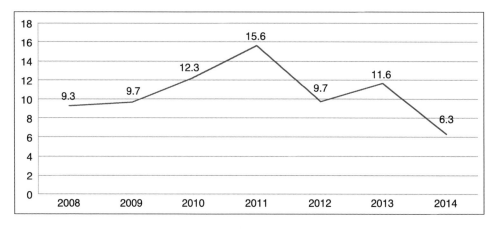

Figure 24.2   Percentile Point Gap Between Women and Men TEA Rates in Iran, 2008–2014

Data extracted from GEM Iran (Zali and Razavi, 2014).

percentile point gap between women and men TEA rates in 2011 was about two and a half times more than that of 2014. Several factors could explain the increase in women's entrepreneurship and hence the reasons for the narrowing of the gender gap in entrepreneurship in the country. Since Iran's Third Economic Development Plans (2000–2004), the concepts of entrepreneurship and women's entrepreneurship have been approached by policy makers in the country. In spite of assigning a special section to 'Women and Economy' in the plans, in practice women in Iran are well below where they should be in terms of economic participation and entrepreneurship. With the help of the government and the awareness of some pioneering women entrepreneurs, NGO's for women and a women's network in entrepreneurship were created in recent years. Moreover, the establishment of the Faculty of Entrepreneurship at the University of Tehran (UT) in 2007 as the first Faculty of entrepreneurship (especially with a Ph.D. programme) in the MENA region and educating women and men in the field of entrepreneurship has promoted entrepreneurship in the country. Currently, women constitute 45.5 per cent of the students who are studying in the field of entrepreneurship at UT; this is promising for the future of women's entrepreneurship.

Established business rates may indicate the sustainability of firms and the low rate of TEA may show a low level of dynamism, particularly when combined with a high rate of established business ownership. Table 24.2 shows that for all the years under study, men have been more likely to be established business-owners than women in Iran.

Countries in the MENA region show lower rates of TEA and established business than average (Kelley et al., 2011). Entrepreneurs are more likely to be prone to failure in developing countries compared with developed economies. GEM tracks the percentage of the adult population who are involved in early-stage entrepreneurial activity and also business-owners who decide to discontinue their businesses.

Female business discontinuance is very low in Iran compared with their male counterparts and the rates in other regions (Table 24.3). This may indicate that when women in Iran decide to start a business, they are relatively well planned. It should also be noted that the

Table 24.2 Female and Male Established Business Owners in Iran, 2008–2014

	2008	*2009*	*2010*	*2011*	*2012*	*2013*	*2014*
Female Established Business Owners	2.2	2.0	3.5	2.6	3.0	3.2	7.78
Male Established Business Owners	11.3	9.8	16.5	15.6	15.9	17.9	10.97

Data extracted from GEM Iran (Zali and Razavi, 2014)

Table 24.3 Business Discontinuance in Iran and Different Regional Averages

	Iran	*Sub-Saharan Africa*	*MENA/ Mid Asia*	*Latin America/ Caribbean*	*Europe: Developing*	*Europe: Developed*	*Asia: Developed*	*Asia: Developing*
Female Business Discontinuance	1	14	10	5	5	3	3	2
Male Business Discontinuance	7	11	10	6	5	5	4	3

Data extracted from GEM Women Report (Kelley et al., 2013) and GEM Iran (Zali and Razavi, 2012).

Table 24.4 Reasons for Business Discontinuance in Iran

Retirement	Opportunity to sell	Exit was planned in advance	Another business opportunity	An incident	Personal reasons	Problems getting finance	Business not profitable
1.46	1.76	3.75	3.75	4.41	15.69	19.46	30.61

Data extracted from GEM Iran (Zali and Razavi, 2010).

early-stage rate of entrepreneurial activity among women in Iran is low and as the GEM survey shows, a lower rate of TEA results in a lower rate of business discontinuance. As a component of entrepreneurial dynamism in an economy, business discontinuance needs to be studied along with TEA and established business rates. Discontinuance may occur for positive or negative reasons.

Some entrepreneurs close their business to open a new one while others may have to shut down their business because they cannot afford to continue for variety of reasons. Table 24.4 displays the reasons for business discontinuance in Iran.

Women's motivation to start a business in Iran

Scholars of entrepreneurship in a variety of disciplines agree that age, work status, education, income and perceptions are all significant factors in a person's decision to start a business (Allen et al., 2007). Galard (2007) identifies financial needs, job satisfaction, achievement of authority and reputation in the society, as the main motivations and driving forces for women entrepreneurs to start a business in Iran. She considers job satisfaction as the most effective one in the startup process. Arasti (2006) found that personal satisfaction (90 per cent), the need to have power (62 per cent), financial needs (54 per cent), and security needs (51 per cent) were the main motivations for women entrepreneurs with higher education to start their own business in Iran.

Women, the same as men, are motivated to start an enterprise either out of necessity or opportunity. The importance of identifying the number of necessity- versus opportunity-motivated entrepreneurs is because of the role played by necessity- and opportunity-driven entrepreneurs in economic development. Opportunity-driven entrepreneurs are generators of new ideas and innovation, and are more likely to contribute to economic growth and poverty reduction by providing jobs to a populace. Necessity-driven entrepreneurs are usually self-employed and start their enterprise in order to have a source of income. Higher rates of opportunity-based entrepreneurship are more likely to be observed as economies develop. For the countries that choose to develop entrepreneurship as a policy for economic development, it is important to improve entrepreneurship of the opportunity-motivated variety. However, for some countries like Iran, where the number of the unemployed female heads of households is increasing, it is also important to empower and enable those needy women who have no job to start and run their business. The more recent statistics released by the Iranian authorities show that the rate of female-headed households has almost doubled from 6.5 per cent in 2006 to 12 per cent in 2011 (Mehr News, 2014). The number of female-headed households has increased from 1.641 million in 2006 to 2.5 million in 2011 (Seddighin, 2014). The rate of unemployment among female-headed households is 88 per cent and only 12 per cent of them were reported to have jobs (Mehr News, 2014). Facilitating

Table 24.5 Necessity-driven and Opportunity-driven Women Entrepreneurs in Iran, 2008–2014

	2008	2009	2010	2011	2012	2013	2014
Necessity-Driven Entrepreneurs (NE)	1.44	1.88	1.77	1.14	2.28	2.34	3.76
Opportunity-Driven Entrepreneurs (OE)	3.07	1.98	2.14	2.82	3.72	3.6	6.6
OE/NE	2.13	1.05	1.35	2.47	1.33	1.5	1.75

Data extracted from GEM Iran (Zali and Razavi, 2014).

necessity entrepreneurship through a series of policies can encourage self-employment for these women and reduce the social problems in the country. Personal and occupational awareness and entrepreneurship training programmes affect the self-esteem and entrepreneurial trends of female heads of households (Tabatabaei and Abedi, 2004).

Table 24.5 shows the proportion of women's entrepreneurial activity that is necessity-driven and opportunity-driven in Iran during 2008–2014. The motivation to start a business out of opportunity among women in Iran has doubled in 2014 compared to 2008. Table 24.5 demonstrates that the tendency towards necessity entrepreneurship among women in Iran has increased during 2011 to 2014. Hence, in spite of the significantly increasing rate of the women who find opportunities to start a business in 2014 compared with 2008, the ratio of women entrepreneurs with an opportunity motivation to women entrepreneurs with a necessity motivation (Table 24.5) has decreased from 2.13 in 2008 to 1.75 in 2014. Figure 24.3 shows that for all the years of study, women in Iran have been more likely to be opportunity-driven entrepreneurs rather than necessity-driven entrepreneurs.

The increase in the rate of necessity-based women entrepreneurs in 2012, 2013 and 2014 (Table 24.5) demonstrates more pressure on women to find a source of income for survival in Iran. While the motivation to find opportunities for Iranian women decreased in 2009 and 2013, in all the years under study, women in Iran were more likely to start their business out of opportunity rather than necessity. This indicates that women in Iran are more likely to be pulled rather than pushed into starting a venture. While in general women are more likely to be pushed into entrepreneurial activity than men, in Iran, England, India and Italy men are more likely to be necessity entrepreneurs than women (Zali et al., 2014). In some countries like Australia, Austria, Denmark, Thailand, Kazakhstan, Netherlands, Singapore,

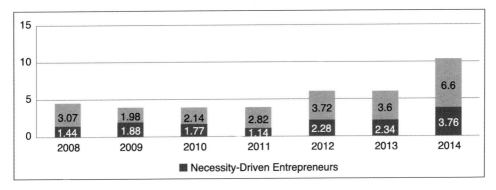

Figure 24.3   Necessity-Driven and Opportunity-Driven Women Entrepreneurs in Iran, 2008–2014

Data extracted from GEM Iran (Zali and Razavi, 2014)

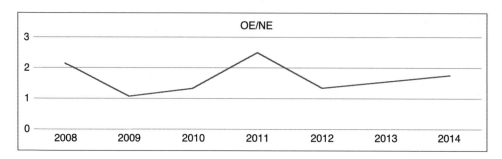

Figure 24.4 Ratio of Opportunity-Driven Women Entrepreneurs (OE) to Necessity-Driven Women Entrepreneurs (NE) in Iran, 2008–2014

Data extracted from GEM Iran (Zali and Razavi, 2014).

Luxembourg and South Africa, men and women have a balanced share of necessity-driven early-stage entrepreneurial activity.

The averages taken from the necessity-driven and opportunity-driven women entrepreneurs in Table 24.5 show that for the period 2008–2014, on average 3.4 per cent of women in Iran were opportunity-driven entrepreneurs and 2.1 per cent of women (on average) were pushed into starting a business.

Figure 24.4 shows the ratio of opportunity-driven women entrepreneurs (OE) to necessity-driven women entrepreneurs (NE) in Iran during 2008–2014. While the increase in the motivation of women to start their business out of necessity led to the decrease of the OE/NE ratio in the years of 2009 and 2011, the increase in the motivation of entrepreneurs to recognize opportunity resulted in the rise of the OE/NE ratio from 2012 to 2014 (Figure 24.4). The significant increase in the women's early-stage entrepreneurship accompanied by the high opportunity-driven women entrepreneurship in 2014 may exhibit a promising future for women entrepreneurship in Iran.

Conclusions

Although a gender gap exists and is significant in women's entrepreneurial activities in Iran, the gap has started narrowing since 2013. While Iran has successfully bridged the gender gap in educational attainment, as well as in health and survival, it has a long way to go to remove the gender disparity in economic participation and political empowerment. Promoting women's participation in various aspects of life can result in a more appropriate entrepreneurial environment for the Iranian women. Even though the GEM survey in Iran shows that Iran has not been successful in providing an appropriate climate for women's entrepreneurial activities, the most recent data published by GEM in 2014 represents a significant improvement in women's entrepreneurship in the country. Fostering women's entrepreneurship in Iran may be attributed to the efforts of women entrepreneurs in recent years to prove their competency and the policy of the government to encourage women's networking in the country. It seems that the educated younger generation does not consider social factors as a key barrier to women's entrepreneurship; this may mean that social change for a better social entrepreneurial environment should be expected in the future. Moreover, the large number of female students at the Faculty of Entrepreneurship at the University of Tehran suggests a promising future for women's entrepreneurship in Iran.

References

Allen, E., Langowitz, N., and Minniti, M. (2007). *Global Entrepreneurship Monitor, 2006, report on women and entrepreneurship*, Babson College, The Center for Women's Leadership at Babson College, and London Business School.

Arasti, Z. (2006). Iranian women entrepreneurs. *Women Research*, 1&2, Spring and Summer, 93–119.

Baughn, C. C., Chua, B. L., and Neupert, K. E. (2006). The normative context for women's participation in entrepreneurship: a multicounty study. *Entrepreneurship Theory and Practice*, 30(5), 687–708.

Bertaux, N., and Crable, E. (2007). Learning about women, economic development, entrepreneurship and the environment in India: A case study. *Journal of Developmental Entrepreneurship*, 12(4), 467–478.

Bosma, N., Acs, Z. J., Autio, E., Coduras, A., and Levie, J. (2009). *Global Entrepreneurship Monitor, 2008 executive report*, Babson College, Universidad Del Desarrollo, London Business School.

Dollar, D., and Gatti, R. (1999). *Gender inequality, income, and growth: are good times good for women?* Gender and Development Working Papers, No. 1. Washington. DC: The World Bank.

Galard, P. (2007). Characteristics, motivations and goals of Iranian women entrepreneurs. *Iran Journal of Trade Studies*, 11(44), 267–295.

Georgeta, I. (2012). Women entrepreneurship in the current international business environment. *Cogito-Multidisciplinary Research Journal*, 1(4), 122–131.

Haussmann, R. (2014*). Gender gap report 2014*, Geneva: World Economic Forum.

Javaheri, F. and Ghozati, S. (2004). Barriers to women's entrepreneurship; Influence of gender inequality on women entrepreneurship in Iran. *Journal of Sociology*, 5(2), 161-178.

Kelley, D. J., Brush, C. G., Greene, P. G. and Litovsky, Y. (2013). *The global Entrepreneurship Monitor report on women's entrepreneurship 2012*. Boston: The Center for Women's Leadership at Babson College and London Business School.

Kelley, D. J., Brush, C. G., Greene, P. G. and Litovsky, Y. (2011). *Global Entrepreneurship Monitor: 2010 women's report*. Boston: The Center for Women's Leadership at Babson College and London Business School.

Landstrom, H. and Lohrke, F. (Eds.) (2010). *Historical foundations of entrepreneurship research*, Cheltenham, UK and Northampton, MA: Edward Elgar Publishing.

Mehr News (2014). Available at http://www.mehrnews.com/news/2210299 (accessed on 5 April 2015).

Minniti, M., and Arenius, P. (2003). Women in entrepreneurship. In *The entrepreneurial advantage of nations: First annual global entrepreneurship symposium* (Vol. 29). New York: United Nations Headquarters.

Mirghafoori, H., Tooranloo, H., and Taheridemneh, M. (2010). Investigating the barriers of women's entrepreneurship in Iran society. *Journal of Management Transformation*, 2(1), 47–64.

Nedelcheva, S. (2012). Female entrepreneurship in Denmark. M.Sc. Thesis, in International Business, Business and Social Sciences, Aarhus University, Denmark.

OECD Week (2012). Gender equality in education, employment and entrepreneurship: Final Report to the MCM 2012, Meeting of the OECD Council at Ministerial Level, Paris, 23–24 May 2012.

Revenga, A., and Sudhir, S. (2012). Empowering women is smart economics. *Finance and Development*, 49(1), 40.

Roudi, F. (2011). Youth Population and Employment in the Middle East and North Africa: Opportunity or Challenge? Population Reference Bureau. UN/POP/EGM-AYD/2011/06, United Nations Expert Group Meeting On Adolescents, Youth and Development Population Division Department Of Economic And Social Affairs, United Nations.

Saber, F. (2002). *Ways to develop women entrepreneurship in Iran*. Tehran: Women Studies Publishers.

Sarfaraz, L., and Faghih, N. (2011). Women's entrepreneurship in Iran: A GEM based-data evidence. *Journal of Global Entrepreneurship Research*, 1(1), 45–57.

Sarfaraz, L., Mian, S., and Karadeniz, E. E. (2013). Female entrepreneurship, internationalization and trade liberalization: the case of Iran, Pakistan, and Turkey, Proceedings of the 16th Annual McGill International Entrepreneurship Conference, August 1st–5th.

Schumpeter, J. A. (1959). *The theory of economic development*. Cambridge, MA: Harvard University Press.

Seddighin. (2014). Empowering female-headed households, available at http://www.seddighin.com/fapage.aspx?563 (accessed on 10 February 2015).

Tabatabaei, S. and Abedi, Y. (2004). Iranian women's empowerment through promoting awareness and developing entrepreneurship. Department of Psychology, Al-Zahra University, Deputy of Employment, Ministry of Labor and Social Affairs, Tehran. Retrieved from http://info.worldbank. org/etools/mdfdb/doc/WP_ TESEV4.pdf (accessed on 12 March 2015).

Verheul, I., Stel, A.V., and Thurik, R. (2004). Explaining female and male entrepreneurship across 29 countries. SCALES-series report on ongoing research at EIM Business and Policy Research, Netherlands' Ministry of Economic Affairs.

Xavier, S. R., Kelley, D., Kew, J., Herrington, M., and Vorderwülbecke, A. (2013). *Global Entrepreneurship Monitor (GEM) 2012 global report*. London: GERA/GEM.

Zali, M. R. and Razavi, S. M. (2010). *GEM-Iran summary 2010 report*, the University of Tehran, Iran.

Zali, M. R. and Razavi, S. M. (2012). *GEM-Iran summary 2012 report*, the University of Tehran, Iran.

Zali, M. R. and Razavi, S. M. (2014). *GEM-Iran summary 2014 report*, the University of Tehran, Iran.

PART IV

Informal sector entrepreneurship

25

INFORMAL ENTREPRENEURSHIP IN DEVELOPING COUNTRIES

An introductory overview

Colin C. Williams and Anjula Gurtoo

Introduction

Part IV of this handbook addresses the topic of entrepreneurship in the informal sector, or what is often shortened to informal entrepreneurship. This refers to those starting up and/ or owning and managing a business venture which does not register with and/or declare some or all of their production and/or sales to the authorities for tax, benefit, and/or labour law purposes when they should do so (Ketchen et al., 2014; Siqueira et al., 2014; Williams and Martinez, 2014a). In this introductory overview to this new sub-discipline of entre-preneurship scholarship, the aim is to outline the size of this phenomenon along with its nature and motives in developing countries, how there has been steady shift from negative to positive representations of informal entrepreneurship, and a brief review of how policy approaches toward this type of entrepreneurial endeavor have consequently slowly begun to move away from eradicating it and toward harnessing entrepreneurship in the informal sector. The final section of this overview will then introduce each of the chapters and the important contributions they make to advancing understanding of informal entrepreneurship.

Given that entrepreneurship has been a problematic and elusive concept for a long time and, as Anderson and Starnawska (2008: 222) state, 'entrepreneurship means different things to different people', a working definition is here employed appropriate to the task at hand. Hence, an entrepreneur is defined as somebody who is actively involved in starting a business or is the owner/manager of a business (Harding et al., 2006; Reynolds et al., 2002), whilst the informal economy is defined as those activities where monetary transactions are not declared to the state for tax, social security, or labour law purposes but which are legal in all other respects (e.g., Williams, 2006; Williams and Windebank, 1998). The findings suggest that informal entrepreneurs can be classified as those owners/managers who are involved in the starting a new for-profit business and not registered with the state authorities for tax, social security, and labour law purposes, but are legal in all other aspects.

Informal entrepreneurship: size, character, and depictions

For much of the twentieth century, informal entrepreneurship in developing countries, akin to the informal sector in general, was largely viewed as unimportant and unworthy of scholarly attention. This is because a modernization theory dominated that viewed informal endeavor as some minor and declining remnant of an earlier pre-capitalist mode of production which would naturally and inevitably disappear with economic advancement and modernization. As such, the continuing persistence of informality in developing countries was simply a signal of their 'underdevelopment' and 'backwardness' (Geertz, 1963; Gilbert, 1998; Lewis, 1959). It was unworthy of scholarly attention because all countries were viewed as on a universal and linear trajectory toward formalization.

Over the past few decades however, it has been widely recognized that the informal sector in general and informal entrepreneurship in particular, is not only an extensive but also persistent feature of the developing world. The informal sector has remained a sizable and steadfast phenomenon in the developing world which is equivalent to around 40–60 percent of GDP (Schneider and Williams, 2013). Moreover, the proportion of the global workforce to have their main employment in the informal sector is 60 percent and this has remained fairly constant for several decades (Jütting and Laiglesia, 2009). The case with the more particular phenomenon of informal entrepreneurship is the same. Of the 1.8 billion whose main employment is in the informal economy, the majority work on a self-employed basis: 70 percent of all informal workers in sub-Saharan Africa, 62 percent in North Africa, 60 percent in Latin America, 59 percent in Asia (ILO, 2002). There are no signs, moreover, of any significant reduction over time either in the proportion employed in the informal sector in general or informal entrepreneurship more particularly. Little evidence therefore exists to support the modernization thesis that there is a universal natural and inevitable trajectory towards formalization. Instead, the stark reality over the past few decades is that although some developing countries may have undergone a slow process of formalization, others have moved in the opposite direction and witnessed further informalization, whilst many others have simply stagnated and neither undergone a process of formalization nor informalization. The result is that much of the developing world is characterized by what might be termed 'informally dominated' economies (Dibben and Williams, 2012) where the informal economy is not the peripheral realm persisting in a few enclaves and marginal spaces but, rather, the formal economy. Contrary to previous depictions, therefore, it is the informal economy that is extensive, persistent, and omnipresent across much of the developing world and the formal economy only exists in a few marginal enclaves and sectors.

This depiction of the dominance of the informal sector in the developing world is nowhere better seen than in the sphere of new venture formation. The emergence of informal entrepreneurship as a new sub-discipline of entrepreneurship scholarship has significantly advanced understanding of new venture creation. It has been widely recognized that many new ventures do not start up on a wholly legitimate basis but rather, that many commence operations without having all of the necessary licences and permits, or without registering and declaring their income for tax purposes, with some continuing to operate on an unregistered basis for many decades. For many years, this was recognized but widely considered relevant to only a small minority of business start-ups. In recent years however, this has been investigated and a figure has been put on how extensive this is as a phenomenon. In one recent study conducted by Autio and Fu (2015) using the Global Entrepreneurship Monitor, it has been estimated that two-thirds of businesses in developing countries are unregistered at start up. Another study by La Porta and Shleifer (2014) using World Bank Enterprise Survey data, reveals that only some 10 percent of these unregistered start-ups eventually register, some after many years of operating unregistered, and thus start to make the transition to formality. Informal entrepreneurship, therefore, is not some minor phenomenon in developing countries but rather the dominant practice.

In recent years, therefore, the emergence of this new sub-discipline of entrepreneurship scholarship has started to re-represent informal entrepreneurship. First, some commentators have sought to update the conventional modernization theory (La Porta and Shleifer, 2008, 2014). Although they now recognize the persistence and extensiveness of informal entrepreneurship, this nonetheless maintains a depiction that they are two disconnected sectors as well as a representation of informal entrepreneurship as a negative phenomenon, depicting informal entrepreneurs as uneducated people operating small unproductive enterprises in separate 'bottom of the pyramid' markets producing low-quality products for low-income consumers using little capital and adding little value (La Porta and Shleifer, 2014).

A second group of scholars adopting a structuralist perspective however, recognize that the formal and informal realms are not unconnected. Instead, the growth of informal entrepreneurship is depicted as a direct by-product and inherent feature of a deregulated open world economy where subcontracting and outsourcing have emerged as a primary means by which informal enterprises have become integrated into contemporary capitalism in order to reduce production costs (Castells and Portes, 1989; Davis, 2006; Meagher, 2010; Slavnic, 2010; Taiwo, 2013). Furthermore, the weak state involvement in social protection and economic intervention resulting from deregulation in developing countries is depicted as pushing those excluded from formal jobs and social protection into informal entrepreneurship as a survival strategy (Chen, 2012; ILO, 2014; Meagher, 2010; Taiwo, 2013).

Nevertheless, these structuralist commentators, although dissimilar to modernization theorists in that they view informal entrepreneurship as intertwined with the formal economy, are similar in the respect that they depict informal entrepreneurship as having negative impacts. Table 25.1 provides a review of these negative impacts of informal entrepreneurship that are highlighted by both modernization and structural commentators alike. Whether considering informal entrepreneurs, formal entrepreneurs, customers or governments and economies, commentators adopting modernization and structuralist perspectives highlight a range of negative impacts of informal entrepreneurship. Economies are viewed as losing 'natural' competitiveness because productive formal enterprises suffer unfair competition from unproductive informal enterprises (Leal Ordóñez, 2014; Levy, 2008; Lewis, 2004). Governments are viewed as losing both regulatory control over work conditions (ILO, 2014) and tax revenue (Bajada and Schneider, 2005), and customers as lacking legal recourse and certainty that health and safety regulations have been followed (Williams and Martinez, 2014b). Informal entrepreneurs, meanwhile, are viewed as 'necessity-driven' (Castells and Portes, 1989; Gallin, 2001), lacking access to capital, credit, and financial services (ILO, 2014), which when combined with the need to keep their business small to stay 'under the radar' of the authorities (Williams et al., 2012a), lack of advice and support (Barbour and Llanes, 2013), and an inability to secure formal intellectual property rights to process and product innovations (De Beer et al., 2013), means that they become locked in a 'poverty trap' (McKenzie and Woodruff, 2006).

In recent years however, and as Table 25.1 displays, it has been slowly recognized that informal entrepreneurship does not only produce negative impacts. Instead, commentators have begun to draw attention to some positive impacts of informal entrepreneurship. Developing economies and governments have been argued to potentially benefit from the ability of informal entrepreneurs to create jobs (Ketchen et al., 2014) and this sphere has started to be seen as a breeding ground for the micro-enterprise system (Barbour and Llanes, 2013). Formal enterprises are viewed as potentially benefiting from cheaper sources of labour and raw materials (Ketchen et al., 2014), potential formal entrepreneurs from the opportunity of using this realm as a test-bed for their business ventures (Williams and Martinez-Perez,

Table 25.1 Positive and Negative Impacts of Entrepreneurship in the Informal Sector

Negative Impacts	Positive Impacts
For informal sector entrepreneurs:	
Lack of access to credit and financial services, partly due to limited credit history.	A source of income to stay out of poverty.
Difficulty in expanding a business which cannot be openly advertised.	Flexibility in where, when and how to work (especially important for women who remain responsible for child-care).
May face higher barriers of entry to the formal market on account of an inability to provide employment history to back up their skills.	Reduces barriers to entry into work because the majority of informal work starts with close social relations.
For formal entrepreneurs:	
Results in an unfair competitive advantage for informal over formal entrepreneurs	Provides entrepreneurs with escape route from corrupt public sector officials
Results in de-regulatory cultures enticing law-abiding entrepreneurs into a 'race to the bottom' away from regulatory compliance	Provides an exit strategy in contexts where the regulatory burden stifles business development
Results in 'hyper-casualisation' as more legitimate entrepreneurs are forced into the informal economy to compete	Enables outsourcing and sub-contracting to lower production costs
For customers:	
Lack legal recourse if a poor job is done, insurance cover; guarantees in relation to the work conducted, and certainty that health and safety regulations have been followed.	A more affordable product or service can be offered
For governments and economies:	
Causes a loss of revenue for the state in terms of non-payment of taxes owed	Income from informal entrepreneurship spent in the formal economy boosts demand for formal goods and services and contributes to 'official' economic growth.
Reduces state's ability to achieve social cohesion by reducing the money available to governments to pursue social integration and mobility	'On the job' training in informal enterprises alleviates pressure on the state and its agencies during times of reduced public spending.
Leads to a loss of regulatory control over work conditions and service provision in the economy	Breeding ground for the micro-enterprise system
Such endeavor may encourage a casual attitude towards the law more widely	Test-bed for fledgling businesses

Source: derived from Llanes and Barbour (2013), Williams (2006) and Williams and Nadin (2012b).

2014a,b), and informal entrepreneurs as having this as an escape route from corrupt public sector officials and the regulatory burden in developing country contexts where this otherwise stifles business development (Puffer et al., 2010; Tonoyan et al., 2010). Customers, especially those in 'bottom of the pyramid' markets, meanwhile, are viewed as potentially benefiting from more affordable goods and services (Ketchen et al., 2014; London and Hart, 2004).

A catalyst for recognizing these more positive impacts has been the recognition that informal entrepreneurship is not always a necessity-driven endeavor, as modernization and structuralist commentators assume, but often a matter of choice (Cross, 2000; Franck, 2012; Gërxhani, 2004; Maloney, 2004; Perry and Maloney, 2007; Snyder, 2004). The resultant agency-oriented theorizations of informal entrepreneurship have been of two broad varieties. On the one hand, a group of mostly neo-liberal scholars have depicted entrepreneurs voluntarily operating informally as rational economic actors who, after weighing up the costs of informality and benefits of formality, decide not to operate in the formal economy. For these scholars, burdensome regulations, high taxes, and corruption among public sector officials lead entrepreneurs to exit the formal sector and to operate in the informal sector (Becker, 2004; De Soto, 1989, 2001; Nwabuzor, 2005). The greater prevalence of informal entrepreneurship in developing compared with developed countries is therefore due to the higher costs (e.g., time and effort to formally register, burdensome regulations, compliance costs) and lower benefits of formalization (De Soto, 2001; Maloney 2004), which commonly mean that the overall costs of formalizing do not exceed the benefits (Cross, 2000).

On the other hand, and drawing upon institutional theory (North, 1990), another agency-oriented group of scholars adopting a more 'social actor' approach, depict informal entrepreneurs as operating outside of formal institutional prescriptions but within the norms, values, and beliefs of informal institutions and thus as engaged in socially legitimate endeavor (Kistruck et al., 2015; Siqueira et al., 2014; Webb et al., 2009). Informal entrepreneurship is thus depicted as resulting from formal institutional voids, such as relatively weak legal systems and contract enforcement regimes, the absence of social protection and basic infrastructure including water, electricity, and the internet (Puffer et al., 2010; Sutter et al., 2013), and/or 'because of the incongruence between what is defined as legitimate by formal and informal institutions' (Webb et al., 2009: 495). If symmetry exists between formal and informal institutions, informal entrepreneurship only occurs unintentionally such as due to a lack of awareness of the codified laws and regulations. When the formal and informal institutions are not aligned however, the result is more informal entrepreneurship (De Castro et al., 2014; Kistruck et al., 2015; Siqueira et al., 2014; Thai and Turkina, 2014; Vu, 2014; Webb et al., 2009, 2013, 2014). Indeed, the greater the degree of asymmetry, the greater is the level of informal entrepreneurship (Williams and Shahid, 2015).

Given these re-representations of informal entrepreneurship, and especially the recognition of the more positive impacts of this endeavor, recent years have begun to witness questions being raised about the policy approach toward informal entrepreneurship that should be adopted.

Informal entrepreneurship: policy approaches

Considering the full range of possible options toward informal entrepreneurship, policy makers might either: do nothing; eradicate enterprise in the informal economy; move formal enterprises into the informal economy, or formalize enterprises in the informal economy. Here, each is reviewed in turn.

Laissez-faire

A first option is for developing countries to do nothing, or in other words, adopt a laissez-faire approach toward informal entrepreneurship. The rationales for taking no action include that it is a breeding ground for the micro-enterprise system, a seed-bed for new venture creation and test-bed for fledgling enterprises. However, the problem with this approach is that it has significant deleterious implications for formal enterprises (e.g., unfair competition), informal enterprises (e.g., pressure to enter exploitative relationships with the formal economy), customers (e.g., lack of legal recourse if a poor job is done) and governments (e.g., reduced public revenue). Until now however, no rigorous evaluations have been conducted. This is a significant gap to be filled in future studies. Despite this lack of an evidence base however, the strong consensus is that on balance, the deleterious impacts outweigh any beneficial impacts. As such, taking no action is not seen as a feasible option. Interventions are instead viewed as required. What form of intervention is therefore required?

Move formal entrepreneurship into the informal economy

A second possibility is to shift formal enterprise into the informal economy. Although not explicitly argued by any commentators, some advocate a deregulation of the formal economy to tackle informal enterprise based on the belief that informal entrepreneurship results from over-regulation of the market (De Soto, 1989, 2001). The intention is therefore to de-regulate the formal economy so that all activities take place in a manner akin to what is currently the informal economy, although they would not be engaged in informal entre-preneurship since they would be conforming to the regulations that remain. However, growing evidence suggests that decreasing the level of state intervention results not in formal-ization but quite the opposite: greater levels of informal entrepreneurship (Kus, 2010, 2014; Williams, 2013, 2014a,b). In consequence, this way forward is not perhaps viable. Indeed, few currently advocate such an option.

Eradicate informal entrepreneurship

Another option is to eradicate informal entrepreneurship. Indeed, based on the view that informal entrepreneurship has largely negative impacts, this has been conventionally the dominant approach adopted by developing countries. However, whether eradication is desirable is debatable. If informal enterprises are a breeding ground for the micro-enterprise system and a seed-bed for enterprise culture, this realm is a potential asset that needs to be harnessed (e.g., Williams, 2006; Gurtoo and William, 2009). Pursuing its eradication would therefore eliminate precisely the entrepreneurship and enterprise culture governments are seeking to foster. The resultant challenge for developing country governments is thus to 'join-up' their policy approach toward informal entrepreneurship with their agendas to foster enterprise culture and entrepreneurship in order to foster economic development and growth. Unless this is achieved, each new initiative to eradicate informal entrepreneurship will result in governments destroying precisely the entrepreneurship and enterprise culture they wish to nurture in order to pursue economic development and growth.

Formalize informal enterprise

Rather than take no action, transfer formal enterprise into the informal economy or eradicate informal entrepreneurship, a fourth and final possibility is to formalize informal entrepreneur-ship (Aliyev, 2015; Dekker et al., 2010; European Commission, 2007; Renooy et al., 2004; Small Business Council, 2004; Williams, 2006; Williams and Nadin, 2012a,b, 2013, 2014; Williams and Renooy, 2013).

So far as formal enterprises are concerned, this would stop the unfair competitive advantage of informal enterprises over those playing by the rules (Khan and Quaddus, 2015). It would also enable a 'high road' rather than 'low road' approach by shifting toward greater regulatory standards on working conditions such as health and safety and labour standards (Grabiner,

2000; Renooy et al., 2004; Williams and Windebank, 1998). Meanwhile, for informal enterprises, the key benefits are that they escape the pressure to enter exploitative relationships with the formal economy (Gallin, 2001; Williams and Windebank, 1998) and achieve the same levels of legal protection as formal enterprises (Boels, 2014; Bruns et al., 2011; ILO, 2014; Morris and Polese, 2014). They are also able to secure formal intellectual property rights for their products and processes (De Beer et al., 2013) and overcome the structural impediments that prevent them from growing, such as their lack of access to advice and support as well as capital (ILO, 2014). For customers, the advantages are that they benefit from legal recourse if a poor job is done, have access to insurance cover, enjoy guarantees regarding the work conducted, and have more certainty that health and safety regulations are being followed (Williams and Martinez, 2014c). Finally, for governments, the benefits are that it improves the level of public revenue (Williams and Windebank, 1998) and joins up the policy approach toward informal enterprise with the more general policy approach toward harnessing entrepreneurship and enterprise culture (Dekker et al., 2010; European Commission, 2007; Small Business Council, 2004).

Therefore, formalizing informal entrepreneurship is starting to be widely recognized by governments as the most viable policy choice. How, therefore, can this be achieved?

Formalizing informal entrepreneurship: direct versus indirect controls

Table 25.2 provides a summary of the different approaches available for formalizing informal entrepreneurship. This distinguishes two contrasting approaches. On the one hand, there is a 'hard' direct controls approach. This treats enterprise owners as rational economic actors

Table 25.2 Policy Approaches for Tackling Formalizing Informal Entrepreneurship

Approach	Tools	Policy measures
Hard approach: deterrents	Improved detection	Data matching and sharing Joined up strategy Joint operations
	Increased penalties	Increased penalties
	Increase perception of risk	Advertise penalties Advertise effectiveness of detection procedures
Hard approach: 'bribes'	For start-ups	Simplification of compliance Direct and indirect tax incentives Support and advice
	For existing informal enterprises	Supply-side incentives (e.g., society-wide amnesties; voluntary disclosure; smoothing transition to formalization) Demand-side incentives (e.g., targeted direct and indirect taxes)
Soft approach: reduce asymmetry between state and citizens	Change citizens (informal institutions)	Tax education Normative appeals Awareness raising of benefits of declaring full salaries
	Change state (formal institutions)	Procedural and redistributive fairness and justice Wider economic and social developments

and seeks compliance by ensuring that the costs of operating in the informal economy are outweighed by the benefits of operating in the formal economy. This is accomplished either by increasing the costs of non–compliance ('sticks') and/or by increasing the benefits of formalization, including making the conduct of work in the formal economy easier ('carrots'). On the other hand, the soft indirect controls approach shifts away from using 'sticks' and 'carrots' to elicit behavior change and instead focuses upon developing the social contract between the state and enterprise owners by nurturing a high trust high commitment culture.

To harness this endeavor using direct controls, therefore, one potential way forward is to reduce the costs and improve the benefits of formalization since at present these remain insufficient to outweigh the benefits of informality in many developing countries. Studies of how simplifying and reducing the cost of formalization result in an increase in registration for example, have been reported in Uganda (Sander, 2003), Bolivia (Garcia-Bolivar, 2006), and Peru (Jaramillo, 2009), although De Mel et al. (2012) in Sri Lanka find that even a financial offer equivalent to two months' profits led to only 50 percent of firms registering. This has been explained as due to the benefits of formalization not being high enough to be an incentive to formalize, the limited ambitions of entrepreneurs, mistrust in governments, and fear of the high recurrent costs of formalization (Maloney, 2004; McKenzie and Woodruff, 2006).

However, reducing the costs and improving the benefits of formalization is not the only means of harnessing this sphere. It assumes that informal entrepreneurs are purely rational economic actors. In recent years nevertheless, we have witnessed the emergent recognition, grounded in institutional theory, that informal entrepreneurs are also often social actors (De Castro et al., 2014; Vu, 2014; Webb et al., 2009, 2013, 2014; Williams and Shahid, 2015). Based on the view that informal entrepreneurship arises when entrepreneurs' norms, values, and beliefs are not in symmetry with the codified laws and regulations of formal institutions, consideration also needs to be given to better aligning entrepreneurs' norms, values, and beliefs with those of the formal institutions as a means of harnessing this sphere. On the one hand, this will require measures to alter the norms, values, and beliefs regarding the accept-ability of operating in the informal sector so that institutional asymmetry (and thus informal entrepreneurship) is reduced, such as by raising awareness about the benefits of taxation and the public goods received. On the other hand, this re-alignment also requires alterations in the formal institutions. These are of two types. First, improvements are needed in the processes of formal institutions in terms of tax fairness, procedural justice, and redistributive justice. Fairness here refers to the extent to which entrepreneurs believe they are paying their fair share compared with others (Wenzel, 2004), redistributive justice to whether they receive the goods and services they feel that they deserve given the taxes that they pay (Richardson and Sawyer, 2001), and procedural justice to the degree to which they believe that the tax authority has treated then in a respectful, impartial, and responsible manner (Braithwaite and Reinhart, 2000; Murphy, 2005). Second, improvements are also required in the products of formal institutions, by which is meant wider economic and social develop-ments. In recent years, institutional theorists have begun to identify the nature of these economic and social developments, revealing that informal entrepreneurship declines as for example, the quality of governance improves and public sector corruption decreases, and the level of government intervention increases (Autio and Fu, 2015; Dau and Cuervo-Cazurra, 2014; Klapper et al., 2007; Thai and Turkina, 2014; Tonoyan et al., 2010).

These different policy measures to harness this sphere based on rational economic actor and social actor approaches, or what can be seen as direct and indirect controls, however, are not mutually exclusive. Indeed, there are at least two ways of combining them. First, a responsive regulation approach starts out by openly engaging entrepreneurs to consider their obligations and take responsibility for regulating themselves in a manner consistent with the law rather than external rules. This facilitating of voluntary self-regulated compliance is then followed by persuasion through incentives and only as a last resort for the small minority refusing to be compliant does it use punitive measures (Braithwaite, 2009; Job et al., 2007). A second approach is the 'slippery slope framework' (Kirchler et al., 2008) which pursues both voluntary and enforced compliance concurrently by developing both greater trust in authorities and the greater power of authorities (Kogler et al., 2015; Muehlbacher et al., 2011; Wahl et al., 2010). Until now however, there has been little comparative evaluation of which sequencing and/or combination is the most appropriate and/or effective means of harnessing this sphere. Further research will be required in developing countries to determine which sequences and/or combinations are most appropriate and effective to use for formalizing informal entrepreneurship.

Contributions of the chapters

Given this introductory overview of informal entrepreneurship in developing countries, attention here turns to a brief review of the contributions of each of the chapters in this handbook.

In chapter 26, 'Entrepreneurship at the base of the pyramid: the case of Nicaragua', Michael Pisani contributes toward the emergence of more positive accounts of the contributions of informal entrepreneurship, both for customers and for those operating informal enterprises. Examining the business and household income outcomes of base of the pyramid (BOP) in-home convenience store entrepreneurs through a census-like business survey conducted during 2012 in Nicaragua, he finds that in-home convenience stores or *pulperías* are ubiquitous BOP businesses that serve BOP consumers. Utilizing a cross-sectional and nationally representative business-focused micro data set, 470 pulperos are examined. Most *pulperías* are found to be operated by female entrepreneurs and contribute positively toward poverty reduction at the BOP. This chapter, therefore, contributes significantly to the advancement of more positive representations of the impacts of informal entrepreneurship at the BOP.

In chapter 27 entitled 'Determinants of participation in the informal sector in Sri Lanka: evidence from a recently conducted special survey', Chandani Wijebandara and N. S. Cooray identify the factors affecting an individual's decision to engage in the informal sector in Sri Lanka; cross-sectional household survey data from 2008/2009, together with the Sri Lanka Quarterly Labour Force Survey, is analyzed using logistic regression analysis. The results indicate that participation in the informal sector is significantly greater in rural areas, amongst men, Moors (an ethnic minority group), and older age groups. Interestingly, a strong negative relationship exists between level of education as well as labour market conditions and informal sector participation. The outcome is a call for increasing investment in human capital and strengthening social security systems as ways forward.

In chapter 28 entitled 'Understanding informal entrepreneurship in Sub-Saharan Africa and its implications for economic development: the Ghanaian experience', Kwame Adom reflects and reinforces the recognition that informal entrepreneurship is not solely a necessity-driven endeavor and is often conducted more out of choice rather than being due to a lack of choice. His additional finding, however, suggests a lack of understanding of the character of informal entrepreneurship, which has resulted in a negative attitude being adopted by the government and a desire to eradicate it. To move forward therefore, he calls for more research into informal entrepreneurship so as to provide a clearer understanding of the positive and negative impacts of this endeavor so as to aid evidence-based policy formulation.

Chapter 29 entitled 'Levels of informality and characteristics of micro-entrepreneurs in Pakistan' by Muhammad Shehryar Shahid, Halima Shehryar, and Minha Akber Allibhoy, meanwhile, significantly advances understanding of the nature of informal entrepreneurship. Until now, too much of the scholarship has adopted a dualistic view of enterprises as either formal or informal. As these authors reveal through face-to-face interviews with 300 informal entrepreneurs in the city of Lahore in Pakistan, however, the vast majority of enterprises are not either wholly formal or wholly informal but rather, display varying degrees of informalization. They then reveal that not all these informal entrepreneurs are driven by economic necessity but that a range of additional motives exist that drive them to voluntarily operate in the informal economy, such as public sector corruption, low tax morality, and lack of awareness regarding the registration process. Importantly, they then reveal that entrepreneurs' rationales for operating informally differ according to the level of formality of their enterprise and the sector in which they operate. The outcome is a call for policy makers to move beyond a one-size-fits-all approach toward formalizing informal entrepreneurship and to develop different pragmatic interventions depending upon the level of formality and nature of the business.

In chapter 30 entitled 'Characteristics and structures of informal entrepreneurship in Botswana', Léo-Paul Dana and Vanessa Ratten contribute to the shift toward developing context-bound understandings of informal entrepreneurship by unpacking the particular conditions in Botswana that have influenced the decision of entrepreneurs to operate on an informal basis. They reveal that in this relatively affluent and stable African country, the government recognizes the need to harness informal entrepreneurship as a means of fostering economic development and growth, and is seeking to nurture such enterprise as a way forward, thus reflecting the overarching but slow shift in the developing world away from an eradication approach and toward an approach that is seeking the formalization of informal entrepreneurship.

Finally, in chapter 31, 'The influence of credit and formalization on the growth of SMEs in Tanzania' by Joseph A. Kuzilwa and Prof. Ganka D. Nyamsogoro, seeks to assess whether the formalization of SMEs increases access to formal financial institutions and external financing, and whether this increased access influences business growth. The finding is that the formalization of SMEs does indeed improve their access to credit and that the existence of a current loan has a positive contribution to SMEs' capital and profitability growth, but not on sales growth.

Given the shift in both understandings of informal entrepreneurship away from depicting it in a purely negative manner and toward recognizing that it can have more positive impacts, coupled with the shift away from eradication and toward formalizing informal entrepreneurship, we hope that you enjoy these contributions that start to put greater flesh on these broad trends.

References

Aliyev, H. (2015). Post-Soviet informality: towards theory-building. *International Journal of Sociology and Social Policy*, 35(3–4), 182–198.

Anderson, A. R. and Starnawska, M. (2008). Research practices in entrepreneurship: problems of definition, description and meaning. *International Journal of Entrepreneurship and Innovation*, 9(4), 221–230.

Autio, E. and Fu, K. (2015). Economic and political institutions and entry into formal and informal entrepreneurship. *Asia Pacific Journal of Management*, 32(1), 67–94.

Bajada, C. and Schneider, F. (2005).Introduction. In C. Bajada and F. Schneider (Eds.), *Size, Causes and Consequences of the Underground Economy: an international perspective* (pp. 1–14). Aldershot: Ashgate.

Barbour, A. and Llanes, M. (2013). *Supporting People to Legitimise their Informal Businesses*. York: Joseph Rowntree Foundation.

Becker, K.F. (2004). *The Informal Economy*. Stockholm: Swedish International Development Agency.

Boels, D. (2014). It's better than stealing: informal street selling in Brussels. *International Journal of Sociology and Social Policy*, 34(9/10), 670–693.

Braithwaite, V. (2009). *Defiance in Taxation and Governance: resisting and dismissing authority in a democracy*. Cheltenham: Edward Elgar.

Braithwaite, V. and Reinhart, M. (2000). The Taxpayers' Charter: does the Australian Tax Office comply and who benefits. Canberra: Centre for Tax System Integrity Working Paper no.1, Australian National University.

Bruns, B., Miggelbrink, J. and Müller, K. (2011). Smuggling and small-scale trade as part of informal economic practices: Empirical findings from the Eastern external EU border. *International Journal of Sociology and Social Policy*, 31(11/12), 664–680.

Castells, M. and Portes, A. (1989). World underneath: the origins, dynamics and effects of the informal economy. In A. Portes, M. Castells and L. Benton (Eds.), *The Informal Economy: studies in advanced and less developing countries* (pp. 1–19). Baltimore, MD: John Hopkins University Press.

Chen, M. (2012). *The Informal Economy: definitions, theories and policies*. Manchester: Women in Informal Employment: Globalizing and Organising.

Cross, J.C. (2000). Street vendors, modernity and postmodernity: conflict and compromise in the global economy. *International Journal of Sociology and Social Policy*, 20(1), 29–51.

Dau, L.A. and Cuervo-Cazurra, A. (2014) To formalize or not to formalize: entrepreneurship and pro-market institutions. *Journal of Business Venturing*, 29(4), 668–686.

Davis, M. (2006). *Planet of Slums*. London: Verso.

De Beer, J., Fu, K. and Wunsch-Vincent, S. (2013). The informal economy, innovation and intellectual property: concepts, metrics and policy considerations, Economic Research Working Paper no. 10, World Intellectual Property Organization, Geneva.

De Castro, J.O., Khavul, S. and Bruton, G.D. (2014). Shades of grey: how do informal firms navigate between macro and meso institutional environments? *Strategic Entrepreneurship Journal*, 8(1), 75–94.

De Mel, S., McKenzie, D. and Woodruff, C. (2012). The demand for, and consequences of formalization among informal firms in Sri Lanka. Washington DC: Policy Research Working Paper 5991, World Bank.

De Soto, H. (1989). *The Other Path: the economic answer to terrorism*. London: Harper and Row.

De Soto, H. (2001). *The Mystery of Capital: why capitalism triumphs in the West and fails everywhere else*. London: Black Swan.

Dekker, H., Oranje, E., Renooy, P., Rosing, F. and Williams, C.C. (2010). *Joining up the Fight against Undeclared Work in the European Union*. Brussels: DG Employment, Social Affairs and Equal Opportunities.

Dibben, P. and Williams, C.C. (2012). Varieties of capitalism and employment relations: informally dominated market economies. *Industrial Relations: a Review of Economy and Society*, 51(S1), 563–582.

European Commission (2007) *Stepping Up the Fight Against Undeclared Work*. Brussels: European Commission.

Franck, A.K. (2012). Factors motivating women's informal micro-entrepreneurship: experiences from Penang, Malaysia. *International Journal of Gender and Entrepreneurship*, 4(1), 65–78.

Gallin, D. (2001). Propositions on trade unions and informal employment in time of globalization. *Antipode*, 19(4), 531–549.

Garcia-Bolivar, O. (2006). *Informal Economy: Is it a problem, a solution or both? The perspective of the informal business*. Berkeley, CA: Bepress Legal Series.

Geertz, C. (1963). *Old Societies and New States: the quest for modernity in Asia and Africa*. Glencoe, IL: Free Press.

Gërxhani, K. (2004). The informal sector in developed and less developed countries: a literature survey. *Public Choice*, 120(3/4), 267–300.

Gilbert, A. (1998). *The Latin American City*. London: Latin American Bureau.

Grabiner, L. (2000). *The Informal Economy*. London: HM Treasury.

Gurtoo, A. and Williams, C.C. (2009). Entrepreneurship and the informal sector: Some lessons from India. *International Journal of Entrepreneurship and Innovation*, 10(1), 55–62.

Harding, R., Brooksbank, D., Hart, M., Jones-Evans, D., Levie, J., O'Reilly, J. and Walker, J. (2006). *Global Entrepreneurship Monitor United Kingdom 2005*. London: London Business School.

ILO (2002). *Decent Work and the Informal Economy*. Geneva: International Labour Office.

ILO (2014). Transitioning from the Informal to the Formal Economy. Report V (1), International Labor Conference, 103rd Session (2014), ILO, Geneva.

Jaramillo, M. (2009). Is there demand for formality among informal firms? Evidence from microfirms in downtown Lima. Bonn: German Development Institute Discussion Paper 12/2009, German Development Institute.

Job, J., Stout, A. and Smith, R. (2007). Culture change in three taxation administrations: from command and control to responsive regulation. *Law and Policy*, 29(1), 84–101.

Jütting, J. and Laiglesia, J. (2009). Employment, poverty reduction and development: what's new? In J. Jütting and J. Laiglesia (Eds.), *Is Informal Normal? Towards more and better jobs in developing countries* (pp. 129–52). Paris: OECD.

Ketchen, D.J., Ireland, R.D. and Webb, J.W. (2014). Towards a research agenda for the informal economy: a survey of the Strategic Entrepreneurship Journal's Editorial Board. *Strategic Entrepreneurship Journal*, 8(1), 95–100.

Khan, E. A. and Quaddus, M. (2015). Examining the influence of business environment on socio-economic performance of informal microenterprises: Content analysis and partial least square approach. *International Journal of Sociology and Social Policy*, 35(3/4), 273–288.

Kirchler, E., Hoelzl, E. and Wahl, I. (2008) Enforced versus voluntary tax compliance: the 'slippery slope' framework'. *Journal of Economic Psychology*, 29(2), 210–225.

Kistruck, G.M., Webb, J.W., Sutter, C.J. and Bailey, A.V.G. (2015).The double-edged sword of legitimacy in base-of-the-pyramid markets. *Journal of Business Venturing*, 30(3), 436–451.

Klapper, L., Amit, R., Guillen, M.F. and Quesdada, J. M. (2007). Entrepreneurship and firm formation across countries. Washington DC: Policy Research Working Paper series 4313, World Bank.

Kogler, C., Muehlbacher, S. and Kirchler, E. (2015). Testing the 'slippery slope framework' among self-employed taxpayers. *Economics of Governance*, 16(2), 125–142.

Kus, B. (2010). Regulatory governance and the informal economy: cross-national comparisons. *Socio-Economic Review*, 8(3): 487–510.

Kus, B. (2014). The informal road to markets: neoliberal reforms, private entrepreneurship and the informal economy in Turkey. *International Journal of Social Economics*, 41(4), 278–293.

La Porta, R. and Shleifer, A. (2008). The unofficial economy and economic development. *Brookings Papers on Economic Activity*, 47(1), 123–135.

La Porta, R. and Shleifer, A. (2014). Informality and development. *Journal of Economic Perspectives*, 28(3), 109–126.

Leal Ordóñez, J.C. (2014). Tax collection, the informal sector and productivity. *Review of Economic Dynamics*, 17(2), 262–286.

Levy, S. (2008). *Good Intentions, Bad Outcomes: social policy, informality and economic growth in Mexico*. Washington DC: Brookings Institution.

Lewis, A. (1959). *The Theory of Economic Growth*. London: Allen and Unwin.

Lewis, W.W. (2004). *The Power of Productivity: wealth, poverty, and the threat to global stability*. Chicago: University of Chicago Press.

Llanes, M. and Barbour, A. (2007). *Self-Employed and Micro-Entrepreneurs: informal trading and the journey towards formalization*, London: Community Links.

London, T. and Hart, S.L. (2004). Reinventing strategies for emerging markets: beyond the transnational model. *Journal of International Business Studies*, 35(5), 350–370.

Maloney, W.F. (2004). Informality revisited. *World Development*, 32(7), 1159–1178.

McKenzie, D. and Woodruff, C. (2006). Do entry costs provide an empirical basis for poverty traps? Evidence from microenterprises. *Economic Development and Cultural Change*, 55(1), 3–42.

Meagher, K. (2010). *Identity Economics: social networks and the informal economy in Nigeria*. New York: James Currey.

Morris, J. and Polese, A. (2014). Introduction: informality – enduring practices, entwined livelihoods. In J. Morris and A. Polese (Eds.), *The Informal Post-Socialist Economy: embedded practices and livelihoods*. (pp. 1–18). London: Routledge.

Muehlbacher, S., Kirchler, E. and Schwarzenberger, H. (2011). Voluntary versus enforced tax compliance: empirical evidence for the 'slippery slope' framework. *European Journal of Law and Economics*, 32(1), 89–97.

Murphy, K. (2005). Regulating more effectively: the relationship between procedural justice, legitimacy and tax non-compliance. *Journal of Law and Society*, 32(4), 562–589.

North, D.C. (1990). *Institutions, Institutional Change and Economic Performance*. Cambridge: Cambridge University Press.

Nwabuzor, A. (2005). Corruption and development: new initiatives in economic openness and strengthened rule of law. *Journal of Business Ethics*, 59(1/2), 121–138.

Perry, G.E. and Maloney, W.F. (2007). Overview – informality: exit and exclusion, In G.E. Perry, W.F. Maloney, O.S. Arias, P. Fajnzylber, A.D. Mason and J. Saavedra-Chanduvi (Eds.), *Informality: exit and exclusion* (pp.1–20). Washington DC: World Bank.

Puffer, S.M., McCarthy, D.J. and Boisot, M. (2010). Entrepreneurship in Russia and China: the impact of formal institutional voids. *Entrepreneurship Theory and Practice*, 34(3), 441–467.

Reynolds, P., Bygrave, W.D., Autio, E. and Hay, M. (2002). *Global Entrepreneurship Monitor: 2002 Executive Monitor*. London: London Business School.

Renooy, P., Ivarsson, S., van der Wusten-Gritsai, O. and Meijer, R. (2004). *Undeclared Work in an Enlarged Union: An Analysis of Shadow Work – an in-depth study of specific items*. Brussels: European Commission.

Richardson, M. and Sawyer, A. (2001). A taxonomy of the tax compliance literature: further findings, problems and prospects. *Australian Tax Forum*, 16(2), 137–320.

Sander, C. (2003). Less is more: Better compliance and increased revenues by streamlining business registration in Uganda: a contribution to WDR 2005 on investment climate, growth and poverty. London: Department for International Development.

Schneider, F. and Williams, C.C. (2013). *The Shadow Economy*. London: Institute of Economic Affairs.

Siqueira, A.C.O., Webb, J. and Bruton, G.D. (2014). Informal entrepreneurship and industry conditions. *Entrepreneurship Theory and Practice*, 40(1), 177–200.

Slavnic, Z. (2010). Political economy of informalization. *European Societies*, 12(1), 3–23.

Small Business Council (2004). *Small Business in the Informal Economy: Making the Transition to the Formal Economy*. London: Small Business Council.

Snyder, K.A. (2004). Routes to the informal economy in New York's East village: crisis, economics and identity. *Sociological Perspectives*, 47(2), 215–240.

Sutter, C.J., Webb, J.W., Kistruck, G.M. and Bailey, A.V.G. (2013). Entrepreneurs' responses to semi-formal illegitimate institutional arrangements. *Journal of Business Venturing*, 28(5), 743–758.

Taiwo, O. (2013). Employment choice and mobility in multi-sector labour markets: theoretical model and evidence from Ghana. *International Labour Review*, 152(3–4), 469–492.

Thai, M.T.T. and Turkina, E. (2014). Macro-level determinants of formal entrepreneurship versus informal entrepreneurship. *Journal of Business Venturing*, 29(4), 490–510.

Tonoyan, V., Strohmeyer, R., Habib, M. and Perlitz, M. (2010). Corruption and entrepreneurship: how formal and informal institutions shape small firm behaviour in transition and mature market economies. *Entrepreneurship Theory and Practice*, 34(5), 803–831.

Vu, T.T. (2014). Institutional Incongruence and the Informal Economy: an Empirical Analysis. Paper presented at the European Public Choice Society meeting, Cambridge. http://www.econ.cam.ac.uk/epcs2014/openconf/modules/request.php?module=oc_programandaction=summary.phpandid=54 (accessed on 1 January 2015).

Wahl, I., Kastlunger, B. and Kirchler, E. (2010). Trust in authorities and power to enforce tax compliance: an empirical analysis of the 'slippery slope framework'. *Law and Policy*, 32(4), 383–406.

Webb, J.W., Bruton, G.D., Tihanyi, L. and Ireland, R.D. (2013). Research on entrepreneurship in the informal economy: framing a research agenda. *Journal of Business Venturing*, 28(1), 598–614.

Webb, J.W., Ireland, R.D. and Ketchen, D.J. (2014). Towards a greater understanding of entrepreneurship and strategy in the informal economy. *Strategic Entrepreneurship Journal*, 8(1), 1–15.

Webb, J.W., Tihanyi, L., Ireland, R.D. and Sirmon, D.G. (2009). You say illegal, I say legitimate: entrepreneurship in the informal economy. *Academy of Management Review*, 34(3), 492–510.

Wenzel, M. (2004). An analysis of norm processes in tax compliance. *Journal of Economic Psychology*, 25(2), 213–228.

Williams, C.C. (2006). *The Hidden Enterprise Culture: entrepreneurship in the underground economy*. Cheltenham: Edward Elgar.

Williams, C.C. (2013). Tackling Europe's informal economy: a critical evaluation of the neo-liberal de-regulatory perspective. *Journal of Contemporary European Research*, 9(3), 261–279.

Williams, C.C. (2014a). *Confronting the Shadow Economy: evaluating tax compliance behaviour and policies*. Cheltenham: Edward Elgar.

Williams, C.C. (2014b). Out of the shadows: a classification of economies by the size and character of their informal sector. *Work, Employment and Society*, 28(5), 735–753.

Williams, C.C. and Martinez, A. (2014a). Do small business start-ups test-trade in the informal economy? Evidence from a UK small business survey. *International Journal of Entrepreneurship and Small Business*, 22(1), 1–16.

Williams, C.C. and Martinez, A. (2014b). Is the informal economy an incubator for new enterprise creation? a gender perspective. *International Journal of Entrepreneurial Behaviour and Research*, 20(1), 4–19.

Williams, C.C. and Martinez, A. (2014c).Why do consumers purchase goods and services in the informal economy? *Journal of Business Research*, 67(5), 802–806.

Williams, C.C. and Windebank, J. (1998). *Informal Employment in the Advanced Economies: implications for work and welfare*. London: Routledge.

Williams, C.C. and Nadin, S. (2012a). Tackling entrepreneurship in the informal economy: Evaluating the policy options. *Journal of Entrepreneurship and Public Policy*, 1(2), 111–124.

Williams, C.C. and Nadin, S. (2012b). Tackling the hidden enterprise culture: Government policies to support the formalization of informal entrepreneurship. *Entrepreneurship and Regional Development*, 24(9–10), 895–915.

Williams, C.C. and Nadin, S. (2013). Harnessing the hidden enterprise culture: Supporting the formalization of off-the-books business start-ups. *Journal of Small Business and Enterprise Development*, 20(2), 434–447.

Williams, C.C. and Nadin, S. (2014). Facilitating the formalization of entrepreneurs in the informal economy: Toward a variegated policy approach. *Journal of Entrepreneurship and Public Policy*, 3(1), 33–48.

Williams, C.C. and Renooy, P. (2013). *Tackling Undeclared Work in 27 European Union Member States and Norway: approaches and measures since 2008*. Dublin: European Foundation for the Improvement of Living and Working Conditions.

Williams, C.C. and Shahid, M.S. (2015). Informal entrepreneurship and institutional theory: Explaining the varying degrees of (in)formalization of entrepreneurs in Pakistan. *Entrepreneurship and Regional Development*, 27(1–2), 1–25.

26

ENTREPRENEURSHIP AT THE BASE OF THE PYRAMID

The case of Nicaragua

Michael J. Pisani

Introduction

Over a decade ago, C.K. Prahalad argued that multinational corporations (MNCs) could help themselves by helping those at the "bottom of the pyramid" (Prahalad, 2004). As a consequence of his academic stature, Prahalad brought renewed global attention to the plight of those around the world earning just a few dollars or less a day. However, his message suggesting that MNCs could and should drive the process of poverty alleviation in the developing world missed and excluded a vast reservoir of entrepreneurship already present at the base of the pyramid[1] and capable of serving the needs of those located there (Pisani and Patrick, 2002). These base of the pyramid entrepreneurs—farmers, store keepers, trades people, and the like—have been present all along, but have been persistently and largely overlooked in their potential to assist in the sustainable development of the base of the pyramid (BOP). While these BOP entrepreneurs are not of course the sole solution to reducing poverty in the poorest regions of the world, the argument of this chapter is that they have an important role to play in any comprehensive policy approach toward poverty mitigation. Hence, a better understanding of the entrepreneurial talent at the BOP will help construct meaningful policy approaches. As such, this chapter focuses on one popular and widespread business segment of entrepreneurs at the BOP operating in Nicaragua, namely those operating an in-house convenience store or *pulpería*.

The *pulpería* or alternatively named *tiendita*,[2] located in most of Latin America, more closely resembles a microenterprise than a small business because very few tienditas employ more than a single employee, although most utilize unpaid family members as helpers within the microenterprise (Pisani and Yoskowitz, 2012). Academic researchers have classified microenterprises as business entities with typically five or fewer employees, engaged in non-primary activities, and selling at least 50 percent of their output (Mead and Liedholm, 1998).[3] Mead and Liedholm (1998) found that working proprietors or one-person shops accounted for over half of all microenterprise employment in the developing world. Extending the analysis to unpaid family members within working proprietorships accounts for over 75 percent of all workers engaged in microenterprise establishments (Mead and Liedholm, 1998).

The pulpería is situated precisely at the crossroads between BOP entrepreneurship and BOP consumers. This crossroads embraces the ability to serve the BOP while improving one's own economic standing within the BOP. In this chapter, the aim is to seek to better understand the BOP entrepreneur—including their base characteristics and business outcomes—through the entrepreneurial lens of pulpería owners in Nicaragua. To do this, answers are sought to two questions: "What are the personal characteristics of and business outcomes for pulperos in Nicaragua?" and "How are the outcomes related to poverty reduction at the BOP?'"

To answer these questions, this chapter is organized as follows. The second section describes pulperías (the sampling unit) and the associated microenterprise literature. The third section explains the research methodology and context of the study. The fourth section presents the results concerning the segmentation of tienditas and the poverty reduction impact of tiendita ownership on the household while the fifth section provides a discussion of the results. The last section draws conclusions.

Pulperías

Pulperías (tienditas) are pervasive throughout Latin America. The in-house convenience or tiny grocery store is typically found in the relatively poorer or underdeveloped sections of the country—such as shantytowns, rural hamlets, and urban barrios. The pulpería caters to a nearby clientele that is bound to the neighborhood by location, primarily the result of mobility constraints resulting from a lack of financial resources, inadequate transportation alternatives, and poor job prospects. In Nicaragua, more than half of urbanites and roughly three-quarters of rural residents chose tienditas as their primary shopping outlet (D'Haese et al., 2008).

The in-house convenience store typically devotes and converts the front section of the home to a selling space or retail outlet. The basic stock of a pulpería includes staple food supplies, hygienic products, junk food, school supplies, and other specialty items depending upon the pulpería. Start-up costs for pulperías may be relatively small, often less than $100 (Pisani and Yoskowitz, 2012).[4] The typical pulpería is open from six in the morning until eight in the evening, seven days per week. For the best and most regular customers, pulperías may extend credit. The workforce principally comes from the family unit, typically under the direction of the wife, who is almost always at home because of the home-based location of the business, and is generally supported by other family members in the household (Haase, 2007).

Pulperos are micro-entrepreneurs and as such are self-employed where entrepreneurship refers to own-account employment (Blanchflower and Oswald, 1998). Entrepreneurs at the BOP have been described as lying on a continuum between necessity-driven entrepreneurs (own-account business owners without other employment options) and opportunity-driven entrepreneurs (own-account business owners by choice, exploiting a market niche [Kirzner, 1973]). For example, Williams (2007, 2008) and Williams and Youssef (2014) observed that both necessity and opportunity drive many into informal entrepreneurship. Gurtoo and Williams (2009) find that in India self-employed informals may be necessity and/ or opportunity driven over time, illustrating microenterprise life cycle dynamism as the motivation to participate in the informal economy.

Tienditas are mostly informal business concerns as are the majority of the microenterprises in developing countries and Central America (Funkhouser, 1996; Jain and Pisani, 2008; Pisani and Pagán, 2004; Pisani and Ysokowitz, 2012). The retail function of tienditas may be performed under the auspices of government regulators and tax collectors, but more often than not, the government is absent from tiendita oversight. This hidden from government purview employment has been referred to as informal employment (Hart, 1973, 1970). In essence work "activities that avoid state regulation" best describes informality (Itzigsohn, 2000, p. 11).

Recent scholarship has revealed the importance of the macroeconomic climate at the BOP in combination with microenterprise health (Daniels, 2003; Khan and Quaddus, 2015; Pisani and Patrick, 2002), microfinance and microenterprise development (Baptista et al., 2006; Pisani and Yoskowitz, 2005), the returns to small start-up investment (McKenzie and Woodruff, 2006), and as dynamic or disadvantaged enterprises (Fajnzylber et al., 2006; Nichter and Goldmark, 2009). The literature is mixed with regards to micro-entrepreneurship and the sectoral maximization of earnings (Daniels, 2003; Pisani and Pagán, 2004; Fajnzylber et al., 2006).

Research methodology

The cross-sectional dataset, bases de datos de la encuesta continua de hogares (http://www. inide.gob.ni/) utilized in this paper was accessed through the Nicaraguan Instituto Nacional de Información de Desarrollo (INIDE). Partial external support for the survey came from the Economic Commission for Latin American and the Caribbean and the International Labour Office. The ECH survey was deployed by INIDE and completed in Nicaragua from April to June 2012 with a primary focus on economic activity. The household questionnaire contains categorical and ratio data concerning the household roster and demographics and employment. The random national household survey included 6,811 households spread representatively across the country and included 31,281 persons.[5] Pulperías were identified utilizing two ECH survey questions in combination: occupation as shop keeper (vendedores y demostradores de tiendas y almacenes) and location of business (en su propia vivienda). Hence only stores located in one's home were included. As the weighting mechanism was not adequately described in the ECH survey documentation, no weighting was used in the empirical analysis reported in the results section of the paper. However, preliminary weighting may suggest a national total of 213,500 Nicaraguans employed in 91,313 pulperías across the country.[6] Nonetheless, the final results utilized in this paper display information from 1,079 employed (owners and employees) in 470 pulperías.

The Nicaraguan context

Contemporary Nicaragua has faced many challenges including natural disasters (e.g., earthquakes and hurricanes), social, economic, and political upheaval (e.g., revolution and counter-revolution), external pressures and shifting alliances (e.g., the oscillating roles of the US, socialism, the Nicaraguan diaspora, and Venezuela), and widespread poverty (e.g., about three-quarters of the current population lives on $2 or less per day) (World Food Programme, 2014; Walker and Wade, 2011). More recently, the political landscape has been dominated by Sandinista Daniel Ortega who has held the presidency since 2007. Under Ortega's leadership, the nation's foreign policy has tilted to the left and aligned the state with the Bolivarian alliance centered in Venezuela. Economically, the nation is tied to the capitalist global market, in particular the United States and the CAFTA region plus Venezuela.

Nicaragua, with approximately six million inhabitants, is the second poorest country in the Western Hemisphere with a 2011 per capita GDP of $1,510, with 42.5 percent of households living below the national poverty line (World Bank, 2013). Presently, the economy is growing between 3 and 5 percent per year with moderate inflation under 10 percent

(Banco Central de Nicaragua, 2013). Informal employment remains persistently high at about 75 percent of all employed Nicaraguans. There is a direct relationship between informality and self-employment which are both inversely related to per capita income (Xavier et al., 2012). Hence, self-employment remains an important economic employment outlet and driver of the economy with self-employment comprising roughly one-third of the economically active population (Banco Central de Nicaragua, 2013; Pisani and Pagán, 2004). The composition of the $10 billion economy is about 35 percent services, 35 percent manufacturing, and 30 percent agriculture. The economy is very open to global trade with imports and exports comprising 105 percent of GDP and overseas remittances accounting for 15 percent of GDP (Banco Central de Nicaragua, 2013). Lastly, the capital city, Managua, is a classic Latin American primate city containing about half of the nation's population and is the hub of the nation's economic activity.

Results

In this section, results are presented to provide insight into the two research questions which are focused on the personal characteristics of and business outcomes for pulperos in Nicaragua and how these outcomes relate to poverty reduction. To begin this section, I contrast and contextualize pulperos from their employees. Previous research has shown tenderos to be highly segmented by gender; hence tenderos are next disaggregated and described by female and male owned tienditas. Subsequently, multivariate analyses as to the determinants of business profits are presented. Lastly, household income in relation to potential poverty outcomes is offered.

Pulpería owners and workers

Table 26.1 provides a demographic profile of pulpería entrepreneurs and workers. Entrepreneurs are overwhelmingly female while the majority of employees are also female and many are children. The survey is national in scope with all of the regions represented noting the principle importance of Managua. Urban areas house about two-thirds of tiendita owners and workers in households holding around five people. Pulperos are nearly twice as old as their workers. The workers are nearly all (98.9 percent) part of the larger family structure and receive almost no explicit monetary remuneration for their assistance in the pulpería. Most of the owners and nearly all of the workers proclaim literacy, yet the workers have generally more education than the pulperos, perhaps indicating improved educational outcomes for pulpero children. The tiendita owner typically resides in a married household with the younger workers more likely to be single.

Gender-based comparison of pulpería firm characteristics

As already noted, the vast majority of pulpería owners are female. This reality deserves further explanation. Pisani and Yoskowitz (2012) and Haase (2007) suggest the gendered nature of pulpería ownership is a result of the convergence of women's work and women's role in the home, socially constructed. That is, "in this view, female business proprietorship undertaken in the home is acceptable, perhaps moral, because 'good' women remain at home under the watchful eye of husband, family, and community" (Pisani and Yoskowitz, 2012, p. 124). Hence, the pulpería "is situated at the junction of public and private spaces, where the home dually serves as a business establishment literally adjacent to the street, and as the hearth of

Table 26.1 Pulpería Demographics: Entrepreneurs and Employees

Variable	Entrepreneurs	Employees (paid and unpaid)
Gender (percent)		
Female	85.1	65.8
Male	14.9	34.2
Region* (percent)		
Segovias	11.1	10.7
Western	6.2	14.9
Managua	29.8	26.3
Southern	10.4	11.0
Central	6.8	4.9
Northern	11.7	16.7
Atlantic	12.8	15.4
Urban/Rural		
Urban	67.2	68.0
Rural	32.8	32.0
Mean Household Size (std. dev.)	4.8 (2.5)	5.5 (2.4)
Mean Age (std. dev.)	46.3 (15.4)	24.1 (16.0)
Literate (percent)		
Yes	83.4	95.6
No	16.6	4.4
Education – Last School Attended (percent)		
None	19.1	4.6
Primary	42.1	43.9
Secondary	26.2	40.9
Technical	3.5	1.2
University	9.1	0.2
Mean Education – Years (std. dev.)	6.0 (4.6)	7.1 (3.8)
Civil Status (percent)		
Single	4.5	61.6
Married (includes unions)	65.1	27.6
Separated/Divorced	21.5	8.7
Widowed	8.9	2.1
Earned Income/Paid in the Pulpería (percent)		
Yes	99.1	3.9
No	0.9	96.1
N=	470	609

*Region is grouped as Segovias: Estelí, Madriz, Nueva Segovia; Western: León, Chinandega; Managua; Southern: Granada, Masaya, Carazo, Rivas; Central: Boaco, Chontales; Northern: Jinotega, Matagalpa; Atlantic: Río San Juan, RAAN, RAAS.

the family where the most intimate family affairs are conducted" (Pisani and Yoskowitz, 2012, p. 124).

Most, but not all, pulperos operate their microbusiness as a year-round endeavor (see Table 26.2). When in operation, the microenterprise generates business income; reported mean monthly profits were $85.17 for female tenderas and $156.23 for male tenderos.[7]

Table 26.2 Pulpería Firm Characteristics – Entrepreneurs (as Primary Occupation)

Variable	Female	Male
Work as a Pulpero Year Round?★ *(percent)*		
Yes	*83.8*	*94.3*
No *(seasonal/other)*	*16.3*	*5.7*
Earned Pulpería Income Over the Past Month? (percent)		
Yes	99.5	98.6
No	0.5	1.4
Amount Earned in Pulpería – Monthly Profits ($US)		
Mean	*85.17*	*156.23*
Standard Deviation	*85.38*	*311.39*
Hours Worked per Week		
Mean	40.57	42.74
Standard Deviation	23.27	22.22
Keep Bookkeeping Records? (percent)		
Yes	29.0	20.0
No	71.0	80.0
Number of Employees (percent)		
0	27.8	22.9
1–4	71.8	75.7
5–8	0.5	1.4
Enrolled in Social Security? (percent)		
Yes	0.0	0.0
No	100.0	100.0
Do you wish to change jobs? (percent)		
Yes	31.5	41.4
No	68.5	58.6
Rationale for those indicating they wish to change jobs: (percent)		
Increase income	94.4	89.7
Better use my skills	0.8	6.9
Other	4.8	3.4
Have you looked for other work over the past 3 months? (percent)		
Yes	7.0	12.9
No	93.0	87.1
Do you have a second job? (percent)		
Yes	30.2	31.4
No	69.8	68.6
Hours Worked per Week in Second Job		
Mean	11.01	15.77
Standard Deviation	7.43	10.67
N=	400	70

★*Italics = significant difference at the .10 level.*

A significant profit gap thus exists between female and male pulperos where female owners earn profits just over half (54.5 percent) of their male counterparts. Most tenderos average just a bit more than 40 hours per week working in the tiendita. Active record keeping takes place in about one in five tienditas. Few employees work in the tiendita; most that do help in the tiendita are family members working without pay and all report an absence of enrollment in social security, a clear sign of informal work conditions.

A majority of pulperos wish to remain in their present occupations, though a substantial minority would change occupations if they were able to increase their income by doing so. Yet very few sought new employment elsewhere. However, about one-third of tenderos earn income through a second job (though participation in a second job is not correlated with those seeking to change jobs) averaging between 11 and 15 hours a week, respectively for women and men.[8,9] Of the pulperos with a second occupation, two-thirds (66.4 percent) owned a second business. The account of second businesses include: bakeries/cooks (33.7 percent); street vendors (29.2 percent); laundry (9.0 percent); tiendita (7.9 percent); agriculture (7.9 percent); seamstress (5.6 percent); and others (5.6 percent). Those not owning a second business almost exclusively earned a second income through agricultural employment.

Multivariate analysis for principal business ownership profits

To better understand the determinants of business profits, I estimated a multiple regression analysis utilizing 15 preselected (a priori) variables. These include gender (female =1), region (Managua [=1] or rest of the country), location (urban [=1] or rural), household size (number of persons living in the household), potential experience (this estimates the amount of potential work experience, calculated as age minus years of education minus 6), potential experience squared divided by 100 (to uncover any nonlinear returns to experience), literacy (literacy = 1), years of education, civil status (married [=1] or not married), foreign remittances (=1 if household receives foreign remittances), keep business records (=1 if tiendita keeps separate business records), have employees (=1 if tiendita has employees), wish to change jobs (=1 if pulpero indicated a desire to change jobs), have a second job (=1 if tendero possess a second job), and number of hours worked per week. The dependent variable is business profits per hour (constructed from monthly business profits and hours worked per week variables).

For all tiendita owners, the following five independent variables were significant in determining monthly profits: gender, region, business record keeping, wish to change jobs, and hours worked (see Table 26.3). Female pulperas earned $0.45 less per hour than their male counterparts; a gender earnings penalty. Pulpería location in Managua enhanced hourly earnings by $0.29. Those tienditas that keep business records and accounts increased their hourly profit by $0.24. Tenderos wishing to change jobs earned $0.26 less per hour than those tenderos seemingly happy in their current occupation. Lastly, tenderos who worked more hours found themselves earning $0.02 less per hour.

Given that women are the clear majority of all pulperos, a separate multiple regression with only female pulperas was estimated. Five independent variables significantly impact tendera profits: region, potential experience squared/100, business record keeping, the wish to change jobs, and hours worked (see Table 26.4). Tenderas located in Managua earned a $0.26 per hour premium over those tenderas located throughout the rest of the country. The returns to potential work experience were nonlinear and negative for women indicating diminishing profits the longer one stayed in business. Business record keeping boosted hourly

Table 26.3 Multiple Regression *Pulpería* hourly Profits

Variable	β	Standard Error	t statistic	Significance
Constant	1.891	.384	4.927	.000***
Gender (Female=1)	−.449	.132	−3.412	.001***
Region (Managua=1)	.291	.114	2.559	.011**
Location (Urban=1)	−.050	.112	−.451	.652
Household Size	−.007	.019	−.387	.699
Potential Experience (PE)	.009	.010	.904	.367
PE Squared/100	−.018	.013	−1.328	.185
Literacy (Yes=1)	.111	.155	.713	.476
Years of Education	.012	.015	.817	.414
Civil Status (Married=1)	.020	.104	.194	.847
Foreign Remittances (Yes=1)	.128	.212	.606	.545
Keep Business Records (Yes=1)	.241	.108	2.224	.027**
Have Employees (Yes=1)	.130	.112	1.158	.248
Wish to Change Jobs (Yes=1)	−.264	.101	−2.614	.009***
Have Second Job (Yes=1)	.011	.102	.112	.911
Hours Worked	−.016	.002	−7.327	.000***

Adjusted R^2 = .119
Model ANOVA: F= 4.916, df=15, p=.000***

***, **, * represent statistical significance at the .001, .05, and .10 levels, respectively.

Table 26.4 Multiple Regression *Pulpería* hourly Profits – Female Owners

Variable	β	Standard Error	t statistic	Significance
Constant	1.005	.253	3.970	.000***
Region (Managua=1)	.262	.097	2.694	.007***
Location (Urban=1)	.107	.095	1.122	.263
Household Size	−.009	.016	−.600	.549
Potential Experience (PE)	.011	.009	1.197	.232
PE Squared/100	−.020	.012	−1.723	.086*
Literacy (Yes=1)	.071	.134	.531	.596
Years of Education	.004	.013	.289	.773
Civil Status (Married=1)	−.011	.088	−.125	.900
Foreign Remittances (Yes=1)	.139	.176	.790	.430
Keep Business Records (Yes=1)	.160	.092	1.740	.083*
Have Employees (Yes=1)	.142	.094	1.508	.132
Wish to Change Jobs (Yes=1)	−.227	.089	−2.566	.011**
Have Second Job (Yes=1)	−.049	.088	−.556	.579
Hours Worked	−.016	.002	−8.359	.000***

Adjusted R^2 = .144
Model ANOVA: F= 5.726, df=14, p=.000***

***, **, * represent statistical significance at the .001, .05, and .10 levels, respectively.

profits $0.16 for pulperas. Tenderas wishing to change jobs saw diminished hourly profits of $0.23. Finally, the longer tenderas worked in the tiendita the less they profited per hour by $0.02 per hour.[10] Too few observations for men made a separate analysis of this type unviable.

Household income, poverty reduction, and pulpería ownership

Previous research has shown that microenterprise ownership may be a viable poverty reduction strategy for individuals for whom the formal educational system has passed by (Pisani, 2013). As educational opportunities are limited in many developing world contexts, entrepreneurship at the BOP becomes an important path toward poverty reduction. Incomes of tendero households in this ECH sample reveal three main sources of income: principal occupation, secondary occupation, and monetary transfers. Household income for tendero households is displayed in Table 26.5. As already noted, male pulperos earn a substantially higher business profit than their female counterparts. Secondary occupational income is comparable between the sexes, averaging just over $10 per month. Monthly transfer income, for those households that receive it, is substantial. In fact transfer income to the tendero household is more than the monthly business profits for female pulperas and more than half of the monthly business profits for male pulperos. In all, total monthly household income rises above $100 for female-owned tienditas and nearly $200 for male owned tienditas. On a per capita household basis, incomes average $32.02 for tendera households and $60.00 for tendero households.

Table 26.5 Pulpero household Income ($US)

Income Source	Female	Male	All
Principal Occupation			
Monthly Mean Amount (std. dev.)	85.17 (85.38)	156.23 (311.39)	95.67 (144.90)
F=14.552, p=.000			
Hourly Mean Amount (std. dev.)	0.67 (0.83)	1.06 (1.79)	0.73 (1.04)
F=9.093, p=.005			
Secondary Occupation			
Monthly Mean Amount (std. dev.)	10.87 (38.88)	13.97 (43.70)	10.87 (39.60)
F=0.494, p=.482			
Hourly Mean Amount (std. dev.)	0.25 (0.97)	0.13 (0.43)	0.24 (0.91)
F=1.023, p=.312			
Transfer Income^			
Monthly Mean Amount (std. dev.)	96.21 (97.18)	117.84 (59.80)	99.72 (92.18)
F=0.597, p=.442			
Total Income			
Monthly Mean Amount (std. dev.)	111.70 (114.57)	192.40 (313.88)	123.62 (162.42)
F=14.950, p=.000			
Per Capita Household Income			
Monthly Mean Amount (std. dev.)	32.02 (47.39)	60.00 (103.49)	36.15 (59.79)
F=13.214, p=.000			

Note: 67 female households received transfer income, 13 male households received transfer income, and 80 total households received transfer income.

Discussion

Recently, Nichter and Goldmark (2009) advanced our understanding of the structural challenges and opportunities facing micro and small enterprises (MSEs) in the developing world. They lumped together the most challenged or "survivalist" firms as firms (and households) on the margins of life, literally interpreted. Nichter and Goldmark (2009) found that the most disadvantaged survivalist firms happen to be those MSEs that are female-owned, informal, and home-based within developing country economic contexts. While not all tenderos are female, clearly women dominate the tiendita business landscape in Nicaragua. No tiendita in the survey reported enrollment in social security, a signal of informality. And by definition, only storefronts embedded within households were selected for analysis; hence in a classic sense, Nicaraguan female pulperas match Nichter and Goldmark's description of a survivalist firm—where average business income falls under $3 per day.

Additionally, tenderos are limited in educational achievement where nearly one-fifth have never attended school and collectively over 60 percent possess an elementary school education or less. As the average pulpero is middle-aged and married, the possibility of acquiring additional education is highly improbable in a developing market context. Within this disadvantaged environment, the good news surrounds the economic returns to entrepreneurship even where the educational system and accompanying opportunities have passed tenderos by. In a country where 75 percent earn $2 a day or less, tenderos earn nearly one-third more than this perilous benchmark (and some quite a bit more). Additionally, the workers in tienditas, who are mostly family members, have a much higher rate of educational achievement suggesting that the children and extended family members of tendero households have the ability to pursue greater levels of education—where greater levels of education translate into higher paying work. Even so, about one-third of tenderos desire a change of occupational scenery hoping that another job would be higher paying. Second occupations for those tenderos who have them suggest few viable alternatives for higher paying work; in essence, many tenderos are doing relatively well considering their occupational alternatives.

The gendered nature of work for pay is evident in the substantial earnings gap between female- and male-owned pulperías. Gender accounts for the largest differential among all of the variables estimated to determine profits. This gap reflects the severe undervaluing of female work in Nicaraguan business society (Babb, 2001). Other earnings penalties were associated with dissatisfaction with tiendita work, hours worked, and length of time worked at a pulpería (females only). Work dissatisfaction and lower earnings are complementary and expected. Working longer in time and experience defies earnings strategies, but reflects the low value placed upon "women's time" especially that time spent in the home. Nevertheless, earnings premiums are associated with location in Managua and with business record keeping. As Managua is the economic hub of the nation, it is expected that neighborhood businesses would perform better in the economic magnet of the country. Keeping business records—recording business transactions—separates home accounts from business accounts, assists in the acquisition of business acumen, and facilitates business decision making (e.g., pricing, margin development, and cost control). Importantly, bookkeeping is a transferable skill that may help mitigate other uncontrollable earning penalties (e.g., gender, location).

Pulpero ownership is clearly a step forward toward reducing poverty at the BOP as the average returns for a full day's work translates into potential business profits of $5.36 for women and $8.48 for men. When combined with other sources of income, such as a second job and transfer income (e.g., remittances, pensions), monthly household income exceeds $100 for pulperas and $190 for pulperos. Of course monthly per capita household incomes reflect the number of persons living in the household, but the threshold number in which per capita income dramatically falls off is four household members for pulperas (from $43.12 for a four-person household and $28.11 for a five-person household) and five household members for pulperos (from $111.39 for a four-person household and $26.04 for a five-person household). As compared to other employment and earnings alternatives for relatively unskilled labor at the BOP, the economic profits associated with pulpero ownership provide a stable and above average means of income.

Conclusions

Pulperías, in-home convenience stores, are ubiquitous in Nicaragua where the total number may exceed 100,000 firms employing 200,000 Nicaraguans. This is not an inconsequential business sector. Indeed more than half of Nicaraguans shop frequently at pulperías, more so in rural areas and in the urban periphery reaching base of the pyramid consumers. In meeting this consumer market niche, pulperías fulfill a Kirznerian or incremental market approach (and market need) toward entrepreneurship.

Pulpería ownership in Nicaragua is the primary (though not the exclusive) domain of female entrepreneurs at the BOP. For most pulperos, profits achieved through self-employment most likely surpass other realistic employment options. This financial outcome is good news for most pulperos who have little or no education. Moreover, business income from pulpería ownership is relatively stable in the region, another benefit of tiendita ownership (Pisani and Yoskowitz, 2012). This is so in spite of the triple disadvantage of the majority of pulperías: female-owned, informal, and based in the home (Nichter and Goldmark, 2009).

Challenges remain, however, for pulperas who suffer a large profit penalty on account of their gender. While gender roles and economic equality are a larger societal issue, this sector may be enhanced through the targeting of pulperas for training in bookkeeping. Pulperas who kept a separate accounting of the business earned nearly a 25 percent profit premium. Public resources could be arranged for basic bookkeeping training at the BOP in order to improve the earnings outcomes of pulperas. Other policy initiatives, such as access to financing and investment capital, business planning, and ease of governmental regulation, may also be helpful in sustaining and improving pulpera businesses.

Self-employed pulperos play an important role at the BOP, not only serving BOP consumers, but also achieving some modicum of relative good fortune for themselves and households given the available alternatives. Hence, work as a pulpero may be as good a self-employment option as possible for adult women and men to reduce poverty and move beyond survival at the BOP in a challenging emerging market like Nicaragua.

Acknowledgments

I would like to thank the participants of the "Leveraging Innovative and Cross-Country Learning for Poverty Reduction: Climbing the Economic Ladder—Examples from and for Nicaragua" Conference, sponsored by the PRME Working Group on Poverty and INCAE, held at the Francisco de Sola Campus of INCAE, Managua, Nicaragua, July 28–30, 2014, for their helpful comments on an earlier draft of this chapter.

Notes

1 More recently, the phrase "base of the pyramid" has mostly replaced the more pejorative expression "bottom of the pyramid."
2 The term *pulpería* is commonly used in Nicaragua to describe these in-home convenience stores. Throughout much of Latin America, however, the more often used term is *tiendita*. Both terms as well as *tendero/a* and *pulpero/a* (owner of a *tiendita* or *pulpería*) are used interchangeably in this chapter.
3 This is in contrast to SMEs which usually allow for firm size to include up to 50 employees.
4 All monetary amounts in this chapter have been converted to U.S. dollars.
5 The representative national sample of households, or sampling frame, was selected randomly from approximately the same number of households from each department of Nicaragua except the capital city of Managua, where that number was tripled. Care was taken to include both urban and rural households in the same proportion as the population in the region. The universe of households (7,460) was derived from previous censuses, voter registration rolls, and validated with field observation. The non-response rate was 8.7 percent. Overall, the quality of the data and sample are considered good.
6 No specialized government census of tienditas exists for Nicaragua.
7 The conversion rate used is 22.9840 Nicaraguan córdobas per \$1US as recorded on July 1, 2012 on Oanda.com.
8 Female *pulperas* earned \$85.17 in their primary occupation and \$10.87 in their second occupation monthly. Male *pulperos* earned \$156.23 in their primary occupation and \$13.97 in their second occupation monthly. The number of hours worked on the second job was significantly different between men and women (ANOVA, $F=6.606$, $df=1$, $p=.011$).
9 In contrast, only 11.0 percent of employees of *tienditas* held a second job. Representative second jobs include: agricultural work (25.4 percent), *tiendita* (23.9 percent), street vendor (19.4 percent), cook (13.4 percent), laborer (11.9 percent), and other (6.0 percent).
10 Additionally, the multiple regression model for monthly profits for second business ownership proved insignificant. Nevertheless, one variable impacted second business profits: receipt of foreign remittances. Indeed, foreign remittances augmented hourly profits by \$1.48. Hence, assistance from abroad may help create and sustain a notable secondary income. Nevertheless, this result is only to be understood as illustrative of the potential impact remittances may have on second business income.

References

Babb, F. E. (2001). *After Revolution, Mapping Gender and Cultural Politics in Neoliberal Nicaragua*, Austin, TX, University of Texas Press.

Baptista, José, Ramalho, J. J. S. and Vidigal da Silva, J. (2006). Understanding the Microenterprise Sector to Design a Tailor-made Microfinance Policy for Cape Verde. *Portuguese Economic Journal*, 5(3), 225–241.

Banco Central de Nicaragua. (2013). Nicaragua en Cifras – 2012, [Nicaragua in Figures] http//www.bcn.gob.ni/estadisticas/economicas_anuales/nicaragua_en_cifras/2012/Nicaragua_cifras_2012.pdf, accessed on May 29, 2013.

Blanchflower, D. G. and Oswald, A. J. (1998). What Makes an Entrepreneur? *Journal of Labor Economics*, 16(1), 26–60.

Daniels, L. (2003). Factors that Influence the Expansion of the Microenterprise Sector, Results from Three National Surveys in Zimbabwe. *Journal of International Development*, 15(6), 675–692.

D'Haese, M., Van de Berg, M., and Speelman, S. (2008). A Country-wide Study of Consumer Choice for an Emerging Supermarket Sector, A Case Study of Nicaragua. *Development Policy Review*, 26(5), 603–615.

Fajnzylber, P., Maloney W. and Rojas, G. M. (2006). Microenterprise Dynamics in Developing Countries, How Similar are They to Those in the Industrialized World? Evidence from Mexico. *The World Bank Economic Review*, 20(3), 389–419.

Funkhouser, E. (1996). The Urban Informal Sector in Central America, Household Survey Evidence. *World Development*, 24(11), 1731–1751.

Gurtoo, A. and Williams, C. C. (2009). Entrepreneurship and the Informal Sector. *International Journal of Entrepreneurship and Innovation*, 10(1), 55–62.

Haese, D. (2007). Closing the Gender Gap. *ESR Review*, 9(2), 4–9.

Hart, K. (1970). Small Scale Entrepreneurs in Ghana and Development Planning. *Journal of Development Planning*, 6(4), 104–120.

Hart, K. (1973). Informal Income Opportunities and Urban Employment in Ghana. *Journal of Modern African Studies*,11(1), 61–89.

Itzigsohn, J. (2000). *Developing Poverty, The States, Labor Market Deregulation, and the Informal Economy in Costa Rica and the Dominican Republic*, University Park, PA, The Pennsylvania State University Press.

Jain, A. and Pisani, M. J. (2008). Small and Microenterprise Business Development in Costa Rica, An Examination of Domestic and Foreign Born Entrepreneurs. *Latin American Business Review*, 9(2), 149–167.

Johnson, M. A. (1998). An overview of basic issues facing microenterprise practices in the United States. *Journal of Developmental Entrepreneurship*. 3(1), 5–22.

Khan, E.A. and Quaddus, M. (2015). Examining the Influence of Business Environment on Socio-economic Performance of Informal Microenterprises, Content Analysis and Partial Least Square Approach. *International Journal of Sociology and Social Policy*, 35 (3/4), 273–288.

Kirzner, I. M. (1973).*Competition and Entrepreneurship*, Chicago, IL, University of Chicago Press.

McKenzie, D. J. and Woodruff, C. (2006). Do Entry Costs Provide an Empirical Basis for Poverty Traps? Evidence from Mexican Microenterprises. *Economic Development and Cultural Change*, 55(1), 3–42.

Mead, D. C. and Liedholm, C. (1998). The Dynamics of Micro and Small Enterprises in Developing Countries. *World Development*, 26(1), 61–74.

Nichter, S. and Goldmark, L. (2009). Small Firm Growth in Developing Countries. *World Development*, 37(9), 1453–1464.

Pisani, M. J. (2013). Informal Entrepreneurship in Central America, A Labor of Love or Survival? in Mai Thi Thanh Thai and Ekaterina Turkina (Eds.). *Entrepreneurship in the Informal Economy, Models, Approaches and Perspectives for Economic Development*, New York, Routledge, pp. 127–142.

Pisani, M. J. and Pagán, J.A. (2004). Self-Employment in the Era of the New Economic Model in Latin America, A Case Study from Nicaragua. *Entrepreneurship and Regional Development*, 16(4) July, 335–350.

Pisani, M. J. and Patrick, J. M. (2002). A Conceptual Model and Propositions for Bolstering Entrepreneurship in the Informal Sector, The Case of Central America. *Journal of Developmental Entrepreneurship*, 7(1), 95–111.

Pisani, M. J. and Yoskowitz, D. W. (2005). In God We Trust: A Qualitative Study of Church-Sponsored Microfinance at the Margins in Nicaragua. *Journal of Microfinance*, 7(2), 1–41.

Pisani, M. J. and Yoskowitz, D. W. (2012). A Study of Small Neighborhood Tienditas in Central America. *Latin American Research Review*, 47(4), 116–138.

Prahalad, C. K. (2004). *Fortune at the Bottom of the Pyramid, Eradicating Poverty through Profits*, Upper Saddle River, NJ, Prentice Hall.

Walker, T.W. and Wade, C. J. (2011). *Nicaragua, Living in the Shadow of the Eagle*, Boulder, CO, Westview Press.

Williams, C. C. (2007). Entrepreneurs Operating in the Informal Economy, Necessity or Opportunity Driven? *Journal of Small Business and Entrepreneurship*, 20(3), 309–320.

Williams, C. C. (2008). Beyond Necessity-driven versus Opportunity-driven Entrepreneurship, A Study of Informal Entrepreneurs in England, Russia and Ukraine. *International Journal of Entrepreneurship and Innovation*, 9(3), 157–165.

Williams, Colin C. and Youssef, Youssef. A. (2014). Is Informal Sector Entrepreneurship Necessity- or Opportunity-driven? Some Lessons from Urban Brazil. *Business and Management Research*, 3(1), 41–53.

World Bank (2013). Nicaragua, http://data.worldbank.org/country/nicaragua, accessed on May 29, 2013.

World Food Programme (2014). Nicaragua, accessed at http//www.wfp.org/countries/nicaragua on February 11, 2014.

Xavier, S. R., Kelley, D., Kew, J., Herrington, M. and Vorderwülbecke, A. (2012). Global Entrepreneurship Monitor 2012 Global Report, available at, http//www.gemconsortium.org/docs/download/2645, accessed May 31, 2013.

27

DETERMINANTS OF PARTICIPATION IN THE INFORMAL SECTOR IN SRI LANKA

Evidence from a recently conducted special survey

Chandani Wijebandara and N. S. Cooray

Introduction

The informal sector is crucial for developing economies as a means of employment generation when the public sector or formal private sector cannot absorb the total labour force (Gupta, 1993; Sethuraman, 1997; ILO, 2002). The informal sector in many South Asian countries is characterized as small, unorganized household based enterprises where usually only one person, with a few members of a household or a few hired casual labourers, works. In India for example, of a total workforce of 397 million, only 28 million are employed in the organized sector, meaning that 92 per cent of the Indian workforce are employed in the unorganized sector (Kalirajan et al., 2010, p. 3). Similarly, some 62 per cent of the employed population are engaged in the informal sector in Sri Lanka. It is widely believed that entry to this sector is easy and the utilization of human capital and physical capital are comparatively low. Informal sector enterprises generally are not subject to government regulations, and are unrecognized or unobservable as they are not included in business registries or statistical frames, with no or little social protection for those working in them. The sector comprises a wide range of economic activities, including agricultural, small-scale commercial and production activities, which mostly produce intermediate goods for the formal sector (Chaudhuri, 1989).

Non-competitive labour markets and formal sector wages above labour-market clearing levels in less developed countries were earlier argued to have resulted in informal sector activities, such as subsistence farming or employment in the agriculture sector (Harris and Todaro, 1970; Gërxhani, 2004; Blau, 1985). This traditional belief has been challenged by a number of scholars. They have argued that engagement in the informal sector is a voluntary choice and therefore that this sector is economically efficient (Williams, 2007, 2008, 2009; Williams and Youssef, 2014). Some sceptics, nevertheless, have asserted that the existence of the informal sector will disappear as a positive outcome of modernization, although others believe that its disappearance will not occur, not least due to its production linkages with the formal sector (Maloney, 1999).

The latest views on the existence of the informal sector thus consist of two arguments. First, the assertion that people voluntarily decide to be employed and second, that people join this sector as they have no opportunity to be employed in the formal sector (Fields, 2005). Universally, nevertheless, it is believed that persons employed in the informal sector are highly vulnerable due to a lack of job security, lack of income security and lack of opportunities or advantages compared to their counterparts in formal sector. Moreover, studies relating to poverty argue that these unfavourable conditions of employment may lead to the existence of in-work poverty. Having identified the importance of decent work and full and productive employment for all to overcome poverty and hunger, the United Nations Development Program (UNDP) pledged to achieve the same for all by setting up the Millennium Development Goals.[1]

According to the Department of Census and Statistics in Sri Lanka, informal sector employment accounts for 62 per cent of total employment of the 7.7 million workers in the country. Official statistics further reveal that the informal sector consists of employees (35 per cent), employers (2 per cent), own account workers (47 per cent) and contributing family workers (16 per cent). Moreover, available data suggests that 86 per cent of employment in the agricultural sector is in the informal sector and 51 per cent in the non-agricultural sector. Evidently, therefore, the informal sector plays an important role in the Sri Lankan economy. The Sri Lanka government and International Labour Organization have been making joint efforts to eradicate poverty by developing the 'Decent Work Country Programme 2008–2012'. The three main priorities of this programme were job security, productivity and competitiveness (ILO, 2008).

Although there have been previous studies on the informal sector in Sri Lanka using either a qualitative approach (Sandaratne, 2001) or more quantitative methods (Banda, 1997; Gunatilaka, 2008), no attempt has been made to critically examine, using quantitative tools, the determinants of the informal sector in Sri Lanka in line with the definition of the International Labour Organisation (ILO).[2] This is the aim of this chapter.[3] To do this, data from a national household survey conducted in 2008/2009 is used; the main sources of data are the Sri Lanka Quarterly Labour Force Survey (QLFS) 2008/2009 and a parallel survey on Household Unincorporated Enterprises with Market production (HUEM), which was specially conducted on a pilot basis under a project on informal sector.[4] The study uses descriptive statistics, bivariate and multivariate methods for the analysis. Logistic regression analysis is utilized to determine the factors that affect participation in the informal sector using QLFS data. The main objectives of the chapter are: (a) to critically examine the current status of informal sector employment; (b) to identify the various socio-economic determinants of informal sector labour participation; and (c) to draw policy recommendations on informal sector employment in Sri Lanka.

The chapter is organised as follows. Following this introduction, the second section provides a review of the key concepts and determinants. The third section provides an overview of characteristics of informal sector employment in Sri Lanka, while the fourth section provides an econometric model specification of the results. In the final section some policy inferences are drawn.

Concepts and determinants: a review

The genesis of the informal sector concept

The term informal sector was used for the first time by the International Labour Organization during their first broad employment mission to Kenya in 1972. In their report on 'Employment, incomes and equality', they defined informality as a 'way of doing things characterized by (a) ease of entry; (b) reliance on indigenous resources; (c) family ownership; (d) small scale operations; (e) labour intensive and adaptive technology; (e) skills acquired outside of the formal sector; and (g) unregulated and competitive markets'. Moreover, by considering the situation of Kenya the study explains, 'Informal sector activities are largely ignored, rarely supported, often regulated and sometimes actively discouraged by the Government' (ILO, 1972: 4). From this starting point, different authors have used different concepts and definitions to define the informal sector. This diversity depends on the nature of the informal sector of a specific country.

Some studies defined the informal sector using the legal status of the organization by focusing on the regulatory framework (de Soto, 1989). In De Soto's book based on Peru, he identifies this sector as enterprises which are 'outside of law' since in Peru this sector was not supported by the government. However, the Peruvian context is different from the state of the informal sector in Sri Lanka, where this sector is supported and promoted by various government policies. In Sri Lanka moreover, the procedure of business registration is comparatively easier and simple. Hence the definition of 'outside of law' is not valid for Sri Lanka.

Other studies use 'business registration' to define the sector, but using only the 'business registration' criteria is also insufficient since many small-scale registered enterprises are functionally not different from unregistered enterprises, especially when the registration is not a company registration. However, Sandaratne (2001) defines the informal sector in Sri Lanka as individual activities and small production units where there are no formal/ written accounts or no written labour contracts, and also as household economic activities (Sandaratne, 2001).

Some studies also use the size of the enterprise, such as the numbers of persons employed, as a threshold to define informal sector. As a result, small-scale operations are identified as in the informal sector. Other studies use the professional status of the individual such as, 'self-employed persons' or 'own account workers'. Yet it is obvious that not all small enterprises, self-employed people or own account workers need to be by definition employed in the informal sector.

While a comparable and a concrete definition for the informal sector for all countries is still under discussion, the definition developed by the ILO and included in the System of National Accounts 1993 is widely used. As described by Hussmanns (2004), this definition is based on the characteristics of the production unit (enterprises) in which activities take place, rather than in terms of the characteristics of the persons involved or of their jobs (labour approach). Hussmann's report further explained that there are conceptual differences between the informal sector (15th ICLS) and informal employment (17th ICLS). In 2006, the Department of Census and Statistics of Sri Lanka (DC&S), the national statistical organization, started to collect information to identify the informal sector of the country through a Quarterly Labour Force Survey. DC&S used the ILO guidelines to define the informal sector and as such examines the three key aspects regarding a production unit, namely its registration status, accounts-keeping practices and the number of regular employees. In this chapter therefore, the ILO definition of an informal sector enterprise is used to explore the informal sector in Sri Lanka.

Determinants of the informal sector

Traditional labour market theories highlight the dualistic nature of the economy viewing it as composed of a modern urban sector and a traditional agricultural sector, or a covered sector and a non-covered sector, where the informal sector is the disadvantaged sector into which workers enter to escape urban unemployment. Moreover, these studies explain that when the wages are set above market-clearing prices, some part of labour is rationed out of the formal sector and the urban informal sector absorbs that fraction of labour (Harris and Todaro, 1970). Hence, the earnings in the informal sector are arguably less compared with the formal sector and people move from informal to formal when there are no entry barriers. Later, some studies on the informal sector argued differently, such as that informal sector employment is a voluntary decision of an individual (Maloney, 1999; Williams and Horodnic, 2015).

The latest argument on informal sector employment is even more nuanced. Fields (2005) divides the informal sector into two distinct categories, namely an 'upper tier' and 'lower tier'. The 'upper tier' represents the competitive part where individuals enter voluntarily while maximizing their utilities and when they expect to earn more than they would earn in the formal sector. The 'lower tier' consists of individuals who were rationed out of the formal labour market. Past research shows that one segment of the informal sector (the 'upper-tier' informal sector) is superior to the other (the 'lower-tier' informal sector) in terms of significantly higher earnings as well as higher returns to education and experience. Moreover, their results clearly show that testing for labour market competitiveness in developing economies can be less precise because it ignores either the employment decision of individuals (leading to selection bias) or the heterogeneity of the informal sector.

Blau (1985) analyzed the influence of unobservable factors such as managerial ability on individual's choice between self and waged employment. He found that managerial ability is positively correlated with an individual's choice to be self-employed. Furthermore, managerial ability has different effects for self-employment in farm and non-farm sectors. Funkhouser (1996), in his study using five Spanish-speaking countries, explained that the level of development and institutional arrangement of a country are vital factors influencing the informal sector. Furthermore, his study explains human capital as a strong determinant of informal sector earnings.

Moreover, the existing literature in developing countries reveals some important determinants of informal sector workers. Maloney (2004) explained in his study that women are over-represented in the informal labour market, both as salaried workers and self-employed. This may be linked to the limited opportunities for women in some countries or, for example, to the downsizing in many countries of public employment, which traditionally has been the main destination of women in the labour market. Furthermore, his study explained that one reason is that women value the flexibility and autonomy that informal work offers as it allows them to combine work and family responsibilities more easily. Perry et al. (2007), meanwhile, show that single women are the most likely to engage in formal employment relative to married women and men. However, among married women, those with more young children are more likely to be self-employed in the informal sector, which also suggests a link between family responsibilities and the choice of informal work, in particular self-employment. Maloney (2004) shows, using evidence from Argentina, Mexico, Costa Rica and Brazil, that women with young children are more likely to be self-employed than formal sector employees. Gërxhani (2011) found a strong negative relationship between education and informal sector participation in his study of Albania.

Characteristics of the informal sector in Sri Lanka: an overview

Understanding the size, distribution, changes over time and characteristics of the informal sector in Sri Lanka is important before proceeding to the analytical methods.

An overview of the informal sector in Sri Lanka

The Sri Lanka Quarterly Labour Force Survey (QLFS) is the main source of labour force statistics in the country. This survey has been conducted annually since 1990. All individuals aged 10 years and above are considered as the working age population. The definition of the informal sector chosen for the QLFS, adopted in 2006, uses the 15th ICLS guidelines, where the distinction between the informal and formal sector employs the characteristics of the enterprises. The three main characteristics are the account-keeping practice, tax registration and the number of those employed in the enterprise.

Table 27.1 presents the estimated labour force statistics for the period 1990–2010. During this period, annual household population growth was 1.5 per cent. The data reported in the table excludes the Northern and Eastern provinces in order to keep the same domain for consistency. The data clearly demonstrates that the labour force has been gradually increasing since 1990, and by 2010, it was 7.6 million. However, from the available data, it is apparent that the labour force participation rate has remained constant or stagnant at around 50 per cent for the last two decades.

Therefore, if the current employment participation rate remains constant or declines further, the Sri Lankan labour force is expected to shrink around 2030 as result of on–going demographic changes of the country. As explained by Arunathilake and Jayawardene (2010), population aging is one of the foremost demographic concerns in the country. Moreover, a significant increase in the proportion of youth in education is also identified as a reason for the decrease in the youth labour force of the country. The available data shows that the employed population grew by 2.2 million between 1990 and 2010, while the unemployed population decreased by 0.58 million.

The percentage of informal sector employment is around 62 per cent of total employment and grew about 1 percentage point from 2006 to 2010. Moreover, the statistics reveal that this sector is highly male dominated (70 per cent) (DC&S D. O., 2010). As Table 27.1 shows, the majority (87 per cent) of agricultural employment in the country is in the informal sector. The formal agriculture sector (13 per cent) comprises the estate sector and large holdings, where formal labour is employed.

The informal sector in Sri Lanka comprises a wide range of activities in both urban and rural areas. Non-agricultural informal sector activities are mainly comprised of construction, small-scale manufacturing, restuarants, retail trade and so on. Proprietors of small-scale economic activities, craft and related workers, elementary occupations, plant and machinery operators and sales and service activities are particularly prevalent.

The distribution of the informal sector varies among administrative districts and some studies explain this as resulting from the uneven distribution of industries. The informal sector can be divided into two main segments: the agricultural sector and non-agricultural sector. Figure 27.1 clearly shows the distribution of the non-agricultural informal sector participation rate in different districts, although the northern part of the country was not covered in the survey due to prevailing unsettled political conditions over this time period. The Western Province consists of the Colombo, Gampaha and Kalutara ditricts, where most of the formal sector organizations are located; these show a lower level of informal sector activity. Moreover, the Anuradhapura and Polonnaruwa districts where mostly agricultural activities are located show a lower level of non-agriculture informal sector participation while the other districts, which are situated away from Colombo, show higher non-agricultural informal sector participation. This may be a result of the uneven distribution of formal sector enterprises in the country.

Table 27.1 Distribution of Age 10 and Above Household Population (1990–2010)

Characteristic	Year								
	1990	1995	2000	2006	2007	2008	2009	2010
HH Population – Age 10 and above (millions)	11.57	12.74	13.17	14.83	15.05	15.08	15.39	15.65
Labour Force Population (millions)	6.00	6.11	6.83	7.59	7.49	7.56	7.57	7.61
Not in Labour Force Population (millions)	5.57	6.63	6.74	7.23	7.56	7.51	7.82	8.04
Unemployed Population (millions)	0.95	0.75	0.52	0.49	0.45	0.39	0.43	0.37
Employed Population (millions)	5.05	5.36	6.31	7.10	7.04	7.17	7.14	7.23
Formal Sector Employment (percent)	NA	NA	NA	38.4	38.1	39.8	38.1	37.4
Informal Sector Employment (percent)	NA	NA	NA	61.6	61.9	60.2	61.9	62.6
Labour Force Participation Rate	51.90	47.90	50.30	51.20	49.80	50.20	49.20	48.60
Unemployment Rate	15.90	12.30	7.60	6.50	6.00	5.20	5.70	4.90

Source: Department of Census and Statistics, QLFS, *Annual Report – 2010*.

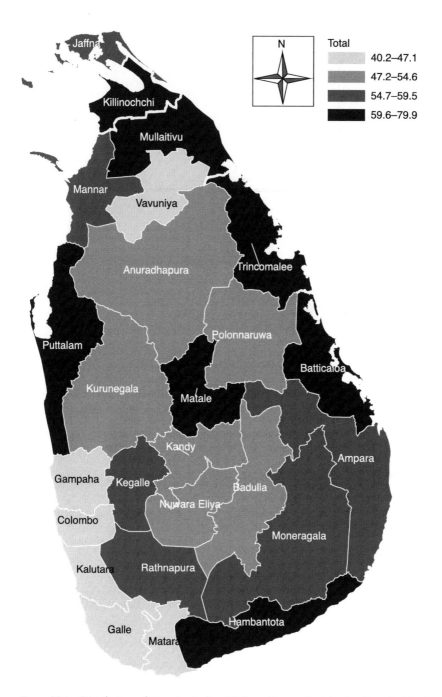

Figure 27.1 Distribution of Non-Agricultural Informal Sector Participation Rate by Districts – 2008

Background to the data of the current study

The study uses data from the Sri Lanka Labour Force Survey (QLFS), which was conducted from the fourth quarter of 2008 until the third quarter of 2009. This is a special data set, since during this period a special survey was conducted to identify informal sector acivities in detail through a survey module attached to the regular Labour Force Survey. This survey module is called 'A survey on Household Unincorporated Enterprises with Market Production' (HUEM). The current study uses this data set in order to conduct an analysis of the informal sector. The survey covered the whole country, excluding the Northern Province, and data was collected for 12 monthly rounds from October 2008 until September 2009. The total sample consists of 20,000 housing units. The sampling design is the same as the QLFS. It is a two-stage stratified sample; the primary sampling unit (PSU) is a census block (a list of housing units in an enumeration area during the 2001 population census) and the secondary sampling unit (SSU) is a housing unit; information was collected from all individuals of the selected household. The HUEM survey consisted of two phases. The first phase (Phase 1) is a module attached to the QLFS to identify HUEMs. The second phase (Phase 2) is a separate questionnaire to get more information on identified HUEMs. The data set used for this study consists of data from the QLFS and from Phase 1 and Phase 2 of the HUEM survey. To identify informal sector employment in the country, the QLFS part of the data is used.

Descriptive analysis

The estimated employed population using the data sample is about 7.6 million, which is almost equal to the published official figure for 2009. This study uses the same definition which is used in the QLFS to define informal sector employment. The estimated informal sector employment is about 61 per cent of the total employed population. It also reveals, as displayed in Table 27.2, that more employed males are engaged in the informal sector than women.

The rural sector of the country, which consists mostly of agricultural activities, small-scale industries, retail trade activities, small-scale construction activities and household economic activities, shows high informal sector employment. The descriptive statistics clearly demonstrate that the agricultural sector and those with lower levels of eduaction show higher levels of informal sector participation. Among the ethnic groups of the country 'Sri Lanka Moor' shows comparatively higher participation in the informal sector while 'Indian Tamils' show higher formal sector partipation since they are employed in the estate sector, where the country's formal sector agriculture is located. There are four categories of employment status and it is obvious from the statistics that own account workers and contributing family worker are highly concentrated in the informal sector.

The survey results reported in Table 27.3 reveal that the average age of a person engaged in the informal sector is higher compared with a person in the formal sector. For the formal sector, there is an upper age limit for retirement but for the informal sector no upper age limit is applicable. Moreover, some of those who are retired from the formal sector enter the informal sector as an additional income source. This may result in the higher average age for informal sector workers. The results also show that formal sector workers are employed for more hours than informal workers. Generally, there is a standard work norm for the formal sector, but for the workers in the informal sector such conditions do not usually apply and the hours worked also depend on the sector in which they are employed. The average household sizes of those employed in the informal and formal sectors are also different.

Table 27.2 Distribution of Employment by Various Charateristics and by Institutional Sector (2008/2009)

Variables	Formal sector (percent)	Informal sector (percent)	Total
Sex			
Male	35.6	64.3	100
Female	43.9	56.0	100
Level of education			
No schooling	23.8	76.2	100
Primary or less	20.6	79.4	100
Junior secondary	28.7	71.3	100
Pass O/L	51.1	48.9	100
Pass A/L and above	78.9	21.1	100
Ethnicity			
Sinhala	37.4	62.6	100
Sri Lanka Tamil	44.6	55.4	100
Indian Tamil	70.5	29.5	100
Sri Lanka Moor	27.6	72.4	100
Other	56.2	43.8	100
Residential Sector			
Urban	53.6	46.4	100
Rural	34.5	65.5	100
Estate	72.4	27.6	100
Industrial Sector			
Agriculture	15.5	84.5	100
Industry	42.9	57.1	100
Services	54.0	46.0	100
Employment status			
Employee	60.5	39.5	100
Employer	44.4	55.6	100
Own Account Worker	5.2	94.8	100
Contributing Family Worker	8.1	91.9	100

Note: Statistics are estimated using the sample data.

Table 27.3 Mean Comparison for Selected Variables

Variable	Mean		Mean Difference
	Formal Sector (Std.Err.)	Informal Sector (Std.Err.)	
Age	38.07	42.17	★★★
	(0.1152)	(0.1051)	
Number of hours usually work per week	49.14	44.08	★★★
	(0.1372)	(0.1270)	
Household size	4.48	4.36	★★★
	(0.0158)	(0.0121)	

***- *Statistically significant at 1 percent level of significance*

In sum, the above results clearly identify some important differences between the informal and formal sector in Sri Lanka. To explore whether these remain significant differences when other variables are held constant, a binary logit analysis will be performed.

Data and model

The main objective of the study is to identify factors which determine individuals to be employed in the informal sector using an econometric model. This section presents the econometric model using individual level cross-sectional survey data.[5]

The empirical framework of the econometric model

The focus group of this study is the employed sample. The employed sample size is 28,088 individuals. Each employed person is identified as working in either the formal sector or informal sector. This is used as the dependant variable for the model. The logistic regression analysis is well suited for studying the relationship between dichotomous dependants and independent variables.

Binary logistic regression model

Model specification

There are multiplicities of macroeconomic and microeconomic variables that decide whether an individual is employed in the formal sector or informal sector. A general function is considered.

$$Y_i = f(X_1, X_2, X_3, \ldots \ldots, X_n) \tag{1}$$

where, Y_i shows the individual's participation decision in an informal sector employment. Y_i is equal to '1' if a worker is employed in the informal sector and equal to zero if the worker is employed in the formal sector.

In the probit and logit model, we assume that there is an unobserved variable (latent variable) $y^\star$ that depends on x:

$$y^\star = \beta_0 + \beta_1 x + u \tag{2}$$

$y^\star$ can be considered as the utility from participating in the informal sector employment. However $y^\star$ cannot be observed and only the actual sector participation outcome can be observed. That is,

$Y = 0$ if the person is not working in the informal sector (working in formal sector)
$Y = 1$ if the person is working in the informal sector

Then it is assumed that,

If $Y = 0$ (the person is not working in the informal sector), then $y^\star$ must have been negative.
If $Y = 1$ (the person is working in the informal sector), then $y^\star$ must have been positive.

$$\begin{cases} \text{If } Y = 0, \text{ then } y\star < 0 \\ \text{If } Y = 1, \text{ then } y\star \geq 0 \end{cases}$$

Given the data about x and Y, we can compute the likelihood contribution for each person in the data by making the distributional assumption about the error term u.

The model:

$$y_i\star = \beta_0 + \beta_1 x_i + u_i, \qquad\qquad\qquad\qquad (3)$$

where i denotes the ith observation.

If error term u_i follows the standard normal distribution $\sim N$ (0, 1) then the model is a probit model. If error term u_i follows a logistic distribution then the model is a logit model.

If u_i follows a logistic distribution, the likelihood contributions are

$$\begin{cases} L_i = \dfrac{1}{1 + e^{\beta_0 + \beta_1 x_i}} \text{ if } Y_i = 0 \\ L_i = \dfrac{e^{\beta_0 + \beta_1 x_i}}{1 + e^{\beta_0 + \beta_1 x_i}} \text{ if } Y_i = 1 \end{cases}$$

Hence, the likelihood function is,

$$L = \prod_{i=1}^{n} L_i = \prod_{i=1}^{n} \left[\frac{1}{1 + e^{\beta_0 + \beta_1 x_i}} \right]^{(1 - Y_i)} \left[\frac{e^{\beta_0 + \beta_1 x_i}}{1 + e^{\beta_0 + \beta_1 x_i}} \right]^{Y_i} \qquad\qquad (4)$$

The coefficient estimates of the logistic model can be obtained by maximizing Log(L). To maximize the log-likelihood, one can differentiate with respect to the β s to find out the $\beta\wedge$. Similarly, coefficients for all independent variables can be obtained using numerical or iterative procedures. The method known as 'Newton Raphson Method' is used to solve the equations to obtain coefficients.

Selection of independent variables

Two groups of factors affect the individual's decision to select the informal sector (Gërxhani and van de Werfhorst, 2013), namely opportunity factors and structural factors. The structural factors consist of financial pressure; socio-psychological pressure; and (formal) institutional constraints. The opportunity factors consist of such individual characteristics as: skills, education, contacts and living situation, or non-individual factors: environment, cultural tradition, values and standards, and geographical factors. Table 27.4 shows the independent variables used for the analysis.

The variables are limited and qualitative in nature, since the objective of the Labour Force Survey is much broader compared to this study. This is one of the limitations of using secondary data for the analysis. All the variables are categorical other than age and district unemployment rate.

Robustness statistics

There are a number of important issues to be considered before estimating the logistic regression model for the analysis such as,

Table 27.4 The Independent Variables Used for the Analysis

Group	Independent Variable
Opportunity Factors	**Individual factors**
	Sex
	Age
	Level of education
	Literacy in English
	Marital status
	Currently attend in any education
	Relationship to head of household
	Ethnicity
	Non-individual factors
	Residential Sector
Structural factors	District Unemployment rate

a) The data comes from a national household survey and therefore sampling weights need to be applied to generalize the results.

b) This is a household survey and the data set includes information collected from all members of the household. Members of the household may have more unobservable similarities than non-members and this is often called intra-class correlation. This violates the assumption of independence between observations; hence this may lead to incorrect standard errors. In order to minimize this error, this study identifies each household as a cluster and the model estimation is done using clustered robust standard errors in STATA.

c) The study focuses only on the employed sample but the other two groups, inactive and unemployed, cannot be neglected due to the problem of sample selection bias, which results due to the self-selection of individuals to the labour force (Heckman, 1979). Therefore this study performs the econometric analysis by considering sample selection bias using the Heckman method. As explained in Heckman's model two kinds of equations are utilized: equation for the self-selection and equation for the problem of interest.

Self-selection equation

This study assumes that the individual's employment decision is a function of individual, household and some social characteristics. It also assumes that an individual's selection is either employed or inactive. The unemployed are also a part of the labour force, which accounts for 0.4 million, or 6 per cent of the total labour force. The inactive population is about 8 million and is almost half of the working age population of the country. Given the statistics, it is clear that the unemployed population is very small; hence this study includes the involuntary unemployed individuals into the inactive group, who voluntarily stay out of labour market. Only 5 per cent of the inactive population is actively looking for employment and therefore without loss of information unemployment can be included in voluntary inactive group.

The selection equation is generally a probit equation (Heckman, 1979). By considering the assumptions explained above, the independent and dependent variables for the model are specified. The dependant variable is a dichotomous type variable, which identifies each individual as 1 if he/she is employed and 0 if he/she is inactive. The independent variables are individual, household and social characteristics available in the QLFS survey data. Selection of independent variables is done with the gained knowledge from background statistics and from literature with the limitation of available information of the survey. These independent variables are consistent with variables from Table 27.4 and with exclusion variables specified below.

To specify the self-selection equation of entering the labour market some additional variables are required; these are called exclusion variables from the problem of interest equation. This study uses the following exclusion variables:

  i. Number of children (age five years and below) in the household
 ii. Number of inactive older persons (age 70 years and above) in the household
iii. Household size

There are two reasons to select the above variables. First, clearly, these variables should collect household-specific reasons that influence the individual's decision to participate in the labour market by considering the opportunity cost of staying out of the labour market. Also these variables have no direct impact on the participation in the informal sector, when the participation decision comes earlier. For example having very young children or older persons at home raises the problem of care taking, since in Sri Lanka day care centres are not so popular; at the same time having elderly persons in the household may be a positive factor for a person to participate in the labour force. It is well known that the size of the household is positively correlated with poverty and may have positive effects for members to participate in the labour force. The other reason, selected variables for the selection model, should provide sufficient exclusion restriction.

By considering all the above issues, separate regressions were estimated to find the most suitable equation, which can be used to discuss the results. The results in Table 27.5 show the estimated coefficients and robust standard errors for each regression equation. The regressions with the Heckman method show little evidence of having sample selection bias in data. The 'lamda' statistic is not significantly different from zero. Therefore we can assume the employed sample is randomly chosen. Moreover the signs of the independent variables do not change for different models and estimated coefficients are almost equal. The most important thing is that statistical significance of the estimated coefficients does not change over the models. After giving careful consideration it is decided that binary logistic regression on the weighted sample and corrected for intra-class correlation is acceptable for presenting final results. Also the extra variables used in the self-selection equation show expected signs and coefficients, which are highly statistically significant. The number of children (age<=5) and the number of inactive old persons at home show negative significant relationship for participating in the labour force, while the household size positively affects labour force participation.

Results and discussion

Table 27.5 presents the estimated coefficients, signs and the statistical significance of explanatory variables. The following discussion is based on the results of Equation–2, but

Table 27.5 The Regression Coefficients and Robust Standard Errors for Different Equations Dependant Variable of the self selection equation: 1 - Economically active, 0 - Economically inactive Dependant Variable of the problem of interest equation: 1 - Employed in informal sector, 0 - Employed in formal sector

Independent Variables	Problem of Interest					
	Equation 1	Equation 2	Equation 3	Equation 4	Equation 5	Equation 6
	Coefficient (Robust Std.Err.)					
Sex						
Male (Reference group)	–	–	–	–	–	–
Female	−0.4525 (0.0417)★	−0.4312 (0.0464)★	−0.4940 (0.1118)★	−0.0872 (0.0195)★	−0.0885 (0.0178)★	−1.0778 (0.0194)★
Age Age in years	0.0191 (0.0014)★	0.0182 (0.0016)★	0.0171 (0.0024)★	0.0030 (0.0004)★	0.0032 (0.0004)★	−0.0221 (0.0006)★
Level of education						
No schooling (Reference group)	–	–	–	–	–	–
Primary or less	0.0413 (0.0898)	−0.0892 (0.0957)	−0.0816 (0.0967)	−0.0144 (0.0136)	0.0040 (0.0148)	0.1284 (0.0335)★
Junior secondary	−0.3869 (0.0870)★	−0.5701 (0.0945)★	−0.5670 (0.0947)★	−0.0858 (0.0134)★	−0.0590 (0.0144)★	0.0403 (0.0326)
Pass O/L	−1.2227 (0.0920)★	−1.3919 (0.1001)★	−1.3889 (0.1003)★	−0.2704 (0.0157)★	−0.2444 (0.0156)★	0.0507 (0.0364)
Pass A/L and above	−2.2692 (0.0966)★	−2.4121 (0.1058)★	−2.3881 (0.1129)★	−0.4781 (0.0181)★	−0.46016 (0.0174)★	0.4763 (0.0400)★
Literacy in English						
Not literate (Reference group)	–	–	–	–	–	–
Literate	−0.8525 (0.0441)★	−0.8942 (0.0502)★	−0.8939 (0.0502)★	−0.1789 (0.0103)★	−0.1698 (0.0083)★	0.0018 (0.0219)
Marital Status						
Never married (Reference group)	–	–	–	–	–	–
Married	−0.1382 (0.0491)★	−0.1204 (0.0548)★★	−0.1013 (0.0635)	−0.0182 (0.0117)	−0.0223 (0.0103)★★	0.4605 (0.0262)★
Separated/Widowed	0.1772 (0.0841)★	0.1861 (0.0913)★★	0.1952 (0.0929)★★	0.0343 (0.0158)★★	0.0325 (0.0147)★★	0.2696 (0.0374)★

(Continued)

Table 27.5 (Continued)

Independent Variables	Problem of Interest					
	Equation 1	Equation 2	Equation 3	Equation 4	Equation 5	Equation 6
	Coefficient (Robust Std.Err.)					
Currently attend in education						
Not attending (Reference group)	–	–	–	–	–	–
Attending	1.0918 (0.1252)★	1.1156 (0.1254)★	0.9363 (0.3087)★	0.1779 (0.0548)★	0.1812 (0.0513)★	-2.4468 (0.0409)★
Relationship to head of household						
Head of household (Reference group)	–	–	–	–	–	–
Spouse	0.4339 (0.0530)★	0.4433 (0.0551)★	0.4331 (0.0568)★	0.0789 (0.0102)★	0.0779 (0.0097)★	-0.2863 (0.0221)★
Child	0.0352 (0.0504)	0.0206 (0.0554)	0.0023 (0.0624)	-0.0016 (0.0115)	0.0011 (0.0103)	-0.3546 (0.0275)★
Relative	-0.03108 (0.0561)	-0.0626 (0.0613)	-0.0949 (0.0796)	-0.0207 (0.0144)	-0.0137 (0.0129)	-0.5560 (0.0250)★
Other	0.4679 (0.1632)★	0.4322 (0.2239)★★★	0.4737 (0.2376)★★	0.0816 (0.0402)★★	0.0857 (0.0304)★	0.9020 (0.1125)★
Ethnicity						
Sinhalese (Reference group)	–	–	–	–	–	–
Sri Lanka Tamil	-0.0563 (0.0602)	-0.0484 (0.0809)	-0.0536 (0.0814)	-0.0097 (0.0144)	-0.0117 (0.0108)	-0.1118 (0.0289)★
Indian Tamil	-0.5635 (0.0945)★	-0.5518 (0.1328)★	-0.5546 (0.1327)★	-0.1102 (0.0258)★	-0.1149 (0.0174)★	-0.0366 (0.0639)
Sri Lanka Moor	0.6804 (0.0610)★	0.6479 (0.0763)★	0.6276 (0.0822)★	0.1053 (0.0128)★	0.1108 (0.0112)★	-0.3932 (0.0244)★
Other	-0.1584 (0.2100)	-0.2583 (0.2504)	-0.2643 (0.2505)	-0.0499 (0.0458)	-0.0353 (0.0382)	-0.1123 (0.0943)
Residential Sector						
Urban (Reference group)	–	–	–	–	–	–
Rural	0.4699 (0.0462)★	0.4495 (0.0568)★	0.4579 (0.0583)★	0.0846 (0.0107)★	0.0876 (0.0085)★	0.1676 (0.0217)★
Estate	-1.3530 (0.0833)★	-1.3840 (0.1226)★	-1.3620 (0.1271)★	-0.2988 (0.0249)★	-0.2953 (0.0164)★	0.4329 (0.0481)★

	Equation 1	Equation 2	Equation 3	Equation 4	Equation 5	Equation 6
District Unemployment rate	0.0415 (0.0067)★	0.0524 (0.0080)★	0.0511 (0.0083)★	0.0089 (0.0014)★	0.0071 (0.0012)★	-0.0258 (0.0031)★
Exclusion variables						
No. of children age <= 5						-0.1990 (0.0120)★
No. of inactive persons age>=70						-0.2785 (0.0163)★
Housuhold size						0.0309 (0.0049)★
Lamda			0.1047 (0.1654)	0.0145 (0.0289)	0.0098 (0.0267)	
Constant	0.2140 (0.1316)	0.3395 (0.1455)★★	0.3379 (0.1456)★★	0.5935 (0.0242)★	0.5785 (0.0227)★	1.5116 (0.0599)★

★ – Statistically significant at 1 % level of significance

★★ – Statistically significant at 5 % level of significance

★★★ – Statistically significant at 10 % level of significance

Equation 1 :- Logit with sample weight for problem of interest (Informal sector)

Equation 2 :- Logit with sample weight and cluster option for problem of interest (Informal sector)

Equation 3 :- Probit for selection equation and Logit with sample weight and cluster option for problem of interest (Informal sector)

Equation 4 :- Probit for selection equation and simple Linear regression with sample weight and cluster option for problem of interest (Informal sector)

Equation 5 :- STATA inbuit command ("hecman")

Equation 6 :- The self selection equation

more attention is paid to the direction and significance of the predictors rather than the magnitude of the coefficients when explaining the results.

The effects of non-individual factors on participation in informal sector employment

Males and females in the labour market have different attitudes. Usually males sell their labour more than females due to opportunity costs. This is especially so in developing economies. The selection equation results show the labour force participation of females is lower compared to males. Similarly, when informal sector participation is considered, the regression results prove a lower level of female participation in comparison to males providing evidence of the male-dominated informal sector of the country.

Generally with increasing age labour force participation is decreasing and the selection equation results support this argument. But when the normal sector participation is considered it is clear that while age is increasing the participation is also increasing. Since there is no retirement age limit for the informal sector, any person can work until he/she is unable to work. Moreover inadequate social security benefits for retired persons may also direct them to join informal sector activities to earn sufficient income.

Education or achievement in human capital is a very important decision factor for labour force participation, usually as the level of education increases the participation increases. However, the results clearly show that informal sector participation is decreasing as the level of education increases. These results are consistent with many of the findings in the literature. Gërxhani and van de Werfhorst (2011) in their study explain various roles of education in occupational choices of persons, such as education itself increases the likelihood of getting a good job with a high income; the higher the education higher the moral attitude and usually these persons refuse to enter the informal sector. More importantly level of education satisfies the formal sector requirements hence more formal sector opportunities are for educated persons. In this competitive situation people with lower levels of education are automatically directed to engage in informal sector activities.

Literacy level is also an outcome of education; in Sri Lanka the literacy rate is reported as 91 per cent in 2009 (DC&S D. O., 2010). This is high in comparison to neighbouring countries in Asia. But literacy in the English language is around 18 per cent. The results show a strong negative relationship between informal sector participation and literacy in English. One of the main requirements of the formal private sector recruitment of employees is English literacy. Lack of English proficiency partly blocks a person entering the formal sector, therefore meaning that they may enter informal sector activities.

Marital status of persons usually indicates their household responsibilities, decision-making abilities or independence. The results indicate that informal sector participation of a married person decreases compared with a never married person. Moreover, informal sector participation of a separated/widowed person increases compared with a never married person. This result is interesting since the separated/widowed group might have a lot of responsibilities to face alone without a partner, as compared with never-married with lower responsibilities. A separated/widowed person will be willing to work in the informal sector, where there is a lack of entry barriers and comparatively lower qualifications requirements.

If a person is currently obtaining education, then he/she cannot participate in a full-time economic activity. Usually formal sector activities are full-time economic activities while there are many part-time activities in the informal sector. The informal sector is thus a good opportunity for them to earn while they are studying. Flexibility in time arrangements and lack of rules or regulations may be positive factors to join the informal sector.

The relationship to the head of the household usually indicates the family structure of the household. Sri Lanka is a patriarchal society and the descriptive statistics revealed that there is a higher number of households headed by males than headed by females. Usually, the head of the household is the main earner. However, the results reveal that compared with the head of household, the spouse's informal sector participation is higher. The results also demonstrate that the 'other' group mainly consisting of non-relatives, boarders or servants show higher informal sector participation rates compared with the head of household. These results display the general conditions of the country, such as that some wives engage in informal sector activities including small retail shops, tailoring, etc. to earn additional income for the family while the husband is in another job. Moreover, housemaids and automobile chauffeurs live in the households, employed informally by the household.

Ethnicity is also a factor. The results show only two ethnic groups display a statistically significant difference in informal sector participation rates compared with the majority 'Sinhalese'. The 'Sri Lankan Tamil' main minority does not show any significant difference in participation rates in informal sector activities compared to the 'Sinhalese' and as such, it is hard to find any discrimination against them at least in this respect. It is believed that 'Moors' usually engage in retail and wholesale trade activities. Furthermore, the data clearly reveals that most of the retail trade activities in the country are placed within the informal sector.

The residential sectors of urban, rural and estate have geographical as well as economic variations. The urban sector comprises large-scale enterprises as well as small-scale enterprises. Much of the agriculture is concentrated in the rural sector; also the rural population of the country is comparatively larger. The estate sector comprises the formal agricultural enterprises, such as tea plantations, rubber plantations and some other large-scale farms. It is concentrated in the central hilly areas of the country. The results show that informal sector participation is higher for a person who lives in the rural sector compared with a person who lives in the urban sector while this is opposite for a person in the estate sector. These results indicate that the geographical distribution of industries affects informal sector participation.

The effects of district unemployment level on participation in informal sector employment

Socio-economic conditions such as poverty levels, GDP contribution, industrial composition and unemployment level vary from district to district. This study uses the district unemployment rate as an indicator for local labour market conditions. The available data clearly shows that youth unemployment is considerably high at around 19 per cent for the 15–24 age group, although the overall unemployment rate is low (5 per cent). Moreover, unemployment rates vary among districts (DC&S D. O., 2010). Unemployment can be considered as an indicator for the mismatching in labour supply and demand. Also, district unemployment can be considered as an indicator of the lack of job opportunities in the area and less favourable labour market conditions.

The regression results show a strong positive relation between informal sector participation rates and district unemployment rates. This indicates a high concentration of the informal sector where unemployment is high, proving either the lack of opportunities in the formal sector or the mismatching with formal sector requirements. Hence, the observed high informal sector may be a result of involuntary informal sector employment in those districts.

Findings and policy recommendations

Using the latest Labour Force Survey data from the special survey conducted by the Department of Census and Statistics, this chapter has critically examined the current character of the informal sector and identified the various socio-economic determinants of informal sector labour participation in Sri Lanka.

Our estimated figure of a 7.6 million total labour force, using 73,000 individual sample data, is almost equal to the published official figure in 2010. Of the 7.6 million, 61 per cent of people are engaged in the informal sector and the majority are male. It is generally believed that the informal sector is less privileged with more female participation, indicating gender discrimination in the sector (Wamuthenya, 2010). However, Sri Lanka shows a different picture, as females participate less, providing no evidence for any gender discrimination in the informal sector labour market.

The rural sector, which consists of most of the agricultural activities, small-scale industries and construction, retail trade, and household economic activities, shows high informal sector employment compared with the urban and estate sectors. The poverty level in the estate sector is higher compared with urban and rural areas. Among the ethnic groups of the country, 'Sri Lanka Moors' shows comparatively higher rates of participation in the informal sector while 'Indian Tamils' show higher formal sector partipation since they are employed in the estate sector, where the country's export agriculture is located. Such districts as Kurunegala, Ampara and Nuwara Eliya have more informal sector employment, indicating a regional bias, due to the heavy concentration of agricultural activities.

The results significantly support the previous findings that higher levels of education lead to lower participation in the informal sector. Many with a low level of schooling go into the informal sector. This trend paves the way for further lowering quality and inefficient outcomes. Education is an entry barrier to the formal sector but not for the informal sector. Literacy in English has become very important to enter the formal sector. Despite those entry barriers, the informal sector still absorbs a large part of the labour force with lower levels of education, reducing the unemployment level and social unrest to some extent. As indicated earlier, persons with lower levels of education are highly concentrated in the informal sector; therefore it is important to establish some institutional mechanism to provide training in management, accounting and book keeping, business opportunities, etc. if the government wishes to improve the livelihood of the rural masses. These could be improved using currently available systems such as 'Vidhata' through local administrative systems.

Another finding is that if people are currently engaged in education, their participation is high in the informal sector, which shows the time allocation flexibility and how part-time informal employment is engaged in by those in education. These results show that the level of education or human capital attainment supports both voluntary and involuntary entry into the informal sector.

Age plays a vital role in participation in the informal sector. This study finds that informal sector participation has a positive relationship with age. Since there is no upper age limit for people to work in the informal sector, it provides some solution to the dependency burden. The results further reveal that the informal sector is supportive of those who either cannot enter the formal sector or who left the formal sector at retirement age. Hence, the observed increase in informal sector employment with increasing age can be identified as voluntary engagement.

The Sri Lankan informal sector has been supported by various social security measures during the last two decades or so. However, those measures are not functioning effectively due to operational weaknesses. This study identifies that the informal sector is very vital for the country in generating employment.

The agriculture sector consists of 87 per cent of informal sector employment while the formal agriculture sector, with large-scale tea and rubber plantations, accounts for only 13 per cent. Those who are working on the plantations are provided with some benefits and also included in social security systems compared with other agricultural activities. The government started a farmers' pension scheme (1987) and a fishermen's pension scheme (1990). However most of the agricultural employment still does not have any social security, due to strict eligibility requirements and the unsupportive nature of the existing systems. Given the importance of the informal sector, the implementation of such pension schemes covering the entire agricultural sector of the country is desirable.

The agricultural sector is crucial for the livelihood of many people, but more than 85 per cent of working persons in the sector are informally employed. For their welfare, it is important to increase the productivity of those people through government spending, not only on research and development (R&D) in agriculture or agriculture extension services but also on research, development, innovation and commercialization (RDI&C) of informal sector activities, as converting informal to formal jobs is not a short-term reality.

Acknowledgements

The authors would like to thank Prof. Kaliappa Kalirajan, Crawford School of Economics and Government, The Australian National University and Prof. Eiji Mangyo, Graduate School of International Relations, International University of Japan for their invaluable comments but the remaining errors are entirely ours.

Notes

1 In 2000, 189 nations made a promise to free people from extreme poverty and multiple deprivations. This pledge became the eight Millennium Development Goals to be achieved by 2015. In September 2010, the world recommitted itself to accelerate progress towards these goals. Goal 1: Eradicate extreme poverty and hunger; Target 1b: Achieve full and productive employment and decent work for all, including women and young people (for more details please see www.undp.org).
2 ILO adopted an international statistical definition of the informal sector at the Fifteenth International Conference of Labour Statisticians (15th ICLS) in 1993. And this definition was immediately included in the System of National Accounts 1993 (SNA93).
3 According to ILO informal sector employment includes the following types of jobs:
(i) own-account workers employed in their own informal sector enterprises; (ii) employers employed in their own informal sector enterprises; (iii) contributing family workers, irrespective of whether they work in formal or informal sector enterprises; (iv) members of informal producers' cooperatives; (v) employees holding informal jobs in formal sector enterprises, informal sector enterprises, or as paid domestic workers employed by households; (vi) own-account workers engaged in the production of goods exclusively for own final use by their household.
4 The Department of Census and Statistics conducted a Special Survey on Household Unincorporated enterprises with the collaboration of UNESCAP in year 2008. This was done parallel to the Quarterly Labour Force Survey.
5 The sample data set consists with individual level data and it records about 73,000 individuals. The statistical analysis packages STATA 12 and PASW Statistics 18 (SPSS) are utilized for the analysis.

References

Arunathilake, N. P. and Jayawardene, P. (2010). *Labour Market Trends and Outcomes in Sri lanka. The Challenge of Youth Unemployment in Sri Lanka*. Washington, DC: The World Bank

Banda, O. D. (1997). *Informal Trade in Sri Lanka*. University of Peradeniya: Department of Economics and Statistics.

Bangasser, P. E. (2000). *The ILO and the Informal Sector:An Institutional History*. Geneva: ILO Publications Bureau.

Blau, D. M. (1985). Self-Employment and Self-Selection in Developing Country Labor Markets. *Southern Economic Journal*, 52(2), 351–363.

Chaudhuri, T. D. (1989). A Theoretical Analysis of the Informal Sector. *World Development*, 17(3), 351–355.

DC&S D. O. (2010). *Sri Lanka Labour Force Survey: Annual Report-2010*. Colombo, Sri Lanka: Department of Census and Statistics.

de Soto, H. (1989). *The Other Path: The Invisible Revolution in the Third World*. New York: Harper & Row.

Ferrer-i-Carbonell, A. and Gërxhani, K. (2011). Financial Satisfaction and (In)formal Sector in a Transition Country. *Social Indicators Research*, 102(2), 315–331.

Fields, G. (2005). *A Guide to Multisector Labour Market Models*. Washington D.C., World Bank.

Funkhouser, E. (1996). The Urban Informal Sector in Central America: Household Survey Evidence. *World Development*, 24(11), 1737–1751.

Gërxhani, K. (2004). The Informal Sector in Developed and Less Developed Countries: A Literature Survey. *Public Choice*, 120(3–4), 267–300.

Gërxhani, K. and Van de Werfhorst, H. G. (2013). The Effect of Education on Informal Sector Participation in a Post-Communist Country. *European Sociological Review*, 29(3), 464–476.

Gunatilaka, R. (2008). *Informal Employment in Sri Lanka: Nature, Probability of Employment, and Determinants of Wages*. New Delhi: International Labour Organization.

Gupta, M. R. (1993). Rural-Uraban Migration, Informal Sector and Development Policies: A Theoretical Analysis. *Journal of Development Economics*, 41(1), 137–151.

Harris, J. and Todaro, M. (1970). Migration, Unemployment and Development: A Two-Sector Analysis. *The American Economic Review*, 60(1), 126–142.

Heckman, J. (1979). Sample selection bias as a specification error. *Econometrica*, 47(1), 153–161.

Hussmanns, R. (2004). Measuring the informal economy: From employment in the informal sector to informal employment, Working Paper No. 53. Policy Integration Department, Bureau of Statistics, International Labour Office, Geneva.

ILO. (2002). *Decent Work and the Informal Economy*. Geneva: International Labour Office.

ILO. (2008). *Decent Work Country Programme Sri Lanka: 2008–2012*. Colombo: ILO.

Kalirajan, K., Drysdale, P. and Singh, K. (2010). Impact of Big Shopping Malls and Retailers on Employment and Consumer Prices in India. *Journal of International Economics (JIE)*, 1(2), 41–56.

Maloney, W. (1999). Does Informality Imply Segmentation in urban Labor Markets? Evidence from Sectoral Transitions in Mexico. *The World Bank Economic Review*, 13(2), 275–302.

Maloney, W. (2004). Informality Revisited. *World Development*, 32(7), 1159–1178.

Perry, G. E. et al. (2007). *Informality: Exit and Exclusion*. Washington, DC: The World Bank.

Sandaratne, N. (2001). *The Informal Sector in Sri Lanka: Its Nature and the Impact of Globalization*. Geneva: International Labour Organisation.

Sethuraman, S. (1997). *Urban Poverty and the Informal Sector:A Critical Assessment of Current Strategies*. Geneva: International Labour Office.

Wamuthenya, W. R. (2010). *Determinants of Employment in the Formal and Informal Sectors of the Urban Areas of Kenya. Nairobi 00200*. Kenya: The African Economic ResearchConsortium.

Williams, C. C. (2007). Entrepreneurs Operating in the Informal Economy: Necessity or Opportunity Driven? *Journal of Small Business and Entrepreneurship*, 20(3), 309–320.

Williams, C. C. (2008). Beyond Necessity-driven versus Opportunity-driven Entrepreneurship: A Study of Informal Entrepreneurs in England, Russia and Ukraine. *International Journal of Entrepreneurship and Innovation*, 9(3), 157–165.

Williams, C.C. (2009). The Motives of Off-the-Books Entrepreneurs: Necessity- or Opportunity-driven? *International Entrepreneurship and Management Journal*, 5(2), 203–217.

Williams, C.C. and Horodnic, I. (2015). Self-employment, the Informal Economy and the Marginalisation Thesis: Some Evidence from the European Union. *International Journal of Entrepreneurial Behaviour and Research*, 21(2), 224–242.

Williams, Colin C. and Youssef, Youssef. A. (2014). Is Informal Sector Entrepreneurship Necessity- or Opportunity-driven? Some Lessons from urban Brazil. *Business and Management Research*, 3(1), 41–53.

28

UNDERSTANDING INFORMAL ENTREPRENEURSHIP IN SUB-SAHARAN AFRICA AND ITS IMPLICATIONS FOR ECONOMIC DEVELOPMENT

The Ghanaian experience

Kwame Adom

Introduction

Contrary to what some originally envisaged, informal entrepreneurship has not receded or disappeared from view since its discovery over four decades ago. Instead, quite the opposite is the case (Adom and Williams, 2012; Adom, 2014; Debrah, 2007; Palmer, 2007; Hanson, 2005). It is today one of the major lifelines for dwellers in both rural and urban economies especially in developing countries, but also in transition economies and the developed world (Aliyev, 2015; Boels, 2014; Williams, 2013, 2014a; Williams and Martinez-Perez, 2014). This is nowhere more obvious than in the birthplace of the 'informal sector' concept, Ghana itself. At present, the existence of a robust and vibrant informal economy is widely noted in Ghana (Adom and Williams, 2012; Debrah, 2007; Haan and Serriere, 2002). Not only are most enterprises and entrepreneurs widely recognised to be operating in the informal economy (Debrah, 2007; Palmer, 2007; UNDP/ISSER, 2007) but some 89 per cent of the labour force in the Ghanaian economy work in the informal economy (Debrah, 2007; Hanson, 2005; ISSER, 2007; Palmer, 2007; Xaba et al., 2002) and just as evident in urban as in rural areas (Boapeah, 1996; Dzisi, 2008; Palmer, 2007). Indeed, and as Palmer (2007, p. 400) asserts, 'informal entrepreneurship in Ghana is the primary destination for all school leavers'.

Yet over 40 years since the informal sector as a concept came into the development economics literature (Hart, 1973), there remains little understanding of informal entrepreneurship and its relationship with the formal economy. To some writing from a modernisation, or what is sometimes called a dual economy, perspective, it represents the other sector of the economy where the economically disadvantaged survive. To others writing from a struc-turalist perspective, it is an offshoot and by-product of the neoliberal economic policies adopted by sub-Saharan African countries under the auspices of the Bretton Woods institu-tions in the 1980s. Despite the widespread recognition of its magnitude and even growth, therefore, there remain competing views on the relationship between the formal economy and informal entrepreneurship and what should be done about it.

Until now, evaluations of these contrasting views have tended to concentrate on western economies, the transition economies of East-Central Europe and Latin America (Williams, 2014a,b,c; Williams and Martinez, 2014; Williams and Youssef, 2013, 2014). Few have evaluated them in relation to Africa, especially Sub-Saharan Africa (Adom and Williams, 2014). As a consequence, this chapter seeks to fill this knowledge gap by examining the relationship between the formal and informal work in Koforidua in Ghana. To evaluate these different views, evidence is here reported that was collected in Koforidua in the Greater Accra and Eastern Region over a period of six months during 2009. This chapter, therefore, first reports these data and then evaluates their implications for the competing views of the relationship between formal and informal entrepreneurship.

Conceptions of informal entrepreneurship in Ghana

Despite the extensiveness of informal entrepreneurship, this sector remains widely depicted by numerous commentators as an arena in which marginalised populations make a living. It is also widely viewed as possessing largely negative attributes, as expressed in its depiction as a 'traditional', 'outmoded' and 'leftover' sphere (Chen et al., 2004; ILO, 2002; Leonard, 2000; Williams, 2005, 2006). The outcome is that informal entrepreneurship is commonly portrayed as a remnant, marginal and sweatshop-like activity which often impairs economic development and social unity (Williams, 2007). Governments, development partners, donors, international and local non-governmental organisations as well as academic commentators, have over the years tried to change this perception but with limited success. Informal entrepreneurship continues to be seen as a space of hopelessness and an arena for the disadvantaged who are not able to secure a formal job. This is what Williams and Windebank (1998) and Williams (2006, 2007) describe as the 'marginality thesis'. In 2007, The World Bank's Country Director for Ghana, Mats Karlson, encapsulated such a view:

> What is left for Ghana to do is to embark on action programmes that would lead to the movement of Small and Medium Scale Enterprises from the informal to formal sector in order for there to be more permanent jobs for the youth. That way, both the economic and social dimensions of development would have been properly taken care of and then we can talk of economic development.
>
> *(http:www.myjoyonline.com/archives/business/2007/02/2743.asp)*

Rather than simply accepting the commonly held assumption that the formalisation of economic life is the only route to progress, modernity and advancement, this study seeks to evaluate this assumption critically.

It also seeks to understand whether the dualist and marginality theses remain relevant, or whether one of the alternative theorisations of the relationship between formal and informal work is more accurate. For many decades, the dualist school of thought that views the informal and formal spheres as discrete and the accompanying 'marginality thesis' has dominated the debate. At the heart of the dualist debate is the view that the separate formal economy is inevitably and irrefutably replacing the informal economy and that participants in the informal economy are increasingly largely composed of those populations marginalised from the mainstream economy (formal) and who engage in informal work out of necessity and as a last resort when no other opportunities are open to them (Button, 1984; Rosanvallon, 1980; Sassen, 1997; Williams, 2006, 2007; Williams and Windebank, 1998). In recent decades, however, both the dualist and marginality theses have come under increasing attack, especially in western economies (eg. Barthe, 1988; Howe, 1990; Koopmans, 1989). The argument has been that it is not the marginalised who conduct informal entrepreneurship but rather the affluent and the employed. This is less the case, however, in studies of developing nations (Chen et al., 2002; Debrah, 2007). Against this backdrop, therefore, this study evaluates the dualist and marginality theses, together with the other perspectives that have sought to replace these theses. One such common approach has been that which adopts a more agency-oriented perspective and is often associated with the legalist view, which assumes that people do informal work of their own volition and not because of the inability of the state or formal economy to provide adequate jobs (De Soto, 1989). Whether this is the case in Ghana will be analysed.

Occupational characteristics of informal entrepreneurs

The main occupation identified from the empirical study is commerce, confirming the report by the New Juaben Municipal Assembly. Predominantly, the commercial activities range from retailing which is conducted from table-tops (*bodwabodwa*), stores, kiosks, containers and so on dealing in provisions, food, stationery, hardware, mobile phones and accessories and the like. Others also engage in food trading including itinerant traders, chop bar (a traditional restaurant where mainly local dishes are served) and restaurant operators most of whom are women (see Table 28.1). They are mainly illiterate or semi-literate with business knowledge and skills obtained or handed over from generation to generation principally from the family and on the job. The next occupation is construction with workers such as masons, carpenters, steel benders, small-scale plumbers, house-wiring electricians, and others who are more often than not males. Again, some of the respondents are dressmakers, hairdressers and barbers. There are others in garages (locally called 'magazine'), general repairs and electrical trades.

From Table 28.1, it can be seen that retailing has 32.5 per cent food traders, 17.5 per cent construction, with mechanics and repairs recording the lowest percentage. The occupational

Table 28.1 Occupational Characteristics of the Respondents (Informal Workers)

Type of occupation	Percentage
Retail (provision/food stores, stationery, mobile phones etc.)	32.5
Food traders/vending (itinerant traders, 'chop bars', restaurants, etc.)	17.5
Construction (contractors and workers)	17.5
Dressmaking (seamstresses and tailors)	15.0
Hairdressers/barbers, beauticians	10.0
Others (mechanics and auto repairs – 'Magazine', general repairs and electricians)	7.5
Total percentage	**100.0**

Source: Field data.

characteristics also provide evidence that these are largely survival activities conducted by the marginalised population. Though there are a handful of informal entrepreneurs in this area who are not marginalised, on the larger scale informal entrepreneurs remain marginal in Koforidua.

Level of education of informal workers

Low levels of education push people in developing countries into informal entrepreneurship (Baah, 2007; Chen, 2005; Chen, Vanek and Carr, 2004; ILO, 2002; Palmer, 2007). It is also true that in countries where the formal economy is the mainstream economy employing most of the people, their literacy and level of education are high (Baah, 2007). Evidence from Koforidua supports the existing popular view that informal workers have a low level of education (Chen, 2005; Palmer, 2007). In this study, about 80 per cent of all informal entrepreneurs interviewed argued that their low level of education is primarily responsible for their participation in the informal economy. It is sometimes argued that a high level of education opens doors to formal jobs. However, a high level of education may not guarantee a formal job. It depends very much on the number of jobs available. Why should this be an issue of concern? The answer is that a high level of education more often than not is associated with a high level of economic development as evidenced by the western nations. There seems to be a strong connection between a low level of education and informality (ILO, 2002b). It may be contended that people who have no formal education are more likely to become informal entrepreneurs and vice versa. Table 28.2 depicts the educational level and gender of the households (informal workers) interviewed for this study.

The majority of respondents (65 per cent) have an educational level up to Junior High School (JHS)/Ordinary Level. The table data shows female domination (54 per cent) in the primary and middle up to Senior High School, as against males (36 per cent). Higher levels of participation in education encourage higher female participation in employment. And this employment is mostly in the informal sector, which has a long tradition in almost every part of the country. Once upon a time, only a few girls were allowed to go to school and even continue beyond the basic level as alleged by some of the respondents of this study. This study confirms this claim, as female percentage for primary and middle education was 24 per cent compared with 16 per cent for males. Although more females were sampled in this study, only 1 per cent had a tertiary education compared with 3 per cent of males. MEYS (2004) also confirm this changing situation in recent times.

Table 28.2 Respondents (Informal Entrepreneurs) Level of Education, sorted by gender

Respondents level of education	*Sex of respondents*		
	Male	*Female*	*Total*
Never	4 percent	2 percent	6 percent
Primary/	16 percent	24 percent	40 percent
JHS/O Level	9 percent	16 percent	25 percent
SHS/A Level	11 percent	14 percent	25 percent
Tertiary	3 percent	1 percent	4 percent
Total	43 percent	57 percent	100 percent

Source: Field data.

The notion that education is the means to achieve socio-economic development has long been highlighted (Abban and Baafour, 1986; Nkrumah, 1943). However, since independence the emphasis has been greater. The underlying assumption is that all other things being equal, when people are educated they become more skilful and knowledgeable and thus can contribute to the growth of the economy. Immediately after Ghana's self-rule, the president (Nkrumah) had a well-orchestrated educational policy as part of the seven-year development plan (Sutherland-Addy and Causa, 2009). The educational system from that time remained until the 1980s. However, in 1987, there was a wake-up call about the shortcomings of the then educational system which began from basic, secondary (Ordinary and Advanced Levels) and to tertiary level, as it did not produce the needed skilled labour power to grow the formal economy. As a result, there was a key policy change in education in 1987 to improve the significance of the educational system by placing emphasis on vocational subjects (Haan, 2006). It is important to state that this educational reform programme was formulated in the context of an economic reform programme imposed on the country by the Breton Woods institutions (Sutherland-Addy and Causa, 2009).

Gender and informal entrepreneurship

The issue of gender and informality is of vital concern in that certain types of informal work are considered to be the preserve of one gender and not the other. Chen et al. (2004) have emphasised the links between informal employment, poverty and gender. In terms of this study, the interest is centred on the gender variations in relation to the type(s) of informal activity. As Table 28.3 displays, this study shows that females are the principal players in petty trading (street vending, hawking, etc.). This also confirms the wider literature (Thompson, 2009).

It also reveals the dominance of women in the informal entrepreneurship in Ghana. However, this is not unique to the study area as there is evidence across the country from the literature (see, Dovi, 2006; Dzisi, 2008; Thompson, 2009). Traditionally females dominate activities such as food vending, especially cooked food (chop bars) where local dishes are mainly served and also the restaurants where both local and foreign dishes are served. Females again are the dominant force in the dressmaking enterprise. In Koforidua, dressmaking shops owned by females are dotted along the main roads and streets within the communities. This

Table 28.3 Gender and Informal Enterprise Characteristics

Type of business enterprise	Male percent	Female percent	Total percent
Retail (provision/food stores, stationary, mobile phones etc)	12.5	20.0	32.5
Food vending ('chop bars', restaurants, etc)	5.0	12.5	17.5
Construction (contractors and workers)	7.5	10.0	17.5
Dressmaking (seamstresses and tailors)	5.0	10.0	15.0
Hairdressers/barbers, beauticians	7.5	2.5	10.0
Others (mechanics and auto repairs – 'Magazine', general repairs and electricians)	5.0	2.5	7.5
Total percentage	**47.5**	**52.5**	**100.0**

Source: Field data.

is also true for those engaged in hairdressing and beauticians but hairdressing tends to be a male-dominated activity. Female dominance in these activities may be explained with historical and cultural reference.

In a typical Akan community such as Koforidua, higher female education was not encouraged because of the associated stigma attached to female education (Dzisi, 2008). The female was and is still seen as the carer of the family and, therefore, normally ends up in apprenticeship training especially in dressmaking (seamstress) and hairdressing and in some cases 'permanent' housewives. The other reason may be that these businesses normally operate from within the house or a store or space in front of the house. This offers the worker the dual opportunity of working and also taking care of the family concurrently. However, activities such as mechanics and auto repairs, general repairs and electrics are the arena for the males. In recent years though, as a result of technical/vocational education, which was the emphasis of the educational reforms, some females are entering into what used to be a male-dominated field (Haan, 2006; Haan and Serriere, 2002).

As observed during this field study, there were few female apprentices at the garages ('magazine'), learning or training to become mechanics (fitters) and repairers in general. The retail sector is composed of both females and males. However females are the dominant players in the street, vending vegetables, raw foodstuffs, cosmetics, foreign used clothes (locally called *Foos* or *Obroniwawu*), which translated literally means 'the clothes of a dead white person' and others. Men are often seen operating retail shops where provision, grocery and other household items, just to mention a few, are sold.

Knowing the gender and informal enterprise characteristics is a key policy formulation factor. This could be one of the tools for the newly constituted Informal Economy Committee (Thompson, 2009) which has the mandate to address the socio-economic problems of informal workers especially women who make up over 90 per cent of the informal economy far in excess of their share of the general population of about 51 per cent (Thompson, 2009). Having established the relationship between gender and informal work and also confirmed that informal economy is the main work in Ghana, the next section uncovers whether the informal workers in Ghana are entirely poor or whether they can contribute meaningfully to economic growth and development.

Are informal economy entrepreneurs always poor?

The relationship between informal entrepreneurship and poverty is a multifaceted and contentious subject that is continuously being debated (ILO, 2002b). For many years most informal entrepreneurs have been branded as poor relative to formal workers (Chen et al., 2004; Hart, 1973; ILO, 1972; ISSER, 2007). However, evidence from the wider literature suggests that over 80 per cent of the labour force in developing countries especially Sub-Saharan Africa are in the informal economy (Chen et al., 2004; ILO, 2000) and in Ghana the figure is over 90 per cent (Debrah, 2007; Palmer, 2007; ISSER, 2007). Looking at these statistics, the informal economy is by far the typical economy. In Ghana most of these informal actors earn very little income (GoG, 2003) and may be seen as poor and can contribute very little even to their own development let alone the national development. Despite the difficulty in all aspects to define who a poor person is, observing the physical conditions of some of the informal operators witnessed in this study makes it possible to conclude that some of them are poor. However, physical appearance may be deceptive and therefore will not be regarded as a good indicator of poverty. Often these perceived poor informal workers live in deplorable conditions and in the urban areas some of the migrant informal workers live in slums and shantytowns (Hart, 1973). The evidence base of this assertion is very much anecdotal but the reality is that the urban formal economy sees this as a separate economy (informal) operating in its own right. This reflects much of a dualist view of the informal economy, reading the informal economy as old fashioned, often dominated by the poor and marginalised in societies that have no link with the modern market economy (formal sector).

In spite of the income-earning ability of most of the informal workers, the policy makers believe that the contribution of the informal economy towards poverty reduction is immense. According to the policy makers, the informal economy in Koforidua employs around 90 per cent of the potential labour force and therefore has the ability to absorb most of the potential labour force. As a result in Koforidua the informal economy is making a contribution to reducing unemployment. It also contributes to revenue mobilisation in the form of tax, levies, fees and others. In a country where the formal economy has failed to provide adequate jobs for all (Adu-Amankwah, 1999; Palmer, 2007), the informal economy has become the best alternative, providing jobs to augment the public and private sector jobs. The impact may be that, as people are employed, they will be earning some income which means they will be in a position to buy goods and services to satisfy their needs and those of their dependants, thereby reducing their own poverty levels and enhancing their living standards.

Typically the informal paid workers have no contract of employment, lack labour law protection and so forth. As a result, they do not qualify for benefits such as sick pay, maternity leave in the case of women; they are not entitled to pensions and a host of other benefits as compared with the formal workers (simply put, no social protection). The key issue here is that on a larger scale there has been very little impact on poverty reduction by the contribution of the informal entrepreneurs, as claimed by the policy makers. Even in Koforidua (both the regional and municipal capital) poverty can be seen and felt in some areas among some people. The high incidence of poverty among the informal entrepreneurs may well explain why the international community classifies Ghana as a poor country. However, recently, the World Bank has reclassified Ghana as a lower middle-income country; what an irony!

As one of the respondents pointed out,

> the majority of us (informal entrepreneurs) operate on subsistence level especially in agriculture, which is basically from hand to mouth, and little or nothing in some cases is left for sale. In situations where people do sell, they do so not because they have excess but to get money to buy other goods and services that they cannot produce from the cash economy.

This is a popular view among those who considered themselves as peasant farmers alongside their petty trading activity. Empirical evidence shows that the informal economy in Koforidua is not only composed of the poor and the marginalised but there are some who are perceived to be rich or have high income.

Significantly, these 'rich' informal workers have been overshadowed by the poor majority. The evidence is that some informal enterprises do employ others on a paid informal work basis: for example, a self-employed construction worker who employs four permanent workers and other casual workers as and when they are needed. Although employing others may not necessarily make one a rich person, in this context they are seen as rich people. The reason is that in Ghana the popular view is that owning a business and employing others is an indication that the owner of that business is rich. This may be seen as another socially constructed reality in Ghana that is also taken for granted. The widespread representation is that these self-employed with employees are not poor though they failed to disclose their actual monthly or annual income. In contrast to the poor informal entrepreneurs, the physical appearance of the perceived (by the society) rich informal entrepreneurs bears witness to that. It is not being argued here that everybody in this sort of situation is a 'rich' informal worker. The perceived rich informal workers are the people who believe the informal work is an alternative to formal and can generate an income more than the formal. This therefore makes it difficult to accept the claim that informal actors are largely destitute and entirely poor. Evidence from the case studies shows that those who are in the hardware business, 'big' retail operators, contractors and others are not poor compared with street vendors, petty traders, hawkers, porters and so on.

Motives of informal workers in Ghana

In developing economies, it is extremely difficult to find evidence that informal entrepreneurs are not acting out of necessity but participate in the informal economy by choice (Chen et al., 2002; Hanson, 2005; Palmer, 2007). Although there may well be a handful of informal entrepreneurs in developing economies who undertake informal activity based on choice, the proportion of those who are driven by necessity and for survival is very significant (Adom and Williams, 2012; Morris et al., 1996). The necessity-driven motive suggests that people are pushed into the informal economy to become informal entrepreneurs. This is especially so in the period of structural changes in an economy. It also means that the informal participants who come as a consequence of this are often motivated by their socio-economic disadvantaged position. In sharp contrast, opportunity-driven situations are those where there exists an opportunity to satisfy a need within the informal economy and this acts as an incentive or a pull factor or a 'magnet' to attract potential informal workers to take advantage of the perceived opportunity. Here, these entrepreneurs are not in the informal economy for survival purposes but to do business with a self-motivated interest and conviction. As confirmed by Jütting et al. (2008), some people who conduct informal work do the cost-benefit analysis before concluding that doing informal work is better than formal work. But what is the proportion of necessity and opportunity informal workers in Ghana?

Evidence from Koforidua reveals that some informal entrepreneurs choose to participate by operating their own business because they enjoy the independence, flexibility, potential for making more money, etc. Others also do so because of their inability to find job in the formal economy, which may be attributed to the low level of education as claimed by the majority of the respondents. Putting informal workers into free will or determinism ends of the divide is extremely difficult. The reason is that there are some informal workers who share both motives. Notwithstanding, in this study, the responses were so clear that it posed little or no difficulty in classifying them as either free will or determinism. Respondents who constantly throughout the survey emphasised issues such as a low level of education, inability to secure formal jobs and the like were classified as necessity-driven. On the contrary, those accepting that more benefits accrue in doing informal work were seen as the free will informal workers. It is not being suggested here that all the free will informal workers had a relatively high level of education. What makes them free will-oriented is the recognition that the informal economy has the potential for making working life more rewarding than the formal.

A key observation is that while the factors which push people (necessity-driven) into the informal economy are connected to or emanate from one another the free will factors are independent of each other. For example, low education has resulted in the inability to secure formal jobs but the high prospect of financial opportunity has no link with independence/flexibility.

In order to appreciate these findings, there is a need to compare them with others elsewhere. In research conducted by Williams and Round (2008) in Ukraine in which they looked at the motives for doing informal work, the finding was that about 53 per cent conducted informal work out of necessity. The finding of this (Koforidua) study is that 31 per cent said people do informal work due to the difficulty in getting a formal job. When this is added to those who do informal work as a last resort, it suggests that they are doing informal work out of necessity and this is consistent with what is happening elsewhere though the proportion in this study is low. Another reason why people operate wholly or partly in informal work is to reduce the costs of production by sub-contracting part or whole to cash-in-hand (Chen et al., 2004; Williams and Windebank, 1998; Williams, 2006, 2007). Even though this is not the general case in this research, sub-contracting in the informal economy cannot be relegated to the background across the country. Private formal enterprises especially in construction do sub-contract part or the whole of their work to informal contractors who also employ labourers on a day-to-day basis on cash-in-hand to complete the contract. As indicated by a carpenter who works for a construction worker,

> I work as a carpenter for a road construction company. I'm not a permanent worker for this company but I'm paid anytime I work for the company. This is what is known locally as 'by-day'. I have been working for this firm for some time now but I am not sure if they would make me permanent.

Likewise the changing structure of educational systems, the way computers are used in modern organisations, amongst other factors, have also priced some people out of the formal job market. The outcome is that some of these people join the informal economy. The formal and the informal ends of the economic continuum are often strongly linked (Chen et al., 2002) and lots of informal enterprises have production or distribution relations with formal enterprises, supplying inputs, finished goods or services either through direct transactions or sub-contracting arrangements. Moreover, some formal enterprises hire wageworkers under informal employment relations (Chen et al., 2002). For example, in Koforidua some of the established informal workers employ part-time workers, temporarily through contracting or sub-contracting arrangements. The finding in this case is consistent with the literature (Gërxhani, 2004). The work of Snyder (2004) in the United States of America also supports that it is not the marginalised who are the workers in the informal economy, but those who work out of choice (see also Cross, 1997, 2000). Others including Fields (2005) have argued that in the urban informal labour market in developing countries there exist two situations; these are 'the upper tier' and the 'lower tier'. The explanation Fields offers is that the 'upper tier' consists of those who out of their own free will decide to work informally and the 'lower tier' is made up of those who cannot afford to be un-employed but have no hope of getting a formal job (Jütting et al., 2008). Although there are some cases of those working informally out of choice, the majority (75 per cent) of participants in the informal economy in Koforidua are necessity-driven and do so as a survival practice. This sits in stark contrast to developed nations where informal entrepreneurs tend to be more opportunity- than necessity-driven (Gërxhani, 2004; Williams, 2004, 2007).

Evaluating views of the informal economy in Ghana

Evaluating the dualist view in Ghana

Proponents of this theory claim that there is a 'big' formal economy which is perceived to be expanding through industrialisation or modernisation, and a separate small (traditional/outmoded) informal economy made up of diverse activities conducted by marginalised populations, which is disappearing over time. It may also be argued that the dualist view is the oldest theorisation of the relationship between the formal and informal economy. This whole idea of dualism is deeply rooted in the works of Furnivall (1939, 1941), Boeke (1942, 1961) and Lewis (1954). Historically, the informal economy in Ghana was in existence before the colonisation of the country (Ninsin, 1991).

This dualist theoretical perspective hinges on the view that there are two distinct economies (i.e. informal and formal) where the informal economy is read as having negative attributes (depicted as traditional, backward and so forth) and the formal economy as having positive attributes portrayed as representing progress, modernity, etc. (Chen et al., 2004; Potts, 2008; Williams, 2007). Another important assumption is that the informal economy will disappear from the economic landscape as nations attain certain levels of economic development (Hart, 1973; ILO, 1972; Lewis, 1954; Sethuraman, 1976; Tokman, 1978; Chen et al., 2004; Williams, 2006, 2007). This is, therefore, portrayed to be a universal trajectory of economic development towards formalisation that all nations must follow.

In Ghana, government rhetoric regarding the informal economy is commonly grounded in this dualist perspective. In the past, successive governments have tried to pursue formalisation by establishing more state-owned enterprises. Nkrumah's policies, aimed at mass job creation by rapid industrialisation, led him towards distinct views concerning employment and informal micro and small enterprise (IMSEs) development at the dawn of independence (Palmer, 2007). Nkrumah saw subsistence farming as backward and instead supported mechanised agriculture on state farms (Palmer, 2007). These state farms (plantations) specialised in the production of mainly cash crops and raw materials for export to the neglect of the informal sector. The formalisation view dominated Nkrumah's thinking at the time and encouraged the thinking that any component of the economy that was not aimed at industrialisation was peripheral and not concerned with the national, or state-led, economy (Palmer, 2007).

Notwithstanding Nkrumah's concerns about economic development through industrialisation (formalisation), it became clear that informal work was the most widespread form of work for the people of Ghana even before and after independence. Years of intensive formalisation policy could not transform the informal economy into the formal economy. Almost all of these state enterprises (formal) have been sold through privatisation policy or public sector reforms since the late 1980s and 1990s. Privatisation or public sector reforms were some of the neoliberal terms and conditions attached to the acceptance of the adjustment programmes necessitated by external force (i.e. IMF/World Bank) in the 1980s and 1990s. The outcome is that most formal workers have become unemployed through voluntary or compulsory redundancy and have taken solace in informal entrepreneurship. As a result, the informal economy has grown (Osei et al., 1993; Sowa et al., 1992).

Analysing further policy makers' views, clearly there are divergent views about the formalisation of the informal economy as a government policy. Some do not envisage how one can formalise the informal economy. The view of a municipal planning officer reinforces this position. As he proclaims, 'once it is an informal economy, it will remain an informal economy'. However, he suggests that any attempt to formalise the informal economy may be achieved through education about the need to pay proper tax and social security; but this will largely depend on the profitability of the businesses. If people, through education, come to accept the need to formalise their activities then there may be some hope for formalisation. Recently moreover, there has been the establishment of the Informal Economy Committee (IEC) with the main responsibility of promoting decent work in the informal economy (Thompson, 2009).

In spite of the policy makers' position on formalisation, they believe that the two economies (formal and informal) are not necessarily distinct from each other and the relationship between them is far from what is portrayed by the dualists. Rather, the two economies interact at all levels within the national economy. Again there was a consensus about the permanent nature of the informal economy as the mainstream economy in Ghana by all the policy makers interviewed. However, the major concern for the Municipal Assembly is the unorganised nature of the broader aspect of the informal economy because of its associated urban planning and management problems and also its potential for reducing revenue to the Assembly. The Assembly has been organising training workshops for the informal actors so that they can move them towards the decent job end of the continuum thereby preparing them in the direction of formalisation. As noted earlier the key underlying factor of the dualists is the formalisation of the informal economy. As a government policy formalization is repeated by the policy makers to encourage more people to go into the private sector but there is little arrangement for people to adhere to the formal way(s) of doing business, thereby ensuring that the formalisation policy may be achieved. In recent years the government of Ghana continues its rhetoric about formalising the informal economy but there is little or no measure put in place to ensure that new entrants into the private sector are registered properly.

A number of the policy makers and other commentators are also of the view that a section of the informal entrepreneurs must go into manufacturing as a way of making the informal economy more diverse and can thus contribute 'better' to the economic development of the country. According to Thompson (2009), Ghana has moved backwards over the years in terms of manufacturing, as its share of manufacturing, for example, has gone down from a historical 14 per cent of GDP in 1975 to as low as 8 per cent in 2009. The reason for less manufacturing activities may be attributed to globalisation and liberalisation which make it easier for local importers than exporters. Imported goods are often cheaper than the locally manufactured goods. The reason may be due to low import tariffs, and other relaxed trade restriction tools and high unit cost of production within the local economy which can be linked to lack of economies of scale and scope. Aside from this, it is believed that Ghanaians have developed a taste for foreign goods to the detriment of the made-in-Ghana goods as they are popularly called.

Evaluating the structuralist perspective in Ghana

The structuralist, unlike the dualist, perspective believes that there exists a relationship between the formal and informal economy but that the informal economy is seen as subordinate to or an offshoot of the formal economy. This view about the informal economy was prominent in the 1970s and 1980s. The underlying assumption is that the informal economy is seen as composed of small economic units (Chen et al, 2004) and workers that serve to reduce input and labour costs. As Chen (2005) argues, structuralists see the informal and formal economies as intrinsically linked. That is, they are mutually inclusive and beneficial with different levels of association with each other. To enhance competitiveness, some capitalist firms in the formal economy are perceived to reduce their input costs, including labour costs, by encouraging informal production and employment relationships with subordinated economic units and workers (Chen et al., 2004). According to structuralists, both informal enterprises and informal wageworkers are subordinated to the interests of capitalist development, providing cheap goods and services (Moser, 1978; Portes et al., 1989).

One of the prime costs of structural adjustment in Ghana since the mid-1980s has been the dwindling formal sector and a corresponding growth and expansion of the informal economy. This has come about as a result of public sector reform which had massive cutbacks of labour as an important element (Adu-Amankwah, 1999). As indicated by Adu-Amankwah (1999), total formal employment fell from 464,000 in 1985 to 186,000 in 1991 demonstrating a loss of 278,000 jobs over a six-year period.

Based on the assumptions underlying this theoretical perspective the question is: does this structuralist perspective apply to the Koforidua informal economy? At present, over 90 per cent of the workers are in the informal economy; of which women constitute around 57 per cent of the informal labour force in Koforidua. A careful observation of the informal economy in Koforidua also reveals that it is widespread across nearly all sectors of the economy, but in the popular imagination, it is particularly acute in four broad realms, namely retailing, services such as hairdressing and dressmaking, car repair and maintenance (locally called 'magazine') and the construction sector.

What is common across both the dualist and structuralist views is that both attribute the informal economy with negative characteristics. The structuralist, like the dualist, believes that the informal economy is the arena for the marginalised population. However, there is a difference in the interpretation of marginality. According to this view (structuralist), the nature of capitalist development (rather than lack of growth) accounts for the continuous growth of informal production. The departure of public sector jobs and the shutting down of unproductive businesses have forced many laid-off workers to find other ways to survive (Becker, 2004). This claim has a lived experience in Ghana; during the period of the IMF/World Bank-led Structural Adjustments and Economic Recovery Programmes (Bello, 2004), most of the State Owned Enterprises (SOEs) were sold through privatisation. Therefore, some people became redundant as the new enterprise owners sought to reduce their costs by downsizing. In order to be able to cope with the situation most of these people ended up in the informal economy.

Conclusions and policy implications

In this chapter, empirical evidence from a study of 80 households in Koforidua, the regional capital of the eastern region of Ghana, has been reported. As the dualist view is rejected and the informal economy is seen as a major component of the national economy a need for an attitudinal change towards the informal economy should be initiated. The informal economy must have a new image. Over the years, government policy on the informal economy has not been the best. Inherent within the informal economy is low earning resulting in high levels of poverty among many in the country and therefore policies must be directed to address these issues. If the contribution of over 90 per cent to the national economy is far below expectation then measures to improve on this status quo are the way forward to make the informal economy more vibrant. Public policy must also take into account the diversity of the informal work and workers when considering policy options and directions for the economy. Women are seen to be at the lower end of the continuum conducting more low paid informal work. As decent work is at the centre of the government's formalisation policy, steps should be taken to address the inherent problems with formalisation such as bureaucracy. Again, the formalisation policy of the government lacks clear-cut definition. What constitutes formalisation presently is very ambiguous. In some sense, formalisation is concerned with informal workers registering their enterprises. Others also emphasise the need to practise basic book keeping principles by recording all activities and the like. Therefore evidently the government must have a clear-cut meaning of formalisation. This policy has the advantage of providing a means to evaluate the policy to find out its worthiness for pursuit in the interest of the nation.

In terms of policy formulations both government and private employment policies should have in them measures to address the low female participation in the formal economy. Back in the late 1990s women's empowerment was a topical issue on the national agenda but there is still a long way to go. Although women form the largest population they are marginalised in all aspects of human endeavour. Policies that have women as the focus may well address the overall issues inherent in the informal economy because women make up over 90 per cent of the informal economy, far in excess of their share of general population of about 51 per cent (Thompson, 2009).

The Assembly's main concern is that the act of selling and buying goods and services along the streets is overwhelming the intended function of streets and this has a severe impact on the city planning. In Ghana, in the cities, it is common to find drains (gutters) that are not covered. Street vendors who sit along these drains often dump all sorts of rubbish into the drains and this poses a severe health challenge for the city dwellers, especially the street vendors and their customers. What the Assembly needs to do is to intensify public health education for these people so that they become fully aware of the health dangers their actions pose. The long-term policy must be to reduce if not totally eliminate street vending along these open drains to ensure the health and safety of both sellers and buyers. The National Youth Employment Programme is one of the means to curb the street vending through training and giving them employment after the training.

Government policy on children who drop out of school must be intensified. Currently, children who dropped out of school as a result of financial difficulty are now being sponsored by the Assembly to go back to school (if they wish to do so) through what is called 'capitation grant'. It is imperative to recognise that getting people off the streets today may not solve the problem because they will come back tomorrow. The reason may be that these people are not catered for most of the time in the physical development planning or existing regulatory frameworks and therefore have to vend informally (Carr and Chen, 2001). Controlling street vending is a very difficult task to pursue. What needs to be done according to the municipal planning officer is 'to find out why they are on the streets and develop measures to address the problems they may have'.

The way forward in terms of policy is not to look at these issues as problems but rather turning them into opportunities for economic development by engaging and working with them regardless of how they are organised. This is the key success factor. The notion of partnership is vital in bringing the formal and informal economy together. It has become clearer that different people are motivated by different factors in terms of conducting informal work. So how do these diverse motives affect policy direction?

Most informal participants assert that low level of education is the main cause for doing informal work. An in-depth evaluation of major educational policies suggests that education has indeed played a vital role in growing the informal economy in Ghana. From EFA to FCUBE the formal economy continues to dwindle in real terms. The educational system in Ghana tends to place more emphasis on numeracy and literacy, leaving vocational skills development behind. The current globalised and commodified market makes it easier and prudent to outsource for the technology or skills that may be lacking from the local economy for economic development. As a consequence any educational policy that aims to produce 'just graduates' will contribute to the graduate unemployment and underemployment in that country thus increasing the numbers in the informal economy. There should be a conscious effort from the government to make education more relevant to the changing needs of the world of work (capitalist economy) so as to be abreast with time and its changing needs. Effort must be intensified in providing technical and vocational education and skill training at all levels. Higher institutions of learning must diversify in terms of academic curricula by providing more enterprise and entrepreneurship programmes aimed at producing graduates who would take delight in working in the informal economy as free will entrepreneurs rather than necessity-driven workers. Most importantly, however, there should be a deliberate effort on the part of policy makers to de-emphasise the norm that the formal economy is the only trajectory to achieve one's socio-economic objectives and to a better life.

Bibliography

Acheampong, K., Djangmah, J., Oduro, A., Seidu, A. and Hunt, F. (2007). Access to Basic Education in Ghana: The Evidence and the Issues, Country Analytic Report: CREATE: University of Sussex.

Abban, J. B. (1986). *Prerequisite of Manpower and Educational Planning in Ghana*. Accra: Baafour Educational Enterprises.

Adom, K. (2014). Beyond the marginalization thesis, an examination of the motivations of informal entrepreneurs in Sub-Saharan Africa: Insights from Ghana. *International Journal of Entrepreneurship and Innovation*, 15(2), 113–125.

Adom, K. and Williams, C. C. (2012). Evaluating the motives of informal entrepreneurs in Koforidua, Ghana. *Journal of Developmental Entrepreneurship*, 17(1), 1–17.

Adom, K. and Williams, C.C. (2014). Evaluating the explanations for the informal economy in third world cities: some evidence from Koforidua in the eastern region of Ghana. *International Entrepreneurship and Management Journal*, 10(10), 427–445.

Adu-Amankwah, K. (1999). *Trade Unions in the Informal Sector: Finding the bearing (The case of Ghana)*. Geneva: Labour Education Review No.116, International Labour Organization.

Adu-Amankwah, K. (2000). Organising in the Informal Sector. Online at: http//www.streetnet.org.za (accessed on 18 September 2009).

Aliyev, H. (2015). Post-Soviet informality: towards theory-building. *International Journal of Sociology and Social Policy*, 35(3–4), 182–198.

Baah, A. Y. (2007). *Organising the Informal Economy; Experiences and Lessons from Africa and Asia*. Accra: Ghana Trade Union Congress.

Barthe, M. A. (1988). *L'economie cachée*. Paris: Syros Alternatives.

Becker, K. F. (2004). *Fact Finding Study: The Informal Economy*. Stockholm: Swedish International Development Cooperation Agency.

Bello, W. (2004). *Deglobalization: Ideas for a New World Economy*. London: Zed.

Boapeah, S. N. (1996). Financing small rural enterprises through informal arrangements: a case study of the Ahanta West District of Ghana. In E. Aryeetey (Ed.) *Small Enterprise Credit in West Africa*. London: British Council and ISSER.

Boeke, J. (1942). *The Structure of the Netherlands Indian Economy*. New York: Institute of Pacific Relations.

Boeke, J. (1961). *Indonesian Economics: The Concept of Dualism in Theory and Policy*. The Hague: W van Hoeve.

Boels, D. (2014). Its better than stealing: informal street selling in Brussels. *International Journal of Sociology and Social Policy*, 34 (9/10), 670–693.

Button, K. (1984). Regional variations in irregular economy: a study of possible trends. *Regional Studies*, 18(2), 385–392.

Carr, M. and Chen, M. A. (2001). *Globalisation and the Informal Economy: How Global Trade and Investment Impact on the Working Poor.* ILO Employment Sector. Geneva: ILO.

Chen, M. A. (2005). *Rethinking the Informal Economy: Linkages with the Formal Economy and the Formal Regulatory Environment.* Geneva: ILO.

Chen, M. A., Jhabvala, R. and Lund, F. (2002). Employment Sector: Supporting Workers in the Informal Economy, A policy Framework: Working Paper on the Informal Economy. Geneva: International Labour Office.

Chen, M. A., Vanek, J. and Carr, M. (2004). *Mainstream Informal Employment and Gender in Poverty Reduction.* London: The Commonwealth Secretariat.

Cross, J. C. (1997). Entrepreneurship and exploitation: measuring independence and dependence in the informal economy. *International Journal of Sociology and Social Planning*, 17(3/4), 37–63.

Cross, J. C. (2000). Street vendors, modernity and postmodernity: Conflict and compromise in the global economy. *International Journal of Sociology and Social Policy*, 20(1), 29–51.

de Soto, H. (1989). *The Other Path.* London: Harper and Row.

Debrah, Y. A. (2007). Promoting the informal sector as a source of gainful employment in developing countries: insights from Ghana. *International Journal of Human Resource Management*, 18(6), 1063–1084.

Dovi, E. (2006). Tapping women's entrepreneurship in Ghana: Access to credit, technology vital for breaking into manufacturing. *Africa Renewal*, 20(1), 12–15.

Dzisi, S. (2008). Entrepreneurial activities of indigenous African women: a case of Ghana. *Journal of Enterprising Communities*, 2(3), 254–264.

Fields, G. (2005). A Guide to Multisector Labour Market models, World Bank Social Protection Discussion Paper Series No. 0505. Washington D.C.: World Bank,

Furnivall, J. (1939). *Netherlands India: a study of plural economies.* Cambridge: Cambridge University Press.

Furnivall, J. (1941). *Progress and Welfare in Southeast Asia: a comparison of colonial policy and practice.* New York: Secretariat, Institute of Pacific Relations.

Gërxhani, K. (2004). The informal sector in developed and less developed countries: A literature survey. *Public Choice*, 120(2), 267–300.

GoG. (2003). Ghana poverty reduction strategy paper (GPRS I).An agenda for growth and prosperity 2003–2005. Country Report No. 03/56: IMF.

Haan, H. C. (2006). *Training for Work in the Informal Micro-Enterprise Sector, Fresh Evidence from Sub-Saharan Africa.* Dordrecht: Springer.

Haan, H. C. and Serriere, N. (2002). Training for Work in Informal Sector: Fresh Evidence from West and Central Africa, Occasional Papers, International Training Centre of the ILO Turin.

Hanson, K. T. (2005). Landscape of survival and escape: social networking in urban livelihoods in Ghana. *Environment and Planning*, 37(7), 1291–1310.

Hart, K. (1973). Informal income opportunities and urban employment in Ghana. *Journal of Modern African Studies*, 11(1), 61–89.

Howe, L. (1990). *Being Unemployed in Northern Ireland: an ethnographic study.* Cambridge: Cambridge University Press.

ILO. (1972). *Employment, Incomes and Equity: a strategy for increasing productivity in Kenya.* Geneva: ILO.

ILO. (2002). *Decent Work and the Informal Economy.* Geneva: International Labour Organization.

ISSER. (2007). *Ghana Human Development Report 2007.* Worldwide Press Accra: UNDP/ISSER.

Jütting, J., Parlevliet, J. and Xenogiani, T. (2008). *Informal Employment Re-loaded.* Paris: OECD Development Centre

Koopmans, C. C. (1989). *Informelearbeid: vraag, aanbod, participanten, prijzen.* Amsterdam: Proefschrift Universitiet van Amsterdam.

Leonard, M. (2000). Coping strategies in developed and developing societies: The workings of the informal economy. *Journal of International Development*, 12(8), 1069–1085.

Lewis, A. (1954). Economic development with unlimited supplies of labour. *Manchester School of Economics and Social Studies*, 22(2), 139–192.

MEYS. (2004). White Paper on the Report of the Education Reform Review Committee, Accra: Ministry of Education Youth and Sports.

Morris, M., Pitt, L. F. and Berthon, P. (1996). Entrepreneurial activity in the Third World informal sector. *International Journal of Entrepreneurial Behaviour and Research*, 12(1), 59–76.

Moser, C. N. (1978). Informal Sector or Petty Commodity Production: Dualism or independence in urban development. *World Development*, 6(9–10), 1041–1064.

Ninsin, K. (1991). *The Informal Sector in Ghana's Political Economy*. Accra: Freedom Publications.

Nkrumah, K. (1943). Education and nationalism in Africa. *Educational Outlook*, 18(1), 32–40.

Osei, B., Baah-Nuakoh, A., Tutu, K. and Sowah, N. K. (1993). Impact of structural adjustment on small scale enterprises in Ghana. In A. J. H. Helmsing and T. Kolstee (Eds.), *Small Enterprise and Changing Policies, Structural Adjustment, financial policy and assistance programmes in Africa*. London: Intermediate Technology Publication.

Pahl, R. E. (1984). *Divisions of Labour*. Oxford: Blackwell

Palmer, R. (2007). Skills for work? From skills development to decent livelihoods in Ghana's rural informal economy. *International Journal of Educational Development*, 27(4), 397–420.

Portes, A., Castells, M., and Benton, L. (1989). *The Informal Economy: Studies in Advanced and Less Developed Countries*. Baltimore and London: Johns Hopkins University Press.

Potts, D. (2008). The urban informal sector in sub-Saharan Africa: from bad to good (and back again). *Development Southern Africa*, 25(2), 151–167.

Rosanvallon, P. (1980). Le développement de l'économie souterraine et l'avenir des sociétés industrielles. *Le Débat*, 2, 15–27.

Sassen, S. (1997). Informalisation in advance market economies. Issues in Development Discussion Paper 20, Geneva.

Schneider, F. and Enste, D. (2003). *The Shadow Economy: An International Survey*. Cambridge: Cambridge University Press.

Sethuraman, S. V. (1976). The urban informal sector: concept, measurement and policy. *International Labour Review*, 114(1), 69–81.

Snyder, K. A. (2004). Routes to the informal economy in New York's East Village: Crisis, economics and identity. *Sociological Perspectives*, 47(2), 215–240.

Sowa, N. K., Baah-Nuakoh, A., Tutu, K. A. and Osei, B. (1992). *Small Enterprises and Adjustment: The Impact of Ghana's Economic Recovery Programme*. London: Overseas Development Institute

Sutherland-Addy, E. and Causa, D. L. H. (2009). *Ideology and Educational Policy: The vision of Osagyefo Dr. Kwame Nkrumah*. Winneaba: University of Education.

Thompson, N. M. (2009). Why the Hawkers are back on the Pavement. Accra: http://news.myjoyonline.com/features/200907/33352.asp (accessed on 15 July 2009).

Tievant, S. (1982). Vivre autrement: échanges et sociabilité en ville nouvelle. CahiersdelOCS vol. 6. Paris: CNRS.

Tokman, V. (1978). An exploration into the nature of the informal–formal relationship. *World Development*, 6(9/10), 1065–1075.

Williams, C.C. (2004) *Small businesses in the informal economy: the evidence base*. London: Small Business Council.

Williams, C. C. (2005). *A Commodified World? Mapping the limits of capitalism*. London: Zed.

Williams, C. C. (2006). *The Hidden Enterprise Culture: Entrepreneurship in the Underground Economy*. Cheltenham: Edward Elgar.

Williams, C. C. (2007). The nature of entrepreneurship in the informal sector: evidence from England. *Journal of Development Entrepreneurship*, 12(2), 239–254.

Williams, C.C. (2013). Beyond the formal economy: evaluating the level of employment in informal sector enterprises in global perspective. *Journal of Developmental Entrepreneurship*, 18(4). doi: 10.1142/S1084946713500271.

Williams, C.C. (2014a). Explaining cross-national variations in the commonality of informal sector entrepreneurship: an exploratory analysis of 38 emerging economies. *Journal of Small Business and Entrepreneurship*, 27(2), 191–212.

Williams, C.C. (2014b). Tackling enterprises operating in the informal sector in developing and transition economies: a critical evaluation of the neo-liberal policy approach. *Journal of Global Entrepreneurship Research*, 2(9), doi: 10.1186/2251-7316-2-9, http://www.journal-jger.com/content/2/1/9.

Williams, C.C. (2014c). Out of the shadows: a classification of economies by the size and character of their informal sector. *Work, Employment and Society*, 28(5), 735–753.

Williams, C.C. and Martinez-Perez, A. (2014). Do small business start-ups test-trade in the informal economy? Evidence from a UK small business survey. *International Journal of Entrepreneurship and Small Business*, 22(1), 1–16.

Williams, C. C. and Round, J. (2008). A critical evaluation of romantic depictions of the informal economy. *Review of Social Economy*, 66(3), 297–323.

Williams, C.C. and Windebank, J. (1998). *Informal Employment in the Advanced Economies: Implications for Work and Welfare*. Routledge: London.

Williams, C.C. and Youssef, Y. (2013). Evaluating the gender variations in informal sector entrepreneurship: some lessons from Brazil. *Journal of Developmental Entrepreneurship*, 18(1), 1–16.

Williams, C.C. and Youssef, Y. (2014). Tackling informal entrepreneurship in Latin America: a critical evaluation of the neo-liberal policy approach. *Journal of Entrepreneurship and Organization Management*, 3(1), 1–9. http://dx.doi.org/10.4172/2169-026X.1000112.

Xaba, J., Horn, P. and Motala, S. (2002). The informal sector in Sub-Saharan Africa. Working Paper on Informal Economy. Geneva: ILO.

29

LEVELS OF INFORMALITY AND CHARACTERISTICS OF MICRO-ENTREPRENEURS IN PAKISTAN

Muhammad Shehryar Shahid, Halima Shehryar and Minha Akber Allibhoy

Introduction

In recent decades, the persistent portrayal of the informal economy as a negative phenomenon (Gallin, 2001; Sassen, 1997) and declining sphere (Ranis, 1989; Williams and Windebank, 1998) has been largely refuted, and it has been recognized that not only is the informal sector extensive and growing, but the rate of its growth in developing countries has been far more rapid than is the case in advanced economies (Burki and Afaqi, 1996; Gennari, 2004; Kemal and Mahmood, 1998). The prevalence of the informal economy can be gauged from a report by OECD according to which out of the total global working population of 3 billion, nearly two-thirds (1.8 billion) are employed in the informal economy (see Jütting and Laiglesia, 2009), a majority of whom work on a self-employed basis: 70 percent of all informal workers in sub-Saharan Africa, 62 percent in North Africa, 60 percent in Latin America, 59 percent in Asia (ILO, 2002a), and 77 percent in the European Union (Williams and Windebank, 2011). This depicts that the informal economy is now an integral part of the entrepreneurial landscape. This is even more so in the context of developing economies (Schneider and Williams, 2013). Consequently, literature on both entrepreneurship (Evans et al., 2006; Katungi et al., 2006; Williams, 2006) and the informal economy (Cross and Morales, 2007; De Soto, 2001; ILO, 2002b) has examined whether entrepreneurs engage wholly or partially on an off-the-books basis.

In Pakistan, 74 percent of the total labor force operates in the informal economy according to the Labor Force Survey 2010–2011 (Pakistan Bureau of Statistics, 2011). However, other varying size estimates of the informal economy have been made as well. For instance, Kemal (2003) estimated the size of the informal economy as a percentage of GDP at 64.3 percent, Yasmin and Rauf (2004) at 29.9 percent, and Schneider and Williams (2013) at 33.5 percent. Despite these discrepancies, the prevalent consensus is that the size of the informal sector is large and steadily expanding (Burki and Afaqi, 1996; Gulzar et al., 2010). However, though many studies have focused on the size of this sector, the motives of those participating in it have remained largely uninvestigated. Since such information is crucial to be able to draft effective policies, this dearth of studies exploring the motives of informality has resulted in conflicting opinions about the ways in which this sector can be tackled; whilst numerous studies recommend heavier penalties, lower tax rates, frequent tax audits, and a simpler tax system (e.g. Aslam, 1998; Yasmin and Rauf, 2004), others assert that there is a need to provide informal enterprises with subsidies and exemptions in order for them to expand and enter the sphere of the formal sector (e.g. Burki and Afaqi, 1996). Furthermore, very few direct surveys have been conducted to explore the informal economy in Pakistan. Of the few direct surveys that have been carried out, most were done during the period 1985–1993 (e.g. Burki, 1989; Guisinger and Irfan, 1980; Kazi, 1990; Nadvi, 1990), and were small-scale surveys whose findings cannot be generalized (Kemal and Mahmood, 1998). It is precisely these gaps that this study undertakes to fill.

At the outset however, informal entrepreneurship needs to be defined. For the purposes of this chapter, informal entrepreneurship is defined as involving somebody who is actively engaged in starting a business or is the owner/manager of a business, who participates in the paid production and sale of goods and services that are unregistered by or hidden from the state for tax, social security and/or labor law purposes, but which are legal in all other respects (Williams, 2014b; Williams and Windebank, 1998; Williams and Nadin, 2010; Williams and Martinez, 2014). Hence, businesses producing and/or selling illegal goods and services, such as smuggling, pirated products, and illicit drugs fall outside the ambit of this definition.

The formal/informal dichotomy of entrepreneurship

For most of the twentieth century, informal entrepreneurship was portrayed as a residue of a pre-modern era that was shrinking with the irrevocable advance of formalization. Seen through this lens, the presence of informal economic activities signalled traditionalism, whereas the formal economy indicated progress (Gilbert, 1998; Packard, 2007). This exemplifies what Derrida (1967) called a "binary hierarchy," which depicted both these economic activities as belonging to entirely discrete opposing realms, and normatively sequenced in a way that endowed the super-ordinate (formal economy) with positive, and the subordinate (informal economy) with negative attributes. However, this binary hierarchical discourse, so far firmly entrenched in the literature, began to be contested with the advent of new explanations. Initially, this was done by simply inverting this binary hierarchy by asserting that informal entrepreneurship was not small and dwindling but extensive and growing (OECD, 2002; Schneider, 2008; Williams, 2006); by replacing the depiction of the formal and the informal economies as discrete with a view of informal entrepreneurship as embedded within the formal economy (Slavnic, 2010); and by transcending the negative portrayal of the informal economy and celebrating informal entrepreneurs as heroes defying state oppression (De Soto, 1989; Sauvy, 1984).

Such attempts to contest this binary hierarchy, however, not only adopted an erroneous approach, they also failed to challenge the binary itself. Other literature on informal entrepreneurship has consequently focused its attention on moving beyond the formal/informal dichotomy toward what is called the "degrees of informalization" approach (see, Williams and Shahid, 2015). Thus, challenging the conventional discourse whereby the formal and informal entrepreneurial activities occupy discrete spaces in the economic landscape, a continuum of spaces from fully formal to fully informal spaces is envisaged (Jones et al., 2006; Smith and Stenning, 2006; Williams, 2014a). Likewise, in recent years not only has it been recognized that a distinct bifurcation between formal and informal workers (Williams, 2004; Williams and Windebank, 1998) and jobs (Williams, 2007, 2013; Woolfson, 2007) is no longer possible, but more importantly for our analysis, the dichotomous depiction of entrepreneurs as operating on either a fully formal or fully informal basis has also been contested by a growing stream of literature which asserts that the vast majority of informal work is not conducted by wholly informal businesses, rather, it is conducted by formal businesses conducting some of their trade off-the-books (Ram et al., 2002a,b; Small Business Council, 2004; Williams, 2006). Resultantly, a continuum of enterprise types has surfaced, ranging from wholly formal to wholly informal enterprises with enterprises with varying levels of formality in between.

Rationales for informal entrepreneurship

Turning to the rationales for informality, two distinct sets of motives for participating in informal entrepreneurship have surfaced, which we here call economic and non-economic rationales. Economic rationales encapsulate motives rooted in economic necessity, as well as motives rooted in an urge to maximize profits. On the one hand the structuralist perspective, refuting the view that informal enterprise is a remnant of the past and endorsing the view that it is extensive and growing (ILO, 2002b; OECD, 2002; Williams, 2006), interprets informal entrepreneurship as a survival strategy, a last resort (Castells and Portes, 1989; ILO, 2002b), and informal entrepreneurs as driven by economic necessity. For these structuralists, informality is seen as an offshoot of the new subcontracting and outsourcing culture of late capitalism, which pushes individuals into the "exploitative" realm of informality (Barsoum, 2015; Castells and Portes, 1989; Davis, 2006; Hudson, 2005). According to the neo-liberals on the other hand, the decision to participate in informal entrepreneurship arises due to a voluntary exit rather than an involuntary exclusion from the formal economy (Gërxhani, 2004; Perry and Maloney, 2007; Williams and Gurtoo, 2011; Williams and Horodnic, 2015). We further extend this argument by asserting that the neo-liberal rationales underlying this voluntary exit can be further bifurcated into two categories: those governed by profit maximizing motives, and those governed by non-economic reasons, to which we shall shortly return. Seen through an economic lens, entrepreneurs are propelled by a desire to maximize profits, and engage in the informal economy for purely material reasons, such as to avoid the high costs of registration arising due to a burdensome regulatory environment (Gulzar et al., 2010; Iqbal, 1998; Kemal, 2007; Khan and Quaddus, 2015; Shabsigh, 1995), or due to high tax rates levied by the state (Ahmed and Ahmed, 1995; Arby, 2010; Hussain and Ahmed, 2006; Kemal, 2003, 2007).

Turning to the non-economic rationales of engaging in informal entrepreneurship, as put forth by the neo-liberals, it is argued that the decision of informal entrepreneurs to participate in the informal economy is not always driven by an urge to maximize profits; rather, there may be other non-economic drivers underlying this decision, such as perceptions of rampant public sector corruption and intricacies of the registration process (De Soto, 1989; Ahmed, 2009; Friedman et al., 2000; Gulzar et al., 2010). With the turn of the millennium, moreover, a post-structuralist perspective came to the fore. In this perspective, individuals are no longer depicted as rational economic actors, basing their livelihood choices on purely economic rationales. Rather, informal entrepreneurship is seen as a "social artefact" resulting due to resentment against the state (Ahmed, 2009; Aliyev, 2015; Boels, 2014; Federal Board of Revenue, 2008; Hodosi, 2015; Kemal, 2003), shared norms and tax morality of the industry (Torgler, 2003), an individual's desire for a particular work identity (Snyder, 2004), and a need to help one's kin, neighbors, relatives, and acquaintances for social and redistributive reasons (Round and Williams, 2008; Smith and Stenning, 2006; Williams, 2004).

Having reviewed the economic and non-economic rationales that drive informal entrepreneurs, we now begin to evaluate how certain characteristics and rationales are more prevalent amongst the micro-entrepreneurs of Lahore with respect to their participation in the informal economy, and how these rationales and characteristics may vary according to the different levels of informality of the entrepreneurs.

Methodology

Data pertaining to the level of informality of enterprises and the rationales behind it was collected through face-to-face interviews conducted with 300 micro-entrepreneurs in Lahore during October 2012 to January 2013, following a pilot study of 30 micro-enterprises in September 2012. The interviews were conducted in either Urdu or the local dialect of Punjabi. To avoid selecting respondents from a specific cohort or place who might have similar rationales behind their level of formality, maximum variation sampling was employed (Adom and Williams, 2012; Williams and Nadin, 2012). At the outset, the city was split into seven contrasting zones ranging from high-, middle-, to low-income localities, followed by a spatially stratified sampling method to select micro-entrepreneurs employed in retail, manu-facturing, and instantly consumable food (ICF) sectors from within each locality. The relative sample size for each sector was assessed using its relative size, which was inferred using proxy indicators obtained from the 2001 census of population and the Labor Force Survey 2010–2011 (Pakistan Bureau of Statistics, 2011). The resultant sample consisted of a heterogeneous mix of micro-entrepreneurs from various sectors across a broad range of localities. The structured face-to-face interview schedule commenced with socio-demographic questions and gradually progressed to more sensitive questions pertaining to the characteristics of the business, registration issues, the type of customers and suppliers of the business, and the problems they faced as a business. Furthermore, in early 2013 a qualitative survey consisted of semi-structured in-depth interviews, lasting between 90 to 120 minutes each, were con-ducted with 15 micro-entrepreneurs (randomly selected from the main survey respondents) with the intention of probing into the rationales behind their informality.

Results and Discussion

Scale of Informality

Before discussing the findings of the survey, it is important to describe the scale of informality as constructed for the purpose of this study. The level of informality is here defined in terms of the number of "actual" registrations that an enterprise holds with respect to the total number of registrations it is liable to acquire according to the given laws. Referring to the definition of informal entrepreneurship (Williams and Windebank, 1998) given at the start of the chapter, we have considered four basic mandatory registrations, namely tax, labor, social security, and food, that a micro-enterprise operating in the city of Lahore within the given three sectors must enrol for in order to be classified as a fully formal enterprise. In Pakistan, each of these registrations is governed by a different department and a separate code of law, as given in Table 29.1.

According to the parameters given in Table 29.1, a first-of-its-kind "scale of informality" is constructed to place the micro-enterprises in this study at varying levels of informality. Consequently, four different categories of micro-enterprises are created: fully formal (FF), largely formal (LF), largely informal (LI) and fully informal (FI). A fully formal enterprise, for instance, is the one that completely complies with all the laws applicable to it given its employment size and sector, and hence possesses all the registrations it is legally obliged to

Table 29.1 Types of Business Registrations in Lahore, Pakistan

Registration type	Governing Body	Governing Law	Registration Criteria	Sectors Applied to:
Tax	Federal Bureau of Revenue (FBR)	Income Tax Ordinance 2001	Any business/individual engaged in paid or self-employed economic activity in Pakistan	Retail Manufacturing ICF
Labour	Punjab Labour and Human Resource Department	The Punjab Shops and Establishment Ordinance, 1969	Establishments employing 2 or more than 2 employees, including part- and full-time workers	Retail Manufacturing ICF
Social Security	Punjab Employees Social Security Institution	The Provincial Employees' Social Security Ordinance, 1965	Establishments employing 5 or more than 5 employees, including part- and full-time workers	Retail Manufacturing ICF
Food	Punjab Food Authority	Punjab Food Authority Act, 2011	Any undertaking, whether or not for profit, carrying out any of the activities related to any stage of manufacturing, processing, packaging, storage, transportation, distribution of food, import, export and includes food services, catering services, sale of food or food ingredients	Only ICF

Table 29.2 Scale of Informality

Scale of formality	A/B:	percentage of formality
	Number of registrations acquired (A) as a fraction of total mandatory registrations (B)	
Fully Formal (FF)	4/4; 3/3; 2/2; 1/1	100 percent
Largely Formal (LF)	3/4; 2/3; 1/2; 2/4	50–75 percent
Largely Informal (LI)	1/4; 1/3	Less than 50 percent
Fully Informal (FI)	0/4; 0/3; 0/2; 0/1	0 percent

acquire under the purview of those laws. A fully informal enterprise, in contrast, is one that does not possess any of the registrations that it essentially requires to acquire. Accordingly, the largely formal and largely informal enterprises are placed somewhere in between these two extremes on the scale of informality. These contain the micro-enterprises that show some level of compliance with the law by obtaining a certain fraction of registrations out of those they are legally obliged to acquire. For instance in percentage terms (see Table 29.2), if the enterprise holds 50 percent–75 percent of the registrations required, it is termed as largely formal, whereas if it complies with less than 50 percent of the registrations applicable to the business, the firm is largely called an informal enterprise.

Extent of informal micro-entrepreneurship in Lahore

Having defined the scale of informality, we will now turn to how many of the micro-entrepreneurs surveyed in this study would fall along this scale and the overall magnitude of informal entrepreneurship in Lahore. The survey conducted with the owners of 300 micro-enterprises across different sectors and regions of the city of Lahore, revealed a high level of informality amongst entrepreneurs (see Table 29.3). Of these, a vast majority of entrepreneurs (61 percent) had not opted for any of the mandatory registrations, not having their firms registered with any government department whatsoever and operating on a fully informal basis. On the contrary, very few of the entrepreneurs surveyed (approx. 18 percent), were fully formal entrepreneurs having acquired all the obligatory registrations for their firms. After fully informal entrepreneurs, the second largest majority of them comprised those who were conducting just a portion of their transactions on an informal basis. They had opted for some of the mandatory registrations for their businesses while ignoring the rest. In our

Table 29.3 Level of Formality: by Sector Type (Percentage)

Level of formality	Sector			
	Retail	Manufacturing	ICF	Total
Full Formal	12.0	4.3	1.3	17.7
Fully Informal	15.7	19.0	26.3	61.0
Largely Formal	4.3	5.3	4.3	14.0
Largely Informal	1.3	4.7	1.3	7.3
Total	33.3	33.3	33.3	100.0

sample, almost one in every four entrepreneurs (23 percent) would fall in the category of either largely formal or largely informal, that is, they had their enterprises registered with at least one and at most three of the four government departments mentioned above. Consequently, while these were not fully ghost entrepreneurs and had their existence on some official records, there was a part of their business that still remained undeclared.

In terms of the registration type, registration with the tax department has turned out to be the most popular compliance amongst the entrepreneurs surveyed, while the registration with the social security department remained extremely dismal. Out of the 300 entrepreneurs we surveyed, only 114 (38 percent) had registered their businesses with the Federal Board of Revenue for tax purposes. For the Punjab Food Authority, out of the 100 entrepreneurs who were liable to register their businesses with this department, only 20 entrepreneurs had in fact registered. As far as the Labour Department is concerned, for a total of 146 entrepreneurs liable to register with it, only 15 (10 percent) had registered their businesses. The rate of registration with the Social Security Institution was deplorably low, where only three out of the 41entrepreneurs (7 percent) who were legally obliged to acquire this registration had in fact registered their businesses with this department.

Crosscutting these different levels of informality across the three sectors surveyed in this study (see Table 29.3) one can observe some interesting trends. In all three sectors the maximum concentration of entrepreneurs were comprised of those operating fully informal enterprises. Nevertheless, the ICF sector seems to have by far the largest concentration of such entrepreneurs as opposed to the manufacturing and retail sectors. Almost one in every two of the fully unregistered enterprises belonged to the ICF sector. On the contrary, the retail sector had got an astonishingly high percentage of fully formal entrepreneurs relative to the other two sectors. Of the total 18 fully formal entrepreneurs reported in the survey, 12 were part of the retail sector, having acquired all the mandatory registrations for their businesses. The higher level of formality amongst retail entrepreneurs is perhaps attributed to the fact that most of them are part of distribution channels for medium or large enterprises that makes it indispensible for them to acquire the basic business registrations. The manu-facturing sector entrepreneurs fall in the middle as far as the level of informality is concerned, having by far the maximum number of entrepreneurs in the categories of largely formal and largely informal when compared with the ICF and retail sectors. Almost one in every three (30 percent) of the manufacturing entrepreneurs was operating a partially informal enter-prise that was usually registered with either the tax and/or labor department, while being unregistered for social security purposes.

Characteristics of informal micro-entrepreneurs in Lahore

Examining the characteristics of the 300 micro-entrepreneurs interviewed in Lahore, Table 29.4 presents very interesting insights about the financing and employment structures of these informal enterprises as they relate to the number of business registrations that these enterprises hold, which is here a sign of their level of informality. Clearly, the gross income of the entrepreneur increases as he tends to acquire more of the mandatory registrations for his business. While the majority (40 percent) of the enterprises having no registration earn less than PKR20,000 (USD195–200[1]) per month, the majority of those with at least one or more than one registrations were on average earning twice of that income (USD400–430), which is significantly higher than the national minimum wage (USD135) earned by a formal employee in Pakistan. Similarly, more educated entrepreneurs are likely to comply with more business regulations and hence be more formal. Overall the majority of these

Table 29.4 Characteristics of Informal Micro-Entrepreneurs/Enterprises in Lahore, Pakistan (Percentage)

	No registration	One registration	More than one registrations
Gross Income			
< 20,000	39.9	5.6	8.3
20,000–30,000	36.4	31.5	20.8
30,000–50,000	15.6	49.4	37.5
> 50,000	8.1	13.5	33.3
Educational Level			
No education	22.4	3.3	3.8
Primary	31.1	22	15.4
Secondary	36.1	41.8	57.7
Diploma	4.4	20.9	3.8
University	6	12.1	19.2
Financing Structure			
Sources of Funding:			
Friends/family	19.5	0	0
Self-funding	71.9	75	88.9
Credit purchases from the suppliers	5.4	15.4	7.4
Advance payments by the customers	3.2	8.7	3.7
Other	0	1	0
Ever Applied for a Bank Loan:			
No	95.6	73.6	80.8
Yes	4.4	26.4	19.2
Reason for not Applying for a Bank Loan:			
Complicated procedures	10.9	1	3.4
High interest rates	19.2	13.7	10.3
High guarantee/collateral requirements	12	9.8	0
Amount of loan offered was insufficient	1.5	8.8	0
Did not need a loan	40.6	42.2	51.7
Religious reasons	15.8	24.5	34.5
Employment Structure			
Employment Size:			
No employee	49.2	36.3	0
1–5 employees	49.2	47.3	57.7
6–10 employees	1.6	16.5	42.3
Sources of Hiring:			
Not willing to hire anyone	20.8	20.9	3.8
Relatives/recommended people	46.4	44	46.2
Employees from other small businesses	14.8	8.8	26.9
Former apprentice	3.8	18.7	7.7
Anyone (no particular preference)	13.1	6.6	11.5
Other	1.1	1.1	3.8

(Continued)

Table 29.4 (Continued)

	No registration	One registration	More than one registrations
Contract Type:			
Written	0.8	12.7	9.8
Verbal	91.8	74.2	77.4
No contract	7.4	13.1	12.8
Payment Method:			
By cheque	1.9	19	2.3
By cash	98.1	81	97.7
Payment Structure:			
Fixed monthly	38.3	48.3	56.4
Daily wage	42.6	21	32.3
Per job	12.9	18.9	7.5
Commission based	2.3	7.6	0
Profit sharing	2.7	3.8	3.8
Payment-in-kind	0.4	0	0
No payment	0.8	0.4	0

micro-entrepreneurs seem to have acquired secondary (6–10 years) education, which is also more than the average level of education in Pakistan, i.e. 5years.[2] Hence, one may assert that most of the informal micro-entrepreneurs surveyed in this study were not only more educated than an average Pakistani, but were also economically better off than many of their counterparts in formal employment.

Talking about the financing structures of these micro-enterprises, in most of the cases (> 70 percent) the business was funded by the entrepreneur's own money with very little reliance on external sources of funding whatsoever, regardless of their level of informality. Nevertheless, the entrepreneurs operating totally unregistered businesses seemed to rely on friends/family as a source of funding more often than the ones with registered businesses, who rather tend to draw their working capital more by maintaining good credit terms with their suppliers. When asked if they had ever applied for a bank loan, a heavy majority of entrepreneurs replied in defiance, with most of them (> 40 percent) did not reckon it needful for their businesses to get a loan. It perhaps is indicative of their un-ambitious growth plans, which some of them expressed quite assertively in the survey. Other factors, such as high interest rate and religious motives were also mentioned as significant reasons to avoid applying for bank loan. Religious motives in this case refer to an Islamic school of thought that believes charging and paying of interest is a prohibited (*haram*) economic activity. Meanwhile, however, only 4.4 percent of the totally unregistered entrepreneurs said to have once applied for a bank loan versus 26.4 percent and 19.2 percent of those who possessed one or more than one registrations respectively. It implies that as entrepreneurs become more formal, they are more likely to seek funding from banks.

As is also evident from Table 29.4, enterprises with some employees are more likely to comply with business regulations as compared to those who had none. While nearly half (49 percent) of the micro-entrepreneurs who were operating totally unregistered enterprises reported to have no employees, a significant percentage (42 percent) of those who had registered their businesses with multiple government departments had employed 6–10 employees in their firms. Overall, most of the hiring by these micro-entrepreneurs was restricted only to people previously known to them, either friends or relatives. However, as they acquire more registrations and hence become more formal, they tend to start hiring from the open labor market. About 27 percent of the entrepreneurs with multiple registrations, for example, reported to have hired ex-employees of other small businesses, usually not known to them. Interestingly, a heavy majority of the employees hired by these micro-enterprises did have some form of contractual arrangement with the employer, although most of them (> 80 percent) only comprised informal verbal agreements.[3] The survey, however, identified a slight shift toward written job agreements as the entrepreneurs become more formal. Cash-in-hand happened to be a unanimously preferred mode of payment instead of cheques regardless of the entrepreneurs' level of informality. Nevertheless, the level of informality does seem to have an impact on the way these entrepreneurs structure the payment of their employees. While most of the entrepreneurs (43 percent) who were operating totally unregistered enterprises paid their employees on a daily wage basis, the bulk of those having one (48 percent) or more than one registrations (56 percent) rather paid their employees through fixed monthly wages. Hardly ever did these entrepreneurs use payment-in-kind as a substitute of monetary remuneration.

Reasons for participation in informal entrepreneurship

So why do these Pakistani micro-entrepreneurs in Lahore operate in the informal economy, and that too at varying levels of informality? As discussed in the literature review, the motives due to which informal entrepreneurship prevails in developing countries like Pakistan can be broadly divided into two major categories: economic and non-economic reasons. Table 29.5 outlines the classification of these motives and their corresponding reasons as chosen by the respondents of this study.

Starting with economic reasons, this study contests the popular discourse that in developing countries, informal entrepreneurship is initiated out of necessity. As Table 29.5 presents, when asked about the motives to start an informal business, only a minority of the entrepreneurs (40 percent) mentioned economic necessity, i.e. inability to find a formal job (34 percent) and/or need for additional income (6 percent), as a prime reason to do so. In contrast, for most of these micro-entrepreneurs, starting up their current businesses was largely a product of certain entrepreneurial ambitions, such as to choose a more lucrative livelihood than simply working for someone else as a salaried person (56 percent), or pursue a flexible lifestyle by being their own boss (50.5 percent). These results are strongly counterintuitive to the general structuralist perception prevailing in developing countries, which tends to underplay the entrepreneurialism of those starting up in the informal sector.

The second set of economic reasons mainly relates to the profit maximization motive. Here the results are quite eccentric too. Akin to most developing countries, a strong assumption exists in Pakistan that higher tax rates lead to greater levels of informality, which in turn acts as the premise for predominant policies regarding business formalization in the country (e.g. Ahmed and Ahmed, 1995; Arby, 2010; Hussain and Ahmed, 2006; Kemal, 2003, 2007). This study, however, has revealed that only a small proportion of the micro-entrepreneurs surveyed (45 out of 300) cited high tax rates as one of the key reasons for their informality. As a grocery retailer and a motorbike mechanic said respectively, "tax rates are quite reasonable, we can afford to pay them" and "the government believes we do it to save taxes, it's not that." Other financial motives, such as the fear of losing competitiveness and profitability to a rival business as a result of formalization are undermined to an even larger

Table 29.5 Motives of Pakistani Entrepreneurs to Participate in Informal Entrepreneurship

	percent age of sample
Economic Motives	
A- Economic Marginality Reasons:	
I could not get a salaried job	34 percent
Need additional income	6 percent
It is more profitable than salaried job	56 percent
B- Profit Maximization Reasons:	
Registration cost is high	4 percent
Tax rates are too high	15 percent
I may lose competitiveness and profitability	6 percent
Non-Economic Motives	
A- Structural/Institutional Reasons:	
1- Lack of awareness	
Do not know if I have to register	26 percent
2- Weak Enforcement of Law	
I do not perceive it risky to run an unregistered business in Pakistan	56 percent
3- Registration system is complicated	19 percent
4- Public sector corruption	21 percent
B- Socio-Cultural Reasons:	
1- Industrial/Social Norms	
All the similar businesses are not registered	25 percent
Non registration is a common practice in my industry	8 percent
	33 percent
2- Resentment against the state and big businesses	
The state does not do anything for us so why should we obey the law	29 percent
Big businesses are not paying taxes so why should we	9 percent
	38 percent
3- Tax morality	
It is highly acceptable to run an unregistered business in Pakistan	85 percent
4- Lifestyle and Identity	
I started this business because I prefer to be my own boss	50.5 percent

extent in the survey. Only a negligible fraction of the entrepreneurs (6 percent) mentioned these as key reasons for their participation in the informal economy. All in all, the economic motives are profoundly underrepresented amongst the micro-entrepreneurs of Lahore as a reason for informality. However, as mentioned earlier, a majority of them did signify their profit-motive at the time for starting up their current ventures.

Clearly, neither do most of the micro-entrepreneurs in Lahore view themselves as what Williams and Gurtoo (2012) call "survivalists," i.e. driven out of economic necessity into informal entrepreneurship, nor do they fully comply with what they call "rational economic actors" in the sense that although they viewed their entrepreneurial endeavors as a more lucrative livelihood option than a formal job, they very meekly represent their informality as a means of profit maximization and competitiveness by evading taxes and registration costs. So what is then the main motive for these micro-entrepreneurs to keep their businesses informal?

As per the survey, the major tilt has been toward the non-economic motives. Starting with intuitional/structural reasons, a considerable portion of these entrepreneurs (21 percent) cited public sector corruption as one of the key reasons for keeping their businesses informal. For example, a small shoe shop owner stated, "Superior officers are like dons and small officers are fully corrupt, they collect and give it to the superiors." Of the total problems encountered with the various government departments by these micro-entrepreneurs vis-a-vis business operations, around 24 percent were said to be resolved "by the payment of a gift (bribe)". This clearly reflects the level of corruption prevailing in the system. The refusal to pay the "gift," meanwhile, would have led to more severe implications. As stated by a street hawker, "last year I bribed a municipal corporation official but this time I refused . . . he put up such a huge fine that I think it's better just to bribe him." Related to corruption is the perceived riskiness of operating informally amongst these micro-entrepreneurs. Strikingly, more than half (56 percent) of them perceive it "not risky at all" to run an unregistered business in Pakistan, while another 34 percent identify it as only "somewhat risky" to do so. The low riskiness of operating informally is an epitome of weak enforcement of business laws in the country that leads to a widespread belief on the part of these micro-entrepreneurs that the likelihood of them being detected and punished is dismally low, and even if such an event occurs they can easily escape the litigation by bribing the officials, which tends to encourage them to remain informal.

Amongst institutional/structural reasons, a widespread lack of awareness on the part of these micro-entrepreneurs about the type and process of registrations has also surfaced as another important factor; one in every four entrepreneurs surveyed (26 percent) mentioned it as a main reason for their non-registration. When asked, most of them had a wrong or a very vague idea about the kind of registrations applicable to their businesses, in fact, some of them did not know that such regulations even existed, let alone the process of registration. The situation is further aggravated due to the perceived complication of the registration system. Expressions like "the system is very vague and confusing" and "they make you go in circles for a simple task," as shared by an electronics shop owner and a biryani[4] seller respectively, were fairly recurring amongst survey respondents. Almost one-fifth (19 percent) of the micro-entrepreneurs cited the intricacies of the registration system as a main reason for their informality. This finding is aligned with the World Bank's latest ranking on ease of doing business that has ranked Pakistan at 127[5] out of 189 countries in terms of the number of processes and time involved in acquiring basic business registrations in the country.

Moving on to socio-cultural reasons, this study has identified a massive impact of the prevailing industrial norms on the entrepreneurs' level of informality. Almost one in every three (33 percent) of the micro-entrepreneurs in the survey attributed his engagement in the informal economy to what he perceived was a norm amongst businesses like him. An electronics retailer, for instance, asserted, "everyone is doing 'do numberian' (hidden transactions), and if you do it the right way you look like a fool." For many of these entrepreneurs, their level of informality would largely depend on how they compare themselves with their counterparts in the immediate market in particular and in the industry at large. As expressed by a stall owner selling street food, "If the entire market will get properly registered so will we." Interestingly, this study identified that at times such normative forces may also exist by virtue of the customers that these micro-entrepreneurs served. As explained by a shoe retailer, "If we bill them with tax inclusive, most of my customers themselves demand for a 'kacha' (non-taxed) bill because a 'kacha' bill makes the goods cheaper for them." Similarly, a timber manufacturer selling wood to small furniture shops expressed, "All my customers are unregistered. They will not do business with me if I go by the books … they only pay you cash-in-hand."

Furthermore, the findings of this survey corroborated earlier studies which assert that the level of informality is high in some populations owing to a deep resentment toward the state (e.g. Leonard, 1994; Torgler, 2003); almost 40 percent of those interviewed in this study believed that the Pakistani state has perpetually failed to deliver its promise of public goods and services, which they cited as a key reason for their informality (also see, Ahmed, 2009; Kemal, 2003). Painfully remembering his experience at a government hospital, for example, the owner of a small restaurant stated, "I lost my eye forever because I was given an expired medicine by the staff at a state-run hospital with no compensation whatsoever ... I will never pay them taxes." This deep resentment toward the state results in these entrepreneurs being less acquiescent toward its laws and hostile toward the big businesses due to the per-ceived preferential treatment they get from the authorities. An automobile spare parts retailer, for example, thinks that "the law saves only the powerful and the rich; they know how to use the loopholes." Also, an owner of a shoe shop asserted, "Big guys are untouchable."

This resentment against the state, combined with the shared norms of informality in the industry, has caused a direct implication on the tax morality of the micro-entrepreneurs of Lahore; of the 300 entrepreneurs interviewed, 105 were of the opinion that it was "highly acceptable" to run an informal business in Pakistan, 150 said it was "somewhat acceptable," and only 46 entrepreneurs considered it "not acceptable" to operate outside the fringes of law. Therefore, low tax morality has made it legitimate (see, Webb et al., 2009) for most of them to operate in the informal economy despite being in contradiction with the given rules and regulations. Now let's have a look at how these motives may vary according to the entrepreneurs' level of informality.

Table 29.6 presents the crosscutting of various reasons as cited by these micro-entrepreneurs with respect to their level of informality. Many insightful trends can be observed. Most striking of all is the fact that the non-economic motives seem to predominate as reasons for informality regardless of the entrepreneurs' level of informality. Clearly a much higher percentage of entrepreneurs in all the three categories seem to have chosen a non-economic motive as a main reason for their informality than those who rather cited an economic reason.

Table 29.6 Motives to Participate in Informal Entrepreneurship and the Level of Informality

	Largely Formal (percent)	*Largely Informal (percent)*	*Fully Informal (percent)*
Economic Motives			
Economic Marginality	11.90	27.27	48.08
Registration cost is high	2.38	9.09	4.40
Tax rates are too high	19.04	22.73	13.18
I may lose competitiveness	7.14	18.18	3.30
Non-Economic Motives			
Lack of awareness of the registration process	76.19	54.54	77.05
Registration system is complicated	21.42	31.82	18.68
Industrial/Social Norms	50	72.72	53.55
Public sector corruption	9.52	22.73	25.82
Resentment against the state/big businesses	33.33	50	27.47
Low tax morality	80.95	86.36	88.46
Low risk of detection	59.52	90.90	92.85

For fully informal entrepreneurs, the three main factors driving their participation in the informal economy are low tax morality, weak enforcement of law (i.e. perceived risk of detection), and their insufficient awareness of the registration process. For largely informal, it is primarily the normative forces of informality in the industry, causing a deteriorating effect on their tax morality also, and the weak enforcement of law that prevents their urge to further reduce their informality. Lastly, for largely formal entrepreneurs, it is their low tax morality, insufficient information of the registration process and weak enforcement of law that hinder their move toward full formalization. Although low tax morality appears to be the leading cause of informality for entrepreneurs regardless of the fact that they operate at varying levels of informality, this study observes a gradual increase in the entrepreneurs' tax morality, as they tend to become more formal. So too is the case with economic marginality. While for almost 50 percent of fully informal entrepreneurs it was their incapacity to find a formal job that pushed them into starting an informal business, only about 12 percent of largely formal entrepreneurs cited similar reasons. Meaning, the entrepreneurs starting off their businesses as a matter of voluntary choice are more likely to acquire mandatory business registrations and be more formal. There is also a significant increase in the entrepreneurs' perceived risk of detection for their informal practices as they graduate from fully informal through largely informal to largely formal. The more formal an entrepreneur becomes, the riskier he believes it is for him to engage in informal activities. As he gets more formal, which by definition here means opting for more registrations, his business becomes more transparent and easier to detect by law enforcement authorities as opposed to someone running a totally unregistered enterprise. Moreover, as entrepreneurs move from fully and largely informal to largely formal, they tend to ascribe a significantly less value to public sector corruption as a key reason for their informality. Apparently, an increased interaction with public sector authorities as a result of getting one's business registered with more government departments seems to improve the entrepreneurs' perception of the prevalent corruption in such departments, or perhaps they are now less vulnerable to the harassment by these government authorities that a relatively less formal business would generally face.

Conclusions

This study has many important conclusions to offer. Theoretically, it has sought to transcend the depiction of entrepreneurs as people who always adhere to the state laws and operate in a fully legitimate manner. Instead, this study has put forth a contrasting reality of entrepreneurs, where a vast majority of them is found to keep certain aspects of their business hidden from the state authorities. However, although it recognizes a widespread participation of entrepreneurs in the informal economy, it refutes the dichotomous depiction of them as either formal or informal by recognizing the fact that entrepreneurs actually operate at different levels of (in)formality, ranging from fully informal through largely informal and largely formal to fully formal entrepreneurs. It would, therefore, be erroneous to place them neatly into formal or informal classifications. Furthermore, the results of this study also call for a more nuanced characterization of informal entrepreneurship in terms of the traits associated with the entrepreneurs and their enterprises. This study has concluded that while there are certain similarities in informal micro-enterprises, they seem to differ significantly in terms of the entrepreneur's income and education, and the enterprise's employment and financial structures. The variations in these characteristics, however, can have a strong correlation with the number of registrations acquired by a particular entrepreneur for his business, which is indicative of a firm's level of (in)formality. Any stereotypical portrayal of informal micro-enterprises, therefore, shall be deceptive.

Another counterintuitive conclusion of this study is the fact that participation of entrepreneurs in the informal economy is not always motivated by economic gains, be it for necessity or profit-maximization reasons, as generally perceived by the structuralist and a faction of the neo-liberal schools of thought. Instead, one can see a strong prevalence of more socially driven and certain structural reasons, such as industrial norms, low tax morality, resentment against the state, public sector corruption, poor knowledge of the registration system, and weak enforcement of law, lending support to the post-structuralist perspective of informal entrepreneurship. Interestingly, the non-economic motives remain the predominant cause of informality amongst the micro-entrepreneurs of Lahore regardless of their level of informality as explained by a cross-tabulation above.

Therefore, this study calls for the policy makers in developing countries like Pakistan to look beyond their typical narrative where the solutions to fix the informal economy tend to revolve round a few particular measures (e.g. reducing taxes, offering tax holidays, increasing detection and penalties). Such initiatives, in Pakistan, have perpetually failed over the last three decades to meet the desired objective, i.e. to regularize informal enterprises and widen the tax net. Clearly, a multipronged approach is required that will rather focus on the very root cause of what motivates entrepreneurs to abstain from full formality. For micro-enterprises, as discovered by this research, the root cause of informality mainly lies in certain socially constructed artefacts and structural loopholes of the state's regulatory system. The orientation of policy measures, therefore, must be changed accordingly.

Acknowledgements

This research was funded by USAID under the Competitive Grants Program (CGP), a joint initiative of the Planning Commission of Pakistan and Pakistan Strategy Support Program (PSSP).

Notes

1 PKR103 = 1USD.
2 An Analysis of Educational Indicators of Pakistan – 2011 by NEMIS-AEPAM (AEPAM Publication No 244). Accessed at: http://www.aepam.edu.pk/Files/EducationStatistics/PakistanEducationStatistics 2010-11.pdf
3 Verbal agreement refers to a non-written mutual understanding between the entrepreneur and his employees in terms of working hours, wage rates, bonuses, and leave entitlement, etc.
4 A special form of a rice dish widely consumed in the sub-continent region.
5 Doing Business in Pakistan (2015). Accessed at: http://www.doingbusiness.org/data/exploreeconomies/ pakistan.

References

Adom, K., and Williams, C.C. (2012). Evaluating the explanations for the informal economy in third world cities: some evidence from Koforidua in the eastern region of Ghana. *International Entrepreneurship and Management Journal*, 8(3), 309–324.
Ahmed, A. M. (2009). Underground economy in Pakistan: how credible are estimates? *NUST Journal of Business and Economics*, 2(1), 1–9.
Ahmed, M., and Ahmed, Q. A. (1995). Estimation of black economy of Pakistan through the monetary approach. *The Pakistan Development Review*, 34(4), 791–807.
Aliyev, H. (2015). Post-Soviet informality: towards theory-building. *International Journal of Sociology and Social Policy*, 35(3–4), 182–198.

Arby, M. (2010). The Size of the Informal Economy in Pakistan. Lahore: State Bank of Pakistan. SBP Working Paper No. 33.

Aslam, S. (1998). The underground economy and tax evasion in Pakistan: annual estimates (1960–1998) and the impact of dollarization of the economy. *The Pakistan Development Review*, 37(4), 621–631.

Barsoum, G. (2015). Striving for job security: the lived experience of employment informality among educated youth in Egypt. *International Journal of Sociology and Social Policy*, 35(5/6), 340–358.

Boels, D. (2014). It's better than stealing: informal street selling in Brussels. *International Journal of Sociology and Social Policy*, 34(9/10), 670–693.

Burki, A. A. (1989). Urban Informal Sector in Pakistan: some selected issues. *Pakistan Development Review*, 28(4), 911–924.

Burki, A. A., and Afaqi, U. (1996). Pakistan's informal sector: review of evidence and policy issues. *Pakistan Journal of Applied Economics*, 12(1), 1–30.

Castells, M., and Portes, A. (1989). World underneath: the origins, dynamics and effects of the informal economy. In A. Portes, M. Castells and L. A. Benton (Eds.), *The informal economy: studies in advanced and less developing countries* (1–19). Baltimore, MD: Johns Hopkins University Press.

Cross, J., and Morales, A. (2007). Introduction: locating street markets in the modern/postmodern world. In J. Cross and A. Morales (Eds.), *Street Entrepreneurs: People, Place and Politics in Local and Global Perspective*. London: Routledge.

Davis, M. (2006). *Planet of Slums*. London: Verso.

Derrida, J. (1967). *Of Grammatology*. Baltimore, MD: Johns Hopkins University Press.

De Soto, H. (1989). *The Other Path: The Economic Answer to Terrorism*. London: Harper and Row.

De Soto, H. (2001). *The Mystery of Capital: Why Capitalism Triumphs in the West and Fails Everywhere Else*. London: Black Swan.

Evans, M., Syrett, S., and Williams, C. C. (2006). *Informal Economic Activities and Deprived Neighbourhoods*. London: Department of Communities and Local Government.

Federal Board of Revenue Pakistan. (2008). Informal Economy in Pakistan. DirectorateGeneral of Training and Research, Syndicate Report 36th STP. http://www.dgtrdt.gov.pk/html/Papers.html.

Friedman, E., Johnson, S., Kaufmann, D., and Zoido-Lobaton, P. (2000). Dodging the grabbing hand: the determinants of unofficial activity in 69 countries. *Journal of Public Economics*, 76(3), 459–493.

Gallin, D. (2001). Propositions on trade unions and informal employment in time of globalization. *Antipode*, 19(4), 531–549.

Gennari, P. (2004). The Estimation of Employment and Value Added of Informal Sector in Pakistan. Paper presented at the 7th Meeting of the Expert Group on Informal SectorStatistics, Delhi Group, New Delhi, February 2–4.

Gërxhani, K. (2004). The informal sector in developed and less developed countries: a literature survey. *Public Choice*, 120(2), 267–300.

Gilbert, A. (1998). *The Latin American City*. New York, NY: Monthly Review Press.

Guisinger, S., and Irfan, M. (1980). Pakistan's informal sector. *The Journal of Development Studies*, 16(4), 412–426.

Gulzar, A., Junaid, N., and Haider, A. (2010). What is hidden, in the hidden economy of Pakistan? Size, causes, issues and implications. *Pakistan Development Review*, 49(4).

Hodosi, A. (2015). Perceptions of irregular immigrants' participation in undeclared work in the United Kingdom from a social trust perspective. *International Journal of Sociology and Social Policy*, 35(5/6), 375–389.

Hudson, R. (2005). *Economic Geographies: Circuits, Flows and Spaces*. London: Sage.

Hussain, M. H., and Ahmed, Q. M. (2006). Estimating the Black Economy Through Monetary Approach: A Case Study of Pakistan. Munich: Munich Personal RePEc Archive. MPRA Paper No. 8153.

International Labor Office. (2002a). *Women and Men in the Informal Economy: A Statistical Picture*. Geneva: International Labor Office.

International Labor Office. (2002b). *Decent Work and the Informal Economy*. Geneva: International Labor Office.

Iqbal, A. Q. (1998). *The Underground Economy and Tax Evasion in Pakistan: A Fresh Assessment*. Lahore: Pakistan Institute of Development Economics. PIDE Research Report No. 158.

Jones, T., Ram, M., and Edwards, P. (2006). Shades of grey in the informal economy. *International Journal of Sociology and Social Policy*, 26(9/10), 357–373.

Jütting, J. P., and Laiglesia, J. R. (2009). Employment, poverty reduction and development: What's new? In J. P. Jütting and J. R. Laiglesia (Eds.), *Is Informal Normal? Towards More and Better Jobs in Developing Countries*. Paris: OECD.

Katungi, D., Neale, E., and Barbour, A. (2006). *People in Low-Paid Informal Work: Need Not Greed*. York: Joseph Rowntree Foundation.

Kazi, S. (1987). Skill formulation, employment and earnings in the urban informal sector. *The Pakistan Development Review*, 26(4).

Kemal, M. A. (2003). Underground Economy and Tax Evasion in Pakistan: A Critical Evaluation. Lahore: Pakistan Institute of Development Economics. PIDE Research Report No. 184.

Kemal, M. A. (2007). Fresh Assessment of the Underground Economy and Tax Evasion in Pakistan: Causes, Consequences and Linkages With the Formal Economy. Lahore: Pakistan Institute of Development Economics. PIDE Working Paper No. 13.

Kemal, A. R., and Mahmood, Z. (1998). The Urban Informal Sector of Pakistan: Some Stylized Facts. Lahore: Pakistan Institute of Development Economics. PIDE Research Report No. 161.

Khan, E. A. and Quaddus, M. (2015). Examining the influence of business environment on socio-economic performance of informal microenterprises: content analysis and partial least square approach. *International Journal of Sociology and Social Policy*, 35(3/4), 273–288.

Leonard, M. (1994). *Informal Economic Activity in Belfast*. Aldershot: Avebury.

Nadvi, K. (1990). Multiple Forms of Subcontracting Arrangements: Implications for the Growth of the Informal Manufacturing Sector. QAU/FES, National Workshop on the Informal Sector of Pakistan: Problems and Policies. September 12–14.

OECD. (2002). *Measuring the Non-Observed Economy*. Paris: OECD.

Packard, T. (2007). *Do Workers in Chile Choose Informal Employment? A Dynamic Analysis of Sector Choice*. Washington DC: World Bank Latin American and the Caribbean Region Social Projection Unit.

Pakistan Bureau of Statistics. (2011). *Labor Force Survey of Pakistan*. Lahore: Government of Pakistan.

Perry, G. E., and Maloney, W. F. (2007). Overview: informality – exit and exclusion. In G. H. Perry, W. F. Maloney, O. S. Arias, P. Fajnzylber, A. D. Mason, and J. Saavedra-Chanduvi (Eds.), *Informality: Exit and Exclusion* (1–19). Washington DC: World Bank.

Ram, M., Edwards, P., and Jones, T. (2002a). *Employers and Illegal Migrant Workers in the Clothing and Restaurant Sectors*. London: DTI Central Unit Research.

Ram, M., Jones, T., Abbas, T., and Sanghera, B. (2002b). Ethnic minority enterprise in its urban context: South Asian restaurants in Birmingham. *International Journal of Urban and Regional Research*, 26(1), 24–40.

Ranis, G. (1989). The role of institutions in transition growth: The East Asian newly industrializing countries. *World Development*, 17(9), 1443–1453.

Round, J. and Williams, C. C. (2008). Everyday tactics and spaces of power: The role of informal economies in post-Soviet Ukraine. *Social and Cultural Geography*, 9(2), 171–185.

Sassen, S. (1997). Informalization in Advanced Market Economies. Geneva: ILO. Issues in Development Discussion Paper No. 20.

Sauvy, A. (1984). *Le Travail Noir et l'Economie de Demain*. Paris: Calmann-Levy.

Schneider, F. (Ed.). (2008). *The Hidden Economy*. Cheltenham: Edward Elgar Publishing.

Schneider, F., and Williams, C.C. (2013). *The Shadow Economy*. London: Institute of Economic Affairs.

Shabsigh, F. (1995). The Underground Economy: estimation, and economic and policy implications – the case of Pakistan. Washington DC: International Monetary Fund, IMF Working Paper No. 101.

Slavnic, Z. (2010). Political economy of informalization. *European Societies*, 12(1), 3–23.

Small Business Council. (2004). *Small Business in the Informal Economy: Making the Transition to the Formal Economy*. London: Small Business Council.

Smith, A., and Stenning, A. (2006). Beyond household economies: articulations and spaces of economic practice in post socialism. *Progress in Human Geography*, 30(2), 190–213.

Snyder, K. A. (2004). Routes to the informal economy in New York's East village: crisis, economics and identity. *Sociological Perspectives*, 47(2), 215–240.

Torgler, B. (2003). To evade taxes or not: that is the question. *Journal of Socio-Economics*, 32, 283–302.

Webb, J. W., Tihanyi, L., Ireland, R. D., and Sirmon, D. G. (2009). You say illegal, I say legitimate: Entrepreneurship in the informal economy. *Academy of Management Review*, 34(3), 492–510.

Williams, C. C. (2004). *Cash-in-Hand Work: The Underground Sector and the Hidden Economy of Favors.* Basingstoke: Palgrave Macmillan.

Williams, C. C. (2006). *The Hidden Enterprise Culture: Entrepreneurship in the Underground Economy.* Cheltenham: Edward Elgar Publishing.

Williams, C. C. (2007). Entrepreneurs operating in the informal economy: necessity or opportunity driven? *Journal of Small Business and Entrepreneurship*, 20(3), 309–320.

Williams, C. C. (2013). Tackling Europe's informal economy: a critical evaluation of the neo-liberal de-regulatory perspective. *Journal of Contemporary European Research*, 9(3), 261–279.

Williams, C. C. (2014a). Out of the shadows: a classification of economies by the size and the character of their informal sector. *Work, Employment and Society*, 28(5), 735–753.

Williams, C. C. (2014b). Explaining cross-national variations in the commonality of informal sector entrepreneurship: an exploratory analysis of 38 emerging economies. *Journal of Small Business and Entrepreneurship*, 27(2), 191–212.

Williams, C. C., and Gurtoo, A. (2011). Evaluating women entrepreneurs in the informal sector: Some evidence from India. *Journal of Developmental Entrepreneurship*, 16(3), 351–369.

Williams, C. C., and Gurtoo, A. (2012). Evaluating competing theories of street entrepreneurship: some lessons from a study of street vendors in Bangalore, India. *International Entrepreneurship and Management Journal*, 8(4), 391–409.

Williams, C. C. and Horodnic, I. (2015). Self-employment, the informal economy and the marginalisation thesis: some evidence from the European Union. *International Journal of Entrepreneurial Behaviour and Research*, 21(2), 224–242

Williams, C. C. and Martinez-Perez, A. (2014). Entrepreneurship in the informal economy: a product of too much or too little state intervention?, *International Journal of Entrepreneurship and Innovation*, 15(4), 227–237.

Williams, C. C., and Nadin, S. (2010). Entrepreneurship and the informal economy: an overview. *Journal of Developmental Entrepreneurship*, 15(4), 361–378.

Williams, C. C., and Nadin, S. (2012). Work beyond employment: representations of informal economic activities. *Work, Employment and Society*, 26(2), 1–10.

Williams, C. C., and Shahid, M. S. (2015). Informal entrepreneurship and institutional theory: explaining the varying degress of (in)formalization of entrepreneurs in Pakistan. *Entrepreneurship and Regional Development*, 1–2.

Williams, C. C., and Windebank, J. (1998). *Informal Employment in the Advanced Economies: Implications for Work and Welfare.* London: Routledge.

Williams, C. C., and Windebank, J. (2011). Regional variations in the nature of the shadow economy: evidence from a survey of 27 European Union member states. In H. Schneider (Ed.), *Handbook of the Shadow Economy* (177–200). Cheltenham: Edward Elgar Publishing.

Woolfson, C. (2007). Pushing the envelope: The 'informalization' of labour in post communist new EU member states. *Work, Employment and Society*, 21(3), 551–564.

Yasmin, B., and Rauf, H. (2004). Measuring the underground economy and its impact on the economy of Pakistan. *The Lahore Journal of Economics*, 9(2), 93–106.

30

CHARACTERISTICS AND STRUCTURES OF INFORMAL ENTREPRENEURSHIP IN BOTSWANA

Léo-Paul Dana and Vanessa Ratten

Introduction

The role of the informal economy in global society has increased in significance in recent years due to its importance in developing as well as transitional countries (Dana, 2010; Williams and Horodnic, 2015). The public revenue losses incurred by the informal economy makes this a key issue for governments around the world (Williams, 2014). The informal economy is a socially legitimate activity that is legal in most aspects apart from tax and labour purposes (Dana, 2010; Williams et al., 2015). Most of the participation in the informal economy has been amongst marginalised populations particularly in the developing world context (Sasunkevich, 2014). This trend has been prevalent in geographical rural areas in developing countries, which are more likely to participate in informal businesses. An informal entrepreneur's culture influences their perception of entrepreneurial opportunity (Dana, 1995) and this is important in the context of informal businesses (Dana, 1993b). In this chapter, we focus on Botswana's informal economy with an emphasis on the characteristics and structures of the business environment.

The informal economy has emerged so business can be conducted outside the observance of current laws in order to offer employment and income for people (Dana, 2010). Informal business activities often operate under the inadequacy of local regulation, which is influenced by the complex social customs of a country. In Africa, the informal economy impacts on the daily lives of people due to the perception of it as an alternative economic development model (Ayande, 2013). More interest is being placed on the informal economy in Africa because of the impact it has on local and international organisations. The importance of the informal economy to developing countries is evident in Ayande (2013: 226) who states 'in Africa, informal work during the past decade is estimated to have accounted for almost 80 percent of non-agricultural employment, over 60 percent of urban employment and over 90 percent of new jobs'.

In the African context of the developing world, the government impact on entrepreneurship directly and indirectly depends on the existing regulatory frameworks (Naude and Havenga, 2005). Some countries in Africa have deregulated their market to promote informal entrepreneurship and encourage the innovative ecosystem that results from this activity

(Dana, 1996). Botswana due to its geographic location is part of the Southern African customs union, which is the world's oldest customs union. The other countries comprising this union are Lesotho, Namibia, South Africa and Swaziland. Botswana has similar averages for the sub-Saharan African region in terms of overall entrepreneurial activities (GEM, 2012). However, compared with other sub-Saharan African countries, Botswana's job growth expectation is higher. This is partly due to Botswana being a market-orientated economy with Africa's highest sovereign credit rating and having one of the most competitive banking sectors in Africa, with financial resources available for entrepreneurs based on market rates. The Botswana government does provide some subsidised loans. In addition, Botswana has abundant natural resources and has one of the world's largest and richest diamond mines. Diamonds account for one-third of the Gross Domestic Product of Botswana and have helped transform it into a middle-income country. Botswana is considered a middle-income country because of its relatively high standard of living.

Botswana is a land-locked country but has been one of the fastest growing economies in the world; it is a developing country that is transitioning from a poor country to a middle-income one and the considerable economic progress of Botswana has been supported by education expenditure being amongst the highest in the world (World Bank, 2015). Despite the development of the Botswana economy there is still high unemployment and income inequality.

Botswana is the most stable democracy in Southern Africa and gained its independence in 1966 from the United Kingdom. The Botswana Democratic Party has governed the country ever since. In order to diversify the Botswana economy, the government has focused on building other industry segments such as those focusing on entrepreneurship and creativity. This is due to Botswana being rated amongst the least corrupt countries and there being economic freedom for entrepreneurs to pursue their own business activities. Despite the market orientation of the Botswana government, the legal system to enforce business dealings is lengthy and time consuming, leading to the presence of informal entrepreneurship.

Botswana is famous for its tourist attractions including the Kalahari Desert and Okavango Delta. The traditional industries of Botswana focus on mineral wealth in the form of diamonds. The revenue Botswana receives from its diamond mines has been invested in education.

In developing countries, informal entrepreneurship is popular as it avoids taxation (Dana, 2013). The governments in some African countries including Namibia have followed a strategic interventionist policy to promote entrepreneurship (Dana, 1993a). In contrast to other African countries that have encouraged socialist principles, Botswana has pursued more of an entrepreneurial spirit. In Botswana, informal entrepreneurship is necessary because of the need for internal subsistence activity.

Whilst mining and especially minerals in the form of diamonds account for a large percentage of Botswana's government's revenues, more than half the population still has middle class status. Botswana needs entrepreneurs in order to transition from an economy focused on mining to a vibrant country focused on innovation. This is important largely due to the mining industry running out in approximately 2030. In order to change the economy, the government needs to improve the private sector by encouraging entrepreneurial communities.

What are the characteristics and structures of informal entrepreneurship in Botswana? We are especially interested in the role of Botswana as a sub-Saharan developing country that has achieved a high level of economic and social growth over the past decade. The primary aim of this chapter is to examine informal entrepreneurship within a developing country context that is growing in the international trading environment. The way informal business operates in Botswana will be discussed and the importance of entrepreneurship in developing countries highlighted.

Our overall objective is to evaluate informal entrepreneurship in Botswana. To do this, the first section will provide an overview of the informal economy with a focus on the developing country context. This leads to a discussion of marginalisation, reinforcement and institutional theory, which are important in explaining informal economies. An examination of these theories is then discussed in the Botswana context, which reveals the need for a better understanding of informal entrepreneurship in developing countries, particularly those in Africa that are likely to engage in the informal economy. The last sections conclude by discussing the implications of informal entrepreneurship in Botswana for the theory and policy for developing countries.

Literature review

The informal economy is delineated in the developing country context by focusing on enterprise- and jobs-based definitions (Williams and Lansky, 2013). Rezaei et al. (2013) suggest that the informal economy is contextual, situational, gradual and conditional. The contextual environment includes the national culture and ways of doing business in a country. In Botswana, due to the high number of middle-class people, informal entrepreneurs can offer services at a higher rate depending on the availability of resources. The situations that lead them into the informal sector can include the lack of employment opportunity which makes informal employment the only option or alternatively, informal entrepreneurs in Botswana may be encouraged to enter the sector due to excessive government restrictions and requirements on establishing a formal business. The gradual refers to the increase in informal entrepreneurs due to economic conditions and living situations. In Botswana, the migration from rural to urban settings has meant that the only way to survive for some informal entrepreneurs is to focus on small-scale enterprises. The conditional means the way informal entrepreneurs manage their businesses based on everyday transactions and market need.

Informal entrepreneurs particularly in developing countries have low education rates and rely on social networks mostly in the form of family to survive. The level of financial capital invested in informal enterprises is low and usually little technological expertise is required to run businesses. Informal enterprises are not regulated by the government and operate outside legal channels. Entrepreneurs in developing countries often enter the informal sector due to economic hardships. Ayande (2013: 225) states, 'the informal economy is characterised by a multiplicity of micro, small and medium family businesses, individual and/or collective, which base their rationale on the solutions they provide in meeting the needs of local and proximate customers'.

The informal sector has also been referred to as the underground and subterranean economy. These negative connotations about the informal economy are often based on the illegal activities conducted in the sector but are often not the reason entrepreneurs exist in this informal environment. The dynamics of entrepreneurship are important to support business development by stimulating innovative activity (Naude and Havenga, 2005). The level of economic activity in a country can be influenced by entrepreneurial activity in the form of self-employment (Wennekers and Thurik, 1999). In some developing countries that have a low level of economic activity people revert to self-employment opportunities.

Entrepreneurship should take into account the society in which it is embedded as it impacts on individual, business and government decisions (Ligthelm, 2010). This means that the context in which entrepreneurship operates is inseparable due to the structural changes existing in a society. Entrepreneurship can change society by promoting economic growth and development. The realisation that entrepreneurship is needed to encourage private sector development is at the heart of many developing countries' high economic growth rates (Ligthelm, 2010).

There are a number of different roles that entrepreneurs have including being a leader, implementing innovation and assuming risk (Ligthelm, 2010). These roles involve different types of entrepreneurship ranging from corporate, social, public and non-profit to intra-preneurship. Despite the popularity of entrepreneurship not all types are beneficial for economic development. Productive entrepreneurship involves exploiting profitable business opportunities whereas unproductive or informal entrepreneurship involves business activities resulting from poverty (Ligthelm, 2010). The next section will discuss the main informal economy theoretical perspectives that apply in the developing world context.

Theoretical perspectives

There is no common definition of the informal economy but most refer to it in terms of its structure and characteristics, which are useful in explaining the different theoretical perspectives. The informal economy is defined by Williams and Horodnic (2015: 154) as 'paid activities not declared to the authorities for tax, social security and/or labour law purposes'. This definition is adopted in this chapter as it considers the informal economy to be a kind of legal activity which does not acknowledge the business for monetary reasons. This means that only activities that are completely undeclared for tax reasons, social security including illegal work status and labour law reasons are part of the informal economy definition. Within this definition of the informal economy, the three main theoretical perspectives being marginalisation, reinforcement and institutional will now be discussed in terms of how they apply to Botswana's informal entrepreneurs.

Marginalisation theory

Marginalisation theory focuses on how disadvantaged populations are more likely to work in the informal economy (Williams and Horodnic, 2015). This means that individuals marginalised by society, which include geographic, ethnicity or financial reasons are more likely to participate in the informal economy. There are a variety of reasons people are marginalised by society and they include employment status, gender, disability, literacy rate and educational background (Barbour and Llanes, 2013). This leads to marginalised groups of individuals being more likely to participate in the informal economy as a way of gaining financial independence.

Most informal entrepreneurs usually do not have formal employment so they look to informal enterprises as a way of gaining resources (Taiwo, 2013). In addition, individuals with financial difficulties and coming from poorer social economic backgrounds are more likely to be informal entrepreneurs (Smith and Stenning, 2006). Previous research by Williams (2014) also found that more women are likely to participate in the informal economy. This is due to the role socio-economic background and gender play in being able to obtain finance and access to business resources in the developing world context.

People who are marginalised by their beliefs and values are more likely to participate in the informal sector (Williams and Martinez, 2014). This is due to their inability to conform to formal institutions and associated business practices (Williams and Horodnic, 2015). The different norms and standards of behaviour followed by the marginalised individuals creates difficulties in incorporating them into the everyday business life. This means that they do not know the ways of behaving because of their social position in society.

Reinforcement theory

Reinforcement theory has emerged as a framework to understand informal entrepreneurship (Williams and Horodnic, 2015). This theory unlike the marginalisation perspective argues that informal entrepreneurship is less likely amongst marginalised populations. This means that high-income earners are more likely to participate in the informal economy based on their geographic and educational position (Williams and Lansky, 2013). Past research by Moldovan and Van de Walle (2013) suggests that unemployed people are less likely to be informal entrepreneurs than those with employment. The reinforcement theory supports common stereotypes about men being more entrepreneurial and participating in the informal economy (Williams, 2011). It also reinforces the view that more affluent individuals are both able to gain the resources and time needed to participate in the informal economy (Williams, 2006).

The reinforcement theory suggests that the marginalised socio-economic individuals including the unemployed or uneducated are less likely to be involved in the informal economy than educated individuals coming from more middle-class backgrounds (Williams and Horodnic, 2015). This is due to the reinforcing of entrepreneurial opportunities by individuals who are not in underprivileged areas but using financial motives to be driven to the informal economy as a way to stay in their local regions or encourage them to relocate to higher economic growth areas. There is also a gender issue in informal businesses with women less likely to participate in the informal economy and this reinforces the stereotypes of entrepreneurs in society (Williams and Horodnic, 2015).

Institutional theory

Institutions are part of society as they regulate and codify standards of behaviour (Williams et al., 2015). These institutions help define the legal rules of conduct in a society (North, 1990). Informal institutions are defined as 'socially shared unwritten rules that express the wider values and beliefs of the population' (Williams et al., 2015: 295). Usually the greater the differences between formal and informal institutions, the more likely people are to participate in the informal economy (Gërxhani, 2004).

Informal work is unregulated by societal institutions but acts as a form of income-generated production (Castells and Portes, 1989). The legal and social environment in which informal work is conducted is unregulated by formal institutions and instead regulated by informal institutions (Schneider and Williams, 2013). Sometimes the informal economy is regarded as legitimate by informal institutions but is illegal from the perspective of formal institutions (Webb et al., 2009).

In institutional theory, institutions are cognitive, normative and regulative structures that govern social behaviour (Williams et al., 2015). Institutions offer stability and meaning to a society (Scott, 1995). This means that informal institutions are the unwritten socially shared rules in a society and this reflects people's values (Helmke and Levitsky, 2004). These informal institutions are especially important in the developing world as institutions can be unregulated and set up in different ways to the more traditional and bureaucratic institutions existing in developed countries.

Informal entrepreneurship

The informal economy is characterised by small sized and typically self-employed workers. Most informal businesses have a low level of organisation and structure as their primary goal is to obtain money with low overhead costs. The goal for informal businesses is to generate an income but is typically without formal rules and regulations. The inability of traditional economic market systems to absorb new entrepreneurs has given rise to the informal economy. Some governments see the informal sector as a survival mechanism for those without access to social security. Typically the types of services offered in the informal sector are those requiring less education and are mostly low cost. Despite the common perception that the informal sector focuses on the poor and low income it can also be operated by the middle class depending on the entrepreneurial spirit of the individuals involved. Many governments have ignored the informal sector due to the unsophisticated nature of many businesses involved. Informal businesses usually have low operating costs and so are easy to start in any geographic location. Most are unregulated but are labour intensive types of businesses.

Informal entrepreneurship is often high in developing countries because individuals want to escape from unemployment and improve their living conditions. Informal entrepreneurs can be delineated as either opportunity or necessity driven into such enterprise based on their motivations for establishing a business. Opportunity entrepreneurs are those pursuing a business venture because of a perceived gap in the market. In developing countries, the opportunities might exist due to difficulty in obtaining market access and trade embargoes on certain products. Necessity entrepreneurs are involved in businesses because of money and work requirements (Dana, 1997). These necessity entrepreneurs in developing countries utilise business opportunities as a way to obtain monetary freedom.

Informal entrepreneurship can take a variety of forms including stall or itinerant vending (Dana, 2013). These stall vendors can be popular in developing countries where income levels mean that individuals can only afford small quantities of luxury or non-essential products. In addition, often informal economic activity is used for unrecorded cash sales that bypass regulating channels. Informal businesses circumventing taxes are a motive for the establishment of impromptu stalls in developing regions. This can be because the formal sector becomes unattractive when there is a demand for government bribes.

Informal businesses that are small in size usually dominate in developing countries (Ligthelm, 2010). A priority for the Botswana government is to regulate informal business by enforcing standards of behaviour. This can provide benefits to society that exceed compliance costs of regulating business (Dana, 2013). The informal economy in Botswana includes small-scale enterprises from street merchants, walkers to agricultural vendors. The informal sector has been criticised in developing countries like Botswana for being uncivilised compared to formal businesses with registered premises. The unsupportive regulatory framework for informal businesses has made it hard for these entrepreneurs to enter formal business arrangements that include long-term contracts.

We suggest that more economic policy should be devoted to the informal sector in Botswana in order to capitalise on the entrepreneurial spirit of the people operating these enterprises. The informal sector is a useful part of Botswana's economic growth but this sector remains marginalised due to difficulties faced by informal entrepreneurs in gaining access to financial resources needed to spur growth. The centralised regulatory structure of the Botswana government discourages informal entrepreneurs.

In Botswana, the informal economy is a means of survival for many individuals as it generates employment for those who would otherwise be unemployed (Ntseane, 2004). The

417

informal economy includes activities in agriculture, manufacturing, transport, construction and retail (Ntseane, 2004). In Botswana, a number of people migrate from rural to urban areas and become part of the informal sector. Many of the people employed in the Botswana informal economy are street vendors who operate small businesses (Ntseane, 2004).

Botswana, in order to transform from a society focused on its mineral wealth to a developed country, needs to build its entrepreneurs by investing in education. This is happening at the University of Botswana in the capital of Gaborone in which entrepreneurship education programmes are promoted. Botswana has urbanised quickly with 50 per cent of the country living in urban areas (Havorka, 2004). In addition, the economic development of Botswana has led to more villages and rural areas being classified as urban (Nkate, 2004). This has led to more people in Botswana moving to urban areas for employment opportunities. The perceived better economic lifestyle of Botswana cities has led to Gaborone becoming the centre of informal entrepreneurship.

Gaborone is one of the fastest growing cities in sub-Saharan Africa (Havorka, 2004). In the greater Gaborone area, there are changing settlement patterns that have given rise to more informal entrepreneurs. The Botswana cultural identity is still associated with rural–urban linkages due to the long tradition of agricultural farming (Havorka, 2004). This agrarian-based tradition has meant that some entrepreneurs in Botswana culturally move between urban and rural areas. In Botswana people still have close relationships to their villages despite living in metropolitan areas (Kruger, 1998). These close relationships help encourage networks between informal entrepreneurs to help increase their business activity.

In the past decade, there has been an increase in the literature about informal economics particularly in terms of helping people (Williams et al., 2015). Jütting and Laiglesia (2009) have suggested that 60 per cent of the global workforce is employed in the informal economy. The importance of the informal economy to the Botswana economy is a key policy issue. The informal economy is characterised by poorer working conditions as unfair competition exists (Williams et al., 2013). The important difference between the informal and unpaid economy is that economic activities are legal. The informal economy thereby has mostly socially legitimate activities.

There are many reasons why people participate in the informal economy. Some participate due to exclusion from the labour market and state benefits (Williams et al., 2015). Others see the informal economy as a way for employees to reduce labour costs by subcontracting the use of informal workers who by necessity need to work (Roberts, 2013). Sometimes informal workers are seen by people as representing marginalised populations who conduct economic activities as the only way to be included in monetary gain (Slavnic, 2010).

Snyder (2004) proposes that the informal economy results from individuals who voluntarily decide to exit the formal economy. In other words, some workers in the informal economy are attracted to the sector because they can avoid formally registering their business (De Soto, 2001). This saving in time and cost from the formal registration process may play a part in the increase in popularity of the informal economy. Other research by Williams (2004) suggests that financial gain is not the main motive of informal entrepreneurs as often work is conducted for friends and family.

Williams et al. (2015a) proposed that informal entrepreneurs have either an exit-driven or exclusion-driven reason for entering the sector. This means that exit-driven applies to informal workers who start their own business and come from more affluent groups of society (Gurtoo and Williams, 2009). Exit-driven rationales apply more in developed economies and are more common in males (Williams et al., 2013). On the other hand, exclusion reasons apply more to people in waged informal employment that come from deprived populations (Gurtoo and Williams, 2009). Exclusion is usually more prevalent in developing countries and more common amongst women informal workers (Grant, 2013). Some informal workers have both exit and exclusion reasons for entering the sector (Williams et al., 2011). This is due to there being a number of disadvantages to the informal economy as suggested by Williams et al. (2015a) and these include lower work standards in terms of health and safety, undermining legitimate businesses and decreased social protection systems.

Policy approaches

The prominence of the informal economy has been well observed in Africa (Dana, 2007). Williams et al. (2015b) suggest that there are two major contrasting policy approaches to the informal economy, which involved the use of either direct or indirect controls. This means that in a developing country context like Botswana, direct controls act as deterrents and incentives to informal entrepreneurship whilst indirect controls act to reduce the information asymmetry between the formal and informal institutions. The direct control of deterring informal work means that there are penalties to Botswana entrepreneurs for engaging in this activity. The Botswana government could deter informal entrepreneurship by making it easier for entrepreneurs to conduct business in a recognised manner. Williams et al. (2015b) refer to the goal of governments to make the cost/benefit ratio between formal and informal work biased in favour of formal work. In Botswana, the government could do this by encouraging more people to participate in compliant and legal economic activity that contributes to societal well-being. Botswana informal entrepreneurs might be persuaded to make their activities formal if the costs and risks of informal work outweigh the benefits. The Botswana government can do this by increasing the rate of detection and sanctions for people in the informal economy by offering them a pathway to formal types of entrepreneurial behaviour.

The indirect control approach looks at how to reduce the information asymmetry between formal and informal institutions that can be significant in developing countries like Botswana. In Botswana, as more people become educated, the informal institutions can raise awareness about the benefits of both informal and formal work by placing importance on the value of legitimate economic activities and the resulting societal benefits. The changing of formal institutional practices such as the provision of redistributive justice is an additional way of creating this symmetry. Table 30.1 depicts the different policy approaches for the Botswana government in transforming the informal economy.

Entrepreneurship policy in Botswana can change the status and meaning of informal economic activities to draw more people into the formal rules and regulations of society. The entrepreneurship endemic in many informal businesses in developing countries like Botswana can be mitigated by advertising and marketing campaigns to improve people's awareness of this economic activity. Policy can also align more informal and formal entrepreneurs' code of conduct in Botswana to improve society's perceptions of the benefits of the informal sector rather than the perceived disadvantages. By engendering a greater sense of social purpose it can help informal entrepreneurs comply with expected standards of behaviour (Williams, 2014). This can involve the Botswana government pursuing social policies that encourage compliance for informal entrepreneurs that treat them in a respectful manner. The emphasis on responsibility of informal Botswanian entrepreneurs is part of the fairness that people believe they deserve as being part of the overall society. The main policy-orientated intention for Botswana should be on the role indirect controls play in encouraging informal entrepreneurs to grow and develop. The persistence of the informal economy in

Table 30.1 Policy Approaches for the Botswana Government to Transform the Informal Economy

Approach	Method	Examples
Direct controls: deterrents	Detection, observing, reporting Penalties, fines Risk, occupational hazards	Monitoring bazaars and street markets checking trade certificates Fines, paying government fees Health and safety warnings, educational programs about workplace injuries
Incentives	Preventative Curative	Entrepreneurship education, co-creation tax benefits Start-up competitions, business plan ideas Voluntary business registration, public/private partnerships
Indirect controls	Values, norms and beliefs Laws and regulations	Awareness of benefits of formal work, challenging mindsets, effective monitoring of relationships, strategic partnerships Social development, modelling skills, mentoring programs, leadership seminars

Source: Adapted from Williams et al. (2015b).

Botswana means that as the country shifts from developing to developed world status the creativity and entrepreneurial spirit of informal entrepreneurs can be strengthened and added to create more overall economic benefits.

Botswana, which has delivered substantial economic growth compared to other developing economies in Africa, which have continued to struggle, merits more attention. The combination of different characteristics presents a challenge for the government developing more entrepreneurial activities in Botswana. However, as more economic reform in Botswana takes place, there has been a positive change in the entrepreneurial ecosystem and shift in society's attitude towards entrepreneurs. The Botswana government has increasingly recognised the role of informal entrepreneurship to the economy and the entrepreneurial economy that results from informal entrepreneurs. Both formal and informal institutional arrangements are important to contributing to entrepreneurial growth rates (Zhou, 2011). In the Botswana context, a strengthening of formal and informal institutional arrangements is needed and more regional deregulation in Africa is required. The next section will further discuss the role of informal entrepreneurship by focusing on future research and policy implications for Botswana and other developing countries.

Policy implications and future research suggestions

Policy makers need to be aware of the cultural attributes of the Botswana people that contribute to informal entrepreneurship. These different cultural characteristics mean that policy priorities should be put into place that reduce poverty by liberalising trade in developing countries like Botswana. This will mean policy makers questioning implicit assumptions of the current economic climate for entrepreneurs (Dana, 2013). Our chapter suggests that policy makers pay more attention to building a pro-entrepreneurial socio-cultural environment. The socio-cultural setting of a country particularly in the developing world context is important in explaining the transition process of Botswana as well as other developing countries. An enhanced awareness regarding developing country environments that facilitate entrepreneurship can help entrepreneurs manage their businesses better and encourage export behaviour. To build a functioning entrepreneurial environment in the developing world it is important to bridge the gap between stakeholders and public policy planners. This is important in Botswana as it transitions from a country focused on its mineral wealth from diamonds to an economy incorporating more dynamic entrepreneurial activity.

Due to the popularity of informal entrepreneurship there are a number of research avenues that should focus on developing countries and especially those in Africa. Future research should look into why Botswana women are underrepresented in the informal economy given the increased participation rates of females in the global economy. This is important as non-governmental organisations such as the World Bank are organising efforts to encourage more females to participate in business, particularly in developing countries. Another worthy topic of future research is the solidarity group approach to informal entrepreneurship in which communities come together to foster business projects (Minniti, 2008). In Botswana, community-based entrepreneurship is encouraging these projects but there needs to be more cooperation between individuals and the government to foster this business activity. This chapter has focused on Botswana as a developing country that has an abundance of informal entrepreneurship. As Botswana has one of the highest standards of living in Africa and continues to develop it will be interesting to see how informal entrepreneurship changes society.

Conclusions

In this chapter, we have sought to bring about new insights regarding informal entrepreneurs in Botswana. In doing so, we have focused on Botswana as a developing country that has a thriving informal sector influenced by regulatory and structural policies. The chapter has highlighted how despite Botswana transitioning from a developing country focused on mining to a more diversified economy, there needs to be more protection and respect for informal entrepreneurs. The consequences of this may be to encourage future policy makers to highlight the benefits of informal entrepreneurship as a way to integrate society, rather than as something to be eradicated. Due to the difficulty in complying with formal business practices, it may also be helpful for the Botswana government to encourage a more entrepreneurial ecosystem as a way to further fuel economic and social growth.

References

Ayande, A. (2013). Informal economy and woman entrepreneurs: A case study of Senegal in Africa. In M. Thai and E. Turkina (eds) *Entrepreneurship in the Informal Economy: Models, Approaches and Prospects for Economic Development*. New York: Routledge, 225–240.

Barbour, A. and Llanes, M. (2013). *Supporting People to Legitimise their Informal Businesses*. York: Joseph Rowntree Foundation.

Castells, M. and Portes, A. (1989). World underneath: the origins, dynamics and effects of the informal economy. In A. Portes, M. Castells and L.A. Benton (eds) *The Informal Economy: Studies in Advanced and Less Developing Countries*. Baltimore: Johns Hopkins University Press, 19–41.

Dana, L. P. (1993a). An analysis of strategic intervention policy in Namibia. *Journal of Small Business Management*, 31(3), 90–95.

Dana, L. P. (1993b). The trade facilitation model: Toward the development of an indigenous small business sector in the Republic of Kenya. *Entrepreneurship, Innovation and Change*, 2(4), 335–343.

Dana, L. P. (1995). Entrepreneurship in a remote sub-Arctic community: Nome, Alaska. *Entrepreneurship: Theory and Practice*, 20(1), 57–72.

Dana, L. P. (1996). Small business in Mozambique after the war. *Journal of Small Business Management*, 34(4), 67–71.

Dana, L. P. (1997). Voluntarily socialist culture and small business in the Kingdom of Lesotho. *Journal of Small Business Management*, 35(4), 83–87.

Dana, L. P. (2007). Promoting SMEs in Africa. *Journal of African Business*, 8(2), 151–174.

Dana, L. P. (2010). *When Economies Change Hands: A Survey of Entrepreneurship in the Emerging Markets of Europe from the Balkans to the Baltic States*. Oxford: Routledge.

Dana, L. P. (2013). Informal economy entrepreneurship and policy implications. In M. Thai and E. Turkina (eds) *Entrepreneurship in the Informal Economy: Models, Approaches and Prospects for Economic Development*. New York: Routledge, 259–269.

De Soto, H. (2001). *The Mystery of Capital: Why Capitalism Triumphs in the West and Fails Everywhere Else*. London: Black Swan.

Global Entrepreneurship Monitor (2012). *Women's Report*. Global Entrepreneurship Research Association (GERA), Babson.

Gërxhani, K. (2004). The informal sector in developed and less developed countries: A literature survey. *Public Choice*, 120, 267–300.

Grant, R. (2013). Gendered spaces of informal entrepreneurship in Soweto, South Africa. *Urban Geography*, 34(1), 86–108.

Gurtoo, A. and Williams, C. C. (2009). Entrepreneurship and the informal sector: Some lessons from India. *International Journal of Entrepreneurship and Innovation*, 10(1), 55–62.

Havorka, A. J. (2004). Entrepreneurial opportunities in Botswana: (re) shaping urban agriculture discourse. *Journal of Contemporary African Studies*, 22(3), 367–388.

Helmke, G. and Levitsky, S. (2004). Informal institutions and comparative politics: A research agenda. *Perspectives on Politics*, 2(4), 725–740.

Jütting, J. and Laiglesia, J. (2009). Employment, poverty reduction and development: What's new? In J. Jütting and J. Laiglesia (eds) *Is Informal Normal? Towards More and Better Jobs in Developing Countries*. Paris: OECD, 129–152.

Kruger, F. (1998). Taking advantage of rural assets as a coping strategy for the urban poor: The case of rural-urban interrelations in Botswana. *Environment and Urbanization*, 10(1), 119–134.

Ligthelm, H. A. (2010). Entrepreneurship and small business sustainability, *Southern African Business Review*, 14(3), 131–153.

Minniti, M. (2008). The role of government policy on entrepreneurial activity: Productive, unproductive or destructive? *Entrepreneurship: Theory and Practice*, 32(5), 779–790.

Moldovan, A. and Van de Walle, S. (2013). Gifts or bribes: attitudes on informal payments in Romanian healthcare. *Public Integrity*, 15(4), 383–395.

Naude, W. A. and Havenga, J. J. D. (2005). An overview of African entrepreneurship and small business research. *Journal of Small Business and Entrepreneurship*, 18(1), 1–15.

Nkate, J. (2004). Urbanization in Botswana, Paper presented to the GCA 2000 Policy Forum, Gaborone.

North, D. C. (1990). *Institutions, Institutional Change and Economic Performance*. Cambridge: Cambridge University Press.

Ntseane, P. (2004). Being a female entrepreneur in Botswana: Cultures, values, strategies for success. *Gender and Development*, 12(2), 37–43.

Rezaei, S., Goli, M. and Dana, L-P. (2013). Informal opportunity among SMEs: An empirical study of Denmark's underground economy. *International Journal of Entrepreneurship and Small Business*, 19(1), 64–76.

Roberts, A. (2013). Peripheral accumulation in the world economy: a cross-national analysis of the informal economy. *International Journal of Comparative Sociology*, 54 (5–6), 420–444.

Sasunkevich, O. (2014). Business as casual: shuttle trade on the Belarus-Lithuania border. In J. Morris and A. Polese (eds) *The Informal Post-socialist Economy: Embedded Practices and Livelihoods*. London: Routledge, 135–151.

Schneider, F. and Williams, C. C. (2013). *The Shadow Economy*. London: Institute of Economic Affairs.

Scott, W. R. (1995) *Institutions and Organizations*. Thousand Oaks, CA: Sage.

Slavnic, Z. (2010). Political economy of informalization. *European Societies*, 12(1), 3–23.

Smith, A. and Stenning, A. (2006). Beyond household economies: articulations and spaces of economic practice in postsocialism. *Progress in Human Geography*, 30(1), 1–14.

Snyder, K. A. (2004). Routes to the informal economy in New York's East village: Crisis, economics and identity. *Sociological Perspectives*, 47(2), 215–240.

Taiwo, O. (2013). Employment choice and mobility in multi-sector labour markets: theoretical model and evidence from Ghana. *International Labour Review*, 152 (3–4), 469–492.

Webb, J. W., Tihanyi, L., Ireland, R. D. and Sirmon, D. G. (2009). You say illegal, I say legitimate: Entrepreneurship in the informal economy. *Academy of Management Review*, 34(3), 492–510.

Wennekers, S. and Thurik, R. (1999). Linking entrepreneurship and economic growth. *Small Business Economics*, 13(1), 27–56.

Williams, C. C. (2006). Beyond marketization: rethinking economic development trajectories in Eastern and Central Europe. *Journal of Contemporary European Studies*, 14(2), 241–254.

Williams, C. C. (2011). Reconceptualising men's and women's undeclared work: evidence from Europe. *Gender, Work and Organisation*, 18(4), 415–437.

Williams, C. C. (2014). *Confronting the Shadow Economy: Evaluating Tax Compliance Behaviour and Policies*. Cheltenham: Edward Elgar.

Williams, C. C., Dzhekova, R., Franic, J. and Mishkov, L. (2015a). Evaluating the policy approach towards the undeclared economy in FYR Macedonia. *International Journal of Entrepreneurship and Small Business*, 24(2), 268–286.

Williams, C. C. and Horodnic, I. (2015). Marginalisation and participation in the informal economy in Central and Eastern European nations. *Post-Communist Economies*, 27(2), 153–169.

Williams, C. C., Horodnic, I. A. and Windebank, J. (2015b). Explaining participation in the informal economy: An institutional incongruence perspective. *International Sociology*, 30(3), 294–313.

Williams, C. C. and Lansky, M. (2013). Informal employment in developed and developing economies: Perspectives and policy responses. *International Labour Review*, 152(3–4), 355–380.

Williams, C. C. and Martinez-Perez, A. (2014). Is the informal economy an incubator for new enterprise creation? A gender perspective. *International Journal of Entrepreneurial Behaviour and Research*, 20(1), 4–19.

Williams, C. C., Rodgers, P. and Round, J. (2011). Explaining the normality of informal employment in Ukraine: A product of exit or exclusion? *The American Journal of Economics and Sociology*, 70(3), 729–755.

World Bank (2015). Botswana – Northern Botswana Human Wildlife Coexistence - Implementation Status Results Report: Project P095617. Washington, DC: World Bank.

www.gemconsortium.org/entrepreneurship/botswana, last visited 1st May 2015.

www.heritage.org/index/country/botswana, last visited 1st May 2015.

www.worldbank.org/en/country/botswana, last visited 1st May 2015.

Zhou, W. (2011). Regional deregulation and entrepreneurial growth in Chinas transition economy. *Entrepreneurship and Regional Development*, 23(9–10), 853–976.

31

THE INFLUENCE OF CREDIT AND FORMALIZATION ON THE GROWTH OF SMES IN TANZANIA

Joseph A. Kuzilwa and Ganka D. Nyamsogoro

Introduction

The role of small and medium enterprises (SMEs) in economic growth and eventually poverty reduction has been an issue of concern to many scholars. Financing is considered crucial in supporting any economic activity while formalization of SMEs is thought to break some barriers to accessing credit. This study investigates the influence of formalization and credit on the growth of SMEs. The chapter is based on findings from a survey of 1362 SMEs from two regions in Tanzania. The survey data collected before and after formalization was obtained from the Property and Business Formalization Program (PBFP). In addition, and to supplement the PBFP data set, four years' data were collected from 234 individual SMEs who are customers of a micro-financial institution known as FINCA in Dar es Salaam. The chapter is organized into eight parts. After this general introduction, the second section spells out the roles of SMEs. Section three reviews a resource-based theory and how it applies to SME growth. The link between credit and SME growth is provided in section four. Section five links formalization and SMEs growth. A general overview of SMEs in Tanzania including challenges and government initiatives to promote a vibrant SME sector are discussed in section six. Section seven presents the methodology and is followed by a presentation of empirical findings in section eight. The last section is the conclusion.

The role of SMEs

There is no generally accepted definition of what constitute micro, small, and medium enterprises. Different countries depending on their level of development use different measures to categorize what is micro, small, and medium enterprise. In all aspects however, the number of employees, total investment and annual sales turnover are commonly used. In Tanzania for example, SMEs are defined in accordance with the National SMEs Policy (2002) based on the number of employees and/or total investment. That is, those engaging up to four people are defined as micro enterprises; between 5 and 49 employees or with capital investment from Tshs. 5 million to Tshs. 200 million are defined as small. Medium enterprises are those employing above 50 people but below 100 or with capital investment between Tshs. 200 million and 800 million.

The role of small and medium enterprises (SMEs) in economic growth and eventually poverty reduction cannot be underestimated. SMEs are reported to be an important source of employment, innovation, income generation, and contribution to a country's GDP. According to Kok et al. (2013), small and medium-sized enterprises (SMEs) provide more jobs than larger enterprises. They are estimated to provide over 60 percent of all formal jobs in developing countries and up to 80 percent in low-income countries (ILO, 2011). In the EU, SMEs contribute about 67 percent of total employment and have been reported to have a positive effect on economic growth (Kok et al., 2011). In Ghana, about 92 percent of companies registered are small and medium firms. These SMEs provide 85 percent of manufacturing employment and their contribution to GDP is 70 percent (Asare, 2014). Similar findings have been reported in Tanzania where SMEs play a crucial role in employment creation and income generation (SME Policy, 2003). SMEs contributed about 27 percent of the country's GDP in 2010 and about 62.7 percent of household income (NBSR, 2012).

Despite their contribution to employment, income generation, and GDP, the majority of SMEs all over the world have limited access to formal financial institutions (Babajide, 2012; Shinozaki, 2012). Consequently, most people use informal finance and microfinance as their major source of financing (Muneer and Kulshreshth, 2014; Nyamsogoro, 2011). Lack of finance may affect negatively the investment activities of SMEs, discourage innovations and enterprise growth. In this study, we examine the influence that formalization and credit has on the growth of SMEs.

Resource-based theory and SME growth

This study is informed by the resource-based theory. Although its prominence started with the work of Wernerfelt (1984), the origin of the resource-based view can be traced back to earlier work by Coase (1937), Penrose (1959), Stigler (1961), Chandler (1962, 1977), and Williamson (1975). The theory suggests that a firm can achieve growth if it acquires and effectively manages all its resources using its competitive advantages. The theory views resources in a wider perspective to include non-financial resources that are necessary in production (Wernerfelt, 1984; Barney, 1986, 1991; Peteraf, 1993). It considers resources from their acquisition to how they are collectively being deployed to generate rent or return (Barney, 1986; Conner, 1991). It views a firm as input combiner and as efficiency seeker in production and distribution. Its success depends on the environment in which it operates and how it interacts with that environment (Conner, 1991).

The growth of an SME is commonly measured using some economic indicators such as the change in profitability, asset value, capital and sales revenue (Almus and Nerlinger, 1999; Brown et al., 2004; Masakure et al., 2008; Babajide, 2012). In addition, the creation of extra employment as measured by changes in number of employees is also considered. According to Kuzilwa (2005), self-employment is considered superior to alternative positions elsewhere and a desire to attain work independency are among the factors that promote entrepreneurship. Thus, creation of employment could be considered as a success indicator for an enterprise.

According to Busenitz and Alvarez (2001), entrepreneurs have individual-specific resources that facilitate the recognition of new opportunities and the acquisition and coordination of resources to implement an entrepreneurial idea. Maintaining distinctiveness of their products, or for identical products, their low cost position is the main problem facing firms (Barney, 1986). Entrepreneurial opportunities exist as a result of having different beliefs and perceptions about the relative value of resources when they are converted from input to output (Schumpeter, 1934; Kirzner, 1979; Shane and Venkataraman, 2000; Busenitz and Alvarez, 2001). Firm-specific resources may affect cognitive differences between managers in these firms (Busenitz and Alvarez, 2001). Thus, all things being equal, the growth of firms comes as a result of acquiring, combining, and deploying resources rather than from the structure of the industry in which the firm finds itself (Conner, 1991). The growth may also be influenced by the entrepreneurial vision and intuition. From a resource-based theory perspective, discerning appropriate inputs is essentially a matter of the entrepreneur's vision.

In addition to identifying appropriate inputs, the success of an entrepreneur will be determined by his or her ability to convert the inputs and generate value in excess of their hire-price in a unique way to avoid the possibility of being copied by competitors at least in the short run. It has been argued that all things being equal, growth is highly influenced by SMEs' specific attributes such as learning by doing and organizational culture (Conner, 1991). These are what make a difference in terms of performance between two firms. According to Dierickx and Cool (1989) purchased assets cannot be sources of long-lived rents because the same can be traded in the market. What one does with these assets is what matters most. All this notwithstanding, however, acquisition of these assets is a pre-requisite and this is where the role of financing cannot be overplayed. Finance is essential in two respects. First, in ensuring that key assets are acquired, and second, in supporting the smooth development and coordination of diverse production skills, innovation and integration of multiple streams of technology (Conner, 1991; Dierickx and Cool, 1989).

The ability to extract proper input may, however, be hindered by factors both internal and external to SMEs. External factors include public policy that may not provide a conducive operating environment. Public policy includes regulatory provisions, laws govern-ing establishment of property rights and business formalization. Another factor is limited demand as a result of stiff market competition emanating from less differentiated products and lack of innovation. The ability to operate at the lowest cost possible may position an SME in a better place than its competitors and the same, all things being equal, may influence its growth.

Internal factors include some entrepreneurial attributes and organization culture that may affect decisions made by an entrepreneur. According to Storey (1994), the growth process in a small firm is a result of three things, namely: the characteristics of the entrepreneur, characteristics of the small firm, and the small firm's development strategy. Firm-specific attributes are very important in influencing growth of SMEs. According to Williamson (1975), what helps one firm to out-perform another, all things being equal, is how a firm coordinates its internal network and relationships. This includes specific organization culture. As Conner (1991: 139) puts it, "for any given input the degree to which it will be specific varies from firms because firms themselves are unique." Ownership and development of an input will yield different rent or return from one firm to another as a result of having different asset combinations in a specific firm. That is, as a result of asset interdependence within the firm.

In short, the resource-based theory views a firm as input combiner and as efficiency seeker in production and distribution. Its success depends on the environment in which it operates and how it interacts with that environment. The better the environment and efficiency with which resources are combined in production and distribution, the better growth will be expected and vice versa. Financing is required at all levels to facilitate SME growth.

Credit and SME growth

The role of finance in supporting any economic activity cannot be over-emphasized. Finance is required to support economic activities and makes a significant contribution to growth (Levine and Dermigüç-Kunt, 2001). In this section, we explore the role of finance in fostering SME growth from the resource-based theory perspective. The resource-based theory of the firm (e.g., Barney, 1991) highlights that firm-specific resources are the corner-stone of corporate performance and competitiveness. The firm-specific resources include finance and the ability to attract finance. In this study we focus on examining the role of finance in general and credit in particular in promoting the growth of SMEs.

Credits ensure that SMEs have access to adequate finance or capital. It has been argued that adequate capital aids entrepreneurship performance (Gatewood et al., 2004). This can be seen in improved output, investment, employment, revenue growth, profit growth, and welfare of the entrepreneurs. It can also be indicated by the level of product innovation. For example, the extent to which an SME has improved its existing machines or acquired new ones; introduced new knowledge in its production; introduced new products in its market. Generally speaking, financing is very crucial in supporting any economic activity.

Finance is required to support initial investment for new undertakings. The same is required to support implementations of various activities for an ongoing undertaking. It is also required to support further investment requirement that will enable an enterprise to maintain its operating capacity, adopt new technology, acquire new technical staff, and support enterprise growth.

Entrepreneurs can obtain their finance from three main sources, namely: previous savings, retaining business profits, and loans from friends or financial institutions. The main source of finance to most entrepreneurs, however, is credit financing (why? Due to limited profit levels at initial levels of growth). Access to credit can allow SMEs to make larger investments to support and even improve their operations, adopt new technologies, and expand. Thus, all things being equal, the larger the credit the higher the expected growth. Limited access to bank credit can force an SME to scale down investment plan and reduce production. In this study, we examine the effects of both current and previous loans on SME growth as measured by increase in sales turnover, capital, and profitability.

Formalization and SME growth

Informality in property and business operations causes many challenges to the financing and growth of SMEs. It has been argued that SMEs in the informal sector grow at lower rate compared to SMEs which operate in the formal sector (Nichter, 2009). Among the reasons are their lack of access to finance which requires legal documents or collateral (Winter, 1995; Nichter, 2009). An informal property or business is not recognized in law and therefore cannot be used to guarantee credit and contracts from a financial institution. As a result, huge capital potential remains dead. Informality of property and business ownership and manage-ment is therefore seen to be an obstacle to inclusive economic development and poverty reduction (MKURABITA, 2014).

The lack of separation of owners from their business is an additional challenge for informal sector enterprises. This may pose a higher risk from the lenders' perspective. For example, when there is no separation of ownership and the owner dies, it is not certain that someone will take over the business in a similarly efficient way as the original owner. Responding to this high risk, banks or providers of finance may charge very high interest rates to cover for the high risk of these informal enterprises. This makes financing very expensive and may discourage SMEs in the informal sector from borrowing. It could also make some of the potential businesses unprofitable or marginally profitable with a potential high failure rate. Lack of finance may also lead SMEs to abandon profitable ventures and even discourage innovations as a result.

However, in some countries like Tanzania, formalization processes and procedures are sometimes very complicated and relatively expensive such that they hinder the formalization and growth of SMEs. For example, a long distance to service centers and the high cost of compliance with regulations may cause an unfriendly environment for SMEs to pursue formalization. This may discourage potential entrepreneurs from formally establishing their businesses, and even drive some existing enterprises out of business and those working for them into unemployment. Moreover, SMEs may decide to abandon the formal system altogether and operate in the informal economy, side-stepping taxes and regulations, and thus not make a full contribution to economic growth and job creation (OECD, 2006).

Thus, formalization procedures and processes should ensure that the benefits of form-alization far exceed the costs. In this study, we examine the contribution of business formalization in Tanzania on SMEs' access to external credit. This could provide a significant benefit of formalization and also represent a significant cost of remaining in the informal sector.

SMEs in Tanzania

As we noted above, there is no single generally accepted definition of what constitutes small or medium enterprises. In Tanzania, SMEs Policy (2002) defines micro enterprises as those enterprises engaging up to four people or with capital investment amounting up to Tshs. 5.0 million. Small enterprises are those employing between 5 and 49 employees or with capital investment from Tshs. 5 million to Tshs. 200 million. Medium enterprises employ between 50 and 99 people or use capital investment from Tshs. 200 million to Tshs. 800 million.

According to recent estimates, more than 95 percent of businesses in Tanzania are small enterprises (World Bank, 2014). These are owned by over 2.7 million entrepreneurs of whom 54.3 percent are female. Of all SMEs in Tanzania, approximately 55.5 percent are in the trade sector, 30.4 percent in the service sector, 13.6 percent are in the manufacturing sector and the remaining 0.5 percent are in other sectors (NBSR, 2012). These SMEs generate about 40 percent of total employment and contribute about 35 percent of the country's Gross Domestic Product (GDP). Figure 31.1 indicates allocation of SMEs by sector.

Challenges facing SMEs in Tanzania

Despite SMEs' contribution in terms of employment, number of companies, and overall economic growth, their full potential remains untapped due to the challenges that hamper their growth (Schlogl, 2004; Omar et al, 2009). These challenges include the unfavorable legal and regulatory framework which hinders formalization, the undeveloped infrastructure, poor business development services, and the limited access to external finance (World Bank, 2014).

SMEs in Tanzania also face informality in property and business operations and poor internal financing challenges. According to the National Baseline Survey Report (NBSR) for Micro, Small, and Medium Enterprises (2012) the main distinctive feature of SMEs in Tanzania is the huge number operating in the informal sector. It is estimated that in 2012,

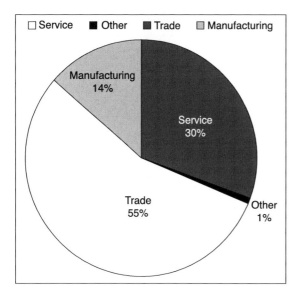

Figure 31.1   SMEs by Sector

less than 5 percent of small business were formally registered by the Business Registrations and Licensing Agency (BRELA). This means that the vast bulk (95 percent) of SMEs in Tanzania operate in the informal sector. This informality hinders the growth of SMEs in the country due to the limited access to external financing.

When attempting to access external financing, SMEs face a financing dilemma. The lack of recognizable security leaves them with limited access to formal financial institutions and cheap credit. Formal financial institutions, especially commercial banks, often find it too expensive and risky to lend to SMEs as the cost of assessing whether an SME is creditworthy is high relative to the return banks could earn by lending to them. Only about 10 percent of the small business owners in the country have access to formal financial services (NBSR, 2012). As a result, semi-formal finance, including micro-financing and informal providers, remains their only hope. About 10.9 percent of small business owners have access to semi-formal providers, 12.1 percent to informal providers and the remaining enterprises (over 65 percent of the total) are excluded from access to financial services (NBSR, 2012). Overall, financing from microfinance institutions is inadequate. SMEs' financial needs often times exceed the small loans that microfinance institutions provide. Some initiatives have been taken by the government of Tanzania to address these challenges and promote a vibrant SME sector. In the next section, we discuss these initiatives.

Government initiatives to promote a vibrant SME sector

Several initiatives have been taken by the government of Tanzania in an attempt to deal with the challenges facing SMEs. Among the initiatives was the formulation of a policy to promote a vibrant SME sector. The policy is intended to put in place a mechanism that would ensure the smooth formalization of informal SMEs. Another initiative was the introduction of property and business formalization in Tanzania. All these were meant to ensure that SMEs attain their full potential.

Formulation of SME development policy

In 2003 the government of Tanzania formulated a policy known as SME Development Policy (2003). Its vision was to ensure that Tanzania has a "vibrant and dynamic SME sector that ensures effective utilization of available resources to attain accelerated and sustainable growth." It was meant to "stimulate development and growth of SME activities through improved infrastructure, enhanced service provision and creation of conducive legal and institutional framework so as to achieve competitiveness" (SME Policy, 2003: 13).

The main objectives of the policy were to foster job creation and income generation through promoting the creation of new SMEs and improving the performance and competitiveness of the existing ones to increase their participation and contribution to the Tanzanian economy (SME Policy, 2003: 13). Specifically, the policy was meant to achieve the following: first, to provide an enabling legal and regulatory framework through simplifying business registration and licensing procedures; review government procurement procedures to facilitate SMEs' participation; establish a window within the commercial court for handling SME disputes; train and sensitize SMEs on property rights. Second, improve physical and work places through allocating land for SMEs by local authorities; and identify and allocate under-utilized public buildings to SMEs. Third, to strengthen entrepreneurial culture and markets for sustainable business development through inculcating values and attitudes that are conducive to development of entrepreneurship; set up business centers for SMEs; promote business linkages between large and small enterprises. Fourth, improve SME access to finance through facilitating establishment of SME window within existing banks and encourage simplification of procedures; mobilize resources and promote establishment of new financial institutions for SME development (SME Policy, 2003: 31–33).

The implementation of this policy is ongoing and progressive achievements are being recorded. These include: the increase in number of households running a business as primary or secondary activity from 35 percent in 2000 to 40 percent in 2006. A further increase since then is expected; enterprise creation from 22,780 (2002/03–2005/06) to 83,441 (2008/09 – 2010/11), increase in the number of registered taxpayers (with tax identification numbers [TIN] including individual and enterprise registrations) from 190,000 in July 2003 to 1,035,281 in June 2012 (UNIDO, 2013: 18). The business registration period has been substantially reduced from three months, especially for SMEs far from Dar es Salaam, to just five days. As a result, there has been an increase in the number of registered business names from 2,480 in 1997 to 16,500 in 2012 and an increase in the number of formalized businesses from 1,892 in 1996/97 to 7,000 in 2011/12 (BRELA, 2012).

Implementation, reviewing, and reconsidering public policies and regulations to ensure that they offer full support to SMEs' growth is a continuous process. Although there could be so many factors responsible for the positive change and some hindrances, still much has to be done to ensure a vibrant SME sector is flourishing in the country. All this notwithstanding, it is important to note that the government and key stakeholders are committed to ensure an environment conducive for SMEs to start and develop is maintained.

Property and business formalization in Tanzania

To unlock the potential of enterprises operating in the informal sector, in 2004 the government of Tanzania embarked on a property and business formalization program popularly known in Swahili language as *Mpango wa Kurasimisha Rasilimali na Biashara za Wanyonge* (MKURABITA). MKURABITA was meant to facilitate formalization of properties and business assets in the country through registering and licensing businesses. It was designed to empower owners of the formalized assets to use the said capital and other social economic opportunities available in the expanded market (MKURABITA, 2014). Through formalization, owners could be empowered to access capital from formal financial institutions. Access to capital was in turn expected to influence the growth of SMEs in the country. The target was to formalize informal business from three different informal categories. First, the formalization of unregistered businesses operating informally was sought; second, registered businesses operating without following proper procedures; and third, registered and authorized businesses operating inconsistently with legal provisions.

Although MKURABITA was introduced in 2004, its effective implementation started formally in 2009 by establishing a "One Stop Centre" that brought together all key stakeholders responsible for one or more aspects of formalization. This reduced the time required for formalization and the costs of formalizing. The key stakeholders included: Business Registration and Licensing Authority (BRELA) for registration of business names and private companies; Tanzania Revenue Authority (TRA) for tax identification and assessment; Council Trade Department (CTD) for business licensing; Finance Service Providers (FSP) for banking and financial services; Tanzania Chamber of Commerce, Industry and Agriculture (TCCIA) for marketing system information.

It has been some years since the implementation of formalization. Data of initial assessment indicates some successes being recorded (MKURABITA, 2014). Since 2009, 40 percent (2,160 businesses) of the target SMEs have been registered as formal businesses and 49 percent (2,668 businesses) obtained formal business licenses. This study aims at assessing whether the formalization of SMEs increases access to formal financial institutions and external financing. In addition, the study investigates whether increased access, if any, influences business growth.

Methodology

The study uses a combination of both quantitative and qualitative analysis techniques. While the quantitative analysis was meant to establish whether the results are statistically significant, the qualitative analysis aimed at finding in-depth explanations of the quantitative results.

A comparative analysis was conducted to assess the influence of formalization on financial access. We compared financing levels before and after formalization. The aggregate means were compared and a two-sample t-test was conducted to determine whether the difference between the two groups is statistically significant. Regression analysis was used in determining the effects of credit on SMEs' growth.

Data collection

The empirical data used in this study was drawn from a survey data set of 1,362 SMEs from Arusha and Dar es Salaam regions in Tanzania. The survey data was collected before and after formalization. Initially, five regions were covered in a base-line study that was conducted before formalization under the Property and Business Formalization Program (PBFP) in Tanzania. However, only two regions, Arusha and Dar es Salaam were covered in post-formalization evaluations. Thus the two regions were selected due to data availability. Additional data, linking credit and SMEs' performance, was obtained from a local MFI indicating amount of loan, sales, capital, and profit over four years from 234 MFI clients in Dar es Salaam and Arusha making a total of 936 observations. In addition, interviews were conducted with 10 MFI clients to gain an insight on quantitative figures.

Statistical analysis

This study employed two types of statistical analysis namely bivariate and multivariate analysis. The bivariate analysis involved comparing mean difference between two groups: access to finance before and after formalization. A non-parametric analysis was used for this case. The multivariate analysis employed an autoregressive panel regression model to determine the influence of credit on SME growth.

Variables and model specification

Three indicators of growth are used as dependent variables in this study when determining the influence of credit on SMEs' growth. These are changes in sales, changes in capital, and changes in profitability. Credit, measured by the amount of loan and its lagged values, is used as a dependent variable. Lagged values are introduced in an attempt to determine when specifically credit influences SME growth. Thus both current and previous loan amounts are used as variables in the autoregressive model.

As noted before, growth as a process is influenced by, among others, the characteristics of the entrepreneur. All things being equal, education shapes one's understanding and decision-making style which in turn may influence how effective one is in pursuing new inventions. Individual characteristics are sources of competitive advantage in the entrepreneurial domain (Busenitz and Alvarez, 2001). Thus in this study, entrepreneurs' education as one of the characteristics of an entrepreneur is used as a control variable. Education is measured in terms of years spent in formal education. In addition to education we also use business location as a control variable. All things being equal, a good business location means more business and could imply growth and vice versa. It has been argued that firms are more likely to grow faster in some locations than in others (Storey, 1994).

Three autoregressive models were tested as indicated below.

$$Y_1 = a + \beta_1 X_1 + \beta_2 X_2 + \beta_3 X_3 + \beta_4 X_4 + e \ldots \quad \ldots \quad \ldots \quad \ldots \tag{1}$$

$$Y_2 = a + \beta_1 X_1 + \beta_2 X_2 + \beta_3 X_3 + \beta_4 X_4 + \beta_5 X_5 + e \ldots \quad \ldots \quad \ldots \tag{2}$$

$$Y_3 = a + \beta_1 X_1 + \beta_2 X_2 + \beta_3 X_3 + \beta_4 X_4 + e \ldots \quad \ldots \quad \ldots \quad \ldots \tag{3}$$

Where Y_1 is change in sales value; Y_2 is change in capital; and Y_3 is change in profitability as dependent variables. Independent variables are: X_1 which represents the current loan amount; X_2 is previous or lagged loan amount; X_3 is entrepreneur's education; X_4 is business location as control variable; X_5 is profit and e is an error term. Profit variable is added in the autoregressive model for capital growth to check whether SMEs in Tanzania have a profit reinvestment plan that can influence capital growth.

Model diagnostics

This study used an autoregressive panel regression model to estimate the relationship between credit and SME performance. We conducted several model diagnostic tests to ensure that our model is properly specified. These included tests for multicollinearity, heteroscedasticity, and autocorrelation. We found that only the heteroscedasticity problem existed in our three models. As a remedy to the problem, we estimated the models using heteroscedasticity robust standard errors (Cameron and Trivedi, 2009).

To deal with omitted variable bias a random effect (RE) panel regression model was used (Hsiao, 2007). An alternative would have been a fixed effect model. However, due to data characteristics the FE was ruled out; that is, the entrepreneurs' education was observed to be constant over time while FE would require it to change over time. Thus being constant over time throughout the study period the FE model would have dropped the education variable all together. This wouldn't have been a good idea as variable "education" is a key control variable that we cannot afford missing in the models.

Findings

In this section, the findings are presented. We first analyze the effects of property and business formalization on SMEs' access to credit. This is followed by an analysis of the effects of credit on SMEs' growth as measured by sales growth, capital growth, and profit growth.

Effects of formalization on SMEs access to credit

The effects of SMEs' formalization on access to finance is examined by comparing SMEs' access before and after formalization. Three aspects are examined. First, whether formalization has influenced SMEs to open bank accounts for their business. Second, whether formalization has enabled SMEs to increase their access to bank borrowing. Finally, we analyze whether formalized SMEs' capital is higher after formalization than before. The following three hypotheses were tested:

1. Ho: Formalization has not influenced SMEs to open bank accounts for their businesses.
   Hi: Formalization has influenced SMEs to open bank accounts for their businesses.
2. Ho: Formalized SMEs do not have better access to bank loans than before.
   Hi: Formalized SMEs have increased their access to bank loans.
3. Ho: SMEs' capital remains the same after formalization.
   Hi: SMEs' capital improves after formalization.

We find very strong evidence to support the assertion that business formalization improves access to finance as indicated in Table 31.1.

Test statistics for the three indicators of access are statistically significant at a 1 percent significance level. We therefore reject all three null hypotheses that formalization has no effect on opening bank accounts, obtaining loans from banks, and increasing capital. This

Table 31.1 Two-Sample T-Test Results

Variable of interest	Mean Before	Mean After	p-value
1. Opening bank account	0.2323978	0.5440115	0.000★★★
	(0.0093742)	(0.0189334)	
2. Access to bank loan	0.0256032	1.49062	0.000★★★
	(0.0035056)	(0.0248941)	
3. Increase in capital	2.343688	3.066378	0.000★★★
	(0.0289257)	(0.0466796)	

★★★significant at 1%

indicates that after formalization, more SMEs opened a bank account, had access to bank loans and finally their capital increased as a result. Of course there could be some other factors responsible for the improvements. One of the factors is the requirement by most banks that before they offer a loan one must open an account with them. This was evident during a personal interview.

> yes, I didn't have a bank account for my business before but now I have one. I was using my personal bank account for business and personal transactions. When I wanted to borrow, my business name and my name were different . . . it was a requirement by the bank that I must open an account with them for my business for the loan to be deposited. I had to comply because I needed the money . . . but all the same, I don't regret as I came to realize that for business accounts there are more bank services and payment flexibility which I never knew before . . . it is safe and convenient. It has also taught me to have financial discipline.

From the interview reply above, formalization was evidently important. The entrepreneur would not have been allowed to open a business bank account without having at least registered the business. It also reveals how separation of business and private transactions could now be possible. Access to bank loans has also enabled SMEs to increase their capital.

Effects of credit on SMEs growth

Indicators of SMEs' growth used in this study are the increase in sales turnover, increase in capital, and SME profitability. The findings on how credit affects the growth of SMEs are presented in this section on each of these indicators respectively.

Sales Growth

Econometric results on the effects of credit on sales growth (Equation 1) indicate that there isn't any strong evidence to support the hypothesis that amount of credit (loan amount) influences SMEs' growth as measured by increase in sales (see Table 31.2). These findings for SMEs in Tanzania tend to support findings by Babajide (2012) that access to credit does not influence sales growth. His study was based on panel data analysis of 502 SMEs in Nigeria. However, the findings in this study contradict the findings by Brown et al. (2004) on 297 SMEs in Romania that access to finance increases the growth of sales.

Table 31.2 Econometric Results on the Effect of Credit on Sales Growth

Variable	Coefficient	Robust Std. Err.	P>z
Current loan	0.4942844	0.4027454	0.220
Previous loan	−0.743889	0.5996171	0.215
Business location	177698.2	121713.6	0.144
Education	337107.1	200322.5	0.092★
R–Sq	Within: 0.0023; Between: 0.1747; Overall: 0.0094		

★ Significant at 10%

The amount of money borrowed by an SME during the current period appears to have positive influence on sales growth while the amount borrowed in previous periods seems to have negative influence on sales growth. All notwithstanding however, the relationship is not statistically significant. A possible explanation for the negative coefficient of the previous loan is that previous loan implies today's repayment which may in effect reduce the level of sales. This is also supported by Babajide (2012).

The insignificant influence of loans, both current and previous, in enhancing sales growth implies many things. First, the increase in financing may not necessarily influence sales turnover. It only does this when the same is invested in promoting sales and in making sales effective. This can be seen on the R-squared value which is very small, meaning that this model cannot predict changes in sales growth. Sales depend much on demand conditions rather than financing itself. Indeed, credit may improve the amount of supply and therefore could influence a change in sales if demand is not a limiting factor. However, if credit cannot change customer choices and preferences and therefore influence their demand, it will be difficult for it to influence sales growth.

Second, it could imply the existence of the misdirecting of the borrowed funds to other activities. It has been reported that due to the fungible nature of financial resources, borrowers sometimes spend the money on activities not directly related to their business. That is, the loan may be transferred from a borrower to someone else or when the loan is not used on the planned activities (Hulme, 2000; Kuzilwa, 2005).

The results presented in Table 31.2 indicate weak evidence that the entrepreneur's characteristic as measured by education influences sales growth positively. Its coefficient is statistically significant at the 10 percent significance level. This supports the findings by Babajide (2012) that the entrepreneur's education influences sales growth positively. However, contrary to the findings by Almus and Nerlinger (1999) and Babajide (2012), although the coefficient is positive, there is no evidence that business location does influence sales growth.

Capital Growth

Econometric results summarized in Table 31.3 show the overall Wald statistic for the capital growth model is statistically significant at 1 percent significance level. Thus, we reject the hypothesis that all coefficients are equal to zero.

The results show that both current and previous loans have significant effect on SMEs' capital growth. The current loan has a positive effect while the previous loan has a negative

Table 31.3 Econometric Results on the Effect of Credit on Capital Growth

Variable	Coefficient	Robust Std. Err.	P>z
Current loan	1.330498	0.2577392	0.000★★★
Previous loan	−1.472876	0.4093179	0.000★★★
Business location	−5085.135	88065.920	0.954
Education	25711.41	119281.60	0.829
Profit	1.229155	0.6216458	0.048★★
R–Sq	Within: 0.1421; Between: 0.6753; Overall: 0.3405		

★★★significant at 1%; ★★significant at 5%; ★significant at 10%

effect. Their coefficients are both statistically significant at 1 percent significance level. As noted before, a possible explanation for the negative coefficient is loan repayments, which may reduce part of the capital. Evidence from the field supports this.

> the business environment isn't always friendly. Sometime we borrow to support the current operations at the same time use the borrowed funds to repay previous loan. It is not easy but we are managing. Sometimes what we get from the business is not enough to cover for the costs involved . . . in such cases borrowing for repayment is inevitable.

Special attention was paid to analyzing the contribution of the positive and negative effects of credit on capital growth. To determine which one of the two has a strong effect, we applied beta or standardized coefficients of the loan amount. It was revealed that the current loan's positive effect is stronger than the negative one for the previous loan. The overall effect therefore should be positive. The beta coefficient for the current loan is 0.7935836 while that of previous loan is −0.594976.

The ability of accumulating and saving own generated funds improves SMEs' access to internal funding for further investment (Hossain, 1988). In this study, strong evidence is found to support the assertion that SMEs use generated profits to increase their capital. The profit variable is statistically significant at 5 percent significance level. This may imply the separation of business and personal resources when it comes to spending. This was also revealed during personal interviews with one of the respondents:

> For years my business was not growing. Each day I would gather what was obtained on the same day and use part of it to meet various family needs. The needs list grew bigger and money was never enough . . . One day I attended a seminar on "keeping business records" organized by a local MFI and discovered that what I was doing was deadly wrong . . . Since then, things have changed completely. At first I struggled but eventually managed . . . Today, my business and I are two different persons. Even my wife knows it . . .

There is, however, no evidence to support the effect of entrepreneurs' education and business location on capital growth. This is contrary to Masakure et al. (2008) and Babajide (2012) who argue that the level of education is important in determining the condition at start-up such as in the form of capital saved from earlier employment and ability to access more capital and accumulate wealth. Indeed the level of education is important. However, if entrepreneurs are just doing similar business and no creativity or application of education is evident then education may have no effect at all.

Profit growth

The findings on the effect of credit on profit growth are summarized in Table 31.4. The overall Wald statistic for the profit growth model is statistically significant at 1 percent significance level. Thus, we reject the hypothesis that all coefficients are equal to zero. The R-squared indicates the model is good at predicting relationships between SMEs more than within an SME.

As with capital growth, both current and previous loans significantly influence profit growth. Their coefficients are statistically significant at a 1 percent significance level. Again,

Table 31.4 Econometric Results on the Effect of Credit on Profit Growth

Variable	Coefficient	Robust Std. Err.	P>z
Current loan	0.0919423	0.0197864	0.000★★★
Previous loan	−0.1077890	0.0267249	0.000★★★
Business location	21587.850	10548.890	0.052★
Education	35212.680	18083.240	0.041★★
R–Sq	Within: 0.0049; Between: 0.4720; Overall: 0.0402		

★★★significant at 1%; ★★significant at 5%; ★significant at 10%

previous loans affect profit growth negatively. An analysis of their beta coefficients reveals once again that the positive effect is stronger than the negative one. The beta coefficient for the current loan is 0.3239498 while the one for the previous loan is −0.2572121.

While credit does not affect sales growth, it does strongly affect growth in profitability. A possible explanation for this is that, with access to credit, entrepreneurs have enough capital to support their initiatives and daily business undertakings. Enough capital assists entrepreneurs to source their supplies in bulk and therefore enables them to enjoy economies of scale. This was evident in the field as indicated by one of the respondents.

> I am very much thankful for the finance access that an MFI has extended to me. Before having this access my capital was very small, as a result, I had to source all my supplies from local shops at a relatively higher price. This limited my profitability as we are operating at a very competitive environment. A slight price increase can assure you that you are losing your customer to the neighboring outlet . . . Now my capital has increased to a reasonable amount. I buy all my supplies in bulk at a relatively cheaper price. I can still sell at the same price. Sometime I even reduce prices to encourage customers to buy more from my shop especially those who buy in bulk.

In addition, the effects of entrepreneurs' education and business location are statistically significant when examining profit, unlike for capital and sales growth. The coefficient for education is significant at a 5 percent significance level while the one for business location is significant at a 10 percent significance level. This implies that, when it comes to change in profitability, entrepreneurs' education and business location matters. There could be many reasons, some of which are: the possibility of proper record keeping and proper cost determination.

Conclusions

This study has sought to determine the effects of business formalization on improving SMEs' access to external financing. It has also sought to determine the effect of credit on SMEs' growth. The finding is a strong association between credit and indicators of SME growth. We conclude that business formalization has a positive effect on SMEs' access to services offered by formal financial institutions. These are opening a business bank account, obtaining loans, and increased capital. We also conclude that access to credit has a strong effect on SMEs' capital and profitability growth. In addition, entrepreneurs' education and location strongly affect profit growth. However, there is no evidence to support the effects of credit on sales growth.

References

Almus, M., and Nerlinger, E. (1999). Growth of Technology Based Firms: Which Factors Matter? *Small Business Economics*, 13(2), 141–154.

Asare, A. O. (2014). Challenges Affecting SMEs Growth in Ghana. *OIDA International Journal of Sustainable Development*, 7(6), 23–28.

Babajide, A. (2012). Effects of Microfinance on Micro and Small Enterprises (MSEs), Growth in Nigeria. *Asian Economic and Financial Review*, 2(3), 463–477.

Barney, J. (1991). Firm Resources and Sustained Competitive Advantage. *Journal of Management*, 17(2), 99–120.

Barney, J. B. (1986). Strategic Factor Markets: Expectations, Luck, and Business Strategy, *Management Science*, 35(10), 1231–1241.

BRELA. (2012). Step by step guide to access, services and brochures, Business Registration and Licensing Agency (BRELA) 2011/2012 BRELA.

Brown, J. D, Earle, J. S., and Lup, D. (2004). What makes small firms grow? finance, human capital, technical assistance, and the business environment in Romania (October). IZA Discussion Paper No. 1343; Upjohn Institute Staff Working Paper No. 03–94.

Busenitz, L. W., and Alvarez, S. A. (2001). The Entrepreneurship of Resource-Based Theory. *Journal of Management*, 27(6), 755–775.

Cameron, A. C., and Trivedi, P. K. (2009). *Microeconometric Using Stata*. College Station, TX: Stata Press.

Chandler, A. D. (1962). *Strategy and Structure*. Cambridge: The MIT Press

Chandler, A. D. (1977). *The Visible Hand*. Cambridge, MA: Harvard University Press

Coase, R. H., (1952). The Nature of the Firm. In G. J. Stigler and K. E. Boulding (Eds.), *Readings in Price Theory*, pp. 331–351. Chicago: Irwin. Reprinted from *Econometrica* (1937), 4, pp. 386–405.

Conner, K. R (1991). A Historical Comparison of Resource-Based Theory and Five Schools of Thought within Industrial Organization Economics: Do We Have a New Theory of the Firm? *Journal of Management*, 17(1), 121–154.

Dierickx, I., and Cool, K. (1989). Asset Stock Accumulation and Sustainability of Competitive Advantage. *Management Science*, 35(12), 1504–1511.

Gatewood, E. J., Brush, C. G., Carter, N. M., Greene, P. G., and Hart, M. M. (2004). Women entrepreneurs, growth and implications for the classroom, USA: Coleman foundation whitepaper series for the USA, Association for small business and Entrepreneurship

Hossain, M. (1988). Credit for Alleviation of Rural Poverty: the Grameen Bank in Bangladesh. IFPRI Research Report 65. Washington, DC: International Food Policy Research Institute.

Hsiao, C. (2007). *Analysis of Panel Data*. 2nd edn. Econometric Society Monographs No. 34, New York: Cambridge University Press.

Hulme, D. (2000). Impact Assessment Methodologies for Microfinance: Theory, Experience and Better Practice. *World Development*, 28(1), 79–98.

ILO (2011). *Statistical Update on Employment in the Informal Economy*. Geneva: Department of Statistics.

Kirzner, I. (1979). *Perception, Opportunity, and Profit*. Chicago: University of Chicago Press.

Kok, J., Christi, C. D., and Veldhuis-Van, E. (2013). Is Small Still Beautiful? Literature Review of Recent Empirical Evidence on the Contribution of SMEs to Employment Creation, International Labour Organisation (ILO), Available at: http://www.ilo.org/wcmsp5/groups/public/—ed_emp/—emp_ent/—ifp_seed/documents/publication/wcms_216909.pdf. Accessed: 15th May 2015.

Kok, J., Vroonhof, P., Verhoeven, W., Timmermans, N., Kwaakh, T., Snijders, J., and Westhof, F. (2011). Do SMEs create more and better jobs? EIM Research Reports, EIM Business & Policy.

Kuzilwa, J. A. (2005). The Role of Credit for Small Business Success: A Study of the National Entrepreneurship Development Fund in Tanzania. *Journal of Entrepreneurship*, 14(2), 131–161.

Levine, R., and Demirgüç-Kunt, A. (2001). *Financial Structure and Economic Growth: A Cross-Country Comparison of Banks, Markets and Development*. Cambridge, MA: MIT Press.

Masakure, O., Cranfield, J., and Henson, S. (2008). The financial performance of non-farm microenterprises in Ghana. *World Development*, 36(12), 2733–2762.

MKURABITA. (2014). *Mpango wa Kurasimisha Rasilimali na Biashara za Wanyonge* (MKURABITA). United Republic of Tanzania

Muneer, B. M., and Kulshreshth, P. (2014). Productivity Change and Technical Efficiency in Indian Microfinance Institutions. *Studies in Microeconomics*, 2(2), 165–200.

NBSR. (2012). National Baseline Survey Report (NBSR) for Micro, Small, and Medium Entreprises, Financial Sector Deepening Trust, Ministry of Industry and Trade: United Republic of Tanzania.

Nichter, S. (2009). Small Firm Growth in the Developing Countries. *World Development*, 37(9), 1453–1464.

Nyamsogoro, G. D. (2011). Factors Influencing Financial Sustainability of Rural Microfinance Institutions in Tanzania. *The Accountant*, 27(2), 5–19.

OECD. (2006). *Small Businesses, Job Creation and Growth: Facts, Obstacles and Best Practices*. Paris: Organisation for Economic Co-operation and Development (OECD).

Omar, S., Arokiasamy, L., and Ismail, M. (2009). The Background and Challenges Faced by the Small Medium Enterprises. A Human Resource Development Perspective. *International Journal of Business and Management*, 4(10), 95–102.

Penrose, E. T. (1959). *The Theory of the Growth of the Firm*. New York: John Wiley.

Peteraf, M. (1993). The Cornerstones of Competitive Advantage: A Resource-based View. *Strategic Management Journal*, 13(5), 363–380.

Schlogl, H. (2004). Small and Medium Enterprises: Seizing the Potential. *Organizational for Economic Cooperation and Development*, 243, 46–48.

Schumpeter, J. (1934). *The Theory of Economic Development*. Cambridge, MA: Harvard University Press.

Shane, S., and Venkataraman, S. (2000). The Promise of Entrepreneurship as a Field of Research. *Academy of Management Review*, 25(1), 217–226.

Shinozaki, S. (2012). A New Regime of SME Finance in Emerging Asia: Empowering Growth-Oriented SMEs to Build Resilient National Economies, ADB Working Paper Series on Regional Economic Integration, No. 104 (Publication Stock No.WPS125308) Available at: http://www.aric.adb.org/pdf/workingpaper/WP104_Shinozaki_SME_Finance.pdf. Accessed 21st July 2015.

SME Policy. (2003). *Small and Medium Enterprise Development Policy*. Ministry of Industry and Trade, United Republic of Tanzania.

Stigler, G. K. (1961). The Economics of Information. *Journal of Political Economy*, 69(3), 213–225.

Storey, D. (1994). *Understanding the Small Business Sector*. New York: Routledge.

UNIDO. (2013). *Tanzania SME Development Policy 2003: Ten Years After Implementation Review*. United Nations Industrial Development Organization (UNIDO).

Wernerfelt, B. (1984). The Resource-Based View of the Firm. *Strategic Management Journal*, 5(2), 171–180.

Wernerfelt, B. (1984). A Resource-based View of the Firm. *Strategic Management Journal*, 5(2), 171–180.

Williamson, O. E. (1975). *Markets and Hierarchies: Analysis and Antitrust Implications*. New York: Free Press.

Winter, S. G (1995). Small and Medium Enterprises in Economic Development: Possibilities for research and policy, World Bank Policy Research working Paper No. 1508, World Bank, Washington, DC.

World Bank (2014). *Country Economic Memorandum, Tanzania: Productive Jobs Wanted*. Washington, DC: World Bank.

PART V

Entrepreneurship education and learning

32

ENTREPRENEURSHIP EDUCATION IN DEVELOPING COUNTRIES

An introductory overview

Colin C. Williams and Anjula Gurtoo

In recent years, based on the belief that fostering entrepreneurship and an enterprise culture is a key means of promoting economic development and growth, many developing countries have sought to shift beyond the traditional conception that entrepreneurs are born and not made, by developing entrepreneurship education. The hope is that this will help stimulate the entrepreneurship and thus economic development and growth so badly sought by these countries. Part V contains chapters on entrepreneurship education in various countries and global regions.

These chapters deal with how entrepreneurship education, which seeks to provide people with the knowledge, skills and motivation to encourage entrepreneurship, is being implemented in a variety of settings across the developing world from the primary and secondary school level to graduate university programmes. The intention in doing so is to enhance the level of entrepreneurship based on the belief that wealth and a large proportion of jobs in economies are created by small businesses started by entrepreneurial individuals, and that entrepreneurship is therefore a key driver of economic development and growth.

The intention in doing so is not only to create an entrepreneurial mind-set amongst a greater number of individuals but also to increase an entrepreneurial intention as well as the skill-sets required by entrepreneurially minded individuals. How this entrepreneurship education and learning has been implemented in different contexts, as well as the barriers to implementing such entrepreneurship education, is therefore the subject matter of the chapters in Part V of this handbook. These chapters deal with multifarious issues ranging from organisation learning in family firms and the role of social networks, examinations of the problems involved in developing the capacity for entrepreneurship education in war-torn conflict zones to how entrepreneurship education is taught and whether it has any real impact on the learners regarding their entrepreneurial intentions and business creation. The somewhat worrying finding, albeit from a limited range of developing world contexts, is that entrepreneurship education programmes currently appear to have an insignificant impact on the attitudes and entrepreneurial intentions of those subject to them. Whether this is due to the client groups served, the nature of the entrepreneurship education programmes being offered or other barriers is now badly in need of investigation.

443

Contributions of the chapters

In chapter 33, 'Capacity building for entrepreneurship education and research in the conflict zone of Peshwar', Lorraine Warren presents reflections on an ongoing eight-year relationship with staff of the Institute of Management Sciences (IMS) in Peshawar in Khyber Pakhtunkhwa (KPK). The purpose of the relationship from a strategic point of view is to develop research capacity and develop the curriculum in IMS, with a view to benefitting the region as it seeks to develop its economy despite ongoing conflict, natural disasters and infrastructural problems. The chapter is a personal reflection that goes further than identifying aims and objectives, met and unmet, looking deeper at why the relationship persists.

Alan A. Ndedi, in chapter 34, 'Entrepreneurship education in Cameroon matters: reorganizing the teaching of the subject', presents the limitations of entrepreneurship education in Cameroon and proposes a new direction. Reporting an empirical study involving a questionnaire of 100 graduates, policy makers and recruitment personnel regarding the impact entrepreneurial courses have had on learners in Cameroon, the finding is that entrepreneurship training has no real impact on learners regarding their entrepreneurial posture or orientation on business creation. The implications are then discussed.

In chapter 35, 'An evaluation of the impact of entrepreneurship education on the entrepreneurship intentions in the Albanian late transition context', Elvisa Drishti, Drita Kruja and Mario Curcija report a longitudinal assessment of whether and to what extent entrepreneurial education programmes influence the entrepreneurial attitudes and intentions of tertiary education students in Albania over time. Based on a quasi-experimental research design and an Entrepreneurial Intention questionnaire, the results confirm an insignificant impact of the entrepreneurial education programmes on the attitudes and entrepreneurial intentions except for the 'perceived behavioural control' component. Findings also suggest some evidence of the robustness of the theory of planned behaviour for the Albanian context choice and applicable recommendations for policy makers and the educators are derived accordingly.

Finally, in chapter 36, 'Organizational learning in Indian family firms: a social network based approach for entrepreneurship', Nobin Thomas and Neharika Vohra examine organisational learning from a network perspective by examining the sub-processes of organisational learning, namely information acquisition, information distribution, information interpretation and organisational memory in two-family firms in South India. Network measures of organisational learning within firms and between firms were compared to deepen understanding of learning processes across hierarchical levels in organisations. This study advances the use of social network analysis in entrepreneurial firms to evidence organisational learning and processes. Limitations are addressed and future research directions are suggested.

33

CAPACITY BUILDING FOR ENTREPRENEURSHIP EDUCATION AND RESEARCH IN THE CONFLICT ZONE OF PESHAWAR

A personal reflection

Lorraine Warren

Introduction: some history

As academics, why do we do the research projects that we do? Why do we choose certain projects over others, this study over that study, this context over that context? Of course, we do things that we are good at, where we have curiosity, and where we have expertise that can solve a problem, sometimes in collaboration with others. Sometimes the reasons are quite instrumental: projects can be geared to funding initiatives that target specific sectors or regions; or we choose something that is likely to catch the eye of a highly ranked journal, even though it may not capture our heart. Or, sometimes the reasons are located in specific individuals, international Ph.D. students for example, who seek us out at a personal level, sometimes leading to long-term regional collaborations. In this chapter, I discuss the deeper personal reasons behind an ongoing eight-year relationship with staff and students of the Institute of Management Sciences (IMS) in Peshawar in Khyber Pakhtunkhwa (KPK).

I remember precisely the moment when my relationship with IMS began. In 2005, someone gave me a Ph.D. proposal to read; there had been delay in finding a supervisor for a student from that institution – mismatches in expertise, the right people not available – would I be interested? It was important to respond quickly, as apparently we (University of Southampton) had a Memorandum of Understanding (MoU) with them, and we (the School of Management) were not looking good due to the delay. As I always do, I began to flick quickly through it checking out the topic, the theory, the methodology: is there a match, a fit? IMS was ranked the top business school in KPK and in the top 10 (currently number five) in Pakistan overall so that was promising. I did not get very far with my rational analysis before I saw that the project was about marble mining and processing, with data collection located in Peshawar, the home city of IMS, and wider, in the Khyber Pakhtunkhwa (KPK) region and the bordering tribal areas, where the mines were located. I was immediately hooked. My reasons were nothing to do with the actual project; just a rapid mental cascade back to childhood romances, dreams, and latter-day fascinations about visiting that part of the world. That led to a long-term relationship that I value greatly, and I will continue to treasure, even though many obvious objectives remain unmet. Ironically, to this day, I have still never been to the Peshawar region.

Being born in the 1950s into an unprepossessing council house in an industrial village on the edge of the Pennine moors, with constantly rowing parents, lent a greyness to life that was partially alleviated by extensive reading fed by the local library. In the 1960s, the town libraries monopolised the blockbuster paperbacks of the time by authors such as Harold Robbins. My little village library was much further down the pecking order, filled with older, more battered, faded hardbacks that chronicled the golden age of polar exploration, and the imperial doings of Rudyard Kipling, Henry Morton Stanley and Stamford Raffles. Some of these eagerly devoured books were really aimed at adults, but there were some 'junior' versions where imperial conquest was linked to finding treasure chests, with beautiful illustrations of gold and gems. All fuelled my childish dreams of escape, of founding cities and finding unlimited gemstones in untravelled regions, away from the constant rain. I looked on fascinated as a wave of Asian immigrants made their home in the milltowns of North East Lancashire. Later on, in my teenage years in the 1970s, older friends lived out my dreams, or so I imagined, dressing as latter-day 'hippies' in 'Afghan' coats, and travelling by bus from Amsterdam to Iran, Afghanistan, North West Frontier Province, Pakistan, and through to Kathmandu and Nepal. Peshawar was a frequent and much-loved stopover. I began to read modern-day authors, travellers and historians such as Dervla Murphy and Victoria Schofield, tales of the Indus and the Pashtun people. Although my dreams now took on a more practical form, my yearning deepened as I waited to grow up and take my turn. That dream ended in 1978 when Russian tanks rode into Kabul, sparking conflict in the region that persists to this day, with thousands of Afghan refugees making their home in Peshawar. Alongside the long-time conflicts of Shia versus Sunni, are newer anti-Western sentiments, all sparking repeated terrorist incidents, such as the infamous Army Public School shootings, where seven gunmen killed 145 people, including 132 schoolchildren, ranging between eight and 18 years of age in December 2014. Added to that are problems of infrastructure, with repeated power cuts, and natural disasters such as the floods of 2010, where monsoon rains flooded the Indus basin, one-fifth of the land area of Pakistan, killing an estimated 2,000 people. Thirty years later, Western tourism to the region has plummeted, with repeated warnings not to travel there from government travel advisories. Rightly so – while the majority of visits to Pakistan take place without incident, there have been some targeted killings. For example a group of 10 Western climbers were shot in the head in June 2013, in retaliation for US drone strikes.

This was a very frustrating situation, because as I had now become a researcher in entrepreneurship and innovation. I was, potentially, in a position to help small businesses in the region, through education and training, working with staff in the region, thus moving on from childhood dreams. But despite KPK still having much to offer in terms of businesses that manage mineral resources, crafts, textiles and leather goods, and active SME business support programmes, University insurers have never sanctioned a visit to the KPK region for me due to the advisory travel warnings which are still in place, usually framed in terms of extreme risk, due to the significant threat from terrorism, risk of kidnapping and the unpredictable security situation. At one point, I did manage to visit Islamabad, though I was only able to access security cleared (and indeed very beautiful) areas. While some academics have been sanctioned to go, they have typically been engineers, offering on the ground support to, for example, water management projects. It is difficult to imagine that a dam project could be undertaken from afar, so a business case can be made that travel is essential, particularly where large-scale, well-funded projects are at stake. Staff of Non-Government Organisations (NGOs) too, such as aid agencies, can get sanction, and also, limited insurance from their employers, drafted around complex risk assessment and management, again undertaken in the knowledge that the job cannot be carried out without a physical presence. For a university project involving entrepreneurship and SME support, the sums of money involved tend to be relatively small, and the case for on-site work less clear. It is argued that staff and students on both sides of the agreements can work together online, or at conferences outside the region, without detriment to the quality of the work produced.

Still, in 2005 there was new hope. A delegation from the University's International Office had travelled to IMS in Peshawar, via Islamabad, during a time when the conflict temperature was relatively low, and the then Vice Chancellor was less risk averse than many a latter-day counterpart. Having experienced wonderful hospitality in the region, and having seen the quality of the institution (currently fifth best Business School in Pakistan, first in KPK), they drew up an MoU to enable institution-wide staff exchanges, and, which is where I started this story, split-site Ph.D. programmes targeted at IMS staff. And so, I agreed to the supervision. Rationally, I took some time over it, carrying out the requisite checks. Emotionally, it probably took no more than a split second.

Muhammad Nouman, now Dr. Nouman, and Associate Professor at IMS, turned out to be an excellent student, successfully completing his Ph.D. on innovation systems surrounding the marble mining and processing industry in KPK/FATA in three years. He spent three months in Southampton each year working on the literature, methodological development and the write-up. He also became a valued colleague and friend, undertaking some teaching on a Level 3 Innovation course, achieving good feedback and results from students, in his understated and efficient way. It is no surprise to me that in 2014 he was awarded a 'Best Teacher' award from the Pakistan Higher Education Council. By this time, the IMS MoU had a good reputation across the Management School, and indeed across the University, as other students performed well during their Ph.D.s. Based on this growing warmth, in 2010, we applied for and won a three-year £60K British Council INSPIRE Strategic Partnership Grant, 'Strategic Partnership for Knowledge Exchange and Research on Sustainable Entrepreneurship and Innovation North West Pakistan', which took the partnership to the next level, as we moved from a Ph.D. relationship to full capacity development for IMS, and opportunities for knowledge exchange and data collection for the UK side too. Dr. Nouman was the Pakistan Principal Investigator (PI), I was PI on the UK side and another academic from Southampton joined me as Co-Investigator. The aims of INSPIRE, as well as part-funding two new split-site Ph.D. students are:

- Develop the existing relationship between the Southampton Business School (SBS) and IMS Peshawar to a new strategic level that will fully realise the benefits of existing links.
- Identify and explore areas for collaboration within curriculum development, joint research, doctoral studies and faculty exchange in the fields of innovation and sustainable entrepreneurship.
- Facilitate relationships between HEIs, industry, and relevant governmental organisations.
- Create new research/evidence-based knowledge concerning the sustainability, governance, leadership and development of SMEs in Pakistan.
- Facilitate outreach to improve performance, management practice of SMEs and enhance their relationships with HEIs in the region.

Laudable aims, and much was achieved. However the difficulties in working with a troubled region, despite best intentions on both sides, compromised the success of the programme, although strong relationships between the institutions and individuals persist to this day. In the next section, the literature discussing entrepreneurship in conflictual regions is presented. Then the outcomes of the INSPIRE project and the overall relationship with IMS are discussed. In the conclusions, recommendations for future practice for academics are made.

Entrepreneurship: the context of turbulent times in Pakistan

The last decade has seen a surge of interest in entrepreneurship in developing and emerging economies, because of its potential to support economic growth and productivity, as well as social improvement. In Pakistan however, entrepreneurial activity remains low, following the implementation of a heavily planned economy post-partition in 1947 (Ul Haque, 2007; Chemin, 2010). Successive policies tended to favour large-scale industries until the 1990s when the focus began to turn to SMEs, with the establishment of the Small And Medium Enterprise Development Authority (SMEDA) in 1998, although Chemin (2010) notes that SMEDA has few mechanisms or resources through which they can effect any impact. Small businesses do, of course, play an important role in Pakistan, providing the bulk of employment and contributing over 35 per cent of GDP. Yet while they produce a quarter of manufacturing exports, most SMEs produce low-value-added products which rely on traditional technologies. In addition, entry rates for new businesses are low, which Chemin (2010) attributes to a challenging economic and socio-cultural environment for entrepreneurship generally. While starting a business is relatively easy, obtaining credit, enforcing contracts and hiring workers is onerous.

Similarly, the development of entrepreneurship education has lagged in Pakistan, with Khan (2011) noting that only in recent years (2010/11) have such programmes been introduced, particularly in the better business schools. Neglect for six decades has of course led to a capacity gap, particularly the lack of well-qualified teaching staff, and evidence-based educational research too, to support pedagogical development that connects the existing literature to the local context. Development at Masters and Ph.D. level is weak, and entrepreneurship centres of the kind typical in most Western universities remain rare, although the establishment of 60 Offices of Research, Innovation & Commercialization (ORICs) suggest that this is changing. Further, positive portrayals of entrepreneurship as a career have been appearing in the media in Pakistan only recently. The emphasis has been on career development envisaged as progress through the ranks in a large firm or government body. Thus, when entrepreneurship was taught, it tended to be through a macro-economic lens rather than the dynamics and behaviours associated with start-ups. Now, a small but vocal 'start-up scene' is beginning to take hold, with, for example *Startup Magazine* and Expo 2015 making entrepreneurship seem cool and attractive as a career, albeit still with a city focus. Women entrepreneurs however, continue to face particular challenges (Roomi and Harrison, 2010) due to gender and tradition, which is a loss as their entrepreneurial activities make a significant contribution to the development of communities, regions and countries elsewhere (Brush et al., 2002; Dionco-Adetayo et al., 2005). Typically, women in higher social strata are able to pursue entrepreneurial opportunities, mainly because they have greater access to education and because their husbands and families tend to be less discouraging of women entrepreneurs (Roomi and Harrison, 2010).

Despite many green shoots, the limitations of this still low base are exacerbated in regions where conflictual circumstances pertain, such as in KPK and surrounding regions. Bruck et al. (2006) note that the majority of research on entrepreneurship has dealt with economic growth and development in relatively stable contexts. Situations where countries or regions get mired down in economic decline and conflict tend to be neglected. Bruck et al. (2006) argue that entrepreneurs are impacted by conflictual situations in different ways and to different extents due to the nature and extent of the conflict in question. Conflicts can deplete the capital stock of a country and its firms; they can also deplete the human capital, impacting on how individuals or communities perceive potentially profitable opportunities and create new value from these opportunities. Of course, value creation initiated through entrepreneurial behaviour takes place in a particular social context, and is not always positive. Entrepreneurship in conflictual situations may provide economic opportunity, which aids recovery, or contribute to peacekeeping activities. Alternatively, there may be a more low level manifestation of criminal activity, such as the classic stereotypical image of the 'spiv', emanating from World War II. Or, entrepreneurial actions of various kinds may inflame turbulent situations towards more violence. This potentially negative outcome is a sobering thought for those seeking to stimulate entrepreneurship. And of course conflict impacts on educators too.

So to summarise, although entrepreneurship education is likely to be desirable, to provide economic opportunity of the right kind, there are capacity needs that must be addressed:

- Teaching staff development particularly at the higher levels
- Curriculum development that is sensitive to cultural issues

A further issue is the need to encourage outreach to develop the 'start-up' practice-based culture. As well as being unusual as a desired career path, experiential learning through the practice of start-up activity is also novel in a region where teaching styles tend to be didactic and expert-driven. These capacity needs drove the development and success of our proposal. While we were developing the proposal, crafting sophisticated aims, objectives, outputs, budgets, there was a stark reminder of the fragility of the endeavour. On the last day prior to submission, I had arranged to email the final draft to Dr. Nouman, my fellow Investigator, to hand deliver to British Council offices in Peshawar – but he did not respond in time. Vaguely irritated and feeling let down, I did the necessary emailing and couriering to make sure we made the Friday deadline. When I got home, news of the terrible 2010 floods was on TV and I was appalled at my selfishness, and now desperately worried about his safety. On Monday I heard he was safe and well and had just been delayed in travelling for many days, and was now involved in the international relief effort. I still feel ashamed of myself.

Aspects of building capacity?

In this section, I draw on elements of the project objectives to discuss different facets of my relationship with IMS. It should be understood that these are personal reflections that extend beyond the boundaries of the project, in time, place and structure. The sections are intended as a guide to key activities and this should not be seen as a project evaluation of INSPIRE.

Develop the existing relationship between SBS and IMS

The initial relationship began from an MoU at UoS that embraced SBS and led to my involvement initially as a split-site Ph.D. supervisor, and later as PI on INSPIRE, a joint

SBS/IMS strategic partnership. A lot of complex organisational relationships needed to inter-act to ensure success, and it is the nature of organisational life that people and projects move on. While IMS continued to send excellent Ph.D. and Masters students to SBS, the Faculty Dean, the SBS Head of School, and the Vice Chancellor involved with the establishment of the initial MoU all left within a short space of time. Organisational memories are short and the original goodwill began to fade as systemic difficulties arose such as the provision of accommodation for split-site students who were in the UK for three months, a period which did not align with either university or private providers. Of course, these factors occur in any institutional relationship, but were exacerbated in this case by the conflictual situation, which prevented the reciprocal visits to Pakistan that would have repaired and cemented the bonds. One particular issue was the speed at which a situation could flare up in Pakistan. Even video conferencing events could be disrupted as IMS closed without warning for the day if passions were high, for example around certain religious festivals. A more high profile failure was the cancellation of a seminar in Islamabad where six UK staff were expected to attend, as were a busload of participants travelling in from Peshawar about two hours' drive away. This was cancelled the day before, as riots took place in Islamabad over the 'Muhammad video' incident in 2012, where crowds stormed the supposedly secure diplo-matic enclave where the hotel and venue were located. Fires were set and tear gas was used. This disruption caused loss of money, but more importantly, 'face' and credibility for all concerned on both sides. This was a watershed moment for further development of institu-tional relations, which in my view, never recovered in terms of developing the institutional partnership. Personal relationships remain strong to this day, though this is collegial rather than institutional. In turn, I too left UoS a year ago. We persuaded the British Council to allow us to replace frequent faculty exchanges, as planned, with a one-off 'capstone' confer-ence in Dubai, that was very successful, attracting a number of participants from northern Pakistan, not just IMS academics. The MoU still pertains, but as UoS seeks to improve and maintain its high international rankings, partnerships with institutions that are lower ranked, that are more developmental in nature, are prioritised less, particularly those that have the potential for high profile failure.

Identify and explore areas for collaboration within curriculum development

Many discussions took place over curriculum and several course/module profiles provided to IMS at both Masters and Bachelors level; at the time, SBS had some well-developed programmes that were recruiting well. These were taken through IMS's validation proce-dures, but for reasons that are unclear, no actual programmes in entrepreneurship or innova-tion are recruiting under that banner. It is of course IMS's choice as to how they organise their curriculum, and the reasons are likely to just be around space and crowded programmes, rather than anything sinister. A decision to embed behaviour and thinking into existing pro-grammes rather than creating separate programmes seems most likely. An unexpected area of influence for me at this time was that I was contacted by two academics from other institutions in northern Pakistan who were also developing entrepreneurship programmes. We had many detailed discussions about how to configure material derived from Western pedagogies to suit local needs, including concepts such as Islamic finance and more discussions of individualistic versus collectivist behaviour. Again the lack of meeting people in person, *in situ*, prevents the detailed discussions that might allow these initiatives to be taken further in any form of partnership, though it seems that progress has been made in the institutions.

One of the best received elements of the INSPIRE project was a series of video-conferences aimed at Masters level and above focussing on specialist areas of research methods, including grounded theory, systems modelling and qualitative methods, alongside Ph.D. process matters such as developing research questions, aims and objectives. Staff at SBS typically ran these though we also had a contribution from Professor Robert Smith, then at The Robert Gordon University, Aberdeen. Typically, these had audiences of around 60 and supported good follow-up discussions.

Doctoral studies in the fields of innovation and sustainable entrepreneurship

A steady stream of Ph.D. students, around 10 in total, have registered at SBS, with two completions in entrepreneurship and innovation and one in corporate social responsibility. I still contribute to the supervision of three students, two on split-site agreements and one full time on secondment from IMS. The topics in questions are, legitimacy questions for NGOs supporting small business, power relations in ORICs and social enterprise in delta regions (although this latter is actually situated in Bangladesh due to circumstances surrounding a partnership with the School of Geography). The students have been able to collect good data, even in the case of Dr. Muhammad Nouman, accessing remote mining areas. He managed this through the use of enumerators and personal connections. Closer to home, the data collection activities of the students are risk-assessed by IMS.

Generally the students have a good performance record, though there are some conflict-related issues. There are many bombings and shootings in central Peshawar and its surrounds, most of which do not make the international news. Terrorist incidents such as the APS shootings referred to above are particularly traumatising, taking place in the middle-class heartlands, and being more likely to affect directly individual staff and students from IMS and their immediate families. Ph.D.s and research take a very low priority mentally when personal safety is threatened. Another less obvious effect, referred to above, is the closure of IMS for security reasons when such disturbances occur. Such closures disrupt classes that have to be rescheduled when the students return, as they are aiming at public exams where dates cannot be changed. At these times, staff can end up teaching very long hours at short notice, which again is not conducive to research. Another difficulty has occurred around publication strategies and mixed messages from the Pakistan Higher Education Council (HEC). Journal publication is directly linked to promotion, which is obviously very impor-tant for the newly qualified Ph.D.s. Back in 2011, it was necessary to just publish 10 articles in pretty much any journal. This strategy obviously favours quantity over quality. Abruptly, two years ago, the position changed to a requirement of a smaller number of articles, but from the Thompson-Reuters list, which sets the bar very high – many mid-ranking, respect-able 2 star journals (in the Association of Business Schools ranking), that might suit early career researchers, are not on it.

In the longer term, this requirement may soften, but if a student graduated in 2011 and spent a year or two writing in unranked (and at times, even disreputable, 'vanity' journals) then the moment has been missed and it becomes much harder to get into the higher ranked journals when memory of the work is fading, and the data is getting old. This loss of momen-tum affected one of my supervisions where the data was excellent, but the publication strategy followed the pattern above and I have never published anything beyond a conference paper from that Ph.D., despite the quality of the work. Nor has the student found the time to address the follow-up with the degree of mental energy necessary; this is disappointing and fuels the fears of the university managers in the UK who must meet rankings targets and thus discourage such collaborations. You can see their point! Of course, this is the issue of a country with weak institutions, rather than a conflictual situation *per se*. Despite all these difficulties, it is possible to claim that through these doctoral studies, we have created new research/evidence-based knowledge concerning the sustainability, governance, leadership and development of SMEs in Pakistan, which was one of the original INSPIRE aims. Unfortunately it has not had the international audience that it deserved, beyond conferences (although I did provide a TEDx Southampton talk on the project overall). Of course, other supervisors may have had a different trajectory; the matter is very time- and individual-sensitive. The most competent individuals who might be expected to publish at the highest levels tend to be the ones who get most loaded down with other administrative, teaching and developmental activities. In fact, my proposed co-author pulled out of writing this book chapter for reasons of workload related to APS disruption and the view that book chapters are now worthless. I am fortunate in being able to enjoy this luxury.

Facilitate relationships between HEIs, industry, and relevant governmental organisations

This is difficult to assess in the absence of travel to the region, and it is clear that the contribution here is weak. I personally have met and interacted with many members of the Pakistani British Council, HEC, SMEDA and the KPK Women Chamber of Commerce. The successful completion of the INSPIRE project created good networks and relationships at least at that level. It seems optimistic to conclude that we facilitated outreach to improve performance, management practice of SMEs and enhance their relationships with HEIs in the region.

Conclusions

From the above analysis we can conclude that

1. Build capacity in entrepreneurship and innovation through a cluster of academics in IMS who have strong research-based knowledge, in relation to the wider ecosystem
2. Maintain and develop capacity through an ongoing network of Ph.D. students with a commonality of experience and thus stronger network bonds than might be expected
3. Initiate and engage a wider academic network through the Dubai conference
4. Engage with a large number of Masters and above staff and students through the medium of videoconferencing, building research methods capacity
5. At least influence curriculum development, in IMS and beyond
6. Disseminate positive messages from the region internationally; in several informal conversations, I was told that having managed to complete the INSPIRE project with at least some degree of success, showing that it could be done, was my most impactful contribution in terms of capacity development.
7. Encourage ongoing relations with the British Council, supporting the valuable work that they do in the region.

Of course, any meaningful reflection must be critical, and there have been negative aspects too; some of these difficulties are actually related to the issues that might face anyone working with a developing country. In the list below, I focus on conflict-related concerns:

1. The lack of travel due to the security situation has marred every aspect of the relationship and my initial reason for taking up this strand of work. I did manage to get out to Islamabad for a research conference, staying in security-cleared buildings; though I have to say I was still anxious when travelling around the city, due to certain comments relating to the fact that we had a veneer of security, rather than actual security. My continued absence, though readily explained, may not be readily understood by all – nuances of university insurance policy are not obvious, and Pakistan colleagues do see a few Westerners around – so if they can make it, why not I? Of course I could go on holiday there and avoid the issue altogether, but then that is bringing a security issue into the homes of friends and I could not in all conscience do that. Even staying in security-cleared buildings has its dangers – the Islamabad Marriott was bombed in 2008, and the sister hotel of the flagship Islamabad Serena in Kabul suffered a shooting attack. Plus, living in a security enclave, however beautiful – and it was beautiful – does not give access to daily life in Pakistan. So, one might ask, why take the risk?

2. The turbulent situation impacts across any planning, and it is easy to lose confidence and money in continuing to try to set up events and contacts. The temptation then, particularly if you are confined to hotels anyway, is to just go somewhere else, like Dubai, or some other middle ground. This does enable contact and progress – at least at a distance – but fails to connect 'on the ground' in Pakistan.

3. There is a personal cost to promoting positive messages about Pakistan. At various times, I have been accused of:

   a. Promoting terrorism, as if saying anything positive at all is evidence of being a dupe, or a 'useful idiot'
   b. Supporting gender imbalance; of course, many of my closer colleagues are men, but some are women. IMS has a good gender balance and the videoconferences often had around 40–50 per cent attendance by women.
   c. Supporting middle-class hegemony in the region; this may indeed be true, but the alternative would be not to act at all
   d. Having colonial aspirations; I try not to, through engaging where possible with local cultural needs, such as influencing the curriculum to reflect the local context.

Beyond those concerns, the greatest criticism of course comes from HE managers in the UK who regret, on my behalf, the amount of time spent on what might seem to them to be a quixotic endeavour yielding little further ongoing funding or research ranking benefits.

In writing this chapter, I have added to the small amount of literature on the development of entrepreneurship education capacity in KPK and north-western Pakistan. More importantly, I have perhaps added something to the understanding of the difficulties of HE project management in conflict-ridden regions. The writing of the chapter has been an almost cathartic experience trying to summarise an emotional roller-coaster that has impacted me more at the personal level than any other, and will stay with me always. Longer term, what will be the impact? That will be determined by what lies in the future for this troubled part of the world with so many riches and wonderful people. When people ask me why I bother, I come back to the opening sentence of this chapter, why as academics do we do what we do? I described a deep-seated emotional pull; I then recalled a more rational intention to help through development of SMEs and the local economy. I am left with the feeling that all I have really done is to create some positive interactions between individuals who tell me that I will always be their friend, and of course, they will be mine. An infinitesimally small contribution. Maybe peace is made up of enough people doing that.

References

Brück, T., Haisten-DeNew, J.B. and Zimmermann, K.F. (2006). Creating low-skilled jobs by subsidizing market contracted household work. *Applied Economics*, 38(4), 899–911.

Brush, C.G., Carter, N.M., Greene, P.G., Hart, M.M. and Gatewood, E. (2002). The role of social capital and gender in linking financial suppliers and entrepreneurial firms: a framework for future research. *Venture Capital*, 4(4), 305–323.

Chemin, M. (2010). Entrepreneurship in Pakistan: government policy on SMEs, environment for entrepreneurship, internationalisation of entrepreneurs and SMEs. *International Journal of Business and Globalisation*, 5(3), 238–247.

Dionco-Adetayo, E.A., Makinde, J.T. and Adetayo, J.O. (2005). *Evaluation of Policy Implementation in Women Entrepreneurship Development*. Ecevit, Yıldız. 2007.

Khan, I.M. (2011). *Entrepreneurship Education: Emerging Trends and Issues in Developing Countries*, Uluslararas› Yükseköretim Kongresi: Yeni Yönelifller ve Sorunlar (UYK-2011), 27–29 May 2011, Istanbul; 2. Cilt/Bölüm VIII/Sayfa, 742–750.

Roomi, M.A. And Harrison, P. (2010). Behind the veil: women-only entrepreneurship training in Pakistan. *International Journal of Gender and Entrepreneurship*, 2(2), 150–172.

Ul Haque, N. (2007). Entrepreneurship in Pakistan, PIDE Working Papers 2007: 29.

34

ENTREPRENEURSHIP EDUCATION IN CAMEROON MATTERS

Reorganizing the teaching of the subject

A.A. Ndedi

Introduction

The promotion of entrepreneurship education in Cameroon has not played an important role in the discussion on education or on entrepreneurship since the early years of the teaching of the subject in national higher learning institutions. International institutions such as The African Development Bank (ADB), UNESCO and the World Bank have commissioned various studies aimed at identifying and investigating provisions for the integration of entrepreneurship training in the technical higher educational system. At the same time, some attempts have also been made to promote technology transfer and regional innovation. The education and the training of students in the various stages of entrepreneurship is a key aspect of the main areas of intervention including the creation and development of enterprises, access to finance, the regulatory framework, and governance (Kiggundu, 2002). A great number of studies have focused on technical and vocational training in selected countries as well as the promotion of entrepreneurial activities for the formal and informal sectors of the economy (McGrath and King, 1999). Most of these studies have approached entrepreneurship education from multi-levels of analysis aimed at fostering the creation and development of small-scale businesses among various economic sectors including farmers, artisans, small food producers, rural mineworkers, and vendors. The main objective of this chapter is twofold:

- To further investigate the impact of entrepreneurship education in Cameroon from a survey of various stakeholders involved in entrepreneurship training;
- To propose a road map on effective entrepreneurship education and training in Cameroon.

Entrepreneurship training

According to Nieman (2000), there exists confusion between entrepreneurship training and small business training. All business owners may not necessarily be entrepreneurs. Significant numbers of small businesses are started as a means to survive, therefore, referred to as survivalist entrepreneurs. The word entrepreneurship is derived from the French *entreprendre*, meaning to undertake, to pursue opportunities, to fulfil needs and wants through innovation; this may include starting businesses inside or outside an established organization. The dictionary definition of entrepreneur is one who undertakes to organize, manage, and assume the risks of a business enterprise. Thus, the entrepreneur is someone who undertakes to accomplish, to make things happen, and does so. As a consequence, the entrepreneur disturbs the status quo and may thus be regarded as a change agent. In such a capacity, he or she does not just work for him or herself in a small firm but may be employed in a large organization (Kirby, 2002). The entrepreneur is somebody who can see an opportunity and exploit it. Even during times of economic depression, real entrepreneurs will always find a use for their skills. According to Timmons (1994), entrepreneurship refers to an individual's ability to turn ideas into action and is therefore a key competence for all, helping young people to be more creative and self-confident in whatever they undertake.

In simple terms, Antonites (2003) and Ndedi (2011) define an entrepreneur as an individual with the potential to create a vision from virtually nothing. Timmons (1994, 7) regards the process of entrepreneurship as creating and building something of value from practically nothing; a human creative act. It involves finding personal energy by initiating and building an enterprise or organization, rather than by just watching, analyzing, or describing one. It requires vision and passion, commitment, and motivation to transmit this vision to other stakeholders. In the view of other scholars in the field, entrepreneurship can be defined as follows. Entrepreneurship requires a willingness to take calculated risks, both personal (time, intellectual) and financial, and then doing everything possible to fulfil one's goals and objectives. It also involves building a team of people with complementary needed skills and talents; sensing and grasping an opportunity where others see failure, chaos, contradiction, and confusion; and gathering and controlling resources to pursue the opportunity, making sure that the venture does not run out of finance when it needs it most (Timmons, 1994; Van Aardt et al., 2002).

According to Davies (2001), to introduce entrepreneurship as a discipline especially in tertiary institutions is problematic due to different mindsets, funding mechanisms, and confusion between entrepreneurship training and the creation of small business managers. The vast majority of academic departments do not offer entrepreneurship training; it is packaged as part of other business programs. SMME research output is also very low, with very little if any on entrepreneurship. Research is required to document the training programs offered and the effectiveness of these programs offered.

Entrepreneurship in education includes development both of personal qualities and attitudes and of formal knowledge and skills that will give students competence in entrepreneurship. Personal qualities and attitudes increase the probability of a person seeing opportunities and doing something to transform them into reality. Work on entrepreneurship in education must primarily place emphasis on the development of personal qualities and attitudes. In that way a basis is laid for later utilization of knowledge and skills in active value creation (Ndedi and Ijeoma, 2008). Knowledge and skills concerning the establishment of a new enterprise, and concerning successful development of an idea into a practical, goal-oriented enterprise, are required.

According to ODEP (2009), in order to be able to concentrate on the objectives of entrepreneurship in the education system, there are several factors that apply to all levels of the education system:

- Entrepreneurship as an integrated part of instruction: Entrepreneurship must be defined as an objective in education, and be included in the instruction strategy.

- Collaboration with the local community: Instruction in entrepreneurship requires close collaboration between schools and the local business and social sector. A need, therefore, exists for more arenas for contact between educational institutions and various players in society. In such arenas educational institutions and the local social and business sectors will get to know one another better, and cultural barriers may be dismantled.
- This will result in mutual benefit inasmuch as it will increase the quality and relevance of education and strengthen recruitment to the local business sector and development of competence.
- Teachers' competence: Teachers are important role models. A positive attitude among young people in schools toward entrepreneurship, innovation, and reorientation requires that teachers have knowledge of this. It is therefore important to focus on entrepreneurship in teacher training, and also provide courses in competence development to working teachers.
- The attitudes of school-owners and school managers: School-owners must follow up the focus on entrepreneurship in curricula and management documents, and build competence and insight among school managers.
- Educational institutions should be given legitimacy and motivation to work on entrepreneurship. School managers must be able to follow up, encourage, and motivate teachers to be good role models and disseminators of knowledge. Both school-owners and school managers must take the initiative in collaborating with the business sector and other agencies in the municipality.

In summary, entrepreneurship education seeks to prepare people, particularly youth, to be responsible enterprising individuals who become entrepreneurs or entrepreneurial thinkers by immersing them in real-life learning experiences where they can take risks, manage the results, and learn from the outcomes (ODEP, 2009).

Entrepreneurship education seeks to provide students with the knowledge, skills, and motivation to encourage entrepreneurial success in a variety of settings. Variations of entrepreneurship education are offered at all levels of schooling through to graduate university programs. What makes entrepreneurship education distinctive is its focus on the realization of opportunity, whereas management education is focused on the best way to operate within existing hierarchies. Both approaches share an interest in achieving "profit" in some form (which in non-profit organizations or government can take the form of increased services or decreased cost or increased responsiveness to the customer/citizen/client).

As for entrepreneur training, it is designed to teach the skills and knowledge that a potential individual needs to know before embarking on a new business venture. While the program may not guarantee success, it should enable the future entrepreneur to avoid more of the pitfalls awaiting him or her than a person who has not received any training. Entrepreneurship training may be initially perceived as a cost, in terms of time and money. However, future rewards can erase all these expenses.

Advantages of entrepreneurship education

Through entrepreneurship education, young people learn organizational skills, including time management, leadership development, and interpersonal skills, all of which are highly transferable skills sought by employers. According to NEPAD (2011), other positive outcomes include:

- improved academic performance, school attendance, and educational attainment
- increased problem-solving and decision-making abilities
- improved interpersonal relationships, teamwork, money management, and public speaking skills
- job readiness
- enhanced social psychological development (self-esteem, ego development, self-efficacy), and perceived improved health status

Additional research commissioned by the same Non Profit Organisation (NPO) for Teaching Entrepreneurship to evaluate the effectiveness and impact of its programs found that when youth participated in entrepreneurship programs:

- interest in attending college increased at about 75 percent
- occupational aspirations increased 60 percent
- independent reading increased 10 percent
- leadership behavior increased 15 percent
- belief that attaining one's goals is within one's control (locus of control) increased.

Benefits of entrepreneurship education

Research regarding the impact of entrepreneurship education on youth shows the following benefits: namely the opportunity for work-based experiences, the opportunity to exercise leadership and develop interpersonal skills, and finally the opportunity to develop planning, financial literacy, and financial management skills:

Opportunity for work-based experiences

Work experiences for youth with disabilities during high school, both paid and unpaid, help them acquire jobs at higher wages after they graduate. Also, students who participate in occupational education and special education in integrated settings are more likely to be competitively employed than students who have not participated in such activities.

Opportunity to exercise leadership and develop interpersonal skills

By launching a small business or school-based enterprise, youth with disabilities can lead and experience different roles. In addition, they learn to communicate their ideas and influence others effectively through the development of self-advocacy and conflict resolution skills. Moreover, they learn how to become team players, and to engage in problem solving and critical thinking—skills valued highly by employers in the competitive workplace of the twenty-first century. Mentors, including peer mentors both with and without disabilities, can assist the youth in developing these competencies.

Opportunity to develop planning, financial literacy, and money management skills

The ability to set goals and to manage time, money, and other resources are important entrepreneurship skills which are useful in any workplace. For youth with disabilities, learning about financial planning, including knowledge about available work incentives is critical for budding entrepreneurs with disabilities who are currently receiving cash benefits from the Supplemental Security Income Program (SSI).

Data collection and methodology

The approach used to collect data for the chapter was twofold; first desk research was conducted on selected work both local and international in the area of entrepreneurial education. This was done to select best practices in entrepreneurship education programs aimed at developing entrepreneurs. The second source of information was collected from empirical investigations on the impact made by the various programs for supporting small, medium and micro enterprises (SMEs).

A tool used during this research in reviewing entrepreneurial education programs is suggested by Fayolle (1999). The tool identifies three critical areas or stages crucial for entrepreneurial development. The same tool gave the results that are going to be developed in the next section. During the empirical research, this tool was used on the selected list of institutions. The institutions were obtained from the Cameroonian Ministry of Higher Education (MINESUP) website, and an in-depth search of other websites. Based on the fact that entrepreneurship education has been intensely analyzed in the context of South African Colleges and Universities (Co and Mitchell, 2006), the research was just a duplication of these previous studies conducted in that country. Many institutions were taken into account for the purpose of this study. Originally, four colleges and universities from about nine that are conducting courses in entrepreneurship were considered in the study. Only four institutions out of nine institutions (44 percent) originally assessed had to be taken out of the study for the following reasons: websites were not accessible; course catalog was unavailable online; data were not sufficient to determine the existence of an entrepreneurship course; data were not available, and officials did not want to be associated to the research. Data of the study were obtained from the remaining five colleges and universities with available online course catalogs. This group represents 40 percent of the whole population. In this study, we broke down the sample into four categories: age, ownership, primary focus of institutions of higher education, and location of entrepreneurship courses.

In the first group, there were managers of recruitment agencies representing 30 percent of the whole population under study. The main question raised with them is whether an entrepreneurial background of a candidate influences their decision during the recruitment selection. Finally, decision makers were part of the sample, representing 30 percent of the whole population.

Findings and discussion

If entrepreneurship is understood to be based on the needed behavioral patterns which are influenced by social, economic, and psychodynamic forces, any attempts aimed at supporting entrepreneurs should recognize these forces and develop effective interventions to increase the total entrepreneurial activity in South Africa (Bbenkele and Ndedi, 2010). In this research, it is understood that entrepreneurial education should be underpinned in the learnerships and the structured learning programs offered by these higher learning institutions. To some extent, new venture creation or entrepreneurship are interchangeably used during the whole discussion. In terms of challenges faced in implementing the skills development programs, the results show a number of issues raised:

- 75 percent said that entrepreneurship training has no real impact on them regarding their entrepreneurial posture or orientation in business creation.
- 40 percent saw no challenges in implementing skills development programs.

- 60 percent of learners said that they are not comfortable with current entrepreneurship trainers and there is lack of roles models.
- 15 percent mention cost factors as an impediment. These costs related to training staff who would then leave the firm or become too expensive to retain; too small to do training (time) and to bear the administrative burdens.
- With industry manuals not available, firms are not sure of courses to put staff on. It was also pointed out that some of the unit standards are not applicable to the industry (11 percent).
- 20 percent reported that in some cases trainees are not interested in being trained.
- 10 percent mentioned problems of company culture, lack of management support, organizational demands, and cultural issues as problems.
- Almost all recruitment agencies said a candidate with a background in entrepreneurship does not influence their decision during the recruitment process.

Recommendations and conclusion

Therefore, the real challenge encountered during this research is to build inter-disciplinary approaches, making entrepreneurship education accessible to all students, and where appropriate creating teams for the development and exploitation of business ideas, mixing students from technical and business studies; thus with different backgrounds.

Innovation and effectiveness stem primarily from action-oriented and student-inclusive teaching forms, teaching students "how to" so that they can understand the more theoretical aspects more easily, and pushing them into action. This approach needs learners and capabilities necessary to achieve these goals. Further, educators should be to some extent entrepreneurs themselves, building their input on real-life experiences. There is a need to cross the university boundaries and explore the world outside with teaching that is very different from the traditional teaching experience in higher education. Finally, considering educators, they should have a background in academia, and recent experience in business, such as in consulting for, or initiating, entrepreneurial initiatives. Ideally they should maintain strong personal links with the business sector. The best professors are teachers who have the required teaching competences as well as real professional experience in the private sector. For those with no experience in the private sector, specific teaching modules should be integrated into the curriculum of future professors, such as "How to devise and teach a case study."

Another recommendation arising from this research is the need to support students' business ideas. A distinction needs to be made between awareness raising and education, and actual business support. An entrepreneurial venture starts with opportunity recognition. The current way of teaching must focus primarily on building awareness (opportunity recognition), and not on offering education programs, courses and activities; because the emphasis is on creating the entrepreneurial mindsets and capacity of learners. Support for university spin-offs is a vast and complex issue, for which a specific think tank needs to be created for the fostering of these spin-offs. Moreover, the concept of innovative spin-offs is not particularly relevant for businesses started by students, who do not have formal links with the university. It seems therefore more appropriate to speak of innovative, knowledge-based businesses launched by students and university graduates. Such students would benefit from dedicated advisory and support programs, like those from the Ministries of Agriculture, Innovation and Small and Medium Enterprises.

In summary, an appropriate scheme of what needs to be done has been suggested in terms of cultivating an entrepreneurial spirit providing training and concentrating efforts on supporting the growth of new ventures. Most appropriate institutions and what needs to be concentrated on have been identified in the suggested model. The model is drafted along the following lines.

In universities, courses in entrepreneurship must be implemented at all levels and in all fields. The course "entrepreneurship" focusing on the management of creativity and innovation develops the nature of creativity and innovation, and how entrepreneurship involves the ability to identify a market opportunity based on new ideas. The course may assist the student to recognize any opportunity around him. However, the courses on Entrepreneurship and New Venture Creation are intended to build personal appreciation for the challenges and rewards of entrepreneurship; and to foster continued development of venture ideas, suitable as career entry options or for investments (Löwegren, 2006). A social sciences or engineering student needs the same entrepreneurial skills as the business student; the same with the medical doctor student. A business plan is needed to open a clinic or a law firm. Opportunity recognition is important not only for business students, but to all those who are willing to embark on any entrepreneurial activities.

This chapter concludes that Cameroon has established well-intentioned government departments and agencies, most of them attached to the Ministry of Small and Medium Enterprises. However, very little coordination has taken place and worse is the fact that entrepreneurial development has been overshadowed by skills development. This study concludes that the government through its Ministry of Small and Medium Enterprises needs to re-examine their role to take up the challenge of developing entrepreneurs and collaborating with other government ministries to provide the needed support services.

References

Antonites, A. J. (2003). An action learning approach to entrepreneurial creativity, innovation and opportunity finding. Unpublished D.Com. Business Management thesis. Pretoria: University of Pretoria.

Bbenkele, E. K. and Ndedi, A. A. (2010). Fostering entrepreneurship education in South Africa: the role of Sector Education Training Authorities (SETA). African Entrepreneurship in Global Contexts. Retrieved from www/slideshare.net/alain. ndedi/entrepreneurship. Accessed in December 15, 2010.

Co, M. J. and Mitchell, B. (2006). Entrepreneurship education in South Africa. *Education + Training*, 48(5), 348–359.

Davies, T. A. (2001). *Entrepreneurship development in South Africa: redefining the role of tertiary institutions in a reconfigured higher education system.* Cape Town: Natal Technikon.

Fayolle, A. (1999). L'enseignement de l'entrepreneuriat dans les universités françaises: analyse de l'existant et propositions pour en faciliter le développement, Ministry for National Education, Research y Technology (MENRT), París.

Kiggundu, E. (2007). Teaching practice in the Greater Vaal Triangle Area: the student teachers experience. *Journal of College Teaching and Learning*, 4(6), 25-35.

Kiggundu, M. N. (2002). Entrepreneurs and entrepreneurship in Africa: What is known and what needs to be done. *Journal of Developmental Entrepreneurship*, October 2002. Retrieved from http://findarticles.com/p/articles/mi_qa3906/is_200210/ai_n9100245. Accessed on March 10, 2015.

Kirby, D, A. (2004). Entrepreneurship education: can business schools meet the challenge? *Education + Training*, 46(8/9), 510-519

Löwegren, M. (2006). Reflection within Entrepreneurship Education – Using Learning Logs. Paper presented at the 16th Internationalizing Entrepreneurship Education and Training Conference, July 2006, Sao Paolo, Brazil.

McGrath S. and King, K. (1999). Learning to grow? The importance of education and training for small and micro-enterprise development. In Kenneth King and Simon McGrath (Eds.), *Enterprise in*

Africa: between poverty and growth. London: Intermediate Technology Development Group Publishing, 246–249.

Ndedi, A A. (2011). *An analysis of corporate entrepreneurship within an advertising organisation*. Saurbrücken: Lambert Academic Publishing.

Ndedi, A. A. and Ijeoma, E. O. C. (2008). Addressing the problem of graduate unemployment in South Africa: the roles of tertiary institutions. Paper presented during the Ronald H. Brown Institute for Sub-Saharan Africa conference in Addis Ababa, Ethiopia, August 20–22, 2008.

NEPAD (2011). Logic Models and Outcomes for Youth Entrepreneurship Programs in Africa. Report to the DC Children and Youth Investment Trust Corporation. Midrand: NEPAD Agency.

Nieman, G. (2000). *Training in entrepreneurship and small business enterprises in South Africa: a situational analysis*. South Africa: University of Pretoria.

ODEP. (2009). Encouraging future innovation: youth entrepreneurship education. Available at http://www.dol.gov/odep/pubs/fact/entrepreneurship.htm Accessed on April 10, 2015.

Timmons, J. A. (1994). *New venture creation: entrepreneurship for the 21st century*. Burr Ridge, IL: Irwin, 7–8.

Van Aardt, I., Van Aardt, C. and Bezuidenhout, S. (2002). *Entrepreneurship and New Venture Management*. Oxford: Oxford University Press.

35

AN EVALUATION OF THE IMPACT OF ENTREPRENEURSHIP EDUCATION ON THE ENTREPRENEURSHIP INTENTIONS IN THE ALBANIAN LATE TRANSITION CONTEXT

Elvisa Drishti, Drita Kruja and Mario Curcija

Introduction

The investigation of entrepreneurship behaviour is motivated by the desire to boost economic performance (Audretsch and Keilbatch, 2004; Van Praag and Versloot, 2007). Whereas in classical economic theory only labour and capital were considered as key factors of production, awareness of the importance of entrepreneurial capital with respect to economic performance dates back to the beginning of the twentieth century (Schumpeter 2008) (Baumol, 1968; Foster, 1984; Lewis, 1955). Given its particular prominence in the last two decades, entrepreneurship capital has been attributed the 'factor of production' status, yielding as a result a growing body of literature and being distinguished as one of the most important aspects of modern economic theory (Matlay, 2005).

Entrepreneurship capital is accrued whenever there is an increased attractiveness towards the self-employment option related with the intention to set up a new venture which clearly manifests itself in a higher incidence of entrepreneurship behaviour amongst a nation's population. According to Gartner and Carter (2003) entrepreneurship behaviour involves those individuals' activities who are associated with the creation of new organizations as a definitive and intentional action (Audretsch and Keilbatch, 2004). The major strand of research in entrepreneurship psychology is accomplished throughout the lenses of the cognitive approach which extensively calls on entrepreneurial intentions (EIs) to predict and explain such behaviour therefore positioning EIs as a powerful theoretical tool (Omorede et al., 2014; Shaver, 2003) that can be applied to this field.

Recent systematic literature reviews of EIs' studies (Linan and Fayolle, 2015) and of entrepreneurship education (Lorze et al., 2013) reveal that the most used intention-based frameworks are: (i) the theory of planned behaviour (TPB) (Ajzen, 1991) which proposes that behaviour is explained by intentions, while intentions are explained by attitudes (personal attitudes, perceived social norms, and perceived behaviour control or self-efficacy

[Bandura, 1997]), and (ii) the Entrepreneurial Event Model (EEM) (Shapero and Sokol, 1982) which suggests that EIs are directly influenced by perceived desirability and feasibility. Taking into consideration the resemblance of TPB and EEM, the authors of this study will employ an integration of both these models, namely the Entrepreneurial Intention Model (EIM) (Linan, 2004) which reconfirms EIs as the best and immediate predictor of entrepreneurial behaviour. Notwithstanding the fact that their initial objective is to predict entrepreneurial behaviour, Fayolle and Gailly (2015) argue that both these intention models, but in particular TPB, can also be used as assessment tools of the impact of entrepreneurship education. Analogously, Fayolle et al. (2006), Fayolle and Degeorge (2006) and Hannan et al. (2006) agree that both frameworks are suitable for the evaluation of Entrepreneurship Education Programs (EEP).

The study is concentrated in Albania. The country still suffers a severe deficiency in terms of entrepreneurial culture that is perhaps partly attributed to the previous Marxist-Leninist system based solely upon centralized decision making and control. On the one hand, as Matlay (2001: 379) suggests, 'the attitudes inherited from a half century of one-party domination proved more detrimental to socio-economic change and development than most observers predicted in the euphoric aftermath of the Communist collapse.' On the other hand, we also believe that entrepreneurial education has a share in improving this matter. Knight (1987) suggests that entrepreneurship education provided in business schools will have a vital effect on the number and the quality of graduate entrepreneurs entering an economy. As a late transition nation going through the first stages of capitalism, the fostering of entrepreneurship education in Albania is mainly provided in business schools but as Umas and Mets (2010) argue, entrepreneurship education offered in higher educational institutions in post-communist nations is primarily taught in classrooms and lacks practice-orientation.

Therefore, considering entrepreneurship education as an exogenous factor (Souitaris et al., 2007), the primary scope of this study is to provide a rigorous assessment of whether and to what extent entrepreneurial education affects the EIs of the new generations of would-be entrepreneurs in Albania. In other words, it sets out to evaluate the impact that EEPs have on students' EIs through the TPB's antecedents in order to derive applicable recommendations for the educators and policy makers with the purpose of emphasizing the nature of corrective actions to be taken in order to increase the engagement of universities and entrepreneurship education with respect to economic growth contribution (European Commision, 2006).

Entrepreneurship and entrepreneurial education in Albania

The EU member states have recognized the necessity to insert entrepreneurial education in all sectors of education including non-formal learning (European Commision, 2013) and in particular, given the post-crisis events, actions are being taken to implement inclusive entrepreneurship in Europe (OECD/European Union, 2014). A similar concern has been expressed in less developed European countries, such as the post-communist ones sometimes labelled as the late transition countries. Albania, as a late transition country, experienced the most severe and long-lasting communist regime in Europe where entrepreneurial activities were suppressed for almost 50 years. In the case of a developing nation, there should be an encouragement of new entrepreneurs to search for new opportunities and take the risk of a start-up (Lewis, 1955). Mitra and Matlay (2004) argue that much of the new thinking and hopes for economic regeneration in Central and Eastern Europe have centred on entrepreneurship and small business development.

In 2014, Albania received EU candidate country status and in order to catch up with other developed countries, public policy has called on entrepreneurial education to pave the path towards the EU requirements of the 'Entrepreneurship 2020 Action Plan' (Ministry of Education and Sports, 2014). For instance, since 2003, within the framework of the European Charter of Small Enterprises membership and Oslo Agenda for Entrepreneurship Education, actions have been taken in entrepreneurship policies amongst which the first goal of Education and Training for Entrepreneurship has been emphasized in order to nurture the entrepreneurial spirit and skills throughout the education system and promote the entrepreneurial efforts of young entrepreneurs-to-be (OECD, 2007). Moreover, since 2009, Albania is member of South East European Centre for Entrepreneurial Learning, a non-profit institution supported by the European Commission, and recently in January 2015 joined the EU programme COSME, a financial instrument created by the European Union and the European Commission to assist SMEs of EU member and candidate countries.

Tackling the issues associated with the newly established entrepreneurial sector in the context of post-communist economies of Poland, Czech Republic and Hungary, Winecki (2003) argued that entrepreneurial activity usually has been initiated by the privatization and spin-offs of large firms which led to a decentralization of the economic production from the state-owned factories to a larger number of small firms. In a broad sense this is the case for all post-communist countries. However, each country should be addressed in an individualized way (Umas and Mets, 2010) because the enterprise and entrepreneurship developments in post-communist nations have undergone their own individual 'brand' of transition (Matlay, 2001) leading to different results (Smallbone and Welter, 2001; Berkowitz and Jackson, 2006). Therefore a summary of the distinctive post-communist developments in Albania is provided below:

- *Political* – In Albania, after the collapse of the communist regime, the newly elected democratic government, in collaboration with and following the recommendations of international institutions such as the International Monetary Fund and the World Bank (Blejer, 1992; Pano, 2001) undertook reforms towards the liberalization, deregulation, privatization, and the reduction of subsidies to public enterprises.
- *Socio-Economical* – The immediate effect during 1990–1992 was the contraction of the production activity by about 30–40 per cent while unemployment followed by increasing up to 27 per cent. The demand for entrepreneurial skills and the deficiencies inherent in the new labour markets exposed post-communist Albania to external shocks. Presumably high unemployment is considered as one of the main push factors of entrepreneurship behaviour and as EEM suggests, it represents one of the major negative disruptions in a person's everyday life that is highly correlated to the new-venture creation. The absence of other options led to the consideration of self-employment hence making it the main driver of new venture creation. As a result, in the case of Albania, entrepreneurship was considered a necessity (Audretsch, 2001; Carree, 2006; Thurik, 2014). On the other hand, lack of the rule of law, problems with property rights, an ever-rising informal economy and a massive and uncontrolled internal migration persist to this day and impose negative bearings on entrepreneurship.
- *Cultural* – Referring to cultural dimensions (Hofstede, 2001), the Albanian national culture is collectivist in nature and persuaded by uncertainty avoidance. The South-Eastern European countries fall under the entrepreneurial regional regime characterized by low propensity to start a business, causing low incidence of local entrepreneurship behaviour. The entrepreneurial spirit lies dormant in Europe when compared with the

USA (Blanchflower et al., 2001) which as regional difference affects the propensity to start a business (Audretsch et al., 2012).

In conclusion, after the 1990s, the upsurge of newly created ventures which contributed to the capitalization and democratization of the society and fostered the first glimpses of the 'entrepreneurial spirit' (Parker, 2004) was driven by the historical background associated with political, socio-economical and cultural differences generating a unique entrepreneurial activity pathway that excludes the possibility of a positive approach to entrepreneurship (Mitra and Matlay, 2004).

Entrepreneurship education, as distinct from general education, in particular has been widely researched in terms of effects on entrepreneurial activity in developed countries as well as in developing countries. Of particular interest to this study are the studies in post-communist countries (Solesvnik et al., 2012, 2013; Umas and Mets, 2010; Varblane and Mets, 2010; Winecki, 2003). Like any other factor of production, entrepreneurship is scarce and the dominating belief is that increased entrepreneurial education will contribute to an increase in the quantity and quality of entrepreneurs in a given economy (Matlay, 2005). De Forest (1965) argued decades ago that the problem of a small quantity (scarcity) of entrepreneurial individuals in underdeveloped economies is in part a consequence of inferior educational facilities. For instance, Solesvik et al. (2013) found that in Ukraine, universities' business students who attended a compulsory entrepreneurship-specific course had a higher propensity to become entrepreneurs. Nevertheless, the relative importance of entrepreneurship-oriented curricula compared with the total curricula is still small in Albania. In most universities, most modules are small business-oriented and use passive teaching methods of entrepreneurship which provide little or no training in entrepreneurship. Umas and Mets (2010) mapped the entrepreneurship education delivered across 774 higher education institutions in 22 post-communist European countries and concluded that among the Southern European countries, the coverage of entrepreneurship teaching was much lower; the current number of centres of entrepreneurship in the region is small, and the research-oriented model of entrepreneurship education is used in three to five institutions only; the best coverage of entrepreneurship-oriented teaching among the countries in the region was in Slovenia and Croatia, followed by the Baltic countries, the Czech Republic and Slovakia.

Theoretical development and hypotheses

A substantial number of studies in social psychology use intention to predict behaviour, especially if this behaviour is rare, hard to observe, and evolves with irregular time lags (MacMillan and Katz, 1992). For a person to perform certain behaviours he/she must previously have formed the intention to do so. Intention indicates a state of mind directing a person's attention (and therefore experience and action) towards a specific (goal) path in order to achieve something (means) (Bird, 1988).

Complex intentional behaviour we seek to investigate in this study is the entrepreneurial behaviour which is embedded in the profile of the (i) potential entrepreneur, a person who is aware of and interested in the option of self-employment (Linan et al., 2011) and when a personally attractive opportunity emerges he/she surfaces and takes the initiative (Krueger and Brazeal, 1994), and in that of the (ii) nascent entrepreneur, a person who is actively involved in setting up a business which he/she will own or co-own; this business has no paid salaries, wages, or any other payments to the owners for more than three months, as described by Global Entrepreneurship Monitor. According to Gartner and Carter (2003), entrepreneurship behaviour involves the activities of individuals who are linked with creating new organizations as a definitive intentional action (Audretsch and Keilbatch, 2004).

Starting up a new firm clearly falls into the category of planned behaviour, as few firms are started by accident (Autio et al., 2001). Entrepreneurship is a process that evolves with time (becoming, rather than being). Omorede et al. (2014), following the work of Shaver (2003), have found the main researched theme in entrepreneurship psychology – comprising a total number of 517 relevant entries under the cognition research approach – investigated questions concerning entrepreneurial intentions. The 'intentionality' of would-be entrepreneurs has in this sense long been stressed as an important variable in understanding the creation of new business ventures (Bird, 1988; Fayolle and Degeorge, 2006). Thompson (2009) defines individual entrepreneurial intent as a self-acknowledged conviction by a person that he/she intends to set up a new business venture and consciously plans to do so at some point in the future. In parallel with research on entrepreneurial cognition, a stream of enquiry has developed with regard to entrepreneurs' attitudes as immediate determinants of individual intentions of entrepreneurial behaviour. Within the framework of entrepreneurship, attitudes (personal attitudes, perceived social norms, and perceived behaviour control or self-efficacy) have been researched by means of famous theories and conceptual frameworks of psychology. Lorze et al. (2013) found that among quantitative studies, the vast majority used theoretical frameworks such as the theory of planned behaviour (Ajzen, 1991), the concept of self-efficacy (Bandura, 1997) and the Model of Entrepreneurial Events (Shapero and Sokol, 1982). In their systematic literature review of more recent research on EIs, Linan and Fayolle (2015) also identified the aforementioned contributions as the major strands in analyzing entrepreneurship behaviour which address the mental process initiated by attitudes and finalized with effective action.

The critical importance of EIs and the use of TPB to capture this notion was initially suggested by Krueger and Carsud (1993) and thereafter became a recognized and established theoretical anchor (Linan and Fayolle, 2015) in entrepreneurship study in Kolvereid's (1996a, 1996b) work. The contribution of TPB can be gauged under a more practical perspective as not only does it represent a suitable tool for the study of entrepreneurial behaviour but also an effective evaluation framework of the impact of EEP (Autio et al., 2001; Fayolle and Degeorge, 2006; Fayolle et al., 2006). Fayolle and Gailly (2015) argue that both intention models, but in particular TPB, can be diverted from their primary task in order to be used as assessment tools to estimate the impact of entrepreneurship education. Similarly, Hannan et al. (2006) approve that both frameworks are suitable for the evaluation of EEPs.

TPB is an expansion of the original study 'The Theory of Reasoned Action' (Ajzen and Fishbein, 1980) that has been tested and validated extensively in the field of entrepreneurship. As Linan (2004) summarizes, entrepreneurial intent can be explained by the three personality inventories: (i) personal preference or attraction towards entrepreneurship; (ii) the perceived social norms regarding that career option; and (iii) perceived entrepreneurial control or self-efficacy. Here, the concept of perceived behavioural control is considered equivalent in many aspects to the self-efficacy suggested by Bandura (1997) in 'The Theory of Social Learning and Self-efficacy'. However, Ajzen (2002) suggests that this similarity is only in terms of perceived ability to perform the (entrepreneurial) behaviour and must not be taken to infer that the performance of behaviour affords control over the attainment of the desired outcome (being able to successfully establish a new venture). In this study we will use these concepts interchangeably, nevertheless we are aware of the ongoing debates on whether to use the construct of perceived behavioural control or self-efficacy. From one perspective, perceived behavioural control is argued to be wider than self-efficacy (Ajzen, 2005) and on the other hand self-efficacy is preferred because it has a clear definition (Kolvereid and Isaksen, 2006). A very similar concept can be distinguished in the EEM (Shapero and Sokol, 1982) denoted as perceived feasibility. This is yet another intentional model that is focused in the entre-preneurship domain and emphasizes the need of a negative/positive disruption in a person's everyday life (i.e. job loss, divorce, inheritance, winning the lottery, etc.) in order for his/ her perceptions of desirability and feasibility of founding a new business to surface (Krueger and Brazeal, 1994). Perceived desirability is the personal attractiveness of starting a venture, including both intrapersonal and extrapersonal, while perceived feasibility is the degree to which one feels personally capable of starting a venture (Krueger et al., 2000).

Consequently, major overlaps of these two models are evident not only in their inclusion of the antecedent conceptually associated with perceived self-efficacy but also for the com-patibility of TPB's personal attitude and perceived social norms with the model of the entrepreneurial event's perceived desirability (Krueger and Brazeal, 1994). As Linan and Fayolle (2015: 9) argue, 'in practice sometimes these models are integrated de facto, because perceived desirability and feasibility are considered as substitutes of personal attitude and behavioural control.' In the present an integration of both these models will be used, namely the 'Entrepreneurial Intention Model' (EIM) suggested by Linan (2004) (see Figure 35.1) which reconfirms EIs as the best and immediate predictor of entrepreneurial behaviour.

What the EIM articulates is that the more favourable the attitude (towards starting a new business) and perceived social norms (with respect to this career choice) and the greater the perceived self-efficacy, the stronger the person's intention to found the new business. Even though these three antecedents comprise the explanatory variables of intention, their relative significance to the prediction of intention is not established in the model as it is expected to vary across different cases (Linan et al., 2011). Empirical studies have revealed that the three antecedents do actually account for a considerable amount of variance of intention (Armitage and Conner, 2001; Tkashev and Kolvereid, 1999; Kolvereid, 1996b) where social norms had the weakest predicting power (Autio et al., 2001; Krueger et al., 2000) often leading to an omission of this antecedent from the model (Veciana et al., 2005; Peterman and Kennedy, 2003). However, the role of social norms is found to be significant in terms of interaction

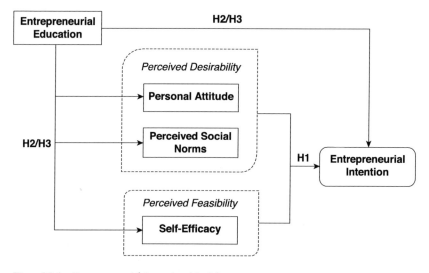

Figure 35.1   Entrepreneurial Intention Model

468

with the two other antecedents (Linan and Chen, 2009). Perceived behavioural control on the other hand emerged as the most important predictor (Autio et al., 2001).

Notwithstanding the fact that the robustness of the TPB in different settings has been confirmed cross-culturally (Linan and Fayolle, 2015), different approaches have been applied to explain entrepreneurial intention and behaviour. A number of studies suggesting that EIs are influenced by personality traits comprise a largely subscribed approach of the personality-trait theory of entrepreneurship. A more recent systematic literature review of EI studies (Linan and Fayolle, 2015) revealed that during the last decade the largest number of papers (148) addressed the personal-level variables, including gender, as the main determinants of EIs thus emphasizing a recent shift from the cognitive approach towards the personality-trait approach of entrepreneurship research. Other authors who engaged in entrepreneurship psychology reviews (Omorede et al., 2014) evidenced that the second most researched theme within the domain of entrepreneurship was with respect to personality-level variables, which comprise a relevant entry of 454 articles. The main significant variables found within the personal-level category are the *big five personality traits* (Saeed et al., 2013; Brandstatter, 2011; Zhao et al., 2010; Zhao and Seibert, 2006). Consequently, Rauch and Frese (2007) extend the breadth of coverage by including additional and more specific personality traits to agree with the aforementioned authors that the common variance of traits contributes to the prediction of entrepreneurial behaviour.

Other personal-level characteristics such as demographic characteristics (including gender) have also been pointed out as possible predictors of EIs (Teemu et al., 2014; Haus et al., 2013; Strobl et al., 2012; Mazzarol et al., 2001; Kolvereid, 1996a). The contextual factors, which in economic geography suggest that entrepreneurship is considered a regional event and that the entrepreneurial opportunities emerge from the adjacent regional environment (Feldman, 2001), have also had their share on the matter at hand (Audretsch et al., 2012; Lee et al., 2011; Enge et al., 2010; Turker and Selcuk, 2009; Veciana et al., 2005; Kristiansen and Indarti, 2004; Luthje and Franke, 2003). Yet, the explanatory power and predictive validity of these variables (personality traits, demographics and contextual factors) has been criticized as being moderate and failed to establish any strong relationships (Autio, et al., 2001; Gartner, 1989) suggesting that the cognition approach (EIs and attitudes) addressed enquiries that personality-trait approach previously failed to answer (Omorede et al., 2014) hence repositioning intentions as the most appropriate, unbiased and superior predictor of planned behaviour (Krueger et al., 2000; Lent et al., 1994; Bagozzi et al., 1989). It is argued that these factors in reality do represent a set of indirect predictors of entrepreneurial intention via their influence on the intention's antecedents (Marques et al., 2012; Wilson et al., 2007).

In this position therefore the first hypothesis is raised to test for the robustness of TPB:

H1: The more favourable the personal attitude and perceived social norms towards new venture creation and the greater the perceived self-efficacy, the stronger the student's intention to found the new venture.

Research on entrepreneurship education (the independent variable)

The belief that entrepreneurship education is linked with the creation of entrepreneurial capital is perhaps as old as the concept of entrepreneurship itself. The underlying assumption here is that entrepreneurship is a process of becoming rather than being (nurture versus nature); previous research suggests that the decision to create a new venture can be influenced by *entrepreneurial education* (TorBjorn, 2012; Von Graevenitz et al., 2010;

Franke and Luthje, 2004). More precisely, the creation of a new venture is considered as a final planned behaviour that is initiated by the entrepreneurial intention and on the other hand, entrepreneurial intention is influenced indirectly by entrepreneurial education. Pittaway and Cope (2007) in their systematic literature review of 185 academic papers focused on the effect of EEP on EIs which were published in the 1970–2004 time span, and found that entrepreneurship education generally has a positive impact on student propensity and intentionality to create a new business. This is also confirmed by Solesvik et al. (2013).

EIs can be enhanced by entrepreneurial education (Franke and Luthje, 2004). Not only does general education as an exogenous factor widely influence the students' decision process towards the creation of a new venture (Bechard and Toulouse, 1998), but studies have also shown significant positive effects of entrepreneurship education, as distinct from general education, on entrepreneurship intentions (Fayolle and Gailly, 2015; Pittaway and Cope, 2007; Souitaris et al., 2007). The major proportion of entrepreneurship education in universities is designed and delivered in business schools (Matlay, 2008) with the underlying assumption here being that entrepreneurship or at least some aspects of it can be taught. Yet the results of the reviewed studies' findings have been controversial in many aspects due to the limitations imposed by their methodological choice. As Linan and Fayolle (2015) conclude, the recent studies that use a methodology of assessing the participants' EIs ex-ante and ex-post the EEP (Shahidi, 2012) report a higher intention level due to the programme. Nevertheless, this positive impact according to Lorze et al. (2013) comprises only 31 per cent of the reviewed studies while 69 per cent relied solely on ex-post data which means that most of the research in this field is cross-sectional in nature. Moreover the majority of these studies do not involve control groups.

Similarly, a positive impact is also reported by studies in which authors have employed a control group (Pihie and Bagheri, 2009) but still there is a fallacy in terms of excluding all types of variables that might have an influence on the students' intentions towards new venture creation and self-employment throughout time but are not related to the EEPs' exposure. The former one represents the key variable whose variance needs to be estimated because otherwise the lack of a control group would lead to ambiguous findings.

Another deficiency is regarding the investigated sample which usually has comprised students who voluntarily chose to attend an entrepreneurship education programme (e.g. elective module, MBA students). This means that their propensity towards a start-up is significant even before the exposure to entrepreneurial education happens. Including only students who had willingly chosen to attend an EEP is restrictive as the findings favour entrepreneurial education (Von Graevenitz et al., 2010) due to the self-selection biases effect (Fayolle and Gailly, 2015).

Moreover, the few empirical studies that overcome at least two of these methodological insufficiencies do again report controversial finds. For instance, disagreements are raised when considering Sanchez (2013) and Byabashaija and Kotono's studies (2011) who report respective positive and moderate impacts of EEP on EIs while other authors found insignificant (Chen et al., 2013) or even a negative (Oosterbeek et al., 2010; Von Graevenitz et al., 2010) influence of entrepreneurial education on the decision to engage in a new business creation. The most instructive example perhaps refers to the most cited and referenced article (Linan and Fayolle, 2015) in the field of entrepreneurship education written by Souitaris et al. (2007) which reports no significant influence of a semester-long EEP on attitudes, perceived behavioural control and pre-venture nascency. From this perspective therefore, the effectiveness of entrepreneurial education programmes is still an under-researched topic (Zhao et al., 2005).

Exceptions perhaps can be made when considering long-term studies such as Degeorge and Fayolle (2008) in which the stability of EIs is assessed during a seven-year time horizon after the first EEP exposure, or as in the case of Liao and Gartner (2008) in which a true panel dataset with three waves of measurements was employed to evaluate new business creation efforts over a five-year time horizon for a sample of entrepreneurs who were in the process of starting businesses, which allows for the derivation of exceptions.

The aforementioned findings suggest that, positioning entrepreneurship education as an exogenous factor, the second and third hypothesis can be raised:

H2: At the end of the entrepreneurship education programme, the (average) students' intentions, personal attitudes, perceived social norms and perceived behavioural control to start a new venture are stronger than at the beginning of the programme.

H3: The greater the learning from the EEP, the higher the increase in the students' attitudes, social norms, perceived behavioural control and intention to start a new venture.

By setting out to test these hypotheses this study seeks to address the call for more hypothesis-driven impact studies and increase the rigour of entrepreneurship research by allowing for a more standardized, reliable, and focused approach to research (Lorze et al., 2013).

Methodology and methods

The quality and rigorousness in entrepreneurship research is as good as the chosen research methods and the choice of the related sample (Matlay, 2005). In terms of theoretical perspective, this study is dominated by a positivist spirit and relies heavily on a quantitative approach. This tradition is compatible with the authors' intentions to provide standardization, generalizability and replicability of results. Similar with an intervention study, this is an impact study which seeks to confirm or reject the existence of causality relationships. The proposed methodology is to capture the changes of the dependent variable – attitudes, social norms, and perceived self-efficacy, and EIs – of tertiary education-level students enrolled in business administration programmes (experimental groups), with two waves of survey data. We exploit the fact that students pursuing other programmes of study are not required to attend a compulsory EEP (control groups) to establish the much desired quasi-experimental research setting (Cohen and Manion, 1989) (Figure 35.2).

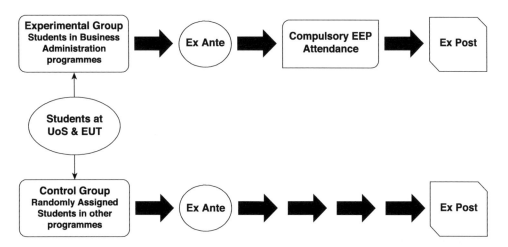

Figure 35.2   Ex-Ante/Ex-Post Control Group Design

Table 35.1 EEP Teaching Components

Component	Activities Included	UoS	EUT
Taught or theoretical part	One or more modules	X	X
Business-Planning	Business plan competitions	X	X
	Advice on developing a specific business idea	X	X
Interaction with Practice	Market-research resources		X
	Talks from practitioners	X	X
	Networking events	X	X
University Support	Space for meetings		X
	A pool of technology with commercial potential		
	Funding to student-teams		

Source: Gartner and Vesper (1994).

The independent variable therefore is the 'treatment' with the attendance of a compulsory semester-long EEP. It is important that students who have no preferences are included in the sample to avoid the self-selection problem (Fayolle and Gailly, 2015; Von Graevenitz et al., 2010). In terms of objectives of the programmes, the definition of EEP suggested by Fayolle et al. (2006: 702) was chosen that considers EEP as any pedagogical programme or process of education for entrepreneurial attitudes and skills, which involves developing certain personal qualities and is not solely focused on the immediate creation of new business. In this study the compulsory EEP is aimed at raising awareness of entrepreneurship as a potential career path that ultimately leads to self-employment. This module is only delivered as part of the business–administration curricula at the business schools of the respective universities and is delivered along 15 weeks from March to June. The applied pedagogies at both universities are compatible and offer a partial combination of the 'good practice' teaching components suggested by Gartner and Vesper (1994) (see Table 35.1). Amongst the listed activities the theoretical part delivered via classroom teaching is the main pedagogical tool.

Sample

The sampling procedure for the experimental group targeted solely students enrolled in business administration programmes at the public University of Shkodra 'Luigj Gurakuqi' and at the private European University of Tirana. The latter is a newly established university and was chosen to diminish the sampling biases (Umas and Mets, 2010) following indications that in general entrepreneurship-oriented education is much better developed in new and private universities. For the control group, we relied on a random selection of students across the campuses of both universities who were attending other programmes of study. A total of 186 valid questionnaires (from students that submitted in March and June) were collected where 106 comprised the experimental group and 80 the control group.

Table 35.2 displays the descriptive statistics of the total sample and of the experimental and control groups. This sample is representative in terms of the demographic features of the population of students registered in business-administration studies and public and private universities (Ministry of Education and Sports, 2014).

Table 35.2 Descriptive Statistics

	Total		Experimental		Control	
	N = 186		N = 106		N = 80	
	Absolute	Relative	Absolute	Relative	Absolute	Relative
Gender						
Female	96	52 percent	50	47 percent	46	57 percent
Male	90	48 percent	56	53 percent	34	43 percent
Age						
18–21	137	74 percent	69	65 percent	68	85 percent
22–25	30	16 percent	22	21 percent	8	10 percent
26–29	7	4 percent	4	4 percent	3	4 percent
30–33	4	2 percent	3	3 percent	1	1 percent
34–37	5	3 percent	5	5 percent	0	0 percent
38+	2	1 percent	2	2 percent	0	0 percent
LegalMarital Status						
Single	163	88 percent	86	81 percent	77	96 percent
Married	21	11 percent	18	17 percent	3	4 percent
Divorced	2	1 percent	2	2 percent	0	0 percent
Relationship to Head of Household						
Head of HH	4	2 percent	2	2 percent	2	3 percent
Son/Daughter	165	89 percent	88	83 percent	77	96 percent
Spouse	17	9 percent	16	15 percent	1	1 percent
Mode of attendance						
Full–time	163	88 percent	85	80 percent	78	98 percent
Part–time	23	12 percent	21	20 percent	2	2 percent
Work experience (t1)						
Yes	88	47 percent	50	47 percent	38	48 percent
No	98	53 percent	56	53 percent	42	53 percent
Self-employment experience (t1)						
Yes	38	31 percent	22	21 percent	16	20 percent
No	128	69 percent	84	79 percent	64	80 percent

Data collection method

The data collection method is the Entrepreneurial Intention Questionnaire (EIQ), developed and cross-culturally validated by Linan and Chen (2009), Linan and Chen (2006) and Linan (2005). EIQ builds on TPB's components and the choice of this standard instrument is convenient as not only does it allow for comparisons of findings but fundamentally addresses the call for more theory-driven impact studies that build on the most influential theoretical frameworks in entrepreneurship education (Lorze et al., 2013).

Whereas the demographic and human capital features are easily assessed for each individual, the measurement of TPB's personality inventories – the dependent variables comprising personal attitudes, perceived social norms, perceived self-efficacy, and EIs – as hypothetical constructs is inaccessible to direct observation, and therefore they are often collected via self-reports (Ajzen, 2005). The EIQ uses multiple items that are adjusted to 7-point Likert-type scales to directly assess each of the major TPB constructs (Ajzen, 2014).

Control variables

The subsequent control (dummy) variables were considered: (i) Whether the student had work experience at t1 as students are more inclined to discover opportunities when they already have information on the sector (Shane, 2000); (ii) Whether the student had self-employment experience at t1 as prior entrepreneurial exposure imposes more realistic perceptions of feasibility and desirability (Fayolle and Gailly, 2009; Krueger, 1993; Shapero and Sokol, 1982); and (iii) the value at t1 of TPB's antecedents and intentions, as students with higher initial values are predicted to experience a lower improvement margin (Souitaris et al., 2007).

Reliability and validity

The reliability α obtained for each of the EIQ's constructs at t1 and t2 was above 0.75. Ex-ante/ex-post study designs (Figure 35.2) offer a higher level of internal validity compared to cross-sectional ones and sampling from universities in different cities with which adds external validity to our findings. Therefore the most important validity procedure was the inclusion of the control group.

Findings

There were no significant violations of the assumptions required for the t-test, one-way ANOVA, repeated measures ANOVA, or regression analysis. The variance inflation factor values of the independent variables were lower than 5 and low bivariate correlations were present, suggesting that multicollinearity was not an issue. The findings, in general, show significant support of TPB robustness except for the social norms construct which was found non-significant in the prediction of intentions (t1: *standardized beta* = 0.066, $p > 0.05$; t2: *standardized beta* = 0.063, $p > 0.05$) (see Table 35.5). This result is compatible with the findings of Linan (2005), Fayolle and Gailly (2004), Autio et al. (2001) and Krueger et al. (2000). On the contrary, the Pearson correlation of social norms was non-significantly correlated with the respective t1 and t2 personal attitude and perceived behavioural control component which is an opposite finding compared to Linan and Chen's (2009) results where the role of social norms was found to be significant in terms of interaction with the two other antecedents. As a result, we followed the Veciana et al. (2005) and Peterman and Kennedy (2003) approach and simply omitted this component from the model. This implies that H1 is reformulated to

H1: The more favourable the *personal attitude* towards new venture creation and the greater the perceived *self-efficacy*, the stronger the student's intention to found the new venture.

The ex-ante/ex-post differences between the control and experimental group using the independent samples t-test are displayed in Table 35.3. There were no significant differences between the control and the experimental groups in the ex-ante measurement. In the ex-post, the experimental group was significantly higher than the control group in all the estimated components.

Table 35.3 Ex-Ante/Ex-Post Differences between the Control and Experimental Group

	Ex-Ante		Ex Post	
	Control 80	Experimental 106	Control 80	Experimental 106
Personal Attitude	5.62	5.75	5.59★	5.71★
Perceived Behavioural Control	4.28	4.41	4.26★	4.77★
Entrepreneurial Intentions	4.16	4.91	4.18★	5.00★

★*Significance level at 0.05*

In Table 35.4 we have summarized the descriptive statistics and Pearson correlations for the total sample. Table 35.5 shows the regression model results while Table 35.6 the one-way ANOVA results regarding the differences scores for the total sample controlling for the control versus experimental group participation. In Table 35.7 the descriptive statistics and Pearson correlations of the experimental group are displayed. Lastly, Table 35.8 displays the effect of categorical variables upon personal attitudes, perceived behavioural control, and intentions resulting from the repeated measures ANOVA for the experimental group.

Control variables

For each of the three ex-ante/ex-post variables, the t1 values had significant negative correlation with the differences (t2 − t1). For personal attitude $r = -0.469$, $p < 0.001$, for perceived behavioural control $r = -0.632$, $p < 0.001$, and for entrepreneurial intention $r = -0.506$, $p < 0.001$. These results confirmed the expected role of the initial values of TPB's antecedents, excluding social norms, and intentions as control variables (Table 35.7).

Work experience prior to the participation in EEP was correlated positively with the difference in personal attitude and perceived behavioural control (for personal attitude $r = 0.262$, $p < 0.01$, and for perceived behavioural control $r = 0.213$, $p < 0.05$) implying that these students increased their personal attitude and perceived behavioural control more in favour of new venture creation. This might be explained by the fact that, before the EEP, they had lower expectation of their success in establishing a new venture and hence lower EIs (for perceived behavioural control at t1 $r = -0.315$, $p < 0.001$ and for entrepreneurial intention at t1 $r = -0.247$, $p < 0.05$).

Table 35.4 Descriptive Statistics and Pearson Correlations of TPB Components (N = 186)

Variable	Mean	S.D	1	2	3	4	5
1. Personal Attitude (t1)	5.69	0.10					
2. Perceived Behavioural Control (t1)	4.30	1.31	.334★★				
3. Entrepreneurial Intentions (t1)	4.64	1.34	.520★★	.660★★			
4. Personal Attitude (t2)	5.58	1.15	.358★★	.294★★	.265★★		
5. Perceived Behavioural Control (t2)	4.55	1.06	.245★★	.369★★	.365★★	.314★★	
6. Entrepreneurial Intentions (t2)	4.72	1.46	.379★★	.469★★	.537★★	.619★★	.677★★

★*Significance level at 0.05*
★★*Significance level at 0.01*

Table 35.5 Regression Models of TPB Antecedents upon Intentions at Time 1 and Time 2 (N=186)

Explanatory Variables	Entrepreneurial Intentions (Model at Time 1)	Entrepreneurial Intentions (Model at Time 2)
	Standardized Coefficients	Standardized Coefficients
Personal Attitude	0.086★	0.074★
Perceived Social Norms	0.066	0.063
Perceived Behavioural Control	0.065★	0.082★
Adjusted R Square	0.473★	0.552★

★ *Significance level at 0.05*

Likewise, prior self-employment experience was correlated negative with the difference in perceived behavioural control ($r = -0.219$, $p < 0.05$) implying that students with entrepreneurial experience increased their perceived behavioural control less. This is due to the fact that these students have higher levels of initial perceived behavioural control and entrepreneurial intention already before the EEP which leaves little room for improvement after the course (for PBC $r = 0.278$, $p < 0.001$, and for EI $r = 0.245$, $p < 0.05$). The GLM procedure (Table 35.8) showed that the only significant differences in terms of TPB's components (excluding social norms) controlling for the categorical variables (work experience and self-employment experience at t1) was evidenced for the perceived behavioural control component.

Hypothesis 1: At both t1 and t2, the intention to create a new venture was positively and significantly correlated with the personal attitude favouring new venture creation (t1: $r = 0.520$, $p < 0.001$; t2: $r = 0.619$, $p < 0.001$) and to the perceived behavioural control (t1: $r = 0.534$, $p < 0.001$; t2: $r = 0.514$, $p < 0.001$) (Table 35.4). The regression models showed significant adjusted regression coefficients (t1: $R2 = 0.473$, $p < 0.05$; t2: $R2 = 0.552$, $p < 0.05$) and significant standardized coefficients for the two TPB antecedents (t1: 0.086, 0.065, $p < 0.05$; t2: 0.074, 0.082, $p < 0.05$) (Table 35.5). Therefore, Hypothesis 1 was accepted.

Hypothesis 2: For the experimental group, paired samples' t-tests (for $p < 0.05$) showed that we could accept the null hypothesis that students had equal ex-ante and ex-post means for intentions ($t = -0.902$, $p = 0.369$) and personal attitude ($t = 0.417$, $p = 0.677$) and reject it for perceived behavioural control ($t = -3.547$. $p = 0.001$). On the other hand, for the control group, t-tests showed non-significant difference between the ex-ante and the ex-post means for all the three variables. Similarly, the GLM procedure (simple time effects, Table 35.8) confirmed an insignificant difference between the ex-ante and the ex-post values for entrepreneurial intention ($F = 0.813$, $p = 0.369$) and personal attitude ($F = 0.174$, $p = 0.677$) and a significant difference for perceived behavioural control ($F = 12.58$, $p = 0.001$). The ANOVA for the whole sample (Table 35.6) showed significant association

Table 35.6 Mean Difference Values between the Experimental and Control Group (N = 186)

Difference in	F	P
Personal Attitude (t2 − t1)	0.743	0.390
Perceived Behavioural Control (t2 − t1)	4.414	0.037
Entrepreneurial Intentions (t2 − t1)	0.132	0.717

Table 35.7 Descriptive Statistics and Pearson Correlations of the Experimental Group (N = 106)

Variable	Mean	S.D	1	2	3	4	5	6	7	8	9	10	11
1. Personal Attitude (t1)	5.747	.921											
2. Perceived Behavioural Control (t1)	4.409	1.014	.359**										
3. Entrepreneurial Intentions (t1)	4.909	1.414	.574**	.697**									
4. Personal Attitude (t2)	5.706	1.006	.438**	.161	.299**								
5. Perceived Behavioural Control (t2)	4.769	.882	.301**	.402**	.351**	.399**							
6. Entrepreneurial Intentions (t2)	5.005	1.278	.455**	.431**	.673**	.635**	.620**						
7. Personal Attitude (t2 – t1)	-.041	1.025	-.469**	-.255**	-.223*	.589**	.220*	.215*					
8. Perceived Behavioural Cont. (t2– t1)	.359	1.043	-.192*	-.632**	-.382**	.266**	.455**	.106	.434**				
9. Entrepreneurial Intentions (t2 – t1)	.096	1.095	-.211*	-.398**	-.506**	.355**	.271**	.297**	.538**	.616**			
10. Entrepreneurial Education (t2 – t1)	.429	1.273	-.072	-.406**	-.322**	.089	.008	-.028	.152	.402**	.154		
11. Work Experience (t1)			-.178	-.315**	-.247*	.103	-.111	-.170	.262**	.213*	.121	.255**	
12. Self-Employment Experience (t2)			.108	.278**	.245*	-.044	-.054	-.132	.145	-.219*	.164	.109	.181

*Significance level at 0.05
**Significance level at 0.01

Table 35.8 The Effect of Categorical Variables on Personal Attitudes, Perceived Behavioural Control and Intentions: GLM Repeated Measures ANOVA (N = 106)

	Personal Attitude			Perceived Behavioural Control			Entrepreneurial Intention		
	F	p	η^2	F	p	η^2	F	p	η^2
Time	0.174	0.677	0.002	12.583	0.001	0.107	0.813	0.369	0.008
Interaction Effects									
Time x Work Experience	4.743	0.032	0.048	7.651	0.007	0.069	1.538	0.218	0.015
Time x Self-Employment	2.012	0.159	0.021	4.925	0.029	0.045	2.589	0.111	0.027

between groups (experimental vs. control) and difference in the ex–ante/ex–post values only for perceived behavioural control ($F = 4.414$, $p = 0.037$) but not for personal attitude ($F = 0.743$, $p = 0.390$) and entrepreneurial intention ($F = 0.132$, $p = 0.717$). Therefore, we do not find support for Hypothesis 2 and reject it.

Hypothesis 3: The change in entrepreneurial education (learning) (t2 − t1) was positively and significantly correlated with the difference in perceived behavioural control ($r = 0.402$, $p < 0.001$) (Table 35.7). Therefore we found partial support for Hypothesis 3.

Discussion

This study attempted to establish whether the following statements held true for the Albanian setting: There is evidence that the theory of planned behaviour robustness and entrepreneurial education programmes have an impact on the theory of planned behaviour components for students enrolled in business administration studies. To accomplish this, we employed a quasi-experimental research design, with hypotheses founded on the components of the theory of planned behaviour.

In terms of the first statement we found support for the theory of planned behaviour robustness except for the 'perceived social norms' construct which emerged as non-significant in the prediction of intentions therefore we proceeded by simply omitting it from the analysis.

Interestingly, for the second statement the results showed that, between the two remaining components of the theory of planned behaviour only the 'before' mean values for 'perceived behavioural control' (self-efficacy) increased significantly with respect to the 'after' ones. This was also confirmed by the fact that the change in 'entrepreneurial knowledge' was positively and significantly correlated with the change in perceived behavioural control. This result is compatible with findings of Autio et al. (2001) where perceived behavioural control emerged as the most important predictor and also of Peterman and Kennedy (2003) who found a positive effect of entrepreneurship programmes on perceived feasibility for high-school students. In summary, the study illustrated that entrepreneurship education programmes contribute only to the increase in the participants' perceived ability to perform the (entrepreneurial) behaviour of starting a new venture.

The fact that there was a lack of a positive attitude towards entrepreneurial behaviour after the programme can be interpreted by the culturally determined beliefs and beliefs inherited from the Communist regime, beliefs (imposed on their children too) of poorly educated individuals who share a fatalistic view of life and prefer to have job security rather than engage in the risky endeavour of new venture creation and self-employment. This is also confirmed by the fact that students with prior work experience had lower expectation of their success in establishing a new venture and hence a lower entrepreneurial intention at the beginning of the programme. On the other hand, students with prior self-employment experience experienced a lower increase in perceived behavioural control implying that they were more self-confident even before attending the programme, therefore there was less room for a change attributed to the programme.

Contribution

The contribution of this study can be gauged under two perspectives. First, it contributes to the generation of empirical knowledge in terms of the specific relationship patterns of the theory of planned behaviour's antecedents and intentions. It is associated with the provision of a new regional context to empirically validate the theory's constructs by demonstrating the robustness of its proposed cognitive approach in such context. Exceptions are made in terms of the weak influence of the 'general acceptability of entrepreneurship as a career choice' on intentions which is supported by previous studies. Second, it also contributes to fill the paucity of empirically rigorous research that seeks to confirm or decline whether the entrepreneurial education programmes delivered to business administration students do in effect equip them with the necessary skills and abilities needed for the creation of profitable new ventures upon finishing their studies.

The literature on entrepreneurship education for the Albanian case in particular remains sparse and while reviewing the few existing studies on this topic the conclusion was that they were overly descriptive, methodologically limited, and cross-sectional in nature.

Conclusion and implications

This evaluative and longitudinal study has indicated the impact of entrepreneurship education on attitudes and intentions. We have shown that even though students who recei-ved entrepreneurship education exhibit higher levels of attitudes (personal attitudes and perceived behavioural control) and intentions compared to those who did not, the former reported only a significant increase in terms of perceived behavioural control. We found no evidence that would support the inclusion of entrepreneurial knowledge as a direct pre-dictor of intention, but only as a direct predictor of the perceived behavioural (self-efficacy) antecedent.

This study has limitations that should be recognized and addressed in future research. First, choosing attitudes and intention to assess the influence of entrepreneurship education allows for the estimation of the immediate impact of a programme but due to the lag time between this moment and the actual venture creation, we were not able to address the association of entrepreneurial intentions and entrepreneurial behaviour. Second, a wider sample would benefit the scope of the study. Moreover, the entrepreneurship education programmes com-prising the 'treatment', even though they are compatible in most teaching components, are delivered by different lecturers who might differ in terms of module delivery. Finally, only the control group was assigned randomly while the experimental group was determined by whether the student was enrolled in business administration programmes which include the compulsory module of entrepreneurship education. This means that their participation in this module is grounded by prior knowledge in the field in general and this might bias the findings.

The main practical implication for policy makers and educators is that while entrepreneurship education programmes can increase the student's self-confidence to perform entrepreneurial behaviour, their personal preference or attraction towards entrepreneurship is not affected. For policy makers, it is important to be aware that strategic memberships and alliances with EU organizations and programmes alone will not necessarily translate into better entrepreneurship education impact unless contextually adapted. This means that an evaluation of the context of universities and institutions should be made to acknowledge how this translates into what is meant by enterprise and entrepreneurship education within the investigated context (Pittaway and Cope, 2007). The Albanian national culture is collectivist in nature and imbued with uncertainty avoidance. The cultural dimension should be of critical importance in this process as regional differences affect the propensity to start a business. Moreover, the fostering of entrepreneurship education should be backed up by empirical research that assesses entrepreneurship education in terms of the desired outputs.

Finally, relevant implications for educators in terms of the pedagogy can be derived. We believe that our results display that students participating in entrepreneurship education do not alter their evaluative response in terms of new venture creation. The attributes linked to entrepreneurial behaviour are in general valued negatively in the Albanian context and only the few who have prior self-employment experience have more realistic expectations of the perceived desirability and feasibility. Given this, entrepreneurship education programmes should focus not only on the creation of new ventures but also on the desirable status and consequences that are associated with such career path. Using more positive role models and addressing the students' acceptability of such a career path should be given more relative importance while designing the modules' content.

Bibliography

Acs, Z. (2006). How is Entrepreneurship Good for Economic Growth? *Innovations: Technology, Governance, Globalization,* 1(1), 97–107.

Ajzen, I. (1991). The Theory of Planned Behaviour. *Organizational Behaviour and Human Decision Processes,* 50(2), 179–211.

Ajzen, I. (2002). Perceived Behavioural Control, Self-Efficacy, Locus of Control, and the Theory of Planned Behaviour. *Journal of Applied Social Psychology,* 32(1), 1–20.

Ajzen, I. (2005). *Attitudes, Personality and Behaviour* (2nd ed.). Milton Keynes: Open University Press.

Ajzen, I. (2014). The Theory of Planned Behaviour is Alive and Well, and Not Ready to Retire: A Commentary on Sniehotta, Presseau, and Araújo-Soares. *Health Psychology Review,* 9(2), 131–137.

Ajzen, I., and Fishbein, M. (1980). *Understanding Attitudes and Predicting Social Behaviour.* Englewood Cliffs, NJ: Prentice-Hall.

Akerlof, G. A. (1970). The Market for "Lemons": Quality Uncertainty and the Market Mechanism. *The Quarterly Journal of Economics,* 84(3), 488–500.

Antoncic, B., Scarlat, C., and Erzetic, B. H. (2005). The Quality of Entrepreneurship Education and Intention to Continue Education: Slovenia and Romania. *Managing Global Transitions,* 3(2), 197–212.

Armitage, C. J., and Conner, M. (2001). Efficacy of the Theory of Planned Behaviour: A Meta-analytic Review. *British Journal of Social Psychology,* 40(4), 471–499.

Audretsch, D. B., and Keilbatch, M. (2004). Entrepreneurship Capital and Economic Performance. *Regional Studies,* 38(8), 949–959.

Audretsch, D. B., Falck, O., Feldman, M. P., and Heblich, S. (2012). Local Entrepreneurship in Context. *Regional Studies,* 46(3), 379–389.

Audretsch, D. C. (2001). Does entrepreneurship reduce unemployment? Tinbergen Institute Discussion Paper, 074 (3). Amsterdam: Tinbergen Institute.

Autio, E., Keeley, R. H., Klofsten, M., Parker, G. G., and Hay, M. (2001). Entrepreneurial Intent Among Students in Scandinavia and in the USA. *Entreprise and Innovation Management Studies*, 2(2), 145–160.

Bagozzi, R., Baumgartner, J., and Yi, Y. (1989). An Investigation Into the Role of Intentions as Mediators of the Attitude-Behaviour Relationship. *Journal of Economic Psychology*, 10(1), 35–62.

Bakotić, D., and Kružić, D. (2010). Students' Perceptions and Intentions towards Entrepreneurship: The Empirical Findings from Croatia. *The Business Review*, Cambridge, 14(2), 209–215.

Bandura, A. (1997). *Self-efficacy: The Exercise of Control*. New York: Freeman.

Baumol, W. J. (1968). Entrepreneurship in Economic Theory. *The American Economic Review*, 58(2), 64–71.

Bechard, J. P., and Toulouse, J. M. (1998). Validation of a Didactic Model for the Analysis of Training Objectives in Entrepreneurship. *Journal of Business Venturing*, 13(4), 317–332.

Berkowitz, D., and Jackson, J. (2006). Entrepreneurship and the Evolution of Income Distributions in Poland and Russia. *Journal of Comparative Economics*, 34(2), 338–356.

Bird, B. (1988). Implementing Entrepreneurial Ideas: The Case for Intention. *The Academy of Management Review*, 13(3), 442–453.

Blanchflower, D. G., Oswald, A., and Stutzer, A. (2001). Latent Entrepreneruship Across Nations. *European Economic Review*, 45(5), 680–691.

Blejer, M. (1992). *Albania: From Isolation toward Reform*. Washington, DC: International Monetary Fund.

Bosma, N., and Schutjens, V. (2011). Understanding Regional Variations in Entrepreneurial Activity and Entrepreneuriak Attitude in Europe. *The Annals of Regional Science*, 47(3), 711–742.

Brandstatter, H. (1997). Becoming an Entrepreneur – A Question of Personality Structure? *Journal of Economic Psychology*, 18(2–3), 157–177.

Brandstatter, H. (2011). Personality Aspects of Entrepreneurship: A look at Five Meta-Analyses. *Personality and Individual Differences*, 51(3), 222–230.

Broadman, H. G., Anderson, J., Claessens, C. A., Ryterman, R., Slavova, S., Vagliasindi, M., et al. (2004). *Building Market Institutions in South Eastern Europe: Comparative Prospects for Investment and Private Sector Development*. Washington, DC: World Bank.

Bufi, Y. (2001). Anetaresimi i Shqiperise ne FMN dhe fillimet e reformes ekonomike. *Shqiperia midis reformave te brendshme dhe integrimit europian* (pp. 16–27). Tirane: Banka e Shqiperise.

Byabashaija, W., and Kotono, I. (2011). The Impact of College Entrepreneurial Education on Entrepreneurial Attitudes and Intention to Start a Business in Uganda. *Journal of Developmental Entrepreneurship*, 16(1), 127–144.

Carree, M. T. (2006). *Understanding the Role of Entrepreneurship for Economic Growth*. Cheltenham, UK and Northampton, MA, US: Edward Elgar Publishing Limited.

Chen, S.-C., Hsiao, H.-C., Chang, J.-C., Chou, C.-M., Chen, C.-P., and Shen, C.-H. (2013). Can The Entrepreneurship Course Improve the Entrepreneurial Intentions of Students? *International Entrepreneurship and Management Journal*, 1–13.

Cohen, L., and Manion, L. (1989). *Research Methods in Education* (3rd ed.). London: Routledge.

De Forest, J. D. (1965). Entrepreneurship and Economic Development. *Challenge*, 13(5), 27–31.

De Tienne, D. R., and Chandler, G. N. (2004). Opportunity Identification and Its Role in the Entrepreneurial Classroom: A Pedagogical Approach and Empirical Test. *Academy of Management Learning and Education*, 3(3), 242–257.

Degeorge, J. M., and Fayolle, A. (2008). Is Entrepreneurial Intention Stable Through Time? First Insights From a Sample of French Students. *International Journal of Entrepreneurship and Small Business*, 5(1), 7–27.

Delmar, F., and Davidsson, P. (2000). Where Do They Come From? Prevalence and Characteristics of Nascent Entrepreneurs. *Entrepreneurship and Regional Development*, 12(1), 1–23.

D'Orlando, F., and Ferrante, F. (2009). The Demand for Job Protection: Some Clues form Behavioural Economics. *The Journal of Socio-Economics*, 38(1), 104–114.

Drishti, E., and Kruja, D. (2014). Analysing the Gap of Public Debt (Un)Sustainability: The Albanian Case. *International Journal of Economics, Commerce and Management*, 2(9), 1–15.

Enge, R. L., Dimitriadi, N., Gavidia, J. V., Schlaegel, C., Delanoe, S., Alvarado, I., et al. (2010). Entrepreneurial Intent: A Twelve-Country Evaluation of Ajzen's Model of Planned Behaviour. *International Journal of Entrepreneurial Behaviour and Research*, 16(1), 36–58.

European Commision. (2006). *Implementing the Community Lisbon Programme: Fostering Entrepreneurial Mindsets Through Education and Learning*. Brussels: European Commission.

European Commision. (2013). *Entrepreneurship Education: A Guide for Educators*. Brussels: European Commission. Brussels: European Commission.

Fayolle, A., and Degeorge, J. M. (2006). Attitudes, Intentions and Behaviour: New Approaches to Evaluating Entrepreneurship Education. In A. Fayolle and H. Klandt (Eds.), *International Entrepreneurship Education: Issues and Newness* (pp. 74–93). Cheltenham: Edward Elgar Publishing Limited.

Fayolle, A., and Gailly, B. (2004). *Using the Theory of Planned Behaviour to Assess Entrepreneruship Teaching Programs: A First Experimentation*. IntEnt2004. Naples, Italy.

Fayolle, A., and Gailly, B. (2009). Évaluation d'une formation en entrepreneuriat: predispositions et impact sur l'intention d'entreprendre. *Management*, 12(3), 175–203.

Fayolle, A., and Gailly, F. (2015). The Impact of Entrepreneurship Education on Entrepreneurial Attitudes and Intention: Hysteresis and Persistence. *Journal of Small Business Management*, 53(1), 75–93.

Fayolle, A., Gailly, B., and Narjisse, L.-C. (2006). Assessing the Impact of Entrepreneurship Education Programmes: A New Methodology. *Journal of European Industrial Training*, 30(9), 701–720.

Feldman, M. P. (2001). The Entrepreneurial Event Revisited: An Examination of New Firm Formation in the Regional Context. *Industrial and Corporate Change*, 10(4), 861–891.

Fishbein, M., and Ajzen, I. (1975). *Belief, Attitude, Intention, and Behaviour: An Introduction to Theory and Research*. Reading, MA: Addison-Wesley.

Foster, J. B. (1984). The Political Economy of Joseph Schumpeter: A Theory of Capitalist Development and Decline. *Studies in Political Economy*, 15, 5–42.

Franke, N., and Luthje, C. (2004). Entrepreneurial Intentions of Business Students: A Benchmarking Study. *International Journal of Innovation and Technology Management*, 1(3), 269–288.

Galindo, M.-A., and Mendez-Picazo, M.-T. (2013). Innovation, Entrepreneurship and Economic Growth. *Management Decision*, 51(3), 501–514.

Galloway, L., and Brown, W. (2002). Entrepreneurship Education at University: A Driver in the Creation of Highgrowth Firms? *Education and Training*, 44(8/9), 398–404.

Galloway, L., Anderson, M., Brown, W., and Wilson, L. (2005). Enterprise Skills for the Economy. *Education e Training*, 47(1), 7–17.

Gartner, W. B. (1989). 'Who is an Entrepreneur?' Is the Wrong Question. *Entrepreneurship Theory and Practice*, 12(2), 47–68.

Gartner, W. B., and Carter, N. M. (2003). Entrepreneurship Behaviour: Firm Organizing Process. In Z. J. Acs and D. B. Audretsch (Eds.), T*he International Handbook of Entrepreneurship* (pp. 195–221). Dordrecht: Kluwer.

Gartner, W. B., and Vesper, K. H. (1994). Experiments in Entreperneurship Education: Success and Failures. *Journal of Business Venturing*, 9(3), 179–187.

Hannan, M., Leitch, C., and Hazlett, S.-A. (2006). Measuring the Impact of Entrepreneurship Education: A Cognitive Approach to Evaluation. *International Journal of Continuing Engineering Education and Life-Long Learning*, 16(5), 400–419.

Haus, I., Steinmetz, H., Isidor, R., and Kabst, R. (2013). Gender Effects on Entrepreneurial Intentions: A Meta-Analytical Structural Equation Model. *International Journal of Gender and Entrepreneurship*, 5(2), 130–156.

Hofstede, G. (2001). *Culture's Consequences: Comparing Values, Behaviors, Institutions and Organizations Across Nations* (2nd ed.). Thousand Oaks, CA: Sage Publications.

Iakovleva, T., Kolvereid, L., and Stephan, U. (2011). Entrepreneurial intentions in developing and developing countries. *Education + Training*, 53(5), 353–370.

INSTAT. (2012). *Students Registered in All Universities According to Programme of Study 2011–2012*. Tirana: Institute of Statistics.

Jakopec, A., Krecar, I. M., and Susanj, Z. (2013). Predictors of Entrepreneurial Intentions of Students of Economics. *Studia Psychologica*, 55(4), 289–297.

Jing, S., Qinghua, Z., and Landstrom, H. (2014). Entrepreneurship Research in Three Regions – The USA, Europe and China. *International Entrepreneurship and Management Journal*, 11(4), 1–30.

Knight, R. M. (1987). Corporate Innovation and Entrepreneurship: A Canadian Study. *Journal of Product Innovation Management*, 49(4), 284–297.

Kolvereid, L. (1996a). Organizational Employment versus Self-Employment: Reasons for Career Choice Intentions. *Entrepreneurship Theory and Practice*, 21(3), 23–31.

Kolvereid, L. (1996b). Prediction of Employment Status Choice Intentions. *Entrepreneurship Theory and Practice*, 21(1), 47–56.

Kolvereid, L., and Isaksen, E. (2006). New Business Start-up and Subsequent Entry Into Self-Employment. *Journal of Business Venturing*, 21(6), 866–885.

Kolvereid, L., and Moen, O. (1997). Entrepreneurship among Business Graduates: Does a Major in Entrepreneurship Make a Difference? *Journal of European Industrial Training*, 21(4), 154–160.

Kristiansen, S., and Indarti, N. (2004). Entrepreneurial Intention Among Indonesian and Norwegian Students. *Journal of Enterprising Culture*, 12(1), 55–78.

Krueger, N. F. (1993). The Impact of Prior Entrepreneurial Exposure on Perceptions of New Venture Feasibility and Desirability. *Entrepreneurship Theory and Practice*, 18(1), 5–21.

Krueger, N. F., and Brazeal, D. V. (1994). Entrepreneurial Potential and Potential Entrepreneurs. *Entrepreneurship Theory and Practice*, 18(1), 91–104.

Krueger, N. F., and Carsud, A. L. (1993). Entrepreneurial Intentions: Applying the Theory of Planned Behaviour. *Entrepreneurship and Regional Development*, 5(4), 315–330.

Krueger, N. F., Reilly, M. D., and Carsud, A. L. (2000). Competing Models of Entrepreneurial Intentions. *Journal of Business Venturing*, 15(5–6), 411–432.

Kume, A., Kume, V., and Shahini, B. (2013). Entrepreneurial Characteristics amongst University Students in Albania. *European Scientific Journal*, 9(16), 206–225.

Lee, L., Wong, P. K., Foo, M. D., and Leung, A. (2011). Entrepreneurial Intentions: The Influence of Organisational and Individual Factors. *Journal of Business Venturing*, 26(1), 124–136.

Lent, R., Brown, S., and Hackett, G. (1994). Toward a Unifying Social Cognitive Theory of Career and Academic Interest, Choice, and Performance. *Journal of Vocational Behaviour*, 45(1), 79–122.

Lewis, W. A. (1955). *The Theory of Economic Growth*. London: Allen and Unwin.

Liao, J., and Gartner, W. B. (2008). The Influence of Pre-Venture Planning on New Venture Creation. *Journal of Small Business Strategy*, 18(2), 1–21.

Linan, F. (2004). Intention-based Models of Entrepreneurship Education. *Picolla Impresa/Small Business*, 3(1), 11–35.

Linan, F. (2005). *Development and Validation of an Entrepreneurial Intention Questionnaire (EIQ)*. IntEnt05. Guildford, United Kingdom.

Linan, F., and Chen, Y. (2006). *Testing the Entrepreneurial Intention Model on a Two-Country Sample*. University Autonoma de Barcelona: Departament d'Economia de l'Empresa.

Linan, F., and Chen, Y.-W. (2009). Development and Cross-Cultural Application of a Specific Instrument to Measure Entrepreneurial Intentions. *Entrepreneurship Theory and Practive*, 33(3), 593–617.

Linan, F., and Fayolle, A. (2015). A Systematic Literature Review on Entrepreneurial Intentions: Citation, Thematic Analyses, and Research Agenda. *International Entreprenurship and Management Journal*, 11(4), 1–27.

Linan, F., Rodrigues-Cohard, J. C., and Rueda-Cantuche, J. M. (2011). Factors Affecting Entrepreneurial Intention Levels: A Role for Education. *International Entrepreneurship Management Journal*, 7(2), 195–218.

Lorze, M., Mueller, S., and Volery, T. (2013). Entrepreneurship Education: A Systematic Review of the Methods in Impact Studies. *Journal of Entreprising Culture*, 21(2), 123–151.

Luthje, C., and Franke, N. (2003). The 'Making' of an Entrepreneur: Testing a Model of Entrepreneurial Intent Among Engineering Students at MIT. *RandD Management*, 33(2), 135–147.

MacMillan, I., and Katz, J. (1992). Idiosyncratic Milieus of Entrepreneurship Research: The Need for Comprehensive Theories. *Journal of Business Venturing*, 7(1), 1–8.

Marques, C. S., Ferreira, J., Gomes, D. N., and Rodrigues, R. G. (2012). Entrepreneurship Education: How Psychological, Demographic and Behavioural Factors Predict the Entrepreneurial Intention. *Education + Training*, 54(8/9), 657–672.

Matlay, H. (2001). Entrepreneurial and Vocational Education and Training in Central and Eastern Europe. *Education + Training*, 43(8/9), 395–404.

Matlay, H. (2005). Researching Entrepreneurship and Education: Part 1: What is Entrepreneurship and Does it Matter? *Education + Training*, 47(8/9), 665–677.

Matlay, H. (2008). The Impact of Entrepreneurship Education on Entrepreneurial Outcomes. *Small Business and Entreprise Development*, 15(2), 382–396.

Mazzarol, T., Volery, T., Doss, N., and Thein, V. (1999). Factors Influencing Small Business Start-ups. *International Journal of Entrepreneurial Behavior and Research*, 5(2), 48–63.

Mazzarol, T., Volery, T., Doss, N., and Thein, V. (2001). Forces Motivating Small Business Start Up Among Nascent Entrepreneurs. *Small Enterprise Research*, 9(1), 3–18.

Ministry of Education and Sports. (2014). *Entrepreneurship, a Key Competence in Education*. Tirana: Ministry of Education and Sports.

Mitra, J., and Matlay, H. (2004). Entrepreneurial and Vocational Education and Training: Lessons from Eastern and Central Europe. *Industry and Higher Education*, 18(1), 53–61.

Nelson, R. E. (1977). Entrepreneurship Education in Developing Countries. *Asian Survey*, 17(9), 880–885.

Nelson, R. E., and Johnson, S. D. (1997). Entrepreneurship Education as a Strategic Approach to Economic Growth in Kenya. *Journal of Industrial Education*, 35(1), 7–21.

OECD. (2007). *Report on the implementation of the European Charter for Small Enterprises in the Western Balkans*. Paris: OECD Publishing.

OECD/European Union. (2014). *The Missing Entrepreneurs 2014: Policies for Inclusive Entrepreneurship in Europe*. Paris: OECD Publishing.

Omorede, A., Thorgen, S., and Wincent, J. (2014). Entrepreneurship Psychology: A Review. *International Entrepreneurship and Management Journal*, 11(4), 1–26.

Oosterbeek, H., Van Praag, M., and Ijsselstein, A. (2010). The Impact of Entreprenurship Education on Entrepreneurship Skills and Motivation. *European Economic Review*, 54(3), 442–454.

Pano, V. (2001). Privatizimi dhe Efikasiteti i tij ne Shqiperi. *Shqiperia midis reformave te brendshme dhe integrimit europian* (pp. 154–192). Tirane: Banka e Shqiperise.

Parker, S. C. (2004). *The Economics of Self-Employment and Entrepreneurship*. Cambridge: Cambridge University Press.

Peterman, N. E., and Kennedy, J. (2003). Enterprise education: Influencing students' perceptions of entrepreneurship. *Entrepreneurship Theory and Practice*, 28(2), 129–145.

Pihie, Z. A., and Bagheri, A. (2009). Developing Future Entrepreneurs: A Need to Improve Science Students' Entrepreneurial Participation. *International Journal of Knowledge, Culture and Change Management*, 9(2), 45–57.

Piperopoulos, P. (2012). Could Higher Education Programmes, Culture and Structure Stifle the Entrepreneurial Intentions of Students? *Journal of Small Business and Enterprise Development*, 19(3), 461–483.

Pittaway, L., and Cope, J. (2007). Entrepreneurship Education – A Systematic Review of the Evidence. *International Small Business Journal*, 25(5), 479–510.

Pittaway, L., and Thorpe, R. (2012). A Framework for Entrepreneurial Learning: A Tribute to Jason Cope. *Entrepreneurship and Regional Development*, 24(9–10), 837–859.

Porter, M. E., Sachs, J. D., and McArthur, J. W. (2002). Executive Summary: Competitiveness and Stages of Economic Development. In *The Global Competitiveness Report 2001–2002* (pp. 16–17). Oxford: Oxford University Press.

Qosja, E. (2014). Innovation, SMEs, and the Entrepreneurship Education Related to Them. *Journal of Educational and Social Research*, 4(6), 69–74.

Rauch, A., and Frese, M. (2007). Let's Put the Person Back into Entrepreneurship Research: A Meta-Analysis on the Relationship Between Business Owners' Personality Traits, Business Creation, and Success. *European Journal of Work and Organizational Psychology*, 16(4), 353–385.

Reynolds, P. D., Hay, M., and Camp, S. M. (1999). *Global Entrepreneurship Monitor*. Kansas City, MO: Kauffman Center for Entrepreneurial Leadership.

Saeed, R., Nayyab, H., Rashied, H., Lodhi, R. N., Musawar, S., and Iqbal, A. (2013). Who is the Most Potential Entrepreneur? A Case of Pakistan. *Middle East Journal of Scientific Research*, 17(9), 1307–1315.

Sanchez, J. (2013). The Impact of an Entrepreneurship Education Program on Entrepreneurial Competencies and Intention. *Journal of Small Business Management*, 51(3), 447–465.

Schumpeter, J. A. ([1911] 2008). In *The Theory of Economic Development: An Inquiry into Profits, Capital, Credit, Interest and the Business Cycle* (R. Opie, Trans.). London: Transaction Publishers.

Shahidi, N. (2012). Les Jeunes Entrepreneurs Nécessitent-ils un Accompagnement Particulier? Le cas Français. *Journal of Small Business and Entrepreneurship*, 25(1), 57–74.

Shane, S. (2000). Prior Knowledge and the Discovery of Entrepreneurial Opportunities. *Organization Science*, 11(4), 448–469.

Shapero, A., and Sokol, L. (1982). Social Dimension of Entrepreneurship. In C. A. Kent, D. L. Sexton, and K. H. Vesper (Eds.), *Encyclopedia of Entrepreneurship* (pp. 72–99). Englewood Cliffs, NJ: Prentice Hall.

Shaver, K. G. (2003). The Social Psychology of Entrepreneurial Behaviour. In Z. J. Acs and D. B. Audretsch (Eds.), *Handbook of Entrepreneurship Research* (pp. 331–357). New York: Springer.

Smallbone, D., and Welter, F. (2001). The distinctiveness of entrepreneurship in transition economies. *Small Business Economics*, 16(4), 249–262.

Solesvik, M., Westhead, P., Matlay, H., and Parsyak, V. (2013). Entrepreneurial Assets and Mindsets. *Education + Training*, 55(8/9), 748–762.

Solesvik, M. Z., Westhead, P., Kolvereid, L., and Matlay, H. (2012). Student Intentions to Become Self-Employed: the Ukrainian Context. *Journal of Small Business and Entreprise Development*, 19(3), 441–460.

Souitaris, V., Zerbinati, S., and Al-Laham, A. (2007). Do Entrepreneurship Programmes Raise Entrepreneurial Intentions of Science and Engeneering Students? The Effects of Learning, Inspiration and Resources. *Journal of Business Venturing*, 22(4), 566–591.

Strobl, A., Kronenberg, C., and Peters, M. (2012). Entrepreneurial Attitudes and Intentions: Assessing Gender Specific Differences. *International Journal of Small Business*, 15(4), 452–468.

Taymans, A. C. (1951). Marx's Theory of the Entrepreneur. *American Journal of Economics and Sociology*, 11(1), 75–90.

Teemu, K., Down, S., and Minniti, M. (2014). Ageing and Entrepreneurial Preferences. *Small Business Economics*, 42(3), 579–594.

Thompson, E. R. (2009). Individual Entrepreneurial Intent: Construct Clarification and Development of an Internationally Reliable Metric. *Entrepreneurship Theory and Practice*, 33(3), 669–694.

Thurik, R. (2014). *Entrepreneurship and the Business Cycle*. London: Bloomsbury, Institute for the Study of Labor (IZA)

Tkashev, A., and Kolvereid, L. (1999). Self-employment Intentions among Russian Students. *Entrepreneurship and Regional Development*, 11(3), 269–280.

Tomic, I., and Domadenik, P. (2012). Matching, Adverse Selection and Labour Market Flows in (Post) Transition setting: The Case of Croatia. *Post-Communist Economies*, 24(1), 39–72.

TorBjorn, N. (2012). Entrepreneurship Education – Does It Matter? *International Journal of Business and Management*, 7(13), 40–48.

Turker, D., and Selcuk, S. (2009). Which Factors Affect Entrepreneurial Intention of University Students? *Journal of European Industrial Training*, 33(2), 142–159.

Umas, V., and Mets, T. (2010). Entrepreneurship Education in Higher Educations Institutions (HEIs) of Post-Communist European Countries. *Journal of Entreprising Communities*, 4(3), 204–219.

Ute, S., and Uhlaner, L. M. (2010). Performance-based vs Socially Supportive Culture: A Cross-national Study of Descriptive Norms and Entrepreneurship. *Journal of International Business Studies*, 41(8), 1347–1364.

Van der Sluis, J., Van Praag, M., and Vijverberg, W. (2005). Entrepreneurship selection and performance: A meta-analysis of the impact of education in developing economies. *The World Bank Economic Review*, 19(2), 225–261.

Van Praag, M., and Versloot, P. H. (2007). What is the Value of Entrepreneurship? A Review of Recent Research. *Small Business Economics*, 29(4), 351–382.

Varblane, U., and Mets, T. (2010). Entrepreneurship education in the higher education institutions (HEIs) of post-communist European countries. *Journal of Enterprising Communities: People and Places in the Global*, 4(3), 204–219.

Veciana, J. M., Aponte, M., and Urbano, D. (2005). University Students' Attitudes Towards Entrepreneurship: A Two Country Comparison. *International Entrepreneurship and Management Journal*, 1(2), 165–182.

Von Graevenitz, G., Harhoff, D., and Weber, R. (2010). The Effects of Entrepreneurship Education. *Journal of Economic Behavior and Organization*, 76(1), 90–112.

Wilson, F., Kickul, J., and Marlino, D. (2007). Gender, Entrepreneurial Self-Efficacy, and Entrepreneurial Career Intentions: Implications for Entrepreneurship Education. *Entrepreneurship: Theory and Practice*, 31(3), 387–406.

Winecki, J. (2003). The Role of the New, Entrepreneurial Private Sector in Transition and Economic Performance in the Light of the Successes in Poland, the Czech Republic and Hungary. *Problems of Economic Transition*, 45(11), 6–38.

Zhao, H., and Seibert, S. E. (2006). The Big Five Personality Dimension and Entrepreneurial Status: A Meta-Analysis Review. *Journal of Applied Psychology*, 91(2), 259–271.

Zhao, H., Hills, G. E., and Seibert, S. E. (2005). The Mediating Role of Self-Efficacy in the Development of Entrepreneurial Intentions. *Journal of Applied Psychology*, 90(6), 1265–1272.

Zhao, H., Seibert, S. E., and Lumpkin, G. T. (2010). The Relationship of Personality to Entrepreneurial Intentions and Peformance: A Meta-Analytic Review. *Journal of Management*, 36(2), 381–404.

36

ORGANIZATIONAL LEARNING IN INDIAN FAMILY FIRMS

A social network based approach to entrepreneurship

Nobin Thomas and Neharika Vohra

Introduction

Organizational learning has been recognized as one of the most powerful enablers in the transition to help firms gain a competitive advantage (Flores et al., 2012). A plethora of studies have shown that organizational learning is the key towards organizational success in future (Alegre and Chiva, 2008). Still, organizational learning for family firms is very much abstruse as is evident in Moores' (2009: 176) words, 'The manner in which units interact with each other from a learning theoretical perspective in the context of the business family domain is still very much in a nascent stage of understanding . . . less has been done here with respect to family businesses'. Similarly, Zahra (2012) points out that the relationship between family ownership and organizational learning in a family firm is still unexplored. Despite the vast literature on the organizational learning process operating in a firm, few studies have tried to analyze family firms (Basly, 2007). To assume that there is no difference between organizational learning processes in a family and non-family firm would be a gross underestimation of the influence of the 'family' in business (Patel and Fiet, 2011). The presence of 'noneconomic goals' and 'socio-cognitive bonds' that are unique to family firms, and developed through 'family' interactions, suggests that learning in family businesses is different.

The significance of this study becomes evident when we realize that two out of every three enterprises in the world are either managed or owned by families (Gersick et al., 1997). According to Kets de Vries et al. (2007), family firms account for 95 percent of all firms in Asia and the Middle East. The CII[1] (Confederation of Indian Industry) data shows 95 percent of registered firms in India are family businesses and together contribute 60–70 percent of Indian GDP. When studies have established that a firm's competitiveness and future success are highly dependent on organizational learning (see Alegre and Chiva, 2008), it is quite unfortunate that family firms, hailed as 'the backbone of corporate life, across nations' (Poutziouris et al., 2006, p. 1), have not yet found their foothold on unfolding organizational learning.

To understand this irony, it is important to understand the dynamics under which a family firm operates. The 'family' in the family firm interacts with both 'family' system and 'business' system and these two systems are not necessarily compatible. Their dual membership in the overlapping systems becomes problematic because of the inherent struggle between 'stability' and 'continuity' espoused by the 'family' system and 'change' and 'adaptation' central to the 'business' system (Nordqvist and Melin, 2010; Smith and Lewis, 2011). Most often, the family's socio-emotional factors (cf. Gomez-mejia et al., 2007) override the learning needs of the 'business' system and as a result, the 'business' system suffers. Zahra (2012) discusses some of the inhibitors of organizational learning in family firms. The domination of family members in decision-making processes often leaves out the non-family members from core activities of the firm. This adversely affects the information flow in the firm that is critical to organizational learning, as non-family members may find it difficult to express their views. Sibling rivalries may also hamper knowledge sharing in family firms. Excessive cohesion among family members might also restrain some of them from dissenting or putting up a counter view (Zahra, 2012).

In this chapter, it is argued that for the possibility of overcoming some of the gaps in measuring the organizational learning process for a family firm we have to view learning as a relational phenomenon. The relational aspect becomes important because a significant part of a member's information and knowledge environment revolves around the relationships or ties an individual can tap into at times of need. Cross and Parker (2004) talk about the value of social networks essential for making the process of learning more effective. The network perspective assumes that relationships are important because they provide access to and control of informational resources. Organizational learning is seen as multiple with distinct sub-processes occurring at different levels of the organization (Huber, 1991). Accordingly, organizational learning begins with some form of information acquisition. The information then gets distributed across the organization. Interpretation and integration of the information would typically follow. During the information interpretation process, people make sense of the information that they receive and try to reach a shared understanding. The process concludes as information gets stored in organizational memory. The next section examines each of the sub-processes of organizational learning in greater detail with respect to entrepreneurial family firms.

Information acquisition

According to the behavioral theory of the firm, it can be postulated that family firms put a cap on their search capabilities in the long run (Cyert and March, 1963). It is also known that family firms tend to become inward focused as they gain experience and information acquisition gets limited to internal search (i.e., within the firm). These inward withdrawal symptoms have been much more pronounced in the case of family businesses (Zahra, 2012). Studies have also shown that family firms tend to lose their entrepreneurial zeal and start laying emphasis on 'continuity' and 'stability' as soon as they get established. The family firms become more inclined toward conservative strategies to keep themselves afloat rather than sink their head in innovation and growth opportunities (Shepherd and Zahra, 2003). The family firm's stiff resistance to change and strong inward focus, breeds inertia that may turn out to be fatal for the family firm's learning capabilities (Zahra, 2008). It has also been found that family members are prone to keep outsiders away from decision making and thereby limit the learning opportunities that could happen through the involvement of non-family members (Zahra, 2012). The high cohesion that exists between family members is a precursor to the increased loyalty that demands conformity to the consensual view of the family. This in turn puts a cap on the ability of family members to come up with diverse views, thereby limiting the information acquisition process (Zahra, 2012). The over-dependence on family members may also hamper the prospects of looking at other resources from which the firm can seek a wide range of complementary information (Greve and Salaff, 2003). It has also been noted that family firm members limit the quality of human capital through their forced interventions, only to promote nepotism. In support of this argument, Covin (1994) found that qualified managers avoided family firms and Sirmon and Hitt (2003) found that it was the habit of family members to undervalue managers considered well trained by most standards.

Information distribution

As defined earlier, information distribution is the sub-process of organizational learning that allows for dissemination of information across the family firm. Information distribution is found to be efficient when there are frequent, repeated, and significant interactions between family and non-family members (Ghoshal and Bartlett, 1990) of the family firm. A strong sense of identity, socio-emotional wealth, informality, and 'familiness' in a family firm (Habbershon et al., 2003; Denison et al., 2004) expedites the dissemination of information among family members (Miller and Le Breton-Miller, 2006).

The information distribution process is contingent upon the types of ties that exist between its members. The social tie can be only instrumental, or only expressive, or a combination of both (Ibarra, 1995). Instrumental ties originate in the workplace and develop in the context of formal work relationships (Manev and Stevenson, 2001). The instrumental ties between family and non-family members would be subject to the extent of inclusivity offered to non-family members.

The existence of family rivalries may sometimes act as a deterrent for information sharing (Lansberg, 1999). Jealousy, owing to the desire to occupy someone else's position, has been common among members of the family firm. The jealousies found in family firms can become a hindrance for efficient information distribution (Grote, 2004). In family firms, the information flow gets affected if there are certain family members who either lack interest in doing business or do not have the propensity to learn (Breton-Miller et al., 2004). A common critique about family firms is that the most valuable knowledge in the firm gets concentrated on a single individual or a group of individuals in the family, namely the owner or his/her family (Zahra et al., 2007) and that can act as barrier for the flow of information.

Interpretation

The presence of strong ties between family members has a strong impact on organizational learning in the case of family firms. The 'strength of tie' has been defined by Granovetter (1973: 61) as a 'combination of the amount of time, the emotional intensity, the intimacy (mutual confiding) and the reciprocal services which characterize that tie'. Consistent with Granovetter's (1973) definition, scholars who have studied tie strength between family members have found evidence for higher levels of trust and affect, increase in the frequency of interactions and a greater sense of reciprocity and obligations among family members (Leana and Van Buren, 1999). It also needs to be emphasized that strong ties between family members may incur in them the need to have similar views, beliefs, and mental maps. As a result, the family members may be constrained in their ability to come up with different viewpoints when faced with a problem.

Studies have shown that members of the same family develop a stable mental schema owing to the similarity in their cognitive skills (Arregle et al., 2007). The norms and traditions followed in a family firm play a significant role in the development of shared interpretation and common understanding (Bettenhausen and Murnighan, 1991). Organizational learning is distinguished from individual-level learning through these shared insights, knowledge, and mental models.

Organizational memory

Organizational memory refers to storing knowledge in repositories that persists over time (Argote et al., 2003). The stored knowledge gets embedded into organizational structures, systems, and cultures through the process of institutionalization (Crossan et al., 1999).

Method

In developing a relational framework for measuring organizational learning in family firms, we use the social network measures developed by Thomas and Vohra (2015). The social network comprises of a set of actors with relationships amongst themselves (Hanneman and Riddle, 2005). The actors in our study were family and non-family members in the family firm and the link between the actors represents the flow of information.

Two family firms of medium size were chosen. To be able to study the organizational learning processes, all members of the top management team and managers at different levels were included in the study.

The first firm where we conducted social network analysis of the organizational learning process was Vismaya,[2] a family firm specialized in spice extraction. The company was established in the year 1992 and is closely held and managed by the promoter and his family. Vismaya had around 300 employees during the time of data collection, including 40 scientists who work full-time in research and monitoring clinical studies. This privately owned company is based in South India, and has won several awards and achievements for its quality research work. We found that there were four hierarchical levels at Vismaya. The first level comprised the top management including Managing Director, Director (Technical), and Director (Marketing). They were members of the owning family. The second level consisted of Assistant General Managers in charge of Research and Development, and Operations. The third level had Senior Managers belonging to different functions. The fourth level comprised Managers. The list of managers and their abbreviations is given in Appendix 36.1.

The second family firm where we conducted social network analysis of the organizational learning sub-processes was Peoples,[3] one of India's leading automobile dealers based in South India. Peoples have diverse business interests and car dealership is one of their core businesses that was started in the 1980s. The group had its origin in the year 1940 as an entrepreneurial venture. We found that there were four hierarchical levels at Peoples. The first level comprised the top management including the Director, Head (Sales), Head (Marketing and Strategy), Chief Financial Officer, General Manager, and Deputy General Manager (HR). The second level consisted of Senior Managers. The third level was Training and Sales Managers. The fourth level had Managers. The list of managers and their abbreviations is given in Appendix 36.2.

As typical in network research, we use a whole-network (socio-centric) approach for network analysis. To identify the network ties, we gave the respondents a roster that included the names of all the four levels of managers in the firm. We asked them questions to find their relationship with others (Marsden, 1990). The network data was collected using a single item for two reasons. The use of multi-item scales is difficult in network research because of time- and fatigue-related concerns. The response rate may be lower and there could be more errors in data collection if we use multi-items (Ibarra and Andrews, 1993). We entered the participant responses from the network survey questionnaire into the software package UCINET 6.488 (Borgatti et al., 2002) to calculate the network measures.

Based on the network measures of organizational learning developed by Thomas and Vohra (2015), we used three network measures to capture the information acquisition process, the first sub-process of organizational learning. The number of nodes seeking information directly from a focal node is captured by the network measure 'Reach Index'. Another network measure for information acquisition called 'Seek Index' calculates the number of people the focal nodes goes out seeking information. We calculate 'Mediation Index' for all the nodes in the information acquisition network. Mediation Index measures the extent to which a node falls between the other nodes that are not directly connected to each other. For information distribution, we used two network measures. The number of actors to whom a node disseminates information directly is represented by the network measure 'Dissemination Index'. The 'Power Index' is another network measure that represents the power of individuals in controlling the flow of information in the network. For information interpretation, we used the network measure 'Similarity Index' which captures the extent of similarity in perspectives among people in the network. If there are many individuals in the network who have a high similarity index, it enhances the direct interaction between members, which in turn results in increased shared understanding (Burt, 2005). We also calculated 'Reciprocity Index' for each of the nodes in the information interpretation network as a measure of information interpretation. For organizational memory, a network measure called 'Expertise Index' captures the number of people who are seen as experts in the organization, irrespective of the domain.

Results and discussion

Information acquisition as defined in this study captures the patterns of behavior in seeking information from others in the family firm to address their work-related queries. In the two firms where we collected data for this study, we found that the individuals at each hierarchical level interacted with people outside their closed group to bring in new information not only from their own levels, but also from other levels. The new information from this interaction helps to increase shared expertise within the group, which, in turn, impacts on group performance. Most likely the shared expertise will make individuals at respective levels more visible to each other. This can potentially build more confidence and trust among individuals and can possibly result in greater organizational learning. The network measures of information acquisition for Vismaya and Peoples are shown in Figure 36.1 and Figure 36. 2.

We found that across levels, the Reach Index was highest for members of the top management (level 1) in both the firms and it gradually reduced as we moved down the hierarchical levels. What it means is that the number of people coming to a manager seeking information was influenced by their position in the hierarchy. We found that the mean value for the Reach Index for level 1 was higher than the mean value of the Reach Index for the

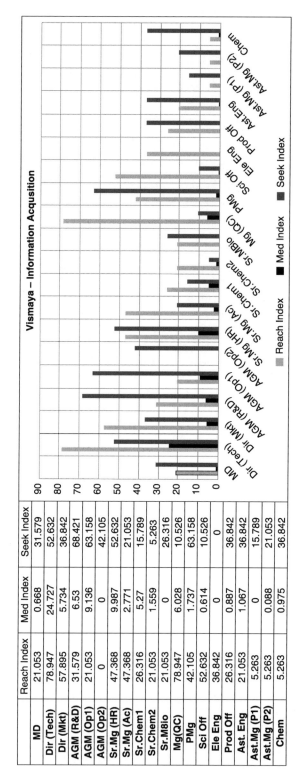

	Reach Index	Med Index	Seek Index
MD	21.053	0.668	31.579
Dir (Tech)	78.947	24.727	52.632
Dir (Mkt)	57.895	5.734	36.842
AGM (R&D)	31.579	6.53	68.421
AGM (Op1)	21.053	9.136	63.158
AGM (Op2)	0	0	42.105
Sr.Mg (HR)	47.368	9.987	52.632
Sr.Mg (Ac)	47.368	2.771	21.053
Sr.Chem1	26.316	5.27	15.789
Sr.Chem2	21.053	1.559	5.263
Sr.MBio	21.053	0	26.316
Mg(QC)	78.947	6.028	10.526
PMg	42.105	1.737	63.158
Sci Off	52.632	0.614	10.526
Ele Eng	36.842	0	0
Prod Off	26.316	0.887	36.842
Ast. Eng	21.053	1.067	36.842
Ast.Mg (P1)	5.263	0	15.789
Ast.Mg (P2)	5.263	0.088	21.053
Chem	5.263	0.975	36.842

Figure 36.1   Vismaya – Information Acquisition

	Reach Index	Mediation Index	Seek Index
Dir	36.84	0.35	31.58
Head (Sales)	68.42	13.02	47.37
Head (M&S)	73.68	14.98	52.63
CFO	47.37	5.26	10.53
GM	68.42	14.78	57.90
DGM (HR)	73.68	4.57	26.32
Sr.Mg1	52.63	8.87	31.58
Sr.Mg2	63.16	10.29	47.37
Sr.Mg3	52.63	5.26	5.26
Mg1 (Sal)	21.05	0.13	15.79
Mg2 (Sal)	26.32	0.00	21.05
Mg1 (Tr)	42.11	3.79	36.84
Mg2 (Tr)	31.58	0.00	10.53
Mg3 (Tr)	47.37	0.00	5.26
Mg1 (L1)	47.37	10.63	31.58
Mg2 (L2)	68.42	16.70	63.16
Mg4 (L3)	21.05	0.04	10.53
Mg3 (L2)	42.11	0.00	10.53
Mg5 (L4)	42.11	3.60	26.32
Mg6 (L5)	15.79	0.00	15.79

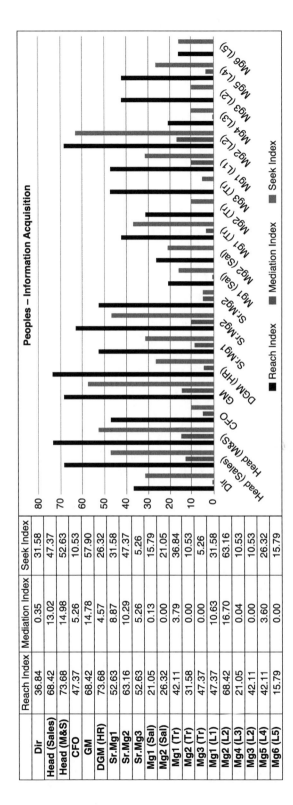

Figure 36.2   Peoples – Information Acquisition

whole organization in the case of both the family firms. This clearly indicates that members of the top management (primarily family members) were the primary source of information for other senior- and middle-level managers in the network. Studies have shown that family members have been found to work long hours to build new ties and maintain the existing ones (Pearson et al., 2008). The motivation for doing so can be attributed to what Tsai and Ghoshal (1998: 465) say, namely 'frequent and close social interactions permit actors to share important information'. Family firms maintain a strong relationship with their clients (Lyman, 1991) for being privy to the unique information that that their client possesses and gain competitive advantage out of it. Studies have also shown that family members seek information from external agents like professional organizations, community groups, religious organizational members (Jack, 2005).

It was also observed that the family member (MD for Vismaya and Director for Peoples), occupying the top position in the organizational chart, had the lowest Reach Index among level 1 members. This might be because of the perceived cost associated with seeking information from the head of the organization. It has been noted that there are costs involved in the process of acquiring information. The costs may be in the form of interpersonal risks or obligations incurred. The interpersonal risk an individual accrues in seeking information from others is by admitting his/her ignorance on the topic he/she is seeking information on. Esteem and reputation of the person is at stake when he/she admits his/her ignorance. Moreover, the norms of reciprocity may place the individual who is seeking information in debt because the other person can always come back to the individual for information in future (Borgatti and Cross, 2003). The perceived high cost deterred managers from approaching the family member who is at the head of the organization. Alternatively, it is also their lack of domain expertise (e.g., Vismaya MD) or other commitments (e.g., Peoples Director), as found during the interviews with managers in various networks, that stops managers approaching the head of the organization. Esteem and reputation issues become dominant in information seeking, as people try to maintain positive self-images and hence, seek out information only from others who confirm a positive sense of self (Lee, 1997). In a study conducted by O'Reilly (1982), he observed that people looked into the source quality while tapping information from their co-workers.

In the case of Vismaya and Peoples, the mean value of the Reach Index for lower levels was comparatively less than that of level 1. Since the lower levels comprised mainly functional managers for both the family firms, the low values of the Reach Index may signify that cross-functional information acquisition was low among members. It may also be that the non-family members become passive employees when there are constant disagreements with family members. Studies have shown that non-family managers may then resort to 'strategic simplicity', which is defined as 'a pathological cognitive condition that causes some managers to overuse ready-made solutions without probing the assumptions underlying the decisions they make' (Zahra, 2005, p. 26) and the net result is that the 'routines that worked well in the past are used again and again regardless of the strategic challenges facing the family firm' (p. 24). If the managers in a family firm take pride in 'strategic simplicity', it would severely limit the family firm's organizational learning sub-processes.

Figure 36.1 shows that the Seek Index was highest for members of the top management and it varied across hierarchical levels. In the case of Vismaya, their products were highly research oriented and had to consistently meet the safety standards set by the health administrator in various countries. The managers during their interviews emphasized the fact that Dir (Tech) made it a point to converse regularly with organizational members to track progress and offered help when they encountered difficulties. Being a member of the owning family, Dir (Tech) was also involved in the administration of the firm and sought information regularly from family and non-family members. The high values for Seek Index, especially for level 1 in both the firms (most often functional heads), indicates is the practice of senior managers of seeking information from lower levels. Studies have shown that as people move higher up within an organization, their work begins to entail more administrative tasks which make them both less accessible and less knowledgeable about the day-to-day work of their subordinates (Cross, Borgatti and Parker, 2002). We also noted that the average Seek Index for level 1 was higher than the mean Seek Index for the whole organization in the case of both firms. This suggests the positive learning attitude of the members of the top management and their willingness to remain immersed in the day-to-day activities of the firm.

In the case of Vismaya, the Seek Index for level 2 was higher than other levels. The members in level 2 were AGM's—Operations and R and D. Since they were heading important functions, they sought information from other levels in order to aid them in their decision making. For Peoples, the Seek Index was comparatively low for lower levels.

As displayed in Figure 36.1 and Figure 36.2, we found that Mediation Index for level 1 was highest for Dir (Tech) for Vismaya and Head (M and S) for Peoples. What was notable was that they were the second or third in line among members of the top management in their respective organizations. It became clear to us that when somebody has to acquire information from an unknown person, they channel it to the person who has a high Mediation Index. It also establishes their role as information broker. By becoming an intermediary in the process of information acquisition, the person who has a high Mediation Index also becomes a storehouse of knowledge. This could be the reason why such individuals had a high Reach Index and high Seek Index. In other words, their high Reach Index could have been influenced by the Mediation Index because when someone needed information not available through their direct contacts, they approached these middlemen and sought information through them.

For level 2, managers had relatively high values for Mediation Index in the case of Vismaya and Peoples. Except for certain individuals, the Mediation Index was low for level 3 and level 4. It suggests that a high Mediation Index can be seen as a property of the top management and clearly signifies their influence on information acquisition.

The network measures of information distribution for Vismaya and Peoples are shown in Figure 36.3 and Figure 36.4. All four levels of Vismaya had high values for Dissemination index. When it comes to Peoples, level 1 and level 2 had high values for the Dissemination Index, but the values for level 3 and level 4 reduced gradually.

Studies have shown that a major inhibitor of information distribution is that information can be considered a source of power and superiority (Szulanski, 1996). In such a scenario, the manager has little incentive to share information with others as it would become a public good and the uniqueness attached to it gets lost. Research also suggests that organizational trust exerts a greater impact on information sharing due to the difficulty in predicting how the shared information would be used (Bock et al., 2005). Going by the same argument, the low Dissemination Index for certain levels in our study may be because of perceptions of trust, privacy, and safety attached to sharing information. The non-family members have little incentive to share information within the family firm because, any time a non-family member takes a decision that has an overall impact on the firm, he/she has to justify his/her decision to the family members (Kang, 1998). As a result, some of the non-family managers remain defensive when it comes to decision making and adopt 'strategic simplicity' explained earlier. The non-family managers' indifference toward the information distribution process may also be attributed to the lack of trust between family and non-family members.

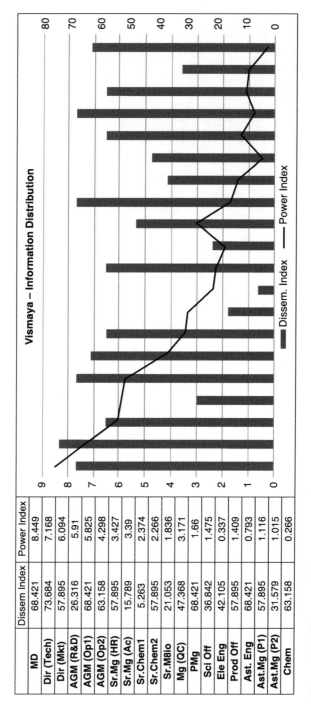

	Dissem Index	Power Index
MD	68.421	8.449
Dir (Tech)	73.684	7.168
Dir (Mkt)	57.895	6.094
AGM (R&D)	26.316	5.91
AGM (Op1)	68.421	5.825
AGM (Op2)	63.158	4.298
Sr.Mg (HR)	57.895	3.427
Sr.Mg (Ac)	15.789	3.39
Sr.Chem1	5.263	2.374
Sr.Chem2	57.895	2.266
Sr.M8io	21.053	1.836
Mg (QC)	47.368	3.171
PMg	68.421	1.66
Sci Off	36.842	1.475
Ele Eng	42.105	0.337
Prod Off	57.895	1.409
Ast. Eng	68.421	0.793
Ast.Mg (P1)	57.895	1.116
Ast.Mg (P2)	31.579	1.015
Chem	63.158	0.266

Figure 36. 3 Vismaya – Information Distribution

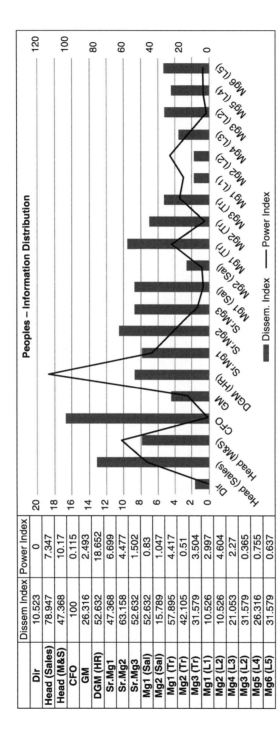

	Dissem Index	Power Index
Dir	10.523	0
Head (Sales)	78.947	7.347
Head (M&S)	47.368	10.17
CFO	100	0.115
GM	26.316	2.493
DGM (HR)	52.632	18.652
Sr.Mg1	47.368	6.699
Sr.Mg2	63.158	4.477
Sr.Mg3	52.632	1.502
Mg1 (Sal)	52.632	0.83
Mg2 (Sal)	15.789	1.047
Mg1 (Tr)	57.895	4.417
Mg2 (Tr)	42.105	0.51
Mg3 (Tr)	31.579	3.504
Mg1 (L1)	10.526	2.997
Mg2 (L2)	10.526	4.604
Mg4 (L3)	21.053	2.27
Mg3 (L2)	31.579	0.365
Mg5 (L4)	26.316	0.755
Mg6 (L5)	31.579	0.637

Figure 36.4   Peoples – Information Distribution

We borrow Zand's (1972) 'spiral reinforcement model of the dynamics of trust' to explain this anomaly. According to this model, when two individuals decide to share information, there exists an initial trust expectation between them. The sharing of information reinforces the initial trust and the resultant trust so developed leads to further sharing of information. Thus, a spiral of trust gets built up and information sharing increases with higher levels of trust. However, if the initial expectation itself is of mistrust, the spiral deteriorates into one of reduced information flow and declining trust. Since the non-family members do not share blood or married relations to family members in the firm, the development of initial trust itself would be difficult. When there is no initial trust, we know that information sharing becomes extremely difficult and the spiral of trust further weakens.

Studies have shown that family members employed in a family firm have greater opportunities for interactions outside of work (e.g., family get-together) than non-family members (Mustakallio, Autio and Zahra, 2003). Moreover, the boundary between work and family is blurred in the case of family members which gives them access to information not available to non-family members. It can also be argued that when non-family managers get access to information that they think would either give them an added advantage or tarnish their image, there are chances that they would withhold it for the predilection of being indispensable or fear of being vulnerable. On the other hand, family members possessing such information would cross structural boundaries and hierarchies to deliver the information to individuals or groups that they believe can potentially use or benefit from them. Such altruistic behavior among family members can lead to the formation of an efficient information distribution system within the family firm.

The Power Index in Vismaya varied across levels. For Peoples, the value for the Power Index gradually became less as we moved down the hierarchy. Knowledge of the organization helped us in identifying the actors who were acting as intermediaries and aiding the flow of information in the network. For example, in the case of Vismaya and Peoples, Dir (Tech) and Head (M and S) were the power nodes. They all had a high Power Index and were instrumental in helping people share information in the network.

One of the reasons for poor information sharing that we found during interviews was that information distribution represents a cost to the source, in terms of time and efforts. Both individuals and social boundaries might inhibit the effective flow of information within organizations. The network indices that we have developed for information distribution gave a clear indication of the individuals who aid information flow and who can become a bottleneck for information to flow in the distribution network.

The network measures of information interpretation for Vismaya and Peoples are shown in Figure 36.5 and Figure 36.6. The members of the top and senior management at Vismaya had high values for Similarity Index. Since high values for Similarity Index reduce uncertainty and anxiety about social acceptance, and promote interpersonal attraction and cohesiveness, they also foster the rapid coordination and integration of knowledge, and speeds mutual understanding (Akgün et al., 2005). The case of Vismaya is a good example. The high value of the Similarity Index for members of the top management reflects the shared understanding among them, and is instrumental in developing a shared vision among members at different levels. To put to practice what Wegner (1987, p. 189) said, 'One person has access to information in another's memory by virtue of knowing that the other person is a location for an item with a certain label. This allows both people to depend on communication with each other for the enhancement of their personal memory storage'; high values for Similarity Index could be the first step. In the case of Peoples, the Similarity Index varied across levels.

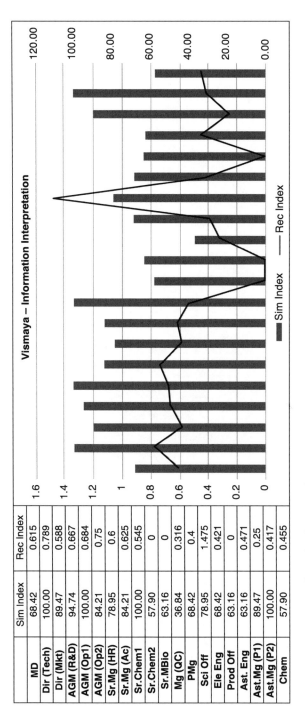

Figure 36.5 Vismaya – Information Interpretation

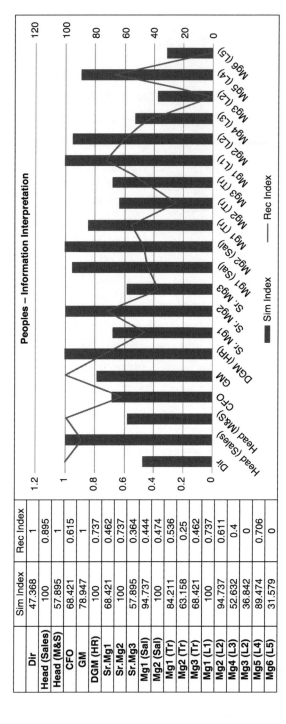

	Sim Index	Rec Index
Dir	47.368	1
Head (Sales)	100	0.895
Head (M&S)	57.895	1
CFO	68.421	0.615
GM	78.947	1
DGM (HR)	100	0.737
Sr.Mg1	68.421	0.462
Sr.Mg2	100	0.737
Sr.Mg3	57.895	0.364
Mg1 (Sal)	94.737	0.444
Mg2 (Sal)	100	0.474
Mg1 (Tr)	84.211	0.536
Mg2 (Tr)	63.158	0.25
Mg3 (Tr)	68.421	0.462
Mg1 (L1)	100	0.737
Mg2 (L2)	94.737	0.611
Mg4 (L3)	52.632	0.4
Mg3 (L2)	36.842	0
Mg5 (L4)	89.474	0.706
Mg6 (L5)	31.579	0

Figure 36.6 Peoples – Information Interpretation

The network measures of organizational memory for Vismaya and Peoples are shown in Figure 36.7 and Figure 36.8. In the case of Vismaya, except for the lowest level of managers, the Expertise Index was found to be high for most of the managers. For Peoples, the means the hierarchical levels for Expertise Index were somewhat near to the organizational mean. To get a clear indication of where expertise lies in the network from a transactive memory perspective, the Expertise Index that we calculated as a measure of organizational memory is very useful. The knowledge of 'who knows what' within an organization helps to locate specialized knowledge. This perspective assumes that though knowledge resides in the organization as a whole, the primary area of interest is in the individuals who contribute knowledge-as-object to the organization as a whole (Contractor and Monge, 2002; Brandon and Hollingshead, 2004). Studies have shown that organizations with transactive memory systems can easily pinpoint where expertise lies in an organization and can access that knowledge and can complete tasks more effectively over time (Lewis, 2004). 'Individuals are capable of capturing and transferring subtle nuances and tacit knowledge. By contrast, organizational routines and technologies are less "sensitive" repositories. Knowledge embedded in organizational routines and technologies, however, is more resistant to depreciation and more readily transferred than knowledge embedded in individuals. Organizations can use the strengths of one knowledge repository to offset the weaknesses of another' (Argote, 1999, p. 108).

As illustrated, social network analysis may be seen as a new way of examining topics currently explored in family firm literature and opens up new avenues for additional areas for future research. Though the two cases illustrated are mainly based on empirical research carried out in two family firms, it needs to be emphasized that the scope of social network analysis is more than just an analytical approach. Social network analysis is based on a strong theoretical foundation that has the potential to address specific issues in family firms.

For entrepreneurial family firms, social network analysis can explain their inner- and outer-family dynamics. Studies have shown that sometimes non-family members tend to be treated as family members in family firms (Karra et al., 2006). The power of social network analysis lies in mapping the internal network among the family and non-family members, and further identifying the associated clusters and cliques that can strengthen our understanding of such phenomenon. Our study clearly maps the relationship between various members of the family firm hierarchy and provides ample evidence about the nature of relationships and its effect on organizational learning. Social network analysis provides accurate description of how information is acquired, disseminated, and interpreted by family and non-family members through mapping the flow of information in the network and use of social network measures. The centrality-based network measures for organizational learning clearly depict how information can become an enabler or hindrance in decision making, based on the relationships between people in the network.

Future studies need to look at how networks between family firms and various other stakeholders (like suppliers and buyers) can affect the learning process as well as performance measures. Likewise, the relationship between different family firms (cf. Padgett and Ansell, 1993) may offer considerable promise.

Conclusion

This research tested an alternative model for measuring organizational learning in family firms using social network analysis. This research is particularly significant as learning is fast becoming a key driver of competitive advantage for family firms. The theoretical contribution

	Expertise Index
MD	84.211
Dir (Tech)	89.474
Dir (Mkt)	68.421
AGM (R&D)	63.158
AGM (Op1)	78.947
AGM (Op2)	73.684
Sr.Mg (HR)	57.895
Sr.Mg (Ac)	57.895
Sr.Chem1	89.474
Sr.Chem2	42.105
Sr.M8io	36.842
Mg (QC)	47.368
PMg	78.947
Sci Off	63.158
Ele Eng	63.158
Prod Off	15.789
Ast. Eng	47.368
Ast.Mg (P1)	36.842
Ast.Mg (P2)	52.632
Chem	36.842

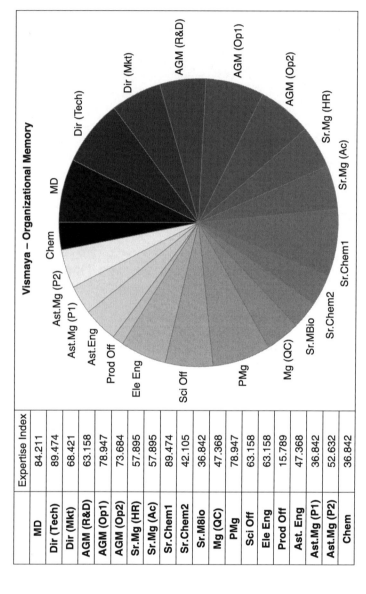

Vismaya – Organizational Memory

Figure 36.7 Vismaya – Organizational Memory

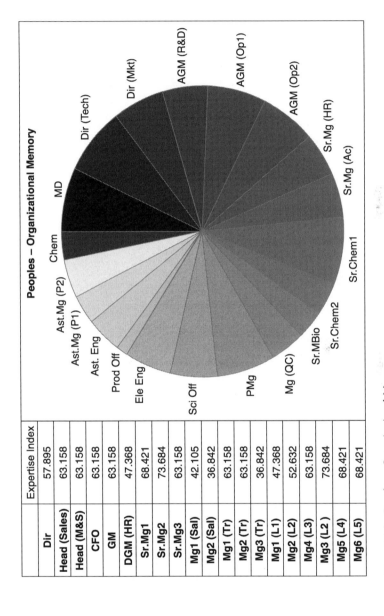

Peoples – Organizational Memory

	Expertise Index
Dir	57.895
Head (Sales)	63.158
Head (M&S)	63.158
CFO	63.158
GM	63.158
DGM (HR)	47.368
Sr.Mg1	68.421
Sr.Mg2	73.684
Sr.Mg3	63.158
Mg1 (Sal)	42.105
Mg2 (Sal)	36.842
Mg1 (Tr)	63.158
Mg2 (Tr)	63.158
Mg3 (Tr)	36.842
Mg1 (L1)	47.368
Mg2 (L2)	52.632
Mg4 (L3)	63.158
Mg3 (L2)	73.684
Mg5 (L4)	68.421
Mg6 (L5)	68.421

Figure 36.8 Peoples – Organizational Memory

includes a better understanding of the various sub-processes of organizational learning in family firms, which had remained unexplored. This study also contributes to the literature on organizational learning and family firms by taking the first step in developing a relational view of organizational learning that is long overdue for family firms.

Notes

1 http://www.cii.in/CII_FBN_India_Chapter.aspx. Accessed January 23, 2015.
2 Name changed for anonymity.
3 Name changed for anonymity.

Bibliography

Akgün, A. E., Byrne, J., Keskin, H., Lynn, G. S., and Imamoglu, S. Z. (2005). Knowledge networks in new product development projects: A transactive memory perspective. *Information and Management*, 42(8), 1105–1120.

Alegre, J., and Chiva, R. (2008). Assessing the impact of organizational learning capability on product innovation performance: An empirical test. *Technovation*, 28(6), 315–326.

Argote, L. (1999). *Organizational learning: creating, retaining, and transferring knowledge.* Boston, MA: Kluwer Academic.

Argote, L., McEvily, B., and Reagans, R. (2003). Managing knowledge in organizations: An integrative framework and review of emerging themes. *Management Science*, 49(4), 571–582.

Arregle, J., Hitt, M.A., Sirmon, D.G., and Very, P. (2007). The development of organizational social capital: Attributes of family firms. *Journal of Management Studies*, 44(1), 73–95.

Basly, S. (2007). The internationalization of family SME: An organizational learning and knowledge development perspective. *Baltic Journal of Management*, 2(2), 154–180.

Bettenhausen, K. L., and Murnighan, J. K. (1991).The development of an intragroup norm and the effects of interpersonal and structural challenges. *Administrative Science Quarterly*, 36(1), 20–35.

Bock, G. W., Zmud, R. W., Kim, Y. G., and Lee, J. N. (2005). Behavioral intention formation in knowledge sharing: Examining the roles of extrinsic motivators, social-psychological forces, and organizational climate. *MIS Quarterly*, 29(1), 87–111.

Borgatti, S. P., and Cross, R. (2003). A relational view of information seeking and learning in social networks. *Management Science*, 49(4), 432–445.

Borgatti, S. P., Everett, M. G., and Freeman, L. C. (2002). *Ucinet for Windows: Software for social network analysis.* Collegeville, PA: Analytic Technologies.

Brandon, D. P., and Hollingshead, A. B. (2004). Transactive memory systems in organizations: Matching tasks, expertise, and people. *Organization Science*, 15(6), 633–644.

Breton-Miller, I. L., Miller, D., and Steier, L. P. (2004). Toward an integrative model of effective FOB succession. *Entrepreneurship Theory and Practice*, 28(4), 305–328.

Burt, R. (2005). *Brokerage and closure: An introduction to social capital.* Oxford: Oxford University Press.

Contractor, N. S., and Monge, P. R. (2002). Managing knowledge networks. *Management Communication Quarterly*, 16(2), 249–258.

Covin, T. J. (1994). Profiling Preference for Employment in Family-Owned Firms. *Family Business Review*, 7(3), 287–296.

Cross, R., and Parker, A. (2004). *The hidden power of social networks: Understanding how work really gets done in organizations.* Boston, MA: Harvard Business Press.

Cross, R., Borgatti, S. P., and Parker, A. (2002). Making invisible work visible: Using social network analysis to support strategic collaboration. *California Management Review*, 44(2), 25–46.

Crossan, M., Lane, H., and White, R.E. (1999). An organizational learning framework: from intuition to institution. *Academy of Management Review*, 24(3), 522–537.

Cyert, R., and March, J. (1963). *A Behavioral Theory of the Firm.* Englewood Cliffs, NJ: PrenticeHall.

Davenport, T. H., and Prusak, L. (1998). *Working knowledge: Managing what your organization knows.* Boston MA: Harvard Business School Press.

Denison, D., Lief, C., and Ward, J. L. (2004). Culture in family-owned enterprises: recognizing and leveraging unique strengths. *Family Business Review*, 17(1), 61–70.

Flores, L. G., Zheng, W., Rau, D., and Thomas, C. H. (2012). Organizational learning: Subprocess identification, construct validation, and an empirical test of cultural antecedents. *Journal of Management*, 38(2), 640–667.

Gersick, K. E., Davis, J. A., McCollom-Hampton, M. M., and Lansberg, I. (1997). Choosing the right ownership structure. In M. Fischetti (Ed.), *The Family Business Succession Handbook* (pp. 7–8). Philadelphia: Family Business Publishing.

Ghoshal, S., and Bartlett, C. A. (1990).The multinational corporation as an interorganizational network. *Academy of Management Review*, 15(4), 603–625.

Gómez-Mejía, L. R., Haynes, K. T., Núñez-Nickel, M., Jacobson, K. J. L., Moyano-Fuentes, J., Haynes, K. T., and Núñez-Nickel, M. (2007). Socioemotional wealth and business risks in family-controlled firms: evidence from Spanish Olive Oil Mills. *Administrative Science Quarterly*, 52(1), 106–137.

Granovetter, M. (1973). The strength of weak ties. *American Journal of Sociology*, 78(6), 1360–1380.

Greve, A., and Salaff, J. W. (2003). Social networks and entrepreneurship. *Entrepreneurship theory and practice*, 28(1), 1–22.

Grote, J. (2004). Conflicting generations: A new theory of family business rivalry. *Family Business Review*, 16(2), 113–124.

Habbershon, T. G., Williams, M., and MacMillan, I. C. (2003). A unified systems perspective of family firm performance. *Journal of Business Venturing*, 18(4), 451–465.

Hanneman, R. A., and Riddle, M. (2005). Introduction to social network methods [Electronic text]. Retrieved from http://faculty.ucr.edu/~hanneman/nettext. Accessed October 12, 2014.

Huber, G. P. (1991). Organizational learning: The contributing processes and literatures. *Organization Science*, 2(1), 88–115.

Ibarra, H. (1995). Race, opportunity, and diversity of social circles in managerial networks. *Academy of Management Journal*, 38(3), 673–703.

Ibarra, H., and Andrews, S. B. (1993). Power, social influence, and sense making: Effects of network centrality and proximity on employee perceptions. *Administrative Science Quarterly*, 38(2), 277–303.

Jack, S. (2005). The role, use and activation of strong and weak network ties: a qualitative study. *Journal of Management Studies*, 42(6), 1233–1259.

Kang, D. (1998). The impact of ownership type on performance in public corporations: a study of the U.S. textile industry 1983–1992.Working paper. Boston: Harvard Business School.

Karra, N., Tracey, P., and Phillips, N. (2006). Altruism and agency in the family firm: Exploring the role of family, kinship, and ethnicity. *Entrepreneurship Theory and Practice*, 30(6), 861–877.

Kets de Vries, M. F. R., Carlock, R. S., and Florent-Treacy, E. (2007). *Family business on the couch: A psychological perspective*. Chichester, England: John Wiley and Sons Publications.

Lansberg, I. (1999). *Succeeding generations: Realizing the dream of families in business*. Boston: Harvard Business Press.

Leana, C. R., and Van Buren, H. J. (1999). Organizational social capital and employment practices. *Academy of Management Review*, 24(3), 538–555.

Lee, F. (1997). When the going gets tough, do the tough ask for help? Help seeking and power motivation in organizations. *Organizational Behavior Human Decision Processes*, 72(3), 336–363.

Lewis, K. (2004). Knowledge and performance in knowledge-worker teams: A longitudinal study of transactive memory systems. *Management Science*, 50(11), 1519–1533.

Lyman, A. R. (1991). Customer service: Does family ownership make a difference? *Family Business Review*, 4(3), 303–324.

Manev, I. M., and Stevenson, W. B. (2001). Nationality, cultural distance, and expatriate status: Effects on the managerial network in a multinational enterprise. *Journal of International Business Studies*, 32(2), 285–303.

Marsden, P. V. (1990). Network data and measurement. *Annual Review of Sociology*, 16(1), 435–463.

Miller, D., and Le Breton-Miller, I. (2006). Family governance and firm performance: Agency, stewardship, and capabilities. *Family Business Review*,19(1), 73–87

Moores, K. (2009). Paradigms and theory building in the domain of business families. *Family Business Review*, 22(2), 167–180.

Mustakallio, M., Autio, E., and Zahra, S. A. (2003). Relational and contractual governance in family firms: Effects on strategic decision making. *Family Business Review*, 15(3), 205–222.

Nordqvist, M., and Melin, L. (2010). Entrepreneurial families and family firms. *Entrepreneurship and Regional Development*, 22(3), 1–29.

O'Reilly, C. A. (1982). Variations in decision makers' use of information sources: The impact of quality and accessibility of information. *Academy of Management Journal*, 25(4), 756–771.

Padgett, J. F., and Ansell, C. K. (1993). Robust action and the rise of Medici: 1400-1434. *American Journal of Sociology*, 98(6), 1259–1319.

Patel, P. C., and Fiet, J. O. (2011). Knowledge combination and the potential advantages of family firms in searching for opportunities. *Entrepreneurship Theory and Practice*, 35(6), 1179–1197.

Pearson, A., Carr, J. C., and Shaw, J. C. (2008). Toward a theory of familiness: A social capital perspective. *Entrepreneurship Theory and Practice*, 32(6), 949–969.

Poutziouris, P. Z., Smyrnios, K., and Klein, S. (2006). *Handbook of Research on Family Business*. Cheltenham: Edward Elgar Publishing.

Shepherd, D., and Zahra, S. (2003). From conservatism to entrepreneurialism: The case of Swedish family firms. Unpublished paper. Boulder, CO: University of Colorado.

Sirmon, D. G., and Hitt, M. A. (2003). Managing resources: Linking unique resources, management and wealth creation in family firms. *Entrepreneurship Theory and Practice*, 27(4), 339–358.

Smith, W. K., and Lewis, M. W. (2011). Toward a theory of paradox: A dynamic equilibrium model of organizing. *Academy of Management Review*, 36(2), 381–403.

Szulanski, G. (1996). Exploring internal stickiness: Impediments to the transfer of best practice within the firm. *Strategic Management Journal*, 17(S2), 27–43.

Thomas, N., and Vohra, N. (2015). Development of Network Measures for Knowledge Processes: A Relational Framework. *Knowledge and Process Management*, 22(2), 126–139.

Tsai, W., and Ghoshal, S. (1998). Social capital and value creation: The role of intrafirm networks. *Academy of Management Journal*, 41(4), 464–476.

Wegner, D. M. (1987). Transactive memory: A contemporary analysis of the group mind. In B. Mullen and G. R. Goethals (Eds.), *Theories of group behavior* (pp. 185–208). New York: Springer.

Zahra, S. (2008). The virtuous cycle of discovery and creation of entrepreneurial opportunities. *Strategic Entrepreneurship Journal*, 2(3), 243–257.

Zahra, S. A. (2005). Entrepreneurial risk taking in family firms. *Family Business Review*, 18(1), 23–40.

Zahra, S. A. (2012). Organizational learning and entrepreneurship in family firms: exploring the moderating effect of ownership and cohesion. *Small Business Economics*, 38(1), 51–65.

Zahra, S. A., Neubaum, D. O., and Larraneta, B. (2007). Knowledge sharing and technological capabilities: The moderating role of family involvement. *Journal of Business Research*, 60(10), 1070–1079.

Zand, D. E. (1972). Trust and managerial problem solving. *Administrative Science Quarterly*, 17(2), 229–239.

Appendix 36.1   List of Vismaya managers who participated in the survey and their abbreviations

1. Managing Director	MD
2. Director–Technical	Dir (Tech)
3. Director–Marketing	Dir (Mkt)
4. Assistant General Manager–R and D	AGM (R & D)
5. Assistant General Manager–Operations1	AGM (Op1)
6. Assistant General Manager–Operations2	AGM (Op2)
7. Senior Manager–HR and Admin	Sr.Mg (HR)
8. Senior Manager–Accounts	Sr.Mg (Ac)
9. Manager–Quality Control	Mg (QC)
10. Senior Chemist1	Sr.Chem1
11. Senior Chemist2	Sr.Chem2
12. SeniorMicrobiologist	Sr.MBio
13. Plant Manager	PMg
14. Scientific Officer	Sci Off
15. Production Officer	Prod Off

16.	Assistant Manager–Production1	Ast.Mg (P1)
17.	Assistant Manager–Production2	Ast.Mg (P2)
18.	Assistant Engineer	Ast.Eng
19.	Electrical Engineer	EleEng
20.	Chemist	Chem

Appendix 36.2 List of Peoples managers who participated in the survey and their abbreviations

1.	Director	Dir
2.	Head–Sales	Head (Sales)
3.	Head–Marketing and Strategy	Head (M & S)
4.	Chief Financial Officer	CFO
5.	General Manager	GM
6.	Deputy General Manager – Human Resources	DGM (HR)
7.	Senior Manager1	Sr.Mg1
8.	Senior Manager2	Sr.Mg2
9.	Senior Manager3	Sr.Mg3
10.	Manager–Sales1	Mg1 (Sal)
11.	Manager–Sales2	Mg2 (Sal)
12.	Manager–Training1	Mg1 (Tr)
13.	Manager–Training2	Mg2 (Tr)
14.	Manager–Training3	Mg3 (Tr)
15.	Manager1–L1	Mg1 (L1)
16.	Manager2–L2	Mg2 (L2)
17.	Manager3–L3	Mg3 (L3)
18.	Manager4–L4	Mg4 (L4)
19.	Manager5–L5	Mg5 (L5)
20.	Manager6–L6	Mg6 (L6)

PART VI

Policy implications and synthesis

37

POLICY EFFORTS TO FOSTER INNOVATIVE SMES IN SOUTH KOREA

Lessons for developing countries

Taehyun Jung and Jungbu Kim

Introduction

Since its industrialization began in the 1960s and during the developmental process from an economy of abject poverty, the Korean economy has been driven by large conglomerates such as Samsung, Hyundai, and LG, to list just a few. Fortunately, these large firms had well adapted themselves to rapidly changing competitive business environments over the tumultuous decades. Some of them, such as Samsung Electronics, even succeeded in restructuring themselves from a follower through a fast follower to an innovator. The economic development model heavily dependent on large firms at the expense of small and medium-sized enterprises (SMEs), however, was confronted with its limitation. From the late 1990s till the early 2000s several symptoms emerged as an indicator of such limits: (slowed down) economic growth without employment growth; heavy dependence on foreign firms for essential parts and materials; and the weakening competitiveness of SME sectors.

Alerted by such symptoms, Korean industrial policy hawks now turn their eyes to the growth potentials that can be exploited through promoting SMEs. From the turn of the century Korean industrial and technology policies have put ever more emphasis than before on promoting startups and beefing up SMEs. This chapter looks back on the process of this policy transition. A main focus of the review is to draw lessons for developing countries that are making strenuous efforts to bolster their respective SMEs. In particular, we highlight the following policy elements among others:

- Rationales and importance of SMEs in innovative capability-building;
- Government-endorsed certification as an instrument for dual purposes (i.e. chaffing out ineligibles and incentivizing self-fulfillment);
- Designated government organization which plays central roles in implementing diverse policy packages;
- Importance of political sponsorship and well-framed slogans; and
- Public–private partnerships.

In the subsequent sections, we discuss each of these policy elements with its potential policy implications for other developing countries.

Rationale and importance of SMEs in innovative capability-building

Support policies for SMEs in Korea have been gradually moving into the industrial policy field since the turn of the century. Both societal and economic concerns drove this transition. One telltale observation is that fruits from the laudable successes by big conglomerates have not been fully savored by SMEs. While SMEs in total account for more than 99.9 percent of total business establishments, employing about 93.4 percent of total employees in 2013,[1] revenue generated by an average employee from SMEs is only about ₩200 million in 2010, which is a mere 40 percent of large firms (₩513.4 million).[2] Beyond statistics, there is a wide-spread public concern that the general weakness of the Korean SME sectors will seriously undermine Korea's overall economic competitiveness.

This concern is not just about the size or scale of SMEs, but also about the structure of the industrial value chain. When large firms sell final goods in global markets, they import materials and parts from foreign countries. Without domestic SMEs taking on producing globally competitive parts, a substantial portion of values attached to the final goods go to SMEs in foreign countries. More than that, globally distributed value chains sometimes hinder a firm from enjoying invisible benefits such as localized knowledge spillovers, a rapid development process and a short time-to-market, and/or possible communication benefits stemming from cultural proximity. This is what happened in Korea during its industrialization and continues to be a woe for policy-makers and industrialists. However, parts and materials oftentimes do not reach a minimum efficient scale in production for large firms, while SMEs lack technological capabilities to develop a competitive product on par with foreign suppliers. Market mechanisms alone could not help SMEs catch up with global technological competition, and brought forth government intervention in subsidizing R&D to SMEs. Thanks to various supporting policies during the last decade, materials and parts sectors have continued to improve their competitiveness in export markets. Still, the trade deficit for Japan in these sectors amounted to $20.5 billion in 2003.[3]

Weak SME sectors bring forth more serious issues regarding the labor market and the Korean society in general. Different from the previous eras during which large firms expanded their production capability by increasing the labor force, large firms nowadays focus more on building up innovative capability and maintaining their labor productivity at a globally competitive level. Consequently, economic growth without growth in employment represented the public sentiment toward the Korean economy in the early 2000s. There is a local satirical acronym "Yi Tae Baek," meaning that more than one half of the youth population (mostly in their 20s) are unemployed. In fact, the employment rate for those in their early 20s (aged between 20 and 24) decreased by 10.1 percent points from 2003 (52.2 percent) to 2013 (42.1 percent). The youth unemployment rate fluctuated around 5.5 percent during the 1990s, peaked at 12.2 percent just after the financial crisis in 1997, and then recorded 9 percent in 2014, the highest rate since 1999. Young people rather choose to go to schools than to work as indicated by the ratio of students in youth (aged between 15 and 29) which increased from 33.3 percent in 1990 to 51.2 percent in 2010 (Korea National Statistical Office 2013).

At the same time, SMEs find themselves struggling to recruit new workforce. The rate of labor force shortage is progressively higher for smaller firms (for example, 0.6 percent for firms with 500 or more employees, and 4.6 percent for firms with less than 30 employees)

(Ministry of Trade, Industry and Energy 2013). Moreover, bright young people choose to work for established large firms rather than to start their own businesses. Now, the Korean public as well as policy-makers are seriously concerned that the Korean economy may have lost its dynamism and future growth momentum by surrendering the potential of millions of people for 'creative destruction' to scores of large firms. Moreover, labor market volatility, especially for young people, incurs huge social costs and possible political costs to Korean society. With such an obvious market failure and the increasingly lackluster economy due to the weak SME sectors, the Korean government has been increasingly restless in resuscitating them and helping them play the role of a new growth momentum.

Government-endorsed certification as an instrument for dual purposes

Different from any other countries, the Korean government institutionalized a system for certifying and promoting 'venture firms'. A law for Special Remedy for Promoting Venture Firms (SRPVF) went into effect in October, 1997. The law and a following rule for Certifying Venture Firms by the Small and Medium Business Administration (SMBA) define certified venture firms using investment criteria and R&D expenditure in combination with business assessment. The first type of venture firms are those that have received a certain amount of investment, loan or credit guarantee from certified semi-public organizations such as Korea Venture Capital Association (KVCA), Korea Technology Finance Corporation (KIBO), or Small and Medium Business Corporation (SBC). The second type of firm (R&D firms) is certified when their R&D intensity is over 5 percent (or greater than KRW 50 million) and passes through assessment from either KIBO or SBC. In 2015, certified venture firms number 30,480 among which firms with technology-credit guarantee account for 84 percent (Table 37.1).

Now, let us look at the trends of venture firms for the last two decades as shown in Figure 37.1. From 1998 when the SRPVF went effective to 2001 when the dotcom bubble burst, the number of venture firms quadrupled. With the opening of KOSDAQ, a stock exchange made after NASDAQ of the U.S., in 1996 and active policy supports including SRPVF, the late 1990s was the first boom for venture firms in Korea. The number of venture firms then slowly and monotonically increased since 2003.

According to a recent survey on SMEs (Ministry of Trade, Industry and Energy, 2013), about 51 percent of the surveyed SMEs are either innovative SMEs or venture firms. In addition to laws supporting venture firms, the Korean government designated innovative SMEs (called 'Inno-Biz firms') and supported them. Inno-Biz firms are SMEs active in business for three years and longer and assessed to be innovative. The assessment criteria are

Table 37.1 Breakdown of Certified Venture Firms in 2015

	Firms with KVCA Investment	Firms with technology-credit guarantee	Firms with loans based on technology assessment	R&D firms	Preliminary venture firms	Sum
Number	882	25,586	2,293	1,647	72	30,480
Share (percent)	2.9	83.9	7.5	5.4	0.2	100

Data: Venture Statistics System from Venturein retrieved on August 10, 2015 from https://www.venturein. or.kr/venturein/data/C61100.do.

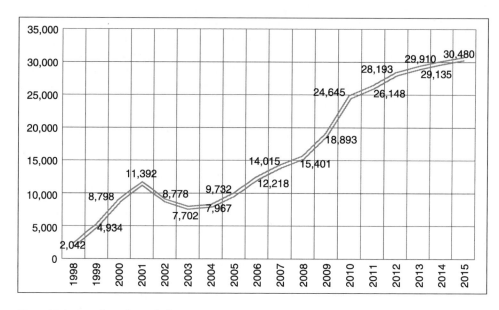

Figure 37.1   Number of Certified Venture Firms in Korea: 1998–2015

Data: Venture Statistics System from Venturein retrieved on August 10, 2015 from https://www.venturein. or.kr/venturein/data/C61100.do.

based on the Oslo Manual (OECD and Eurostat, 2005) and include capabilities in technology innovation, commercialization, managing innovation, and innovation performance. The Inno-Biz firms are eligible for Small Business Innovative Research projects run by SMBA and for many other support packages. Currently, 17,398 SMEs are designated as Inno-Biz.

The government-endorsed certification system of venture and Inno-biz firms serves three goals in supporting policies for SMEs. First, by certifying a firm that satisfies a certain set of criteria, support is more accurately and effectively targeted to those firms who are not only eligible but also willing and capable to follow the policy guidance. Selecting the right recipients of funding or R&D support can effectively mitigate risks of adverse selection and information asymmetry. By limiting the range of eligible applicants to those already certified as Venture or Inno-Biz, the government-funded support packages effectively target the early-stage startups or innovative small firms. Second, the certification system can benefit market participants by signaling and advertising governmental policy directions to the stakeholders. Delineating a formal boundary for a certain group of firms from others and funneling supports to those certified firms, in themselves, effectively shepherd firms around the borderline to get certified. Related to this, lastly, certification does not enforce but incentivizes firms to voluntarily develop themselves into what policy measures intend them to develop. To be certified as an Inno-biz firm, for example, it must show that it has capabilities in technology innovation, commercialization, managing innovation, and innovation performance.

Designated government organization for SME policies

The institutional protagonist of SME support policies in Korea is Small and Medium Business Administration (SMBA) which was established in 1996 and is dedicated to supporting SMEs

Table 37.2 Governmental Projects and Expenditures for Supporting Venture Startups

Responsible Ministries	2014		2015 Budget	
	Expenditures (# of Projects)	*Share (percent)*	*Expenditures (# of Projects)*	*Share (percent)*
Small and Medium Business Administration (SMBA)	20,534.4(18)	94.80	18,141.0(18)	94.90
Ministry of Science, ICT and Future Planning (MSIP)	791.2(7)	3.65	721.4(7)	3.78
Ministry of Trade, Industry and Energy	20.0(1)	0.09	20.0(1)	0.10
Ministry of Culture, Sports and Tourism	137.6(2)	0.64	154.7(2)	0.81
Ministry of Education	15.0(1)	0.07	13.5(1)	0.07
Ministry of Employment and Labor	163.3(3)	0.75	64.9(3)	0.34
Total	21,661.5(32)	100	19,115.5(32)	100

Source: Lim and Jeong (2014: 5).

Unit: 100 million KRW.

and startups. The central role of SMBA as a perpetrator of startup support policies is clearly shown in the breakdown of government expenditures (Table 37.2). In 2014, more than ₩2 trillion of the government budget was allocated for supporting venture firms and startups. A similarly structured but slightly reduced budget was appropriated for year 2015. SMBA commands about 95 percent of the budget in startup support policies in both years. Various ministries of Science, ICT and Future Planning (MSIP), of Culture, Sports and Tourism (MCST), of Trade, Industry and Energy (MTIE), of Employment and Labor (MEL), and of Education (ME) are also involved in supporting startups but to a limited extent.

The Korean government has been expanding policies for SMEs and startups by streamlining the startup process and providing better opportunities for attracting investment (Lee 2015). The overall policy packages cover the life-cycle of startups and consist of two parts: R&D and support for commercialization. As shown in the Figure 37.2, the gamut from identifying ideas to commercialization is composed of at least six distinct stages (business ideas, product concept development, R&D planning, R&D, commercialization, and marketing). The left four stages require R&D support and so their budget and programs are substantially coordinated by the Ministry of Science, ICT and Future Planning (MSIP), the flagship ministry for the Korean government's SandT, R&D, and innovation policies. The rightmost two stages are related to marketing and commercializing technologies and products. Because these activities do not belong to traditional areas of R&D, their budget and programs are ultimately coordinated by the Ministry of Strategy and Finance. Despite separate coordination, most programs for supporting startups and ventures are perpetrated by SMBA.

Now, let us overview the detailed programs targeting startups and ventures. We list programs, projects, and sub-projects related to startups and ventures by detailing the programs from the ministry in Table 37.3. As of 2014, there are at least 63 different projects and programs that support and facilitate starting a new business (Lee 2015), two-thirds of which are implemented by MSIP and SMBA. These programs/projects have distinct emphases; entrepreneurial spirit, generation and substantiation of ideas, commercialization, and globalization, but about half of the programs are focusing on identifying and leveraging ideas.

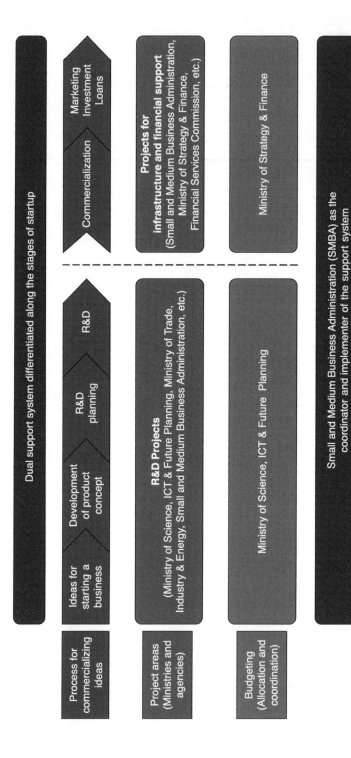

Figure 37.2 Dual Support System Differentiated along the Stages of the Startup Process

Source: Adapted from Kim and Jeong (2014, p. 27).

Table 37.3 Governmental Projects for Supporting Venture Startups

Programs	Projects	Sub-projects
Small and Medium Business Administration	Facilitation of Startup-Friendly Environment	Facilitation of startups	Nurturing startup environment
			Support for startup business models
			Nurturing leading universities for startups
			Support for SMB revival
		Startup infra support	Support for startup infrastructure
		Preferential loans for startups	Preferential loan for startups
	Stabilization support for SMB growth	Performance improvement in support policies	Performance improvement in preferential loans
	Support for Corporate Partnership	Support for businesses owned by women and/or the disabled	Nurturing female-owned businesses
			Nurturing disabled-owned businesses
	Support for small enterprises and traditional markets	Support for small enterprises	Strengthening management capacity of small enterprise owners
	Support for SMB technology development	Support for technology development	Technology development for startup and growth
	Support for promoting startup business activities	Support for venture growth infrastructure	Modernization of venture capital
			Strengthening venture competitiveness
			Support for Merger and Acquisition (M&A) facilitation
		Investment in Cooperatives for the Fund for Funds (seed money)	Investment in SMB Cooperatives for the Fund for Funds (seed money)
		Establishment of business conversion infrastructure	Facilitation of business conversion
		Fund for loans for business conversion	Loans for business conversion
		Fund for the development of leisure gear industry	Support for the development of leisure gear industry

Ministry			
Ministry of Science, ICT and Future Panning	Facilitation of broadcasting-telecommunications conversion	Establishment of infrastructure for nurturing SMBs in the broadcasting and telecommunications industry	Nurturing ICT-based creative firms
	Promotion of the ICT industry	Promotion of contents for broadcasting and telecommunications	Establishment of infrastructure for creative contents production; Korea Fund for Digital Contents
			Establishment and operation of total support packages for creative economy
	Advancement of science/technology infrastructure	Establishment of infrastructure for nurturing creative economy	Support for technology diffusion in ICT
		Support for technology diffusion	Establishment of infrastructure for creative economy
		Establishment of infrastructure for creative economy	Support for commercialization of technologies by research communities
		Support for commercialization of technologies by research communities	
Ministry of Trade, Industry and Energy	Establishment of the energy supply system	Preferential loans for promoting mining towns	Preferential loans for startups in alternative industries
Ministry of Employment and Labor	Employment policy	Support for job creation	Support for job creation
		Youth internships at SMBs	Youth internships for job creation
	Industrial accident compensation insurance	Preferential loans for welfare services for victims of industrial accidents	Preferential loans for the startups for victims of industrial accidents
Ministry of Education	Strengthening higher education capacity	Nurturing leading universities in university-industry cooperation	Nurturing leading universities in university-industry cooperation
Ministry of Culture, Sports and Tourism	Nurturing of the content development industry	Promotion of cultural contents	Operation of the Contents Korea Laboratory
	Nurturing of the tourism industry	Support for nurturing domestic tourism	Nurturing creative tourism

Source: Adapted from Lim and Jeong (2014: 139–140).

SMBA is involved in broad and diverse areas of programs. They include direct funding programs for startup R&D (e.g. 'Support for SMB technology development'), business model development (e.g. 'Support for startup business models'), and financial support for startup operation (e.g. 'Preferential loans for startups' and 'Support for businesses owned by women and/or the disabled'). SMBA is also in charge of indirect support policies to improve the business environment and infrastructure for startups. Most support policies in this category fall under the program named 'Support for promoting startup business activities,' which aims to enhance venture capital industry and Merger and Acquisition (M&A) environment. The Korean government also established 'the Fund for Funds' to provide seed money for venture and patent-based financing and to lubricate startup investment by compensating for a portion of possible loss resulting from it.

MSIP policies center on promoting and commercializing ICT-based innovation as well as enhancing overall infrastructure for nurturing ideas and facilitating commercialization. The other ministries are responsible for supporting niche areas related to startups and ventures but under their substantive areas. For example, MTIE supports startups in the energy sector (in particular, those startups that can rejuvenate the declining mining industry). MCST, on the other hand, supports startups and SMEs in cultural contents and tourism industries.

In sum, supporting policies for startups, ventures, and SMEs in Korea seem diverse and comprehensive. They cover all the stages of the startup life-cycle including nurturing ideas and R&D to supporting commercialization and marketing. The protagonist in policy implementation is SMBA. MSIP plays important roles in R&D stages and in particular areas of technology such as ICT. Coordination between different programs as well as different ministries is, however, still an issue. Among others two powerful ministries—MSF and MSIP—split the responsibility in budgeting and coordinating the policies for startups. Some say that this structural division of responsibility makes streamlining and integrating relevant policies difficult and causes serious inefficiencies and ineffectiveness in policy implementation (Lim and Jeong 2014).

Importance of political sponsorship and slogan

The current administration led by President Park Geun-hye put forth 'Creative Economy' as a political platform and an overarching policy orientation. As might be guessed from its nomenclature, policy packages for entrepreneurship and new venture creation play central roles in it. Creative Economy (CE) is a political rhetoric (Kim and Park 2013) to spearhead new economic development, as promoted by the current Park Geun-hye administration (since 2013). However, it does go beyond the rhetoric and incorporate a full policy package covering R&D, infrastructural support, and nurturing of business startups.

As a policy 'guiding theme,' or a paradigm for economic policies, it intends to address 'fundamental challenges within Korea's innovation ecosystem,' that cut across regulatory, structural, educational and cultural dimensions and restrict Korea's ability to renew its growth dynamism (Connell 2013, p. 1). The policy package of CE foremost recognizes the critical importance of creative assets in boosting the Korean economy. Creative assets in the economy combine 'creative idea, imagination/communication technology (ICT) (that) plays a pivotal role in stimulating startups' (Ministry of Science, ICT and Future Planning 2015a). The CE policy package also embraces that Korea's new growth engine be grounded on the convergence of top notch science and technology, especially ICT, with the traditional industries, based on creative ideas and imagination. The CE policy roadmap also pays particular attention to the critical roles that can be played by ICT-savvy SME startups imbued with creative ideas and challenging spirits. Therefore, the CE policy package includes further support for basic and applied science research, measures of transferring knowledge from public research institutes and universities to businesses, especially SMEs, and a total package of nurturing SMEs (including infrastructure, property rights, venture capital, and marketing).

The CE policy initiative, as driven by Madam President herself, intends ultimately to create an ecosystem that facilitates and brims over with startups and SMEs that are based on creative and synergistic combinations of scientific knowledge, technology, and ICT. For this purpose, the Korean political leadership is committed to: 1) breaking down obstacles that hinder startups and their foray into new markets, beefing up the intellectual property right system for safer circulation of creative ideas and knowledge, and creating stronger resilience after a failure; 2) support for, and cultivation of, venture and SMEs with financial support, preferential tax treatment, and measures to encourage partnerships between large companies and SMEs to share benefits from economic growth; 3) creation of new industries and markets by developing new products and services leveraging the convergence of knowledge and technology, especially in agriculture, culture, health, and marine sectors; 4) development of creative talents who, exuding with entrepreneurial spirit, can compete globally, by helping them fully realize their professional capabilities abroad; 5) strengthening the capacities in science and technology and ICT by increasing public expenditures in R&D and building the world's best Internet and network environment; and 6) creation of inclusive and creative culture, a social environment where the public can express their creative ideas without any reservations, with more opportunities for the creation and innovation of new values, and where the government engages the public to work together and innovate in its own operation (Ministry of Science, ICT and Future Planning 2015b).

Public–private partnership

The CE policy orientation is substantiated through the leadership of President Park and MSIP and by engaging private stakeholders, as depicted in Figure 37.3. Under the MSIP minister, the Chief Coordinator for Creative Economy is responsible for managing and coordinating the key program initiatives for the CE policy packages. Three key program initiatives, Creative Economy Town (CET), Centers for Creative Economy and Innovation (CCEI), and Idea Innovation 6 Months Challenge (Inno 6+) Platform, are all geared toward swiftly identifying and translating ICT-based promising business ideas into startups, through better nurturing partnerships between public institutions and private enterprises and individuals. Such public leadership, however, is incorporating, and complemented by, private inputs through an advisory forum and the public–private task force. Another key characteristic of the governance for the CE policy packages is that at both the national and regional levels, inputs from private firms and experts assume critical importance in the operation of the regional CCEIs and the mentoring process for the proposers of innovative ideas in the Inno 6+ Platform.

As the current Park administration struggles to redefine and transform Korea's growth engine leveraging the conversion of science, technology, and ICT, the CE packages have been paid special attention by budgeters who make it an all-out governmental endeavor. There are four broad program areas that involve multiple projects and ministries/agencies: creative culture; ecosystem for startups and support for SMEs; capacity building in Science and Technology (S&T) and ICT; and spearheading new industries and new markets. These program areas cover diverse projects implemented by the ministries/agencies for industrial, educational, cultural, R&D, fiscal planning, SMEs, agricultural and food policies. That is,

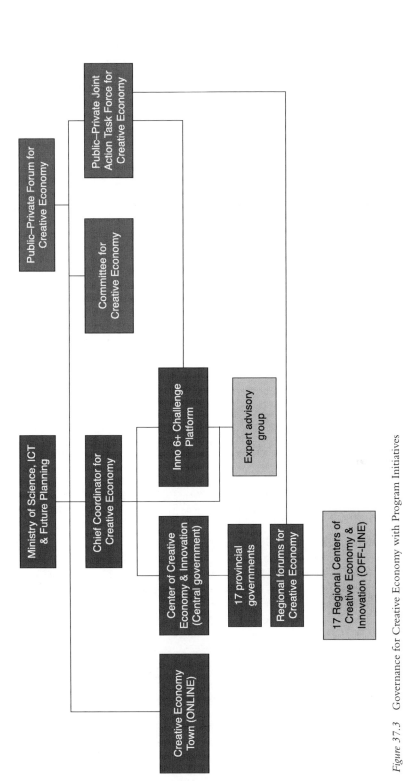

Figure 37.3 Governance for Creative Economy with Program Initiatives

Source: Adopted from Lee (2015, p. xvi).

policies embracing the CE initiative go beyond a particular ministry/agency and stretch across almost the entire central and sub-national governments and the public–private partnership forum plays a critical role in bringing together private firms and individuals with ideas and supporting public institutions.

The Korean government has increased its budgetary expenditures for the CE initiative by 17.1 percent to ₩8,330 billion (about US$7 billion) in 2015, which is about 4 percent[4] of the central government's expenditures from the general account. Of the ₩8,330 billion CE budget, 43 percent is for blazing the trail for new industries and market; and 23 percent for strengthening S&T and ICT capacity. More notable are the expenditure hikes for establishing the ecosystem of startups and SMEs (by ₩486 billion, an increase of 38.5 percent) and for spearheading new industries and markets (by ₩561 billion, an increase of 18.8 percent). As summarized by Table 37.4, these expenditures finance R&D by SMEs, R&D in culture, provision of infrastructure (facilities), networking and nurturing partnerships among stakeholders, and facilitation of conversion of SandT and ICT across diverse industries.

These projects and the policy roadmap hinge upon the facilitation of an ecosystem of startups based on creative ideas. Such facilitation of the startup process will depend on the roles played by *an intermediary organization (accelerator) that serves as a broker*, given that the innovative networks most likely lack information or suffer from information asymmetry. The broker can solve such problems by linking the generators of ideas, founders, venture capitals, and other supporting institutions. The Park administration implements three distinct programs for this purpose: 1) Online Creative Economy Town; 2) Centers for Creative Economy and Innovation (CCEI); and 3) Idea Innovation 6 Months Challenge (Inno 6+) Platform. In what follows, each of these three initiatives will be introduced with some critical and evaluative discussions. All of these initiatives are taking issue with the criticisms that the previous startup support policies tend to ignore the initial process of clarifying and translating ideas into business models and practices and that the support policies have yet to tap into the full potential of various stakeholders such as universities, individual firms, and venture capitals.

The *Centers for Creative Economy and Innovation* (CCEI) is another key policy measure to build regional innovation hubs by linking large companies, local startups, and ventures. Through each CCEI, a large company with global presence can help startups and SMEs in the development of business models and products based on creative ideas and technologies, marketing, and/or investing in them. This is a sharp departure from the previous practices in that the large conglomerates with top-notch business expertise take the initiative in guiding the startups and SMEs in navigating through the gamut of entrepreneurialism.

As summarized in Table 37.5, each of Korea's 17 regional (or provincial) jurisdictions has one CCEI established, starting from the Daegu Metropolitan city in September 2014. Korea's regional jurisdictions are all distinctive in terms of historical experiences, presence of higher education institutions, industrial structures and clusters, location of public research institutes, and ultimately their respective regional innovation systems which have been shaped through a long series of strong industrial and regional policies over the last 50 years. At each Center, a Korean conglomerate or a comparable big company serves as the prime facilitator in the region providing innovative dynamism for the regional innovation system. Some of those conglomerates include *Samsung, LG*, and *Hyundai Motor Company*. Each CCEI has also its own fund for supporting SMEs and encouraging startups, totaling ₩1,770 billion (or, about US$1.5 billion), excluding the Seoul CCEI. Each CCEI also has supporting staff of variable size. In total, the regional CCEIs employ 226 staff members.

The *Idea Innovation Six Months Challenge Platform* (Inno 6+ Platform) Project is a policy platform designed to accelerate the startup process to be full-circled in six months, aiming

Table 37.4 Budget for the Creative Economy Policy Packages, 2015

Key program areas (Total budget)	Key projects	Expenditure amount	Responsible ministries
Creative culture (₩1,146)	Centers for Creative Economy and Innovation	₩19.7	MSIP
	Global complex for knowledge-based CE	₩5.5	MSF
	Establishment and operation of Lab for Unlimited Imagination	₩4.6	MSIP
	Nurturing talent in cultural contents	₩2.2	MCST
Ecosystem for startups and support for SMEs (₩1,748)	Six Months Challenge Platform	₩10	MSIP
	Support for SME revitalization	₩20	SMBA
	Building export potential by SMEs	₩66	SMBA
	Technology development for startup and growth	₩147.4	SMBA
	Creation of new industries through the nexus of industry–university–region	₩15	MSIP
	Regional ecosystem for commercializing ideas	₩10.3	MSIP
Capacity building in SandT and ICT (₩1,892)	Promotion of CE Valley	₩30.8	MSIP
	District for Industry–University Conversion	₩23	MTIE
	One Stop Service for Businesses	₩8	MSIP
	Inter-Ministrial Giga Korea	₩41	MSIP
	International Science Business Belt	₩214	MSIP
Spearheading new industries and new markets (₩3,544)	Provision of smart factories	₩5	MTIE
	Building soft power in manufacturing industries	₩1	MTIE
	Facilitation of conversion–based industries in rural areas	₩12.7	MAFRA
	Golden Seed Project	₩40.3	MAFRA, MOF, etc.
	Next generation medical equipment industry	₩11.6	MSIP
	Global market penetration by top-notch bio-medical products	₩15	MSIP, MHW
	System development for spatial big data	₩5.7	MLIT
	R&D in cultural technology	₩27.3	MCST

Source: Adapted from MSIP (2014).

Unit: in ₩ billion.

Table 37.5 Profiles of Centers for Creative Economy and Innovation

Location (region)	Date of establishment	Key supporting conglomerate	Specialization	Expected size of funds (In billions)	Number of full-time staffers
Seoul	July 17, 2015	CJ	Cultural contents	Under consideration	7
Busan	March 16, 2015	LOTTE	Retail and films	₩230	22
Incheon	July 22, 2015	Hanjin	Marine transport, aviation, and logistics hub	₩159	13
Gwangju	January 27, 2015	Hyundai	Automobile	₩68.6	13
Daejeon	October 10, 2014	SK	ICT	₩50	30
Daegu	September 15, 2014	Samsung	Electronics	₩20	20
Sejong	June 30, 2015	SK	ICT for agriculture	₩2.3	11
Ulsan	July 15, 2015	Hyundai Heavy Industry	Shipbuilding and machinery	₩162	10
Gyeonggi	March 30, 2015	KT	IT services	₩105	16
Gangwon	May 11, 2015	NAVER	IT services and big data	₩105	14
Chungbuk	February 4, 2015	LG	Electronics, information, and bio	₩150	20
Chungnam	May 22, 2015	Hanwha	Solar energy and ICT	₩152.5	12
Jeonbuk	November 24, 2014	Hyosung	Carbon fiber	₩40	8
Jeonnam	June 2, 2015	GS	Chemicals and bio energy	₩139	18
Gyungbuk	December 17, 2014	Samsung	Electronics	₩60	21
Gyungnam	April 9, 2015	Doosan	Machinery and maintenance	₩170	16
Jeju	June 26, 2015	Daum Kakao	IT services	₩156.9	11
		Amore Pacific			

to facilitate 100 startups in 2015, from 1,000 selected promising bright ideas from individual citizens and aspiring entrepreneurs (Ministry of Science, ICT and Future Planning 2015b). Launched in June, 2015, by the *Public-Private Joint Action Task Force*, the Inno 6+ Platform is to provide intensified care for commercializing ideas selected from CET (online) and regional CCEIs (off-line). By closely connecting online and off-line sources of ideas to commercialization, the Inno 6+ Platform aims to promote an ecosystem of creative economy brimming with vibrant startups in a close linkage with the regional CCEIs and Dream Enter that supports the CET project. The key point of the Inno 6+ Platform is its intention to provide intensified support by startup specialists over a rather short six-month period, as related to the development of business models based on promising ideas, application and registration for intellectual property rights, and preparation of business plans. To accelerate the startup process, the Inno 6+ Platform project has CCEIs and Dream Enter employ specialists in startup and commercialization as Program Directors (PDs). PDs provide a total package of intensive support for six months for translating ideas into startups.

As illustrated in Figure 37.4, the Inno 6+ Platform picks up what CET has been identifying and accelerates the commercialization process by providing systematic support through networking critical stakeholders in the process of establishing a new business. These include

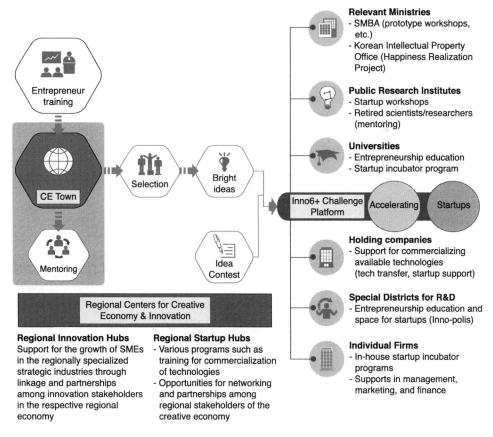

Figure 37.4 Inno 6+ Challenge Platform and the Creative Economy Initiative

Source: http://www.msip.go.kr.

relevant governmental ministries, public research institutes, universities, private holding companies, special districts for R&D, and other individual firms, all of which are to assume indispensable roles. The Inno 6+ Platform endeavors to bring together these stakeholders in the startup process.

Concluding remarks

Korea has been touted as an exemplary case for the government's pivotal roles played for R&D activities as well as for industrial policies. However, with the advent of the new global economic environment since the 1997 Asian financial crisis, Korea has desperately been searching for a new economic growth engine, trying to take advantage of its R&D capacity and infrastructure in information and communication technologies (ICT). This chapter has reviewed Korean policies for supporting new SME startups exploiting science and technology (SandT) capabilities. Our review identifies a couple of key characteristics of Korean SME policy experiences that may have implications for other developing countries. First of all, the Korean government has shifted its attention from big conglomerates to SMEs with the realization that the market has under-tapped their rich potential. When it realized its policy shortcomings toward SMEs, it lost no time in leveraging Korea's strengths in R&D and ICT to nurture an ecosystem of SME startups. While introducing a certification system for venture firms to signal the market, the Korean government has also streamlined its govern-ance for SME policies between SMBA and the MSIP. With more responsibilities on the shoulders of these two entities, the SME policies have been given more focused attention. The Korean policy-makers have long been aware of the importance of close cooperation and partnerships between public institutions and private enterprises (and individual experts). The current administration specifically endeavors to incorporate the ideas and energies of private actors by establishing diverse forums of interactions such as the Inno 6+ Challenge Platform and the Centers for Creative Economy and Innovation. And, most importantly, these SME policies are given close attention and support by the president and the key influential ministers, to the effect that they continue to be on the nation's top policy agenda.

Korea has exerted relentless efforts on multiple fronts to break ground for nurturing an ecosystem of SMEs creation and growth. Korea's public R&D investment and upgrading its efficiency remain the top policy priority over the last two decades. Accordingly, Korea's share of public R&D expenditures out of GDP has been second only to a couple of OECD countries and its R&D performance as measured in scientific publications and patenting has improved substantially over the same period. However, Korea is still struggling to redefine its knowledge- and creativity-based economic growth engine focused on SandT and ICT as indicated by its lackluster overall growth rate and the anemic roles played by its SME sectors. The policy initiatives are impressive; however, their outcomes still in the making are yet to be delivered. The results on the end-of-the-pipe technology are not assumed to be readily available.

The Korean case is also characterized by the policy salience sustained by the top leadership of the successive administrations since 1998. The four successive administrations after the 1997 financial crisis placed different policy emphases regarding the new growth engine and SMEs. For example, the Roh Moo-hyun administration (2003–2008) wholeheartedly embraced the RIS concept and pursued regionally balanced development, still paying attention to the dynamism of SMEs. The Lee Myung-bak Administration (2008–2013) laid its economic development policy platform on the green growth industry, focusing on renewable energy spearheaded by SMEs. The top leadership of those administrations maintained their attention on these initiatives, reshuffled the governance structure among respective players in the public and private sectors, and channeled ever-increasing fiscal resources to establish new projects across the country and/or expand pre-existing programs.

With sustained policy attention, the top leadership of the administrations choreographed the concerted efforts by multiple ministries and agencies. Such administration-wide initiatives have involved partnerships between public and private institutions such as the Ministry of Science, ICT and Future Planning (MSIP), the Small and Medium Business Administration (SMBA), Korea Technology Finance Corporation (KIBO), Small and Medium Business Corporation (SBC), Korea Venture Capital Association (KVCA), and numerous public research institutes and universities. These actors are providing comprehensive support packages along the gamut of ideas generation and identification, business model development, R&D, commercialization, financing, and marketing. These tailor-made policy packages reflect a critical lesson learned over the period that the startup process can be aborted if only one critical link is missing. Therefore, different agencies/ministries are picking up distinct responsibilities along the stages of the startup process, orchestrated by the top leadership and the Minister of MSIP.

The current Park Geun-hye administration moves such policy efforts one step further both by enlisting Korea's traditional economic building blocks, those globally competitive conglomerates such as Samsung, LG, and Hyundai Motors, to help young entrepreneurs start new businesses, and by incorporating online and off-line platforms to expedite the process from ideas inception, business model development, R&D, patenting, commercialization, financing/investment, and marketing. The current SME startup policies, particularly the Creative Economy Policy Initiatives, also incorporate domestic policy concerns for equitable development across the nation. Each of the nation's 17 regional jurisdictions has one conglomerate combined with regional players of innovation into a Center of Creative Economy and Innovation with one or two specialized industries, for example, electronics, ICTs, shipbuilding, big data, machinery, solar energy, and bionics. In its all-out endeavors, the Korean government puts together all relevant actors from the president, numerous ministries/agencies, regional/local governments, public research institutes, private firms, and even individual specialists and citizens. It is, however, yet to be seen how effective such policy initiatives would be since it all depends on how organic and vibrant the respective innovation systems are going to be, where this time the roles by Korean conglomerates, who are increasingly willing and able to brush off governmental arm-twisting, are critical.

The Korean government has also recently realized that the innovation-oriented creative general public can be an indispensable element of the ecosystem for SMEs. Therefore, the government has expanded its SMEs policy purview from the narrowly defined venture firms to Inno-Biz, medium-sized but globally competitive World Class 300, *key chaebols* (conglomerates), and the general public. The current administration's Creative Economy Initiative makes such orientation clear enough. Projects such as the web-based Creative Economy Town and the Inno 6+ Challenge Platform intend to tap into the creative energy of the general public, encouraging them to propose bright ideas for innovation and business creation. Such ideas as evaluated and mentored by experienced startup specialists are fast-tracked to expedite startups. All such policy efforts are under close attention by the Korean president and coordinated by the MSIP.

All in all, with the recognition that SMEs are the engine of Korea's future economic growth, the Korean government has moved the traditional policies for SMEs over a new horizon, beyond the limited sphere of the SMBA. Now, policies for nurturing and supporting SMEs are given top policy attention; they involve key central ministries, all of the regional governments, Korea's globally competitive conglomerates, and the attentive general public.

The all-out efforts are also guided by insights offered by studies on regional innovation systems, industrial clusters, knowledge bases, and knowledge transfers across sectors. However, it is premature to show a clear piece of evidence on whether such initiatives have been producing tangible results in terms of new SME establishments, their revenues, employments and growth, or whether they are just another bureaucratic hubbub black-holing public resources.

Notes

1 The definition of SMEs in Korea varies by industry and adopts multiple standards including the number of employees, revenues, and capital. In this calculation we regarded those establishments whose employees are less than 1,000 as SMEs. When we lower the threshold to 300 employees, the figure for employees changes to 86.0 percent while the figure for establishments does not change. We used the Census on Establishments provided by the Statistics Korea (Korea's National Statistics Office).
2 Authors' own calculation based on the 2010 Economic Census available at the online statistics portal: http://kosis.kr. Per the current exchange rate, USD 1.00 is about ₩1,165.
3 A press release by the Ministry of Trade, Industry and Energy, Jan. 17, 2014.
4 It should be noted that the Korean government spends additionally about ₩10 trillion for R&D purposes. Expenditures on R&D and the CE initiative together amounted to ₩18.8 trillion in 2015.

Bibliography

Connell, S. (2013). Building a Creative Economy in South Korea: Analyzing the Plans and Possibilities for New Economic Growth. Academic Paper Series. Korea Economic Institute of America.

Creative Korea. (2015). Introduction to the Creative Economy Town. Available at https://www.creativekorea.or.kr. Accessed on July 4, 2015.

Kim, K-H. and Park, T-W. (2013). The Korean Creative Economy: Terminological Variation and Implication. *Humanities Contents* 31(3), 103–118.

Korea National Statistical Office. (2013). Survey on the Economically Active Population. Available at http://stat.seoul.go.kr/pdf/Fe-webzine79.pdf. Accessed on June 16, 2015.

Lee, D-H. (2015). *Commercializing Excellent Ideas for Creative Economy: Focusing on the Six Months Challenge Platform Project. Research Report 2015–047.* Korea Institute of SandT Evaluation and Planning.

Lim, G-W. and Jeong, Y-H. (2014). *Key Issues in Venture Startup Policies and Some Recommendations. Project Evaluation Report 14–05.* National Assembly Budget Office.

Ministry of Science, ICT and Future Planning. (2014). How to Achieve a Creative Economy? Available at http://www.msip.go.kr/webzine/posts.do?postIdx=62. Accessed on June 16, 2015.

Ministry of Science, ICT and Future Planning. (2015a). Overview of Creative Economy. Available at http://english.msip.go.kr/english/msipContents/contents.do?mId=MjY4. Accessed on June 16, 2015.

Ministry of Science, ICT and Future Planning. (2015b). Launching the 6 Months Platform for Accelerating the Startup Process Utilizing Promising Creative Ideas. June 16, 2015. Available at http://www.msip.go.kr/web/msipContents/contentsView.do?cateId=mssw311andartId=1266545. Accessed on June 16, 2015.

Ministry of Trade, Industry and Energy. (2013). Survey on the Demand and Supply of Human Resources in Industrial Technologies. Available at http://www.motie.go.kr/motie/ne/rt/press/bbs/bbsView.do?bbs_seq_n=78604andbbs_cd_n=16. Accessed on July 10, 2015.

OECD. (2015). Research and Development Statistics (RDS). Available at http://www.oecd.org/innovation/inno/researchanddevelopmentstatisticsrds.htm.

OECD and Eurostat. (2005). *Guidelines for Collecting and Interpreting Innovation Data – Oslo Manual* (Third ed.). Paris: Organization for Economic Co-operation and Development.

World Bank. (2015). *World Development Indicators 2015.* Washington, DC: World Bank. doi: 10.1596/978-1-4648-0440-3. Accessed on July 10, 2015.

38

ENTREPRENEURIAL HETEROGENEITY AND THE DESIGN OF ENTREPRENEURSHIP POLICIES FOR ECONOMIC GROWTH AND INCLUSIVE DEVELOPMENT

Elisa Calza and Micheline Goedhuys

Introduction

After decades of exclusion, since the early 1990s, there has been a renewed policy interest in entrepreneurship. In developing countries, the role of the private sector as a major actor and driver of growth is no longer questioned, after state-led industrialization and development experiences massively failed. In advanced economies similarly, new technological developments and globalization of production have contributed to the rise of an entrepreneurial economy in which smaller-scale production is no longer a disadvantage (Audretsch et al., 2006).

Entrepreneurship—defined as the "discovery and exploitation of profitable opportunities" (Shane and Ventakaraman, 2000) and translated into "the start-up and growth of a business firm" (Hart, 2003; Vivarelli, 2013)—is increasingly considered important for employment, income generation and economic growth at the aggregate level. In advanced economies, the prolonged economic crisis and the slow recovery have fed the idea that entrepreneurship is a potential way to re-boost productivity and employment, especially among youth. In particular, the potential for job creation from new firms and especially "high growth firms" (HGFs) (OECD, 2007) is attracting a lot of interest from policy makers, as reflected in the surge of popularity of related literature on "gazelles" and HGFs (Coad et al., 2014). In developing countries, policy makers embrace entrepreneurship as a way to provide jobs for the large, young, and growing labor force which often faces unemployment due to a lack of formal sector jobs.

This policy ambition with entrepreneurship might lead to ineffective policies if policy action comes without an adequate understanding of the heterogeneity of entrepreneurs and their potential contribution to economic or social development. There are large differences among types of entrepreneurs with respect to their contribution to economic growth and/

or inclusive development. Research has demonstrated that entrepreneurship in developing countries is not a binding constraint (Naudé, 2011). We observe large numbers of entrants in most industries and countries, especially if we include entrepreneurial activity in the informal sector, where entrepreneurship is a survival strategy rather than a positive choice for business profitability. Exit rates are equally large, pointing to a high turnover of firms. When entry and exit rates are significantly correlated, this might be the result of "entry mistakes," poor entrepreneurial skill and low productivity, and the phenomenon of exit being common among young and new firms (Cressy, 2006).

At the same time, the number of small businesses that develop and successfully evolve into medium or larger-sized businesses is very small, worldwide, but especially so in African economies (Sleuwaegen and Goedhuys, 2002). This is problematic, as the growth of small and medium-sized businesses encompasses a process of employment creation, technological upgrading, and a shift toward higher productivity and value addition. SMEs are essential players in a process of structural change and their emergence and growth should be the focus and objective of an economic growth policy in developing countries.

Yet, entrepreneurship policies are still often designed to stimulate entry, through entrepreneurship training, funding or a combination thereof. While this may be justifiable from a social or political perspective, for economic growth, these policies may miss effectiveness. Rather, policies should be developed that facilitate the growth and high growth of existing or young firms, to create formal sector employment, innovation, and structural change to high productivity activities.

Empirical studies indeed provide a much more nuanced picture of the entrepreneurship contribution to economic growth and development. The aim of this chapter is to discuss the heterogeneity of entrepreneurship and to contribute to the debate on entrepreneurial policies in developing countries from this perspective. We start by showing evidence from macro studies which investigate the contribution of entrepreneurship to economic growth in the second section. We argue that innovative growth-oriented entrepreneurship has the largest contribution to growth. In the third section we then logically turn to the micro level to see what can be learned from micro-evidence-based studies with respect to the drivers of growth and high growth of firms, so as to use these insights in the policy discussion in the fourth section.

Entrepreneurship, economic growth, and inclusive development

This role of entrepreneurship in economic development and growth has been discussed in the literature (Wennekers and Thurik, 1999; Audretsch et al., 2006; Van Praag and Verloot, 2007; Naudé, 2008). Entrepreneurial activity is thought to facilitate the structural transformation of an economy toward modern sectors, by favoring the reallocation of resources, such as labor and capital, toward more productive activities (Acs and Storey, 2004; Murphy et al., 2006; Acs, 2006; Dias and McDermott, 2006).[1] Moreover, in line with the Schumpeterian idea of the "innovator entrepreneurs" as actors of "creative destruction" (Schumpeter, 1939), entrepreneurial firms induce technological change and innovation, which leads to higher valued added goods and more efficient production methods (Szirmai, Naudé and Goedhuy, 2011). Quantitatively, this process translates into increases in productivity and per capita income.

The arguments presented would imply that "high measured levels of entrepreneurship will thus translate directly into high levels of economic growth" (Acs, 2006). However, "the accumulated evidence [that entrepreneurial activity is a positive driving force in the economy] remains largely inconclusive" (Nightingale and Coad, 2014), suggesting that the role played by entrepreneurship at the macro level is probably more complex and, sometimes, ambiguous.

Some studies investigate the evidence of a positive relationship between the "magnitude" of entrepreneurial activities and the level of economic development (Reynolds et al., 2001; Wennekers et al., 2005; Amorós et al., 2007; Amorós and Cristi, 2008).[2] Their results show that this relationship does not behave linearly, but rather follows a U-shape pattern where entrepreneurship is larger at the extreme points of low and high levels of per capita income. The existence of this U-shape is supported by the theories of transformation of the economic structure along the process of development (Stam and van Stel, 2011; Nelson and Pack, 1999; Rodrik, 2007; Gries and Naudé, 2010). Entrepreneurial activity is likely to be more relevant during initial stages of agricultural production and small-scale manufacturing, and in later stages of transition to service-based modern sectors, where there is the increased role of human capital, of innovation and knowledge spillovers making the role of small firms more relevant (Audretsch et al., 2013). On the contrary, entrepreneurship tends to be lower in an intermediate stage characterized by physical capital expansion and economies of scale and scope, with large firms driving economic dynamism (Snodgrass and Biggs, 1996; Acs, 2006; van Stel et al., 2005; Carree and Thurik, 2002; Acs et al., 2012).

Other studies explore the relationship between entrepreneurship and economic growth (measured as GDP growth) (Blanchflower, 2000; Carree et al., 2002). An interesting finding is that the direction of this relationship changes across different per capita income levels. Van Stel et al. (2005) show that entrepreneurship has a negative effect on GDP growth rate for poor countries, while this turns positive for rich ones. Similarly, Stam and van Stel (2011) find that the impact of entrepreneurship on economic growth is irrelevant in middle-income countries, while it is larger for transition and high-income ones. They suggest that the stronger impact in high-income countries may be accounted for by the presence of more growth-oriented entrepreneurial activity in this context.

Raising awareness on the risk of assuming an a priori "overoptimistic" positive effect of "all entrepreneurship," these studies do provide evidence of a positive macro impact of entrepreneurship on growth and development, but *not* always and *not* everywhere. Then, the main issue becomes why countries at a lower income and development level seem to benefit less from entrepreneurship in terms of aggregate economic growth—what shapes these different effects on growth?

The answer lies in understanding which kind of entrepreneurship actually contributes more to economic growth in developed and in developing countries, and why. This requires shifting "the focus back to the micro foundations of entrepreneurship" (Quatraro and Vivarelli, 2015: 2), shedding light on how the micro-based heterogeneity of entrepreneurial actors—within and across heterogeneous economic contexts—actually translates into different contributions to macroeconomic growth and employment.

By exploring the sources of economic growth from a micro perspective, various empirical studies try to find evidence for the argument that only certain types of entrepreneurs are accountable for most of the effect of entrepreneurship on economic growth and employment. These studies investigate which type of entrepreneurial performance is more conducive to economic growth. Focusing mainly on "high-growth firms" (HGFs), growth-oriented entrepreneurs[3] with high-aspiration, past studies find these entrepreneurial groups to consistently have a significant positive impact on economic growth, being accountable in large part for the higher effect of entrepreneurship on growth in high-income countries (Autio, 2011; Stam et al., 2011; Stam and van Stel, 2011).

The findings of these studies point out that considering entrepreneurial heterogeneity is crucial for "a more realistic evaluation of the impact of entrepreneurs by avoiding a composition fallacy that assigns the benefits of entrepreneurship to the average firm" (Nightingale and Coad, 2004). Thus, a last step is looking at the composition of entrepreneurship in developing countries.

In low-income countries, the weaker contribution of entrepreneurship to growth is the product of an entrepreneurial universe, where "opportunity"-driven and "ambitious" entrepreneurs are scarce, but coexist with a multitude of marginal, unproductive, and low-skilled entrepreneurs in informal micro and small businesses, whose total contribution to aggregate growth is limited (Fields, 1990; House, 1984; Mead and Liedholm, 1998; Wennekers and Thurik, 1999; Beck et al., 2005; Grimm et al., 2012). Rather, entrepreneurship might have a social value (Acs et al., 2013),[4] as entrepreneurs can perform functions that go beyond economic rationales and that are instead oriented toward livelihood, social inclusion, and poverty alleviation (Schramm, 2004).[5] This argument has relevant implications for policies, reflected in the design of programs based more on social and political targets rather than economic motivations (Audretsch and Thurik, 2004).

Two fundamental lessons can be drawn from this section. First, between as well as within economic contexts, there is a relevant heterogeneity across entrepreneurial actors—in terms of performances, features, aspirations, opportunities, and contexts. Second, it is clear that this heterogeneity accounts for the different effect on economic growth. There is a kind of entrepreneurship—growth-oriented start-ups and firms—that seems to be driving the growth impact at macro level. Therefore the following section will turn to the micro level, to delve deeper into the factors that the literature has identified as triggering firm growth in developing countries.

The microeconomics of growth: critical factors and lessons from empirical studies

Growth is measured as changes in size, usually measured by employment, sales, assets, or capital. Growing firms are crucial for stable formal employment generation, which is a relevant policy issue in developing countries given the serious problem of youth unemployment. Related to this, there is large interest—both from academia and policy makers—in understanding the phenomenon of "high growth" firms (HGFs) and "gazelles." These firms are characterized by a rapid growth (in term of employees or sales) in a short span of time (three–five years). The Eurostat/OECD (2007) definition for "high growth firms" and for "gazelles" is currently the most followed,[6] but the definition has been often adjusted to the specific context (see for example Goedhuys and Sleuwaegen, 2010). A similar concept is Wong et al.'s (2005) definition of high potential entrepreneurial activity (TEA) based on GEM data, that considers the criteria of innovation and export activity as well.[7] Knowing under which conditions HGFs or high impact firms are likely to occur can help to tailor policies that boost employment. Equally important is to understand the determinants of average firm growth for a more broad-based development perspective.

The literature on firm growth has indicated that there are many unidentified and unobservable factors that are responsible for the growth of firms. There is a lot of randomness to the growth of firms. Yet, a growing number of studies find that there are systematic observable factors—such as firm size, age, innovation, capabilities, and resources; entrepreneur characteristics; and contextual factors and institutions—that systematically and significantly shift the growth perspectives of firms. These are the factors policy makers can consider in the design of policies. We briefly discuss them below.[8]

Firm characteristics

Size and age

A large body of empirical studies[9] find a significant negative relationship between firm growth and size—thus, small firms grow faster than large firms—and between the variability in growth and firm size—small firms have very high but also very low growth rates. These findings are stylized facts. A similar negative relationship between firm growth and firm age is also observed as is a negative relationship between the variability in growth and age. Hence, smaller and younger firms grow faster than larger and older ones, but the volatility in their growth rates is also higher, as are their hazard rates.

This observation lends support to Jovanovic's (1982) theoretical passive "Bayesian" learning model of, which states that entrepreneurs have different efficiency levels when they start firms, but the efficiency level is not known a priori. Later, once established and absorbing knowledge from the market, the entrepreneurs learn about their own efficiency. The more successful (efficient) firms get positive feedback from the market and expand up to a size that corresponds with their efficiency level; the least efficient firms by contrast stagnate or are even forced to exit. This process takes place in the earliest years after start-up. It is a critical phase young starters go through.

The size–age–growth relationships have been tested in the context of African firms. Goedhuys and Sleuwaegen (1999) and Sleuwaegen and Goedhuys (2002), Biggs and Srivastava (1996) and Bigsten and Gebreeyesus (2007) provide empirical evidence that younger and smaller firms have higher growth rates than larger and older companies. However, important non-linearities in the size–growth and age–growth relationship have also been found. Sleuwaegen and Goedhuys (2002) found that while small firms grow faster, for the smallest starters these growth rates flatten out quickly. For the Ivorian firms in their sample, firms that started at a larger size tended to regress less fast in growth rate over time than smaller firms. This helped explain the weak representation of medium-sized firms in the economy, as the smallest firms stagnate quickly, while the medium firms grow steadily larger. A similar growth path is described in Grimm et al. (2012), who look at the informal sector in West Africa and find that the returns to capital are fairly high but drop quickly for the larger informal firms. Bigsten and Gebreeyesus (2007) found that both young Ethiopian firms grow faster in their early years of activity, but also older firms grow slightly faster, when firms are likely to benefit increasingly from reputation effects.

These non-linearities are important to understand in a developing country context. They are present because many countries present a duality in their market structure, with survivalist entrepreneurs active in the informal sector, and a more modern economy dominated by larger firms, as described in the second section. The main challenge is therefore to identify factors that can break the informality trap and open up the transition from micro and small firms to small and medium-sized firms. Innovation and capabilities emerge as triggering factors.

Innovation and capabilities

There is broad theoretical reasoning that firm-specific investments in innovation raise competences and open up growth opportunities (Aghion and Howitt, 1992; Geroski, 2000;

see Coad, 2009 for a discussion). The idea is that efficiency levels of firms do not necessarily need to be fixed, as in Jovanovic's (1982) passive learning model, but can be increased over time through research, innovation, and the development of specific competences. These can raise efficiency or productivity levels of firms, and hence firms experience extra growth opportunities.

For developing countries, where a majority of firms operate substantially below the technological frontier, firms' innovation efforts are primarily oriented toward absorbing, adapting, mastering, and eventually improving technologies developed elsewhere. Several authors have pointed at the importance of "technological capabilities" of firms in developing countries as the knowledge and skills—technical, managerial, and institutional—necessary for firms to utilize equipment and technology efficiently (Lall, 1992). Firms build up these technological capabilities, by engaging in a wide variety of activities, such as training of the workforce, investment in new vintage machinery and the use of ICT, technology licensing from abroad, aimed at introducing products and production processes that are new to the firm and reinforce the firm's competitive position.

Evidence demonstrates that innovation and technology development increase the growth potential of firms. Gebreeyesus (2011) found for Ethiopia that innovation triggered employment growth in Ethiopian SMEs. Goedhuys and Sleuwaegen (2010) found that product innovation raised not only the average growth of firms, but especially high-growth firms in Africa. Similar findings are presented in studies on developed economies (Almus, 2002; Coad and Rao, 2008; Stam and Wennberg, 2009; Hölzl and Friesenbichler, 2010; Czarnitzki and Delanote, 2013).

Another strand in the literature investigates innovation and technology development in developing countries in relation to productivity (see a special issue on this topic by Goedhuys, Janz, Mairesse and Mohnen, 2008). The productivity enhancing effect of innovation that is overwhelmingly found in the literature is clearly the underlying mechanism that explains why innovative firms or technologically active firms grow faster.

Resources

Another element that can be included into the firm-level dimension is the firm's availability of resources, both tangible and intangible. Among the elements that can be labelled as intangible resources, social capital, and social networks[10] seem to be valuable assets for firms in developing countries, since they can facilitate access to information and resources (e.g., credit), reduce transaction costs, help contract enforcement and regulation (Nichter and Goldmark, 2009), thus having a possible positive impact on firms' productivity and growth (Barr, 1998).

Among tangible resources, financial assets have been traditionally considered one of the main factors affecting firms' performance in developing countries. It is argued that their availability facilitates productive investment, while their lack limits growth and even undermines firms' survival. This seems to hold especially for micro and small firms in developing countries during early years, since they tend to find it more difficult to prove their reliability and to get credit (Schiffer and Weder, 2001).

Financial resources have been largely studied as a main driver of entrepreneurial entry (Vivarelli, 2013). Many empirical studies show that start-ups tend to be financially constrained in developing countries (Paulson and Townsend, 2004; Beck and Demirgüç-Kunt, 2006; Ayyagari et al., 2007; Klapper et al., 2006). This makes initial wealth conditions more important and implies that in the presence of start-up costs, wealth inequality might play a role in determining the likelihood of becoming an entrepreneur (Naudé, 2008; Cagetti and De Nardi, 2005).

This had a major influence on entrepreneurial policies, in terms of both the aims and types of interventions. Most policies still aim at increasing the number of entrepreneurs by reducing entry barriers, providing start-ups with credits and subsidies (Coad et al., 2014).

Entrepreneur characteristics

Entrepreneur characteristics, such as the age of the entrepreneur, education, work experience, gender, ethnicity, migrant status, and family background, affect the performance of the entrepreneurial firm.

"Entrepreneurial ability" is probably the individual aspect that has attracted more attention as a driver of entrepreneurial activity and performance. A rather complex and multi-dimensional concept, it refers to skills and abilities gained through relevant education and experience, but also to some specific attitudes and qualities that are recognized as typical of entrepreneurial behavior, such as the ability to perceive opportunities and to learn, risk aversion and risk-taking, desire for independence, perseverance, focus on achievement, optimism and internal *locus* of control (Licht, 2007). The multidimensionality of the concept poses a clear challenge for empirical investigation. In practice ability is often proxied by education, experience, and other observable indicators.

Education might affect entrepreneurship in two ways: by raising the entrepreneurial ability of the individual, stimulating entry, but also by increasing opportunities on the job market, reducing entry (Giannetti and Simonov, 2004; Naudé, 2008). Thus, the net effect of education on entry is not easily predicted. In developing countries, the level of education of the entrepreneur is often observed to be low especially in the large group of survivalist small and micro firms, since waged alternatives are likely to be more attractive for better educated individuals (Nichter and Goldmark, 2009).

Van Der Sluis et al. (2004) summarized evidence from at least 20 African countries and investigated the impact of schooling and experience on entrepreneurial performance. They find evidence supporting the idea that more educated entrepreneurs show superior growth performance. Yet others find no effect of schooling on growth in Latin America (Alvarez and Crespi, 2003). Again, these ambiguous results reinforce the idea of the importance of looking at the context, and of considering context- or country-specific thresholds for education level, below which no effects on growth and productivity can be observed (Nichter and Goldmark, 2009). Moreover, it is also likely that the effect of education on firms' entry and growth could be industry- and sector-specific, thus expected to be positive and much stronger in sectors with higher knowledge and technological intensity.

Empirical studies show that experience gained in previous jobs and activities may have a positive impact on performance in entrepreneurial firms, through increasing both the entrepreneur's ability and his/her relationship and social network (Biggs and Shah, 2006). Other studies have pointed out that experience may not play a role *per se*, but may depend on the entrepreneurs' capacity to actually learn from past experiences (Stam et al., 2007). The argument that entrepreneurial ability can be developed through learning is particularly relevant for the specific debate about the role of "serial" and "habitual entrepreneurs"[11] in affecting entrepreneurial performance (Naudé, 2008).

The age of the entrepreneur is supposed to have an indirect effect on performance through affecting entrepreneurial ability in two opposing ways: on one side, younger entrepreneurs might underestimate the risk and overestimate their abilities, resulting in a higher risk profile and an expected negative impact on survival and growth; on the other hand, young entrepreneurs are also likely to be more innovative and better able to perceive opportunities (Naudé, 2008).

Gender is a variable often used in modeling firm performance in developing countries. The relevance of this feature is clearly understood when looking at the share of women that own or run entrepreneurial firms (between 40 percent and 80 percent of small businesses) (Nichter and Goldmark, 2009). Empirical analyses found that women entrepreneurial firms grow slower than those owned by men. This might be related to the fact that some women entrepreneurs are constrained by the lack of alternative opportunities in wage employment (Rubio, 1991), also given their lower education and literacy level. For many, entrepreneurship fulfills the double need of diversifying household income and allocating time to household duties and family responsibilities, which women have to perform alongside entrepreneurial activities (Downing and Daniels, 1992). If on one hand this might provide them more flexibility in their time management (Grimm et al., 2012), it is often a constraint on growth of their entrepreneurial firms (Kevane and Wydick, 2001). Moreover, women-owned firms tend to operate in slow-growing sectors, and the firms are more often located within the household than men-owned firms (Nichter and Goldmark, 2009; Grimm et al., 2012).

In some developing countries, some ethnic groups have been recognized to be particularly entrepreneurially active, thus increasing the likelihood of their members to succeed as entrepreneurs (Ramachandran and Shah, 1999; Biggs and Shah, 2006). However, ethnicity does not have an effect *per se*, but through the possibility of being part, without incurring entry costs, of an existing and functioning network.

Finally, among other individual-level features, entrepreneurs' aims and *motivations* in running an entrepreneurial activity might also influence the firm's final performance. Some individuals might decide to become entrepreneurs due to preference for non-pecuniary benefits associated with this activity compared to a waged job, such as independence and autonomy (Moskowitz and Vissing-Jorgensen, 2002; Licht, 2007). Others might be driven by social motivations and ambitions (e.g., gaining the "status" of entrepreneurs in cultures and societies that reward this economic condition; strengthening their social network) and different economic aims (e.g., subsistence of the household; innovate) (Bosma et al., 2005; Naudé, 2008).

Contextual factors affecting firm growth

Context-related and socio-economic environment factors also affect entry and performance, representing external constraints or setting opportunities for entrepreneurial firms. Macroeconomic conditions are generally recognized to be relevant for entrepreneurial activity. Positive growth rates associated with rising demand generate market opportunities that favor firm growth, and boost the generation of other important factors, such as infrastructural improvements. However, when growth comes with a rise of employment, this might raise the opportunity cost of being an entrepreneur with respect to a salaried job and consequently increase exit and reduce entry rates (Naudé, 2008). Symmetrically, negative growth spans may imply a contraction of employment and a lack of salaried employment alternatives, resulting in a parallel increase of self-employment of low-entrepreneurial quality and mainly "necessity"-driven (Nichter and Goldmark, 2009; Naudé, 2008), whose effects we discuss more in the next section. Macroeconomic stability (such as low price and exchange rate volatility) also plays a positive role by reducing the uncertainty faced by entrepreneurs, favoring access to credit, investment, and business expansion, and thus contributing to a favorable business environment (Nichter and Goldmark, 2009).

Institutions—defined by Baumol (1990) as "rules of the game"—are also particularly important for the generation of an adequate context for entrepreneurial prosperity, especially in developing countries (Naudé, 2008; 2011). The lack of a clear legal framework, certainty of economic rights, enforcement and dispute resolution mechanisms constitute a major obstacle for firms' growth (Beck et al., 2005). Cultural values and beliefs can also play a role in favoring entry and survival of entrepreneurial firms, for example when a high value is attached to independence, or there is no social "stigma" associated with entrepreneurial failure (Licht, 2007).

The presence of specific regulations and standards might affect positively firms' performance, conditional on being able to meet these standards. For example, meeting high quality standards for accessing developed countries' demands forces firms to improve their managerial practices which then increases productivity and stimulates growth (Goedhuys and Sleuwaegen, 2013). At the same time, these can act as an entry barrier for a large number of less competitive entrepreneurial actors, increasing the sunk cost of entry in foreign markets (Kaplinsky, 2010)

Lastly, literature broadly agrees that informality is one of the most typical features of developing contexts, where it includes between 40 percent and 80 percent of the non-agricultural workforce (ILO, 2004). Informality inhibits and slows down entrepreneurial firm growth in developing countries (Nichter and Goldmark, 2009; Sleuwaegen and Goedhuys, 2002). A first explanation of this detrimental effect on performance is the fact that informality is often encountered in traditional non-dynamic sectors and in subsistence and "necessity-driven" entrepreneurial actors, and it is often associated with high vulnerability, illegality, and scarce efficiency (De Paula and Scheinkman, 2007). The empirical literature provides evidence that informality directly constrains firms' growth by limiting the incentives of becoming large and "too visible," with the risk of incurring taxation (Snodgrass and Biggs, 1996), and by limiting access to formal business opportunities (such as participating in public procurement, or competing in high-standards and high-margin international markets) and to other important resources, such as formal credit or alternative inputs (Nichter and Goldmark, 2009).

Given the importance of this issue, one of the main challenges of promoting more productive entrepreneurship in developing countries has to do with reducing barriers to the formal sector. These barriers include red tape, excessive regulation, corruption and bribery in the process of obtaining permits, and lack of support services to formal firms. Related to the dichotomy of formality *versus* informality, another important context-related factor for developing country entrepreneurs is the geographical location, especially in terms of rural versus non-rural entrepreneurs, and the sector and type of activity, whether agricultural versus non-agricultural, and farming versus non-farming (Nagler and Naudé, 2014).

Lessons for the design and implementation of effective entrepreneurship policies

Why are entrepreneurial policies needed? Answering this question is crucial for developing countries, given the scarce availability of resources and the high opportunity cost of possible misuse. Once the rationales and the aims of the policies are clear, a second issue concerns their effective implementation: how can ("good") entrepreneurship be promoted in developing countries?

Rationales for entrepreneurial policies

The economic rationales for policy interventions have traditionally referred to the existence of market failures. First, there are spillovers and positive externalities that the entrepreneurial actor cannot fully appropriate, reducing the incentive to establish a firm. Second, there exists asymmetry of information in the credit market that may lead to adverse selection and may prevent profitable projects from being funded. As a result, the entrepreneurial activity that emerges in a country remains below the level that would be socially optimal (Naudé, 2008).

In addition, in developing countries, entrepreneurial firms face several constraints to growth. Institutional and information failures, poor infrastructure, macroeconomic uncertainty are stringent constraints, both for entry and growth, besides internal constraints like low levels of human capital, education, and entrepreneurial ability (see previous section), all of which have implications for policy.

Finally, the already mentioned possible "social value" of entrepreneurship in a developing context brings into the picture a social rationale for policy intervention, more related to human development goals than directly to productivity, structural change, and growth.

Policy interventions in developing countries

Policy interventions in developing countries should take into account the heterogeneous composition of entrepreneurial actors, and translate it into specific tailored interventions to address the constraints and boost the potential of different entrepreneurial subgroups.

Despite their limited contribution to economic growth and structural transformation, policy action should not disregard the multitude of micro and small "necessity"-driven entrepreneurs, who account for the largest share of the self-employed and that may actually be responding also to social functions, beneficial for vulnerable and marginalized groups too (women and youth). Policies can mainly focus on removing some of the most severe external and internal constraints they face (Grimm et al., 2012). Interventions could facilitate access to credit, such as via microfinance programs (Quatraro and Vivarelli, 2014), as well as foster the formation of human capital and entrepreneurial skills, via education and training programs (Goedhuys and Sleuwaegen, 2000). Often a business start-up training program for micro-entrepreneurs is combined with financial support, which appears to be more successful than separate interventions. Recent evaluations find these programs indeed increase start-ups within a given period of evaluation, even though there is doubt about their effectiveness for firms' survival and potential to generate income for, and beyond its immediate owner (McKenzie and Woodruff, 2014).

Policy makers should also be aware of the unique opportunities offered by internet connectivity and the widespread use of mobile phones in developing countries. Micro-entrepreneurs use their mobile phone applications for financial transactions, such as the successful case of M-Pesa[12] in Kenya and other places in order to access market information and knowledge on production or farming technologies (e.g. M-Farm, iCow[13]), information on health-related issues (e.g. M-Pedigree, Mimba Bora[14]), and so on. The magnitude of the impact of these technologies on entrepreneurs' access to information and cash and the speed at which knowledge spreads among micro-entrepreneurs is unprecedented. Government should take the lead in establishing a well-functioning and competitive market for telecom that facilitates this development. Moreover, reforming the labor market to provide formal stable wage-employment may be an efficient and effective means of alleviating poverty and improving living conditions (Quatraro and Vivarelli, 2014).

"Opportunity"-driven entrepreneurs active in the formal sector have a different profile and face different constraints. Being less internally constrained,[15] they would not benefit too much from basic education and training interventions. The potential of these entrepreneurs could be better tapped by strengthening the business environment and leveling the playing field. Various authors agree on the importance of policies in this direction. Interventions could focus on setting stronger institutions, such as property rights and rule of law (Wiggens, 1995; Parker, 2007) and a more favorable business climate (Dethier et al., 2011; Klapper et al., 2006), fostering formalization (Bruhn and McKenzie, 2013; Williams, 2015a,b; Williams and Martinez-Perez, 2014; Williams and Nadin, 2012a,b, 2013, 2014), reducing uncertainty (economic and political), and increasing information flows and collaboration to reduce transaction costs. Furthermore, a more favorable entrepreneurial context could also stimulate more "positive" entrepreneurship by reducing the relative attractiveness of illegal and predatory activities (Mehlum et al., 2003). With the same purpose, other types of interventions can be found, trying to lower the "cultural barriers" that could also be preventing entry, by promoting an "entrepreneurial culture" and strengthening the non-pecuniary benefits associated with being an entrepreneur—for example, reducing the possible stigma attached to business failure (Cressy, 2006), or increasing the social "status" of entrepreneurs (Naudé, 2008).

Given the severity of the credit constraint faced by small firms and start-ups in developing countries, entrepreneurial policies aimed at fostering formalization have experimented with lowering the cost of formal entry through broad-based direct entry subsidies or facilitating access to credit (Naudé, 2008). However, these general *erga omnes* policies aimed at easing entrepreneurial entry have been strongly criticized as being ineffective.[16] Various studies point out their "perverse" consequences, as they tend to attract also individuals with lower entrepreneurial ability and productivity (Santarelli and Vivarelli, 2002; Shane, 2009; Naudé, 2008; Stam and van Stel, 2011). Furthermore, these policies induce inefficiencies in the use of financial resources: first, there is crowding-out, as some of the beneficiaries of the subsidy would have entered anyway, with their own resources; second, "turbulence" and "entry mistakes" by unproductive and low quality entrepreneurs are more likely, followed by a high rate of firm exit once the support is suspended, thus resulting in a net waste of resources (Vivarelli, 2013). Thus, higher entry rates do not *per se* result in growth, revealing the insufficiency of *erga omnes* policies that only aim at increasing the "quantity" of entrepreneurs.

An alternative is represented by policies aiming at promoting "quality" entrepreneurship by fostering factors whose effects on growth have been recognized in the literature, such as, for example, innovation and adherence to international standards. Innovation is associated with high-impact entrepreneurship, with macro-implications in terms of productivity and structural transformation (Szirmai, Naudé and Goedhuys, 2011; Vivarelli, 2013; Dias and McDermott, 2006). Since innovation is costly (especially when it requires R&D) and involves risk and uncertainty, policies can play a crucial role in bearing part of the risk and costs, supporting start-ups and growth-oriented entrepreneurs to perform innovative activities by stimulating innovation investments in innovative projects and R&D, through tax exemptions, grants and subsidies or other forms of financial assistance (Quatraro and Vivarelli, 2014). This is justified considering the positive externalities that these activities have on capabilities, and the positive spillovers for the whole economy (Cohen and Levinthal, 1990).

Some studies also show the positive impact of adherence to international management and product standards, both in terms of formal employment creation and on poverty alleviation (Goedhuys and Sleuwaegen, 2013; Henson, Masakure and Cranfield, 2011;

Gebreeyesus, 2014; Maertens and Swinnen, 2009). For firms willing to enter foreign markets, the obtaining of standards certificates may be a necessary condition. However, to obtain certification, firms have to go through a process of external auditing, which can be costly for smaller producers. In this sense, policies aimed at helping meet standards, by creating awareness of standards, organizing or subsidizing business consultants, establishing channels of information related to quality of goods and the high-margins international market could provide producers in developing countries with more profitable opportunities, effectively contributing to increasing their income and economic condition, and to creating more formal wage employment.

Some of the interventions oriented at specific firms with innovation, growth or export potential, imply "targeting," which still represents one of the major challenges to the implementation of tailored pro-growth policies in developing countries. Targeting can be controversial, as it may lead policy makers to "pick winners" which would do equally well without support. The problem boils down to being able to identify a priori exactly those firms that have high growth potential, but are somehow constrained to realize it. With targeted support it would be possible to unleash their growth. In practice, and due to the large unpredictability and randomness of a firm's growth path, it is a difficult exercise to identify these firms. In policy therefore, targeting is done on the basis of observable characteristics that the literature identifies in relation to success: small, young, innovative companies with highly educated managers, embedded in a social network, etc. . . . .to reduce the targeting error. Furthermore, even if targeting is possible, the process is costly and the actual effectiveness of targeting should be rigorously assessed.

Dealing with exits

A last consideration is dedicated to a possible further expansion of the scope of action for entrepreneurial policies. Both in developed and in developing countries, policies have focused almost exclusively on fostering entry and/or growth of entrepreneurial firms. In this respect, they have mirrored the scarce interest shown by literature toward other stages of entrepreneurial firms' lifecycle, such as decline, exit, and death (Coad et al., 2014). In fact, despite being a rather common and frequent phenomenon among entrepreneurial firms, an adequate understanding of the processes of decline and exit is still missing; for example, a discussion on which type of interventions could help better address their consequences is still left out of the debate. Among the various reasons that may push entrepreneurs to leave the business and exit, the factors associated with business failure and insufficient profitability have been most frequently considered (Jovanovic, 1982). However, this seems to be an oversimplification of the exit dynamic, and the literature shows that exit is not necessarily due to unsuccessful economic results. Exit and dissolution may have a value *per se* (Taylor, 1999; Abbring and Campbell, 2003) and act as a form of learning experience and "self-assessment" (Jovanovic, 1982; Kanbur, 1979). It could also be the best response to a change in the opportunity costs of being an entrepreneur (Andersson, 2006), or be due to retirement and to transferring of the firm to another generation (Kanniainen and Poutvaara, 2007). A better understanding of the factors driving survival and exit would contribute new and useful insights also to the design and implementation of entrepreneurial policies, especially when it comes to utilizing the knowledge and valuable assets of individuals with unique experience that can benefit the society in a variety of ways. Further analyses of these phenomena and their implications, together with better exploring the role played by "serial" entrepreneurs (Ucbasaran at al., 2006), could provide new insights for more comprehensive and "well-rounded" entrepreneurial policies, effective also in addressing resource redeployment and supporting the re-starting of entrepreneurial activities.

Notes

1 This argument is grounded on the "dual economies models," based on Lewis (1954). For a more specific debate about this issue, see Naudé (2008); Szirmai, Naudé and Goedhuys (2011).

2 These studies use Global Entrepreneurship Monitor (GEM) data for 36 countries in 2002 for the Total Entrepreneurial Activity (TEA) (a measure of nascent entrepreneurs), and per capita income as a measure of the level of economic development.

3 See next section for their detailed definitions.

4 This idea is close to the definition of "social entrepreneurship," a rising issue in development studies. For more discussion of this issue, see Acs et al. (2013).

5 For example, entrepreneurial activity also provides social relations and social interactions, allows diversifying household income, and gives flexibility in the use of time for women to also fulfill household duties (Naudé, 2008; Nichter and Goldmark, 2009; Grimm et al., 2012).

6 This defines "high growth firms" as the enterprises that are originally bigger than 10 employees, and that present a growth rate larger than 20 percent over the previous three years (OECD, 2007).

7 The term "high impact TEA" refers to start-ups that are going to employ at least 20 workers within five years, with a positive market creation and 25 percent of costumers abroad, and that employ technologies that were not available a year previously (Wong et al., 2005, in Naudé, 2008: 3).

8 For more elaborate discussion of this literature we refer to Coad (2009), Quatraro and Vivarelli (2014), Goedhuys and Sleuwaegen (2010) or Naudé (2008).

9 See Coad (2009) for an overview.

10 In this context, the term "social network" refers to interpersonal relationships, or rather "micro-level relationships between agents in an economy" (Nichter and Goldmark, 2009: 1461).

11 For the definitions of these terms, we refer to Ucbasaran at al. (2006: 5) (quoted in Naudé, 2008: 17): "'Serial entrepreneurs' are individuals who have sold or closed at least one business." "Habitual entrepreneur," which includes also "portfolio entrepreneur," are "individuals who currently have minority or majority ownership stakes in two or more independent businesses."

12 M-Pesa is a mobile phone-based money transfer and microfinancing service. Originally started in Kenya, due to its success it has rapidly expanded to Tanzania, Afghanistan, South Africa, India, and Eastern Europe.

13 M-Farm is a SMS (text message) mobile phone tool that helps Kenyan farmers get information on the retail price of their products, buy their farm inputs at favorable prices, and find buyers for their produce. iCow is another Kenyan mobile phone application that provides tips on cow breeding, animal nutrition, milk production efficiency, and gestation to small dairy farmers.

14 M-Pedigree is a mobile platform to track back the origin of drugs and medical products through an exchange of information between manufacturers and consumers, with the aim of increasing health security and reduce counterfeit medicines in Ghana. Mimba Bora is a mobile application that helps expectant women monitor their pregnancy.

15 Some low-performing entrepreneurs might not be so internally constrained as they are perceived to be. These are defined as "constrained gazelles."

16 "*Stimulating entrepreneurship alone will be insufficient as it is likely to attract necessity entrepreneurs with low human capital levels who do not contribute to economic growth*" (Stam and van Stel, 2011). "*Many routinely adopted policies for entrepreneurship, such as provision of credit, are shown to have more subtle effects, not all of which are conducive to growth-enhancing entrepreneurship*" (Naudé, 2008: 24).

Bibliography

Abbring, J. and Campbell, J. R. (2003). A firm's first year. Federal Reserve Bank of Chicago Working Paper WP-03-11. Chicago.

Acemoglu, D. (1995). Reward structures and the allocation of talent. *European Economic Review*, 39: 17–33.

Acs, Z., Boardman, M. and McNeely, C. (2013). The social value of productive entrepreneurship. *Small Business Economics*, 40(3), 785–796.

Acs, Z. (2006). How is entrepreneurship good for economic growth? *Innovations: Technology, Governance, Globalization*, 1(1), 97–107.

Acs, Z. J., Audretsch, D. B. and Lehmann, E. E. (2013). The knowledge spillover theory of entrepreneurship. *Small Business Economics*, 41(4), 757–774.

Acs, Z. J., Audretsch, D. B., Braunerhjelm, P. and Carlsson, B. (2012). Growth and entrepreneurship. *Small Business Economics*, 39(2), 289–300.

Acs, Z. and Storey, D. (2004). Introduction: entrepreneurship and economic development. *Regional Studies*, 38(8), 871–877.

Aghion, P. and Howitt, P. (1992). A model of growth through creative destruction. *Econometrica*, 60(2), 323–351.

Almus, M. (2002). What characterizes a fast-growing firm? *Applied Economics*, 34(12), 1497–1508.

Alvarez, R. and Crespi, G. (2003). Determinants of technical efficiency in small firms. *Small Business Economics*, 20(3), 233–244.

Amorós, J. E., Robin, C. F. and Gertosio, J. T. (2007). Quantifying the Relationship between Entrepreneurship and Competitiveness Development Stages in Latin America. Paper presented at the ICSB World Conference, Turku, 13 June.

Amorós, J. and Cristi, O. (2008). Longitudinal analysis of entrepreneurship and competitiveness dynamics in Latin America. *International Entrepreneurship and Management Journal*, 4(4), 381–399.

Andersson, P. (2006). Determinants of Exits from Self-Employment. Essay IV in a Ph.D. thesis in economics, Swedish Institute for Social Research, Stockholm University.

Audretsch, D. B. (2011) Entrepreneurship policy, in *World Encyclopedia of Entrepreneurship*, 111–121.

Audretsch, D. (2012). Entrepreneurship research. *Management Decision*, 50(5), 755–764.

Audretsch, D. B., Keilbach, M. C. and Lehmann, E. E. (2006). *Entrepreneurship and economic growth*. New York: Oxford University Press.

Audretsch, D. and Thurik, R. (2004). A model of the entrepreneurial economy. Discussion Paper on Entrepreneurship, Growth and Public Policy. Jena: Max Planck Institute.

Autio, E. (2011) High-aspiration entrepreneurship. In M. Minniti (Ed.), *The dynamics of entrepreneurship*. Oxford: Oxford University Press.

Ayyagari, M., Asli, D. K. and Vojislav, M. (2011). Small vs. Young Firms Across the World: Contribution to Employment, Job Creation, and Growth. World Bank Policy Research, Working Paper No. 5631. Washington, DC: World Bank.

Ayyagari, M., Beck, T. and Demirgüç-Kunt, A. (2007). Small and medium enterprises across the globe. *Small Business Economics*, 29(4), 415–434.

Baldwin, J. R. and Gorecki, P. K. (1987). Plant creation versus plant acquisition: The entry process in Canadian manufacturing. *International Journal of Industrial Organization*, 5(1), 27–41.

Baldwin, J. R. and Gorecki, P. K. (1991). Firm entry and exit in the Canadian manufacturing sector, 1970–1982. *The Canadian Journal of Economics*, 24(2), 300–323.

Barr, A. (1998). Enterprise performance and the functional diversity of social capital. Working Paper. Center for Studies on African Economies. Oxford: University of Oxford.

Baumol, W. J. (1990). Entrepreneurship: productive, unproductive, and destructive. *Journal of Political Economy*, 98(5), 893–921.

Beck, T. and Demirgüç-Kunt, A. (2006). Small and medium-size enterprises: access to finance as growth constraint. *Journal of Banking and Finance*, 30(6), 2931–43.

Beck, T., Demirgüç-Kunt, A. and Maksimovic, V. (2005). Financial and legal constraints to growth: does firm size matter? *The Journal of Finance*, 60(1), 137–177.

Beesley, M. E. and Hamilton, R. T. (1984). Small firms' seedbed role and the concept of turbulence. *The Journal of Industrial Economics*, 33(2), 217–231.

Biggs, T. and Srivastava, P. (1996). Structural aspects of manufacturing in Sub-Saharan Africa. The World Bank Disucssion Paper 346. Washington, DC: World Bank.

Biggs, T. and Shah, M. K. (2006). African SMES, networks, and manufacturing performance. *Journal of Banking and Finance*, 30(11), 3043–3066.

Bigsten, A. and Gebreeyesus, M. (2007). The small, the young, and the productive: determinants of manufacturing firm growth in Ethiopia. *Economic Development and Cultural Change*, 55(4), 813–840.

Blanchflower, D. G. and Oswald, A. J. (1998). What makes an entrepreneur? *Journal of Labor Economics*, 16(1), 26–60.

Blanchflower, D. G. (2000). Self-employment in OECD countries. *Labor Economics*, 7(5), 471–505.

Bosma, N., de Wit, G. and Carree, M. (2005). Modelling entrepreneurship: unifying the equilibrium and entry/exit approach. *Small Business Economics*, 25(1), 35–48.

Bruhn, M. and McKenzie, D. (2013). Entry Regulation and Formalization of Microenterprises in Developing Countries. World Bank Policy Research Working Paper 6507. Washington, DC: World Bank: 16.

Cagetti, M. and De Nardi, M. (2005). Wealth Inequality: Data and Models. Federal Reserve Bank of Chicago, Working Paper WP 2005–10. Chicago.

Carree, M. and Thurik, R. (2002). The impact of entrepreneurship on economic growth. In Z.J. Acs and D.B. Audretsch (eds.), *Handbook of Entrepreneurship Research*. New York: Springer, 557–594.

Carree, M. A., van Stel, A. J., Thurik, A. K., and Wennekers, A. R. M. (2002). Economic development and business ownership: an analysis using data of 23 OECD countries in the period 1976–1996. *Small Business Economics*, 19(3), 271–290.

Coad, A. (2009). *The Growth of Firms*. Cheltenham: Edward Elgar.

Coad, A. and Rao, R. (2008). Innovation and firm growth in high-tech sectors: A quartile regression approach. *Research Policy*, 37(4), 633–648.

Coad, A., Daunfeldt, S.-O., Hölzl, W., Johansson, D. and Nightingale, P. (2014). High-growth firms: introduction to the special section. *Industrial and Corporate Change*, 23(1), 91–112.

Cohen, W. M. and Levinthal, D. A. (1990). Absorptive capacity: a new perspective on learning and innovation. *Administrative Science Quarterly*, 35(1), 128–152.

Cressy, R. (2006). Why do most firms die young? *Small Business Economics*, 26, 103–116.

Czarnitzki, D. and Delanote, J. (2013). Young innovative companies: The new high-growth firms? *Industrial and Corporate Change*, 22(5), 1315–1340.

Daunfeldt, S-O., Elert, N. and Johansson, D. (2014). Economic contribution of high growth firms: Do policy implications depend on the choice of growth indicator? *Journal of Industry, Competition and Trade*, 14(3), 337–365.

De Meza, D. and Webb, D. (1987). Too much investment: a problem of asymmetric information. *Quarterly Journal of Economics*, 102(2), 281–292.

Demirgüç-Kunt, A. and Maksimovic, V. (1998). Law, finance, and firm growth. *The Journal of Finance*, 53(6), 2107–2137.

De Paula, A. and Scheinkman, J. A. (2007). The Informal Sector. NBER Working Paper 13486, Cambridge, MA: National Bureau of Economic Research.

Desai, S. (2009). Measuring entrepreneurship in developing countries. Research paper, UNU-WIDER 2009.10.

Dethier, J.-J., Hirn, M. and Straub, S. (2011). Explaining enterprise performance in developing countries with business climate survey data. *The World Bank Research Observer*, 26(2), 258–309.

Dias, J. and McDermott, J. (2006). Institutions, education, and development: The role of entrepreneurs. *Journal of Development Economics*, 80(1), 299–328.

Downing, J. and Daniels, L. (1992). The growth and dynamics of women entrepreneurs in Southern Africa GEMINI Technical Report No. 47PACT Publications, New York.

Evans, D. S. (1987). The relationship between firm growth, size, and age: estimates for 100 manufacturing industries. *The Journal of Industrial Economics*, 35(4), 567–581.

Evans, D. S. and Jovanovic, B. (1989). An estimated model of entrepreneurial choice under liquidity constraints. *Journal of Political Economy*, 97(4), 808–827.

Fields, G. S. (1990). Labour market modelling and the urban informal sector: Theory and evidence. In D. Turnham, B. Salomé, and A. Schwarz (Eds.), *The informal sector revisited*: 49–69. Paris: Organisation for Economic Co-operation and Development.

Freeman, J., Carrol, G. G., and Hannan, M. T. (1983). The liability of newness: age dependence in organization death rates. *American Sociology Review*, 48(5), 692–710.

Gebreeyesus, M. (2011). Innovation and microenterprise growth in Ethiopia. In A. Szirmai (Ed.), *Entrepreneurship, innovation, and economic development*. Oxford: Oxford University Press.

Gebreeyesus, M. (2014). Firms' adoption of international standards: Evidence from the Ethiopian floriculture sector. UNU-MERIT Working Paper 2014–007. The Netherlands.

Geroski, P. A. (2000). Models of technology diffusion. *Research Policy*, 29(4–5), 603–625.

Giannetti, M. and Simonov, A. (2004). On the determinants of entrepreneurial activity: social norms, economic environment and individual characteristics. *Swedish Economic Policy Review*, 11(2), 269–313.

Gibrat, R. (1939). *Les inégalités économiques*, Paris: Librarie du Recueil Sirey.

Ghatak, M., Morelli, M. and Sjöström, T. (2007). Entrepreneurial talent, occupational choice and trickle up policies. *Journal of Economic Theory*, 137(1), 27–48.

Goedhuys, M. and Sleuwaegen, L. (1999). Barriers to growth of firms in developing countries: evidence from Burundi. In D. B. Audretsch and R. Thurik (Eds), *Innovation, industry evolution and employment*. Cambridge University Press.

Goedhuys, M. and Sleuwaegen, L. (2000). Entrepreneurship and growth of entrepreneurial firms in Côte d'Ivoire. *Journal of Development Studies*, 36(3), 123–145.

Goedhuys, M. and Sleuwaegen, L. (2010). High-growth entrepreneurial firms in Africa: A quartile regression approach. *Small Business Economics*, 34(1), 31–51.

Goedhuys, M. and Sleuwaegen, L. (2013). The impact of international standards certification on the performance of firms in less developed countries. *World Development*, 47(3), 87–101.

Goedhuys, M., Janz, N., Mairesse, J. and Mohnen, P. (2008). Micro-evidence on innovation and development (MEIDE), an introduction. *The European Journal of Development Research* 20(2), 167–171.

Gries, T. and Naudé, N. (2010). Entrepreneurship and structural economic transformation. *Small Business Economics* 34(1), 13–29.

Grimm, M., Knorringa, P. and Lay, J. (2012). Constrained gazelles: high potentials in West Africa's informal economy. *World Development*, 40(7), 1352–1368.

Hart, D. M. (2003). Entrepreneurship policy: what it is and where it came from. In D. M. Hart (Ed.), *The emergence of entrepreneurship policy: governance, start-ups and growth in the US knowledge economy*. Cambridge: Cambridge University Press.

Henson, S., Masakure, O., and Cranfield, J. (2011). Do fresh produce exporters in Sub-Saharan Africa benefit from global GAP certification? *World Development*, 39(3), 375–386.

Hölzl, W. and Friesenbichler, K. S. S. (2010). High-growth firms, innovation and the distance to the frontier. *Economics Bulletin*, 30(2), 1016–1024,

House, W. J. (1984). Nairobi's informal sector: dynamic entrepreneurs or surplus labor? *Economic Development and Cultural Change*, 32(2), 277–302.

Jovanovic, B. (1982). Selection and the evolution of industry. *Econometrica*, 50(3), 649–670.

ILO (2004). *A fair globalization: creating opportunities for all*. Geneva: ILO.

Jovanovic, B. (1982). Selection and the evolution of industry. *Econometrica* 50(3), 649–670.

Klapper, L., Laeven, L. and Rajan, R. (2006). Entry regulation as a barrier to entrepreneurship. *Journal of Financial Economics*, 82(3), 591–629.

Kanniainen, V. and Poutvaara, P. (2007). Imperfect transmission of tacit knowledge and other barriers to entrepreneurship. *Comparative Labor Law and Policy Journal*, 28, 675–693.

Kanbur, S. M. (1979). Of risk-taking and the personal distribution of income. *Journal of Political Economy*, 87(4), 769–797.

Kaplinsky, R. (2010). The Role of Standards in Global Value Chains. World Bank Policy Research Working Paper Series. Washington, DC: World Bank.

Kevane, M. and Wydick, B. (2001). Microenterprise lending to female entrepreneurs: sacrificing economic growth for poverty alleviation? *World Development*, 29(7), 1225–1236.

Klapper, L. and Laeven, L. (2006). Entry regulation as a barrier to entrepreneurship. *Journal of Financial Economics*, 82(3), 591–629.

Lall, S. (1992). Technological capabilities and industrialization. *World Development*, 20(2), 165–186.

Lewis, W. A. (1954). Economic development with unlimited supplies of labor. *Manchester School of Economic and Social Studies*, 22(1), pp. 139–91.

Licht, A. N. (2007). The entrepreneurial spirit and what the law can do about it. *Comparative Labor Law and Policy Journal*, 28(4), 817–862.

Maertens, M. and Swinnen, J. F. M. (2009). Trade, standards, and poverty: evidence from Senegal. *World Development*, 37(1), 161–178.

Mason, C. and Brown, R. (2013). Creating good public policy to support high-growth firms. *Small Business Economics*, 40(2), 211–225.

McKenzie, D. and Woodruff, C. (2014). What are we learning from business training and entrepreneurship evaluations around the developing world? *The World Bank Research Observer*, 29(1), 48–82.

Mead, D. C. and Liedholm, C. (1998). The dynamics of micro and small enterprises in developing countries. *World Development*, 26(1), 61–74.

Mehlum, H., Moene, K. and Torvik, R. (2003). Predator or prey? Parasitic enterprises in economic development. *European Economic Review*, 47, 275–294.

Mengistae, T. (1999). Wage Rates and Job Queues: Does the Public Sector Overpay in Ethiopia?. World Bank Policy Research, Working Paper No. 210.

Moskowitz, T. J. and Vissing-Jorgensen, A. (2002). The returns to entrepreneurial investment: a private equity premium puzzle? *American Economic Review*, 92, 745–779.

Murphy, P. J., Liao, J. and Welsch, H. (2006). A conceptual history of entrepreneurial thought. *Journal of Management History*, 12(1), 12–35.

Nagler, P. and Naudé, W. (2014). Non-farm Entrepreneurship in Rural Africa: Patterns and Determinants. IZA Discussion Paper No. 800. South Africa.

Naudé, W. (2007). Peace, prosperity, and pro-growth entrepreneurship. UNU-WIDER Discussion Paper 2007/02., UNU-WIDER Helsinki, Finland, 33p.

Naudé, W. (2008). Entrepreneurship in Economic Development. Research paper/UNU-WIDER 2008/20. Helsinki: UNU-WIDER.

Naudé, W. (2011). Entrepreneurship is not a binding constraint on growth and development in the poorest countries. *World Development*, 39(1), 33–44.

Nelson, R. R. and Pack, H. (1999). The Asian miracle and modern growth theory. *The Economic Journal*, 109(457), 416–436.

Nichter, S. and Goldmark, L. (2009). Small firm growth in developing countries. *World Development*, 37(9), 1453–1464.

Nightingale, P. and Coad, A. (2014). Muppets and gazelles: political and methodological biases in entrepreneurship research. *Industrial and Corporate Change*, 23(1), 113–143.

OECD. (2007). *Eurostat-OECD manual on Business Demography Statistics*. Paris.

Parker, S. C. (2007). Law and the economics of entrepreneurship. *Comparative Labor Law and Policy Journal*, 28(4), 695–716.

Paulson, A. L. and Townsend, R. M. (2004). Financial Constraints and Entrepreneurship: Evidence from the Thai Financial Crisis. FRBC Discussion paper. Chicago: Federal Reserve Bank of Chicago.

Quatraro, F. and Vivarelli, M. (2015). Drivers of Entrepreneurship and Post-entry Performance of Newborn Firms in Developing Countries, Policy Research Working Paper Series 7074, The World Bank.

Ramachandran, V. and Shah, M. K. (1999). Minority entrepreneurs and firm performance in sub-Saharan Africa. *The Journal of Development Studies*, 36(2), 71–87.

Reynolds, P. D., Camp, M. S., Bygrave, W. D., Autio, E. and Hay, M. (2001). *Global Entrepreneurship Monitor, 2001 summary report*. London Business School and Babson College, London.

Rodrik, D. (2007). Industrial development: Some stylized facts and policy directions. In United Nations, *Industrial Development for the 21st Century: Sustainable Development Perspectives*. Department of Social and Economic Affairs. New York: United Nations, 7–28

Rubio, F. (1991). Microenterprise Growth Dynamics in the Dominican Republic: The ADEMI case. GEMINI Working Paper number 21. Washington, DC, USAID.

Santarelli, E. and Vivarelli, M. (2002). Is subsidizing entry an optimal policy? *Industrial and Corporate Change*, 11(1), 39–52.

Schiffer, M. and Weder, B. (2001). Firm Size and the Business Environment: Worldwide Survey Results. IFC Working Paper 43. Washington, DC: World Bank.

Schumpeter, J. (1939). *Business cycles: a theoretical, historical and statistical analysis of the capitalist process*. New York: McGraw-Hill.

Schramm, C. J. (2004). Building entrepreneurial economies. *Foreign Affairs*, 83(4), 104–115.

Shane, S. (2009). Why encouraging more people to become entrepreneurs is bad public policy. *Small Business Economics*, 33(2), 141–149.

Shane, S. and Venkataraman, S. (2000). The promise of entrepreneurship as a field of research. *Academy of Management Review*, 25(1), 217–226.

Sleuwaegen, L. and Goedhuys, M. (2002) Growth of firms in developing countries, evidence from Côte d'ivoire. *Journal of Development Economics*, 68(1), 117–135.

Snodgrass, D. and Biggs, T. (1996). *Industrialization and the small firm*. San Francisco: International Center for Economic Growth.

Stam, E. and Wennberg, K. (2009). The roles of R&D in new firm growth. *Small Business Economics*, 33(1), 77–89.

Stam, E. and van Stel, A. (2011). Types of entrepreneurship and economic growth. In A. Szirmai (Ed.), *Entrepreneurship, innovation, and economic development*. Oxford: Oxford University Press.

Stam, E., Hartog, C., van Stel, A. and Thurik, R. (2011). Ambitious entrepreneurship, high-growth firms, and macroeconomic growth. The dynamics of entrepreneurship. In M. Minniti (Ed.), *The Dynamics of Entrepreneurship: Evidence from the Global Entrepreneurship Monitor Data*. Oxford: Oxford University Press.

Stam, E., Audretsch, D. and Meijaard, J. (2007). Renascent Entrepreneurship: Entrepreneurial Preferences Subsequent to Firm Exit. Unpublished paper presented at the Babson College Entrepreneurship Conference in 2006.

Stiglitz, J. E. and Weiss, A. (1981). Credit rationing in markets with imperfect information. *American Economic Review*, 71(3), 393–410.

Storey, D. J. (1994) *Understanding the small business sector*. London: Routledge.

Szirmai, A., Naudé, W. and Goedhuy, M. (2011). Entrepreneurship, innovation and economic development: an overview, in *Entrepreneurship, innovation, and economic development*. Oxford; New York, Oxford University Press.

Taylor, M. P. (1999). Survival of the fittest? An analysis of self-employment duration in Britain. *The Economic Journal*, 109, C140–C155.

Ucbasaran, D., Westhead, P. and Wright, M. (2006). *Habitual entrepreneurs*. Cheltenham: Edward Elgar.

Van Praag, M. C and Verloot, P. H. (2007). What is the value of entrepreneurship? A review of recent research. *Small Business Economics*, 29(4), 351–382.

van der Sluis, J., van Praag, M. and Vijverberg, W. (2004). Education and Entrepreneurship in Industrialized Countries: A Meta-analysis. Tinbergen Institute Working Paper No. TI 03-046/3.

van Stel, A., Carree, M. and Thurik, R. (2005). The effect of entrepreneurial activity on national economic growth. *Small Business Economics Journal*, 24(3), 311–321.

Vivarelli, M. (2013). Is entrepreneurship necessarily good? Microeconomic evidence from developed and developing countries. *Industrial and Corporate Change*, 22(6), 1453–1495.

Wennekers, S. and Thurik, R. (1999). Linking entrepreneurship and economic growth. *Small Business Economics*, 13(1), 27–56.

Wennekers, S., Van Stel, A., Thurik, R. and Reynolds, P. (2005). Nascent entrepreneurship and level of economic development. *Small Business Economics*, 24(3), 293–309.

Wiggens, S. N. (1995). Entrepreneurial enterprises, endogenous ownership and limits to firm size. *Economic Inquiry*, 33(1), 54–69.

Williams, C. C. (2015a). Entrepreneurship in the shadow economy: a review of the alternative policy approaches. *International Journal of Small and Medium Enterprises and Sustainability*, 1(1), 51–82.

Williams, C. C. (2015b). Tackling entrepreneurship in the informal sector: an overview of the policy options, approaches and measures. *Journal of Developmental Entrepreneurship*, 19(5), 1–18.

Williams, C. C. and Martinez-Perez, A. (2014). Entrepreneurship in the informal economy: a product of too much or too little state intervention? *International Journal of Entrepreneurship and Innovation*, 15(4), 227–237.

Williams, C. C. and Nadin, S. (2014). Facilitating the formalisation of entrepreneurs in the informal economy: towards a variegated policy approach. *Journal of Entrepreneurship and Public Policy*, 3(1), 33–48.

Williams, C. C. and Nadin, S. (2013). Harnessing the hidden enterprise culture: supporting the formalization of off-the-books business start-ups. *Journal of Small Business and Enterprise Development*, 20(2), 434–447.

Williams, C. C. and Nadin, S. (2012a). Tackling entrepreneurship in the informal economy: evaluating the policy options, *Journal of Entrepreneurship and Public Policy*, 1(2), 111–124.

Williams, C. C. and Nadin, S. (2012b). Tackling the hidden enterprise culture: government policies to support the formalization of informal entrepreneurship. *Entrepreneurship and Regional Development*, 24(9–10), 895–915.

Wong, P. K., Ho, Y. P. and Autio, E. (2005). Entrepreneurship, innovation and economic growth: evidence from GEM data. *Small Business Economics* 24(3), 335–350.

Yamada, G. (1996). Urban informal employment and self-employment in developing countries: theory and evidence. *Economic Development and Cultural Change*, 44(2), 289–314.

39

HARNESSING ENTREPRENEURSHIP IN DEVELOPING COUNTRIES

A lived practices approach

Colin C. Williams and Anjula Gurtoo

Introduction

Across the developing and developed world, well-known entrepreneurs such as Roman Abramovich, Richard Branson, Bill Gates, Captain Gobinath, Steve Jobs, Lakshmi Mittal, Alan Sugar and Ratan Tata, are widely revered. They are heralded as heroes and assigned iconic status as the symbolic figureheads of capitalist culture. Until now, the literature on entrepreneurship has done little to challenge this normative ideologically driven ideal-type portrayal of entrepreneurs as objects of desire. Indeed, the entrepreneurship literature is littered with statements that entrepreneurs are 'economic heroes' (Cannon, 1991), even 'super heroes' (Burns, 2001: 24). As Burns (2001: 1) acclaims, they are 'the stuff of "legends" . . . held in high esteem and held up as role models to be emulated'.

The aim of this final chapter is to directly and intentionally contest this dominant depiction of the entrepreneur as a heroic icon and symbolic figurehead that spearheads economic progress and development by calling for a more grounded 'lived practice' approach towards entrepreneurship in developing countries and then exploring the implications of such a grounded approach for harnessing entrepreneurship. This re-representation, that is, recognises and values the existence of other (and 'othered') forms of entrepreneur and entrepreneurship across the global economic landscape, thus opening up entrepreneurship to re-signification as demonstrative of the persistence and resilience of everyday forms of enterprising endeavour that point to the possibility of a diverse array of economic and social futures. The intention in doing so is to display how the chapters in this handbook have started to put flesh on the bones of this 'lived practice' approach towards entrepreneurship in the developing world. Perhaps more contentiously, by highlighting some persistent beliefs about entrepreneurship in developing countries that are based on unfounded assumptions rather than evidence-based findings, we here set out a research agenda for the future that puts these widely held assumptions under the spotlight so as to further develop this 'lived practices' approach.

To commence, therefore, and following the structure of the *Handbook*, this final chapter will set out the need for a lived practices approach in relation to first, the institutional environment of entrepreneurship; second, the motivations of entrepreneurs; third, the gendering of entrepreneurship; fourth, entrepreneurship in the informal sector; fifth, entrepreneurship education; and sixth and finally, policy approaches towards entrepreneurship in developing countries.

Institutional environment of entrepreneurship

As mentioned, for many decades, entrepreneurs have been revered both in popular culture and the entrepreneurship literature as the heroic icons and symbolic figureheads that spearhead economic development and growth (Burns, 2001; Cannon, 1991). As Jones and Spicer (2009: 237) assert, they are portrayed as an 'object of desire' for others to seek to emulate, rather than as lived subjects. This ideal-type representation of the entrepreneur prevails, moreover, across all theoretical approaches to entrepreneurship (see Cunningham and Lischeron 1991: 47). Although it is explicit in the 'great person' school that depicts them as born (rather than made) and portrays them as possessing a 'sixth sense' along with intuition, vigour, energy, persistence and self-esteem and contrasts them with 'mortals' who 'lack what it takes'. This thought is also to the fore in the more socially constructed approaches of the classical, management, leadership or intrapreneurship schools. All portray entrepreneurs as being positive and wholesome heroic figureheads and as possessing virtuous attributes that 'lesser mortals' do not. One outcome acclaims them as spearheading economic development and growth. There is in other words a widely held view that entrepreneurs and entrepreneurship drive economic development and growth. Another outcome is that entrepreneurs and forms of entrepreneurship that do not reinforce this ideal-type have tended to be either ignored, depicted as weak, temporary or disappearing forms of entrepreneurship, or simply classified as being not 'proper' entrepreneurship. In this section, we focus upon the former outcome. The next sections will deal with the latter outcome.

Throughout this book, the assumption in nearly every chapter has been that entrepreneurship drives economic development and growth. Based on this widely held premise, Part I of this handbook recognized that entrepreneurship is a socially constructed behaviour which is a product of its institutional context and sought to understand how various dimensions of the institutional context facilitate and constrain entrepreneurship in developing countries. These chapters reviewed how formal institutions can act as a facilitator and barrier to entrepreneurship, as well as how informal institutions can be either a help or hindrance to the fostering of an 'enterprise culture' and entrepreneurship. For example, when considering developing countries, the emphasis is often placed on the prevalence of over-burdensome regulations, high taxes and corruption in the public sector (De Soto, 1989; Nwabuzor, 2005) and the existence of formal institutional voids such as relatively weak or inadequate legal systems and contract enforcement regimes (Khan and Quaddus, 2015; Puffer et al., 2010; Sutter et al., 2013). As many of the chapters in this handbook on post-communist countries reveal, moreover, such as chapter 35 on entrepreneurship education in Albania by Elvisa Drishti, Drita Kruja and Mario Curcija, the norms, values and beliefs that constitute the informal institutions are also often not conducive to fostering entrepreneurship and an enterprise culture.

However, and as Elisa Calza and Micheline Goedhuys start to uncover in chapter 38, the evidence-base to support the view that entrepreneurship drives economic development and growth is far from solid. The certainty that the relationship between entrepreneurship and economic development is causal and in the direction assumed in the vast majority of the literature, namely that entrepreneurship drives economic development and growth, is very tenuous. It might well be the case, for example, that the relationship is in the other direction. Entrepreneurship may be a result of economic development and growth. With greater wealth and social protection in societies, more people may become entrepreneurs. It may also be the case, alternatively, that entrepreneurship shapes, and is shaped by, economic development and growth in a more mutually iterative manner than has so far been considered. Until now, however, little evidence exists on the direction of this relationship. In future, therefore, research is required that puts under the spotlight this significant gap in our knowledge. Is it the case that entrepreneurship drives economic development and growth? If this is the case, and only if this is so, does it then become relevant to ask the question: what are the institutional conditions that might facilitate the growth of entrepreneurship? It is not just the popular assumption that entrepreneurship drives economic development and growth, however, that needs evaluation in future research on developing countries.

Entrepreneurs' motivations in developing countries

Despite widespread recognition that multifarious factors feed into the decision to start up a business (Baty, 1990; Bolton and Thompson, 2000; Brockhaus and Horowitz, 1986; Burns, 2001; Chell et al, 1991; Cooper, 1981; Kanter, 1983), and warnings not to over-simplify the multiplicity of rationales driving entrepreneurship (Rouse and Dallenbach, 1999), entrepreneurship scholarship has adopted a rather simple classificatory schema when examining entrepreneurs' motives in developing countries and beyond. Entrepreneurs are classified as either 'necessity' entrepreneurs pushed into entrepreneurship as a survival tactic in the absence of alternative means of livelihood, or as 'opportunity' entrepreneurs pulled into this endeavour more out of choice (Aidis et al., 2006; Benz, 2009; Harding et al., 2006; Maritz, 2004; Minniti et al., 2006; Perunović, 2005; Reynolds et al., 2002; Smallbone and Welter, 2004). This structure/agency binary that views some entrepreneurs as forced out of 'necessity' and others as voluntarily engaging has become ever more dominant (Acs, 2006; Bosma et al., 2008; Williams, 2007, 2008, 2009; Williams et al., 2006, 2009, 2010; Williams and Lansky, 2013).

When studying developing countries, the commonly held assumption in both popular portrayals and policy-making circles is that entrepreneurs are largely from marginalized populations and participate in such endeavour out of necessity as a survival practice and last resort in the absence of alternative means of livelihood. This, nevertheless, is an *a priori* assumption rather than an empirical finding. Moreover, it is then assumed that these entrepreneurs are less efficient and unproductive, and at best, do not contribute to economic development and growth and at worst, hinder growth.

As Part II of this handbook has revealed however, studies in developing countries have started to gauge the ratio of necessity-to-opportunity entrepreneurship in different developing country contexts, as well as who engages in such entrepreneurial endeavour out of necessity and who does so voluntarily, as well as to decipher how the activities that they engage in differ. There appears to be a socio-spatial contingency of entrepreneurs' motives in terms of the ratio of necessity-to-opportunity entrepreneurship with greater proportions of necessity-driven entrepreneurship for example in deprived populations and opportunity entrepreneurship in more affluent populations. An emerging recognition finds that necessity- and opportunity-drivers can often combine when considering the motives of individual entrepreneurs and also a recognition that entrepreneurs' motives can change over time, such as from more necessity-oriented to opportunity-oriented rationales.

The issue that has received less attention, however, is the assumption that necessity-driven entrepreneurs are less efficient and unproductive relative to opportunity-driven entrepreneurs. Until now, this has largely been a widespread assumption, rather than grounded in empirical evidence. This now needs to be evaluated. If indeed the necessity-driven entrepreneurs are less productive than opportunity-driven entrepreneurs, then support will be found for focusing attention on those more opportunity-driven as the source of future higher-performing enterprises that will facilitate economic development and growth. However, if it is not the case, or if many entrepreneurs who start up for necessity reasons later become opportunity-driven, then a change in policy approach will be required towards necessity-driven entrepreneurs. Rather than pursue a laissez-faire approach towards them or at worst, seek to eradicate them, policy will need to pay as much attention to fostering such entrepreneurship as it currently does to opportunity-driven entrepreneurs. A key question which needs addressing in future research on developing countries, therefore, is whether necessity-driven entrepreneurs are less productive than opportunity-driven entrepreneurs, measured for example in terms of future sales growth, employment creation and labour productivity.

Based on the view that much entrepreneurship in developing countries is necessity-driven, there has also been an assumption that entrepreneurship at the base of the pyramid and beyond is by definition a profit-driven endeavour conducted for monetary gain. As several chapters in Part II of this handbook have revealed however, there is a small but growing literature that entrepreneurship in developing countries is not always purely a profit-driven endeavour and how entrepreneurs engage in not-for-profit activity. Future research therefore, needs to pay greater attention to examining the existence and nature of social entrepreneurship and how entrepreneurs possess social objectives in developing countries. Until now, this has been relatively absent in a developing world context compared with the burgeoning social entrepreneurship literature in the developed world.

Gender and entrepreneurship

Examining the issue of gender and entrepreneurship in developing countries, it is not only the case that scholarship and discourse on entrepreneurship has sometimes 'written out' women but even when they have been included, women entrepreneurs have been commonly portrayed as necessity-driven and engaging in entrepreneurship purely as a means to earn some extra income for their families (ILO 2005; Bhatt, 2006; Carr and Chen, 2002; Mehrotra and Biggeri, 2002). The chapters in Part III begin to examine the nature of, and rationales for, entrepreneurship of men and women and whether they differ in the manner so far assumed.

Examining the lived practices of entrepreneurship in developing countries through a gender lens is important. It appears that the gender disparities in the wider labour market are often mirrored and reinforced when studying the gendering of entrepreneurship. Not only are recorded participation rates in entrepreneurship sometimes lower for women, but so too do women commonly receive lower incomes from their entrepreneurial endeavour than men despite being better educated, and often face additional barriers to engagement in entrepreneurship and developing their new ventures not suffered by many men. Unless these are evaluated, then half of the world's population will find themselves marginalized from inclusion in the development process by being represented as unworthy of attention and support.

Informal sector entrepreneurship

It is now widely recognized that the informal sector in general and informal entrepreneurship in particular, is extensive and a persistent feature of many developing economies (Autio and

Fu, 2015; Williams, 2014a,b, 2015a,b). In recent years, a new sub-discipline of entrepreneurship scholarship has emerged focused on informal entrepreneurship. On the one hand, this has examined its magnitude, including its varying prevalence cross-nationally (Autio and Fu, 2015; Thai and Turkina, 2014; Williams, 2013), the differing degrees of informalization of entrepreneurs (De Castro et al., 2014; Williams and Shahid, 2015) and the determinants of informal sector entrepreneurship (Dau and Cuervo-Cazurra, 2014; Siqueira et al., 2014; Thai and Turkina, 2014). On the other hand, its character has been analyzed, including who participates (Hudson et al., 2012; Thai and Turkina, 2014; Williams and Martinez, 2014) and their motives, including whether they are necessity- and/or opportunity-driven (Adom, 2014; Barsoum, 2015; Franck, 2012; Maloney, 2004; Perry et al., 2007).

More recently, furthermore, there has been a turn away from analyzing solely its negative impacts and towards highlighting some of the more positive contributions made by this realm. The catalyst for seeking to understand these more positive impacts has been the recognition that informal entrepreneurship is not always a necessity-driven endeavour, but often a matter of choice (Cross, 2000; Franck, 2012; Gërxhani, 2004; Maloney, 2004; Perry and Maloney, 2007; Snyder, 2004).

What has not so far been examined, however, is whether it is the case that informal sector entrepreneurship has lower productivity and is less efficient than formal entrepreneurship. Indeed, given that informal entrepreneurs avoid the burdensome regulations, do not pay tax and avoid other labour laws, there are rationales for assuming that this might not be the case. Until now, nevertheless, this has not been investigated. Future research on informal sector entrepreneurship, therefore, could put under the spotlight the widely held assumption that such endeavour is less productive than formal entrepreneurship.

Indeed, many of the other impacts often attributed to informal entrepreneurship are also based on thin empirics, that is, a flimsy evidence base. Future research, therefore, could also evaluate these other impacts. Developing economies and governments have been asserted to potentially benefit from the ability of informal entrepreneurs to create jobs (Ketchen et al., 2014) and this sphere has started to be viewed as a breeding ground for the micro-enterprise system (Barbour and Llanes, 2013). Formal enterprises are seen as potentially benefiting from cheaper sources of labor and raw materials (Ketchen et al., 2014), potential formal entrepreneurs from the opportunity of using this realm as a test-bed for their business ventures (Williams & Martinez, 2014) and informal entrepreneurs from having this as an escape route from corrupt public sector officials and the regulatory burden in contexts where this stifles business development (Puffer et al., 2010). Customers especially in 'bottom of the pyramid' markets, meanwhile, are viewed as potentially benefiting from more affordable goods and services (Ketchen et al., 2014; London et al., 2014). An evidence-based evaluation of these purported impacts and many more provides an agenda for future research on informal entrepreneurship. If some of these more positive features are identified, then there will be evidence to support a resultant shift in developing economies away from an eradication approach and towards a policy approach which seeks to facilitate the formalization of informal entrepreneurship.

Entrepreneurship education and learning

Based on the assumption that fostering entrepreneurship and an enterprise culture is a key means of promoting economic development and growth, many developing countries have sought to shift beyond the traditional conception that entrepreneurs are born and not made, by developing entrepreneurship education. Part V of this handbook reviewed entrepreneurship education in various countries and global regions.

Despite some evidence existing elsewhere in the world that providing people with the knowledge, skills and motivation to be entrepreneurs facilitates entrepreneurship (see for example chapter 38), the chapters in this handbook have revealed that this can be contested. Across the developing world, based on the unproven assumption that entrepreneurship is a key driver of economic development and growth, there has been the development of entrepreneurship education from the primary and secondary school level to graduate university programmes. The intention has been to enhance both entrepreneurial intention as well as the level of entrepreneurship by creating an entrepreneurial mind-set amongst a greater number of individuals as well as the skill-sets required by entrepreneurially minded individuals.

The somewhat concerning finding in many of the chapters, however, is that entrepreneurship education programmes in numerous developing countries currently appear to have an insignificant impact on the attitudes and entrepreneurial intentions of those subject to them. Much more research is therefore required into why this is the case. Whether due to the client groups served, the nature of the entrepreneurship education programmes being offered or other barriers now requires investigation. Before doing so, nevertheless, whether entrepreneurship is a driver of economic development and growth needs to be evaluated. If found to be a response to, or product of, economic development and growth for example, then the value of pursuing entrepreneurship education programmes in developing countries would be much diminished.

Conclusions

Hopefully, this handbook has provided a useful primer for readers to start to get to grips with understanding entrepreneurship in developing countries. The key finding demonstrates that for progress to be made in understanding entrepreneurship in the developing world, there a more evidence-based approach is required which examines the lived practices of entrepreneurship in developing world contexts.

Unless greater understanding is developed of the magnitude and distribution of entrepreneurship across populations, the multifarious lived practices of entrepreneurship in different contexts, who engages in what kinds of entrepreneurial endeavour, along with their motives and the barriers to participation, then the governments of developing countries will not know what needs to be done. Hopefully, this handbook provides academics, policy makers and others interested in fostering entrepreneurship in the developing world with an improved understanding of entrepreneurship and what questions need to be asked moving forward in order to further advance understanding about the lived practices of entrepreneurship and what needs to be done. If the *Routledge Handbook of Entrepreneurship in Developing Economies* has succeeded in doing this, then its objective has been achieved.

References

Acs, Z. J. (2006). How is entrepreneurship good for economic growth? *Innovations*, 1(1), 97–107.

Adom, K. (2014). Beyond the marginalization thesis, an examination of the motivations of informal entrepreneurs in Sub-Saharan Africa: insights from Ghana. *International Journal of Entrepreneurship and Innovation*, 15(2), 113–125

Aidis, R., Welter, F., Smallbone, D. and Isakova, N. (2006). Female entrepreneurship in transition economies: the case of Lithuania and Ukraine. *Feminist Economics*, 13(2), 157–83.

Autio, E. and Fu, K. (2015). Economic and political institutions and entry into formal and informal entrepreneurship. *Asia Pacific Journal of Management*, 32(1), 67–94.

Barbour, A. and Llanes, M. (2013). *Supporting people to legitimise their informal businesses*. New York: Joseph Rowntree Foundation.

Barsoum, G. (2015). Striving for job security: the lived experience of employment informality among educated youth in Egypt. *International Journal of Sociology and Social Policy*, 35(5/6), 340–358.

Baty, G. (1990). *Entrepreneurship in the nineties*. London: Prentice Hall.

Benz, M. (2009). Entrepreneurship as a non-profit seeking activity. *International Entrepreneurship and Management Journal*, 5(1), 23–44.

Bhatt, E. (2006). *We are poor but so many: the story of self-employed women in India*. Oxford: Oxford University Press.

Bolton, B. and Thompson, J. (2000). *Entrepreneurs: talent, temperament, technique*. Oxford: Butterworth-Heinemann.

Bosma, N., Jones, K., Autio, K. and Levie, J. (2008). *Global Entrepreneurship Monitor: 2007 executive report*. London: Global Entrepreneurship Monitor Consortium.

Burns, P. (2001). *Entrepreneurship and small business*, Basingstoke: Palgrave.

Cannon, T. (1991). *Enterprise: creation, development and growth*, Oxford: Butterworth-Heinemann.

Carr, M. and Chen, M. (2002). Globalization and the informal economy: How global trade and investment impact on the working poor. Geneva: The Informal Economy Working Paper No. 1, Geneva: Policy Integration Department, International Labor Office.

Cross, J. C. (2000). Street vendors, modernity and postmodernity: conflict and compromise in the global economy. *International Journal of Sociology and Social Policy*, 20(1), 29–51.

Cunningham, J. B. and Lischeron, J. (1991). Defining entrepreneurship. *Journal of Small Business Management*, 29(1), 43–51.

Dau, L. A. and Cuervo-Cazurra, A. (2014). To formalize or not to formalize: entrepreneurship and pro-market institutions. *Journal of Business Venturing*, 29(5), 668–686.

De Castro, J. O., Khavul, S. and Bruton, G. D. (2014). Shades of grey: how do informal firms navigate between macro and meso institutional environments? *Strategic Entrepreneurship Journal*, 8, 75–94.

De Soto, H. (1989). *The other path: the economic answer to terrorism*. London: Harper and Row.

Franck, A. K. (2012). Factors motivating women's informal micro-entrepreneurship: experiences from Penang, Malaysia. *International Journal of Gender and Entrepreneurship*, 4(1), 65–78.

Gërxhani, K. (2004). The informal sector in developed and less developed countries: a literature survey. *Public Choice*, 120(3/4), 267–300.

Harding, R., Brooksbank, D., Hart, M., Jones-Evans, D., Levie, J., O'Reilly, J.and Walker, J. (2006). *Global Entrepreneurship Monitor United Kingdom 2005*. London: London Business School.

Hudson, J., Williams, C. C., Orviska, M. and Nadin, S. (2012). Evaluating the impact of the informal economy on businesses in South East Europe: some lessons from the 2009 World Bank Enterprise Survey. *The South-East European Journal of Economics and Business*, 7(1), 99–110.

ILO (2005). *World employment report 2004–05: employment, productivity and poverty reduction*. Geneva: ILO.

Jones, C. and Spicer, A. (2009). *Unmasking the entrepreneur*. Cheltenham: Edward Elgar.

Ketchen, D. J., Ireland, R. D. and Webb, J. W. (2014). Towards a research agenda for the informal economy: a survey of the Strategic Entrepreneurship Journal's Editorial Board. *Strategic Entrepreneurship Journal*, 8(1), 95–100.

Khan, E. A. and Quaddus, M. (2015). Examining the influence of business environment on socio-economic performance of informal microenterprises: content analysis and partial least square approach. *International Journal of Sociology and Social Policy*, 35(3/4), 273–88.

London, T., Esper, H., Grogan-Kaylor, A. and Kistruck, G. M. (2014). Connecting poverty to purchase in informal markets. *Strategic Entrepreneurship Journal*, 8(1), 37–55.

Maloney, W. F. (2004). Informality revisited. *World Development*, 32(7), 1159–1178.

Maritz, A (2004). New Zealand necessity entrepreneurs. *International Journal of Entrepreneurship and Small Business*, 1(3/4), 255–264.

Mehrotra, S and Biggeri, M. (2002). Social protection in the informal economy: Home-based women workers and outsourced manufacturing in Asia. Florence: Innocenti Working Paper no. 97, UNICEF Innocenti Research Unit.

Minniti, M., Bygrave, W. and Autio, E. (2006). *Global Entrepreneurship Monitor: 2005 executive report*. London: London Business School.

Nwabuzor, A. (2005). Corruption and development: new initiatives in economic openness and strengthened rule of law. *Journal of Business Ethics*, 59(1/2), 121–138.

Obeng, B.A., Blundel, R.K. and Agyapong, A. (2013). Enterprise education for small artisanal businesses: a case study of Sokoban Wood village, Ghana. In M. T. Thanh Thai and E. Turkina (Eds.), *Entrepreneurship in the informal economy: models, approaches and prospects for economic development*, Routledge, London, 192–207.

Perry, G. E. and Maloney, W. F. (2007). Overview – informality: exit and exclusion, In G. E. Perry, W. F. Maloney, O. S. Arias, P. Fajnzylber, A. D. Mason and J. Saavedra-Chanduvi (Eds.), *Informality: exit and exclusion* (pp. 1–20). Washington, DC: World Bank.

Perry, G. E., Maloney, W. F., Arias, O. S., Fajnzylber, R., Mason, A. D. and Saavedra-Chanduvi, J. (2007). *Informality: exit and exclusion*. Washington, DC: World Bank.

Perunović, Z. (2005). Introducing Opportunity-Based Entrepreneurship in a Transition Economy. Michigan: Policy Brief 39, William Davidson Institute, University of Michigan.

Puffer, S. M., McCarthy, D. J. and Boisot, M. (2010). Entrepreneurship in Russia and China: the impact of formal institutional voids. *Entrepreneurship Theory and Practice*, 34(3), 441–467.

Reynolds, P., Bygrave, W. D., Autio, E. and Hay, M. (2002). *Global Entrepreneurship Monitor: 2002 executive monitor*. London: London Business School.

Rouse, M. and Dallenbach, U. (1999). Rethinking research methods for the resource-based perspective: isolating sources of sustainable competitive advantage. *Strategic Management Journal* 20(5), 487–494.

Siqueira, A. C. O., Webb, J. W. and Bruton, G. D. (2014). Informal entrepreneurship and industry conditions. *Entrepreneurship Theory and Practice*, doi: 10.1111/etap.12115. Accessed on 21 December 2014.

Smallbone, D. and Welter, F. (2004). Entrepreneurship in transition economies: necessity or opportunity driven? www.babson.edu/entrep/fer/BABSON2003/XXV/XXV-S8/xxv-s8.htm (last accessed 9 April 2013).

Snyder, K. A. (2004). Routes to the informal economy in New York's East village: crisis, economics and identity. *Sociological Perspectives*, 47(2), 215–240.

Sutter, C. J., Webb, J.W., Kistruck, G. M. and Bailey, A.V.G. (2013). Entrepreneurs' responses to semi-formal illegitimate institutional arrangements. *Journal of Business Venturing*, 28(5), 743–758.

Thai, M. T. T. and Turkina, E. (2014). Macro-level determinants of formal entrepreneurship versus informal entrepreneurship. *Journal of Business Venturing*, 29(4), 490–510.

Williams, C. C. (2007). Entrepreneurs operating in the informal economy: necessity or opportunity driven? *Journal of Small Business and Entrepreneurship*, 20(3), 309–320.

Williams, C. C. (2008). Beyond necessity-driven versus opportunity-driven entrepreneurship: a study of informal entrepreneurs in England, Russia and Ukraine. *International Journal of Entrepreneurship and Innovation*, 9(3), 157–166.

Williams, C. C. (2009). The motives of off-the-books entrepreneurs: necessity- or opportunity-driven? *International Entrepreneurship and Management Journal*, 5(2), 203–17.

Williams, C. C. (2013). Tackling Europe's informal economy: a critical evaluation of the neo-liberal de-regulatory perspective. *Journal of Contemporary European Research*, 9(3), 261–279.

Williams, C. C. (2014a). Out of the shadows: a classification of economies by the size and character of their informal sector. *Work, Employment and Society*, 28(5),735–753.

Williams, C. C. (2014b). Explaining cross-national variations in the commonality of informal sector entrepreneurship: an exploratory analysis of 38 emerging economies. *Journal of Small Business and Entrepreneurship*, 27(2), 191–212.

Williams, C. C. (2015a). Explaining cross-national variations in the scale of informal employment: an exploratory analysis of 41 less developed economies. *International Journal of Manpower*, 36(2), 118–135.

Williams, C. C. (2015b). Out of the margins: classifying economies by the prevalence and character of employment in the informal economy. *International Labour Review*, 154(3), 373–392.

Williams, C. C. and Lansky, M. (2013). Informal employment in developed and emerging economies: perspectives and policy responses. *International Labour Review*, 152(3–4), 355–380.

Williams, C. C. and Martinez, A. (2014).Is the informal economy an incubator for new enterprise creation? a gender perspective. *International Journal of Entrepreneurial Behaviour and Research*, 20(1), 4–19.

Williams, C. C. and Shahid, M. S. (2015). Informal entrepreneurship and institutional theory: Explaining the varying degrees of (in)formalization of entrepreneurs in Pakistan. *Entrepreneurship and Regional Development* [dx.doi.org/10.1080/08985626.2014.963889].

Williams, C. C., Round, J. and Rodgers, P. (2006). Beyond necessity- and opportunity-driven entrepreneurship: some case study evidence from Ukraine. *Journal of Business and Entrepreneurship*, 18(2), 22–34.

Williams, C. C., Round, J. and Rodgers, P. (2009). Evaluating the motives of informal entrepreneurs: some lessons from Ukraine. *Journal of Developmental Entrepreneurship*, 14(1), 59–71.

Williams, C. C., Round, J. and Rodgers, P. (2010). Explaining the off-the-books enterprise culture of Ukraine: reluctant or willing entrepreneurship? *International Journal of Entrepreneurship and Small Business*, 10(2), 65–80.

INDEX

For Product Safety Concerns and Information please contact our EU representative GPSR@taylorandfrancis.com Taylor & Francis Verlag GmbH, Kaufingerstraße 24, 80331 München, Germany

Printed and bound by CPI Group (UK) Ltd, Croydon, CR0 4YY

11/05/2025

01866588-0002